CDEV 2010–2011 Edition
Spencer A. Rathus

Sr. Publisher: Linda Schreiber

Editor-in-Chief: Michelle Julet

Senior Editor: Jaime Perkins

Director, 4LTR Press: Neil Marquardt

Developmental Editor: David Ferrell, B-Books, Ltd.

Associate Development Editor: Dan Moneypenny

Assistant Editor: Paige Leeds

Editorial Assistant: Philip Hovanessian

Sr. Project Manager, 4LTR Press: Michelle Lockard

Executive Brand Marketing Manager: Robin Lucas

Executive Marketing Manager: Kimberly Russell

Marketing Manager: Tierra Morgan

Executive Marketing Communications Manager: Talia Wise

Marketing Coordinator: Molly Felz

Production Director: Amy McGuire, B-books, Ltd.

Content Project Manager: Matthew Ballantyne

Media Editor: Mary Noel

Print Buyer: Becky Cross

Production Service: B-books, Ltd.

Sr. Art Director: Vernon Boes

Internal Designer: Ke Design

Cover Designer: Denise Davidson

Cover Images: Getty Images, Veer, Rubberball

Photography Manager: Deanna Ettinger

Photo Researcher: Sam Marshall

For product information and technology assistance contact us at
Cengage Learning Customer & Sales Support, 1-800-354-9706

For permission to use material from this text or product, submit all requests online at **www.cengage.com/permissions**
Further permissions questions can be emailed to
permissionrequest@cengage.com

Library of Congress Control Number: 2009935583

ISBN-13: 978-0-495-90553-0
ISBN-10: 0-495-90553-4

Wadsworth
20 Davis Drive
Belmont CA 94002-3098
USA

Cengage Learning is a leading provider of customized learning solutions with office locations around the globe, including Singapore, the United Kingdom, Australia, Mexico, Brazil, and Japan. Locate your local office at **www.cengage.com/global**.

Cengage Learning products are represented in Canada by Nelson Education, Ltd.

To learn more about Wadsworth visit **www.cengage.com/wadsworth**
Purchase any of our products at your local college store or at our preferred online store **www.cengagebrain.com**

Printed in the United States of America
2 3 4 5 15 14 13 12

BRIEF CONTENTS

PART 1: WHAT IS CHILD DEVELOPMENT? 2

Chapter 1: History, Theories, and Methods of Child Development 3

PART 2: BEGINNINGS 22

Chapter 2: Heredity and Conception 23
Chapter 3: Prenatal Development 41
Chapter 4: Birth and the Newborn Baby: In the New World 57

PART 3: INFANCY 78

Chapter 5: Infancy: Physical Development 79
Chapter 6: Infancy: Cognitive Development 97
Chapter 7: Infancy: Social and Emotional Development 115

PART 4: EARLY CHILDHOOD 132

Chapter 8: Early Childhood: Physical Development 133
Chapter 9: Early Childhood: Cognitive Development 147
Chapter 10: Early Childhood: Social and Emotional Development 163

PART 5: MIDDLE CHILDHOOD 180

Chapter 11: Middle Childhood: Physical Development 181
Chapter 12: Middle Childhood: Cognitive Development 195
Chapter 13: Middle Childhood: Social and Emotional Development 219

PART 6: ADOLESCENCE 234

Chapter 14: Adolescence: Physical Development 235
Chapter 15: Adolescence: Cognitive Development 257
Chapter 16: Adolescence: Social and Emotional Development 275

Listen Up!

CDEV was designed for students just like you – busy people who want choices, flexibility, and multiple learning options.

CDEV delivers concise, focused information in a fresh and contemporary format. And... CDEV gives you a variety of online learning materials designed with you in mind.

At 4ltrpress.cengage.com/cdev, you'll find electronic resources such as printable and interactive flashcards, downloadable study aids, games, quizzes, and PowerVisuals. These resources will help supplement your understanding of childhood and adolescent development concepts in a format that fits your busy lifestyle.

Visit 4ltrpress.cengage.com/cdev to learn more about the multiple CDEV resources available to help you succeed!

CONTENTS

PART ONE WHAT IS CHILD DEVELOPMENT? 2

1 History, Theories, and Methods of Child Development 3

LO1: The Development of the Study of Child Development 3

Pioneers in the Study of Child Development 4

LO2: Theories of Child Development 4

The Psychoanalytic Perspective 5
The Learning Perspective: Behavioral and Social
    Cognitive Theories 7
The Cognitive Perspective 9
The Biological Perspective 11
The Ecological Perspective 12
The Sociocultural Perspective 12

LO3: Controversies in Child Development 15

The Nature–Nurture Controversy 15
The Continuity–Discontinuity Controversy 16
The Active–Passive Controversy 16

LO4: How We Study Child Development 17

Gathering Information 17
Correlation: Putting Things Together 17
The Experiment: Trying Things Out 18
Longitudinal Research: Studying Development
    over Time 19
Ethical Considerations 21

SIGMUND FREUD

ERIK ERIKSON AND HIS WIFE, JOAN ERIKSON

JOHN B. WATSON

B. F. SKINNER

ALBERT BANDURA

LEV SEMENOVICH VYGOTSKY

JEAN PIAGET

PART TWO BEGINNINGS 22

2 Heredity and Conception 23

LO1: The Influence of Heredity on Development 23

Chromosomes and Genes 24
Mitosis and Meiosis 24
Identical and Fraternal Twins 26
Dominant and Recessive Traits 26

LO2: Chromosomal Abnormalities 27

Down Syndrome 28
Sex-Linked Chromosomal Abnormalities 28

LO3: Genetic Abnormalities 29

Phenylketonuria 29
Huntington's Disease 29
Sickle-Cell Anemia 29
Tay-Sachs Disease 29
Cystic Fibrosis 29
Sex-Linked Genetic Abnormalities 30

LO4: Genetic Counseling and Prenatal Testing 30

Amniocentesis and Chorionic Villus Sampling 30
Ultrasound 31
Blood Tests 32

LO5: Heredity and the Environment 32

Canalization 32
Genetic–Environmental Correlation 32
Kinship Studies 34
Twin Studies: Looking in the Genetic Mirror 34
Adoption Studies 34

LO6: Conception: Against All Odds 34

Ova 35
Sperm Cells 35

LO7: Infertility 36

Causes of Infertility 37
Methods Used to Help Infertile Couples Bear Children 37
Selecting the Sex of Your Child 38

3 Prenatal Development 41

LO1: The Germinal Stage: Wanderings 41

LO2: The Embryonic Stage 43

Sexual Differentiation 44
The Amniotic Sac 44
The Placenta 44

LO3: The Fetal Stage 45

Fetal Perception 45
Fetal Movements 46
Birth Rates Around the World 46

LO4: Environmental Influences on Prenatal Development 48

Nutrition 48
Teratogens and Health Problems of the Mother 48
Critical Periods of Vulnerability 48
Sexually Transmitted Infections 48
Rubella 49
Toxemia 50
RH Incompatibility 50
Drugs Taken By the Parents 51
Environmental Hazards 53
Effects of Parents' Age—Do Men Really Have All the Time in the World? 53

4 Birth and the Newborn Baby: In the New World 57

Countdown... 58

LO1: The Stages of Childbirth 58

LO2: Methods of Childbirth 61

Anesthesia 61
Prepared Childbirth 61
Doulas 62
Cesarean Section 62

LO3: Birth Problems 62

Oxygen Deprivation 62
Preterm and Low-Birth-Weight Infants 63

LO4: The Postpartum Period 66

Maternal Depression 66
Bonding 67

LO5: Characteristics of Neonates 67

Assessing the Health of Neonates 67
Reflexes 68

Sensory Capabilities 69
Learning: Really Early Childhood "Education" 72
Sleeping and Waking 73
Sudden Infant Death Syndrome (SIDS) 75

5 Infancy: Physical Development 79

LO1: Physical Growth and Development 79

Sequences of Physical Development 80
Growth Patterns in Height and Weight 80
Failure to Thrive 82
Nutrition: Fueling Development 82
Breast Feeding versus Bottle Feeding 83

LO2: Development of the Brain and Nervous System 84

Development of Neurons 84
Development of the Brain 85
Nature and Nurture in Brain Development 87

LO3: Motor Development 87

Lifting and Holding the Torso and Head 88
Control of the Hands: Getting a Grip 88
Locomotion 89

LO4: Sensory and Perceptual Development 90

Development of Vision 90
Development of Hearing 93
Development of Coordination of the Senses 94
The Active–Passive Controversy in Perceptual Development 94
Nature and Nurture in Perceptual Development 95

6 Infancy: Cognitive Development 97

LO1: Cognitive Development: Jean Piaget 97

The Sensorimotor Stage 98
Development of Object Permanence 100
Evaluation of Piaget's Theory 101

LO2: Information Processing 101

Infants' Memory 102
Imitation: Infant See Infant Do? 102

LO3: Individual Differences in Intelligence among Infants 103

Testing Infants: Why and with What? 103
Instability of Intelligence Scores Attained in Infancy 104
Use of Visual Recognition Memory 105

LO4: Language Development in Infancy 105

Early Vocalizations 105
Development of Vocabulary 107
Development of Sentences 108
Theories of Language Development 109
Views that Emphasize Nurture 109
Views that Emphasize Nature 110

7 Infancy: Social and Emotional Development 115

LO1: Attachment: Bonds That Endure 115

Patterns of Attachment 116
Establishing Attachment 117
Stability of Attachment 117
Stages of Attachment 117
Theories of Attachment 118

LO2: When Attachment Fails 120

Social Deprivation 120
Child Abuse and Neglect 121
Autism Spectrum Disorders 122

LO3: Day Care 124

LO4: Emotional Development 125

*Emotional Development and Patterns of
    Attachment 126*
Fear of Strangers 126
Social Referencing: What Should I Do Now? 126
Emotional Regulation: Keeping on an Even Keel 127

LO5: Personality Development 127

The Self-Concept 127
Temperament: Easy, Difficult, or Slow to Warm Up? 128
Sex Differences 130

8 Early Childhood: Physical Development 133

LO1: Growth Patterns 133

Height and Weight 133
Development of the Brain 134

LO2: Motor Development 136

Gross Motor Skills 136
Physical Activity 136
Fine Motor Skills 137
Children's Drawings 137
Handedness 138

LO3: Nutrition 140

LO4: Health and Illness 140

Minor Illnesses 140
Major Illnesses 140
Accidents 141

LO5: Sleep 141

Sleep Disorders 142

LO6: Elimination Disorders 143

Enuresis 143
Encopresis 144

Early Childhood: Cognitive Development 147

LO1: Jean Piaget's Preoperational Stage 148

Symbolic Thought 148
Symbolic or Pretend Play 148
Egocentrism: It's All About Me 149
Causality: Why? Because. 149
Confusion of Mental and Physical Events 150
Focus on One Dimension at a Time 151

LO2: Factors in Cognitive Development 152

Scaffolding and the Zone of Proximal Development 152
The Home Environment 153
Effects of Early Childhood Education 153
Television 154

LO3: Theory of Mind 154

False Beliefs: Where Are Those Crayons? 155
Origins of Knowledge 155
The Appearance–Reality Distinction 155

LO4: Development of Memory 156

Factors Influencing Memory 156
Memory Strategies: Remembering to Remember 157

LO5: Language Development: Why "Daddy Goed Away" 158

Development of Vocabulary 158
Development of Grammar 159
Pragmatics 160
Language and Cognition 160

10 Early Childhood: Social and Emotional Development 163

LO1: Dimensions of Child Rearing 163

How Parents Enforce Restrictions 164
Parenting Styles: How Parents Transmit Values and Standards 165
Effects of the Situation and the Child on Parenting Styles 166

LO2: Social Behaviors 166

Influence of Siblings 166
Birth Order 167
Peer Relationships 167
Play—Child's Play, That Is 168
Prosocial Behavior 170
Development of Aggression 171
Theories of Aggression 171

LO3: Personality and Emotional Development 174

The Self 174
Initiative versus Guilt 174
Fears: The Horrors of Early Childhood 174

LO4: Development of Gender Roles and Sex Differences 175

Sex Differences 176
Theories of the Development of Sex Differences 176
Psychological Androgyny 178

PART FIVE MIDDLE CHILDHOOD 180

11 Middle Childhood: Physical Development 181

LO1: Growth Patterns 181

Nutrition and Growth 182
Sex Similarities and Differences in Physical Growth 183

LO2: Overweight in Children 183

Causes of Overweight 184

LO3: Motor Development 186

Gross Motor Skills 186
Fine Motor Skills 187
Sex Similarities and Differences in Motor Development 187
Exercise and Fitness 188

Children with Disorders 188

LO4: Attention-Deficit/Hyperactivity Disorder (ADHD) 189

Causes of ADHD 191
Treatment and Outcome 191

LO5: Learning Disorders 192

Origins of Dyslexia 192
Educating Children with Disorders 193

12 Middle Childhood: Cognitive Development 195

LO1: Piaget: The Concrete-Operational Stage 195

Conservation 196
Transitivity 196
Class Inclusion 197
Applications of Piaget's Theory to Education 197

LO2: Moral Development: The Child as Judge 198

Piaget's Theory of Moral Development 198
Kohlberg's Theory of Moral Development 199

LO3: Information Processing 201

Development of Selective Attention 201
Developments in the Storage and Retrieval of Information 201
Development of Recall Memory 204
Development of Metacognition and Metamemory 204

LO4: Intellectual Development, Creativity, and Achievement 205

Theories of Intelligence 205
Measurement of Intellectual Development 206
Patterns of Intellectual Development 210
Differences in Intellectual Development 211
Creativity and Intellectual Development 213
Determinants of Intellectual Development 214

LO5: Language Development and Literacy 215

Vocabulary and Grammar 215
Reading Skills and Literacy 215
Methods of Teaching Reading 216
Bilingualism: Linguistic Perspectives on the World 216

13 Middle Childhood: Social and Emotional Development 219

LO1: Theories of Social and Emotional Development in Middle Childhood 219

Psychoanalytic Theory 219
Social Cognitive Theory 220
Cognitive-Developmental Theory and Social Cognition 220
Development of the Self-Concept in Middle Childhood 220

LO2: The Family 222

Parent–Child Relationships 223
Lesbian and Gay Parents 223
Generation X or Generation Ex? What Happens to Children Whose Parents Get Divorced? 223
The Effects of Maternal Employment 224

LO3: Peer Relationships 225

Peers as Socialization Influences 225
Peer Acceptance and Rejection 225
Development of Friendships 225

LO4: The School 226

Entry into School 226
The School Environment: Setting the Stage for Success or... 227
Teachers 227

LO5: Social and Emotional Problems 229

Conduct Disorders 229
Childhood Depression 230
Childhood Anxiety 231

PART SIX ADOLESCENCE 234

14 Adolescence: Physical Development 235

LO1: Puberty: The Biological Eruption 236

The Adolescent Growth Spurt 237
Pubertal Changes in Boys 239
Pubertal Changes in Girls 240
Early versus Late Maturers 241

LO2: Emerging Sexuality and the Risks of Sexually Transmitted Infections 242

HIV/AIDS 243
Risk Factors 244
Prevention of STIs 244

LO3: Health in Adolescence 244

Risk Taking in Adolescence 246
Nutrition: An Abundance of Food 246
An Abundance of Eating Disorders 247

LO4: Substance Abuse and Dependence 250

Depressants 251
Stimulants 252
Hallucinogenics 252
Prevalence of Substance Abuse 253
Students' Attitudes toward Drugs 254
Factors in Substance Abuse and Dependence 254
Treatment and Prevention 255

15 Adolescence: Cognitive Development 257

LO1: The Adolescent in Thought: My, My, How "Formal" 258

Piaget's Stage of Formal Operations 258
Adolescent Egocentrism: Center Stage 260
Sex Differences in Cognitive Abilities 261

LO2: The Adolescent in Judgment: Moral Development 263

The Postconventional Level 264
Moral Behavior and Moral Reasoning 265
Cross-Cultural Differences in Moral Development 266
Sex Differences in Moral Development 268

LO3: The Adolescent in School 267

Making the Transition from Elementary School 267
Dropping Out 268

LO4: The Adolescent at Work: Career Development and Work Experience 270

Career Development 274
Adolescents in the Workforce 271

16 Adolescence: Social and Emotional Development 275

LO1: Development of Identity: "Who Am I?" 276

Erikson and Identity Development 276
Identity Statuses 276
Ethnicity and Development of Identity 277
Sex and Development of Identity 278
Development of the Self-Concept 278
Self-Esteem 279

LO2: Relationships with Parents and Peers 279

Relationships with Parents 279
Relationships with Peers 280

LO3: Sexuality 282

Sexual Identity 283
Masturbation 283
Male–Female Sexual Behavior 283
Teenage Pregnancy 285

LO4: Juvenile Delinquency 287

Ethnicity, Sex, and Juvenile Delinquency 287
Who Are the Delinquents? 288

LO5: Suicide: When the Adolescent Has Nothing— Except Everything—to Lose 288

Risk Factors in Suicide 289
Ethnicity, Sex, and Suicide 289

LO6: Epilogue: Emerging Adulthood—Bridging Adolescence and the Life Beyond 290

References 293

Name Index 321

Subject Index 329

This book has a story to tell.

An important story. A remarkable story. It is your story.

1

History, Theories, and Methods of Child Development

TRUTH OR FICTION?

T F   During the Middle Ages, children were often treated as miniature adults.

T F   Nail biting and smoking cigarettes are signs of conflict experienced during early childhood.

T F   Research with monkeys has helped scientists understand the formation of attachment in humans.

T F   To learn how a person develops over a lifetime, researchers have tracked some individuals for more than 50 years.

This book has a story to tell. An important story. A remarkable story. It is your story. It is about the remarkable journey you have already taken through childhood. It is about the unfolding of your adult life. Billions of people have made this journey before. You have much in common with them. Yet you are unique, and things will happen to you, and because of you, that have never happened before.

LO1 The Development of the Study of Child Development

Scientific inquiry into human development has proceeded for little more than a century. In ancient times and in the Middle Ages, children often were viewed as innately evil and discipline was harsh. Legally, medieval children were treated as property and servants. They could be sent to a monastery, married without consultation, or convicted of crimes. Children were nurtured until they were 7 years old, which was considered the "age of reason." Then they were expected to work alongside adults in the home and in the field.

Learning Outcomes

LO1 Outline the development of the field of child development.

LO2 Outline and evaluate the various theories of child development.

LO3 Discuss controversies in child development.

LO4 Describe ways in which researchers study child development, including the strengths and weaknesses of each.

T F   During the Middle Ages, children were often treated as miniature adults.
True; they were disciplined harshly and, once they reached the age of 7, were expected to work alongside adults.

The transition to modern thinking about children is marked by the writings of philosophers such as John Locke and Jean-Jacques Rousseau. Englishman John Locke (1632–1704) believed that the child came into the world as a *tabula rasa*—a "blank tablet," or clean slate—that was written on by experience. Locke did not believe that inborn predispositions toward good or evil played an important role in the conduct of the child. Instead, he focused on the role of the environment or of experience. Locke believed that social approval and disapproval are powerful shapers of behavior. But Jean-Jacques Rousseau (1712–1778), a Swiss–French philosopher, argued that children are inherently good and that, if allowed to express their natural impulses, they will develop into generous and moral individuals.

During the Industrial Revolution, family life came to be defined in terms of the nuclear unit of mother, father, and children rather than the extended family. Children became more visible, fostering awareness of childhood as a special time of life. Still, children often labored in factories from dawn to dusk up until the early years of the 20th century.

In the 20th century, laws were passed to protect children from strenuous labor, to require that they attend school until a certain age, and to prevent them from getting married or being sexually exploited. Whereas children were once considered the property of parents to do with as they wished, laws now protect children from abuse by parents and other adults. Juvenile courts see that children who break the law receive appropriate treatment in the criminal justice system.

PIONEERS IN THE STUDY OF CHILD DEVELOPMENT

Various thoughts about child development coalesced into a field of scientific study in the 19th and early 20th centuries. Charles Darwin (1809–1882) is perhaps best known as the originator of the theory of evolution, but he was also one of the first observers to keep a *baby biography* in which he detailed his infant son's behavior. G. Stanley Hall (1844–1924) is credited with founding child development as an academic discipline. He adapted the questionnaire method for use with large groups of children, and it was Hall who labeled adolescence a time of "storm and stress"—which it may not be. The Frenchman Alfred Binet (1857–1911), along with Theodore

Simon, developed the first standardized intelligence test near the beginning of the 20th century. Binet's purpose was to identify public school children who were at risk of falling behind their peers in academic achievement. By the start of the 20th century, child development had emerged as a scientific field of study. Soon major theories of the developing child had begun to emerge, proposed by theorists such as Arnold Gesell, Sigmund Freud, John B. Watson, and Jean Piaget.

LO2 Theories of Child Development

Give me a dozen healthy infants, well-formed, and my own specified world to bring them up in, and I'll guarantee to train them to become any type of specialist I might suggest—doctor, lawyer, merchant, chief, and, yes, even beggar and thief, regardless of their talents, penchants, tendencies, abilities, vocations, and the race of their ancestors.

—Watson, 1924, p. 82

john B. Watson (1878–1958), the founder of American **behaviorism**, viewed development in terms of learning theory. He generally agreed with Locke that children's ideas, preferences, and skills are shaped by experience. There has been a long-standing nature–nurture debate in the study of children. In his theoretical approach to understanding children, Watson came down on the side of nurture—the

importance of the physical and social environments—as found, for example, in parental training and approval.

Arnold Gesell (1880–1961) expressed the opposing idea that biological **maturation** was the main principle of development: "All things considered, the inevitability and surety of maturation are the most impressive characteristics of early development. It is the hereditary ballast which conserves and stabilizes growth of each individual infant" (Gesell, 1928, p. 378). Watson was talking about the behavior patterns that children develop, whereas Gesell was focusing mainly on physical aspects of growth and development.

Theories such as behavioral theory and maturational theory help developmentalists explain, predict, and influence the events they study. Let us consider theories that are popular among developmentalists today. They fall within broad perspectives on development.

THE PSYCHOANALYTIC PERSPECTIVE

A number of theories fall within the psychoanalytic perspective. Each owes its origin to Sigmund Freud (1856–1939) and views children—and adults—as caught in conflict. Early in development, the conflict is between the child and the world outside. The expression of basic drives, such as sex and aggression, conflicts with parental expectations, social rules, moral codes, even laws. But the external limits—parental demands and social rules—are brought inside or *internalized*. Once internalization occurs, the conflict takes place between opposing *inner* forces. The child's observable behavior, thoughts, and feelings reflect the outcomes of these hidden battles.

Let us consider Freud's theory of psychosexual development and Erik Erikson's theory of psychosocial development. Each is a **stage theory** that sees children as developing through distinct periods of life. Each suggests that the child's experiences during early stages affect the child's emotional and social life at the time and later on.

Sigmund Freud's Theory of Psychosexual Development

Sigmund Freud's theory of **psychosexual development** focused on emotional and social development and on the origins of psychological traits such

as dependence, obsessive neatness, and vanity. Freud theorized three parts of the personality: *id, ego,* and *superego*. The id is present at birth and is part of the *unconscious*. It represents biological drives and demands instant gratification, as suggested by a baby's wailing. The ego, or the conscious sense of self, begins to develop when children learn to obtain gratification consciously, without screaming or crying. The ego curbs the appetites of the id and makes plans that are in keeping with social conventions so that a person can find gratification but avoid social disapproval. The superego develops throughout infancy and early childhood. It brings inward the wishes and morals of the child's caregivers and other members of the community. Throughout the remainder of the child's life, the superego will monitor the intentions and behavior of the ego, hand down judgments of right and wrong, and attempt to influence behavior through flooding the person with feelings of guilt and shame when the judgment is negative.

According to Freud, there are five stages of psychosexual development: *oral, anal, phallic, latency,* and *genital*. If a child receives too little or too much gratification during a stage, the child can become *fixated* in that stage. For example, during the first year of life, which Freud termed the *oral stage*, oral activities such as sucking and biting bring pleasure and

maturation The unfolding of genetically determined traits, structures, and functions.

psychosexual development The process by which libidinal energy is expressed through different erogenous zones during different stages of development.

stage theory A theory of development that views changes as occurring in distinct periods of life.

CHECK LiST
Freudian Stages of Psychosexual Development
☐ Oral
☐ Anal
☐ Phallic
☐ Latency
☐ Genital

SIGMUND FREUD

gratification. If the child is weaned early or breast-fed too long, the child may become fixated on oral activities such as nail biting or smoking, or even show a "biting wit." (There is actually no research evidence to support this claim.)

T F Nail biting and smoking cigarettes are signs of conflict experienced during early childhood.
This is true according to psychoanalytic theory, but there is no empirical evidence for it. Therefore, we label it a fiction.

In the second stage or *anal stage,* gratification is obtained through control and elimination of waste products. Excessively strict or permissive toilet training can lead to the development of anal-retentive traits, such as perfectionism and neatness, or anal-expulsive traits, such as sloppiness and carelessness. In the third stage, the *phallic stage,* parent–child conflict may develop over masturbation, which many parents treat with punishment and threats. It is normal for children to develop strong sexual attachments to the parent of the other sex during the phallic stage and to begin to view the parent of the same sex as a rival.

By age 5 or 6, Freud believed, children enter a *latency stage* during which sexual feelings remain unconscious, children become involved with schoolwork, and they typically prefer playmates of their own sex. The final stage of psychosexual development, the *genital stage,* begins with the biological changes that usher in adolescence. Adolescents generally desire sexual gratification through intercourse with a member of the other sex. Freud believed that oral or anal stimulation, masturbation, and male–male or female–female sexual activity are immature forms of sexual conduct that reflect fixations at early stages of development.

Evaluation Freud's views about the anal stage have influenced child-care workers to recommend that toilet training not be started too early or handled punitively. His emphasis on the emotional needs of children has influenced educators to be more sensitive to the possible emotional reasons behind a child's misbehavior. Freud's work has also been criticized. For one thing, Freud developed his theory on the basis of contacts with adult patients (mostly women) (Schultz & Schultz, 2008), rather than direct observations of children. Freud may also have inadvertently guided patients into expressing ideas that confirmed his views.

Some of Freud's own disciples, including Erik Erikson, believed that Freud placed too much emphasis on basic instincts and unconscious motives. Erikson argued that people are motivated not only by drives such as sex and aggression but also by social relationships and conscious desires to achieve, to have aesthetic experiences, and to help others.

Erik Erikson's Theory of Psychosocial Development

Erik Erikson (1902–1994) modified Freud's theory and extended it through the adult years. Erikson's theory, like Freud's, focuses on the development of the emotional life and psychological traits, but emphasizes social relationships rather than sexual or aggressive instincts. Therefore, Erikson spoke of **psychosocial development** rather than of *psychosexual development.* Furthermore, he placed greater emphasis on the ego, or the sense of self.

Erikson (1963) extended Freud's five stages to eight to include the concerns of adulthood. Rather than label his stages after parts of the body, Erikson labeled them after the **life crises** that people might encounter during the stages.

Erikson proposed that social relationships and physical maturation give each stage its character. For example, the parent–child relationship and the infant's dependence and helplessness are responsible for the nature of the earliest stages of development.

Early experiences affect future development. With parental support, most children resolve early life crises productively. Successful resolution of each crisis bolsters their sense of identity—of who they are and what they stand for—and their expectation of future success.

ERIK ERIKSON AND HIS WIFE, JOAN ERIKSON

Erikson's views, like Freud's, have influenced child rearing, early childhood education, and child therapy. For example, Erikson's views about an adolescent **identity crisis** have entered the popular culture and have affected the way many parents and teachers deal with teenagers. Some schools help students master the crisis by means of life-adjustment courses and study units on self-understanding in social studies and literature classes.

Evaluation   Erikson's views are appealing in that they emphasize the importance of human consciousness and choice. They are also appealing in that they portray us as prosocial and helpful, whereas Freud portrayed us as selfish and needing to be compelled to comply with social rules. There is also some empirical support for the Eriksonian view that positive outcomes of early life crises help put us on the path to positive development (Hoegh & Bourgeois, 2002).

THE LEARNING PERSPECTIVE: BEHAVIORAL AND SOCIAL COGNITIVE THEORIES

During the 1930s, psychologists using the behavioral perspective derived an ingenious method for helping 5- and 6-year-old children overcome bed-wetting. Most children at this age wake up and go to the bathroom when their bladders are full. Bed wetters, though, sleep through bladder tension and reflexively urinate in bed. With this behavioral method, the psychologists placed a special pad beneath the sleeping child. Wetness in the pad closed an electrical circuit, causing a bell to ring and waking the sleeping child. After several repetitions, most children learned to wake up before they wet the pad. How? They learned through a process called *classical conditioning,* explained in this section.

The so-called bell-and-pad method for bed-wetting is an exotic example of the application of learning theory in human development. Most applications of learning theory to development are found in everyday events, however. In this section, we consider two theories of learning: behaviorism and social cognitive theory.

Behaviorism

John B. Watson argued that a scientific approach to development must focus on the observable behavior only and not on things like thoughts, fantasies, and other mental images.

Classical conditioning is a simple form of learning in which an originally neutral stimulus comes to bring forth, or elicit, the response usually brought forth by a second stimulus as a result of being paired repeatedly with the second stimulus. In the bell-and-pad method for bed-wetting, psychologists repeatedly pair tension in the children's bladders with a stimulus that awakens them (the bell). The children learn to respond to the bladder tension as if it were a bell; that is, they wake up (see Figure 1.1).

Behaviorists argue that much emotional learning is acquired through classical conditioning. In **operant conditioning** (a different kind of conditioning), children learn to do something because of its effects. B. F. Skinner (1904–1990) introduced the key concept of **reinforcement**. Reinforcers are stimuli that increase the frequency of the

identity crisis According to Erikson, a period of inner conflict during which one examines one's values and makes decisions about one's life roles.

classical conditioning A simple form of learning in which one stimulus comes to bring forth the response usually brought forth by a second stimulus by being paired repeatedly with the second stimulus.

operant conditioning A simple form of learning in which an organism learns to engage in behavior that is reinforced.

reinforcement The process of providing stimuli that follow responses and increase the frequency of those responses.

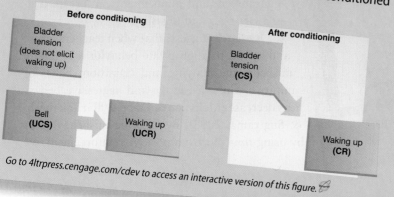

FIGURE 1.1
Schematic Representation of Classical Conditioning

Before conditioning, the bell elicits waking up. Bladder tension, a neutral stimulus, does not elicit waking up. During conditioning, bladder tension always precedes urination, which in turn causes the bell to ring. After conditioning, bladder tension becomes a conditioned stimulus that elicits waking up, which is the conditioned response (CR).

Before conditioning

Bladder tension (does not elicit waking up)

Bell (UCS) → Waking up (UCR)

After conditioning

Bladder tension (CS)

Waking up (CR)

Go to 4ltrpress.cengage.com/cdev to access an interactive version of this figure.

behavior they follow. Most children learn to adjust their behavior to conform to social codes and rules in order to earn reinforcers such as the attention and approval of their parents and teachers. Other children, ironically, may learn to misbehave because misbehavior also draws attention. Any stimulus that increases the frequency of the responses preceding it serves as a reinforcer. Skinner distinguished between positive and negative reinforcers. **Positive reinforcers** increase the frequency of behaviors when they are *applied*. Food and approval usually serve as positive reinforcers. **Negative reinforcers** increase the frequency of behaviors when they are *removed*. Fear acts as a negative reinforcer in that its removal increases the frequency of the

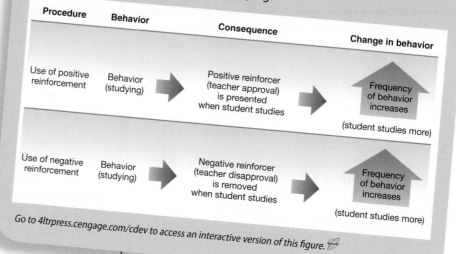

FIGURE 1.2
Positive versus Negative Reinforcers

All reinforcers *increase* the frequency of behavior. In these examples, teacher approval functions as a positive reinforcer when students study harder because of it. Teacher *disapproval* functions as a negative reinforcer when its removal increases the frequency of studying.

Procedure	Behavior	Consequence	Change in behavior
Use of positive reinforcement	Behavior (studying) →	Positive reinforcer (teacher approval) is presented when student studies →	Frequency of behavior increases (student studies more)
Use of negative reinforcement	Behavior (studying) →	Negative reinforcer (teacher disapproval) is removed when student studies →	Frequency of behavior increases (student studies more)

Go to 4ltrpress.cengage.com/cdev to access an interactive version of this figure.

JOHN B. WATSON

B. F. SKINNER

behaviors preceding it. Figure 1.2 compares positive and negative reinforcers.

Extinction results from repeated performance of operant behavior without reinforcement. After a number of trials, the operant behavior is no longer shown. Children's temper tantrums and crying at bedtime can often be extinguished by parents' remaining out of the bedroom after the children have been put to bed. Punishments are aversive events that suppress or *decrease* the frequency of the behavior they follow. (Figure 1.3 compares negative reinforcers with punishments.) Many learning theorists agree that punishment is undesirable in child rearing for several reasons: punishment does not in itself suggest an alternative acceptable form of behavior; punishment tends to suppress behavior only when its delivery is guaranteed; and punishment can create feelings of anger and hostility.

Research suggests that when teachers praise and attend to appropriate behavior and ignore misbehavior, studying and classroom behavior improve while disruptive and aggressive behaviors decrease (McIlvane & Dube, 2003; Takahashi & Sugiyama, 2003). By ignoring misbehavior or by using *time out* from positive reinforcement, we

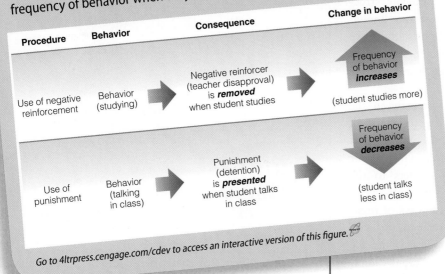

FIGURE 1.3
Negative Reinforcers versus Punishments

Both negative reinforcers and punishments tend to be aversive stimuli. Reinforcers, however, *increase* the frequency of behavior. Punishments *decrease* the frequency of behavior. Negative reinforcers increase the frequency of behavior when they are *removed*.

Procedure	Behavior	Consequence	Change in behavior
Use of negative reinforcement	Behavior (studying)	Negative reinforcer (teacher disapproval) is **removed** when student studies	Frequency of behavior *increases* (student studies more)
Use of punishment	Behavior (talking in class)	Punishment (detention) is **presented** when student talks in class	Frequency of behavior *decreases* (student talks less in class)

Go to 4ltrpress.cengage.com/cdev to access an interactive version of this figure.

can avoid reinforcing children for misbehavior. In using time out, children are placed in drab, restrictive environments for a specified time period such as 10 minutes when they behave disruptively.

Operant conditioning is used every day in the *socialization* of young children. Parents and peers influence children to acquire gender-appropriate behaviors through the elaborate use of rewards and punishments. Thus, boys may ignore other boys when they play with dolls and housekeeping toys but play with them when they use transportation toys.

Social Cognitive Theory

Behaviorists tend to limit their view of learning to conditioning. **Social cognitive theorists** such as Albert Bandura (1925–) (1986, 2006a, 2006b) have shown that much learning also occurs by observing other people, reading, and viewing characters in the media. People may need practice to refine their skills, but they can acquire the basic know-how through observation.

Observational learning occurs when children observe how parents cook, clean, or repair a broken appliance. It takes place when adults watch supervisors sketch out sales strategies on a blackboard or hear them speak a foreign language. In social cognitive theory, the

people after whom we pattern our own behavior are termed *models*.

Evaluation of Learning Theories

Learning theories allow us to explain, predict, and influence many aspects of behavior. The use of the bell-and-pad method for bed-wetting would probably not have been derived from any other theoretical approach. Many of the teaching approaches used in educational TV shows are based on learning theory.

THE COGNITIVE PERSPECTIVE

Cognitive theorists focus on people's mental processes. They investigate the ways in which children perceive and mentally represent the world, how they develop thinking, logic, and problem-solving ability. One cognitive perspective is **cognitive-developmental theory**, advanced by Swiss biologist Jean Piaget (1896–1980) and further developed by many theorists. Another is information-processing theory.

Cognitive-Developmental Theory

During adolescence, Jean Piaget studied philosophy, logic, and mathematics, but years later he took his Ph.D. in biology. In 1920, he obtained a job at the Binet Institute in Paris, where research on intelligence tests was being conducted. Through his studies, Piaget realized that when children answered questions incorrectly, their wrong answers still often reflected consistent—although illogical—mental processes. Piaget regarded children as natural physicists who actively intend to learn about and take intellectual charge of their worlds. In the Piagetian view, children who squish their food and laugh enthusiastically are often acting as budding scientists. They are studying both the texture and consistency of their food, as well as their parents' response.

Piaget used concepts such as *schemes, adaptation, assimilation, accommodation,* and *equilibration* to describe and explain cognitive development. Piaget defines the **scheme** as a pattern of action or mental structure that is involved in acquiring or organizing knowledge. For example, newborn babies might be said to have a sucking scheme (others call this a *reflex*), responding to things put in their mouths as "things I can suck on" versus "things I can't suck on."

Adaptation refers to the interaction between the organism and the environment. According to Piaget, all organisms adapt to their environment. Adaptation consists of assimilation and accommodation, which occur throughout life. Cognitive **assimilation** refers to the process by which someone responds to new objects or events according to existing schemes, or ways of organizing knowledge. Two-year-olds who refer to horses as "doggies" can be said to be assimilating horses into the dog scheme. Sometimes a novel object or event cannot be made to fit into an existing scheme. In that case, the scheme may be changed or a new scheme may be created to incorporate the new event. This process is called **accommodation**. Consider the sucking reflex. Infants accommodate by rejecting objects that are too large, that taste bad, or that are of the wrong texture or temperature.

A SUCKING SCHEME

Things I can't suck on . . .

Things I can suck on . . .

Piaget theorized that when children can assimilate new events to existing schemes, they are in a state of cognitive harmony, or equilibrium. When something that does not fit happens along, their state of equilibrium is disturbed and they may try to accommodate. The process of restoring equilibrium is termed **equilibration**. Piaget believed that the attempt to restore equilibrium lies at the heart of the natural curiosity of the child.

scheme An action pattern or mental structure that is involved in the acquisition and organization of knowledge.

adaptation The interaction between the organism and the environment, consisting of assimilation and accommodation.

assimilation The incorporation of new events or knowledge into existing schemes.

accommodation The modification of existing schemes to permit the incorporation of new events or knowledge.

equilibration The making of an equilibrium, or balance, between assimilation and accommodation.

ALBERT BANDURA

JEAN PIAGET

Piaget's Stages of Cognitive Development

Piaget (1936/1963) hypothesized that children's cognitive processes develop in an orderly sequence, or series, of stages. Piaget identified four major stages of cognitive development: *sensorimotor, preoperational, concrete operational,* and *formal operational.*

Because Piaget's theory focuses on cognitive development, its applications are primarily in educational settings. Teachers following Piaget's views actively engage the child in solving problems. They gear instruction to the child's developmental level and offer activities that challenge the child to advance to the next level.

Piaget's theory ends with formal operational thought. Lifespan theorists such as William Perry note that college students' views on what they know and how they get to know what they know become more complex as they are exposed to the complexities of college thought. Gisela Labouvie-Vief notes that the "cognitively healthy" adult is more willing than the egocentric adolescent to compromise and cope within the world as it is, not the world as she or he would like it to be.

Evaluation Many researchers, using a variety of methods, find that Piaget may have underestimated the ages when children are capable of doing certain things. It also appears that many cognitive skills may develop gradually and not in distinct stages. Nevertheless, Piaget provided a strong theoretical foundation for researchers concerned with sequences in cognitive development.

Information-Processing Theory

Another face of the cognitive perspective is information processing (Flavell et al., 2002; Siegler & Alibali, 2005). Many psychologists speak of people as having working or short-term memory and a more permanent long-term memory (storage). If information has been placed in long-term memory, it must be retrieved before we can work on it. Retrieving information from our own long-term memories requires certain cues, without which the information may be lost.

Thus, many cognitive psychologists focus on information processing in people—the processes by which people encode (input) information, store it (in long-term memory), retrieve it (place it in short-term memory), and manipulate it to solve problems. Our strategies for solving problems are sometimes referred to as our "mental programs" or "software." In this computer metaphor, our brains are the "hardware" that runs our mental programs. Our brains—containing billions of brain cells called *neurons*—become our most "personal" computers. When psychologists who study information processing contemplate cognitive development, they are likely to talk in terms of the *size* of the person's short-term memory and the *number of programs* she or he can run simultaneously.

The most obvious applications of information processing occur in teaching. For example, information-processing models alert teachers to the sequence of steps by which children acquire information, commit it to memory, and retrieve it to solve problems. By understanding this sequence, teachers can provide experiences that give students practice with each stage.

We now see that the brain is a sort of biological computer. Let us next see what other aspects of biology can be connected with development.

THE BIOLOGICAL PERSPECTIVE

The biological perspective directly relates to physical development: gains in height and weight; development of the brain; and developments connected with hormones, reproduction, and heredity. Here we consider one biologically oriented theory of development, *ethology.*

Ethology: "Doing What Comes Naturally"

Ethology was heavily influenced by the 19th-century work of Charles Darwin and by the 20th-century work of ethologists Konrad Lorenz and Niko Tinbergen (Washburn, 2007). Ethology is concerned with instinctive, or inborn, behavior patterns.

The nervous systems of most, and perhaps all, animals are "prewired" to respond to some situations in specific ways. For example, birds raised in isolation from other birds build nests during the mating season even if they have never seen a nest or seen another bird building one. Nest-building could not have been learned. Birds raised in isolation also sing the songs typical of their species. These behaviors are "built in," or instinctive. They are also referred to as **fixed action patterns (FAPs).**

During prenatal development, genes and sex hormones are responsible for the physical development

ethology The study of instinctive, or inborn, behavior patterns.

fixed action pattern (FAP) A stereotyped pattern of behavior that is evoked by an instinct.

ecology The branch of biology that deals with the relationships between living organisms and their environment.

ecological systems theory The view that explains child development in terms of the reciprocal influences between children and environmental settings.

microsystem The immediate settings with which the child interacts, such as the home, the school, and peers.

mesosystem The interlocking settings that influence the child, such as the interaction of the school and the larger community.

exosystem Community institutions and settings that indirectly influence the child, such as the school board and the parents' workplaces.

macrosystem The basic institutions and ideologies that influence the child.

chronosystem The environmental changes that occur over time and have an effect on the child.

of female and male sex organs. Most theorists also believe that in many species, including humans, sex hormones can "masculinize" or "feminize" the embryonic brain by creating tendencies to behave in stereotypical masculine or feminine ways. Testosterone, the male sex hormone, seems to be connected with feelings of self-confidence, high activity levels, and—the negative side—aggressiveness (Archer, 2006; Davis et al., 2005; Geary, 2006).

Evaluation Research into the ethological perspective suggests that instinct may play a role in human behavior. Two questions that research seeks to answer are these: What areas of human behavior and development, if any, involve instincts? How powerful are instincts in people?

THE ECOLOGICAL PERSPECTIVE

Ecology is the branch of biology that deals with the relationships between living organisms and their environment. The **ecological systems theory** of development addresses aspects of psychological, social, and emotional development as well as aspects of biological development. Ecological systems theorists explain development in terms of the interaction between people and the settings in which they live (Bronfenbrenner & Morris, 2006).

According to Urie Bronfenbrenner (1917–2005), for example, we need to focus on the two-way interactions between the child and the parents, not just maturational forces (nature) or child-rearing practices (nurture). Bronfenbrenner (Bronfenbrenner & Morris, 2006) suggested that we can view the settings, or contexts, of human development as consisting of multiple

systems, each embedded within the next larger context. From narrowest to widest, these systems are the microsystem, the mesosystem, the exosystem, the macrosystem, and the chronosystem (Figure 1.4).

The **microsystem** involves the immediate setting in which the child and other people interact, such as the home, the school, or the peer group. Initially, the microsystem is small, involving care-giving interactions with the parents or others, usually at home. As children get older, they do more, with more people, in more places.

The **mesosystem** involves the interactions of the various settings within the microsystem. For instance, the home and the school interact during parent–teacher conferences. The school and the larger community interact when children are taken on field trips. The ecological systems approach addresses the joint effect of two or more settings on the child.

The **exosystem** involves the institutions in which the child does not directly participate but which exert an indirect influence on the child. For example, the school board is part of the child's exosystem because board members put together programs for the child's education, determine what textbooks will be acceptable, and so forth. In similar fashion, the parents' workplaces and economic situations determine the hours during which they will be available to the child, and so on (Kaminski & Stormshak, 2007). Thus, elements of the exosystem affect children's behavior at home and school.

The **macrosystem** involves the interaction of children with the beliefs, values, expectations, and lifestyles of their cultural settings. Cross-cultural studies examine children's interactions with their macrosystem. Macrosystems exist within a particular culture. In the United States, the dual-earner family, the low-income single-parent household, and the family with father as sole breadwinner describe three different macrosystems. Each has its lifestyle, set of values, and expectations (Bronfenbrenner & Morris, 2006; Silbereisen, 2006).

The **chronosystem** considers the changes that occur over time. For example, the effects of divorce peak about a year after the event, and then children begin to recover. The breakup has more of an effect on boys than on girls. The ecological systems approach broadens the strategies for intervention in problems such as teenage pregnancy, child abuse, and juvenile offenses, including substance abuse (Kaminski & Stormshak, 2007).

THE SOCIOCULTURAL PERSPECTIVE

The sociocultural perspective teaches that people are social beings who are affected by the cultures in which

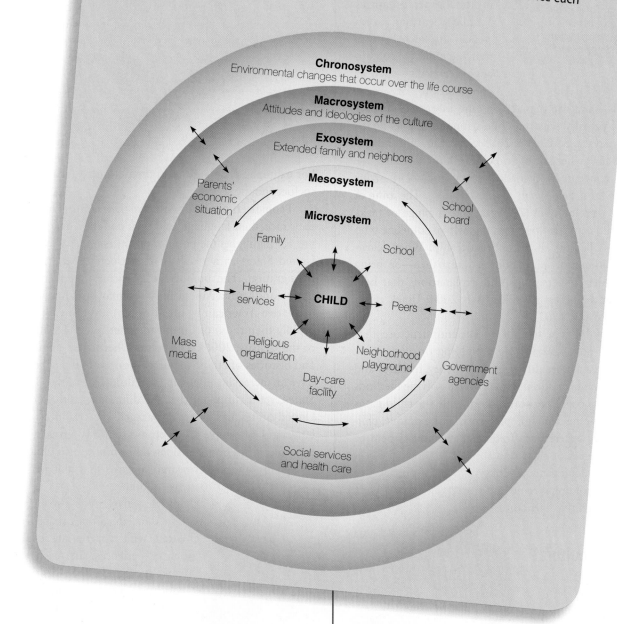

FIGURE 1.4
The Contexts of Human Development

According to ecological systems theory, the systems within which children develop are embedded within larger systems. Children and these systems reciprocally influence each other.

Chronosystem
Environmental changes that occur over the life course

Macrosystem
Attitudes and ideologies of the culture

Exosystem
Extended family and neighbors

Mesosystem

Microsystem

Parents' economic situation

School board

Family

School

CHILD

Health services

Peers

Mass media

Religious organization

Neighborhood playground

Government agencies

Day-care facility

Social services and health care

they live. Developmentalists use the term *sociocultural* in a couple of different ways. One refers quite specifically to the *sociocultural theory* of Russian psychologist Lev Semenovich Vygotsky (1896–1934). The other addresses the effect of human diversity on people, including such factors as ethnicity and gender.

Vygotsky's Sociocultural Theory

Whereas the field of genetics focuses on the biological transmission of traits from generation to generation, Vygotsky's (1978) theory is concerned with the transmission of information and cognitive skills from generation to generation. The transmission of skills involves

zone of proximal development (ZPD) Vygotsky's term for the range of tasks a child can carry out with the help of someone who is more skilled.

scaffolding Vygotsky's term for temporary cognitive structures or methods of solving problems that help the child as he or she learns to function independently.

teaching and learning, but Vygotsky does not view learning in terms of conditioning. Rather, he focuses on how the child's social interaction with adults, largely in the home, organizes a child's learning experiences in such a way that the child can obtain cognitive skills—such as computation or reading skills—and use them to acquire information. Like Piaget, Vygotsky sees the child's functioning as adaptive (Kanevsky & Geake, 2004), and the child adapts through his or her social and cultural interactions.

Key concepts in Vygotsky's theory include the *zone of proximal development* and *scaffolding*. The **zone of proximal development (ZPD)** refers to a range of tasks that a child can carry out with the help of someone who is more skilled, as in an apprenticeship. When learning with other people, children internalize—or bring inward—the conversations and explanations that help them gain the necessary skills (Ash, 2004; Umek et al., 2005; Vygotsky, 1962).

A *scaffold* is a temporary skeletal structure that enables workers to fabricate a building or other more permanent structure. In Vygotsky's theory, teachers and parents provide children with problem-solving methods that serve as cognitive **scaffolding** while the child gains the ability to function independently. For example, children may be offered scaffolding that enables them to use their fingers or their toes to do simple calculations. Eventually, the scaffolding is removed and the cognitive structures stand alone.

The Sociocultural Perspective and Human Diversity

The sociocultural perspective asserts that we cannot understand individuals without awareness of the richness of their diversity (Fouad & Arredondo, 2007).

LEV SEMENOVICH VYGOTSKY

Archives of the History of American Psychology – The University of Akron / © U.P. Images/iStockphoto.com / © graham klotz/iStockphoto.com

For example, people differ in their ethnicity, gender, and socioeconomic status.

People's ethnic groups involve their cultural heritage, their race, their language, and their common history. Figure 1.5 highlights the population shifts under way in the United States as a result of reproductive patterns and immigration. The numbers of African Americans and Latino and Latina Americans (who may be White, Black, or Native American in racial origin) are growing more rapidly than those of European Americans (U.S. Bureau of the Census, 2006). The cultural heritages, languages, and histories of ethnic minority groups are thus likely to have an increasing effect on the cultural life of the United States, yet it turns out that the dominant culture in the United States has often disparaged the traditions and languages of people from ethnic minority groups. For example, it has been considered harmful to rear children bilingually, although research suggests that bilingualism broadens children.

Studying diversity is also important so that educators can provide children with appropriate educational experiences. To teach students and guide their learning, educators need to understand children's family values and cultural expectations. Issues that affect people from various ethnic groups include bilingualism, ethnic differences in intelligence test scores, the prevalence of suicide

© Jani Bryson/iStockphoto.com

FIGURE 1.5

Numbers of Various Racial and Ethnic Groups in the United States, Today versus Year 2050 (in millions)

The numbers of each of the various racial and ethnic groups in the United States will grow in this half-century, with the numbers of Latino and Latina Americans and Asian Americans and Pacific Islanders growing most rapidly.

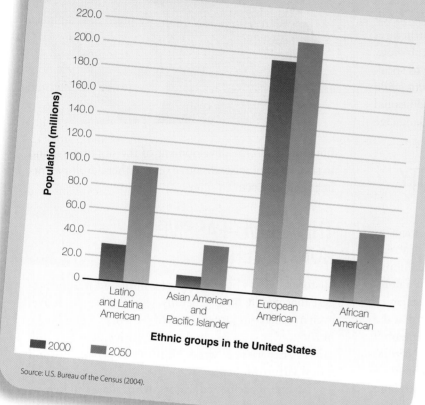

Source: U.S. Bureau of the Census (2004).

inroads into academic and vocational spheres—such as medicine, law, engineering, and the military—that were traditionally male preserves. Today, most college students in the United States are female, but it is worth noting that girls were not considered qualified for education until relatively recent times. Even today, there remain many parts of the world in which women are prevented from obtaining an education.

LO3 Controversies in Child Development

the discussion of theories of development reveals that developmentalists can see things in very different ways. Let us consider how they react to three of the most important debates in the field.

THE NATURE–NURTURE CONTROVERSY

Researchers are continually trying to sort out the extent to which human behavior is the result of **nature** (heredity) and of **nurture** (environmental influences). What aspects of behavior originate in our genes and are biologically programmed to unfold as time goes on, as long as minimal nutrition and social experience are provided? What aspects of behavior can be traced largely to such environmental influences as nutrition and learning?

Scientists seek the natural causes of development in children's genetic heritage, in the functioning of the nervous system, and in maturation. Scientists seek the

among members of different backgrounds, and patterns of child rearing among parents of various groups.

Gender is another aspect of human diversity. *Gender* is the psychological state of being male or being female, as influenced by cultural concepts of gender-appropriate behavior. Expectations of females and males are often polarized by cultural expectations. That is, gender differences may be exaggerated, as in the case of intellectual abilities. Males may differ from females in some respects, but history has created more burdens for women than men as a result. Historically, females have been discouraged from careers in the sciences, politics, and business. Women today are making

environmental causes of development in children's nutrition, cultural and family backgrounds, and opportunities to learn about the world, including cognitive stimulation during early childhood and formal education.

Some theorists (e.g., cognitive-developmental and biological theorists) lean heavily toward natural explanations of development, whereas others (e.g., learning theorists) lean more heavily toward environmental explanations. Today, though, nearly all researchers agree that nature and nurture play important roles in nearly every area of development. Consider the development of language. Language is based in structures found in certain areas of the brain. Thus, biology (nature) plays a vital role. Children also come to speak the languages spoken by their caretakers. Parent–child similarities in accent and vocabulary provide additional evidence for the role of learning (nurture) in language development.

THE CONTINUITY–DISCONTINUITY CONTROVERSY

Some developmentalists view human development as a continuous process in which the effects of learning mount gradually, with no major sudden qualitative changes. In contrast, other theorists believe that a number of rapid qualitative changes usher in new stages of development. Maturational theorists point out that the environment, even when enriched, profits us little until we are ready, or mature enough, to develop in a certain way. For example, newborn babies will not imitate their parents' speech, even when parents speak clearly and deliberately. Nor does aided practice in "walking" during the first few months after birth significantly accelerate the emergence of independent walking. Babies are not ready to do these things.

Stage theorists such as Sigmund Freud and Jean Piaget saw development as discontinuous. They saw biological changes as providing the potential for psychological changes. Freud focused on the ways in which biological developments might provide the basis for personality development. Piaget believed maturation of the nervous system allowed cognitive development.

Certain aspects of physical development do occur in stages. For example, from the age of 2 years to the onset of puberty, children gradually grow larger. Then the adolescent growth spurt occurs as rushes of hormones cause rapid biological changes in structure and

Girls usually spurt in growth before boys do. These dancers are the same age.

© Mark Richards/PhotoEdit, Inc.

function (as in the development of the sex organs) and in size. Psychologists disagree on whether developments in cognition occur in stages.

THE ACTIVE–PASSIVE CONTROVERSY

Historical views of children as willful and unruly suggest that people have generally seen children as active, even mischievous (at best) or evil (at worst). John Locke introduced a view of children as passive beings (blank tablets); experience "wrote" features of personality and moral virtue on them.

At one extreme, educators who view children as passive may assume that they must be motivated to learn by their instructors. Such educators are likely to provide a rigorous traditional curriculum with a powerful system of rewards and punishments to promote absorption of the subject matter. At the other extreme, educators who view children as active may assume that they have a natural love of learning. Such educators are likely to argue for open education and encourage children to explore and pursue their unique likes and talents.

These debates are theoretical. Scientists value theory for its ability to tie together observations and suggest new areas of investigation, but they also follow an **empirical** approach. That is, they engage in research methods, such as those described in the next section, to find evidence for or against various theoretical positions.

LO4 How We Study Child Development

What is the relationship between intelligence and achievement? What are the effects of maternal use of aspirin and alcohol on the fetus? What are the effects of parental divorce on children? What are the effects of early retirement? We all may have expressed opinions on such questions at one time or another, but scientists insist that such questions be answered by research. Strong arguments or reference to authority figures are not evidence. Scientific evidence is obtained only by gathering sound information and conducting research.

GATHERING INFORMATION

Researchers use various methods to gather information about child development. For example, they may ask teachers or parents to report on the behavior of children, use interviews or questionnaires with adults, or study statistics compiled by the government or the United Nations. They also directly observe children in the laboratory, the playground, or the classroom. Let us discuss two ways of gathering information: the naturalistic-observation method and the case-study method.

Natural observation studies are conducted in natural settings where real-life behaviors happen.

Naturalistic Observation

Studies using **naturalistic-observation** are conducted in "the field," that is, in the natural, or real-life, settings in which behaviors occur. In field studies, investigators observe the natural behavior of children in settings such as homes, playgrounds, and classrooms and try not to interfere with it. Researchers may try to "blend into the woodwork" by sitting quietly in the back of a classroom or by observing the class through a one-way mirror.

Naturalistic-observation studies have been done with children of different cultures. For example, researchers have observed the motor behavior of Native American Hopi children who are strapped to cradle boards during their first year. You can read more about this in Chapter 5.

The Case Study

The **case study** is a carefully drawn account of the behavior of an individual. Parents who keep diaries of their children's activities are involved in informal case studies. Case studies themselves often use a number of different kinds of information. In addition to direct observations, case studies may include information from questionnaires, **standardized tests**, and interviews. Information gleaned from public records may be included. Scientists who use the case-study method try to record all relevant factors in a person's behavior, and they are cautious in drawing conclusions about what leads to what.

CORRELATION: PUTTING THINGS TOGETHER

Researchers use the correlational method to determine whether one behavior or trait being studied is related to, or correlated with, another. Consider intelligence and achievement. These variables are assigned numbers such as intelligence test scores and grade point averages. Then the numbers or scores are mathematically related and expressed as a **correlation coefficient**—a number that

naturalistic observation A method of scientific observation in which children (and others) are observed in their natural environments.

case study A carefully drawn account of the behavior of an individual.

standardized test A test of abilities in which an individual's score is compared to the scores of a group of similar individuals.

correlation coefficient A number ranging from +1.00 to −1.00 that expresses the direction (positive or negative) and strength of the relationship between two variables.

positive correlation
A relationship between two variables in which one variable increases as the other increases.

negative correlation
A relationship between two variables in which one variable increases as the other decreases.

experiment A method of scientific investigation that seeks to discover cause-and-effect relationships by introducing independent variables and observing their effects on dependent variables.

hypothesis A proposition to be tested.

varies between +1.00 and −1.00.

In general, the higher people score on intelligence tests, the better their academic performance (or income) is likely to be. The scores attained on intelligence tests are **positively correlated** (about +0.60 to +0.70) with overall academic achievement (and income).

There is a **negative correlation** between adolescents' grades and delinquent acts. The higher an adolescents'

grades, the less likely he or she is to engage in criminal behavior. Figure 1.6 illustrates positive and negative correlations.

Limitations of Correlational Information

Correlational information can reveal relationships between variables, but it does not show cause and effect. It may seem logical to assume that exposure to violent media makes people more aggressive, but it may also be that more aggressive people *choose* violent media. This research bias is termed a *selection factor*.

Similarly, studies report that children (especially boys) in divorced families tend to show more behavioral problems than children in intact families (Greene et al., 2006; Lansford et al., 2006). These studies, however, do not show that divorce causes these adjustment problems. It could be that the factors that led to divorce—such as parental conflict—also led to adjustment problems among the children (Hetherington, 2006). To investigate cause and effect, researchers turn to the experimental method.

THE EXPERIMENT: TRYING THINGS OUT

The experiment is the preferred method for investigating questions of cause and effect. In the **experiment**, a group of subjects receives a treatment and another group does not. The subjects are then observed to determine whether the treatment changes their behavior. Experiments are usually undertaken to test a **hypothesis**. For example, a researcher might hypothesize that TV violence will cause aggressive behavior in children.

© eva serrabassa/iStockphoto.com

FIGURE 1.6
Examples of Positive and Negative Correlations

When two variables are correlated positively, one increases as the other increases. There is a positive correlation between the amount of time spent studying and grades, as shown in Part A. When two variables are correlated negatively, one increases as the other decreases. There is a negative correlation between the frequency of a child's delinquent acts and his or her grades, as shown in Part B. As delinquent behavior increases, grades tend to decline.

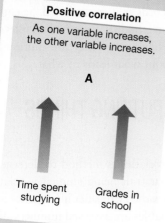

Positive correlation

As one variable increases, the other variable increases.

A

Time spent studying   Grades in school

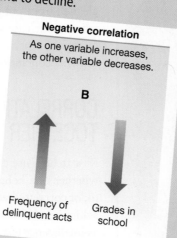

Negative correlation

As one variable increases, the other variable decreases.

B

Frequency of delinquent acts   Grades in school

Independent and Dependent Variables

In an experiment to determine whether TV violence causes aggressive behavior, subjects in the experimental group would be shown a TV program containing violence, and its effects on behavior would be measured. TV violence would be considered an **independent variable**, a variable whose presence is manipulated by the experimenters so that its effects can be determined. The measured result—in this case, the child's behavior—is called a **dependent variable**. Its presence or level presumably depends on the independent variable.

Experimental and Control Groups

Experiments use experimental and control groups. Subjects in the **experimental group** receive the treatment, whereas subjects in the **control group** do not. All other conditions are held constant for both groups. Thus, we can have confidence that experimental outcomes reflect the treatments and not chance factors.

Random Assignment

Subjects should be assigned to experimental or control groups on a chance or random basis. We could not conclude much from an experiment on the effects of TV violence if the children were allowed to choose whether they would be in a group that watched TV violence or in a group that did not. A selection factor rather than the treatment might then be responsible for the results of the experiment.

Ethical and practical considerations also prevent researchers from doing experiments on the effects of many life circumstances, such as divorce or different patterns of child rearing. We cannot randomly assign some families to divorce or conflict and assign other families to "bliss." Nor can we randomly assign parents to rearing their children in an authoritarian or permissive manner. In some areas of investigation, we must settle for correlational evidence.

When experiments cannot ethically be performed on humans, researchers sometimes carry them out with animals and try to generalize the findings to humans. No researcher would separate human infants from their parents to study the effects of isolation on development, yet experimenters have deprived monkeys of early social experience. Such research has helped psychologists investigate the formation of parent–child bonds of attachment.

T F Research with monkeys has helped scientists understand the formation of attachment in humans.
True, and ethics prevent investigators from carrying out the same type of research with humans.

LONGITUDINAL RESEARCH: STUDYING DEVELOPMENT OVER TIME

The processes of development occur over time, and researchers have devised different strategies for comparing children of one age with children or adults of other ages. In **longitudinal research**, the same people are observed repeatedly over time, and changes in development, such as gains in height or changes in mental abilities, are recorded. In **cross-sectional research**, children of different ages are observed and compared at the same time. It is assumed that when a large number of children are chosen at random, the differences found in the older age groups are a reflection of how the younger children will develop, given time. Table 1.1 summarizes the major features of cross-sectional and longitudinal research.

Longitudinal Studies

Some ambitious longitudinal studies have followed the development of children and adults for more than half a century. The Terman Studies of Genius, begun in the 1920s, tracked children with high IQ scores for more than 50 years. Male subjects, but not female subjects, went on to high achievements in the professional world. Why?

independent variable A condition in a scientific study that is manipulated so that its effects can be observed.

dependent variable A measure of an assumed effect of an independent variable.

experimental group A group made up of subjects who receive a treatment in an experiment.

control group A group made up of subjects in an experiment who do not receive the treatment but for whom all other conditions are comparable to those of subjects in the experimental group.

longitudinal research The study of developmental processes by taking repeated measures of the same group of participants at various stages of development.

cross-sectional research The study of developmental processes by taking measures of participants of different age groups at the same time.

TABLE 1.1
Comparison of Cross-Sectional and Longitudinal Research

	CROSS-SECTIONAL RESEARCH	LONGITUDINAL RESEARCH
Description	• Studies children of different ages at the same point in time	• Studies the same children repeatedly over time
Advantages	• Can be completed in short period of time	• Allows researchers to follow development over time • No drop-out or practice effects • Studies the relationships between behavior at earlier and later ages
Disadvantages	• Does not study development across time • Cannot study relationship between behavior displayed at earlier and later ages • Is prey to cohort effect (subjects from different age groups may not be comparable)	• Expensive • Takes a long time to complete • Subjects drop out • Subjects who drop out may differ systematically from those who remain in the study

Contemporary studies of women show that women with high intelligence generally match the achievements of men and suggest that women of the earlier era were held back by traditional gender-role expectations.

T F To learn how a person develops over a lifetime, researchers have tracked some individuals for more than 50 years. *True; the Terman studies provide an example.*

Most longitudinal studies span months or a few years, not decades. For example, briefer longitudinal studies have found that the children of divorced parents undergo the most severe adjustment problems within a few months of the divorce. By 2 or 3 years afterward, many children regain their equilibrium, as indicated by improved academic performance and social behavior (Hetherington et al., 1992).

Longitudinal studies have drawbacks. For example, it can be difficult to enlist volunteers to participate in a study that will last a lifetime. Many subjects fall out of touch as the

cohort effect Similarities in behavior among a group of peers that stem from the fact that group members are approximately the same age.

years pass; others die. The researchers must be patient or arrange to enlist future generations of researchers.

Cross-Sectional Studies

Because of the drawbacks of longitudinal studies, most research that compares children of different ages is cross-sectional. In other words, most investigators gather data on what the "typical" 6-month-old is doing by finding children who are 6 months old today. When they expand their research to the behavior of typical 12-month-olds, they seek another group of children, and so on.

A major challenge to cross-sectional research is the **cohort effect**. A cohort is a group of people born at about the same time. As a result, they experience cultural and other events unique to their age group. In other words, children and adults of different ages are not likely to have shared similar cultural backgrounds. People who are 80 years old today, for example, grew up without TV. Today's children are growing up taking iPods and the Internet for granted.

Children of past generations also grew up with different expectations about gender roles and appropriate social behavior. Women in the Terman studies generally chose motherhood over careers because of the times. Today's girls are growing up with female role models who are astronauts and government officials.

© Polina Lobanova/Shutterstock

In longitudinal studies, we know that we have the same individuals as they have developed over 5, 25, even 50 years or more. In cross-sectional research, we can only hope that they will be comparable.

Cross-Sequential Research

Cross-sequential research combines the longitudinal and cross-sectional methods so that many of their individual drawbacks are overcome. In the cross-sequential study, the full span of the ideal longitudinal study is broken up into convenient segments (see Figure 1.7). Assume that we wish to follow the attitudes of children toward gender roles from the age of 4 through the age of 12. The typical longitudinal study would take 8 years. We can, however, divide this 8-year span in half by attaining two samples of children (a cross-section) instead of one: 4-year-olds and 8-year-olds. We would then interview, test, and observe each group at the beginning of the study (2010) and 4 years later (2014).

An obvious advantage to this collapsed method is that the study is completed in 4 years rather than 8 years. Still, the testing and retesting of samples provides some of the continuity of the longitudinal study. By observing both samples at the age of 8 (a **time-lag comparison**), we can also determine whether they are, in fact, comparable or whether the 4-year difference in their date of birth is associated with a cohort effect.

cross-sequential research An approach that combines the longitudinal and cross-sectional methods by following individuals of different ages for abbreviated periods of time.

time lag comparison The study of developmental processes by taking measures of participants in different groups when they are the same age.

ETHICAL CONSIDERATIONS

Researchers adhere to ethical standards that are intended to promote the dignity of the individual, foster human welfare, and maintain scientific integrity. These standards also ensure that they do not use methods or treatments that harm subjects:

- Researchers are not to use methods that may do physical or psychological harm.
- Participants (and parents, if participants are minors) must be informed of the purposes of the research and about the research methods.
  - Participants must provide voluntary consent to participate in the study.
  - Participants may withdraw from the study at any time, for any reason.
  - Participants should be offered information about the results of the study.
  - The identities of the participants are to remain confidential.
  - Researchers should present their research plans to a committee of their colleagues and gain the committee's approval before proceeding.

These guidelines present researchers with a number of hurdles to overcome before proceeding with and while conducting research, but because they protect the welfare of participants, the guidelines are valuable.

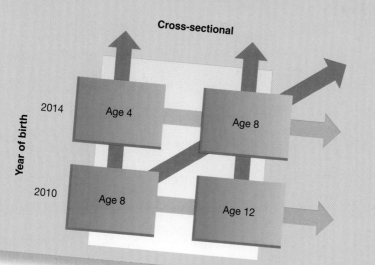

FIGURE 1.7
Example of Cross-Sequential Research

Cross-sequential research combines three methods: cross-sectional, longitudinal, and time lag. The child's age at the time of testing appears in the boxes. Vertical columns represent cross-sectional comparisons. Horizontal rows represent longitudinal comparisons. Diagonals represent time-lag comparisons.

Cross-sectional

Year of birth

2014   Age 4   Age 8

2010   Age 8   Age 12

Heredity makes possible

all things human.

2

Heredity and Conception

Let's talk about the facts of life. Here are a few of them:

- People cannot breathe underwater (without special equipment).
- People cannot fly (without special equipment).
- Fish cannot learn to speak French or dance an Irish jig, even if you raise them in enriched environments and send them to finishing school.

We cannot breathe underwater or fly because we have not inherited gills or wings. Fish are similarly limited by their heredity. **Heredity** defines our nature, which is based on the biological transmission of traits from one generation to another. Because of their heredity, fish cannot speak any language or do a jig.

Learning Outcomes

LO1   Explain the influences of heredity on development, referring to chromosomes and genes, mitosis and meiosis, twins, and dominant and recessive traits.

LO2   Describe the features and causes of various chromosomal abnormalities.

LO3   Describe the features and causes of various genetic abnormalities.

LO4   Discuss methods of detecting genetic abnormalities.

LO5   Describe methods of determining our genotypes and our phenotypes.

LO6   Describe the process of conception.

LO7   Discuss the causes of infertility and alternate ways of becoming parents.

LO1 The Influence of Heredity on Development

heredity makes possible all things human. The structures we inherit make our behavior possible and place limits on it. The field of biology that studies heredity is called **genetics**.

Genetic influences are fundamental in the transmission of physical traits, such as height, hair texture, and eye color. Genetics also appears to play a role in psychological

heredity The transmission of traits and characteristics from parent to child by means of genes.

genetics The branch of biology that studies heredity.

traits such as intelligence, activity level, sociability, shyness, anxiety, empathy, effectiveness as a parent, happiness, even interest in arts and crafts (Johnson & Krueger, 2006; Knafo & Plomin, 2006; Leonardo & Hen, 2006). Genetic factors are also involved in psychological problems such as schizophrenia, depression, and dependence on nicotine, alcohol, and other substances (Farmer et al., 2007; Hill et al., 2007; Metzger et al., 2007).

CHROMOSOMES AND GENES

Traits are transmitted by chromosomes and genes. **Chromosomes** are rod-shaped structures found in cells. Typical human cells contain 46 chromosomes organized into 23 pairs. Each chromosome contains thousands of segments called genes. **Genes** are the biochemical materials that regulate the development of traits. Some

traits, such as blood type, appear to be transmitted by a single pair of genes, one of which is derived from each parent. Other traits are **polygenic**, that is, determined by several pairs of genes.

Our heredity is governed by 20,000 to 25,000 genes (International Human Genome Sequencing Consortium, 2006). Genes are segments of strands of **deoxyribonucleic acid (DNA)**. DNA takes the form of a double spiral, or helix, similar to a twisting ladder (see Figure 2.1). The "rungs" of the ladder consist of one of two pairs of chemical compounds called *bases*, either adenine with thymine (A with T) or cytosine with guanine (C with G). The sequence of the rungs is the genetic code that will cause the developing organism to grow arms or wings, skin or scales.

MITOSIS AND MEIOSIS

We begin life as a single cell, or zygote, that divides repeatedly. There are two types of cell division: *mitosis* and *meiosis*. In **mitosis**, strands of DNA break apart, or "unzip" (see Figure 2.2). The halves move to separate sides of the cell. Each incomplete rung combines with the appropriate base "partner" (i.e., G and C, A and T) to form a new complete ladder. The two resulting identical copies of the DNA strand separate when the cell divides; each becomes a member of a newly formed cell. As a result, the genetic code is identical in

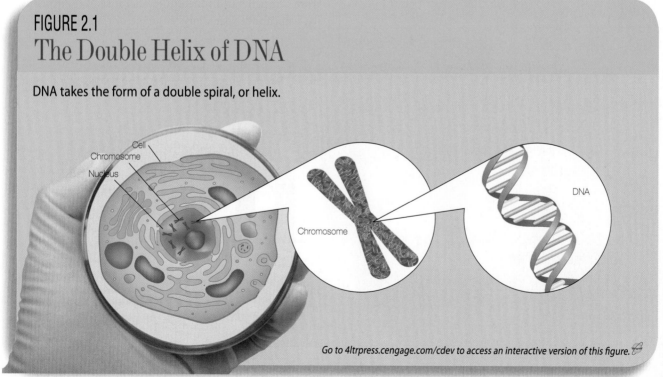

FIGURE 2.1
The Double Helix of DNA

DNA takes the form of a double spiral, or helix.

Cell

Chromosome

Nucleus

Chromosome

DNA

Go to 4ltrpress.cengage.com/cdev to access an interactive version of this figure.

© Linde Stewart/iStockphoto.com

FIGURE 2.2
Mitosis

(a) A segment of a strand of DNA before mitosis. (b) During mitosis, chromosomal strands of DNA "unzip." (c) The double helix is rebuilt in the cell as each incomplete "rung" combines with an appropriate base: A, T, C, or G.

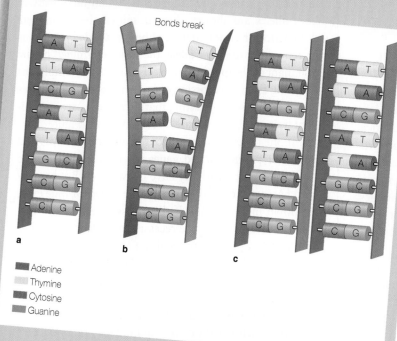

Bonds break

a

b

c

■ Adenine
■ Thymine
■ Cytosine
■ Guanine

new cells unless **mutations** occur through radiation or other environmental influences. Mutations also occur by chance, but not often.

Sperm and ova are produced through **meiosis**, or *reduction division*. In meiosis, the 46 chromosomes within the cell nucleus first line up into 23 pairs. The DNA ladders then unzip, leaving unpaired chromosomes. When the cell divides, one member of each pair goes to each newly formed cell. Each new cell nucleus contains only 23 chromosomes, not 46.

When a sperm cell fertilizes an ovum, the zygote receives 23 chromosomes from the father's sperm cell and 23 from the mother's ovum, and the combined chromosomes form 23 pairs (Figure 2.3). Twenty-two of the pairs are **autosomes**—paired chromosomes that look alike and possess genetic information concerning the same set of traits. The 23rd pair contains **sex chromosomes**, which determine the zygote's sex. Humans receive an X sex chromosome (so called because of its X shape) from their mothers. The father supplies either a Y or an X sex chromosome. If a zygote receives another X sex chromosome from the father, it develops into a female, and if a Y (named after its Y shape), a male.

FIGURE 2.3
The 23 Pairs of Human Chromosomes

People normally have 23 pairs of chromosomes. Females have two X sex chromosomes, whereas males have an X and a Y sex chromosome.

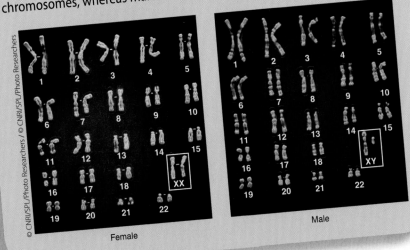

© CNRI/SPL/Photo Researchers / © CNRI/SPL/Photo Researchers

Female

Male

Your father determined whether you are female or male.

True; he did so by supplying a Y or an X sex chromosome. We all receive an X sex chromosome from our mother. If we receive another X sex chromosome from our father, we develop into a female. If we receive a Y sex chromosome from our father, we develop into a male.

IDENTICAL AND FRATERNAL TWINS

Now and then, a zygote divides into two cells that separate so that each develops into an individual with the same genetic makeup. These individuals are identical twins, or **monozygotic (MZ) twins**. If the woman produces two ova in the same month and they are each fertilized by different sperm cells, they develop into fraternal twins, or **dizygotic (DZ) twins**. DZ twins run in families. If a woman is a twin, if her mother was a twin, or if she has previously borne twins, the chances rise that she will bear twins (Office of National Statistics, 2006).

As women reach the end of their child-bearing years, **ovulation** becomes less regular, resulting in a number of months when more than one ovum is released. Thus, the chances of twins increase with parental age (National Guideline Clearinghouse, 2007). Fertility drugs also enhance the chances of multiple births by causing more than one ovum to ripen and be released during a woman's cycle (National Guideline Clearinghouse, 2007).

monozygotic (MZ) twins Twins that derive from a single zygote that has split into two; identical twins. Each MZ twin carries the same genetic code.

dizygotic (DZ) twins Twins that derive from two zygotes; fraternal twins.

ovulation The releasing of an ovum from an ovary.

allele A member of a pair of genes.

homozygous Having two identical alleles.

heterozygous Having two different alleles.

dominant trait A trait that is expressed.

recessive trait A trait that is not expressed when the gene or genes involved have been paired with dominant genes.

carrier A person who carries and transmits a recessive gene but does not exhibit its effect.

DOMINANT AND RECESSIVE TRAITS

Traits are determined by pairs of genes. Each member of a pair of genes is termed an **allele**. When both of the alleles for a trait, such as hair color, are the same, the person is said to be **homozygous** for that trait. When the alleles for a trait differ, the person is **heterozygous** for that trait. Some traits result from an "averaging" of the genetic instructions carried by the parents. When the effects of both alleles are shown, there is said to be incomplete dominance or codominance. When a *dominant* allele is paired with a *recessive* allele, the trait determined by the dominant allele appears in the offspring. For example, the offspring from the crossing of brown eyes with blue eyes have brown eyes, suggesting that brown eyes are a **dominant trait** and blue eyes are a **recessive trait** (Figure 2.4).

If one parent carried genes for only brown eyes and the other parent carried genes for only blue eyes, the children would invariably have brown eyes. But brown-eyed parents can also carry recessive genes for blue eyes, as shown in Figure 2.4. If the recessive gene from one parent combines with the recessive gene from the other parent, the recessive trait will be shown. As suggested by Figure 2.4, approximately 25% of the children of brown-eyed parents who carry recessive blue eye color will have blue eyes. Table 2.1 shows a number of dominant and recessive traits in humans.

People who bear one dominant gene and one recessive gene for a trait are said to be **carriers** of the recessive

If a woman is a twin the chances of her bearing twins increases. Mary Ferrell (bottom right) and her sister Martha Blanton (front middle) are heterozygous twins. Mrs. Ferrell's two daughters (back left and back middle) are homozygous twins.

FIGURE 2.4

Transmission of Dominant and Recessive Traits

These two brown-eyed parents each carry a gene for blue eyes. Their children have an equal opportunity of receiving genes for brown eyes and blue eyes.

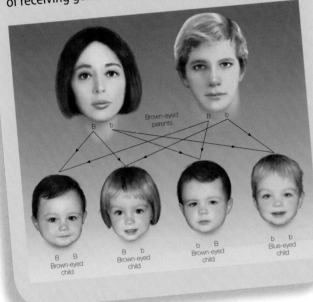

TABLE 2.1

Examples of Dominant and Recessive Traits

DOMINANT TRAIT	RECESSIVE TRAIT
Dark hair	Blond hair
Dark hair	Red hair
Curly hair	Straight hair
Normal color vision	Red-green color blindness
Normal vision	Myopia (nearsightedness)
Farsightedness	Normal vision
Normal pigmentation	Deficiency of pigmentation in skin, hair, and retina (albinism)
Normal sensitivity to touch	Extremely fragile skin
Normal hearing	Some forms of deafness
Dimples	Lack of dimpling
Type A blood	Type O blood
Type B blood	Type O blood
Tolerance of lactose	Lactose intolerance

gene. In the cases of recessive genes that cause illness, carriers of those genes are fortunate to have dominant genes that cancel their effects.

T F You can carry the genes for a deadly illness and not become sick yourself.
True; this occurs when the genes responsible for the illness are recessive and dominant genes cancel their effects.

Chromosomal or genetic abnormalities can cause health problems. Some chromosomal disorders (such as Down syndrome) reflect abnormalities in the 22 pairs of autosomes; others (such as XYY syndrome) reflect abnormalities in the sex chromosomes. Some genetic abnormalities, such as cystic fibrosis, are caused by a single pair of genes; others are caused by combinations of genes. Diabetes mellitus, epilepsy, and peptic ulcers are **multifactorial problems**; they reflect both a genetic predisposition *and* environmental contributors.

LO2 Chromosomal Abnormalities

People normally have 46 chromosomes. Children with more or fewer chromosomes usually experience health problems or behavioral abnormalities. The risk of chromosomal abnormalities rises with the age of the parents (American Fertility Association, 2007).

multifactorial problems
Problems that stem from the interaction of heredity and environmental factors.

DOWN SYNDROME

Down syndrome is usually caused by an extra chromosome in the 21st pair, resulting in 47 chromosomes. The probability of having a child with Down syndrome increases with the age of the parents. People with Down syndrome have characteristic features that include a rounded face, a protruding tongue, a broad, flat nose, and a sloping fold of skin over the inner corners of the eyes (Figure 2.5). They show deficits in cognitive development (Rondal & Ling, 2006) and motor development (Virji-Babul et al., 2006)

FIGURE 2.5
Down Syndrome

The development and adjustment of children with Down syndrome are related to their acceptance by their families. Children with Down syndrome who are reared at home develop more rapidly and achieve higher levels of functioning than those who are reared in institutions.

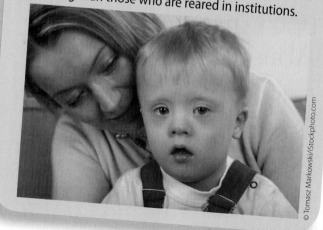

© Tomasz Markowski/iStockphoto.com

and usually die from cardiovascular problems by middle age, although modern medicine has extended life appreciably.

SEX-LINKED CHROMOSOMAL ABNORMALITIES

A number of disorders stem from an abnormal number of sex chromosomes and are therefore called **sex-linked chromosomal abnormalities**. Most individuals with an abnormal number of sex chromosomes are infertile. Beyond that common finding, there are many differences, some of them associated with "maleness" or "femaleness" (Wodrich, 2006).

Approximately 1 male in 700–1,000 has an extra Y sex chromosome. The Y chromosome is associated with maleness, and the extra Y chromosome apparently heightens male secondary sex characteristics. For example, XYY males are somewhat taller than average and develop heavier beards. For these kinds of reasons, males with XYY sex chromosomal structure were once called "supermales." However, XYY "supermales" tend to have more problems than XY males. For example, they are often mildly delayed in language development.

Approximately 1 male in 500 has **Klinefelter syndrome**, which is caused by an extra X sex chromosome (an XXY sex chromosomal pattern). XXY males produce less of the male sex hormone **testosterone** than average males. As a result, male primary and secondary sex characteristics—such as the testes, deepening of the voice, musculature, and the male pattern of body hair—do not develop properly. XXY males usually have enlarged breasts (*gynecomastia*) and are usually mildly mentally retarded, particularly in language skills (van Rijn et al., 2006). XXY males are typically treated with testosterone replacement therapy, which can foster development of sex characteristics and elevate the mood, but they remain infertile.

Approximately 1 female in 2,500 has a single X sex chromosome and as a result develops **Turner syndrome**. The external genitals of such girls are normal, but their ovaries are poorly developed and they produce little **estrogen**. Females with this problem are shorter than average and infertile. Researchers have connected a specific pattern of cognitive deficits with low estrogen levels: problems in visual–spatial skills, mathematics, and nonverbal memory (Hart et al., 2006).

Approximately 1 female in 1,000 has an XXX sex chromosomal structure, known as *Triple X syndrome*. Such females are normal in appearance but tend to show lower-than-average language skills and poorer memory for recent events. Development of external sexual organs appears normal enough, although there is increased incidence of infertility (Wodrich, 2006).

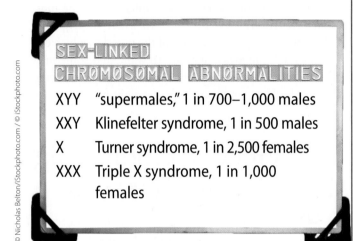

SEX-LINKED CHROMOSOMAL ABNORMALITIES

XYY	"supermales," 1 in 700–1,000 males
XXY	Klinefelter syndrome, 1 in 500 males
X	Turner syndrome, 1 in 2,500 females
XXX	Triple X syndrome, 1 in 1,000 females

LO3 Genetic Abnormalities

 number of disorders have been attributed to genes.

PHENYLKETONURIA

The enzyme disorder **phenylketonuria (PKU)** is transmitted by a recessive gene and affects about 1 child in 8,000. Children with PKU cannot metabolize an amino acid called *phenylalanine*, so it builds up in their bodies and impairs the functioning of the central nervous system, resulting in mental retardation, psychological disorders, and physical problems. There is no cure for PKU, but children with PKU can be placed on diets low in phenylalanine within 3–6 weeks of birth and develop normally (Brazier & Rowlands, 2006).

HUNTINGTON'S DISEASE

Huntington's disease (HD) is a fatal, progressive degenerative disorder that is transmitted by a dominant gene and affects approximately 1 American in 18,000. Physical symptoms include uncontrollable muscle movements

(Jacobs et al., 2006). Psychological symptoms include loss of intellectual functioning and personality change (Robins Wahlin et al., 2007). Because the onset of HD is delayed until middle adulthood, many individuals with the defect have borne children only to discover years later that they and possibly half their offspring will develop it. Medicines can help deal with some symptoms.

phenylketonuria (PKU) A genetic abnormality in which phenylalanine builds up in the body and causes mental retardation.

Huntington's disease A fatal genetic degenerative disorder whose onset is in middle age.

sickle-cell anemia A genetic disorder that decreases the blood's capacity to carry oxygen.

Tay-Sachs disease A fatal genetic neurological disorder.

cystic fibrosis A fatal genetic disorder in which mucus obstructs the lungs and pancreas.

SICKLE-CELL ANEMIA

Sickle-cell anemia is caused by a recessive gene. Sickle-cell anemia is most common among African Americans. Nearly 1 African American in 10 and 1 Latino or Latina American in 20 is a carrier. In sickle-cell anemia, red blood cells take on the shape of a sickle and clump together, obstructing small blood vessels and decreasing the oxygen supply. The lessened oxygen supply can impair cognitive skills and academic performance. Physical problems include painful and swollen joints, jaundice, and potentially fatal conditions such as pneumonia, stroke, and heart and kidney failure.

TAY-SACHS DISEASE

Tay-Sachs disease is also caused by a recessive gene. It causes the central nervous system to degenerate, resulting in death. The disorder is most commonly found among children in Jewish families of Eastern European background. Approximately 1 in 30 Jewish Americans from this background carries the recessive gene for Tay-Sachs. Children with the disorder progressively lose control over their muscles, experience sensory losses, develop mental retardation, become paralyzed, and usually die by about the age of 5.

CYSTIC FIBROSIS

Cystic fibrosis, also caused by a recessive gene, is the most common fatal hereditary disease among European Americans. Approximately 30,000 Americans have the

hemophilia A genetic disorder in which blood does not clot properly.

sex-linked genetic abnormalities Abnormalities resulting from genes that are found on the X sex chromosome. They are more likely to be shown by male offspring (who do not have an opposing gene from a second X chromosome) than by female offspring.

muscular dystrophy A chronic disease characterized by a progressive wasting away of the muscles.

genetic counseling Advice concerning the probabilities that a couple's children will show genetic abnormalities.

prenatal Before birth.

amniocentesis A procedure for drawing and examining fetal cells sloughed off into amniotic fluid to determine the presence of various disorders.

disorder, but another 10 million (1 in every 31 people) are carriers (Cystic Fibrosis Foundation, 2007). Children with the disease suffer from excessive production of thick mucus that clogs the pancreas and lungs. Most victims die of respiratory infections in their 20s.

SEX-LINKED GENETIC ABNORMALITIES

Some genetic defects, such as **hemophilia**, are carried on only the X sex chromosome. For this reason, they are referred to as **sex-linked genetic abnormalities**. These defects also involve recessive genes.

Females, who have two X sex chromosomes, are less likely than males to show sex-linked disorders because the genes that cause the disorder would have to be present on both of a female's sex chromosomes for the disorder to be expressed. Sex-linked diseases are more likely to afflict sons of female carriers because males have only one X sex chromosome, which they inherit from their mothers.

One form of **muscular dystrophy**, Duchenne muscular dystrophy, is sex-linked. Muscular dystrophy is characterized by a weakening of the muscles, which can lead to wasting away, inability to walk, and sometimes death. Other sex-linked abnormalities include diabetes, color blindness, and some types of night blindness.

LO4 Genetic Counseling and Prenatal Testing

it is possible to detect genetic abnormalities that are responsible for many diseases. Genetic counselors compile information about a couple's genetic heritage to explore whether their children might develop genetic abnormalities. Couples who face a high risk of passing along genetic defects to their children sometimes elect to adopt or not have children rather than conceive their own. In addition, **prenatal** testing can indicate whether the embryo or fetus is carrying genetic abnormalities.

AMNIOCENTESIS AND CHORIONIC VILLUS SAMPLING

Amniocentesis is usually performed on the mother at 14–16 weeks after conception, although many physicians now perform the procedure earlier (*early amniocentesis*). In this method, the health professional uses a syringe (needle) to withdraw fluid from the amniotic sac (Figure 2.6). The fluid contains cells that are sloughed off by the fetus. The cells are separated from the amniotic fluid, grown in a culture, and then examined microscopically for genetic and chromosomal abnormalities.

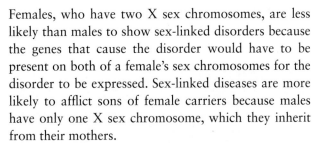

© Photo 12/The Image Works

Queen Victoria was a carrier of hemophilia and transmitted the blood disorder to many of her children, who in turn carried it into a number of the ruling houses of Europe. For this reason, hemophilia has been dubbed the "royal disease."

FIGURE 2.6
Amniocentesis

Amniocentesis allows prenatal identification of certain genetic and chromosomal disorders by examining genetic material sloughed off by the fetus into amniotic fluid.

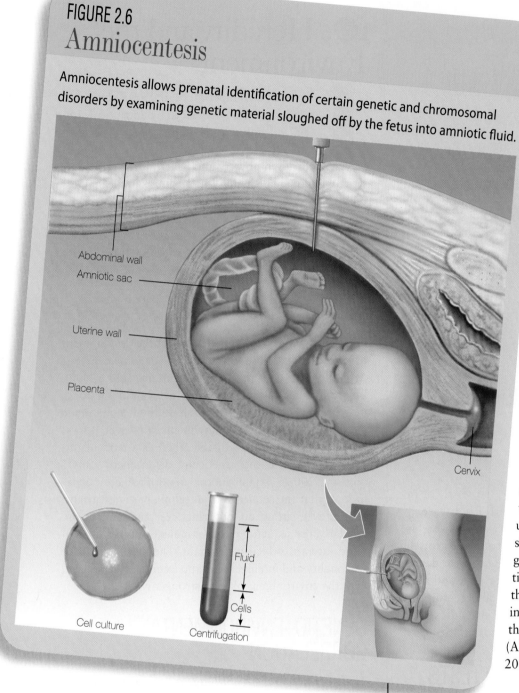

Abdominal wall

Amniotic sac

Uterine wall

Placenta

Cervix

Fluid

Cells

Cell culture

Centrifugation

chorionic villus sampling A method for the prenatal detection of genetic abnormalities that samples the membrane enveloping the amniotic sac and fetus.

uterus The hollow organ within females in which the embryo and fetus develop.

ultrasound Sound waves too high in pitch to be sensed by the human ear.

sonogram An image of an embryo or fetus generated using ultrasound waves.

Amniocentesis has become routine among American women who become pregnant past the age of 35 because the chances of Down syndrome and other chromosomal abnormalities increase dramatically as women approach or pass the age of 40. Amniocentesis also permits parents to learn the sex of their unborn child through examination of the sex chromosomes, but most parents learn the sex of their baby earlier by means of ultrasound. Amniocentesis carries some risk of miscarriage (approximately 1 woman in 100 who undergo the procedure will miscarry), so health professionals would not conduct it just to learn the sex of the child.

Chorionic villus sampling (CVS) is similar to amniocentesis but is carried out between the 9th and 12th week of pregnancy. A small syringe is inserted through the vagina into the **uterus** and sucks out some threadlike projections (villi) from the outer membrane that envelops the amniotic sac and fetus. Results are available within days. CVS has not been used as frequently as amniocentesis because CVS carries a slightly greater risk of spontaneous abortion. More recent studies suggest that both amniocentesis and CVS increase the risk of miscarriage and that the risks might *not* be equal (Alfirevic et al., 2003; Philip et al., 2004).

ULTRASOUND

Health professionals also use sound waves that are too high in frequency to be heard by the human ear—**ultrasound**—to obtain information about the fetus. Ultrasound waves are reflected by the fetus, and a computer uses the information to generate a picture of the fetus. The picture is termed a **sonogram** (see Figure 2.7).

Ultrasound is used to guide the syringe in amniocentesis and CVS by determining the position of the fetus. Ultrasound is also used to locate fetal structures when intrauterine transfusions are necessary

FIGURE 2.7

Sonogram of a 5-Month-Old Fetus

In the ultrasound technique, sound waves are bounced off the fetus and provide a picture that enables professionals to detect various abnormalities.

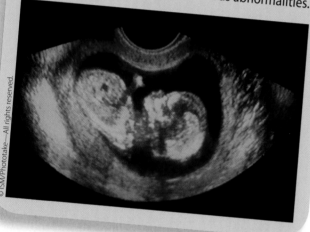

alpha-fetoprotein (AFP) assay A blood test that assesses the mother's blood level of alpha-fetoprotein, a substance that is linked with fetal neural tube defects.

genotype The genetic form or constitution of a person as determined by heredity.

phenotype The actual form or constitution of a person as determined by heredity and environmental factors.

canalization The tendency of growth rates to return to genetically determined patterns after undergoing environmentally induced change.

for the survival of a fetus with Rh disease.

Ultrasound also is used to track the growth of the fetus, to determine fetal age and sex, and to detect multiple pregnancies and structural abnormalities.

BLOOD TESTS

Parental blood tests can reveal the presence of genetic disorders such as sickle-cell anemia, Tay-Sachs disease, and cystic fibrosis. The **alpha-fetoprotein (AFP) assay** is used to detect neural tube defects such as spina bifida and certain chromosomal abnormalities. Neural tube defects cause an elevation in the AFP level in the mother's blood. Elevated AFP levels also are associated with increased risk of fetal death.

LO5 Heredity and the Environment

in addition to inheritance, the development of our traits is also influenced by nutrition, learning, exercise, and—unfortunately—accident and illness. A potential Shakespeare who is reared in poverty and never taught to read or write will not create a *Hamlet.* Our traits and behaviors represent the interaction of heredity and environment. The sets of traits that we inherit from our parents are referred to as our **genotypes**. The actual sets of traits which we exhibit are called our **phenotypes**. Our phenotypes reflect both genetic and environmental influences.

CANALIZATION

Our genotypes lead to **canalization** of the development of various traits, both physical and—to some degree—psychological (Crusio, 2006; Del Giudice et al., 2009). Environmental restrictions, such as scarcity of food, may prevent children from reaching the heights made possible by their genetic endowments. However, if food becomes more readily available, there is a tendency to "snap back" into the genetically determined "canal" (Crusio, 2006). Infant motor development is canalized in that the sequence of development is invariant: rolling over, sitting up, crawling, creeping, and so on. Similarly, the sequence of development of types of two-word utterances is also invariant. The development of personality and intelligence is apparently less canalized, with the environment playing stronger roles.

GENETIC–ENVIRONMENTAL CORRELATION

There is also *genetic–environmental correlation* (Gottlieb, 2007; Narusyte et al., 2008). One of the problems in sorting out the influences of heredity and environment, or nature and nurture, is that genes in part determine the environments to which people are exposed (Weinberg et al., 2004). Developmental psychologist Sandra Scarr (1998) described three types of correlations between genetic and environmental influences, and they are related to the age of the individual.

Passive Correlation

Children's biological parents not only contribute genes to their offspring; they also intentionally and unintentionally place them in certain kinds of environments. Artistically oriented parents are not only likely to transmit genes that predispose children to interest in the arts, but they are also likely to expose their children to artistic activities, such as visits to museums and piano lessons. Athletic parents may enroll their children in soccer lessons and sports camps. The artistic and athletic parents may also ridicule the interests of the other group, purposefully contributing to the development of their children's attitudes. This type of correlation is termed a *passive genetic–environmental correlation* because the children have no choice in the matter.

Evocative Correlation

An *evocative genetic–environmental correlation* exists because the child's genotype is connected with behaviors that evoke, or elicit, certain kinds of responses from others. These responses, in turn, become part of the social environment of the child. A sociable, active, even-tempered infant is likely to receive more positive social stimulation from caregivers and other people than a passive, socially withdrawn infant. A good-looking infant and child is more likely to evoke more attentive and playful responses from others, including his or her mother, and possibly develop more skillful social behavior as a result (Langlois et al., 1995). Teachers are more likely to befriend and smile at children who are interested in their subjects, pay attention, and avoid misbehavior.

Active Correlation

As we mature, we are more likely to take an active, conscious role in choosing or creating our environments. This effect is called an *active genetic–environmental correlation*. The intelligent, highly motivated child may ask to be placed in honors classes. The strong, coordinated, aggressive child may join athletic teams. The child or adolescent with lesser academic and athletic talents may choose to be a "loner" or join a deviant peer group in which

friends reinforce his or her behaviors. At some point, we may ask caregivers to help us attend activities that relate to our genetically inspired interests. Adolescents may also select after-school activities that are connected with their academic, artistic, or athletic interests. Choosing environments that allow us to develop inherited preferences is termed **niche-picking** (Feinberg et al., 2005; Plomin & Daniels, 1987).

niche-picking Choosing environments that allow us to develop inherited preferences.

The Epigenetic Framework

The relationship between genetic and environmental influences is not a one-way street. Instead it is bidirectional. While it is true that our genes affect the development of our traits and behaviors, our traits and behaviors also lead us to place ourselves in certain environments. These environments—specialized schools, after-school activities, museums, the theatre, the films and television programs we choose to watch—all affect the manner in which genes are expressed. According to what developmentalists call *epigenesis,* or the *epigenetic framework,* our development reflects continuing bidirectional exchanges between our genetic heritages and the environments in which we find ourselves or place ourselves (Bateson & Mameli, 2007; Lickliter & Logan, 2007; Rosenblatt, 2007).

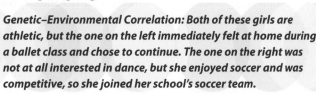

Genetic–Environmental Correlation: Both of these girls are athletic, but the one on the left immediately felt at home during a ballet class and chose to continue. The one on the right was not at all interested in dance, but she enjoyed soccer and was competitive, so she joined her school's soccer team.

autism A developmental disorder characterized by failure to relate to others, communication problems, intolerance of change, and ritualistic behavior.

Researchers have developed a number of strategies to help sort out the effects of heredity and the environment on development.

KINSHIP STUDIES

Researchers study the distribution of a trait or behavior among relatives who differ in degree of genetic closeness. The more closely people are related, the more genes they have in common. Parents and children have a 50% overlap in their genetic endowments, and so do siblings (brothers and sisters). Aunts and uncles have a 25% overlap with nieces and nephews, as do grandparents with grandchildren. First cousins share 12.5% of their genetic endowment. If genes are implicated in a trait, people who are more closely related should be more likely to share it.

TWIN STUDIES: LOOKING IN THE GENETIC MIRROR

Monozygotic (MZ) twins share 100% of their genes, whereas dizygotic (DZ) twins have a 50% overlap, just as other siblings do. If MZ twins show greater similarity on some trait or behavior than DZ twins do, a genetic basis for the trait or behavior is indicated.

MZ twins resemble each other more closely than DZ twins on a number of physical and psychological traits, even when the MZ twins are reared apart and the DZ twins are reared together (Bouchard & Loehlin, 2001). MZ twins are more likely to look alike and to be similar in height (Plomin, 2002). Heredity even affects their preference for coffee or tea (Luciano et al., 2005). MZ twins resemble one another more strongly than DZ twins in intelligence and personality traits (Hur, 2005; Johnson et al., 2004; McCrae et al., 2000). MZ twins are also more likely to share psychological disorders such as **autism**, depression, schizophrenia, and vulnerability to alcoholism (Belmonte & Carper, 2006; Plomin, 2002; Ronald et al., 2006).

But one might ask whether MZ twins resemble each other so closely partly because they are often treated so similarly? One way to answer this question is to find

> The relationship between genetic and environmental influences is not just a one way street.

and compare MZ twins who were reared apart. Except for the uterine environment, similarities between MZ twins reared apart would appear to be a result of heredity. In the Minnesota Study of Twins Reared Apart (T. J. Bouchard et al., 1990; DiLalla et al., 1999; Lykken, 2006), researchers have been measuring the physiological and psychological characteristics of 56 sets of MZ adult twins who were separated in infancy and reared in different homes. The MZ twins reared apart are about as similar as MZ twins reared together on measures of intelligence, personality, temperament, occupational and leisure-time interests, and social attitudes. These traits would thus appear to have a genetic underpinning.

ADOPTION STUDIES

Adoption studies in which children are separated from their natural parents at an early age and reared by adoptive parents provide special opportunities for sorting out nature and nurture. When children who are reared by adoptive parents are nonetheless more similar to their natural parents in a trait, a powerful argument is made for a genetic role in the appearance of that trait.

Traits are determined by pairs of genes. One gene of each pair comes from each parent in the process called *conception.*

LO6 Conception: Against All Odds

On a balmy day in October, Marta and her partner Jorge rush to catch the train to their jobs in the city. Marta's workday is outwardly the same as any other. Within her body, however, a drama is unfolding. Yesterday, hormones had caused an ovarian follicle to rupture, releasing its egg cell, or ovum. Like all women, Marta possessed all the ova she would ever have at birth, each encased in a follicle. How this particular follicle was selected to ripen and release its ovum this month remains a mystery, but for the next day or so, Marta will be capable of conceiving.

The previous morning, Marta had used her ovulation-timing kit, which showed that she was about to ovulate. So later that night, Marta and Jorge made love, hoping that Marta would conceive. Jorge ejaculated hundreds of millions of sperm within Marta's vagina. Only a few thousand survived the journey through the cervix and uterus to the fallopian tube that contained the ovum, released just hours earlier. Of these, a few hundred remained to bombard the ovum. One succeeded in penetrating the ovum's covering, resulting in conception. From a single cell formed by the union of sperm and ovum, a new life begins. The new cell is just 1/175 of an inch across, a tiny beginning for the drama about to take place.

Conception is the union of an ovum and a sperm cell. Conception, from one perspective, is the beginning of a new human life. From another perspective, though, conception is also the end of a fantastic voyage in which one of several hundred thousand ova produced by the woman unites with one of hundreds of million sperm produced by the man in the average ejaculate.

OVA

At birth, women already have all the ova they will ever have: some 400,000. The ova, however, are immature in form. The ovaries also produce the female hormones estrogen and progesterone. At puberty, in response to hormonal command, some ova begin to mature. Each month, an egg (occasionally more than one) is released from its ovarian follicle about midway through the menstrual cycle and enters a nearby fallopian tube. It might take 3 to 4 days for an egg to be propelled by small, hairlike structures called *cilia* and, perhaps, by contractions in the wall of the tube, along the few inches of the fallopian tube to the uterus. Unlike sperm, eggs do not propel themselves.

The 6-inch ostrich egg and the chicken egg are each just one cell.

If the egg is not fertilized, it is discharged from the uterus through the vagina along with the **endometrium** that had formed to support an embryo, in the menstrual flow. During a woman's reproductive years, about 400 ova (that is, 1 in 1,000) will ripen and be released.

Ova are much larger than sperm. The chicken egg and the 6-inch ostrich egg are each just one cell, although the sperm of these birds are microscopic. Human ova are barely visible to the eye, but their bulk is still thousands of times larger than that of sperm cells.

SPERM CELLS

Sperm cells develop through several stages. They each begin with 46 chromosomes, but after meiosis, each sperm has 23 chromosomes, half with X sex chromosomes and half with Y. Each sperm cell is about 1/500 of an inch long, one of the smallest types of cells in the body. Sperm with Y sex chromosomes appear to swim faster than sperm with X sex chromosomes. The main reason that 120 to 150 boys are conceived for every 100 girls is because of this difference. Male fetuses suffer a higher rate of **spontaneous abortion** than females, however, often during the first month of pregnancy. At birth, boys outnumber girls by a ratio of only 106 to 100. Boys also have a higher incidence of infant mortality, which further equalizes the numbers of girls and boys.

T F Approximately 120 to 150 boys are conceived for every 100 girls.
True, but male fetuses suffer a higher rate of spontaneous abortion than females.

The 150 million or so sperm in the ejaculate may seem to be a wasteful investment because only one sperm can fertilize an ovum, but only 1 in 1,000 sperm will ever approach an ovum. Millions deposited in the vagina flow out of the woman's body because of gravity. Normal vaginal acidity kills many more sperm. Many surviving sperm then have to swim against the current of fluid coming from the cervix (see Figure 2.8).

conception The union of a sperm cell and an ovum that occurs when the chromosomes of each of these cells combine to form 23 new pairs.

endometrium The inner lining of the uterus.

spontaneous abortion Unplanned, accidental abortion.

© iStockphoto.com / © Tomasz Zachariasz/iStockphoto.com

FIGURE 2.8
Female Reproductive Organs

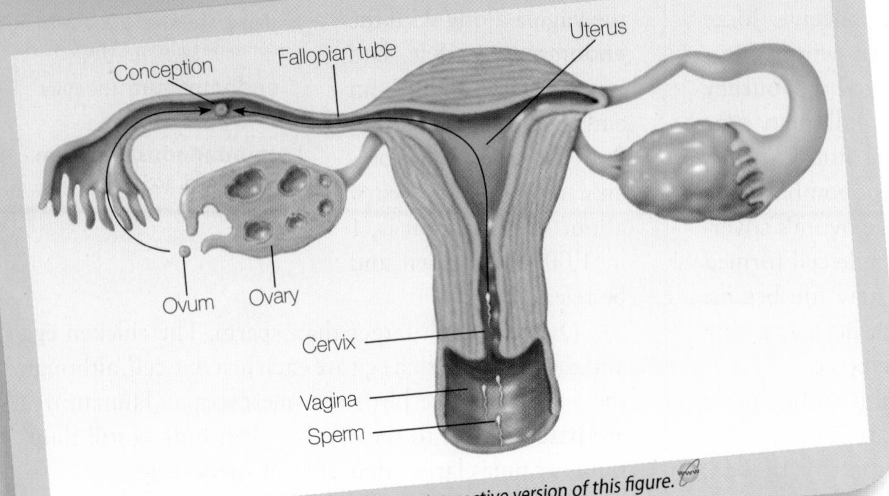

Conception
Fallopian tube
Uterus
Ovum
Ovary
Cervix
Vagina
Sperm

Go to 4ltrpress.cengage.com/cdev to access an interactive version of this figure.

LO7 Infertility

approximately one American couple in six or seven has fertility problems (Rebar & DeCherney, 2004). The term *infertility* usually is not applied until the couple has failed to conceive on their own for 1 year. Infertility was once viewed as a problem of the woman, but it turns out that the problem lies with the man in about 40% of cases.

Sperm that survive these initial obstacles may reach the fallopian tubes 60–90 minutes after ejaculation. About half the sperm enter the tube that contains no egg. Perhaps 2,000 enter the correct tube. Fewer still manage to swim the final 2 inches against the currents generated by the cilia that line the tube.

Although the journey of sperm is literally blind, it is apparently not random. It is *not* true that sperm travel about at random inside the woman's reproductive tract. Sperm cells are apparently "egged on" (pardon the pun) by a change in calcium ions that occurs when an ovum is released by a follicle (Angier, 2007).

T F Sperm travel about at random inside the woman's reproductive tract.
Actually, sperm are apparently attracted to the ovum by chemical changes that occur when it is released.

Of all the sperm swarming around the egg, only one enters (see Figure 2.9). Ova are surrounded by a gelatinous layer that must be penetrated if fertilization is to occur. Many of the sperm that have completed their journey to the ovum secrete an enzyme that briefly thins the layer, but it enables only one sperm to penetrate. Once a sperm cell has entered, the layer thickens, locking other sperm out.

The chromosomes from the sperm cell line up across from the corresponding chromosomes in the egg cell. They form 23 new pairs with a unique set of genetic instructions.

FIGURE 2.9
Human Sperm Swarming Around an Ovum in a Fallopian Tube

Fertilization normally occurs in a fallopian tube. The egg (on the left) is surrounded by millions of yellow hairlike sperm. Only one of the sperm, however, will penetrate the egg to fertilize it.

© Dr. Yorgos Nikas/Photo Researchers, Inc.

CAUSES OF INFERTILITY

The following fertility problems are found in men (American Fertility Association, 2007):

- Low sperm count
- Deformed sperm
- Poor ability of the sperm to swim to the ovum (low sperm motility)
- Infectious diseases, such as sexually transmitted infections
- Chronic diseases, such as diabetes
- Injury of the testes
- An autoimmune response, in which the man's body attacks his own sperm as foreign agents

A low sperm count or a lack of sperm is the most common infertility problem in men. Men's fertility problems have a variety of causes: genetic factors, environmental poisons, diabetes, sexually transmitted infections (STIs), overheating of the testes (which happens now and then among athletes, such as long-distance runners), pressure (as from using narrow bicycle seats), aging, and certain prescription and illicit drugs (Hatcher et al., 2007). Sometimes the sperm count is adequate, but other factors such as prostate or hormonal problems deform sperm or deprive them of their **motility**. Motility can also be impaired by the scar tissue from infections, such as STIs.

Women encounter the following fertility problems (American Fertility Association, 2007):

- Irregular ovulation, including failure to ovulate
- Declining levels of the hormones estrogen and progesterone that occur with aging and that may prevent the ovum from becoming fertilized or remaining implanted in the uterus
- Inflammation of the tissue that is sloughed off during menstruation (endometriosis)
- Obstructions or malfunctions of the reproductive tract, which are often caused by infections or diseases involving the reproductive tract

The most common problem in women is irregular ovulation or lack of ovulation. This problem can have many causes, including irregularities among the hormones that govern ovulation, stress, and malnutrition.

So-called fertility drugs (e.g., *clomiphene* and *pergonal*) are made up of hormones that cause women to ovulate. These drugs may cause multiple births by stimulating more than one ovum to ripen during a month (Legro et al., 2007).

Infections may scar the fallopian tubes and other organs, impeding the passage of sperm or ova. Such infections include **pelvic inflammatory disease (PID)**. PID can result from bacterial or viral infections, including the STIs gonorrhea and chlamydia. Antibiotics are usually helpful in treating bacterial infections, but infertility may be irreversible.

Endometriosis can obstruct the fallopian tubes, where conception normally takes place. Endometriosis has become fairly common among women who delay childbearing. Each month, tissue develops to line the uterus in case the woman conceives. This tissue—the endometrium—is then sloughed off during menstruation. But some of it backs up into the abdomen through the fallopian tubes. It then collects in the abdomen, where it can cause abdominal pain and lessen the chances of conception. Physicians may treat endometriosis with hormones that temporarily prevent menstruation or through surgery.

motility Self-propulsion.

pelvic inflammatory disease (PID) An infection of the abdominal region that may have various causes and that may impair fertility.

endometriosis Inflammation of endometrial tissue sloughed off into the abdominal cavity rather than out of the body during menstruation; the condition is characterized by abdominal pain and sometimes infertility.

artificial insemination Injection of sperm into the uterus to fertilize an ovum.

METHODS USED TO HELP INFERTILE COUPLES BEAR CHILDREN

Many methods are available to help infertile couples become parents. Most are biological, but adoption is also an option.

Artificial Insemination

Multiple ejaculations of men with low sperm counts can be collected and quick-frozen. The sperm can then be injected into the woman's uterus at the time of ovulation. This procedure is one form of **artificial insemination**. Sperm from men with low sperm motility can also be injected into their partners' uteruses so that the sperm can begin their journey closer to the fallopian tubes. When a man has no sperm or an extremely low sperm count, his partner can be artificially inseminated with the sperm of a donor who resembles the man in physical traits. Some women who want a baby but do not have a male partner also use artificial insemination.

In Vitro Fertilization

Have you heard of "test-tube" babies? These babies are not actually grown in a test-tube. In this method, more technically known as **in vitro fertilization (IVF)**, ripened ova are removed surgically from the mother and placed in a laboratory dish. The father's sperm are also placed in the dish. One or more ova are fertilized and then injected into the mother's uterus to become implanted.

T ⓕ "Test-tube" babies are grown in a laboratory dish throughout their 9-month gestation period.
This is not true; they are conceived in laboratory dishes but then implanted in the uterus for gestation.

IVF may be used when the fallopian tubes are blocked because it means that the ova need not travel through them. If the father's sperm are low in motility, they are sometimes injected directly into the ovum. A variation known as **donor IVF** can be used when the intended mother does not produce ova. An ovum from another woman is fertilized and injected into the uterus of the mother-to-be.

Because only a minority of attempts lead to births, it can take several attempts to achieve a pregnancy. Several embryos may be injected into the uterus at once, increasing the odds of pregnancy. IVF remains costly but is otherwise routine, if not guaranteed.

Surrogate Mothers

Surrogate mothers bring babies to term for other women who are infertile. Surrogate mothers may be artificially inseminated by the partners of infertile women, in which case the baby carries the genes of the father. But sometimes—as with 60-year-old singer-songwriter James Taylor and his 54-year-old wife—ova are surgically extracted from the biological mother, fertilized in vitro by the biological father, and then implanted in another woman's uterus, where the baby is brought to term. Surrogate mothers are usually paid and sign agreements to surrender the baby.

Adoption

Adoption is another way for people to obtain children. Despite occasional conflicts that pit adoptive parents against biological parents who change their minds about giving up their children, most adoptions result in the formation of loving new families. Many Americans find it easier to adopt infants from other countries or with special needs.

SELECTING THE SEX OF YOUR CHILD

Today, there is a reliable method for selecting the sex of a child prior to implantation: preimplantation genetic diagnosis (PGD). PGD was developed to detect genetic disorders, but it also reveals the sex of the embryo. In PGD, ova are fertilized in vitro. After a few days of cell division, a cell is extracted from each, and its sex chromosomal structure is examined microscopically to learn of its sex. Embryos of the desired sex are implanted in the woman's uterus, where one or more can grow to term. However, implantation cannot be guaranteed.

Ⓣ F You can select the sex of your child.
True; the method for doing so is preimplantation genetic diagnosis (PGD).

This three year-old girl, originally from China, holds her certificate of U.S. citizenship during a children's citizenship ceremony in Washington, D.C. Opportunities for Americans to adopt foreign children have grown in recent years.

© Alex Wong/Getty Images

Learning Your Way

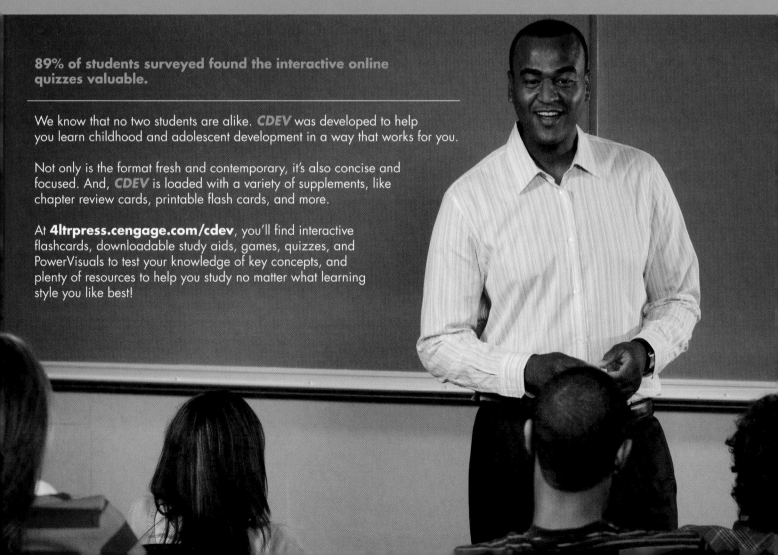

89% of students surveyed found the interactive online quizzes valuable.

We know that no two students are alike. *CDEV* was developed to help you learn childhood and adolescent development in a way that works for you.

Not only is the format fresh and contemporary, it's also concise and focused. And, *CDEV* is loaded with a variety of supplements, like chapter review cards, printable flash cards, and more.

At **4ltrpress.cengage.com/cdev**, you'll find interactive flashcards, downloadable study aids, games, quizzes, and PowerVisuals to test your knowledge of key concepts, and plenty of resources to help you study no matter what learning style you like best!

Within 9 months,

a fetus develops from a nearly microscopic cell to a neonate about 20 inches long.

3

Prenatal Development

TRUTH OR FICTION?

T F Newly fertilized egg cells survive without any nourishment from the mother for more than a week.

T F Your heart started beating when you were only one-fourth of an inch long and weighed a fraction of an ounce.

T F Parents in wealthy nations have more children.

T F The same disease organism or chemical agent that can do serious damage to a 6-week-old embryo may have no effect on a 4-month-old fetus.

T F It is harmless to the embryo and fetus for a pregnant woman to have a couple of glasses of wine in the evening.

The most rapid and dramatic human developments are literally "out of sight" and take place in the uterus. Within 9 months, a fetus develops from a nearly microscopic cell to a **neonate** about 20 inches long. Its weight increases a billionfold.

neonate A newborn baby.

We can date pregnancy from the onset of the last menstrual period before conception, which makes the normal gestation period 280 days. We can also date pregnancy from the assumed date of fertilization, which normally occurs 2 weeks after the beginning of the woman's last menstrual cycle. With this accounting method, the gestation period is 266 days.

Prenatal development is divided into three periods: the germinal stage (approximately the first 2 weeks), the embryonic stage (the third through the eighth weeks), and the fetal stage (the third month through birth). Health professionals also commonly speak of prenatal development in terms of three trimesters of 3 months each.

Learning Outcomes

LO1 Describe the key events of the germinal stage.

LO2 Describe the key events of the embryonic stage.

LO3 Describe the key events of the fetal stage.

LO4 Describe environmental influences on prenatal development, including maternal nutrition, teratogens, infections, parental drug use, environmental hazards, and parents' age.

LO1 The Germinal Stage: Wanderings

Within 36 hours after conception, the zygote divides into two cells. It then divides repeatedly as it undergoes its 3–4 day journey to the uterus. Within another 36 hours, it has

germinal stage The period of development between conception and the implantation of the embryo.

blastocyst A stage within the germinal period of prenatal development in which the zygote has the form of a sphere of cells surrounding a cavity of fluid.

embryonic disk The platelike inner part of the blastocyst that differentiates into the ectoderm, mesoderm, and endoderm of the embryo.

trophoblast The outer part of the blastocyst from which the amniotic sac, placenta, and umbilical cord develop.

umbilical cord A tube that connects the fetus to the placenta.

placenta An organ connected to the uterine wall and to the fetus by the umbilical cord. The placenta serves as a filter between mother and fetus for the exchange of nutrients and wastes.

FIGURE 3.1
The Ovarian Cycle, Conception, and the Early Days of the Germinal Stage

Division of the zygote creates the hollow sphere of cells termed the *blastocyst*, which becomes implanted in the uterine wall.

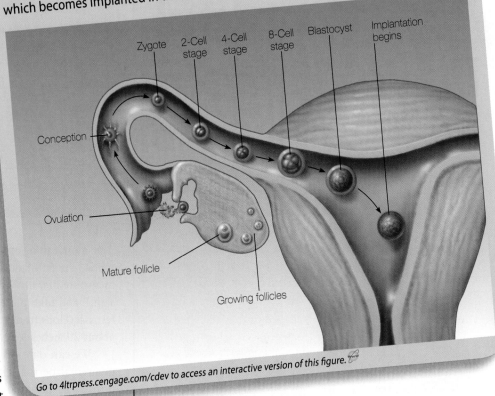

Go to 4ltrpress.cengage.com/cdev to access an interactive version of this figure.

become 32 cells. The mass of dividing cells wanders about the uterus for another 3 to 4 days before it begins to implant in the uterine wall. Implantation takes another week or so. The period from conception to implantation is called the **germinal stage** (see Figure 3.1).

A few days into the germinal stage, the dividing cell mass takes the form of a fluid-filled ball of cells called a **blastocyst**. In the blastocyst, cells begin to separate into groups that will eventually become different structures. The inner part of the blastocyst has two distinct layers that form a thickened mass of cells called the **embryonic disk**. These cells will become the embryo and eventually the fetus.

The outer part of the blastocyst, or **trophoblast**, at first consists of a single layer of cells, but it rapidly differentiates into four membranes that will protect and nourish the embryo. One membrane produces blood cells until the embryo's liver develops and takes over this function. Then it disappears. Another membrane develops into the **umbilical cord** and the blood vessels of the **placenta**. A third develops into the amniotic sac, and the fourth becomes the chorion, which will line the placenta.

The cluster of cells that will become the embryo and then the fetus is at first nourished only by the yolk of the egg cell, like a chick developing in a chicken egg. A blastocyst gains mass only when it receives nourishment from outside. For that to happen, it must be implanted in the uterine wall.

T (circled) F Newly fertilized egg cells survive without any nourishment from the mother for more than a week.

True; they do not receive nourishment from the mother until they become implanted in the uterine wall, which can take about a week and a half.

Implantation may be accompanied by bleeding, which is usually normal and results from the rupturing of small blood vessels that line the uterus. But bleeding can also be a sign of miscarriage. Most women who experience implantation bleeding, however, do not miscarry, but have normal pregnancies. Miscarriage usually stems from abnormalities in the developmental process. Many women miscarry early in pregnancy, but their menstrual flow appears about on schedule so that they may not know they had conceived. About 15–20% of pregnancies in which the woman knows she is pregnant end in miscarriage, with most miscarriages occurring in the first 7 weeks of pregnancy (National Library of Medicine, 2009). Women who have miscarriages tend to experience a good deal of anxiety during the early months of subsequent pregnancies (Geller et al., 2004).

LO2 The Embryonic Stage

the **embryonic stage** begins with implantation and covers the first 2 months, during which the major organ systems differentiate. Development follows **cephalocaudal** (Latin for "head to tail") and **proximodistal** (Latin for "near to far") trends. Growth of the head takes precedence over growth of the lower parts of the body (see Figure 3.2). You can also think of the body as containing a central axis that coincides with the spinal cord. Growth of the organ systems near the spine occurs earlier than growth of the extremities. Relatively early maturation of the brain and the organs that lie near the spine allows them to play key roles in further development.

During the embryonic stage, the outer layer of cells of the embryo, or **ectoderm**, develops into the nervous system, sensory organs, nails, hair, teeth, and outer layer of skin. At approximately 21 days, two ridges appear in the ectoderm and fold toward one another to compose the **neural tube**, from which the nervous system will develop. The inner layer of the embryo, or **endoderm**, forms the digestive and respiratory systems, the liver, and the pancreas. A bit later, the mesoderm, a middle layer of cells, becomes differentiated. The **mesoderm** develops into the excretory, reproductive, and circulatory systems, the muscles, the skeleton, and the inner layer of the skin.

During the third week after conception, the head and blood vessels begin to form. An embryo's heart starts beating when the embryo is only 1/4 of an inch long and weighs a fraction of an ounce. The major organ systems develop during the first 2 months. Arm buds and leg buds begin to appear toward the end of the first month. Eyes, ears, nose, and mouth begin to take shape. By this time, the nervous system, including the brain, has also begun to develop. The upper arms and legs develop before the forearms and lower legs. Next come hands and feet, followed at 6 to 8 weeks by webbed fingers and toes. By the end of the second month, the limbs are elongating and separated, and the webbing is gone from fingers and toes.

> **embryonic stage** The stage of prenatal development that lasts from implantation through the eighth week of pregnancy; it is characterized by the development of the major organ systems.
>
> **cephalocaudal** From head to tail.
>
> **proximodistal** From the inner part (or axis) of the body outward.
>
> **ectoderm** The outermost cell layer of the newly formed embryo from which the skin and nervous system develop.
>
> **neural tube** A structure that forms in the ectoderm during the embryonic stage, from which the nervous system develops.
>
> **endoderm** The inner layer of the embryo from which the lungs and digestive system develop.
>
> **mesoderm** The central layer of the embryo from which the bones and muscles develop.

 T F Your heart started beating when you were only one-fourth of an inch long and weighed a fraction of an ounce.

True.

By this time, the embryo is looking quite human. The head has the lovely, round shape of your own, and the facial features have become quite distinct. Bear in mind that all this detail is inscribed on an embryo that is only approximately 1 inch long and weighs only about 1/30 of an ounce. During the second month, the cells in the

FIGURE 3.2
A Human Embryo at 7 Weeks

Note that the head is oversized in relation to the rest of the body.

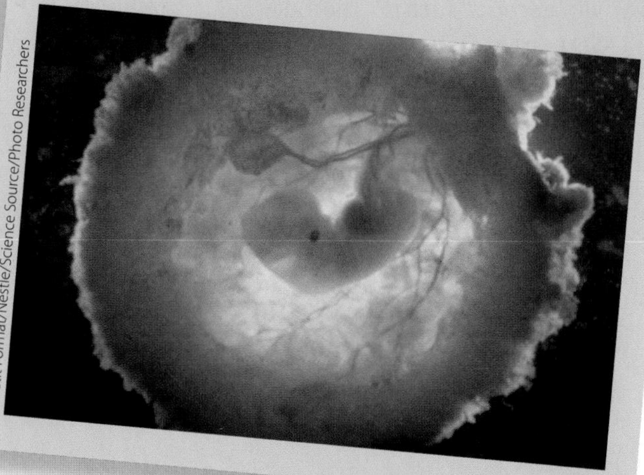

© Petit Format/Nestle/Science Source/Photo Researchers

androgens Male sex hormones.

amniotic sac The sac containing the fetus.

amniotic fluid Fluid within the amniotic sac that suspends and protects the fetus.

nervous system begin to "fire"; that is, they send messages among themselves. Most likely, it is random cell firing, and the "content" of such "messages" is anybody's guess. By the end of the embryonic period, teeth buds have formed. The embryo's kidneys are filtering acid from the blood, and its liver is producing red blood cells.

SEXUAL DIFFERENTIATION

By 5 to 6 weeks, the embryo is only one-quarter to one-half inch long. At this stage of development, both the internal and the external genitals resemble primitive female structures. By about the seventh week, the genetic code (XY or XX) begins to assert itself, causing sex organs to differentiate. Genetic activity on the Y sex chromosome causes the testes to begin to differentiate. The ovaries begin to differentiate if the Y chromosome is *absent*. By about 4 months after conception, males and females show distinct external genital structures. Once the testes have developed in the embryo, they begin to produce male sex hormones, or **androgens**, the most important of which

is testosterone. Female embryos and fetuses produce small amounts of androgens, but they are usually not enough to cause sexual differentiation along male lines. But they are connected with the further development of female sexual organs, and they spur the development of some secondary sexual characteristics in adolescence, such as the appearance of pubic hair and underarm hair. Androgens are also important in the sex drive of females for a lifetime (Morley & Perry, 2003; Nyunt et al., 2005).

THE AMNIOTIC SAC

The embryo and fetus develop within a protective **amniotic sac** in the uterus. This sac is surrounded by a clear membrane and contains **amniotic fluid**. The fluid serves as a kind of natural air bag, allowing the embryo and fetus to move around without injury. It also helps maintain an even temperature.

The placenta is a mass of tissue that permits the embryo (and, later on, the fetus) to exchange nutrients and wastes with the mother. The placenta is unique in origin. It grows from material supplied by both the mother and the embryo. The fetus is connected to the placenta by the umbilical cord. The mother is connected to the placenta by blood vessels in the uterine wall.

THE PLACENTA

Mother and embryo have separate circulatory systems. The pancake-shaped placenta contains a membrane that acts as a filter that permits oxygen and nutrients to reach the embryo from the mother and permits carbon dioxide and waste products to pass to the mother from the embryo. The mother then eliminates them through her lungs and kidneys. Some harmful substances can also pass through the placenta, including various "germs," such as the ones that cause syphilis and German measles, but HIV (the virus that causes AIDS) is more likely to be transmitted through childbirth. Some drugs—aspirin, narcotics, alcohol, tranquilizers, and others—cross the placenta and affect the fetus.

The placenta also secretes hormones that preserve the pregnancy, prepare the breasts for nursing, and stimulate the uterine contractions that prompt childbirth. Ultimately, the placenta passes from the birth canal after the baby; for this reason, it is also called the *afterbirth*.

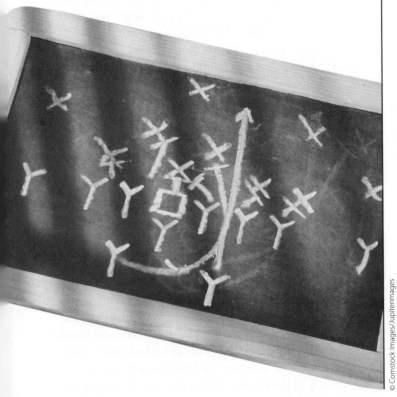

© Comstock Images/Jupiterimages

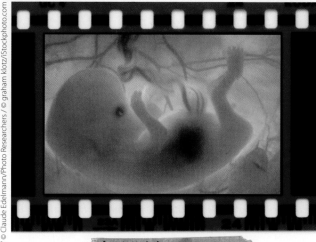

A HUMAN FETUS AT 11 WEEKS

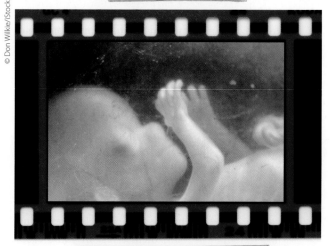

THE HANDS OF A HUMAN FETUS AT 4½ MONTHS

LO3 The Fetal Stage

he **fetal stage** lasts from the beginning of the third month until birth. The fetus begins to turn and respond to external stimulation at about the ninth or tenth week. By the end of the first trimester, the major organ systems have been formed. The fingers and toes are fully formed. The eyes and the genitals of the fetus can be clearly seen.

The second trimester is characterized by further maturation of fetal organ systems and dramatic gains in size. The brain continues to mature, contributing to the fetus's ability to regulate its own basic body functions. The fetus advances from 1 ounce to 2 pounds in weight and grows four to five times in length, from about 3 inches to 14 inches. By the end of the second trimester, the fetus opens and shuts its eyes, sucks its thumb, alternates between wakefulness and sleep, and perceives light and sounds. Soft, downy hair grows above the eyes and on the scalp. The skin turns ruddy because of blood vessels that show through the surface. (During the third trimester, fatty layers will give the skin a pinkish hue.)

During the third trimester, the organ systems mature further. The fetus gains about 5 1/2 pounds and doubles in length. During the seventh month, the fetus normally turns upside down in the uterus so that delivery will be head first. By the end of the seventh month, the fetus will have almost doubled in weight, gaining another 1 pound, 12 ounces, and will have increased another 2 inches in length. The chances of survival for babies born at this point in development are nearly 90%. For babies born at the end of the eighth month, the odds are overwhelmingly in favor of survival. Newborn boys average about 7 1/2 pounds and newborn girls about 7 pounds.

> For babies born at the end of the eighth month, the odds are overwhelmingly in favor of survival.

FETAL PERCEPTION

By the 13th week of pregnancy, the fetus responds to sound waves. Sontag and Richards (1938) rang a bell near the mother's abdomen, and the fetus responded with movements similar to those of the startle reflex shown after birth. During the third trimester, fetuses respond to sounds of different frequencies through a variety of movements and changes in heart rate, suggesting that they can discriminate pitch (Lecanuet et al., 2000).

An experiment by Anthony DeCasper and William Fifer (1980) is even more intriguing. In this study, women read the Dr. Seuss book *The Cat in the Hat* out loud twice daily during the final month and a half of pregnancy. After birth, their babies were given special pacifiers. Sucking on these pacifiers in one way would activate a recording of their mothers reading *The Cat in the Hat*, and sucking on them in another way would activate a recording of their mother reading a book which was written in a very different

fetal stage The stage of development that lasts from the beginning of the ninth week of pregnancy through birth; it is characterized by gains in size and weight and by maturation of the organ systems.

rhythm. The newborns "chose" to hear *The Cat in the Hat*. Fetal learning may be one basis for the development of attachment to the mother (Krueger et al., 2004; Lecanuet et al., 2005).

FETAL MOVEMENTS

The mother usually feels the first fetal movements in the middle of the fourth month (Adolph & Berger, 2005). By 29–30 weeks, the fetus moves its limbs so vigorously that the mother may complain of being kicked. The fetus also turns somersaults, which are clearly felt by the mother. The umbilical cord will not break or become dangerously wrapped around the fetus, no matter how many acrobatic feats the fetus performs.

Fetuses show different patterns of prenatal activity (de Vries & Hopkins, 2005). Slow squirming movements begin at about 5 or 6 months. Sharp jabbing or kicking movements begin at about the same time and increase in intensity until shortly before birth. As the fetus grows, it becomes cramped in the uterus, and movement is constricted, so the fetus becomes markedly less active during the ninth month of pregnancy.

> We are in the middle of a **population explosion**, are we not?

BIRTH RATES AROUND THE WORLD

Let's have a look at some history and some prehistory—that is, some guesstimates of events that might have occurred before records were made. According to the U.S. Census Bureau (U.S. Census Bureau, 2008), which was *not* distributing questionnaires at the time, some 5 million humans walked the Earth about 10,000 years ago. It took another 5,000 years for that number to expand to 14 million. Skipping ahead 2,000 years to the year 1, humans had gained a stronger foothold on the planet, and the number had increased tenfold, to some 170 million. By 1900 the number increased tenfold again, to about 1.7 billion. Estimates place the number in 1950 at about 2.5 billion, and today—with the increase in the food supply, sanitary water supplies,

Improvements in world-wide supplies of sanitary water, such as the drilling of wells like this one in Gambia, have played a role in the dramatic global population growth since 1950.

© Christine Osborne Pictures/Alamy

and vaccinations—the number is estimated to be at about 6.5 billion.

Therefore, we are in the middle of a population explosion, are we not? The answer would seem to depend on where one happens to be. For example, if you check out Table 3.1, you will readily see that it is not true that parents in wealthy nations have more children. Parents need to have slightly in excess of two children to reproduce themselves because some children are lost to illness, accidents, or violence. The table will show you that in countries such as Spain, Greece, Italy, Japan, Canada, Russia, and the United Kingdom, parents are not coming close to reproducing themselves. In some cases, the national birth rates mask major differences within a country. In Israel, for example, the minorities of Orthodox Jews and Arabs out reproduce the majority of less religious or nonreligious Jews, providing an overall somewhat inflated birth rate.

Also consider factors related to birth rates, such as use of modern means of contraception, literacy rates, and education, as measured by numbers of years spent in school. Consider the extremes. How do the birth rates of countries where 30% or fewer of the population use modern means of contraception compare with those where 60% or more use modern means? Similarly, what are the relationships between literacy and birth rate? Between education level and birth rate?

T **F** Parents in wealthy nations have more children.

Actually, parents in wealthy nations tend to have fewer children.

TABLE 3.1
Fertility Rates and Related Factors around the World*

NATION	FERTILITY RATE	RATE OF USAGE OF MODERN METHODS OF CONTRACEPTION (%)	LITERACY RATES (%)		YEARS OF EDUCATION	
			Men	**Women**	**Men**	**Women**
Afghanistan	7.48	3.6	43	13	9	4
Angola	6.75	4.5	83	54	4	3
Australia	1.75	72.2	**	**	20	20
Brazil	2.35	70.3	88	89	14	14
Canada	1.51	73.3	**	**	15	16
China	1.70	83.3	95	87	11	11
Colombia	2.62	67.6	93	93	11	12
Congo	6.70	4.4	81	54	4***	4***
Cuba	1.61	72.1	100	100	14	14
Egypt	3.29	56.5	83	59	12***	12***
France	1.87	69.3	**	**	15	16
Germany	1.32	71.8	**	**	16	16
Greece	1.25	**	98	94	15	16
Guatemala	4.60	34.4	75	63	10	9
India	3.07	42.8	73	48	11	9
Iran	2.12	56.0	84	70	13	12
Iraq	4.83	10.4	84	64	11	8
Ireland	1.94	**	**	**	18	18
Israel	2.85	51.9	98	96	15	16
Italy	1.28	38.9	99	98	16	16
Jamaica	2.44	62.6	74	86	11	12
Japan	1.33	51.0	**	**	15	15
Kenya	5.00	31.5	78	70	10	10
Mexico	2.40	59.5	92	90	13	13
Pakistan	4.27	20.2	63	36	7	5
Palestinian Territories	5.57	37.1	97	88	13	14
Philippines	3.22	33.4	93	93	12	12
Russia	1.33	**	100	99	13	14
Saudi Arabia	4.09	28.5	87	69	10	10
Spain	1.27	67.4	**	**	16	17
Turkey	2.46	37.7	95	80	12	10
United Kingdom	1.66	81.0	**	**	16	17
United States	2.04	70.5	**	**	15	16

*Sources: United Nations Department of Economic and Social Affairs. (2008 December). *Demographic and social statistics. Social indicators.* Retrieved January 1, 2009, from http://unstats.un.org/unsd/demographic/products/socind/default.htm. Total fertility estimates from Population Division of the United Nations Secretariat, *World Population Prospects* (various editions).

**Data missing or unavailable at the United Nations Web site. It is not possible to draw conclusions of any kind.

***Number of years is for males and females combined because the statistics provided by the nation did not permit categorization by sex.

LO4 Environmental Influences on Prenatal Development

the developing fetus is subject to many environmental hazards. Scientific advances have made us keenly aware of the types of things that can go wrong and what we can do to prevent these problems.

NUTRITION

It is a common misconception that fetuses "take what they need" from their mothers. However, maternal malnutrition has been linked to low birth weight, prematurity, retardation of brain development, cognitive deficiencies, behavioral problems, and even cardiovascular disease (Guerrini et al., 2007; Morton, 2006). The effects of fetal malnutrition are sometimes overcome by a supportive, care-giving environment. Experiments with children who suffered from fetal malnutrition show that enriched day-care programs enhance intellectual and social skills by 5 years of age (Ramey et al., 1999). Supplementing the diets of pregnant women who might otherwise be deficient in their intake of calories and protein also shows modest positive effects on the motor development of infants (Morton, 2006). On the other hand, maternal obesity is linked with a higher risk of **stillbirth** (Fernandez-Twinn & Ozanne, 2006) and neural tube defects. Over the course of pregnancy, women who do not restrict their diet will normally gain 25–35 pounds. Overweight women may gain less, and slender women may gain more. Regular weight gains of about 1/2 pound per week during the first half of pregnancy and 1 pound per week thereafter are desirable. Sudden large gains or losses in weight should be discussed with a doctor. Inadequate weight gain in pregnancy increases the chances of having a premature or low-birth-weight baby (Christian et al., 2003; Hynes et al., 2002).

stillbirth The delivery of a dead fetus.

teratogens Environmental agents that can damage the embryo or fetus.

critical period In this usage, a period during which an embryo or fetus is particularly vulnerable to a certain teratogen.

syphilis A sexually transmitted infection that, in advanced stages, can attack major organ systems.

congenital Present at birth; resulting from the prenatal environment.

TERATOGENS AND HEALTH PROBLEMS OF THE MOTHER

Teratogens are environmental agents that can harm the embryo or fetus. They include drugs taken by the mother, such as thalidomide and alcohol, and substances that the mother's body produces, such as Rh-positive antibodies. Another class of teratogens is the heavy metals, such as lead and mercury, which are toxic to the embryo. Hormones are healthful in countless ways—for example, they help maintain pregnancy—but excessive quantities are harmful to the embryo. Exposure to radiation can harm the embryo. Of course, disease-causing organisms—also called *pathogens*—such as bacteria and viruses are also teratogens.

CRITICAL PERIODS OF VULNERABILITY

Exposure to particular teratogens is most harmful during **critical periods** that correspond to the times when organs are developing. For example, the heart develops rapidly in the third to fifth weeks after conception. As you can see in Figure 3.3, the heart is most vulnerable to certain teratogens at this time. The arms and legs, which develop later, are most vulnerable in the fourth through eighth weeks. Because the major organ systems differentiate during the embryonic stage, the embryo is generally more vulnerable to teratogens than the fetus. Even so, many teratogens are harmful throughout the entire course of prenatal development.

T F The same disease organism or chemical agent that can do serious damage to a 6-week-old embryo may have no effect on a 4-month-old fetus.
True; certain harmful agents have their effects during so-called critical periods, when specific organs are developing.

Let us consider the effects of various health problems of the mother. We begin with sexually transmitted infections (STIs).

SEXUALLY TRANSMITTED INFECTIONS

The **syphilis** bacterium can cause miscarriage, stillbirth, or **congenital** syphilis. Routine blood tests early in preg-

FIGURE 3.3
Critical Periods in Prenatal Development

Specific teratogens are most harmful during certain periods of prenatal development.

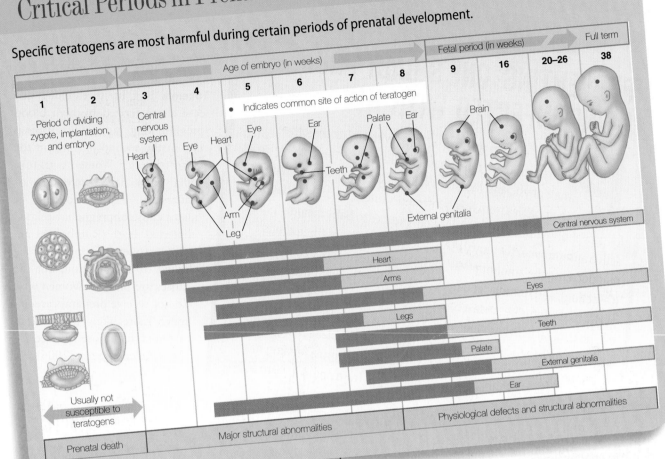

nancy can diagnose syphilis. The syphilis bacterium is vulnerable to antibiotics. The fetus will probably not contract syphilis if an infected mother is treated with antibiotics before the fourth month of pregnancy (Centers for Disease Control and Prevention, 2006b). If the mother is not treated, the baby may be infected in utero and develop congenital syphilis. About 12% of those infected die.

HIV/AIDS (human immunodeficiency virus/acquired immunodeficiency syndrome) disables the body's immune system and leaves victims prey to a variety of fatal illnesses, including respiratory disorders and cancer. HIV/AIDS is lethal unless treated with a "cocktail" of antiviral drugs. Even then, the drugs do not work for everyone, and the eventual outcome remains in doubt (Rathus et al., 2008).

HIV can be transmitted by sexual relations, blood transfusions, sharing hypodermic needles while shooting up drugs, childbirth, and breast feeding. About one-fourth of babies born to HIV-infected mothers become infected themselves (Coovadia, 2004). During childbirth, blood vessels in the mother and baby rupture, enabling an exchange of blood and transmission of HIV. HIV is also found in breast milk. An African study found that the probability of transmission of HIV through breast milk was about 1 in 6 (16.2%) (Nduati et al., 2000).

RUBELLA

Rubella (German measles) is a viral infection. Women who are infected during the first 20 weeks of pregnancy stand at least a 20% chance of bearing children with birth

HIV/AIDS HIV stands for *human immunodeficiency virus*, which cripples the body's immune system. AIDS stands for *acquired immunodeficiency syndrome*, a condition in which the immune system is weakened and the body becomes vulnerable to a variety of fatal illnesses.

rubella A viral infection that can cause retardation and heart disease in the embryo. Also called *German measles*.

PREVENTING ONE'S BABY FROM BEING INFECTED WITH HIV

Pregnant women who are infected with HIV or any other sexually transmitted disease should discuss this issue with their physicians. Measures can be taken that will help prevent their babies from being infected. Current recommendations for preventing transmission of HIV from mother to baby include highly active antiretroviral therapy (HAART), a combination of three drugs that decrease the amount of HIV in the bloodstream; cesarean section (C-section), and formula feeding. C-sections help prevent transmission of HIV to the fetus because it is not exposed to the mother's blood during vaginal delivery, when blood vessels rupture. HIV is also found in breast milk (hence the recommendation for formula feeding). All in all, the combination of HAART, C-section, and formula feeding has reduced mother-to-infant transmission of HIV from about 25% to 1–2% (Coovadia, 2004).

For up-to-date information on HIV/AIDS, call the National AIDS Hotline at 1-800-342-AIDS. If you want to receive information in Spanish, call 1-800-344-SIDA. You can also visit the Centers for Disease Control and Prevention website at http://www.cdc.gov/hiv.

© Image Source

caused by rubella, from approximately 2,000 cases in 1964–1965 to 21 cases in 2001 (Food and Drug Administration, 2004; Reef et al., 2004).

TOXEMIA

Toxemia is a life-threatening disease characterized by high blood pressure that may afflict women late in the second or early in the third trimester. Women with toxemia often have **premature** or undersized babies. Toxemia is also a cause of pregnancy-related maternal death (Rumbold et al., 2006). Toxemia appears to be linked to malnutrition, but the causes are unclear. Women who do not receive prenatal care are much more likely to die from toxemia than those who receive prenatal care (Scott, 2006).

RH INCOMPATIBILITY

In **Rh incompatibility**, antibodies produced by the mother are transmitted to a fetus or newborn infant and cause brain damage or death. Rh is a blood protein found in the red blood cells of some individuals. Rh incompatibility occurs when a woman who does not have this factor—and is thus Rh negative—is carrying an Rh-positive fetus, which can happen if the father is Rh positive. The negative–positive combination occurs in approximately 10% of American couples and becomes a problem in some resulting pregnancies. Rh incompatibility does not affect a first child because women will not have formed Rh antibodies. The chances of an exchange of blood are greatest during childbirth. If an exchange occurs, the mother produces Rh-positive antibodies to the baby's Rh-positive blood. These antibodies can enter the fetal bloodstream during subsequent deliveries, causing anemia, mental deficiency, or death.

If an Rh-negative mother is injected with Rh immunoglobulin within 72 hours after delivery of an Rh-positive baby, she will not develop the antibodies. A

defects such as deafness, mental retardation, heart disease, or eye problems, including blindness (Food and Drug Administration, 2004; Reef et al., 2004).

Many adult women had rubella as children and became immune in this way. Women who are not immune are best vaccinated before they become pregnant, although they can be inoculated during pregnancy, if necessary. Inoculation has led to a dramatic decline in the number of American children born with defects

toxemia A life-threatening disease that can afflict pregnant women; it is characterized by high blood pressure.

premature Born before the full term of gestation. Also referred to as *preterm*.

Rh incompatibility A condition in which antibodies produced by the mother are transmitted to the child, possibly causing brain damage or death.

fetus or newborn child at risk of Rh disease may receive a blood transfusion to remove the mother's antibodies.

DRUGS TAKEN BY THE PARENTS

Rh antibodies can be lethal to children, but many other substances can have harmful effects. Even commonly used medications, such as aspirin, can be harmful to the fetus. If a woman is pregnant or thinks she may be, it is advisable for her to consult her obstetrician before taking any drugs, not just prescription medications. A physician usually can recommend a safe and effective substitute for a drug that could potentially harm a developing fetus.

Thalidomide

Thalidomide was marketed in the 1960s as a treatment for insomnia and nausea. It was available in Germany and England without prescription. Within a few years, more than 10,000 babies with missing or stunted limbs were born in these countries and elsewhere as a result of their mothers using thalidomide during pregnancy (Ances, 2002).

Thalidomide provides a dramatic example of a teratogen that has its effect during a critical period of vulnerability. A fetus's extremities undergo rapid development during the second month of pregnancy. Thalidomide taken during this period almost invariably causes birth defects, such as missing or stunted limbs.

Hormones

Women at risk for miscarriages have been prescribed hormones to help maintain their pregnancies. **Progestin** is chemically similar to male sex hormones and can masculinize the external sex organs of female embryos. **DES** (short for *diethylstilbestrol*), a powerful estrogen, was given to many women during the 1940s and 1950s to help prevent miscarriage (Centers for Disease Control and Prevention, 2005), but it has caused cervical and testicular cancer in some of the offspring. Among daughters of DES users, about 1 in

1,000 will develop cancer in the reproductive tract. Daughters are also more likely to have babies who are premature or low in birth weight. Daughters and sons of mothers who took DES have high rates of infertility and immune system disorders (Centers for Disease Control and Prevention, 2005).

Vitamins

Although pregnant women are often prescribed multivitamins to maintain their own health and to promote the development of their fetuses, high doses of vitamins A and D have been associated with central nervous system damage, small head size, and heart defects (National Institutes of Health, 2002).

Heroin and Methadone

Maternal addiction to heroin or methadone is linked to low birth weight, prematurity, and toxemia. Narcotics such as heroin and methadone readily cross the placental membrane, and the fetuses of women who use them regularly can become addicted (Lejeune et al., 2006). Addicted newborns may be given the narcotic or a substitute shortly after birth so that they will not suffer serious withdrawal symptoms. The drug is then withdrawn gradually. Addicted newborns may also have behavioral effects, such as delays in motor and language development at the age of 12 months (Bunikowski et al., 1998).

Marijuana (Cannabis)

Smoking marijuana during pregnancy apparently poses a number of risks for the fetus, including slower growth (Hurd et al., 2005) and low birth weight (Visscher et al., 2003). The babies of women who regularly used marijuana show increased tremors and startling, suggesting immature development of the nervous system (Huestis et al., 2002).

Research into the cognitive effects of maternal use of marijuana during pregnancy

> **thalidomide** A sedative used in the 1960s that has been linked to birth defects, especially deformed or absent limbs.
>
> **progestin** A hormone used to maintain pregnancy that can cause masculinization of the fetus.
>
> **DES** Diethylstilbestrol, an estrogen that has been linked to cancer in the reproductive organs of children of women who used the hormone when pregnant.

It's a Boy!

© Julie Masson Deshaies/iStockphoto.com / © Masterfile

shows mixed results. Some studies suggest that there may be no impairment (Fried & Smith, 2001). Others suggest that cognitive skills, including learning and memory, may be impaired (Huizink & Mulder, 2006). One study assessed the behavior of 10-year-olds who had been exposed prenatally to maternal use of marijuana (Goldschmidt et al., 2000) and suggested that prenatal exposure to marijuana was significantly related to increased hyperactivity, impulsivity, problems in paying attention, and increased delinquency and aggressive behavior. The researchers suggested that the pathway from prenatal exposure to marijuana to delinquency involves the effects of marijuana on attention, impairing the abilities to learn in school and to conform to social norms.

Cocaine

Pregnant women who abuse cocaine increase the risk of stillbirth, low birth weight, and birth defects. Their infants are often excitable and irritable, or lethargic; sleep is disturbed (Schuetze et al., 2006). There are suggestions of delays in cognitive development even at 12 months of age (Singer et al., 2005).

Children who are exposed to cocaine prenatally also show problems at later ages. One study compared 189 4-year-olds who had been exposed to cocaine in utero with 185 4-year-olds who had not (Lewis et al., 2004). The children exposed to cocaine had much lower receptive and expressive language abilities.

Alcohol

Because alcohol passes through the placenta, drinking by a pregnant woman poses risks for the embryo and fetus. Heavy drinking can be lethal and is also connected with deficiencies and deformities in growth. Some children of heavy drinkers develop **fetal alcohol syndrome (FAS)** (Connor et al., 2006; see Figure 3.4). Babies with FAS are often smaller than normal, and so are their brains. They have distinct facial features: widely spaced eyes, an underdeveloped upper jaw, and a flattened nose. There may be malformation of the limbs, poor coordination, and cardiovascular problems. Psychological characteristics appear to reflect dysfunction of the brain: mental retardation, hyperactivity, distractibility, lessened verbal fluency, and learning disabilities (Guerrini et al., 2007).

T (F) It is harmless to the embryo and fetus for a pregnant woman to have a couple of glasses of wine in the evening.
False; even light drinking by the mother puts the fetus at risk of developing fetal alcohol syndrome (FAS).

The facial deformities of FAS diminish as the child moves into adolescence, and most children catch up in height and weight, but the intellectual, academic, and behavioral deficits of FAS persist (Guerrini et al., 2007). Maladaptive behaviors such as poor judgment, distractibility, and difficulty perceiving social cues are common (Schonfeld et al., 2005). FAS is part of a broader group of fetal alcohol-related problems referred to as *fetal alcohol spectrum disorders* (Connor et al., 2006).

It cannot be guaranteed that even one glass of wine a day is harmless to the embryo and fetus. Although some health professionals allow pregnant women a glass of wine with dinner, research suggests that even moderate drinkers place their offspring at increased risk for a less severe set of effects known as *fetal alcohol effect*. Preg-

FIGURE 3.4
Fetal Alcohol Syndrome (FAS)

The children of many mothers who drank alcohol during pregnancy exhibit FAS. This syndrome is characterized by developmental lags and such facial features as an underdeveloped upper jaw, a flattened nose, and widely spaced eyes.

© George Steinmetz

nant women who have as few as one or two drinks a day may be more likely to miscarry and have growth-delayed babies than pregnant women who do not drink alcohol (Newburn-Cook et al., 2002).

Caffeine

Many pregnant women consume caffeine in the form of coffee, tea, soft drinks, chocolate, and nonprescription drugs. Research findings on caffeine's effects on the developing fetus have been inconsistent (Signorello & McLaughlin, 2004). Some studies report no adverse findings, but other studies do (Weng et al., 2008).

Cigarettes

Cigarette smoke contains many ingredients, including the stimulant nicotine, the gas carbon monoxide, and hydrocarbons ("tars"), which are carcinogens. Nicotine and carbon monoxide pass through the placenta and reach the fetus. Nicotine stimulates the fetus, but its long-term effects are uncertain. Carbon monoxide is toxic; it decreases the amount of oxygen available to the fetus. Oxygen deprivation is connected with impaired motor development, academic delays, learning disabilities, mental retardation, and hyperactivity (Secker-Walker & Vacek, 2003).

Pregnant women who smoke are likely to deliver smaller babies than nonsmokers (Bernstein et al., 2005). Their babies are more likely to be stillborn or to die soon after birth (Cnattingius, 2004). Secondhand smoke also holds dangers. Men who smoke are more likely to produce abnormal sperm. Babies of fathers who smoke have higher rates of birth defects, infant mortality, low birth weight, and cardiovascular problems (Goel et al., 2004).

ENVIRONMENTAL HAZARDS

Mothers know when they are ingesting drugs, but there are many other substances in the environment they may take in unknowingly. These substances are environmental hazards to which we are all exposed and which are referred to collectively as *pollution*.

Prenatal exposure to heavy metals such as lead, mercury, and zinc threatens to delay mental development at 1 and 2 years of age (Heindel & Lawler, 2006). But the cognitive functioning of these children can improve if there is no longer lead in the home.

Polychlorinated biphenyls (PCBs), used in many industrial products, accumulate in fish that feed in polluted waters. Newborns whose mothers consumed PCB-contaminated fish from Lake Michigan were smaller and showed poorer motor functioning and memory defects (Jacobson et al., 1992).

Experiments with mice show that fetal exposure to radiation in high doses can damage the eyes, central nervous system, and skeleton (e.g., Hossain et al., 2005). Pregnant women exposed to atomic radiation during the bombings of Hiroshima and Nagasaki in World War II gave birth to babies who were likely to be mentally retarded as well as physically deformed (Sadler, 2005). Pregnant women are advised to avoid unnecessary exposure to x-rays. (Ultrasound, which is not an x-ray, has not been shown to harm the fetus.)

Men exposed to heavy metals and radiation can also produce children with abnormalities. For example, children of fathers employed in jobs with high exposure to lead had three times more kidney tumors than children whose fathers were not exposed (Davis, 1991).

EFFECTS OF PARENTS' AGE— DO MEN REALLY HAVE ALL THE TIME IN THE WORLD?

"What if 30-year-old women started looking at 50-year-old men as damaged goods, what with their washed-up sperm, meaning those 50-year-olds might actually have to date (gasp!) women their own age? What if men, as the years passed, began to look with new eyes at Ms. Almost Right?"

—Lisa Belkin, 2009

The artist Pablo Picasso fathered children in his 70s. Former Senator Strom Thurmond fathered a child in his 90s. It has been widely known that women's chances of conceiving children decline as they age. The traditional message has been "Women: you'd better hurry up. Men: you have all the time in the world" (Belkin, 2009). Not so, apparently, as we see here.

From a biological vantage point, the 20s may be the ideal age for women to bear children. Teenage mothers have a higher incidence of infant mortality and children with low birth weight (Phipps et al., 2002; Save the Children, 2008). Pregnancy may place a burden on the bodies of early teens, which may not have adequately matured to facilitate pregnancy and childbirth. Teenage mothers also are less educated and less likely to obtain prenatal care (Berg et al., 2003).

What about women older than 30? Women's fertility declines gradually until the mid-30s, after which it declines more rapidly. Women beyond their middle 30s may have passed the point at which their reproductive systems function most efficiently. Women possess most of their ova in immature form at birth. Over 30 years, these cells are exposed to the slings and arrows of an outrageous environment of toxic wastes, chemical pollutants, and radiation, increasing the risk of chromosomal abnormalities such as Down syndrome (Behrman et al., 2000). Women in their 30s or 40s also increase the likelihood of having stillborn or preterm babies (Berg et al., 2003). But with adequate prenatal care, the risk of bearing an unhealthy baby still is relatively small (Berg et al., 2003). This news should be encouraging for women who have delayed, or plan to delay, bearing children until their 30s or 40s.

Older fathers are more likely to produce abnormal sperm, leading to fertility problems (Belkin, 2009). But that's only the tip of the iceberg. Researchers analyzed data from some 33,000 U.S. children and found that the older the father is at conception, the lower a child's score may be on tests of reading skills, reasoning, memory, and concentration. The ages of 29 and 30 may be a turning point for men, because children conceived past these ages are at greater risk for schizophrenia and bipolar disorder (Perrin et al., 2007). Children born to men past 40 also have a greater risk of autism (Reichenberg et al., 2006), as you can see in Figure 3.5.

These findings do not mean that the majority of children born to men past their reproductive "prime" will develop these problems, but it does mean that a man's age, like a woman's, is related to risks for children. As noted by one of the researchers in schizophrenia, "It turns out the optimal age for being a mother is the same as the optimal age for being a father" (Belkin, 2009).

Whatever the age of the parents, the events of childbirth provide some of the most memorable moments in the lives of parents. In Chapter 4, we continue our voyage with the process of birth and the characteristics of the newborn child.

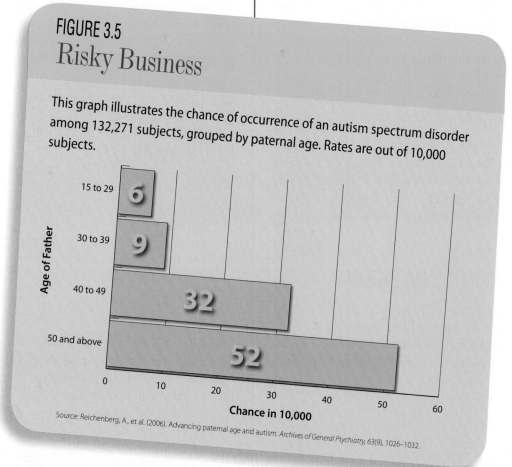

FIGURE 3.5
Risky Business

This graph illustrates the chance of occurrence of an autism spectrum disorder among 132,271 subjects, grouped by paternal age. Rates are out of 10,000 subjects.

Source: Reichenberg, A., et al. (2006). Advancing paternal age and autism. *Archives of General Psychiatry*, 63(9), 1026–1032.

Log In!

CDEV was designed for students just like you—busy people who want choices, flexibility, and multiple learning options.

CDEV delivers concise, focused information in a fresh and contemporary format. And . . . *CDEV* gives you a variety of online learning materials designed with you in mind.

At **4ltrpress.cengage.com/cdev**, you'll find electronic resources such as printable and interactive **flashcards,** downloadable **study aids, games, quizzes,** and **PowerVisuals** to test your knowledge of key concepts. These resources will help supplement your understanding of core childhood and adolescent development concepts in a format that fits your busy lifestyle.

Visit **4ltrpress.cengage.com/cdev** to learn more about the multiple *CDEV* resources available to help you succeed!

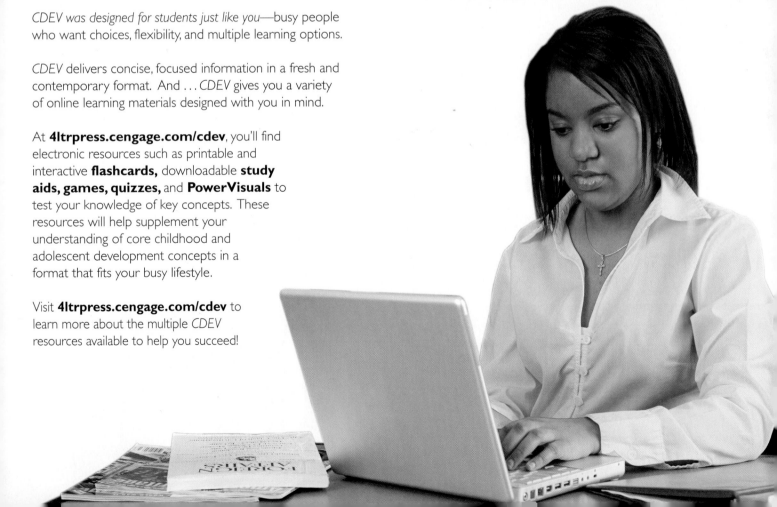

Nearly all first-time mothers

struggle through the last weeks of pregnancy and worry about the mechanics

of delivery.

4

Birth and the Newborn Baby: In the New World

During the few weeks before she gave birth, Michele explained: "I couldn't get my mind off the pregnancy—what it was going to be like when I finally delivered Lisa. I'd had the amniocentesis, so I knew it was a girl. I'd had the ultrasounds, so all her fingers and toes had been counted, but I was still hoping and praying that everything would turn out all right. To be honest, I was also worried about the delivery. I had always been an A student, and I guess I wanted to earn an A in childbirth as well. Matt was understanding, and he was even helpful, but, you know, it wasn't him."

Nearly all first-time mothers struggle through the last weeks of pregnancy and worry about the mechanics of delivery. Childbirth is a natural function, of course, but so many of them have gone to classes to learn how to do what comes naturally! They worry about whether they'll get to the hospital or birthing center on time ("Is there gas in the car?" "Is it snowing?"). They worry about whether the baby will start breathing on its own properly. They may wonder if they'll do it on their own or need a C-section. They may also worry about whether it will hurt, and how much, and when they should ask for anesthetics, and, well, how to earn that A.

Learning Outcomes

LO1 Identify the stages of childbirth.

LO2 Examine different methods of childbirth.

LO3 Discuss potential problems with childbirth.

LO4 Describe the postpartum period.

LO5 Describe the characteristics of a neonate.

full term The amount of time of a normal pregnancy: 266 days from the date of conception.

Braxton-Hicks contractions The first, usually painless, contractions of childbirth.

prostaglandins Hormones that stimulate labor contractions.

oxytocin A hormone that stimulates labor contractions.

efface Thin out.

dilate Widen or enlarge.

Close to **full term**, Michele and other women are sort of frontloaded and feel bent out of shape, and guess what? They are. The weight of the fetus may also be causing backaches. Will they deliver the baby, or will the baby—by being born—deliver them from discomfort? "Hanging in and having Lisa was a wonderful experience," Michele said. "I think Matt should have had it."

Countdown . . .

Early in the last month of pregnancy, the head of the fetus settles in the pelvis. This process is called *dropping,* or *lightening*. Because lightening decreases pressure on the diaphragm, the mother may, in fact, feel lighter.

The first uterine contractions are called **Braxton-Hicks contractions**, or false labor contractions. They are relatively painless and may be experienced as early as the sixth month of pregnancy. They tend to increase in frequency as the pregnancy progresses and may serve to tone the muscles that will be used in delivery. Although Braxton-Hicks contractions may be confused with actual labor contractions, real labor contractions are more painful and regular and are also usually intensified by walking.

© NASA

A day or so before labor begins, increased pelvic pressure from the fetus may rupture superficial blood vessels in the birth canal so that blood appears in vaginal secretions. The mucous tissue that had plugged the cervix and protected the uterus from infection becomes dislodged. At about this time, about 1 woman in 10 has a rush of warm liquid from the vagina. This liquid is amniotic fluid, and its discharge means that the amniotic sac has burst. The amniotic sac usually does not burst until the end of the first stage of childbirth, as described later. Indigestion, diarrhea, an ache in the small of the back, and abdominal cramps are also common signs that labor is beginning.

The fetus may actually signal the mother when it is "ready" to be born, that is, when it is mature enough to sustain life outside the uterus. The adrenal and pituitary glands of the fetus may trigger labor by secreting hormones (Snegovskikh et al., 2006).

Fetal hormones stimulate the placenta (which is a gland as well as a filter for the exchange of nutrients and wastes between mother and fetus) and the uterus to secrete **prostaglandins**. Prostaglandins are the main culprits when women experience uncomfortable cramping before or during menstruation; these hormones also serve the function of exciting the muscles of the uterus to engage in labor contractions. As labor progresses, the pituitary gland releases **oxytocin**, another hormone. Oxytocin stimulates contractions that are powerful enough to expel the baby.

LO1 The Stages of Childbirth

regular uterine contractions signal the beginning of childbirth. Developmentalists speak of childbirth as occurring in three stages.

In the first stage of childbirth, uterine contractions **efface** and **dilate** the cervix. This passageway needs to widen to about 4 inches (10 centimeters) to allow the baby to pass. Dilation of the cervix is responsible for most of the pain during childbirth. If the cervix dilates rapidly and easily, there may be little or no discomfort.

Among women undergoing their first deliveries, the first stage may last from a few hours to more than a day. From a half a day to a day is about average, but some first stages are much briefer, and some last up to a couple of days. In subsequent pregnancies, the first stage may

© graham klotz/iStockphoto.com

take less time and may be surprisingly rapid, sometimes between 1 and 2 hours. The first contractions are not usually all that painful and are spaced 10 to 20 minutes apart. They may last from 20 to 40 seconds each.

As the process continues, the contractions become more powerful, frequent, and regular. Women are usually advised to go to the hospital or birthing center when the contractions are 4 to 5 minutes apart. Until the end of the first stage of labor, the mother is usually in a labor room with her partner or another companion.

If the woman is to be "prepped"—that is, if her pubic hair is to be shaved—it takes place now. The prep is intended to lower the chances of infection during delivery and to facilitate the performance of an episiotomy (described later). A woman may be given an enema to prevent an involuntary bowel movement during labor. Many women, however, find prepping and enemas degrading and seek obstetricians who do not perform them routinely.

During the first stage of childbirth, **fetal monitoring** may be used. An electronic sensing device can be strapped around the woman's abdomen to measure the fetal heart rate as well as the frequency, strength, and duration of the labor contractions. An abnormal heart rate alerts the medical staff to possible fetal distress so that appropriate steps can be taken, such as speeding up the delivery by **forceps**, a **vacuum extraction tube**, or other means.

When the cervix is nearly fully dilated, the head of the fetus begins to move into the vagina (birth canal). This process is called **transition**. During transition, which lasts about 30 minutes or less, contractions usually are frequent and strong.

The second stage of childbirth begins when the baby appears at the opening of the birth canal (see Figure 4.1). The second stage is briefer than the first stage. It may last minutes or a few hours and culminates in the birth of the baby. The woman may be taken to a delivery room for the second stage of childbirth.

The contractions of the second stage stretch the skin surrounding the birth canal farther and continue to propel the baby down the birth canal. The baby's head is said to have *crowned* when it begins to emerge from the birth canal. Once crowning has occurred, the baby normally emerges from the birth canal within minutes.

The physician, nurse, or midwife may perform an **episiotomy** once crowning takes place. The purpose

fetal monitoring Use of an electronic sensing device to track the fetus's vital signs during childbirth.

forceps An instrument that fits around the baby's head to pull the baby through the birth canal.

vacuum extraction tube An instrument that uses suction to pull the baby through the birth canal.

transition Initial movement of the baby's head into the birth canal.

episiotomy An incision between the birth canal and anus that widens the vaginal opening to prevent random tearing during childbirth.

FIGURE 4.1
Stages of Childbirth

In the first stage, uterine contractions efface and dilate the cervix. The second stage begins with movement of the baby into the birth canal and ends with birth of the baby. During the third stage, the placenta separates from the uterine wall and is expelled through the birth canal.

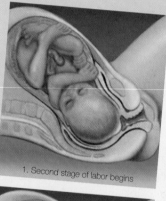

1. Second stage of labor begins

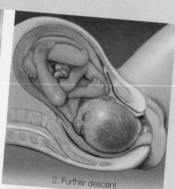

2. Further descent

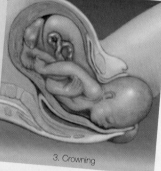

3. Crowning

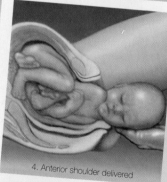

4. Anterior shoulder delivered

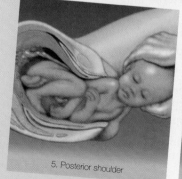

5. Posterior shoulder

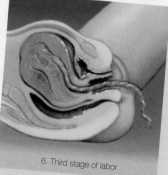

6. Third stage of labor

of the episiotomy is to prevent random tearing when the area between the birth canal and the anus becomes severely stretched. Women are unlikely to feel the incision of the episiotomy because the pressure of the crowning head tends to numb the region between the vagina and the anus. The episiotomy, like prepping and the enema, is controversial and is not practiced in Europe. The incision may cause itching and discomfort as it heals. The incidence of the use of episiotomy in the United States dropped from about 70% in 1983 to 19% in 2000 (Goldberg et al., 2002). Many health professionals believe that an episiotomy is warranted when the baby's shoulders are quite wide or if the baby's heart rate declines for a long period of time. The strongest predictor of whether a practitioner will choose to use episiotomy is not the condition of the mother or the baby, but rather whether the practitioner normally performs an episiotomy.

Whether or not the practitioner performs an episiotomy, the passageway into the world outside is a tight fit, and the baby squeezes through. Sometimes the baby's head and facial features are quite bent out of shape. The baby's head can wind up elongated, its nose can be flattened or pushed to the side, and the ears can be contorted, as though the little thing had gotten caught up in a vicious prizefight. (My wife and I sometimes joke that our second child was born with her nose apparently coming out the side of her cheek.) Parents understandably wonder whether their baby's features will "pop up" properly or return to a more normal shape. Usually they need not worry.

To clear the passageway for breathing, mucus is suctioned from the baby's mouth as soon as the head emerges from the birth canal.

T (F) After birth, babies are held upside down and slapped on the buttocks to stimulate independent breathing.
False; we may see newborns slapped on the buttocks to stimulate breathing in old movies, but suction is the method used in the United States today.

When the baby is breathing adequately on its own, the umbilical cord is clamped and severed about 3 inches from the baby's body (Figure 4.2). At approximately 266 days after conception, mother and infant have finally become separate beings. The stump of the umbilical cord will dry and fall off on its own in about 7 to 10 days.

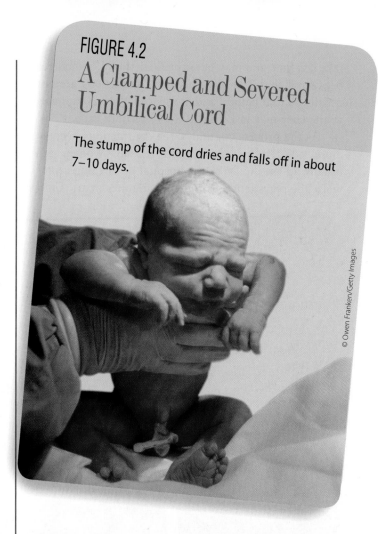

FIGURE 4.2
A Clamped and Severed Umbilical Cord

The stump of the cord dries and falls off in about 7–10 days.

© Owen Franken/Getty Images

T (F) The way the umbilical cord is cut determines whether the baby's belly button will be an "innie" or an "outie."
False; your belly-button status—that is, whether you have an outie or an innie— is unrelated to the methods of your obstetrician.

Now the baby is often whisked away by a nurse, who will perform various procedures, including footprinting the baby, supplying an ID bracelet, putting antibiotic ointment (erythromycin) or drops of silver nitrate into the baby's eyes to prevent bacterial infections, and giving the baby a vitamin K injection to help its blood clot properly if it bleeds (newborn babies do not manufacture vitamin K). While these procedures go on, the mother is in the third stage of labor, which lasts from minutes to an hour or more and is called the *placental stage*. During this stage, the placenta separates from the wall of the uterus and is expelled through the birth canal. Some bleeding is normal. The physician, nurse, or midwife now sews the episiotomy, if one has been performed.

LO2 Methods of Childbirth

Childbirth was once a more intimate procedure that usually took place in the woman's home and involved her, perhaps a **midwife**, and family. This pattern is followed in many less developed nations today, but only rarely in the United States and other developed nations. Contemporary American childbirths usually take place in hospitals, where physicians use sophisticated instruments and **anesthetics** to protect mother and child from complications and discomfort. Modern medicine has saved lives, but childbearing has also become more impersonal. Some argue that modern methods wrest control from women over their own bodies. They even argue that anesthetics have denied many women the experience of giving birth, although many women admit that they appreciate having the experience "muted."

ANESTHESIA

Although painful childbirth has historically been seen as the standard for women, today at least some anesthesia is used in most American deliveries. Two types of anesthetics are used to lessen the pain associated with childbirth. **General anesthesia** puts the woman to sleep, usually by means of an injected barbiturate. Other drugs in common use are **tranquilizers**, oral barbiturates, and narcotics. These drugs reduce anxiety and the perception of pain without causing sleep. General anesthesia reduces the responsiveness of the baby shortly after birth, but there is little evidence that it has long-term negative effects (Caton et al., 2002).

Regional or **local anesthetics** deaden pain without putting the mother to sleep. With a pudendal block, the mother's external genitals are numbed by local injection. With an epidural block or a spinal block, anesthesia is injected into the spinal canal or spinal cord, temporarily numbing the body below the waist. Local anesthesia has minor depressive effects on neonates shortly after birth, but the effects have not been shown to linger (Caton et al., 2002; Eltzschig et al., 2003).

In so-called **natural childbirth**, a woman uses no anesthesia. Instead, a woman is educated about the biological aspects of reproduction and delivery, encouraged to maintain physical fitness, and taught relaxation and breathing exercises.

© Masterfile

PREPARED CHILDBIRTH

In the **Lamaze method**, or prepared childbirth, women perform breathing and relaxation exercises that lessen fear and pain and distract them from discomfort. The mother-to-be attends Lamaze classes with a "coach"—most often, her partner—who will aid her in the delivery room by doing things such as massaging her, timing contractions, offering social support, and coaching her in patterns of breathing and relaxation.

midwife A trained person who helps women in childbirth.

anesthetics Agents that lessen pain.

general anesthesia Putting a person to sleep to prevent her or him from feeling pain.

tranquilizer A drug that reduces feelings of anxiety and tension.

local anesthetic A method that reduces pain in an area of the body.

natural childbirth A method of childbirth in which women use no anesthesia but are educated about childbirth and strategies for coping with discomfort.

Lamaze method A childbirth method in which women learn to relax and breathe to conserve energy and lessen pain and have a coach during childbirth.

T (F) Women who give birth according to the Lamaze method do not experience pain.
False; women who use the Lamaze method experience pain, but they often report less pain and ask for less medication (Meldrum, 2003).

Years ago, the rule of thumb was that pregnant women were not to exert themselves. Today, it is recognized that exercise is healthful for pregnant women because it promotes cardiovascular fitness and increases muscle strength, both of which are assets during childbirth.

DOULAS

Social support during labor can be provided by individuals other than a woman's partner, such as her mother, a sibling, a friend, or an experienced but nonprofessional female companion known as a *doula* (Guzikowski, 2006). Women with doulas present during birth appear to have shorter labors than women without doulas (Campbell et al., 2006).

CESAREAN SECTION

In a **cesarean section** (C-section), the physician delivers the baby by abdominal surgery. The physician cuts through the mother's abdomen and the uterus and physically removes the baby. The incisions are then sewn. Physicians usually perform C-sections so that the incision is more or less hidden by the upper edge of the woman's pubic hair.

T̶ F In the United States, about 3 births in 10 are by cesarean section.

True; some 31% of deliveries are now by C-section, whereas they accounted for only 1 in 20 births (5%) in 1965 (Hamilton et al., 2009). Some of the increase is due to advances in medicine. For example, fetal monitors now allow physicians to more readily detect fetal distress. But physicians also perform C-sections because they are concerned about the possibility of malpractice suits if something goes wrong during a vaginal delivery (Maternity Center Association, 2004).

Physicians prefer C-sections to vaginal delivery when they believe that normal delivery may threaten the mother or child or may simply be more difficult than desired. Typical indications of the C-section are a small pelvis in the mother, maternal weakness or fatigue (e.g., if labor has been prolonged), multiple babies, or a baby that is very large or in apparent distress. C-sections are also performed when the physician

Physicians prefer C-sections to vaginal delivery when they **believe** that normal delivery may threaten the mother or child.

wants to prevent the circulatory systems of the mother and baby from mixing, as might occur when there is (normal) bleeding during vaginal delivery. C-sections in such cases help prevent transmission of the viruses that cause genital herpes or AIDS. The physician may also perform a C-section when it appears that the baby is facing in the wrong direction (not entering the birth canal head first).

LO3 Birth Problems

lthough most deliveries are unremarkable from a medical standpoint, perhaps every delivery is most remarkable from the parents' point of view. Still, a number of problems can and do occur. In this section, we discuss the effects of oxygen deprivation and the problems of preterm and low-birth-weight neonates.

OXYGEN DEPRIVATION

Researchers use two terms to discuss oxygen deprivation: anoxia and hypoxia. **Anoxia** derives from roots meaning "without oxygen." **Hypoxia** derives from roots meaning "under" and "oxygen," the point again being that the baby does not receive enough oxygen throughout pregnancy to develop properly. Prenatal oxygen deprivation can impair the development of the fetus's central nervous system, leading to cognitive and motor problems, especially in memory and spatial relations, and psychological disorders (Golan & Huleihel, 2006; Hogan et al., 2006). Prolonged cutoff of the baby's oxygen supply during delivery can also cause psychological and physical health problems, such as early-onset **schizophrenia** and cerebral palsy (Rees et al., 2006). Of course, severe, prolonged oxygen deprivation is lethal.

Oxygen deprivation can be caused by maternal disorders such as diabetes, by immaturity of the baby's respiratory system, and by accidents that create pressure against the umbilical cord during birth. Passage through the birth canal is tight, and the umbilical cord is usually squeezed during the process. If the squeezing is temporary, the effect is like holding one's breath for a moment, and no problems are likely to ensue. But if constriction of the umbilical cord is prolonged, problems can result. Prolonged constriction is more likely during a **breech presentation**, when the baby enters the birth canal buttocks first and his or her body may press the umbilical cord against the birth canal.

PRETERM AND LOW-BIRTH-WEIGHT INFANTS

A baby is considered premature, or **preterm**, when birth occurs at or before 37 weeks of gestation compared with the normal 40 weeks. A baby is considered to have a low birth weight when it weighs less than 5 pounds (about 2,500 grams). When a baby is low in birth weight, even though it is born at full term, it is referred to as being **small for dates**. Mothers who smoke, abuse drugs, or fail to receive proper nutrition place their babies at risk of being small for dates. Small-for-dates babies tend to remain shorter and lighter than their age-mates and show slight delays in learning and problems with attention (O'Keeffe et al., 2003). Preterm babies who survive are more likely than small-for-dates babies to achieve normal heights and weights. Prematurity is more common with multiple births, including twins (Kogan et al., 2000). Approximately 7% of children are born preterm or low in birth weight (Kogan et al., 2000).

Risks Associated with Prematurity and Low Birth Weight

Neonates weighing between 3.25 and 5.5 pounds are 7 times more likely to die than infants of normal birth weight, whereas those weighing less than 3.3 pounds are nearly 100 times more likely to die (Nadeau et al., 2003). By and large, the lower a child's birth weight, the more poorly he or she fares in neurological development and cognitive functioning throughout the school years (Dorling et al., 2006; Wocadlo & Rieger, 2006). Children whose birth weight is less than 750 grams (1.65 pounds) fare less well at middle-school age than children whose birth weight was 750–1,499 grams (1.65–3.30 pounds) (Taylor et al., 2004). Both low-birth-weight groups perform more poorly than children whose birth weight was normal. There also seem to be sex differences. The cognitive functioning and school achievement

of girls with low birth weight seem to improve more rapidly than those of boys with low birth weight (Hindmarsh et al., 2000).

There are also risks for motor development. One study compared 96 very-low-birth-weight (VLBW) children with normal-term children (Jeng et al., 2000). The median age at which the full-term infants began to walk was 12 months, compared with 14 months for the VLBW infants. By 18 months of age, all full-term infants were walking, compared to 89% of the VLBW infants. Studies overall seem to suggest that the severity of disability reflects the extent of the deficiency in birth weight (Walther et al., 2000).

Signs of Prematurity

Preterm babies are relatively thin because they have not yet formed the layer of fat that gives so many full-term children their round, robust appearance. They often have fine, downy hair, referred to as **lanugo**, and an oily white substance on the skin known as **vernix**. Lanugo and vernix disappear within a few days or weeks after birth. If a baby is born 6 weeks or more before term, the nipples will not yet have emerged. The testicles of boys born this early will not yet have descended into the scrotum. The nipples develop further and the testes descend after birth, however.

The muscles of preterm babies are immature, so their sucking and breathing reflexes are weak. The muscles of some preterm babies may not be mature

> **breech presentation** A position in which the baby enters the birth canal buttocks first.
>
> **preterm** Born at or before completion of 37 weeks of gestation.
>
> **small for dates** Descriptive of full-term neonates who are unusually small for their age.
>
> **lanugo** Fine, downy hair on the body of the neonate, especially preterm babies.
>
> **vernix** An oily white substance that coats the skin of the neonate, especially preterm babies.

This newborn shows lanugo and vernix, both characteristics of prematurity.

© Tracy Dominey/Photo Researchers

enough to sustain independent breathing. In addition, the walls of the tiny air sacs in their lungs may tend to stick together because the babies do not yet secrete substances that lubricate these walls. As a result, babies born more than a month before full term may breathe irregularly or suddenly stop breathing, evidence of **respiratory distress syndrome**. Preterm infants with respiratory distress syndrome show poorer than normal neurological, cognitive, language, and motor development during infancy. Injecting pregnant women at risk for delivering preterm babies with corticosteroids, however, increases the babies' chances of survival (Crowther et al., 2006).

Strides have been made in helping low-birth-weight children survive. Even so, children who survive often show below-average verbal ability and academic achievement and various motor and perceptual impairments (Saigal et al., 2006).

Treatment of Preterm Babies

Because of their physical frailty, preterm infants usually remain in the hospital in **incubators**, which maintain a temperature-controlled environment and afford some protection from disease. The babies may be given oxygen, although excessive oxygen can cause permanent eye injury.

Parents and Preterm Neonates

Parents often do not treat preterm neonates as well as they treat full-term neonates. For one thing, preterm neonates are less attractive than full-term babies. Preterm infants usually do not have the robust, appealing appearance of many full-term babies. Their cries are more high pitched and grating, and they are more irritable (Bugental & Happaney, 2004; Eckerman et al., 1999). The demands of caring for preterm babies can depress parents (Davis et al., 2003; Drewett et al., 2004). Mothers of preterm babies frequently report that they feel alienated from their babies and harbor feelings of failure, guilt, and low self-esteem (Bugental & Happaney, 2004). Fear of hurting preterm babies discourages some parents from handling them, but encouraging mothers to massage their preterm infants can help them cope with fear of handling their babies and with feelings of helplessness and hopelessness (Feijó et al., 2006).

Once they come home from the hospital, preterm infants remain more passive and less sociable than full-term infants (Larroque et al., 2005; McGrath et al., 2005). Parents are more likely to poke at preterm babies, caress them, and talk to them, perhaps to prod them out of their passivity. Preterm infants fare better when they have responsive and caring parents (Dieterich et al., 2004; Lawson & Ruff, 2004).

Intervention Programs

Preterm infants profit from early stimulation just as full-term babies do—being cuddled, rocked, talked to and

Maternal and Infant Mortality around the World

Modern medicine has made vast strides in decreasing the rates of maternal and infant mortality, but the advances are not equally spread throughout the world. Save the Children, a nonprofit relief and development organization, tracks the likelihood that a woman will die in childbirth and that an infant will die during its first year. The likelihood of maternal and infant mortality is connected with factors such as the percentage of births that are attended by trained people, the literacy rate of adult women (which is one measure of the level of education of women), and the participation of women in national government (which is one measure of the extent to which a society empowers women). The safest place for a woman to deliver and for her baby to survive is Sweden, where the chances of the woman dying are about 1 in 30,000, and where only 3 infants in 1,000 die during the first year. In Afghanistan, 1 woman in 6 will die as a result of pregnancy, and 165 children of 1,000 will die during their first year. If you look at Table 4.1, you can see how these two countries compare in terms of the female literacy rate, the percentage of births attended by trained personnel, and the level of female participation in the national government.

TABLE 4.1
Maternal Mortality and Infant Mortality around the World as Related to Access to Medical Assistance and Empowerment of Women

Americans who view charts such as this one may wonder why the United States is not closer to the top of the list. One answer is that the United States is made up of nations within the nation. States with above-average poverty rates, large rural populations, and less-than-average levels of education have the highest maternal mortality and infant mortality rates. Among these states are Texas, Mississippi, Arkansas, Arizona, and New Mexico.

COUNTRY	LIFETIME RISK OF MATERNAL MORTALITY	PERCENTAGE OF BIRTHS ATTENDED BY TRAINED PERSONNEL	ADULT FEMALE LITERACY RATE (%)	PARTICIPATION OF WOMEN IN NATIONAL GOVERNMENT (% OF SEATS HELD BY WOMEN)	INFANT MORTALITY RATE (PER 1,000 LIVE BIRTHS)
Sweden	1 in 29,800	100	99	45	3
Austria	1 in 16,000	100	99	34	6
Denmark	1 in 9,800	100	99	38	4
United Kingdom	1 in 3,800	99	99	18	5
South Korea	1 in 2,800	100	96	6	5
United States	1 in 2,500	99	99	18	5
Israel	1 in 1,800	99	93	15	6
Russia	1 in 1,000	99	99	8	18
China	1 in 830	76	78	22	31
North Korea	1 in 590	97	96	20	42
Turkey	1 in 480	81	77	4	36
Iran	1 in 370	90	69	4	35
Mexico	1 in 370	86	89	23	24
Egypt	1 in 310	61	44	2	35
Brazil	1 in 140	88	87	9	30
Iraq	1 in 65	72	23	8	102
India	1 in 48	43	45	9	67
Pakistan	1 in 31	20	28	22	83
Zambia	1 in 19	43	72	12	108
Afghanistan	1 in 6	12	21	—	165

Source: Save the Children. (2008).

<table><tr><td>postpartum period The period following childbirth.

postpartum depression (PPD) Severe, prolonged depression after delivery that is characterized by feelings of sadness, apathy, and worthlessness.</td></tr></table>

sung to, being exposed to their mothers' voices, and having music and mobiles (Arnon et al., 2006; Hunter & Sahler, 2006). Other forms of stimulation include massage (Field et al., 2006) and "kangaroo care" (Lai et al., 2006), in which the baby spends time lying skin to skin, chest to chest, with a parent. Stimulated preterm infants often gain weight more rapidly, show fewer respiratory problems, and make greater advances in motor, intellectual, and neurological development than control infants (Caulfield, 2000; Dombrowski et al., 2000) (see Figure 4.3).

FIGURE 4.3
Stimulating a Preterm Infant

It was once believed that preterm infants should be left as undisturbed as possible. Today, however, it is recognized that preterm infants usually profit from various kinds of stimulation.

© Louie Psihoyos/Science Faction

LO4 The Postpartum Period

The **postpartum period** refers to the weeks following delivery, but there is no specific limit. "Parting is such sweet sorrow," Shakespeare has Juliet tell Romeo. The "parting" from the baby is also frequently a happy experience. The family's long wait is over. Concerns about pregnancy and labor are over, fingers and toes have been counted, and despite some local discomfort, the mother finds her "load" to be lightened, most literally. According to the American Psychiatric Association (2000, p. 423), however, about 70% of new mothers have periods of tearfulness, sadness, and irritability that the association refers to as the "baby blues."

MATERNAL DEPRESSION

Problems related to maternal depression include the baby blues and more serious mood disorders (postpartum-onset mood episodes), which occasionally include psychotic features (American Psychiatric Association, 2000).

T F It is abnormal to feel depressed following childbirth.

False; it is actually normal to feel depressed following childbirth. The baby blues affect most women in the weeks after delivery (American Psychiatric Association, 2000). Baby blues and other postpartum mood problems are so common that they are statistically normal (Gavin et al., 2005).

Maternal depression is not limited to the United States or even to developed nations. It is far-flung, and researchers find it in China, Turkey, Guyana, Australia, and South Africa with similar frequency (Bloch et al., 2006; Cohen et al., 2006). Researchers believe that the baby blues are common because of hormonal changes that follow delivery (Kohl, 2004).

The baby blues last about 10 days and are generally not severe enough to impair the mother's functioning. Perhaps as many as one in five women encounter the more serious mood disorder, **postpartum depression (PPD)**. PPD begins about a month after delivery and may linger for weeks or months. PPD is characterized by serious sadness, feelings of hopelessness, helplessness, and worthlessness, difficulty concentrating, and major changes in appetite (usually loss of appetite) and sleep patterns (frequently insomnia).

Many researchers suggest that PPD is triggered by a sudden drop in estrogen (Kohl, 2004). The focus is on physiological factors because of the major changes in body chemistry during and after pregnancy and because women around the world seem to experience similar disturbances in mood, even when their life experiences and support systems are radically different from those found in the United States (Cohen et al., 2006).

According to the American Psychiatric Association (2000), postpartum-onset mood episodes are accompanied by a break with reality in as many as 1 woman in 500. Mothers with these symptoms may have delusional thoughts that place the infant at risk. Some women experience delusions that the infant is possessed by the devil. Some women have "command hallucinations" to kill the infant. These psychotic symptoms are rare, however, and when they occur, they do not always place the baby at risk.

Women who experience PPD usually profit from social support and counseling, even if it does little more than explain that many women encounter PPD and it usually eases and ends as time goes on. Drugs that increase estrogen levels or act as antidepressants may help.

BONDING

Bonding—that is, the formation of feelings of attachment between parents and their children—is essential to the survival and well-being of children. Since the publication of controversial research by Marshall Klaus and John Kennell in the 1970s, many have wondered whether extended parent–infant contact is required during the first postpartum hours in order to foster parent–infant bonding (Klaus & Kennell, 1978). In the Klaus and Kennell study, one group of mothers was randomly assigned to standard hospital procedures in which their babies were whisked away to the nursery shortly after birth. Throughout the remainder of the hospital stay, the babies visited their mothers during feeding. The other group of mothers spent 5 hours a day with their infants during the hospital stay. Hospital staff encouraged and reassured the mothers who had extended contact. Follow-ups over 2 years suggested that mothers with extended contact were more likely than control mothers to cuddle their babies, soothe them when they cried, and interact with them. However, critics note that the Klaus and Kennell study did not separate the benefits of extended contact from the benefits attributable to parents' knowledge that they were in a special group and to the extra attention of the hospital staff.

Parent–child bonding has been shown to be a complex process involving desire to have the child, parent–child physical familiarity with one another, and caring. On the other hand, serious maternal depression can delay bonding with newborns (Klier, 2006), and a history of rejection by their parents can interfere with women's bonding with their own children (Leerkes & Crockenberg, 2006).

T F Parents must have extended early contact with their newborn children if adequate bonding is to take place.

False; despite the Klaus and Kennell study, which made a brief splash in the 1970s, it is not necessary that parents have extended early contact with their newborn children for adequate bonding to occur. Many parents, for instance, adopt older children and bond closely with them.

LO5 Characteristics of Neonates

ven though neonates come into the world utterly dependent on others, they are probably more aware of their surroundings than you might imagine. Neonates also make rapid adaptations to the world around them.

ASSESSING THE HEALTH OF NEONATES

The neonate's overall level of health is usually evaluated at birth according to the **Apgar scale** (Table 4.2). Apgar scores are based on five signs of health: appearance, pulse, grimace, activity level, and respiratory effort. The neonate can receive a score of 0, 1, or 2 on each sign. The total Apgar score can therefore vary from 0 to 10. A score of 7 or above usually indicates that the baby is not in danger. A score below 4 suggests that the baby is in critical condition and requires medical attention. By 1 minute after birth, most normal babies attain scores of 8 to 10 (Clayton & Crosby, 2006).

The Brazelton Neonatal Behavioral Assessment Scale measures neonates' reflexes and other behavior patterns. This test screens neonates for behavioral and neurological problems by assessing four areas of behavior: motor behavior, including muscle tone and most reflexes; response to stress; adaptive behavior; and control over physiological state.

bonding The formation of feelings of attachment between caregiver and child.

Apgar scale A measure of a newborn's health that assesses appearance, pulse, grimace, activity level, and respiratory effort.

TABLE 4.2
The Apgar Scale

POINTS	0	1	2
Appearance: Color	Blue, pale	Body pink, extremities blue	Entirely pink
Pulse: Heart rate	Absent (not detectable)	Slow—below 100 beats/minute	Rapid—100–140 beats/minute
Grimace: Reflex irritability	No response	Grimace	Crying, coughing, sneezing
Activity level: Muscle tone	Completely flaccid, limp	Weak, inactive	Flexed arms and legs; resists extension
Respiratory effort: Breathing	Absent (infant is apneic)	Shallow, irregular, slow	Regular breathing; lusty crying

© Brand X Pictures/Jupiterimages

REFLEXES

Reflexes are simple, unlearned, stereotypical responses that are elicited by certain types of stimulation. They occur without thinking. Reflexes are the most complicated motor activities displayed by neonates. Most reflexes are displayed shortly after birth and disappear within a few months. However, if the behaviors still serve a purpose, they are replaced by corresponding voluntary actions.

Pediatricians learn a good deal about the adequacy of a neonate's neural functioning by testing its reflexes. The absence or weakness of a reflex may indicate immaturity (as in prematurity), slowed responsiveness (which can result from anesthetics used during childbirth), brain injury, or retardation.

The rooting and sucking reflexes are basic to survival. In the *rooting reflex*, the baby turns the head and mouth toward a stimulus that strokes the cheek, chin, or corner of the mouth. The rooting reflex facilitates finding the mother's nipple for sucking. Babies will suck almost any object that touches their lips. The sucking reflex grows stronger during the first days after birth and can

reflex An unlearned, stereotypical response to a stimulus.

The Rooting Reflex

© Dan Bryant   © Dan Bryant   © Dan Bryant / © Danilo Comba/iStockphoto.com

be lost if not stimulated. As the months go on, reflexive sucking becomes replaced by voluntary sucking.

In the *startle reflex,* or *Moro reflex,* the back arches and the legs and arms are flung out and then brought back toward the chest, with the arms in a hugging motion. The Moro reflex occurs when a baby's position is suddenly changed or when support for the head and neck is suddenly lost. It can also be elicited by loud noises, bumping the crib, or jerking the baby's blanket. The Moro reflex is usually lost within 6 to 7 months. Absence of the Moro reflex can indicate immaturity or brain damage.

During the first few weeks, babies show an increasing tendency to reflexively grasp fingers or other objects pressed against the palms of their hands. In this *grasping reflex,* or *palmar reflex,* they use four fingers only (not the thumbs). Most babies can be literally lifted into the air as they reflexively cling on with their hands. Absence of the grasping reflex may indicate depressed activity of the nervous system, as from use of anesthetics during childbirth. The grasping reflex is usually lost within 3 to 4 months, and babies generally show voluntary grasping within 5 to 6 months.

Within 1 or 2 days after birth, babies show a reflex that mimics walking. When held under the arms and tilted forward so that the feet press against a solid surface, a baby will show a *stepping reflex* in which the feet advance one after the other. A full-term baby "walks" heel to toe, whereas a preterm infant is more likely to remain on tiptoe. The stepping reflex usually disappears by about 3 or 4 months of age.

In the *Babinski reflex,* the neonate fans or spreads the toes in response to stroking of the underside of the foot from heel to toes. The Babinski reflex normally disappears toward the end of the first year, to be replaced by curling downward of the toes.

The *tonic-neck reflex* is observed when the baby is lying on its back and turns its head to one side. The arm and leg on that side extend, while the limbs on the opposite side flex.

Some reflexes, such as breathing regularly and blinking the eye in response to a puff of air, remain with us for life. Others, such as the sucking and grasping reflexes, are gradually replaced after a number of months by voluntary sucking and grasping. Still others, such as the Moro and Babinski reflexes, disappear, indicating that the nervous system is maturing on schedule.

SENSORY CAPABILITIES

In 1890, William James, a founder of modern psychology, wrote that the neonate must sense the world "as one great blooming, buzzing confusion." The neonate emerges from being literally suspended in a temperature-controlled environment to being—again, in James's words—"assailed by eyes, ears, nose, skin, and entrails at once." We now describe the sensory capabilities of neonates and see that James, for all his eloquence, probably exaggerated their disorganization.

Vision

Neonates can see, but they are nearsighted (Kellman & Arterberry, 2006). Neonates can best see objects that are about 7 to 9 inches from their eyes. They also do not have the peripheral vision of older children (Candy et al., 1998).

Neonates can visually detect movement, and many neonates can visually follow, or track, movement the first day after birth. In fact, they appear to prefer (i.e., spend more time looking at) moving objects to stationary objects (Kellman & Arterberry, 2006). In classic research (Haith, 1966), 1- to 4-day-old neonates were exposed to moving or nonmoving lights while they sucked on a pacifier. The frequency of their sucking decreased significantly when moving lights were presented, suggesting that they preferred this visual stimulus.

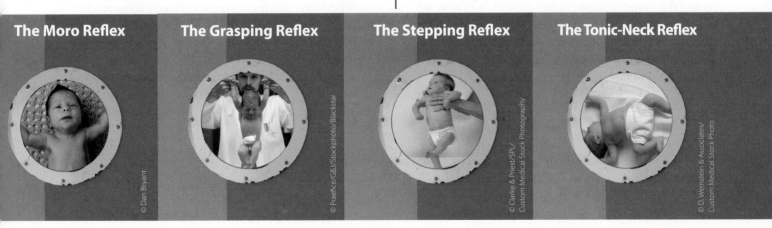

The Moro Reflex
© Dan Bryant

The Grasping Reflex
© Praefice/C&J/Stockphoto/Blackstar

The Stepping Reflex
© Clarke & Priest/SPL/Custom Medical Stock Photography

The Tonic-Neck Reflex
© D. Weinstein & Associates/Custom Medical Stock Photo

Studying Visual Acuity in Neonates: How Well Can They See?

By drawing conclusions based on what they observe babies looking at, researchers can assess the visual acuity of neonates. Robert Fantz and his colleagues (1975) used a "looking chamber" to observe what a baby is looking at. The baby lies on its back in the chamber, with two panels above. Each panel contains a visual stimulus. The researcher records the baby's eye movements to show how much time is spent looking at each panel. In the baby's natural environment, a movie or TV camera can be trained on the baby's eyes. Reflections from objects in the environment indicate what the baby is looking at.

Neonates will stare at almost any nearby object for minutes, be it a golf ball, wheel, checkerboard, bull's-eye, circle, triangle, or even a line (Maurer & Maurer, 1976), but researchers have observed certain preferences. Babies will spend more time looking at black-and-white stripes than at gray blobs. Therefore, one strategy for measuring visual acuity in neonate involves gradually narrowing the stripes until they take on the appearance of a gray blob. We can assume that babies continue to discriminate them as stripes only as long as they spend more time looking at them than at blobs. Studies with the stripes and blobs suggest that neonates are quite nearsighted.

Visual accommodation refers to the self-adjustments made by the eye's lens to bring objects into focus. If you hold your finger at arm's length and bring it gradually nearer, you will feel tension in your eyes as your lenses automatically foreshorten and thicken in an effort to maintain the image in focus. Neonates show little or no visual accommodation; rather, they see as if through a fixed-focus camera. Objects placed about 7–9 inches away are in clearest focus for most neonates, but visual accommodation improves dramatically during the first 2 months (Kellman & Arterberry, 2006).

Bring your finger toward your eyes and try to maintain a single image of the approaching finger. If you do so, it is because your eyes turn inward, or converge on the finger. **Convergence** is made possible by the coordination of the eye muscles. Neonates do not have the muscular control to converge their eyes on a nearby object. For this reason, one eye may be staring off to the side while the other fixates on an object straight ahead. Convergence does not occur until 7 or 8 weeks of age for nearby objects (Kellman & Arterberry, 2006).

The degree to which neonates perceive color remains an open question. By 4 months, however, infants can see most, if not all, colors of the visible spectrum (Franklin et al., 2005).

Even at birth, babies do not just passively respond to visual stimuli. Babies placed in absolute darkness open their eyes wide and actively search the visual field (Kellman & Arterberry, 2006).

Hearing

Fetuses respond to sound months before they are born. Although myelination of the auditory pathways is not complete before birth, fetuses' middle and inner ears

visual accommodation The automatic adjustments made by the lenses of the eyes to focus on objects.

convergence The inward movement of the eyes to focus on a nearby object.

© Design Pics/Leah Warkentin

normally reach their mature shapes and sizes before birth. Normal neonates hear well unless their middle ears are clogged with amniotic fluid (Priner et al., 2003). Most neonates turn their heads toward unusual sounds, such as the shaking of a rattle.

Neonates have the capacity to respond to sounds of different **amplitude** and **pitch**. They are more likely to respond to high-pitched sounds than to low-pitched sounds (Trehub & Hannon, 2006). By contrast, speaking or singing to infants softly, in a relatively low-pitched voice, can have a soothing effect (Volkova et al., 2006). That may explain the widespread practice in many cultures of singing lullabies to infants to promote sleep (Volkova et al., 2006).

The sense of hearing may play a role in the formation of bonds between neonates and their mothers that goes well beyond the soothing potential of the mothers' voices. Research indicates that neonates prefer their mothers' voices to those of other women, but they do not show similar preferences for the voices of their fathers (DeCasper & Prescott, 1984; Freeman et al., 1993). This preference may reflect prenatal exposure to sounds produced by their mothers.

Neonates are particularly responsive to the sounds and rhythms of speech, although they do not show preferences for specific languages. Neonates can discriminate between different speech sounds (Dehaene-Lambertz et al., 2004), and they can discriminate between new speech sounds and those they have heard before (Brody et al., 1984).

Smell: The Nose Knows—Early

Neonates can discriminate distinct odors, such as those of onions and licorice. They show more rapid breathing patterns and increased bodily movement in response to powerful odors. They also turn away from unpleasant odors, such as ammonia and vinegar, as early as the first day after birth (Werner & Bernstein, 2001). The nasal preferences of neonates are quite similar to those of older

children and adults (Werner & Bernstein, 2001).

The sense of smell, like hearing, may provide a vehicle for mother–infant recognition and attachment (Macfarlane, 1975, 1977). Neonates may be sensitive to the smell of milk because, when held by the mother, they tend to turn toward her nipple before they have had a chance to see or touch it. In one experiment, Macfarlane placed nursing pads above and to the sides of neonates' heads. One pad had absorbed milk from the mother, the other was clean. Neonates less than 1 week old spent more time turning to look at their mothers' pads than at the new pads.

Breast-fed 15-day-old infants also prefer their mother's underarm odor to odors produced by other lactating (milk-producing) women and by non-lactating women. Bottle-fed infants do not show this preference (Cernoch & Porter, 1985; Porter et al., 1992). Underarm odor, along with odors from breast secretions, might contribute to the early development of recognition and attachment.

Taste

Neonates are sensitive to different tastes, and their preferences, as suggested by their facial expressions in response to various fluids, appear to be similar to those of adults (Werner & Bernstein, 2001). Neonates swallow without showing any facial expression suggestive of a positive or negative response when distilled water is placed on their tongues. Sweet solutions are met with smiles, licking, and eager sucking, as in Figure 4.4a (Rosenstein & Oster, 1988). Neonates discriminate among solutions with salty, sour, and bitter tastes, as suggested by reactions in the lower part of the face (Rosenstein & Oster, 1988). Sour fluids (Figure 4.4b) elicit pursing of the lips, nose wrinkling, and eye blinking. Bitter solutions (Figure 4.4c) stimulate spitting, gagging, and sticking the tongue out.

Sweet solutions are calming to neonates (Blass & Camp, 2003). One study found that sweeter solutions increase the heart rate, suggesting heightened arousal, but also slow down the rate of sucking (Crook & Lipsitt, 1976). Researchers interpret this finding to suggest an effort to savor the sweeter solution, to make the flavor last.

Touch and Pain

The sense of touch is an extremely important avenue of learning and communication for babies. Not only do the skin senses provide information about the external

amplitude The height of sound waves; the greater the amplitude of sound waves, the louder the sound is.

pitch The highness or lowness of a sound, as determined by the frequency of sound waves.

FIGURE 4.4

Facial Expressions Elicited by Sweet, Sour, and Bitter Solutions

Neonates are sensitive to different tastes, as shown by their facial expressions when tasting (a) sweet, (b) sour, and (c) bitter solutions.

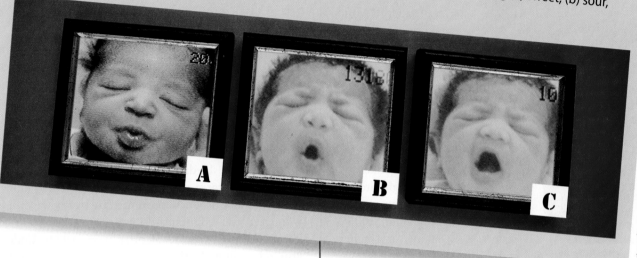

Courtesy of Rosenstein, DS, and Oster, H. (1988) / © Mara Radeva/iStockphoto.com

world, but the sensations of skin against skin also appear to provide feelings of comfort and security that contribute to the formation of bonds of attachment between infants and caregivers. Many reflexes—including the rooting, sucking, Babinski, and grasping reflexes—are activated by pressure against the skin.

> The sense of touch is an extremely important avenue of learning and communication for babies.

LEARNING: REALLY EARLY CHILDHOOD "EDUCATION"

The somewhat limited sensory capabilities of neonates suggest that they may not learn as rapidly as older children do. After all, we must sense clearly those things we

are to learn about. Neonates do, however, seem capable of conditioning.

Classical Conditioning of Neonates

In classical conditioning of neonates, involuntary responses are conditioned to new stimuli. In a typical study (Lipsitt, 2002), neonates were taught to blink in response to a tone. Blinking (the unconditioned response) was elicited by a puff of air directed toward the infant's eye (the unconditioned stimulus). A tone was sounded (the conditioned stimulus) as the puff of air was delivered. After repeated pairings, sounding the tone caused the neonate to blink (the conditioned response). This indicates that neonates can learn that events peculiar to their own environments (touches or other conditioned stimuli) may mean that a meal is at hand (more accurately, at mouth). The conditioned stimuli are culture specific; the capacity to learn is universal.

Operant Conditioning of Neonates

Neonates also learn by operant conditioning. In Chapter 3, we described an experiment in which neonates learned to suck on a pacifier to activate a recording of their mother reading *The Cat in the Hat* (DeCasper & Fifer, 1980; DeCasper & Spence, 1991), which the

© Image Source Black/Jupiterimages

mother had read aloud during the final weeks of pregnancy. In this example, the infants' sucking reflexes were modified through the reinforcement of hearing their mother read a familiar story.

SLEEPING AND WAKING

As adults, we spend about one-third of our time sleeping. Neonates greatly outdo us, spending two-thirds of their time, or about 16 hours per day, in sleep. And, in one of life's basic challenges to parents, neonates do not sleep their 16 hours consecutively.

A number of different states of sleep and wakefulness have been identified in neonates and infants, as shown in Table 4.3 (Cornwell & Feigenbaum, 2006; Salzarulo & Ficca, 2002; Wulff & Siegmund, 2001). Although individual babies differ in the amount of time they spend in each of these states, sleep clearly predominates over wakefulness in the early days and weeks of life.

Different infants require different amounts of sleep and follow different patterns of sleep, but virtually all infants distribute their sleeping throughout the day and night through naps. The typical infant has about six cycles of waking and sleeping in a 24-hour period. The longest nap typically approaches 4½ hours, and the neonate is usually awake for a little more than 1 hour during each cycle.

After a month or so, the infant has fewer but longer sleep periods and will usually take longer naps at night. By the ages of about 6 months to 1 year, many infants begin to sleep through the night. Some infants start sleeping through the night even earlier (Salzarulo & Ficca, 2002). A number of infants begin to sleep through the night for a week or so and then revert to their wakeful ways for a while.

© Adam Przezak/iStockphoto.com

REM and Non-REM Sleep

Sleep can be divided into **rapid-eye-movement (REM) sleep** and **non-rapid-eye-movement (non-REM) sleep** (Figure 4.5). REM sleep is characterized by rapid

TABLE 4.3 States of Sleep and Wakefulness in Infancy	
STATE	**COMMENTS**
Quiet sleep (non-REM)	Regular breathing, eyes closed, no movement
Active sleep (REM)	Irregular breathing, eyes closed, rapid eye movement, muscle twitches
Drowsiness	Regular or irregular breathing, eyes open or closed, little movement
Alert inactivity	Regular breathing, eyes open, looking around, little body movement
Alert activity	Irregular breathing, eyes open, active body movement
Crying	Irregular breathing, eyes open or closed, thrashing of arms and legs, crying

eye movements that can be observed beneath closed lids. The EEG patterns produced during REM sleep resemble those of the waking state. For this reason, REM sleep is also called *paradoxical sleep*. However, we are difficult to awaken during REM sleep. Adults who are roused during REM sleep report that they have been dreaming about 80% of the time. Is the same true of neonates?

Neonates spend about half their time sleeping in REM sleep (Figure 4.5). As they develop, the percentage of sleeping time spent in REM sleep declines. By 6 months or so, REM sleep accounts for only about 30% of the baby's sleep. By 2 to 3 years, REM sleep drops off to about 20–25% of total sleep (Salzarulo & Ficca, 2002). There is a dramatic falling-off in the total number of hours spent in sleep as we develop (Salzarulo & Ficca, 2002), much of which can be attributed to lessened REM sleep.

What is the function of REM sleep in neonates? Research with humans and other animals, including kittens and rat pups, suggests that the brain requires a certain amount of activity for the creation of proteins that are involved in

rapid-eye-movement (REM) sleep A period of sleep during which we are likely to dream, as indicated by rapid eye movements.

non-rapid-eye-movement (non-REM) sleep Periods of sleep during which no rapid eye movements occur.

the development of neurons and synapses (Dang-Vu et al., 2006). Perhaps neonates create this stimulation by means of REM sleep, which most closely parallels the waking state in terms of brain waves. Preterm babies spend an even greater proportion of their time in REM sleep, perhaps because they need relatively greater stimulation of the brain.

Crying

No discussion of the sleeping and waking states of the neonate would be complete without mentioning crying, a comment that parents will view as an understatement. The main reason babies cry seems to be simple enough: pain (Gormally et al., 2001; Zeifman, 2004). Hospital staff often tell parents not to worry when their babies are crying, because crying helps babies clear their respiratory systems of fluids that linger from the amniotic sac and also stimulates the circulatory system. Whether crying is healthful and necessary remains an open question, but at least some crying among babies seems to be universal.

Before parenthood, many people wonder whether they will be able to recognize the meaning of their babies' cries, but it usually does not take them long. Parents typically learn to distinguish cries that signify hunger, anger, and pain. A sudden, loud, insistent cry associated with flexing and kicking of the legs may indicate *colic*, that is, pain resulting from gas or other sources of distress in the digestive tract. The baby may seem to hold its breath for

> Whether **crying** is healthful and necessary remains an open question, but at least some crying among babies seems to be universal.

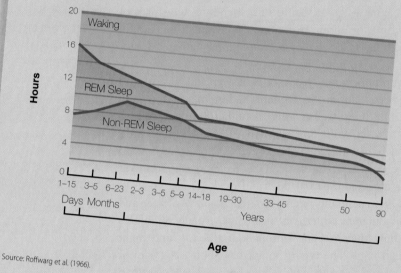

FIGURE 4.5
REM Sleep and Non-REM Sleep

Neonates spend nearly 50% of their time sleeping in rapid-eye movement (REM) sleep. The percentage of time spent in REM sleep drops off to 20–25% in 2- to 3-year-olds.

Source: Roffwarg et al. (1966).

a few moments, then gasp and begin to cry again. Crying from colic can be severe and persistent; it may last for hours, although cries generally seem to settle into a pattern after a while (Barr et al., 2005). Much to the relief of parents, colic tends to disappear by the third to sixth month, as a baby's digestive system matures.

Certain high-pitched cries, when prolonged, may signify health problems. The cries of chronically distressed infants differ from those of nondistressed infants in both rhythm and pitch. Patterns of crying may be indicative of such problems as chromosomal abnormalities, infections, fetal malnutrition, and exposure to narcotics (Zeifman, 2004). Peaks of crying appear to be concentrated in the late afternoon and early evening (McGlaughlin & Grayson, 2001). Although some cries may seem extreme and random at first, they tend to settle into a pattern that is recognizable to most parents. Infants seem to produce about the same number of crying bouts during the first 9 months or so, but the duration of the bouts grows briefer, by half, during this period (van IJzendoorn & Hubbard, 2000). The response of the mother apparently influences infants' crying. It turns out that the more frequently mothers ignore their infants' crying bouts in the first 9 weeks,

© iStockphoto.com

the less frequently their infants cry in the following 9-week period (Ijzendoorn & Hubbard, 2000). This finding should certainly not be interpreted to mean that infant crying is best ignored. At least at first, crying communicates pain and hunger, and these are conditions that it is advisable to correct. Persistent crying can strain the mother–infant relationship (Reijneveld et al., 2004).

Soothing

Sucking seems to be a built-in tranquilizer. Sucking on a **pacifier** decreases crying and agitated movement in hungry neonates (Field, 1999). Therefore, the soothing function of sucking need not be learned through experience. Sucking (drinking) a sweet solution also appears to have a soothing effect (Stevens et al., 2005).

Caregivers soothe infants by picking them up, patting them, caressing and rocking them, swaddling them, and speaking to them in a low voice. Caregivers then usually try to find the specific cause of the distress by offering a bottle or pacifier or checking the diaper. Parents learn by trial and error what types of embraces and movements are likely to soothe their infants, and infants learn quickly that crying is followed by being picked up or other forms of intervention. Parents sometimes worry

that if they pick up the crying baby quickly, they are reinforcing the baby for crying. In this way, they believe, the child may become spoiled and find it progressively more difficult to engage in self-soothing to get to sleep.

Fortunately, as infants mature and learn, crying tends to become replaced by less upsetting verbal requests for intervention. Among adults, of course, soothing techniques take very different forms—a bouquet of flowers or admission that one started the argument.

pacifier An artificial nipple, teething ring, or similar device that, when sucked, soothes babies.

sudden infant death syndrome (SIDS) The death, while sleeping, of apparently healthy babies who stop breathing for unknown reasons.

SUDDEN INFANT DEATH SYNDROME (SIDS)

Ⓣ F More children die from sudden infant death syndrome (SIDS) than from cancer, heart disease, pneumonia, child abuse, AIDS, cystic fibrosis, and muscular dystrophy combined.

True; see Lipsitt (2003).

Sudden infant death syndrome—also known as *SIDS,* or *crib death*—is a disorder of infancy that apparently strikes while a baby is sleeping. In the typical case, a baby goes to sleep, apparently in perfect health, and is found dead the next morning. There is no sign that the baby struggled or was in pain.

SIDS is more common among the following (Hunt & Hauck, 2006; Paterson et al., 2006):

- Babies aged 2–4 months
- Babies who are put to sleep in the prone position (on their stomachs) or their sides (Bruckner, 2008)
- Premature and low-birth-weight infants (Verbeek et al., 2008)
- Male babies
- Babies in families of lower socioeconomic status (Bruckner, 2008)
- Babies in African American families (African American babies are twice as likely as European American babies to die of SIDS) ([NCHS], 2006)
- Babies of teenage mothers

The incidence of **SIDS** has been declining, but some 2,000–3,000 **infants** in the United States still die each year because of this disorder.

- Babies whose mothers smoked during or after pregnancy or whose mothers used narcotics during pregnancy (Shea & Steiner, 2008)

The incidence of SIDS has been declining, but some 2,000–3,000 infants in the United States still die each year because of this disorder. It is the most common cause of death during the first year, and most of these deaths occur between 2 and 5 months of age (Paterson et al., 2006). New parents frequently live in dread of SIDS and check regularly through the night to see if their babies are breathing. It is not abnormal, by the way, for babies occasionally to suspend breathing for a moment.

The Children's Hospital Boston Study

Perhaps the most compelling study to date about the causes of SIDS was led by health professionals at the Children's Hospital Boston (Paterson et al., 2006). The study focused on an area in the brainstem called the **medulla** (Figure 4.6), which is involved in basic functions such as breathing and the sleep-and-wake cycles. The medulla causes us to breathe if we are in need of oxygen. Researchers compared the medullas of babies who had died from SIDS with those of babies who had died at the same ages from other causes. They found that the medullas of the babies who died from SIDS were less sensitive to the brain

medulla A part of the brainstem that regulates vital and automatic functions such as breathing and the sleep–wake cycle.

chemical *serotonin*, a chemical that helps keep the medulla responsive. The problem was particularly striking in the brains of the boys, which could account for the sex difference in the incidence of SIDS.

What should *you* do about SIDS? Bear in mind that the prevention of SIDS begins during pregnancy. Smoking and using other drugs during pregnancy increase the risk of SIDS. Obtain adequate nutrition and health care during pregnancy. Once a baby has arrived, "The Safe Sleep Top Ten," compiled by the National Institute of Child Health and Human Development (NICHD, 2006), can be of help.

FIGURE 4.6
The Medulla

Research by a team at the Children's Hospital Boston suggests that sudden infant death syndrome (SIDS) may be caused by a relatively low level of sensitivity of the medulla to the brain chemical serotonin.

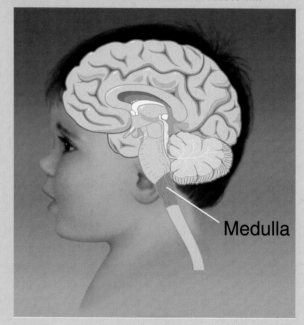

Medulla

Lowering a Baby's Risk of SIDS: "The Safe Sleep Top 10"

What can you do to lower a baby's risk of SIDS? Here are some answers from the National Institute of Child Health and Human Development (NICHD, 2006):

1. Always place your baby on his or her back to sleep, for naps and at night. The back sleep position is the safest, and every sleep time counts.

2. Place your baby on a firm sleep surface, such as on a safety-approved crib mattress, covered by a fitted sheet. Never place your baby to sleep on pillows, quilts, sheepskins, or other soft surfaces.

3. Keep soft objects, toys, and loose bedding out of your baby's sleep area. Don't use pillows, blankets, quilts, sheepskins, and pillow-like crib bumpers in your baby's sleep area, and keep any other items away from your baby's face.

4. Do not allow smoking around your baby. Don't smoke before or after the birth of your baby, and don't let others smoke around your baby.

5. Keep your baby's sleep area close to, but separate from, where you and others sleep. Your baby should not sleep in a bed or on a couch or armchair with adults or other children, but he or she can sleep in the same room as you. If you bring the baby into bed with you to breastfeed, put him or her back in a separate sleep area, such as a bassinet, crib, cradle, or a bedside co-sleeper (infant bed that attaches to an adult bed) when finished.

6. Think about using a clean, dry pacifier when placing the infant down to sleep, but don't force the baby to take it. (If you are breastfeeding your baby, wait until your child is 1 month old or is used to breastfeeding before using a pacifier.)

7. Do not let your baby overheat during sleep. Dress your baby in light sleep clothing, and keep the room at a temperature that is comfortable for an adult.

8. Avoid products that claim to reduce the risk of SIDS because most have not been tested for effectiveness or safety.

9. Do not use home monitors to reduce the risk of SIDS. If you have questions about using monitors for other conditions talk to your health care provider.

10. Reduce the chance that flat spots will develop on your baby's head: provide "Tummy Time" when your baby is awake and someone is watching; change the direction that your baby lies in the crib from one week to the next; and avoid too much time in car seats, carriers, and bouncers.

During the first 2 years,

children make enormous strides in physical growth and development.

5

Infancy: Physical Development

TRUTH OR FICTION?

T F The head of a newborn child doubles in length by adulthood, but the legs increase in length by about five times.

T F Infants triple their birth weight within a year.

T F A child's brain reaches half its adult weight by the age of 1 year.

T F The cerebral cortex—the outer layer of the brain that is vital to human thought and reasoning—is only 1/8 of an inch thick.

T F Native American Hopi infants spend the first year of life strapped to a board, yet they begin to walk at about the same time as children who are reared in other cultures.

What a fascinating creature the newborn is: tiny, delicate, apparently oblivious to its surroundings, yet perfectly formed and fully capable of letting its caregivers know when it is hungry, thirsty, or uncomfortable. And what a fascinating creature is this same child 2 years later: running, playing, talking, hugging, and kissing.

It is hard to believe that only 2 short years—the years of infancy—bring about so many changes. It seems that nearly every day brings a new accomplishment. But as we will see, not all infants share equally in the explosion of positive developments. Therefore, we will also enumerate some developmental problems and what can be done about them.

Learning Outcomes

LO1 Discuss tendencies in physical growth in infancy.

LO2 Examine the development of the brain and neurons in infancy.

LO3 Describe motor development in infancy.

LO4 Discuss sensory and perceptual development in infancy.

LO1 Physical Growth and Development

during the first 2 years, children make enormous strides in physical growth and development. In this section, we explore sequences of physical development, changes in height and weight, and nutrition. As we see next, development is "head first."

SEQUENCES OF PHYSICAL DEVELOPMENT

Three key sequences of physical development are cephalocaudal development, proximodistal development, and differentiation.

Cephalocaudal Development

Development proceeds from the upper part of the head to the lower parts of the body. When we consider the central role of the brain, which is contained within the skull, the cephalocaudal sequence appears quite logical. The brain regulates essential functions, such as heartbeat. Through the secretion of hormones, the brain also regulates the growth and development of the body and influences basic drives, such as hunger and thirst.

The head develops more rapidly than the rest of the body during the embryonic stage. By 8 weeks after conception, the head constitutes half the entire length of the embryo. The brain develops more rapidly than the spinal cord. Arm buds form before leg buds. Most newborn babies have a strong, well-defined sucking reflex, although their legs are spindly and their limbs move back and forth only in diffuse excitement or agitation. Infants can hold up their heads before they gain control over their arms, their torsos, and, finally, their legs. They can sit up before they can crawl and walk.

The lower parts of the body, because they get off to a later start, must do more growing to reach adult size. The head doubles in length between birth and maturity, but the torso, arms, and legs increase in length by three, four, and five times, respectively.

T F The head of a newborn child doubles in length by adulthood, but the legs increase in length by about five times.
True; also, the torso increases by about three times, and the arms by four.

Proximodistal Development

Growth and development also proceed from the trunk outward, from the body's central axis toward the periphery. This proximodistal sequence also makes sense. The brain and spinal cord follow a central axis down through the body, and it is essential that the nerves be in place before the infant can gain control over the arms and legs. Consider also that the life functions of the newborn baby—heartbeat, respiration, digestion, and elimination of wastes—are all carried out by organ systems close to the central axis. These functions must be in operation or ready to operate when the child is born.

In terms of motor development, infants gain control over their trunks and their shoulders before they can control their arms, hands, and fingers. Similarly, infants gain control over their hips and upper legs before they can direct their lower legs, feet, and toes.

Differentiation

As children mature, their physical reactions become less global and more specific. The tendency of behavior to become more specific and distinct is called **differentiation**. If a neonate's finger is pricked or burned, he or she may withdraw the finger but also thrash about, cry, and show general signs of distress. Toddlers may also cry, show distress, and withdraw the finger, but they are less likely to thrash about wildly. Thus, the response to pain has become more specific. An older child or adult is also likely to withdraw the finger, but less likely to wail (sometimes) and show general distress.

GROWTH PATTERNS IN HEIGHT AND WEIGHT

The most dramatic gains in height and weight occur during prenatal development. Within a span of 9 months, children develop from a zygote about 1/175 of an inch long to a neonate about 20 inches in length. Weight increases by a factor of billions.

During the first year after birth, gains in height and weight are also dramatic, although not by the standards of prenatal gains. Infants usually double their birth weight in about 5 months and triple it by the first birthday (Kuczmarski et al., 2000). Their height increases by about 50% in the first year, so that a child whose length at birth was 20 inches is likely to be about 30 inches tall at 12 months.

T F Infants triple their birth weight within a year.
True; infants usually double their birth weight in about 5 months and triple it by the first birthday.

Growth in infancy has long been viewed as a slow and steady process. Growth charts in pediatricians' offices resemble the smooth, continuous curves shown in Figure 5.1, but research suggests that infants actually grow in spurts. About 90–95% of the time, they are not growing at all. One study measured the heights of infants throughout their first 21 months (Lampl et al., 1992). The researchers found that the infants would remain the same size for 2 to 63 days and then would suddenly add from 1/5 of an inch (0.5 centimeter) to a full inch (2.5 centimeters) of length in less than 24 hours.

FIGURE 5.1

Growth Curves for Weight and Height (Length) from Birth to Age 2 Years

The curves indicate the percentiles for weight and length at different ages. Lines labeled "97th," for example, show the height and weight of children who are taller and heavier than 97% of children of a particular age. Lines marked "50th" indicate the height and weight of the average child of a given age.

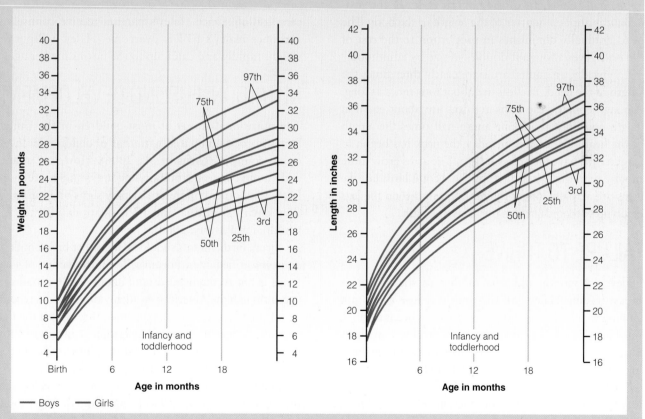

Source: Kuczmarski et al. (2000, Figures 1–4).

Infants grow another 4 to 6 inches during the second year and gain another 4 to 7 pounds. Boys generally reach half their adult height by their second birthday. Girls, however, mature more quickly than boys and are likely to reach half their adult height at the age of 18 months (Tanner, 1989). The growth rates of taller-than-average infants, as a group, tend to slow down. Those of shorter-than-average infants, as a group, tend to speed up. This does not mean that there is no relationship between infant and adult heights or that we all wind up in an average range. Tall infants, as a group, become taller adults than short infants do, but in most cases not by as much as seemed likely during infancy.

Changes in Body Proportions

Development proceeds in a cephalocaudal manner. A few weeks after conception, an embryo is almost all head. At the beginning of the fetal stage, the head is about half the length of the unborn child. In the neonate, it is about a quarter of the length of the body. The head gradually diminishes in proportion to the rest of the body, even though it doubles in size by adulthood.

Typically, an adults' arms are nearly three times the length of the head. The legs are about four times as long. Among neonates, the arms and legs are about equal in length and only about one and a half times the length of the head. By the first birthday, the neck has begun to lengthen, as have the arms and legs. The arms grow more rapidly than the legs at first; by the second birthday, the arms are actually longer than the legs, but soon the legs catch up with and surpass the arms in length.

FAILURE TO THRIVE

Haley is 4 months old. Her mother, as she puts it, is breast-feeding Haley "all the time" because she is not gaining weight. Not gaining weight for a while is normal, but Haley is also irritable and feeds fitfully, sometimes refusing the breast entirely. Her pediatrician is evaluating her for a syndrome called **failure to thrive (FTT)**.

FTT is a serious disorder that impairs growth in infancy and early childhood (Simonelli et al., 2005). Yet FTT is sometimes a fuzzy diagnosis. Historically, researchers have spoken of biologically based (or organic)

FTT versus nonbiologically based (nonorganic) FTT. The idea is that an underlying health problem accounts for organic FTT. Nonorganic FTT (NOFTT) apparently has psychological roots, social roots, or both. In either case, the infant does not make normal gains in weight and size (Simonelli et al., 2005).

Regardless of the cause or causes, feeding problems are central. As in Haley's case, infants are more likely to be described as variable eaters than as hungry (Wright & Birks, 2000). FTT is linked not only to slow physical growth but also to cognitive, behavioral, and emotional problems (Simonelli et al., 2005). At the age of 8 1/2, children who had been diagnosed with FTT in infancy were smaller, less cognitively advanced, and more emotionally disturbed than normal children (Dykman et al., 2001).

Catch-Up Growth

A child's growth can be slowed from its genetically predetermined course by many organic factors, including illness and malnutrition. If the problem is alleviated, the child's rate of growth frequently accelerates until it gets back on its normal course (van IJzendoorn & Juffer, 2006). The tendency to return to one's genetically determined pattern of growth is referred to as **canalization**. Once Haley's parents receive counseling and once Haley's FTT is overcome, Haley will put on weight rapidly and catch up to the norms for her age.

NUTRITION: FUELING DEVELOPMENT

The nutritional status of most children in the United States is good compared with that of children in developing countries (Arija et al., 2006). However, infants and young children from low-income families are more likely than other children to display signs of poor nutrition, such as anemia and FTT (National Center for Children in Poverty, 2004).

From birth, infants should be fed either breast milk or an iron-fortified infant formula. The introduction of solid foods is not recommended until about 4 to 6 months of age, although the American Academy of Pediatrics recommends that infants be fed breast milk throughout the first year and longer if possible (American Academy of Pediatrics, 2007). The first solid food is usually iron-enriched cereal, followed by strained fruits, vegetables, meats, poultry, and fish. Whole cow's milk is normally not included in the diet until the infant is 9 to 12 months old. Finger foods such as teething biscuits are introduced in the latter part of the first year.

Here are some useful guidelines for infant nutrition (National Library of Medicine, 2007):

- Build up to a variety of foods. Introduce new foods one at a time. The infant may be allergic to a new food, and introducing foods one at a time helps isolate such possible effects.

- Pay attention to the infant's appetite to help avoid overfeeding or underfeeding.

- Do not restrict fat and cholesterol too much. Infants need calories and some fat.

- Do not overdo high-fiber foods.

- Generally avoid items with added sugar and salt.

- Encourage eating of high-iron foods; infants need more iron, pound for pound, than adults do.

Parents who are on low-fat, high-fiber diets to ward off cardiovascular problems, cancer, and other health problems should not assume that the same diet is healthful for infants.

BREAST FEEDING VERSUS BOTTLE FEEDING

In many developing nations, mothers have to breast-feed. Even in developed nations, where formula is readily available, breast milk is considered by most health professionals to be the "medical gold standard" (Knaak, 2005). Perhaps for this reason, popular magazines in the United States tend to carry more articles on breast feeding than on bottle feeding (Frerichs et al., 2006).

Over the past few decades, breast feeding has become more popular, largely because of increased knowledge of its health benefits (Sloan et al., 2006). Today, most American mothers—more than 70%—breast-feed their children for at least a while, but only about two women in five continue to breast-feed after 6 months, and only one in five is still breast feeding after 1 year (Centers for Disease Control and Prevention [CDC], 2006a).

Many women bottle-feed because they return to work after childbirth and are unavailable to breast-feed. Their partners, extended families, nannies, or child-care workers give their children bottles during the day. Some mothers pump their milk and bottle it for use when they are away. Some parents bottle-feed because it permits both parents to share in feeding.

There are numerous advantages to breast milk (American Academy of Pediatrics, 2007):

- Breast milk conforms to human digestion processes (i.e., it is unlikely to upset the infant's stomach).

- Breast milk alone is adequate for the first 6 months after birth. Other foods can merely supplement breast milk through the first year (CDC, 2006).

- As the infant matures, the composition of breast milk changes to help meet the infant's changing needs.

- Breast milk contains the mother's antibodies and helps the infant ward off health problems ranging from ear infections, pneumonia, wheezing, bronchiolitis, and tetanus to chicken pox, bacterial meningitis, and typhoid fever.

- Breast milk helps protect against the form of cancer known as childhood lymphoma (a cancer of the lymph glands).

- Breast milk decreases infants' likelihood of developing serious cases of diarrhea.
- Infants who are nourished by breast milk are less likely to develop allergic responses and constipation.
- Breast-fed infants are less likely to develop obesity later in life.
- Breast feeding is associated with better neural and behavioral organization in the infant.

Breast feeding also has health benefits for the mother: It reduces the risk of early breast cancer and ovarian cancer, and it builds the strength of bones, which can reduce the likelihood of the hip fractures that result from osteoporosis following menopause. Breast feeding also helps shrink the uterus after delivery.

There are downsides to breast feeding. For example, breast milk is one of the bodily fluids that transmit HIV. As many as a third of the world's infants who have HIV/AIDS were infected in this manner (Joint United Nations Programme on HIV/AIDS [UNAIDS], 2006). Alcohol, many drugs, and environmental hazards such as polychlorinated biphenyls (PCBs) can also be transmitted through breast milk. Furthermore, for breast milk to contain the necessary nutrients, the mother must be adequately nourished herself. Furthermore, the mother experiences the physical demands of producing and expelling milk, a tendency for soreness in the breasts, and the inconvenience of being continually available to meet the infant's feeding needs.

LO2 Development of the Brain and Nervous System

the nervous system is a system of the brain, spinal cord, and all the **nerves** in the body involved in heartbeat, visual–motor coordination, thought and language, and so on.

DEVELOPMENT OF NEURONS

The basic units of the nervous system are cells called **neurons**. Neurons receive and transmit messages from one part of the body to another. The messages account for phenomena such as reflexes, the perception of an itch from a mosquito bite, the visual–motor coordination of a skier, the composition of a concerto, and the solution of a math problem.

People are born with about 100 billion neurons, most of which are in the brain. Neurons vary according to their functions and locations in the body. Some neurons in the brain are only a fraction of an inch in length, whereas neurons in the leg can grow several feet long. Each neuron possesses a cell body, dendrites, and an axon (see Figure 5.2). **Dendrites** are short fibers that extend from the cell body and receive incoming messages from up to 1,000 adjoining transmitting neurons. The **axon** extends trunklike from the cell body and accounts for much of the difference in length of neurons. An axon can be up to several feet in length if it is carrying messages from the toes upward. Messages are released from axon terminals (branching structures at the ends of axons) in the form of chemicals called **neurotransmitters**. These messages are received by the dendrites of adjoining neurons or by cells in muscles or glands. As the child matures, axons lengthen, and dendrites and axon terminals proliferate.

Myelin

Many axons are wrapped in white, fatty **myelin sheaths** that give them the appearance of a string of white sausages. The high fat content of the myelin sheath insulates the axon from electrically charged atoms in the fluids that encase the nervous system. In this way, leakage of the electric impulses being carried along the axon is minimized, and messages are conducted more efficiently.

The term **myelination** refers to the process by which axons are coated with myelin. Myelination is

© Plainpicture/Jupiterimages

FIGURE 5.2
Anatomy of a Neuron

Nerve impulses enter neurons through dendrites, are transmitted along the axon, and sent through axon terminals to muscles, glands, and other neurons. Neurons develop by proliferation of dendrites and axon terminals and through myelination.

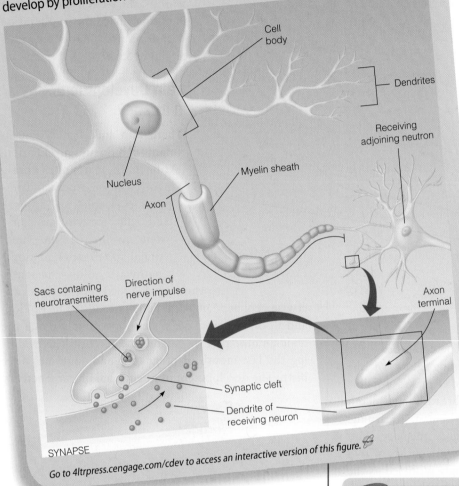

Go to 4ltrpress.cengage.com/cdev to access an interactive version of this figure.

multiple sclerosis A disorder in which hard fibrous tissue replaces myelin, impeding neural transmission.

medulla An area of the brainstem involved in heartbeat and respiration.

cerebellum The part of the hindbrain involved in coordination and balance.

DEVELOPMENT OF THE BRAIN

The brain of the neonate weighs a little less than a pound, or nearly a quarter of its adult weight. In keeping with the principles of cephalocaudal growth, an infant's brain reaches a good deal more than half its adult weight by the child's first birthday. It triples in weight, reaching nearly 70% of its adult weight (see Figure 5.3). Let's look at the brain, as shown in Figure 5.4, and discuss the development of the structures within it.

T F A child's brain reaches half its adult weight by the age of 1 year.
True; by the first birthday, a child's brain has usually tripled in weight, reaching roughly 70% of its adult weight—easily over half.

not complete at birth, but rather is part of the maturation process that leads to the abilities to crawl and walk during the first year after birth. Myelination of the brain's prefrontal matter continues into the second decade of life and is connected with advances in working memory and language ability (Aslin & Schlaggar, 2006; Pujol et al., 2006). Breakdown of myelin is believed to be associated with Alzheimer's disease, a source of cognitive decline that begins later in life.

In the disease **multiple sclerosis**, myelin is replaced by hard, fibrous tissue that disrupts the timing of neural transmission, interfering with muscle control (Stankoff et al., 2006). Phenylketonuria (PKU) causes mental retardation by inhibiting the formation of myelin in the brain (Sirrs et al., 2007).

Structures of the Brain

Many nerves that connect the spinal cord to higher levels of the brain pass through the **medulla**. The medulla is vital in the control of basic functions, such as heartbeat and respiration. The medulla is part of an area called the brainstem. Above the medulla lies the **cerebellum**. The cerebellum helps the child maintain balance, control motor behavior, and coordinate eye movements with bodily sensations.

FIGURE 5.3

Growth of Body Systems as a Percentage of Total Postnatal Growth

The brain will triple in weight by the infant's first birthday, reaching nearly 70% of its adult weight.

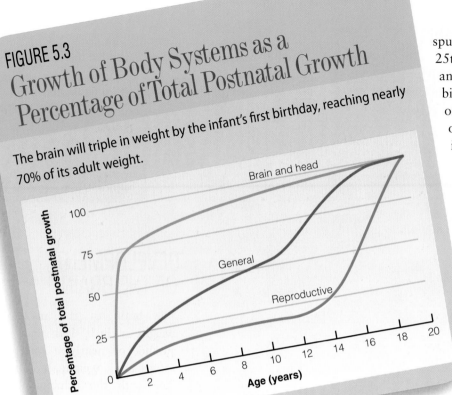

spurt in the brain occurs between the 25th week of prenatal development and the end of the second year after birth. Whereas the first growth spurt of the brain is due to the formation of neurons, the second growth spurt is due primarily to the proliferation of dendrites and axon terminals (see Figure 5.5).

Brain Development in Infancy

There is a link between what infants can do and myelination. At birth, the parts of the brain involved in heartbeat and respiration, sleeping and arousal, and reflex activity are fairly well myelinated and functional. Myelination of motor pathways allows neonates to show stereotyped reflexes, but otherwise neonates' physical activity tends to be random and ill-organized. Myelin develops rapidly along the major motor pathways from the cerebral cortex during the last month of pregnancy and continues after birth. The development of intentional physical activity

cerebrum The part of the brain responsible for learning, thought, memory, and language.

The **cerebrum** is the crowning glory of the brain. It makes possible the breadth and depth of human learning, thought, memory, and language. The surface of the cerebrum consists of two hemispheres that become increasingly wrinkled as the child matures, developing ridges and valleys called *fissures*. This surface is the cerebral cortex. The cerebral cortex is only 1/8 of an inch thick, yet it is the seat of thought and reason. It is here that we receive sensory information from the world outside and command muscles to move.

T (F) The cerebral cortex—the outer layer of the brain that is vital to human thought and reasoning—is only 1/8 of an inch thick.
This is true.

Growth Spurts of the Brain

The first major growth spurt of the brain occurs during the fourth and fifth months of prenatal development, when neurons proliferate. A second growth

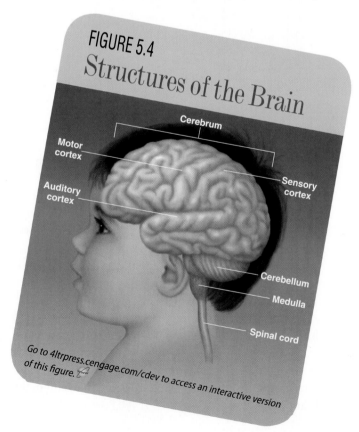

FIGURE 5.4

Structures of the Brain

Go to 4ltrpress.cengage.com/cdev to access an interactive version of this figure.

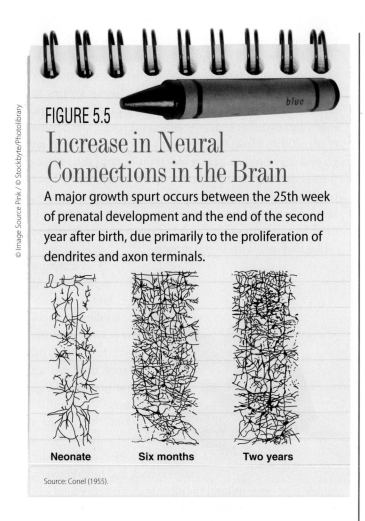

FIGURE 5.5

Increase in Neural Connections in the Brain

A major growth spurt occurs between the 25th week of prenatal development and the end of the second year after birth, due primarily to the proliferation of dendrites and axon terminals.

| Neonate | Six months | Two years |

Source: Conel (1955).

coincides with myelination as the unorganized movements of the neonate come under increasing control. Myelination of the nerves that connect to muscles is largely complete by the age of 2 years, although myelination continues to some degree into adolescence (Wozniak & Lim, 2006).

Although neonates respond to touch and can see and hear quite well, the areas of the cortex that are involved in vision, hearing, and the skin senses are less well myelinated at birth. As myelination progresses and the interconnections between the various areas of the cortex thicken, children become increasingly capable of complex and integrated sensorimotor activities (Wozniak & Lim, 2006).

Myelination of the neurons involved in the sense of hearing begins at about the sixth month of pregnancy. Myelination of these pathways is developing rapidly at full term and continues until about the age of 4 years. The neurons involved in vision begin to myelinate only shortly before full term, but then they complete the process of myelination rapidly. Within 5 to 6 months after birth, vision has become the dominant sense.

NATURE AND NURTURE IN BRAIN DEVELOPMENT

Development of the areas of the brain that control sensation and movement begins as a result of maturation, but sensory stimulation and physical activity during early infancy also spur the development of these areas (Güntürkün, 2006; Posner & Rothbart, 2007).

Research with animals shows how sensory stimulation sparks growth of the cortex. Researchers have given rats "amusement parks" with toys such as ladders, platforms, and boxes to demonstrate the effects of enriched environments. In these studies, rats exposed to the more complex environments develop heavier brains than control animals. The weight differences in part reflect more synapses per neuron (Briones et al., 2004). On the other hand, animals reared in darkness show shrinkage of the visual cortex, impaired vision, and impaired visual–motor coordination (Klintsova & Greenough, 1999). If they don't use it, they lose it.

The brain is also affected by experience. Two-year-olds actually have more connections among neurons than adults do. Connections that are activated by experience survive; the others do not (Tsuneishi & Casaer, 2000; Weinberg, 2004).

The great adaptability of the brain appears to be a double-edged sword. Adaptability allows us to develop different patterns of neural connections to meet the demands of different environments, but lack of stimulation—especially during critical early periods of development—can impair adaptability.

LO3 Motor Development

motor development involves the activity of muscles, leading to changes in posture, movement, and coordination of movement with the infant's developing sensory apparatus. Motor development provides some of the most fascinating changes in infants, because so much happens so fast.

Like physical development, motor development follows cephalocaudal and proximodistal sequences and shows differentiation. Infants gain control of their heads and upper torsos before they can effectively use their arms. This trend is due to cephalocaudal development. Infants also can control their trunks and shoulders before they can use their hands and fingers, reflecting the proximodistal sequence.

LIFTING AND HOLDING THE TORSO AND HEAD

Neonates can move their heads slightly to the side. They can thus avoid suffocation if they are lying face down and their noses or mouths are obstructed by bedding. At about 1 month, infants can raise their heads. By about 2 months, they can also lift their chests while lying on their stomachs.

When neonates are held, their heads must be supported. But by 3 to 6 months of age, infants generally manage to hold up their heads quite well so supporting the head is no longer necessary. Unfortunately, infants who can normally support their own head cannot do so when they are lifted or moved about in a jerky manner; infants who are handled carelessly can thus develop neck injuries.

CONTROL OF THE HANDS: GETTING A GRIP

The development of hand skills is an example of proximodistal development. Infants will

ulnar grasp Grasping objects between the fingers and the palm.

pincer grasp Grasping objects between the fingers and the thumb.

track slowly moving objects with their eyes shortly after birth, but they will not reach for them. Voluntary reaching and grasping require visual–motor coordination. By about 3 months, infants will make clumsy swipes at objects. Between 4 and 6 months of age, infants become more successful at grasping objects (Piek, 2006; Santos et al., 2000). However, they may not know how to let go and may hold an object indefinitely, until their attention is diverted and the hand opens accidentally. Four to 6 months is a good age for giving children rattles, large plastic spoons, mobiles, and other brightly colored hanging toys that can be grasped but are harmless when they wind up in the mouth.

Grasping is reflexive at first. Voluntary holding replaces reflexive grasping by 3 to 4 months. Infants first use an **ulnar grasp**, holding objects clumsily between their fingers and their palm. By 4 to 6 months, they can transfer objects back and forth between hands. The oppositional thumb comes into play at about 9 to 12 months, enabling infants to pick up tiny objects in a **pincer grasp**. By about 11 months, infants can hold objects in each hand and inspect them in turn.

Another aspect of visual–motor coordination is stacking blocks. On average, children can stack two blocks at 15 months, three blocks at 18 months, and five blocks at 24 months (Wentworth et al., 2000).

Pincer Grasp

Crawling

Walking

LOCOMOTION

Locomotion is movement from one place to another. Children gain the capacity to move their bodies through a sequence of activities that includes rolling over, sitting up, crawling, creeping, walking, and running (see Figure 5.6). There is much variation in the ages at which infants first engage in these activities. Although the sequence mostly remains the same, some children will skip a step. For example, an infant may creep without ever having crawled.

Most infants can roll over, from back to stomach and from stomach to back, by about the age of 6 months. By about 7 months, infants usually begin to sit up by themselves. At about 8 to 9 months, most infants begin to crawl, a motor activity in which they lie on their bellies and use their arms to pull themselves along. Creeping, in which infants move themselves along on their hands and knees, usually appears a month or so after crawling.

Standing overlaps with crawling and creeping. Most infants can remain in a standing position by holding on to something at the age of 8 or 9 months. At this age, they may also be able to walk a bit with support. About 2 months later, they can pull themselves to a standing position by holding on to the sides of their cribs or other objects and can stand briefly without holding on. By 12 to 15 months or so, they walk by themselves, earning them the label **toddlers**.

Toddlers soon run about, supporting their relatively heavy heads and torsos by spreading their legs in a bowlegged fashion. Because they are top-heavy and inexperienced, they fall frequently. Many toddlers are skillful at navigating slopes (Adolph & Berger, 2005). They walk down shallow slopes but prudently choose to slide or crawl down steep ones. Walking lends children new freedom. It allows them to get about rapidly and to grasp objects that were formerly out of reach. Give toddlers a large ball to toss and run after; it is an inexpensive and most enjoyable toy.

As children mature, their muscle strength, bone density, and balance and coordination improve (Metcalfe et al., 2005). By the age of 2 years, they can climb steps one at a time, placing both feet on each step. They can run well, walk backward, kick a large ball, and jump several inches.

Both maturation (nature) and experience (nurture) are involved in motor development. Certain voluntary motor activities are not possible until the brain has matured in terms of myelination and the differentiation of the motor areas of the cortex. Although the neonate shows stepping and swimming reflexes, these behaviors are controlled by more primitive parts of the brain. They disappear when cortical development inhibits some functions of the lower parts of the brain; and, when they reappear, they differ in quality.

Infants also need some opportunity to experiment before they can engage in milestones such as sitting up

locomotion Movement from one place to another.

toddler A child who walks with short, uncertain steps.

FIGURE 5.6
Motor Development in Infancy

Motor development proceeds in an orderly sequence, but there is considerable variation in the timing of marker events.

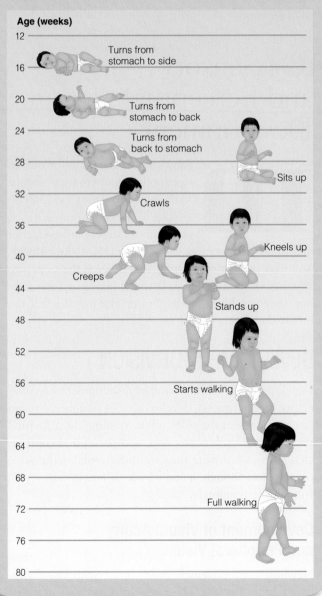

Age (weeks)

- Turns from stomach to side
- Turns from stomach to back
- Turns from back to stomach
- Sits up
- Crawls
- Kneels up
- Creeps
- Stands up
- Starts walking
- Full walking

and walking. Even so, many of these advances can apparently be attributed to maturation. In classic research, Wayne Dennis and Marsena Dennis (1940) reported on the motor development of Native American Hopi children who spent their first year strapped to a cradle board. Although denied a full year of experience in locomotion, the Hopi infants gained the capacity to walk early in their second year, about when other children do.

T F Native American Hopi infants spend the first year of life strapped to a board, yet they begin to walk at about the same time as children who are reared in other cultures.

True; when they are released from the cradle board, Hopi infants learn to move around very quickly and, like most other children, walk in their second year.

Can training accelerate the appearance of motor skills? In a classic study with identical twins, Arnold Gesell (1929) gave one twin extensive training in hand coordination, block building, and stair climbing from early infancy. The other twin was allowed to develop on his own. At first, the trained twin had better skills, but as time passed, the untrained twin became just as skilled. The development of motor skills can be accelerated by training (Adolph & Berger, 2005; Zelazo, 1998), but the effect seems slight.

Although being strapped to a cradle board did not permanently prevent the motor development of Hopi infants, Wayne Dennis (1960) reported that infants in an Iranian orphanage, who were exposed to extreme social and physical deprivation, were significantly retarded in their motor development. They grew apathetic, and all aspects of development suffered. By contrast, however, the motor development of similar infants in a Lebanese orphanage accelerated dramatically in response to such minimal intervention as being propped up in their cribs and being given a few colorful toys (Dennis & Sayegh, 1965).

Nature provides the limits—the *reaction range*—for the expression of inherited traits. Nurture determines whether the child will develop skills that reach the upper limits of the range. Even such a fundamental skill as locomotion is determined by a complex interplay of maturational and environmental factors (Adolph & Berger, 2005). There may be little purpose in trying to train children to enhance motor skills before they are ready. Once they are ready, however, teaching and practice do make a difference. One does not become

an Olympic athlete without "good genes," but one also usually does not become an Olympic athlete without solid training.

LO4 Sensory and Perceptual Development

many things that are obvious to us are not so obvious to infants. You may know that a coffee cup is the same whether you see it from above or from the side, but make no such assumption about the infant's knowledge. You may know that an infant's mother is the same size whether she is standing next to the infant or approaching from two blocks away, but do not assume that the infant shares this knowlege.

DEVELOPMENT OF VISION

Development of vision involves development of visual acuity (or sharpness), development of peripheral vision (seeing things at the sides while looking ahead), visual preferences, depth perception, and perceptual constancies, such as knowing that an object remains the same object even though it may look different when seen from a different angle.

Development of Visual Acuity and Peripheral Vision

Newborns are extremely nearsighted, with visual acuity of about 20/600. The most dramatic gain in visual acuity is made between birth and 6 months of age, when acuity reaches about 20/50 (Haith, 1990; Skoczenski, 2002). By 3 to 5 years, visual acuity generally approximates adult levels (20/20 in the best cases).

Neonates also have poor peripheral vision (Cavallini et al., 2002; Skoczenski, 2002). Adults can perceive objects that are nearly 90 degrees off to the side (i.e., directly to the left or right), although objects at these extremes are unclear. Neonates cannot perceive visual stimuli that are off to the side by an angle of more than 30 degrees, but their peripheral vision expands to an angle of about 45 degrees by the age of 7 weeks. By 6 months, their peripheral vision is about equal to that of an adult.

Let us now consider the development of visual perception. We will see that infants frequently prefer the strange to the familiar and will avoid going off the deep end—sometimes.

Visual Preferences

Neonates look at stripes longer than at blobs. This finding has been used in much of the research on visual acuity. Classic research by Robert Fantz found that by the age of 8 to 12 weeks, most infants also show distinct preferences for curved lines over straight ones (Fantz et al., 1975).

Robert Fantz (1961) also wondered whether there was something intrinsically interesting about the human face that drew the attention of infants. To investigate this question, he showed 2-month-old infants the six disks in Figure 5.7. One disk contained human features, another newsprint, and still another a bull's-eye. The remaining three disks were featureless but colored red, white, and yellow. In this study, the infants fixated significantly longer on the human face.

Some studies suggest that the infants in Fantz's (1961) study may have preferred the human face because it had a complex, intriguing pattern of dots (eyes) within an outline, not because it was a face. But de Haan and Groen (2006) assert that "reading" faces (interpreting facial expressions) is important to infants because they do not understand verbal information as communicated through language.

Researchers therefore continue to ask whether humans come into the world "prewired" to prefer human faces as visual stimuli to other stimuli that are just as complex, and—if so—what it is about human faces that

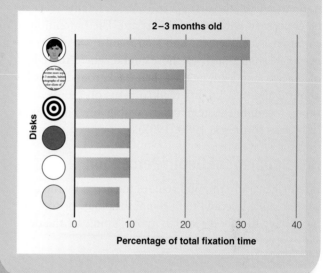

© Jarek Szymanski/iStockphoto.com

FIGURE 5.7
Preferences for Visual Stimuli in 2-Month-Olds

Infants appear to prefer complex to simple visual stimuli. By the time they are 2 months old, they also tend to show a preference for the human face.

draws attention. Some researchers—unlike de Haan and Groen—argue that neonates do not "prefer" faces because they are faces per se but because of the structure of their immature visual systems (Simion et al., 2001). A supportive study of 34 neonates found that the longer fixations on facelike stimuli resulted from a larger number of brief fixations (looks) rather than from a few prolonged fixations (Cassia et al., 2001). The infants' gaze, then, was sort of bouncing around from feature to feature rather than "staring" at the face in general. The researchers interpreted the finding to show that the stimulus properties of the visual object are more important than the fact that it represents a human face. Even so, of course, the immature visual system would be providing some "prewired" basis for attending to the face.

Learning also plays some role. For example, neonates can discriminate their mother's face from a stranger's after 8 hours of mother–infant contact spread over 4 days (Bushnell, 2001).

Neonates appear to direct their attention to the edges of objects. This pattern persists for the first several weeks (Bronson, 1991). When they are given the opportunity to look at human faces, 1-month-old infants tend to pay most attention to the "edges," that is, the chin, an ear, or the hairline. The eye movements of 2-month-old infants move in from the edge (see Figure 5.8). The infants focus particularly on the eyes, although they also inspect other features such as the mouth and nose (Nelson & Ludemann, 1989).

Some researchers (e.g., Haith, 1979) explain infants' tendencies to scan from the edges of objects inward by noting that for the first several weeks, infants seem to be concerned with *where* things are. Their attention is captured by movement and sharp contrasts in brightness and shape, such as those found where the edges of objects stand out against their backgrounds. But by about 2 months, infants tend to focus on the *what* of things, scanning systematically within the boundaries of objects (Bronson, 1990, 1997).

Development of Depth Perception

Infants generally respond to cues for depth by the time they are able to crawl (6 to 8 months of age or so), and most have the good sense to avoid "going off the deep

FIGURE 5.9
The Visual Cliff

This young explorer has the good sense not to crawl out onto an apparently unsupported surface, even when mother beckons from the other side.

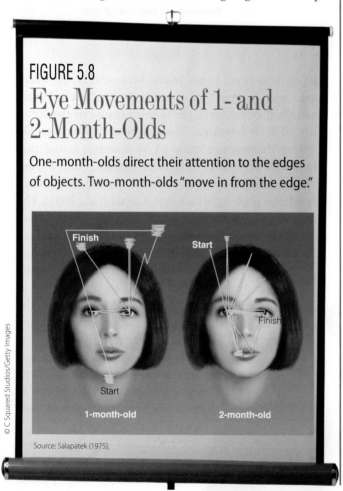

FIGURE 5.8
Eye Movements of 1- and 2-Month-Olds

One-month-olds direct their attention to the edges of objects. Two-month-olds "move in from the edge."

Finish

Start

Start

Finish

1-month-old

2-month-old

Source: Salapatek (1975).

end," that is, crawling off ledges and tabletops into open space (Campos et al., 1978).

In a classic study on depth perception, Gibson and Walk (1960) placed infants of various ages on a clever device called a *visual cliff* (see Figure 5.9). The visual cliff consists of a sheet of Plexiglas that covers a cloth with a checkerboard pattern. On one side, the cloth is placed immediately beneath the Plexiglas; on the other, it is dropped about 4 feet. In the Gibson and Walk study, 8 out of 10 infants who had begun to crawl refused to venture from the supported side of the Plexiglass surface onto the seemingly unsupported side, even when their mothers beckoned encouragingly from the other side.

Psychologists can assess infants' emotional responses to the visual cliff long before infants can crawl. For example, Campos and his colleagues (1970) found that 1-month-old infants showed no change in heart rate when placed face down on the "cliff." They apparently did not perceive the depth of the cliff. At 2 months, infants showed decreases in heart rate when so placed, which psychologists interpret as a sign of interest. But the heart rates of 9-month-olds accelerated on the cliff, which is interpreted as a fear response. The study appears to suggest that infants profit from some experience crawling about (and, perhaps, accumulating some bumps) before they develop fear of heights. The 9-month-olds but not the 2-month-olds had had such experience. Other studies support the view that infants usually do not develop fear of heights until they can move around (Sorce et al., 2000; Witherington et al., 2005).

Development of Perceptual Constancies

It may not surprise you that a 12-inch ruler is the same length whether it is 2 feet or 6 feet away or that a door across the room is a rectangle whether closed or ajar. Awareness of these facts depends not on sensation alone but on the development of perceptual constancies. **Perceptual constancy** is the tendency to perceive an object to be the same, even though the sensations produced by the object may differ under various conditions.

Consider again the example of the ruler. When it is 2 feet away, its image, as focused on the retina, has a certain retinal size. From 6 feet away, the 12-inch ruler is only a third as long in terms of retinal size, but we perceive it as being the same size because of size constancy. *Size constancy* is the tendency to perceive the same objects as being of the same size even though their retinal sizes vary as a function of their distance. From 6 feet away, a 36-inch yardstick has a retinal size equal to that of the 12-inch ruler at 2 feet, but—if recognized as a yardstick—it is perceived as longer, again because of size constancy.

Bower (1974) conditioned 2 1/2- to 3-month-old infants to turn their heads to the left when shown a 12-inch cube from a distance of 3 feet. He then presented them with three experimental stimuli: (1) a 12-inch cube 9 feet away, whose retinal size was smaller than that of the original cube; (2) a 36-inch cube 3 feet away, whose retinal size was larger than that of the original cube; and (3) a 36-inch cube 9 feet away, whose retinal size was the same as that of the original cube. The infants turned their heads most frequently in response to the first experimental cube, although its retinal image was only one-third the length of that to which they had been conditioned, suggesting that they had achieved size constancy. Later studies have confirmed Bower's finding that size constancy is present in early infancy. Some research suggests that even neonates possess rudimentary size constancy (Slater, 2000; Slater et al., 1990).

Shape constancy is the tendency to perceive an object as having the same shape even though, when perceived from another angle, the shape projected onto the retina may change dramatically. When the top of a cup or a glass is seen from above, the visual sensation is in the shape of a circle. When seen from a slight angle, the top of the cup or glass is seen as elliptical. However, because of our familiarity with the object, we still perceive the rim of the cup or glass as being a circle. In the first few months after birth, infants see the features of their caregivers, bottles, cribs, and toys from all different angles so that by the time they are 4 or 5 months old, a broad grasp of shape constancy seems to be established, at least under certain conditions (Slater, 2000).

perceptual constancy Perceiving objects as maintaining their identity although sensations from them change as their positions change.

habituation Becoming used to a stimulus and therefore paying less attention to it.

DEVELOPMENT OF HEARING

Neonates can crudely orient their heads in the direction of a sound (Saffran et al., 2006). By 18 months of age, the accuracy of sound-localizing ability approaches that of adults. Sensitivity to sounds increases in the first few months of life (Saffran et al., 2006). As infants mature, the range of the pitch of the sounds they can sense gradually expands to match the adult's range of 20 to 20,000 cycles per second. The ability to detect differences in the pitch and loudness of sounds improves considerably throughout the preschool years. Auditory acuity also improves gradually over the first several years (Saffran et al., 2006), although infants' hearing can be so acute that many parents complain their napping infants will awaken at the slightest sound. This is especially true if parents have been overprotective in attempting to keep their rooms as silent as possible. Infants who are normally exposed to a backdrop of moderate noise levels become habituated to them and are not likely to awaken unless there is a sudden, sharp noise.

By the age of 1 month, infants perceive differences between speech sounds that are highly similar. In a classic study relying on the **habituation** method, infants of this age could activate a recording of "bah" by sucking on a nipple (Eimas et al., 1971). As time went on, habituation occurred, as shown by decreased sucking so as to hear the "bah" sound. Then the researchers switched from "bah" to "pah." If the sounds had seemed the same to the infants, their lethargic sucking patterns would have continued, but they immediately sucked harder, suggesting that they perceived the difference. Other researchers have found that 2- to 3-month-old infants reliably discriminate three-syllable words such as *marana* and *malana* (Kuhl et al., 2006).

Infants can discriminate the sounds of their parent's voices by 3 1/2 months of age. In classic research, infants of this age were oriented toward their parents as

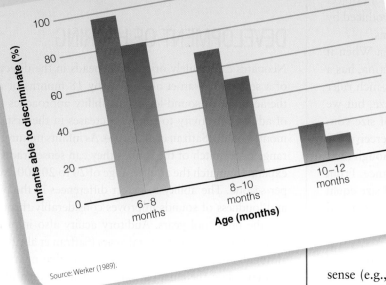

FIGURE 5.10
Declining Ability to Discriminate the Sounds of Foreign Languages

Infants show a decline in the ability to discriminate sounds not found in their native language. At 6 months of age, nearly all infants from English-speaking families could discriminate sounds found in Hindi (red bars) and Salish, a Native American language (blue bars). By 10 to 12 months of age, only a small proportion could do so.

Source: Werker (1989).

they reclined in infant seats.

The experimenters (Spelke & Owsley, 1979) played recordings of the mother's or father's voice while the parents themselves remained inactive. The infants reliably looked at the parent whose voice was being played.

Young infants are capable of perceiving most of the speech sounds present in the world's languages. But after exposure to their native language, infants gradually lose the capacity to discriminate those sounds that are not found in the native language (Werker et al., 2007), as shown in Figure 5.10 (Werker, 1989).

Infants also learn at an early age to ignore small, meaningless variations in the sounds of their native language. Adults do this routinely. For example, if someone speaking your language has a head cold or a slight accent, you ignore the minor variations in the person's pronunciation and hear these variations as the same sound.

Infants can screen out meaningless sounds as early as 6 months of age (Kuhl et al., 2006). Kuhl and her colleagues (1997) presented American and Swedish infants with pairs of sounds in either their own language or

the other one. The infants were trained to look over their shoulder when they heard a difference in the sounds and to ignore sound pairs that seemed to be the same. The infants routinely ignored variations in sounds that were part of their language, because they apparently perceived them as the same sound. But the infants noticed slight variations in the sounds of the other language. Another study demonstrated the same ability in infants as young as 2 months (Marean et al., 1992).

DEVELOPMENT OF COORDINATION OF THE SENSES

Neonates crudely orient their heads toward sounds and pleasant odors. In this way, they increase the probability that the sources of the sounds and odors will also be sensed through visual scanning. Young infants can also recognize that objects experienced by one sense (e.g., vision) are the same as those experienced through another sense (e.g., touch). This ability has been demonstrated in infants as young as 1 month old (Bushnell, 1993). One experiment demonstrating such understanding in 5-month-olds takes advantage of the fact that infants of this age tend to look longer at novel rather than familiar sources of stimulation. Féron and her colleagues (2006) first allowed 5-month-old infants to handle (become manually familiar with) groups of either two or three objects, when they were presented one by one, to their right hand. The infants were then shown visual displays of either two or three objects. The infants looked longer at the group of objects that differed from the one they had become manually familiar with, showing a transfer of information from the sense of touch to the sense of vision.

THE ACTIVE–PASSIVE CONTROVERSY IN PERCEPTUAL DEVELOPMENT

Newborn children may have more sophisticated sensory capabilities than you expected. Still, their ways of perceiving the world are largely mechanical, or passive.

Neonates seem to be generally at the mercy of external stimuli. When a bright light strikes, they attend to it. If the light moves slowly across the plane of their vision, they track it.

As time passes, broad changes occur in the perceptual processes of children, and the child's role in perception appears to become decidedly more active. Developmental psychologist Eleanor Gibson (1969, 1991) noted a number of these changes, listed on the clipboard to the right.

In short, children develop from passive, mechanical reactors to the world about them into active, purposeful seekers and organizers of sensory information.

Changes in Children's Perceptual Processes

1. Intentional action replaces "capture" (automatic responses to stimulation). As infants mature and gain experience, purposeful scanning and exploration of the environment take the place of mechanical movements and passive responses to stimulation.
2. Systematic search replaces unsystematic search. Over the first few years of life, children become more active as they develop systematic ways of exploring the environment. They come to pay progressively more attention to details of objects and people and to make finer and finer discriminations.
3. Attention becomes selective. Older children become capable of selecting the information they need from the welter of confusion in the environment.
4. Irrelevant information becomes ignored. Older children gain the capacity to screen out or deploy their attention away from stimuli that are irrelevant to the task at hand. That might mean shutting out the noise of cars in the street or radios in the neighborhood so as to focus on a book.

NATURE AND NURTURE IN PERCEPTUAL DEVELOPMENT

The nature–nurture issue is found in perceptual development, as in other areas of development.

Evidence for the Role of Nature

Compelling evidence supports the idea that inborn sensory capacities play a crucial role in perceptual development. Neonates arrive in the world with a good number of perceptual skills. They can see nearby objects quite well, and their hearing is usually fine. They are born with tendencies to track moving objects, to systematically scan the horizon, and to prefer certain kinds of stimuli. Preferences for different kinds of visual stimuli appear to unfold on schedule as the first months wear on. Sensory changes, as with motor changes, appear to be linked to maturation of the nervous system.

Evidence for the Role of Nurture

Evidence that experience plays a crucial role in perceptual development is also compelling. Children and other young animals have critical periods in their perceptual development. Failure to receive adequate sensory stimulation during these periods can result in permanent sensory deficits (Greenough et al., 2002). For example, newborn kittens raised with a patch over one eye wind up with few or no cells in the visual area of the cerebral cortex that would normally be stimulated by light

that enters that eye. In effect, that eye becomes blind, even though sensory receptors in the eye itself may fire in response to light. On the other hand, if the eye of an adult cat is patched for the same amount of time, the animal will not lose vision. The critical period will have passed. Similarly, if health problems require that a child's eye must be patched for an extensive period of time during the first year, the child's visual acuity in that eye may be impaired.

Today most developmentalists would agree that nature and nurture interact to shape perceptual development. Nature continues to guide the maturation of the child's physical systems. Yet nurture continues to interact with nature in the development of these systems. In the next chapter, we see how nature and nurture influence the development of thought and language in infants.

© Image Source

Cognitive development focuses

on the development of children's ways of perceiving and mentally representing the world.

6

Infancy: Cognitive Development

TRUTH OR FICTION?

T F For 2-month-old infants, out of sight is out of mind.

T F A 1-hour-old infant may imitate an adult who sticks out his or her tongue.

T F Psychologists can begin to measure intelligence in infancy.

T F Infant crying is a primitive form of language.

T F You can advance children's development of pronunciation by correcting their errors.

T F Children are "prewired" to listen to language in such a way that they come to understand rules of grammar.

Laurent ... resumes his experiments of the day before. He grabs in succession a celluloid swan, a box, etc., stretches out his arm and lets them fall. He distinctly varies the position of the fall. Sometimes he stretches out his arm vertically, sometimes he holds it obliquely, in front of or behind his eyes, etc. When the object falls in a new position, he lets it fall two or three times more on the same place, as though to study the spatial relation; then he modifies the situation.

Is this description one of a scientist at work? In a way, it is. Although Swiss psychologist Jean Piaget (1936/1963) was describing his 11-month-old son Laurent, children of this age frequently act like scientists, performing what Piaget called "experiments in order to see."

Learning Outcomes

LO1 Examine Jean Piaget's studies of cognitive development.

LO2 Discuss the information-processing approach.

LO3 Identify individual differences in intelligence among infants.

LO4 Examine language development in infancy.

LO1 Cognitive Development: Jean Piaget

Cognitive development focuses on the development of children's ways of perceiving and mentally representing the world. Piaget labeled children's concepts of the world *schemes*. He hypothesized that children try to use *assimilation* to absorb new events into existing schemes. When assimilation does not allow children to make sense of novel events, they try to modify existing schemes through *accommodation.*

Piaget (1936/1963) hypothesized that cognitive processes develop in an orderly sequence of stages. Some children may advance more quickly than others, but the sequence remains constant (Flavell et al., 2002; Siegler & Alibali, 2005). Piaget identified four stages of cognitive development: sensorimotor, preoperational, concrete operational, and formal operational. In this chapter, we discuss the sensorimotor stage.

THE SENSORIMOTOR STAGE

Piaget's sensorimotor stage refers to the first 2 years of cognitive development, a time during which infants progress from responding to events with reflexes, or ready-made schemes, to goal-oriented behavior. Piaget divided the sensorimotor stage into six substages. In each substage, earlier forms of behavior are repeated, varied, and coordinated.

Simple Reflexes

The first substage covers the first month after birth. It is dominated by the assimilation of sources of stimulation into inborn reflexes such as grasping and visual tracking. At birth, reflexes seem stereotypical and inflexible. But even within the first few hours, neonates begin to modify reflexes as a result of experience. During the first month or so, however, infants apparently make no connection between stimulation perceived through different sensory modalities. They make no effort to grasp objects that they visually track.

Primary Circular Reactions

The second substage, primary circular reactions, lasts from about 1 to 4 months of age and is characterized by the beginnings of the ability to coordinate various sensorimotor schemes. Infants tend to repeat stimulating actions that first occurred by chance. They may lift an arm repeatedly to bring it into view. **Primary circular reactions** focus on the infant's own body rather than on the external environment. Piaget noticed the following primary circular reaction in his son Laurent:

> *At 2 months 4 days, Laurent by chance discovers his right index finger and looks at it briefly. At 2 months 11 days, he inspects for a moment his open right hand, perceived by chance. At 2 months 17 days, he follows its spontaneous movement for a moment, then examines it several times while it searches for his nose or rubs his eye.*

> —Piaget (1936/1963, pp. 96–97)

Thus, Laurent, early in the third month, visually tracks the behavior of his hands, but his visual observations do not affect their movement. In terms of assimilation and accommodation, the child is attempting to assimilate the motor scheme (moving the hand) into the sensory scheme (looking at it). But the schemes do not automatically fit. Several days of apparent trial and error pass, during which the infant seems to be trying to make accommodations so that the schemes will fit. By the third month, an infant may

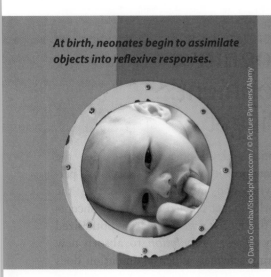

At birth, neonates begin to assimilate objects into reflexive responses.

Infants repeat actions that involve their bodies (primary circular reactions).

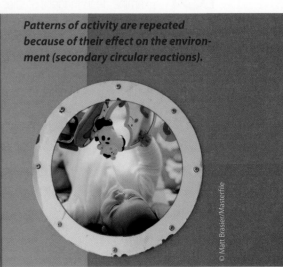

Patterns of activity are repeated because of their effect on the environment (secondary circular reactions).

examine objects repeatedly and intensely. It seems that the infant is no longer simply looking and seeing but is now "looking in order to see."

Because Laurent (and other infants) repeat actions that allow them to see, cognitive developmental psychologists consider sensorimotor coordination self-reinforcing. Laurent acts on his hands to keep them in his field of vision. Piaget considered the desire to prolong stimulation to be as "basic" as the drives of hunger or thirst.

Secondary Circular Reactions

The third substage lasts from about 4 to 8 months of age and is characterized by **secondary circular reactions**, in which patterns of activity are repeated because of their effect on the environment. In the second substage (primary circular reactions), infants are focused on their own bodies, as in the example about Laurent. In the third substage (secondary circular reactions), the focus shifts to objects and environmental events. Infants may now learn to pull strings in order to make a plastic face appear or to shake an object in order to hear it rattle.

Coordination of Secondary Schemes

In the fourth substage, infants no longer act simply to prolong interesting occurrences. Now they can coordinate schemes to attain specific goals. Infants begin to show intentional, goal-directed behavior in which they differentiate between the means of achieving a goal and the goal or end itself. For example, they may lift a piece of cloth to reach a toy that they had seen a parent place under the cloth earlier. In this example, the scheme of picking up the cloth (the means) is coordinated with the scheme of reaching for the toy (the goal or end). This example indicates that the infant has mentally represented the toy placed under the cloth.

During the fourth substage, infants also gain the capacity to imitate gestures and sounds that they had previously ignored. The imitation of a facial gesture implies that infants have mentally represented their own faces and can tell what parts of their faces they are moving through feedback from facial muscles.

Tertiary Circular Reactions

In the fifth substage, which lasts from about 12 to 18 months of age, infants behave in ways that Piaget saw as characteristic of budding scientists. Infants now engage in **tertiary circular reactions**, or purposeful adaptations of established schemes to specific situations. Behavior takes on a new experimental quality, and infants may vary their actions dozens of times in a deliberate trial-and-error fashion to learn how things work.

Piaget reported an example of tertiary circular reactions by his daughter Jacqueline. The episode was an experiment in which Piaget placed a stick outside Jacqueline's playpen, which had wooden bars (Piaget, 1936/1963). At first, Jacqueline grasped the stick and tried to pull it sideways into the playpen. The stick was too long and could not fit through the bars. After days of overt trial and error, however, Jacqueline discovered that she could bring the stick between the bars by turning it upright. In the sixth substage, described next, infants apparently engage in mental trial and error before displaying the correct overt response.

> **secondary circular reactions** The repetition of actions that produce an effect on the environment.
>
> **tertiary circular reactions** The purposeful adaptations of established schemes to new situations.

Infants coordinate their behavior to attain specific goals (coordinating secondary schemes).

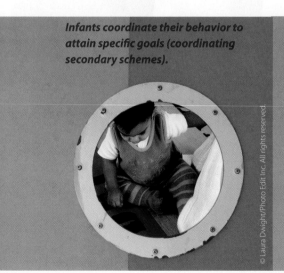

Infants use trial and error to learn how things work (tertiary circular reactions).

The Bayley scales measure an infant's mental and motor development.

object permanence
Recognition that objects or people continue to exist when they are not in view.

Invention of New Means through Mental Combinations

The sixth substage lasts from about 18 to 24 months of age. It serves as a transition between sensorimotor development and the development of symbolic thought. External exploration is replaced by mental exploration. At about 18 months, children may also use imitation to symbolize or stand for a plan of action.

Piaget presented his other children, Lucienne and Laurent, with the playpen and stick problem at the age of 18 months. Rather than engage in overt trial and error, the 18-month-old children sat and studied the situation for a few moments. Then they grasped the stick, turned it upright, and brought it into the playpen with little overt effort. Lucienne and Laurent apparently mentally represented the stick and the bars of the playpen and perceived that the stick would not fit through as it was. They must then have rotated the mental image of the stick until they perceived a position that would allow the stick to pass between the bars.

DEVELOPMENT OF OBJECT PERMANENCE

The appearance of **object permanence** is an important aspect of sensorimotor development. Object permanence is the recognition that an object or person continues to exist when out of sight. For example, your textbook continues to exist when you leave it in the library after

studying for the big test, and an infant's mother continues to exist even when she is in another room. The development of object permanence is tied to the development of infants' working memory and reasoning ability (Aguiar & Baillargeon, 2002; Saiki & Miyatsuji, 2007).

Neonates show no tendency to respond to objects that are not within their immediate sensory grasp. By the age of 2 months, infants may show some surprise if an object (such as a toy duck) is placed behind a screen and then taken away so that when the screen is lifted, it is absent. However, they make no effort to search for the missing object. Through the first 6 months or so, when the screen is placed between the object and the infant, the infant behaves as though the object is no longer there (see Figure 6.1).

FIGURE 6.1
Development of Object Permanence

To the infant who is in the early part of the sensorimotor stage, out of sight is truly out of mind. Once a sheet of paper is placed between the infant and the toy monkey (top two photos), the infant loses all interest in the toy. From evidence of this sort, Piaget concluded that the toy is not mentally represented. The bottom series of photos shows a child in a later part of the sensorimotor stage. This child does mentally represent objects and pushes through a towel to reach an object that has been screened from sight.

Series: © Doug Goodman/Photo Researchers, Inc.

Series: © 2004 George S. Zimbel

T F For 2-month-old infants, out of sight is out of mind.

True; 2-month-olds have not yet developed object permanence.

There are some interesting advances in the development of the object concept by about the sixth month (Piaget's substage 3). For example, an infant at this age will tend to look for an object that has been dropped, behavior that suggests some form of object permanence. There is also reason to believe that by this age the infant perceives a mental representation (image) of an object, such as a favorite toy, in response to sensory impressions of part of the object. This perception is shown by the infant's reaching for an object that is partly hidden.

By 8 to 12 months of age (Piaget's substage 4), infants will seek to retrieve objects that have been completely hidden. But in observing his own children, Piaget (1936/1963) noted an interesting error known as the *A not B error*. Piaget repeatedly hid a toy behind a screen (A), and each time, his infant removed the screen and retrieved the toy. Then, as the infant watched, Piaget hid the toy behind another screen (B) in a different place. Still, the infant tried to recover the toy by pushing aside the first screen (A). It is as though the child had learned that a certain motor activity would reinstate the missing toy. The child's concept of the object did not, at this age, extend to recognition that objects usually remain in the place where they have been most recently mentally represented.

Under certain conditions, 9- to 10-month-old infants do not show the A not B error (Bremner & Bryant, 2001; Marcovitch & Zelazo, 2006). If infants are allowed to search for the object immediately after seeing it hidden, the error often does not occur. But if they are forced to wait 5 or more seconds before looking, they are likely to commit the A not B error (Wellman et al., 1986).

EVALUATION OF PIAGET'S THEORY

Piaget's theory remains a comprehensive model of infant cognition. Many of his observations of his own infants have been confirmed by others. The pattern and sequence of events he described have been observed among American, European, African, and Asian infants (Werner, 1988). Still, research has raised questions about the validity of many of Piaget's claims (Siegler & Alibali, 2005).

First, most researchers now agree that cognitive development is not as tied to discrete stages as Piaget suggested (Krojgaard, 2005; Siegler & Alibali, 2005). Although later developments seem to build on earlier ones, the process appears to be more gradual than discontinuous.

Second, Piaget emphasized the role of maturation, almost to the point of excluding adult and peer influences on cognitive development. However, these interpersonal influences have been shown to play important roles in cognitive development (Kuhn, 2007; Maratsos, 2007).

> **deferred imitation** The imitation of an action that occurred in the past.

Third, Piaget appears to have underestimated infants' competence (Siegler & Alibali, 2005). For example, infants display object permanence earlier than he believed (Wang et al., 2005). Also contrary to Piaget are results of studies on **deferred imitation** (imitation of an action that may have occurred hours, days, or even weeks earlier). The presence of deferred imitation suggests that children have mentally represented behavior patterns. Piaget believed that deferred imitation appears at about 18 months, but others have found that infants show deferred imitation as early as 9 months. In Meltzoff's (1988) study, 9-month-old infants watched an adult perform behaviors such as pushing a button to produce a beep. When given a chance to play with the same objects a day later, many of the infants imitated the actions they had witnessed.

DEFERRED IMITATION

© David Muir/Masterfile

LO2 Information Processing

the information-processing approach to cognitive development focuses on how children manipulate or process information coming in from the environment or already stored in the mind. Infants' tools for processing information include their memory and imitation.

INFANTS' MEMORY

Many of the cognitive capabilities of infants—recognizing the faces of familiar people, developing object permanence, and, in fact, learning in any form—depend on one critical aspect of cognitive development: memory (Daman-Wasserman et al., 2006; Hayne & Fagen, 2003). Even neonates demonstrate memory for stimuli to which they have been exposed previously. For example, neonates adjust their rate of sucking to hear a recording of their mother reading a story she had read aloud during the last weeks of pregnancy, as discussed in Chapter 2 (DeCasper & Fifer, 1980; DeCasper & Spence, 1991).

Memory improves dramatically between 2 and 6 months of age and then again by 12 months (Pelphrey et al., 2004; Rose et al., 2001). The improvement may indicate that older infants are more capable than younger ones of encoding (i.e., storing) information, retrieving information already stored, or both (Hayne & Fagen, 2003).

A fascinating series of studies by Carolyn Rovee-Collier and her colleagues (Rovee-Collier, 1993) illustrates some of these developmental changes in infant memory. One end of a ribbon was tied to a brightly colored mobile suspended above the infant's crib. The other end was tied to the infant's ankle, so that when the infant kicked, the mobile moved. Infants quickly learned to increase their rate of kicking. To measure memory, the infant's ankle was again fastened to the mobile after a period of 1 or more days had elapsed. In one study, 2-month-olds remembered how to make the mobile move after delays of up to 3 days, and 3-month-olds remembered for more than a week (Greco et al., 1986).

ROVEE-COLLIER STUDIES

FIGURE 6.2
Imitation in Infants

These 2- to 3-week-old infants are imitating the facial gestures of an adult experimenter. How are we to interpret these findings? Can we say that the infants "knew" what the experimenter was doing and "chose" to imitate the behavior, or is there another explanation?

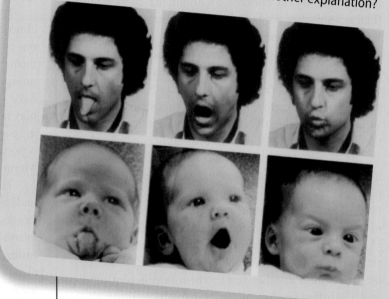

A. N. Meltzoff and M. K. Moore, Imitation of facial and manual gestures by human neonates. *Science*, 1977, 198, 75–78.

Infant memory can be improved if infants receive a reminder before they are given the memory test (Bearce & Rovee-Collier, 2006). In one study that used a reminder (priming), infants were shown the moving mobile on the day before the memory test, but they were not allowed to activate it. Under these conditions, 3-month-olds remembered how to move the mobile after a 28-day delay (Rovee-Collier, 1993).

IMITATION: INFANT SEE, INFANT DO?

Imitation is the basis for much of human learning. Deferred imitation—that is, the imitation of actions after a time delay—occurs as early as 6 months of age (Barr et al., 2005; Campanella & Rovee-Collier, 2005). To help them remember the imitated act, infants are usually permitted to practice it when they learn it. But in one study, 12-month-old infants were prevented from practicing the behavior they imitated. Yet they were able to demonstrate it 4 weeks later, suggesting that they had mentally represented the act (Klein & Meltzoff, 1999).

But infants can imitate certain actions at a much earlier age. Neonates only 0.7 to 71 hours old have been found to imitate adults who open their mouths or stick out their tongues (Meltzoff & Prinz, 2002; Rizzolatti et al., 2002; see Figure 6.2).

Courtesy of Prof. Carolyn Rovee-Collier / © Don Wilkie/iStockphoto.com / © Stefan Klein/iStockphoto.com

Before you become too impressed with this early imitative ability of neonates, you should know that some studies have not found imitation in early infancy (Abravanel & DeYong, 1991). One key factor may be the infants' age. The studies that find imitation generally have been done with very young infants—up to 2 weeks old—whereas the studies that do not find imitation have tended to use older infants. Therefore, the imitation of neonates is likely to be reflexive. Thus, imitation might disappear when reflexes are "dropping out" and re-emerge when it has a firmer cognitive footing.

T F A 1-hour-old infant may imitate an adult who sticks out his or her tongue.
True; this does often occur. Imitation at this age is likely to be reflexive.

Why might newborns possess some sort of imitation reflex? Answers lie in the realm of speculation. One possibility is that such a built-in response would contribute to the formation of caregiver–infant bonding and the survival of the newborn (Meltzoff & Prinz, 2002). Some theorists speculate that the imitation reflex is made possible by *mirror neurons* that are found in human brains. Such neurons are maintained by evolutionary forces because they enhance the probability of survival as a result of caregiving (Oztop et al., 2006; Rizzolatti et al., 2002).

LO3 Individual Differences in Intelligence among Infants

Cognitive development does not proceed in the same way or at the same pace for all infants (Newman et al., 2006; Rose et al., 2001, 2005). Efforts to understand the development of differences in infants' cognitive development have relied on so-called scales of infant development or infant intelligence.

Measuring cognition or intelligence in infants is quite different from measuring it in adults. Infants cannot, of course, be assessed by asking them to explain the meanings of words, the similarity between concepts, or the rationales for social rules. One of the most important tests of intellectual development in infants—

> Imitation might **disappear** when reflexes are "dropping out" and **re-emerge** when it has a firmer cognitive footing.

the Bayley Scales of Infant Development, constructed in 1933 by psychologist Nancy Bayley and revised since—contains very different kinds of items.

The Bayley scales currently consist of 178 mental-scale items and 111 motor-scale items. The mental scale assesses verbal communication, perceptual skills, learning and memory, and problem-solving skills. The motor scale assesses gross motor skills, such as standing, walking, and climbing, and fine motor skills, as shown by the ability to manipulate the hands and fingers. A behavior rating scale based on examiner observation of the child during the test is also used. The behavior rating scale assesses attention span, goal directedness, persistence, and aspects of social and emotional development. Table 6.1 contains sample items from the mental and motor scales and shows the ages at which 50% of the infants taking the test passed the items.

T F Psychologists can begin to measure intelligence in infancy.
True; there are intelligence tests for infants, but their scores do not correlate all that well with scores of tests given at older ages.

TESTING INFANTS: WHY AND WITH WHAT?

As you can imagine, it is no easy matter to test an infant. The items must be administered on a one-to-one basis by a patient tester, and it can be difficult to judge whether the infant is showing the targeted response. Why, then, do we test infants?

One reason is to screen infants for handicaps. A tester may be able to detect early signs of sensory or neurological problems, as suggested by development of visual–motor coordination. In addition to the Bayley scales, a number of tests have been developed to screen infants for such difficulties, including the Brazelton

TABLE 6.1
Items from the Bayley Scales of Infant Development (BSID–II)

AGE	MENTAL-SCALE ITEMS	MOTOR-SCALE ITEMS
1 month	The infant quiets when picked up.	The infant makes a postural adjustment when put to examiner's shoulder.
2 months	When examiner presents two objects (bell and rattle) above the infant in a crib, the infant glances back and forth from one to the other.	The infant holds his or her head steady when being carried about in a vertical position.
5 months	The infant is observed to transfer an object from one hand to the other during play.	When seated at a feeding-type table and presented with a sugar pill that is out of reach, the infant attempts to pick it up.
8 months	When an object (toy) in plain view of the infant (i.e., on a table) is covered by a cup, the infant removes the cup to retrieve the object.	The infant raises herself or himself into a sitting position.
12 months	The infant imitates words that are spoken by the examiner.	When requested by the examiner, the infant stands up from a position in which she or he had been lying on her or his back on the floor.
14–16 months	The infant builds a tower with two cubes (blocks) after the examiner demonstrates the behavior.	The infant walks alone with good coordination.

Neonatal Behavioral Assessment Scale (see Chapter 4) and the Denver Developmental Screening Test.

INSTABILITY OF INTELLIGENCE SCORES ATTAINED IN INFANCY

Researchers have also tried to use infant scales to predict development, but this effort has been less than successful. One study found that scores obtained during the first year of life correlated moderately at best with scores obtained a year later (Harris et al., 2005). Certain items on the Bayley scales appear to predict related intellectual skills later in childhood. For example, Bayley items measuring infant motor skills predict subsequent fine motor and visual–spatial skills at 6 to 8 years of age (Siegel, 1992). Bayley language items also predict language skills at the same age (Siegel, 1992).

One study found that the Bayley scales and socioeconomic status were able to predict cognitive development among low-birth-weight children from 18 months to 4 years of age (Dezoete et al., 2003). But overall scores on the Bayley and other infant scales apparently are not good predictors of school grades or IQ scores among schoolchildren (Colombo, 1993). Perhaps the sensorimotor test items used during infancy are not that strongly related to the verbal and symbolic items used to assess intelligence at later ages.

The overall conclusion seems to be that the Bayley scales can identify gross lags in development and relative strengths and weaknesses. However, they are only moderate predictors of intelligence scores even one year later,

Bayley items measuring infant motor skills predict subsequent fine motor and visual/spatial skills at 6 to 8 years of age.

and are still poorer predictors of scores taken after longer stretches of time.

USE OF VISUAL RECOGNITION MEMORY

In a continuing effort to find aspects of intelligence and cognition that might remain consistent from infancy through later childhood, a number of researchers have recently focused on visual recognition memory (Courage et al., 2004). **Visual recognition memory** is the ability to discriminate previously seen objects from novel objects. This procedure is based on *habituation*.

Let us consider longitudinal studies of this type. Susan Rose and her colleagues (Rose et al., 1992) showed 7-month-old infants pictures of two identical faces. After 20 seconds, the pictures were replaced with one picture of a new face and a second picture of the familiar face. The amount of time the infants spent looking at each face in the second set of pictures was recorded. Some infants spent more time looking at the new face than at the older face, suggesting that they had better memory for visual stimulation. The children were given standard IQ tests yearly from ages 1 through 6. It was found that the children with greater visual recognition memory later attained higher IQ scores.

Rose and her colleagues (2001) also showed that, from age to age, individual differences in capacity for visual recognition memory are stable. This finding is important because intelligence—the quality that many researchers seek to predict from visual recognition memory—is also theorized to be a reasonably stable trait. Similarly, items on intelligence tests are age graded; that is, older children perform better than younger children, even as developing intelligence remains constant. So, too, with visual recognition memory. Capacity for visual recognition memory increases over the first year after birth (Rose et al., 2001).

A number of other studies have examined the relationship between either infant visual recognition memory or preference for novel stimulation (which is a related measure) and later IQ scores. In general, the results show good predictive validity for broad cogni-

tive abilities throughout childhood, including measures of intelligence and language ability (Heimann et al., 2006; Rose et al., 2004).

In sum, scales of infant development may provide useful data as screening devices, as research instruments, or simply as a way to describe the things that infants do and do not do, but their predictive power as intelligence tests has been disappointing. Tests of visual recognition hold better promise as predictors of intelligence at older ages.

Now let us turn our attention to a fascinating aspect of cognitive development, the development of language.

LO4 Language Development in Infancy

a s children develop language skills, they often begin speaking about things closely connected with their environments and their needs. Children enjoy playing with language. In physical development, the most dramatic developments come early—fast and furious—long before the child is born. Language does not come quite as early, and its development may not seem quite so fast and furious. Nevertheless, during the years of infancy, most children develop from creatures without language to little people who understand nearly all the things that are said to them and who relentlessly sputter words and simple sentences for all the world to hear.

EARLY VOCALIZATIONS

Children develop language according to an invariant sequence of steps, or stages, as outlined in Table 6.2. The first stage involves the production of **prelinguistic** vocalizations. True words are symbols of objects and events. Prelinguistic vocalizations, such as cooing and babbling, do not represent objects or events.

visual recognition memory The kind of memory demonstrated by an infant's ability to discriminate previously seen objects from novel objects.

prelinguistic Referring to vocalizations made by the infant before the development of language.

TABLE 6.2
Milestones in Language Development in Infancy

APPROXIMATE AGE	VOCALIZATION AND LANGUAGE
Birth	• Cries.
12 weeks	• Cries less. • Smiles when talked to and nodded at. • Engages in squealing and gurgling sounds (cooing). • Sustains cooing for 15–20 seconds.
16 weeks	• Responds to human sounds more definitely. • Turns head, searching for the speaker. • Chuckles occasionally.
20 weeks	• Cooing becomes interspersed with consonant-like sounds. • Vocalizations differ from the sounds of mature language.
6 months	• Cooing changes to single-syllable babbling. • Neither vowels nor consonants have fixed pattern of recurrence. • Common utterances sound somewhat like *ma, mu, da,* or *di.*
8 months	• Continuous repetition (reduplication) enters into babbling. • Patterns of intonation become distinct. • Utterances can signal emphasis and emotion.
10 months	• Vocalizations mixed with sound play, such as gurgling, bubble blowing. • Makes effort to imitate sounds made by older people with mixed success.
12 months	• Identical sound sequences replicated more often. • Words (e.g., *mama* or *dada*) emerge. • Many words and requests understood (e.g., "Show me your eyes").
18 months	• Repertoire of 3–50 words. • Explosive vocabulary growth. • Babbling consists of several syllables with intricate intonation. • Little effort to communicate information. • Little joining of words into spontaneous two-word utterances. • Understands nearly everything spoken.
24 months	• Vocabulary more than 50 words, naming everything in the environment. • Spontaneous creation of two-word sentences. • Clear efforts to communicate.

Source: Table items adapted from Lenneberg (1967, pp. 128–130).
Note: Ages are approximations. Slower development does not necessarily indicate language problems. Albert Einstein did not talk until the age of 3.

Newborn children, as parents are well aware, have an unlearned but highly effective form of verbal expression: crying and more crying. Crying is about the only sound that infants make during the first month. During the second month, infants begin **cooing**. Infants use their

cooing Prelinguistic vowel-like sounds that reflect feelings of pleasure or positive excitement.

T F Infant crying is a primitive form of language.

False; cries do not represent objects or events. Therefore, crying is a prelinguistic vocalization, not a form of language at all.

tongues when they coo. For this reason, coos are more articulated than cries. Coos are often vowel-like and may resemble extended "oohs" and "ahs." Cooing appears linked to feelings of pleasure or positive excitement. Infants tend not to coo when they are hungry, tired, or in pain.

Cries and coos are innate but can be modified by experience (Volterra et al., 2004). When parents respond positively to cooing by talking to their infants, smiling at them, and imitating them, cooing increases. Early parent–child "conversations," in which parents respond to coos and then pause as the infant coos, may foster infant awareness of taking turns as a way of verbally relating to other people.

By about 8 months of age, cooing decreases markedly. Somewhere between 6 and 9 months, children begin to babble. **Babbling** is the first vocalizing that sounds like human speech. In babbling, infants frequently combine consonants and vowels, as in "ba," "ga,"and, sometimes, the much valued "dada" (Stoel-Gammon, 2002). At first, "dada" is purely coincidental (sorry, dads), despite the family's jubilation over its appearance.

In verbal interactions between infants and adults, the adults frequently repeat the syllables produced by their infants. They are likely to say "dadada" or "bababa" instead of simply "da" or "ba." Such redundancy apparently helps infants discriminate these sounds from others and further encourages them to imitate their parents (Elkind, 2007; Tamis-LeMonda et al., 2006).

After infants have been babbling for a few months, parents often believe that their children are having conversations with themselves. At 10 to 12 months, infants tend to repeat syllables, showing what linguists refer to as **echolalia**. Parents overhear them going on and on, repeating consonant–vowel combinations ("ah-bah-bah-bah-bah"), pausing, and then switching to other combinations.

Toward the end of the first year, infants are also using patterns of rising and falling **intonation** that resemble the sounds of adult speech. It may sound as though the infant is trying to speak the parents' language. Parents may think that their children are babbling in English or in whatever tongue is spoken in the home.

> **babbling** The child's first vocalizations that have the sounds of speech.
>
> **echolalia** The automatic repetition of sounds or words.
>
> **intonation** The use of pitches of varying levels to help communicate meaning.
>
> **receptive vocabulary** The number of words one understands.
>
> **expressive vocabulary** The number of words one can use in the production of language.

DEVELOPMENT OF VOCABULARY

Vocabulary development refers to the child's learning the meanings of words. In general, children's development of **receptive vocabulary** outpaces that of **expressive vocabulary** (Lickliter, 2001; Ouellette, 2006). In other words, at any given time, they can understand more words than they can use. One study, for example, found that 12-month-olds could speak an average of 13 words but could comprehend the meaning of 84 (Tamis-LeMonda et al., 2006). Infants usually understand much of what others are saying well before they themselves utter any words at all. Their ability to segment speech sounds into meaningful units—or words—before 12 months is a good predictor of their vocabulary at 24 months (Newman et al., 2006).

The Child's First Words

Ah, that long-awaited first word! What a milestone! Sad to say, many parents miss it. They are not quite sure when their infants utter their first word, often because the first word is not pronounced clearly or because pronunciation varies from usage to usage.

A child's first word typically is spoken between the ages of 11 and 13 months, but a range of 8 to 18 months is considered normal (Hoff, 2006; Tamis-LeMonda et al., 2006). First words tend to be brief, consisting of one or two syllables. Each syllable is likely to consist of a consonant followed by a vowel. Vocabulary acquisition is slow at first. It may take children 3 or 4 months to achieve a vocabulary of 10 to 30 words after the first word is spoken (de Villiers & de Villiers, 1999).

By about 18 months of age, children may be producing up to 50 words. Many of them are quite familiar, such as *no, cookie, mama, hi,* and *eat.* Others, such as *all gone* and *bye-bye,* may not be found in the dictionary, but they function as words. That is, they are used consistently to symbolize the same meaning.

More than half (65%) of children's first words consist of general nominals and specific nominals (Hoff, 2006; Nelson, 1973). *General nominals* are similar to nouns in that they include the names of classes of objects *(car, ball)*, animals *(doggy, cat)*, and people *(boy, girl)*, but they also include both personal and relative pronouns *(she, that)*. *Specific nominals* are proper nouns, such as *Daddy* and *Rover*. Words expressing movement are frequently found in early speech.

At about 18 to 22 months of age, there is a rapid burst in vocabulary (Tamis-LeMonda et al., 2006). The child's vocabulary may increase from 50 to more than 300 words in only a few months. This vocabulary spurt could also be called a naming explosion because almost 75% of the words added during this time are nouns. The rapid pace of vocabulary growth continues through the preschool years, with children acquiring an average of nine new words per day (Hoff, 2006).

Referential and Expressive Styles in Language Development

Some children prefer a referential approach in their language development, whereas others take a more expressive approach (Hoff, 2006; Nelson, 1981). Children who show the **referential language style** use language primarily to label objects in their environments. Children who use an **expressive language style** use language primarily as a means for engaging in social interactions. Children with an expressive style use more pronouns and many words involved in social routines, such as *stop, more,* and *all gone.* More children use an expressive style than a referential style (Tamis-LeMonda et al., 2006), but most use a combination of the styles.

Overextension

Young children try to talk about more objects than they have words for. To accomplish their linguistic feats, children often extend the meaning of one word to refer to things and actions for which they do not have words (McDonough, 2002). This process is called **overextension.** Eve Clark (1973, 1975) studied diaries of infants' language development and found that overextensions are generally based on perceived similarities in function or form between the original object or action and the new one. She provides the example of the word *mooi,* which one child originally used to designate the moon. The child then overextended *mooi* to designate all round objects, including the letter *o* and cookies and cakes. Overextensions gradually pull back to their proper references as the child's vocabulary and ability to classify objects develop (McDonough, 2002).

DEVELOPMENT OF SENTENCES

The infant's first sentences are typically one-word utterances, but they express complete ideas and therefore can be thought of as sentences. Roger Brown (1973) called brief expressions that have the meanings of sentences **telegraphic speech.** Adults who write telegrams use principles of syntax to cut out all the unnecessary words. "Home Tuesday" might stand for "I expect to be home on Tuesday." Similarly, only the essential words are used in children's tele-

Brief expressions that have the meanings of sentences is known as telegraphic speech.

graphic speech—in particular, nouns, verbs, and some modifiers.

Let us now consider the features of two types of telegraphic speech: holophrases and two-word utterances.

Holophrases

Holophrases are single words that are used to express complex meanings. For example, "Mama" may be used by the child to signify meanings as varied as "There goes Mama," "Come here, Mama," and "You are Mama." Most children readily teach their parents what they intend by augmenting their holophrases with gestures, intonations, and reinforcers. That is, they act delighted when parents do as requested and howl when they do not (Tamis-LeMonda et al., 2006).

Two-Word Sentences

When the child's vocabulary consists of 50 to 100 words (usually somewhere between 18 and 24 months of age), telegraphic two-word sentences begin to appear (Tamis-LeMonda et al., 2006). In the sentence "That ball," the words *is* and *a* are implied.

Two-word sentences, although brief and telegraphic, show understanding of **syntax** (Slobin, 2001). The child will say "Sit chair," not "Chair sit," to tell a parent to sit in a chair. The child will say "My shoe," not "Shoe my," to show possession. "Mommy go" means Mommy is leaving, whereas "Go Mommy" expresses the wish for Mommy to go away.

THEORIES OF LANGUAGE DEVELOPMENT

Since all normal humans talk but no house pets or house plants do, no matter how pampered, heredity must be involved in language. But since a child growing up in Japan speaks Japanese whereas the same child brought up in California would speak English, the environment is also crucial. Thus, there is no question about whether heredity or environment is involved in language, or even whether one or the other is "more important." Instead, ... our best hope [might be] finding out how they interact.

—Steven Pinker

Billions of children have learned the languages spoken by their parents and have passed them down, with minor changes, from generation to generation. But how do they do so? In discussing this question—and so many others—we refer to the possible roles of nature and nurture.

Learning theorists have come down on the side of nurture, and those who point to a basic role for nature are said to hold a nativist view.

VIEWS THAT EMPHASIZE NURTURE

Learning plays an obvious role in language development. Children who are reared in English-speaking homes learn English, not Japanese or Russian. Learning theorists usually explain language development in terms of imitation and reinforcement.

The Role of Imitation

From a social cognitive perspective, parents serve as **models**. Children learn language, at least in part, by observation and imitation. Many vocabulary words, especially nouns and verbs, are learned by imitation. But imitative learning does not explain why children spontaneously utter phrases and sentences that they have not observed (Tamis-LeMonda et al., 2006). Parents, for example, are unlikely to model utterances such as "Bye bye sock" and "All gone Daddy" but children say them. And children sometimes steadfastly avoid imitating certain language forms suggested by adults, even when the adults are insistent. Note the following exchange between 2-year-old Ben and a (very frustrated) adult (Kuczaj, 1982, p. 48):

> *Ben: I like these candy. I like they.*
>
> *Adult: You like them?*
>
> *Ben: Yes, I like they.*
>
> *Adult: Say "them."*
>
> *Ben: Them.*
>
> *Adult: Say "I like them."*
>
> *Ben: I like them.*
>
> *Adult: Good.*
>
> *Ben: I'm good. These candy good too.*
>
> *Adult: Are they good?*
>
> *Ben: Yes. I like they. You like they?*

> **holophrase** A single word that is used to express complex meanings.
>
> **syntax** The rules in a language for combining words in order to form sentences.
>
> **models** In learning theory, those whose behaviors are imitated by others.

© Leah-Anne Thompson/iStockphoto.com

Ben is not resisting the adult because of obstinacy. He does repeat "I like them" when asked to do so. But when given the opportunity afterward to use the objective form *them*, he reverts to using the subjective form *they*. Ben is likely at this period in his development to use his (erroneous) understanding of syntax spontaneously to actively produce his own language, rather than just imitate a model.

The Role of Reinforcement

B. F. Skinner (1957) allowed that prelinguistic vocalizations such as cooing and babbling may be inborn. But parents reinforce children for babbling that approximates the form of real words, such as "da," which, in English, resembles *dog* or *dad*. Children, in fact, do increase their babbling when it results in adults smiling at them, stroking them, and talking back to them. As the first year progresses, children babble the sounds of their native tongues with increasing frequency; foreign sounds tend to drop out. The behaviorist explains this pattern of changing frequencies in terms of reinforcement of the sounds of the adults' language and **extinction** of foreign sounds. Another (nonbehavioral) explanation is that children actively attend to the sounds in their linguistic environments and are intrinsically motivated to utter them.

From Skinner's perspective, children acquire their early vocabularies through **shaping**. That is, parents require that children's utterances be progressively closer to actual words before they are reinforced. In support of Skinner's position, research has shown that reinforcement accelerates the growth of vocabulary in children (August et al., 2005; Kroeger & Nelson, 2006).

But recall Ben's refusal to be shaped into correct syntax. If the reinforcement explanation of language development were sufficient, parents' reinforcement would facilitate children's learning of syntax and pronunciation. However, parents are more likely to reinforce their children for the accuracy, or "truth value," of their utterances than for their grammatical correctness (Brown, 1973). The child who points down and says "The grass is purple" is not likely to be reinforced, despite correct syntax. But the enthusiastic child who shows her empty plate and blurts out "I eated it all up" is likely to be reinforced, despite the grammatical incorrectness of "eated."

Selective reinforcement of children's pronunciation can also backfire. Children whose parents reward proper pronunciation but correct poor pronunciation develop vocabulary more slowly than children whose parents are more tolerant about pronunciation (Nelson, 1973).

T F You can advance children's development of pronunciation by correcting their errors.
False; selective reinforcement of a child's pronunciation can actually backfire by delaying vocabulary development.

Learning theory also cannot account for the invariant sequences of language development and for children's spurts in acquisition. The types of questions used, the passive voice and other features emerge in the same order.

On the other hand, aspects of the child's language environment do influence the development of language. Studies show that language growth in young children is enhanced when adults (Tamis-LeMonda et al., 2006):

- Use a simplified form of speech known as *Motherese*.
- Use questions that engage the child in conversation.
- Respond to the child's expressive language efforts in a way that is attuned; for example, adults relate their speech to the child's utterance by saying "Yes, your doll is pretty" in response to the child's statement "My doll."
- Join the child in paying attention to a particular activity or toy.
- Gesture to help the child understand what they are saying.
- Describe aspects of the environment occupying the infant's current focus of attention.
- Read to the child.
- Talk to the child a great deal.

VIEWS THAT EMPHASIZE NATURE

The nativist view of language development holds that inborn factors cause children to attend to and acquire language in certain ways. From this perspective, children bring an inborn tendency in the form of neurological "prewiring" to language learning. According to Steven Pinker and Ray Jackendoff (2005), the structures that enable humans to perceive and produce language evolved in bits and pieces. Those individuals who possessed these language-related bits and pieces were more likely to reach

"Motherese"

Adults influence the language development of infants through baby talk or *Motherese,* known technically as *child-directed,* or *infant-directed, speech.* But grandparents, fathers, siblings, and older children also use Motherese when talking to infants (Kidd & Bavin, 2007; Snedeker et al., 2007). Motherese occurs in languages as different as Arabic, English, Comanche, Italian, French, German, Xhosa (an African language), Japanese, and Mandarin Chinese (Nonaka, 2004; Trainor & Desjardins, 2002).

Motherese may foster language development. The short, simple sentences and high pitch used in Motherese are more likely to produce a response from the child and enhance vocabulary development than are complex sentences spoken in a lower pitch. Repeating and recasting utterances also promote learning (Tamis-LeMonda et al., 2001; Trevarthen, 2003).

Motherese has several characteristics:
1. Motherese is spoken slowly, at high pitch, and there are pauses between ideas.
2. Sentences are brief.
3. Sentences are simple in grammar.
4. Key words are put at the ends of sentences and are spoken in a higher and louder voice.
5. The diminutive morpheme *y* is frequently used. "Dad" becomes "Daddy," and "horse" becomes "horsey."
6. Adults repeat sentences several times with minor variations: "Show me your nose." "Where is your nose?"
7. Motherese includes reduplication. "Yummy" becomes "yummy-yummy." "Daddy" may alternate with "Da-da."
8. Vocabulary is concrete, referring to objects in the immediate environment. Stuffed lions may be referred to as "kitties."
9. Objects may be overdescribed. Rabbits may become "bunny rabbits," and cats may become "kitty cats."
10. Parents speak for the children, as in "We want to take our nap now, don't we?"

psycholinguistic theory The view that language learning involves an interaction between environmental influences and an inborn tendency to acquire language.

language acquisition device (LAD) An inborn tendency to acquire language, which primes the learning of grammar.

surface structure The superficial features of language, especially vocabulary and grammar.

deep structure The underlying set of rules for transforming ideas into sentences.

aphasia A disruption in the ability to understand or produce language.

Broca's aphasia An aphasia caused by damage to Broca's area and shown by difficulty in speaking.

Wernicke's aphasia An aphasia caused by damage to Wernicke's area and characterized by impaired comprehension of speech and difficulty in producing the right word.

maturity and transmit their genes to another generation because communication ability increased their chances of survival.

Psycholinguistic Theory

According to **psycholinguistic theory**, language acquisition involves an interaction between environmental influences—such as exposure to parental speech and reinforcement—and an inborn tendency to acquire language. Noam Chomsky (1988, 1990) labeled this innate tendency the **language acquisition device (LAD)**. Evidence for an inborn tendency is found in the universality of human language abilities; in the regularity of the early production of sounds, even among deaf children; and in the invariant sequences of language development among all languages (Bloom, 1998; Volterra et al., 2004).

The inborn tendency primes the nervous system to learn grammar. On the surface, languages differ much in vocabulary and grammar. Chomsky labels these elements the **surface structure** of language. However, Chomsky believes that the LAD serves children all over the world because languages share a "universal grammar"—an underlying **deep structure**, or set of rules for transforming ideas into sentences. From Chomsky's perspective, children are genetically prewired to attend to language and deduce the rules for constructing sentences from ideas.

T F Children are "prewired" to listen to language in such a way that they come to understand rules of grammar.

True; this prewiring has been termed a language acquisition device (LAD).

Brain Structures Involved in Language

Many parts of the brain are involved in language development; however, some of the key biological structures that may provide the basis for the functions of the LAD are based in the left hemisphere of the cerebral cortex for nearly all right-handed people and for two out of three left-handed people (Pinker, 1994). In the left hemisphere, the two areas most involved in speech are Broca's area and Wernicke's area (see Figure 6.3). Damage to either area is likely to cause an **aphasia**—a disruption in the ability to understand or produce language.

Broca's area is located near the section of the motor cortex that controls the muscles of the tongue and throat and other areas of the face that are used in speech. When Broca's area is damaged, people speak laboriously in a pattern termed **Broca's aphasia**. But they can readily understand speech. Wernicke's area lies near the auditory cortex and is connected to Broca's area by nerves. People with damage to Wernicke's area may show **Wernicke's aphasia**, in which they speak freely and with proper syntax but have trouble understanding speech and finding the words to express themselves.

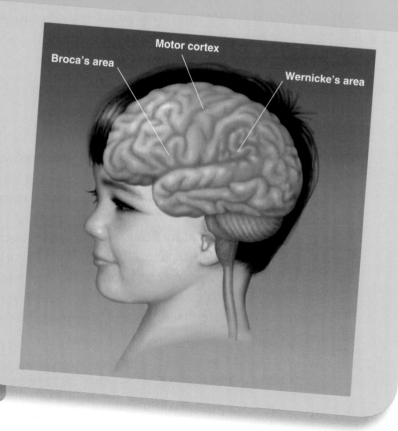

FIGURE 6.3
Broca's and Wernicke's Areas of the Cerebral Cortex

A part of the brain called the *angular gyrus* lies between the visual cortex and Wernicke's area. The angular gyrus "translates" visual information, such as written words, into auditory information (sounds) and sends it on to Wernicke's area. Problems in the angular gyrus can cause problems in reading because it is difficult for the reader to segment words into sounds (Pugh et al., 2000).

The Sensitive Period

Language learning is most efficient during **sensitive periods**, which begin at about 18 to 24 months and last until puberty (Clancy & Finlay, 2001; Uylings, 2006). During these periods, neural development provides plasticity of the brain.

Evidence for a sensitive period is found in recovery from brain injuries in some people. Injuries to the hemisphere that controls language (usually the left hemisphere) can impair or destroy the ability to speak (Werker & Tees, 2005). But before puberty, children suffering left-hemisphere injuries frequently recover a good deal of speaking ability. In young children, left-hemisphere damage may encourage the development of language functions in the right hemisphere. But such adaptive capability wanes in adolescence, when brain tissue has reached adult levels of differentiation (Snow, 2006).

The best way to determine whether people are capable of acquiring language once they have passed puberty would be to run an experiment in which one or more children were reared in such severe isolation that they were not exposed to language until puberty. Of course, such an experiment could not be done, for ethical reasons. However, the disturbing case history of Genie offers insights into whether there is a sensitive period for language development (Fromkin et al., 2004; LaPointe, 2005).

Genie's father locked her in a small room at the age of 20 months and kept her there until she was 13 years old. Her social contacts during this period were limited to her mother, who entered the room only to feed Genie, and to beatings by her father. When Genie was rescued, she weighed only about 60 pounds, did not speak, was not toilet trained, and could barely stand. She was placed in a foster home, and thereafter her language development followed the normal sequence of much younger children in a number of ways. Five years after her liberation, however, Genie's language remained largely telegraphic. She still showed significant problems with syntax, such as failing to reverse subjects and verbs to phrase questions.

Genie's language development provides support for the sensitive-period hypothesis, although her language problems might also be partly attributed to her years of malnutrition and abuse. Her efforts to acquire English after puberty were laborious, and the results were substandard compared even with the language of many 2- and 3-year-olds.

In sum, the development of language in infancy represents the interaction of environmental and biological factors. The child brings a built-in readiness to the task of language acquisition, whereas houseplants and other organisms do not. The child must also have the opportunity to hear spoken language and to interact verbally with others. In the next chapter, we see how interaction with others affects social development.

sensitive periods Time spans from about 18 months of age to puberty when the brain is especially capable of learning language.

---

6 < substages in Piaget's sensorimotor stage of development

8 to 12 months < age range by which object permanence has usually been acquired

0.7 hours < earliest point at which newborns are known to imitate adult facial expressions

50 < number of words children may be producing by 18 months

75% < portion of words which are nouns added to the infant's vocabulary between 18 and 22 months

18 to 24 months < the first "sensitive period" for language learning

Attachment

is a two-way street.

7
Infancy: Social and Emotional Development

When she was 2 years old, my daughter almost succeeded in preventing publication of a book I was writing. When I locked myself into my study, she positioned herself outside the door and called, "Daddy, oh Daddy." At other times she would bang on the door or cry. When I would give in (several times a day) and open the door, she would run in and say, "I want you to pick up me," hold out her arms or climb into my lap. How would I finish the book? One solution was to write outside the home, but this solution had the drawback of distancing me from my family. Another solution was to ignore her and let her cry, but I didn't want to discourage her efforts to get to me. Attachment, you see, is a two-way street.

Learning Outcomes

LO1 Describe the development of attachment in infants.

LO2 Discuss social deprivation, neglect, and other factors that influence attachment.

LO3 Discuss the effects of day care on attachment.

LO4 Examine the emotional development of infants.

LO5 Examine the personality development of infants.

LO1 Attachment: Bonds That Endure

a ttachment is what most people refer to as affection or love. Mary Ainsworth (1989), a preeminent researcher on attachment, defines **attachment** as an enduring emotional bond between one animal or person and another. John Bowlby adds that attachment is essential to the survival of the infant (Bowlby,

> **attachment** An emotional bond shown by seeking closeness with another and feeling distress upon separation.

separation anxiety Fear of separation from an attachment figure.

secure attachment A type of attachment shown by exhibiting mild distress at leave-takings and being readily soothed by reunion.

avoidant attachment A type of insecure attachment shown by apparent indifference to leave-takings by and reunions with an attachment figure.

ambivalent/resistant attachment A type of insecure attachment shown by severe distress at leave-takings by and ambivalent behavior at reunions with an attachment figure.

disorganized–disoriented attachment A type of insecure attachment shown by confusion or disorientation and contradictory behaviors toward an attachment figure.

PATTERNS OF ATTACHMENT

Ainsworth and her colleagues (1978) identified various patterns of attachment. Broadly, infants show **secure attachment** or insecure attachment. Most infants in the United States are securely attached (Belsky, 2006a; McCartney et al., 2004).

Ainsworth developed the *strange-situation method* as a way of measuring the development of attachment (Figure 7.1). In this method, an infant is exposed to a series of separations and reunions with a caregiver (usually the mother) and a stranger who is a confederate of the researchers. In the test, secure infants mildly protest their mothers' departure, seek interaction upon reunion, and are readily comforted by their mothers.

1988). He notes that babies are born with behaviors—crying, smiling, clinging—that stimulate caregiving from adults.

Infants try to maintain contact with caregivers to whom they are attached. They engage in eye contact, pull and tug at them, and ask to be picked up. When they cannot maintain contact, they show **separation anxiety**—thrash about, fuss, cry, screech, or whine.

There are two major types of insecurity, or insecure attachment: **avoidant attachment** and **ambivalent/resistant attachment**. Infants who show avoidant attachment are least distressed by their mothers' departures. They play without fuss when alone and ignore their mothers upon reunion. Ambivalent/resistant babies are the most emotional. They show severe signs of distress when their mothers leave and show ambivalence upon reunion by alternately clinging to their mothers and pushing them away. Additional categories of insecure attachment have been proposed, including **disorganized–disoriented attachment**. Babies showing this pattern seem dazed, confused, or disoriented. They may show contradictory behaviors, such as moving toward the mother while looking away from her.

FIGURE 7.1
The Strange Situation

These historic photos show a 12-month-old child in the strange situation. In (a), the child plays with toys, glancing occasionally at his mother. In (b), the stranger approaches with a toy. While the child is distracted, the mother leaves the room. In (c), the mother returns after a brief absence. The child crawls to her quickly and clings to her when picked up. In (d), the child cries when the mother again leaves the room.

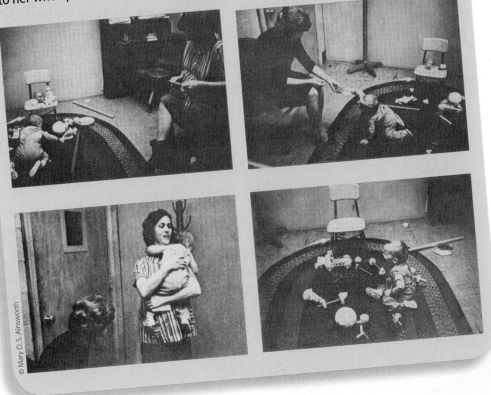

© Mary D. S. Ainsworth

Robert S. Marvin

© U.P. Images/iStockphoto.com / © graham klotz/iStockphoto.com /

MARY D. AINSWORTH

Secure infants and toddlers are happier, more sociable, and more cooperative with caregivers. At ages 5 and 6, they get along better with peers and are better adjusted in school than insecure children (Belsky, 2006a; McCartney et al., 2004; Spieker et al., 2003). Insecure attachment at the age of 1 year predicts psychological disorders at the age of 17 (Blakeslee, 1998; Steele, 2005a).

ESTABLISHING ATTACHMENT

Attachment is related to the quality of infant care (Belsky, 2006a; Coleman, 2003). The parents of secure infants are more affectionate, cooperative, and predictable than the parents of insecure infants. They respond more sensitively to their infants' smiles and cries (Harel & Scher, 2003).

A Japanese study found evidence for the intergenerational transmission of attachment (Kazui et al., 2000). The children of secure mothers showed the most secure patterns of attachment themselves (Cicchetti et al., 2006). Siblings tend to develop similar attachment relationships with their mother (van IJzendoorn et al., 2000). Siblings of the same sex are also more likely than girl–boy pairs to form similar attachment relationships with their mother.

Security is also connected with the infant's temperament (Belsky, 2006a; Kerns et al., 2007). The mothers of "difficult" children are less responsive to them and report feeling more distant from them (Morrell & Steele, 2003; Stams et al., 2002).

Involvement of Fathers

How involved is the average father with his children? The brief answer, in developed nations, is more so than in the past (Grossmann et al., 2002). But mothers engage in more interactions with their infants. Most fathers are more likely to play with their children than to feed or clean them (Laflamme et al., 2002). Fathers more often than mothers engage in rough-and-tumble play, whereas mothers are more likely to play games involving toys, and patty-cake and peek-a-boo (Laflamme et al., 2002).

How strongly, then, do infants become attached to their fathers? The more affectionate the interaction between father and infant is, the stronger the attachment (R. A. Thompson et al., 2003).

indiscriminate attachment The display of attachment behaviors toward any person.

STABILITY OF ATTACHMENT

Patterns of attachment tend to persist when care giving conditions remain constant (Ammaniti et al., 2005; Karavasilis et al., 2003). Byron Egeland and Alan Sroufe (1981) followed infants who were severely neglected and others who received high-quality care from 12 to 18 months of age. Attachment patterns remained stable (secure) for infants receiving fine care. But many insecure neglected infants became securely attached over the 6-month period, either because of a relationship with a supportive family member or because home life grew less tense. Children can also become less securely attached to caregivers when home life deteriorates (Belsky, 2006a). Children adopted at various ages can become securely attached to adoptive parents (Veríssimo & Salvaterra, 2006). Early attachment patterns tend to endure into middle childhood, adolescence, and even adulthood (Ammaniti et al., 2005; Karavasilis et al., 2003).

STAGES OF ATTACHMENT

Cross-cultural studies have led to a theory of stages of attachment. In one study, Ainsworth (1967) tracked the behavior of Ugandan infants. Over a 9-month period, she noted their efforts to maintain contact with the mother, their protests when separated, and their use of the mother as a base for exploring the environment. At first, the Ugandan infants showed **indiscriminate attachment**—no particular preferences for a familiar caregiver. Specific attachment to the mother, as evidenced by separation anxiety and other behavior, began to develop at about 4 months of age and grew intense by about 7 months. Fear of strangers developed 1 or 2 months later.

initial-preattachment phase The first phase in development of attachment, characterized by indiscriminate attachment.

attachment-in-the-making phase The second phase in development of attachment, characterized by preference for familiar figures.

clear-cut-attachment phase The third phase in development of attachment, characterized by intensified dependence on the primary caregiver.

In another study, whose results are displayed in Figure 7.2, Scottish infants showed indiscriminate attachment during the first 6 months or so after birth (Schaffer & Emerson, 1964). Then, indiscriminate attachment waned. Specific attachments to the mother and other familiar caregivers intensified, as demonstrated by the appearance of separation anxiety, and remained at high levels through the age of 18 months. Fear of strangers occurred a month or so after the intensity of specific attachments began to mushroom. In both this study and the Ugandan study, fear of strangers followed separation anxiety and the development of specific attachments by weeks.

From such studies, Ainsworth and her colleagues (1978) identified the following three phases of attachment:

1. The **initial-preattachment phase** lasts from birth to about 3 months and is characterized by indiscriminate attachment.

2. The **attachment-in-the-making phase** occurs at about 3 or 4 months and is characterized by preference for familiar figures.

3. The **clear-cut-attachment phase** occurs at about 6 or 7 months and is characterized by intensified dependence on the primary caregiver, usually the mother.

Most infants have more than one adult caregiver and are likely to form multiple attachments: to the father, day-care providers, grandparents, and other caregivers, as well as the mother.

THEORIES OF ATTACHMENT

There are several theories of the development of attachment.

Cognitive View of Attachment

The cognitive view suggests that an infant must develop the concept of object permanence before specific attachment becomes possible. If caregivers are to be missed when absent, the infant must perceive that they continue to exist. We have seen that infants tend to develop specific attachments at about the age of 6 to 7 months. Basic object permanence concerning objects develops somewhat earlier (see Chapter 6).

Behavioral View of Attachment

Early in the twentieth century, behaviorists argued that attachment behaviors are conditioned. Caregivers feed their infants and tend to their other physiological needs. Thus, infants associate their caregivers with gratification and learn to approach them to meet their needs. From this perspective, a caregiver becomes a conditioned reinforcer.

Psychoanalytic Views of Attachment

According to psychoanalytic theorists, the caregiver, usually the mother, becomes not just a "reinforcer" but also a love object who forms the basis for all later attach-

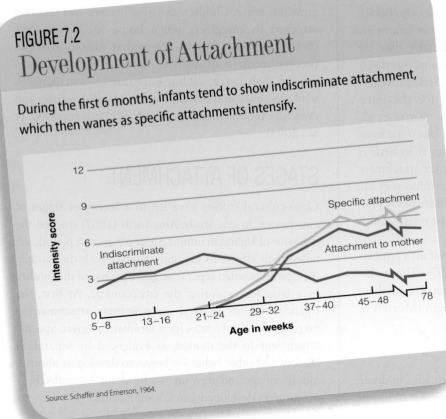

FIGURE 7.2
Development of Attachment

During the first 6 months, infants tend to show indiscriminate attachment, which then wanes as specific attachments intensify.

Source: Schaffer and Emerson, 1964.

ments. Sigmund Freud emphasized the importance of oral activities, such as eating, in the first year. Freud believed that the infant becomes emotionally attached to the mother during this time because she is the primary satisfier of the infant's needs for food and sucking.

Erik Erikson believed that the first year is critical for developing a sense of trust in the mother, which fosters attachment. The mother's general sensitivity to the child's needs, not just the need for food, fosters the development of trust and attachment.

Caregiver as a Source of Contact Comfort

Harry and Margaret Harlow conducted classic experiments to demonstrate that feeding is not critical to the attachment process contrary to what Freud suggested (Harlow & Harlow, 1966). In one study, the Harlows placed rhesus monkey infants in cages with two surrogate "mothers" (see Figure 7.3). One mother was made from wire mesh, from which a baby bottle was extended. The other surrogate mother was made of soft, cuddly terry cloth but was not equipped with a baby bottle. Infant monkeys spent most of their time clinging to the cloth mother, even though she did not offer food. The Harlows concluded that monkeys—and perhaps humans—have a need for **contact comfort** that is as basic as the need for food.

Ethological View of Attachment

Ethologists note that for many animals, attachment is an inborn or instinctive response to a specific stimulus. Some researchers theorize that a baby's cry stimulates caregiving in women. By 2 to 3 months of age, the human face begins to elicit a **social smile** in infants helping to ensure survival by eliciting affection (Ainsworth & Bowlby, 1991; Bowlby, 1988). In circular fashion, the mother's social response to her infant's face can reliably produce infant smiling by 8 months of age (Jones & Hong, 2005). The pattern contributes to a mutual attachment.

In many nonhumans, attachment occurs during a **critical period** of life. Waterfowl become attached during this period to the first moving object they encounter. Because the image of the moving object seems to become imprinted on the young animal, the process is termed **imprinting**.

contact comfort The pleasure derived from physical contact with another.

ethologist A scientist who studies the behavior patterns characteristic of various species.

social smile A smile that occurs in response to a human voice or face.

critical period A period during which imprinting can occur.

imprinting The process by which some young nonhumans become attached to the first moving object they encounter.

FIGURE 7.3
Contact Comfort

Although this rhesus monkey infant is fed by the wire-mesh "mother," it spends most of its time clinging to a soft, cuddly terry-cloth "mother."

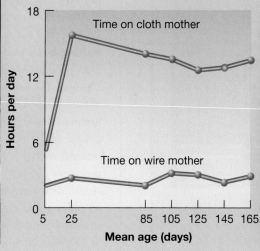

Ethologist Konrad Lorenz (1962, 1981) became well known when pictures of his "family" of goslings were made public. Lorenz acquired his "following" by being present when the goslings hatched and allowing them to follow him. The critical period for geese and ducks begins when they first engage in locomotion and ends when they develop fear of strangers. The goslings followed Lorenz persistently, ran to him when frightened, honked with distress at his departure, and tried to overcome barriers placed between them. If you substitute crying for honking, it sounds quite human.

Ethology, Ainsworth, and Bowlby

Let us return to Ainsworth and Bowlby (1991). They wrote that "the distinguishing characteristic of the theory of attachment that we have jointly developed is that it is an ethological approach" (p. 333). But they addressed several distinctions for humans. They noted that caregiving in humans is largely learned and not inborn. Ainsworth and Bowlby also noted that the critical period for attachment in humans—if one exists—extends to months or years (Ainsworth & Bowlby, 1991; Verissimo & Salvaterra, 2006). Caregiving itself and infant responsiveness, such as smiling, also promote attachment.

Konrad Lorenz with his "family" of goslings. The type of attachment shown here is known as imprinting.

KONRAD LORENZ AND HIS GOSLINGS

© U.P. Images/iStockphoto.com / © graham klotz/iStockphoto.com / © Time Life Pictures/Getty Images

LO2 When Attachment Fails

What happens when children are reared with little or no contact with caregivers? When parents neglect or abuse their children? When children develop autism spectrum disorders?

SOCIAL DEPRIVATION

Studies of children reared in institutions where they receive little social stimulation from caregivers are limited in that they are correlational. In other words, family factors that led to the children's placement in institutions may also have contributed to their developmental problems. Ethical considerations prevent us from conducting experiments in which we randomly assign children to social deprivation. However, experiments of this kind have been undertaken with rhesus monkeys, and the results are consistent with those of the correlational studies of children.

Experiments with Monkeys

The Harlows and their colleagues conducted studies of rhesus monkeys that were "reared" by wire-mesh and terry-cloth surrogate mothers. In later studies, rhesus monkeys were reared without even this questionable "social" support—without seeing any other animal, monkey or human (Harlow et al., 1971).

The Harlows found that rhesus infants reared in this most solitary confinement later avoided other monkeys. In fact, they cowered in the presence of others. Nor did they try to fend off attacks by other monkeys. Rather, they sat in the corner, clutching themselves and rocking back and forth. Females who later bore children ignored or abused them.

Can the damage from social deprivation be overcome? When monkeys deprived for 6 months or more are placed with younger, 3- to 4-month-old females for a couple of hours a day, the younger monkeys attempt to interact with their deprived elders. Many of the deprived monkeys begin to play with the youngsters after a few weeks, and many eventually expand their social contacts to older monkeys (Suomi et al., 1972). Socially withdrawn 4- and 5-year-old children similarly make gains in their social and emotional development when provided with younger playmates (Furman et al., 1979).

Exposure to younger playmates can help withdrawn older children improve socially and emotionally.

Studies with Children

Institutionalized children whose material needs are met but who receive little social stimulation from caregivers encounter problems in all areas of development (Ganesh & Magdalin, 2007; Rutter, 2006). René A. Spitz (1965) found that many institutionalized children show withdrawal and depression. In one institution, infants were maintained in separate cubicles for most of their first year to ward off infectious diseases (Provence & Lipton, 1962). Adults tended to them only to feed them and change their diapers. As a rule, baby bottles were propped up in their cribs. Attendants rarely responded to their cries; they were rarely played with or spoken to. By the age of 4 months, the infants showed little interest in adults. A few months later, some of them sat withdrawn in their cribs and rocked back and forth, almost like the Harlows' monkeys. None were speaking at 12 months.

Why do children whose material needs are met show such dramatic deficiencies? The answer may depend, in part, on the age of the child. Research by Leon Yarrow and his colleagues (Yarrow et al., 1971; Yarrow & Goodwin, 1973) suggests that deficiencies in sensory stimulation and social interaction may cause more problems than lack of love in infants who are too young to have developed specific attachments. But once infants have developed specific attachments, separation from their primary caregivers can lead to problems.

The Capacity to Recover from Social Deprivation

Infants also have powerful capacities to recover from deprivation. One study showed how many children may be able to recover fully from 13 or 14 months of deprivation (Kagan & Klein, 1973). The natives in an isolated Guatemalan village believe that fresh air and sunshine will sicken children. Children are thus kept in windowless huts until they can walk and are played with infrequently. During their isolation, the infants behave apathetically. They are physically and socially deficient when they start to walk. But by 11 years of age they are as alert and active as U.S. children of the same age.

A classic longitudinal study of orphanage children also offers evidence of the ability of children to recover from social deprivation (Skeels, 1966). In this study, a group of 19-month-old intellectually deficient children were placed in the care of older institutionalized girls. The girls spent a great deal of time playing with and nurturing them. Four years after being placed with the girls, the "deficient" children made dramatic gains in IQ scores, whereas children remaining in the orphanage showed declines in IQ.

CHILD ABUSE AND NEGLECT

Consider the following statistics from national surveys (Straus & Field, 2003; U.S. Department of Health and Human Services [USDHHS], 2004): By the time children are 2 years of age, 90% of parents have engaged in some sort of psychological or emotional abuse; 55% of parents have slapped or spanked their children; and 31% of parents have pushed, grabbed, or shoved their children.

According to the USDHHS (2004), some 3 million American children are neglected or abused each year by their parents or caregivers. More than 150,000 of the 3 million are sexually abused (Letourneau et al., 2004; USDHHS, 2004). But researchers believe that 50–60% of cases of abuse and neglect go unreported, so the true incidences are higher (USDHHS, 2004). Neglect causes more injuries and deaths than abuse (USDHHS, 2004).

It is not known how many children are sexually abused (Hines & Finkelhor, 2007). Although most sexually abused children are girls, one quarter to one third are boys (Edwards et al., 2003). A survey at a health maintenance organization (HMO) suggests that the prevalence of sexual abuse is about 18% among boys and 25% among girls (Edwards et al., 2003).

Effects of Child Abuse

Abused children show a high incidence of personal and social problems and psychological disorders (Letourneau et al., 2004). In general, abused children are less securely attached to their parents. They are less intimate with peers and more aggressive, angry, and noncompliant than other children (Joshi et al., 2006). They have lower self-esteem and perform more poorly in school (Shonk & Cicchetti, 2001). Later on, abused children are at greater risk for delinquency, risky sexual behavior, and substance abuse (Haapasalo & Moilanen, 2004). When they reach adulthood, they are more likely to act aggressively toward their partners (Malinosky-Rummell & Hansen, 1993).

Causes of Child Abuse

Various factors contribute to child abuse, including stress, a history of child abuse in at least one parent's family of origin, lack of adequate coping and child-rearing skills, unrealistic expectations of children, and substance abuse (Maluccio & Ainsworth, 2003; Merrill et al., 2004). Stress has many sources, including divorce, loss of a job, moving, and birth of a new family member (Joshi et al., 2006).

Ironically, infants who are already in pain of some kind and difficult to soothe are more likely to be abused (Frodi, 1985). Abusive parents may find the cries of their infants particularly aversive, so infants' crying may precipitate abuse (Schuetze et al., 2003). Children who are disobedient, inappropriate, or unresponsive are also at greater risk (Bugental & Happaney, 2004).

What to Do

Many states require helping professionals such as psychologists and physicians to report any suspicion of child abuse. Some legally require *anyone* who suspects child abuse to report it to authorities.

A number of techniques have been developed to help prevent child abuse. One approach focuses on strengthening parenting skills among the general population (Joshi et al., 2006). Another approach targets groups at high risk for abuse, such as poor, single teen mothers (Joshi et al., 2006). In some programs, home visitors help new parents develop skills in caregiving and home management (Duggan et al., 2004).

© Jeff Hutchens/Getty Images

A third technique focuses on presenting information about abuse and providing support to families. For instance, many locales have child abuse hotlines. Individuals who suspect child abuse may call for advice. Parents having difficulty controlling aggressive impulses toward their children are also encouraged to call.

AUTISM SPECTRUM DISORDERS

Autism spectrum disorders (ASDs) are characterized by impairment in communication skills and social interaction, and by repetitive, stereotyped behavior (Table 7.1). ASDs tend to become evident by the age of 3 and sometimes before the end of the first year. A CDC study of 407,578 children from 14 parts of the United States identified 1 in every 152 children as having an ASD (Rice et al., 2007). There are several variations of ASDs, but autism is the major type. Other forms of ASDs include:

- *Asperger's disorder.* Characterized by social deficits and stereotyped behavior but without the significant cognitive or language delays associated with autism.

- *Rett's disorder.* Characterized by a range of physical, behavioral, motor, and cognitive abnormalities that begin after a few months of normal development.

- *Childhood disintegrative disorder.* Abnormal functioning and loss of previously acquired skills that begins after about 2 years of apparently normal development.

Autism

Autism is four to five times more common among boys than girls. Autistic children do not show interest in social interaction and may avoid eye contact. Attachment to others is weak or absent.

Other features of autism include communication problems, intolerance of change, and ritualistic or stereo-

TABLE 7.1
Characteristics of Autism Spectrum Disorders (ASDs)

KEY INDICATORS

Does not babble, point, or make meaningful gestures by 1 year of age

Does not speak one word by 16 months

Does not combine two words by 2 years

Does not respond to name

Loses language or social skills

OTHER INDICATORS

Poor eye contact

Doesn't seem to know how to play with toys

Excessively lines up toys or other objects

Is attached to one particular toy or object

Doesn't smile

At times seems to be hearing impaired

Source: Adapted from Strock (2004).

typical behavior (Georgiades et al., 2007) (see Table 7.1). Parents of autistic children often say they were "good babies," which usually means they made few demands. But as autistic children develop, they tend to shun affectionate contacts such as hugging, cuddling, and kissing.

 T F Autistic children may respond to people as though they were pieces of furniture. *This is true.*

Development of speech lags. There is little babbling and communicative gesturing during the first year. Autistic children may show **mutism**, echolalia, and pronoun reversal, referring to themselves as "you" or "he." About half use language by middle childhood, but their speech is unusual and labored.

Autistic children become bound by ritual. Even slight changes in routines or the environment may cause distress. The teacher of a 5-year-old autistic girl would greet her each morn-

ing with, "G o o d morning,

mutism Refusal to speak.

Lily, I am very, very glad to see you." Lily would ignore the greeting, but she would shriek if the teacher omitted even one of the *very*s. This feature of autism is termed *preservation of sameness*. When familiar objects are moved from their usual places, children with autism may throw tantrums or cry until the placement is restored. They may insist on eating the same food every day. Autistic children show deficits in peer play, imaginative play, imitation, and emotional expression. Many sleep less than their age-mates (Georgiades et al., 2007).

Some autistic children mutilate themselves, even as they cry out in pain. They may bang their heads, slap their faces, bite their hands and shoulders, or pull out their hair.

Causes of Autism

Contrary to what some theorists say, research evidence shows that there is no correlation between the development of autism and deficiencies in child rearing (Mackic-Magyar & McCracken, 2004).

Various lines of evidence suggest a key role for biological factors in autism. For example, very low birth weight and advanced maternal age may heighten the risk of autism (Maimburg & Væth, 2006). A role for genetic mechanisms is suggested by kinship studies (Constantino et al., 2006; Gutknecht, 2001). The concordance (agreement) rates for autism are about 60% for pairs of identical (MZ) twins, who fully share their genetic heritage, compared with about 10% for pairs of fraternal (DZ) twins, whose genetic codes overlap by half (Plomin et al., 1994).

Biological factors focus on neurological involvement. Many children with autism have abnormal brain wave patterns or seizures (Canitano, 2007; Roulet-Perez & Deonna; 2006). Other researchers have found that the brains of children with autism have abnormal sensitivities to neurotransmitters such as serotonin, dopamine, acetylcholine, and norepinephrine (Bauman et al., 2006). Other researchers note unusually high activity in the motor region of the cerebral cortex (R. Mueller et al., 2001) and less activity in some other areas of the brain (Lam et al., 2006; Penn, 2006).

Treatment of Autism

Treatment for autism is mainly based on principles of learning, although investigation of biological approaches is also under way (Strock, 2004). Behavior modification has been used to increase the child's ability to attend to others, to play with other children, and to discourage self-mutilation. Brief bursts of mild, harmless electric shock rapidly eliminate self-mutilation (Lovaas, 1977). The use of electric shock raises serious moral, ethical, and legal concerns, but O. Ivar Lovaas has countered that failure to eliminate self-injurious behavior places the child at yet greater risk.

Because children with autism show behavioral deficits, behavior modification is used to help them develop new behaviors. Many autistic children can be taught to accept people as reinforcers, rather than objects, by pairing praise with food treats (Drasgow et al., 2001). Praise can then be used to encourage speech and social play.

The most effective treatment programs focus on individualized instruction (Rapin, 1997). In a classic study conducted by Lovaas and his colleagues (1989), autistic children received more than 40 hours of one-to-one behavior modification a week for at least 2 years. Significant intellectual and educational gains were reported for 9 of the 19 children (47%) in the program. Less intensive educational programs have yielded some positive results with autistic toddlers (Stahmer et al., 2004).

Biological approaches for the treatment of autism are under study. Drugs that enhance serotonin activity (selective serotonin reuptake inhibitors, or SSRIs) can apparently help prevent self-injury, aggressive outbursts, depression, anxiety, and repetitive behavior (Kwok, 2003). Drugs that are usually used to treat schizophrenia—so-called major tranquilizers—are useful in reducing stereotyped behavior, hyperactivity, and self-injury, but not cognitive and language problems (Kwok, 2003; McClellan & Werry, 2003).

Autistic behavior generally continues into adulthood to one degree or another. Nevertheless, some autistic people go on to achieve college degrees and function independently (Rapin, 1997).

LO3 Day Care

Looking for a phrase that can strike fear in the hearts of millions of caregivers? Try *day care*. Most parents, including mothers with infants, are in the workforce (Carey, 2007a). As a result, of the more than 10 million American children under the age of 5, more than 20% are cared for in day-care centers.

© liquidlibrary/Jupiterimages

Many parents wonder whether day care will affect their children's attachment to them. Some studies have found that infants who are in full-time day care are more likely than other children to show insecure attachment (Brandtjen & Verny, 2001). Some researchers conclude that a mother who works full time puts her infant at risk for developing emotional insecurity. Others note that infants whose mothers work may simply become less distressed by her departure and less likely to seek her out when she returns as time goes on, thus providing the appearance of being less attached. Moreover, the likelihood of insecure attachment is not much greater in infants placed in day care than in those cared for in the home. Most infants in both groups are securely attached (Timmerman, 2006).

Some studies report that infants with day-care experience are more peer oriented and play at higher developmental levels than do home-reared infants. Children in high-quality day care are more likely to share their toys. They are more independent, self-confident, outgoing, and affectionate as well as more helpful and cooperative with peers and adults (Lamb & Ahnert, 2006; Pierce & Vandell, 2006). Participation in day care is also linked with better academic performance in elementary school (Belsky, 2006b).

A study funded by the National Institute of Child Health and Human Development (NICHD) found that "high-quality" day care can result in scores on tests of cognitive skills that rival or exceed those of the children reared in the home by their mothers (Belsky et al., 2007). The quality of the day care was defined in terms of the richness of the learning environment (availability of toys, books, and other materials), the ratio of caregivers to children (high quality meant more caregivers), the amount of individual attention received by the children, and the extent to which caregivers talked to the children and asked them questions.

However, the researchers also found that children placed in day care may be less cooperative and more aggressive toward peers and adults than children who are reared in the home. The more time spent away from their mothers, the more likely these children were to be rated as defiant, aggressive, and disobedient once they got to kindergarten.

T F Children placed in day care are more aggressive than children who are cared for in the home.
True, although their level of aggression is generally not severe.

Teacher ratings found that once children who were in day care are in school, they are significantly more likely than children cared for in the home to interrupt in class and tease or bully other children (Belsky et al., 2007). The degree of disturbance generally remained "within normal limits." That is, the children who had been in day care could not be labeled criminals and were not being expelled. *The quality of the day-care center made no difference.* Children from high-quality day-care centers were also more likely to be disruptive than children cared for in the home. Moreover, the behavioral difference persisted through the sixth grade.

Now let us note some limitations of the NICHD study. Although the differences in disruptive behavior between children in full time day care and those cared for in the home are statistically significant—meaning that they are unlikely to be due to chance—they are small. The study implies that day care *causes* the later disruptive behavior, but there is no control group (Harris, 2007). Children are *not* assigned at random to day care or care in the home. Therefore, it may be that children placed in day care are those whose caregivers are most stressed by work through their children's primary school years (Taylor, 2007). Also, do we know that the so-called disruptive children become less productive and successful adults (Kulp, 2007)? Perhaps they actually become assertive and entrepreneurial, especially since their cognitive skills and other social skills are intact.

In any case, reality intrudes. Millions of parents do not have the option of deciding whether to place their children in day care; their only choice is where. And some parents, given their financial and geographic circumstances, might not even have that choice.

LO4 Emotional Development

an emotion is a state of feeling with physiological, situational, and cognitive components. Physiologically, when emotions are strong, our hearts may beat more rapidly and our muscles may tense. Situationally, we may feel anger when provoked or pleasure or relief when we are being held by a loved one. Cognitively, anger may be triggered by the idea that someone is purposefully withholding something we need.

It is unclear how many emotions babies have, and they cannot tell us what they are feeling. We can only observe their behavior, including their facial expressions (Oster, 2005). Facial expressions appear to be universal in that they are recognized in different cultures around the world, so they are considered a reliable index of emotion.

Researchers have long debated whether the emotional expression of newborns begins in an undifferentiated state of diffuse excitement or whether several emotions are present (Soussignan & Schaal, 2005). They have asked whether the newborn baby's crying is nothing more than a reflex in response to discomfort. They have even asked whether the facial expressions of infants, which many researchers claim express emotions such as anger, joy, fear, and excitement within a few months after birth, actually reflect internal states of feeling. It seems clear enough that as infants develop through the first year, their cognitive appraisal of events, including their interactions with their caregivers, becomes a key part of their emotional life and their emotional expression (Camras et al., 2007; Soussignan & Schaal, 2005).

Infants' initial emotional expressions appear to comprise two basic states of emotional arousal: a positive attraction to pleasant stimulation, such as hearing the caregiver's voice or being held, and withdrawal from aversive stimulation, such as a sudden loud noise. By the age of 2 to 3 months, social smiling has replaced reflexive smiling. Social smiling is usually highly endearing to caregivers. At 3 to 5 months, infants laugh at active stimuli, such as being repetitively touched on the belly or playing "Ah, boop!"

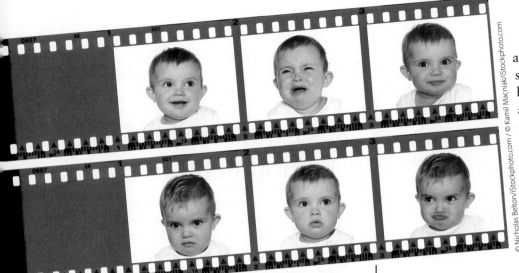

In sum, researchers agree that infants show only a few emotions during the first few months. They agree that emotional development is linked to cognitive development and social experience. They do not necessarily agree on exactly when specific emotions are first shown or whether discrete emotions are present at birth (Camras et al., 2007).

EMOTIONAL DEVELOPMENT AND PATTERNS OF ATTACHMENT

Emotional development has been linked with various histories of attachment. In a longitudinal study of 112 children at ages 9, 14, 22, and 33 months, Kochanska (2001) studied the development of fear, anger, and joy by using laboratory situations designed to evoke these emotions. Patterns of attachment were assessed using the strange-situation method. Differences in emotional development could first be related to attachment at the age of 14 months. Resistant children were most fearful, and they frequently responded with distress even in episodes designed to evoke joy. When they were assessed repeatedly over time, it became apparent that securely attached children were becoming significantly less angry. By contrast, the negative emotions of insecurely attached children rose: Avoidant children grew more fearful, and resistant children became less joyful. At 33 months of age, securely attached children were less likely to show fear and anger, even when they were exposed to situations designed to elicit these emotions.

FEAR OF STRANGERS

social referencing Using another person's reaction to a situation to form one's own response.

When my daughter Jordan was 1 year old, her mother and I needed a nanny for a few hours a day so that we could teach, write, breathe, and engage in other life activities. We hired a graduate social work student who had a mild, engaging way about her. She nurtured Jordan and played with her for about 4 months, during which time Jordan came to somewhat grudgingly accept the nanny, most of the time. Even so, Jordan was never completely comfortable with the nanny and often let out a yowl as if buildings were collapsing around her, although the nanny did nothing except calmly try to soothe her.

Unfortunately, Jordan met the nanny during the period when she had developed fear of strangers. The fear would eventually subside, as these fears do, but during her entire encounter with the nanny, the nanny wondered what she was doing wrong. The answer was simple: She was existing within sight of Jordan.

Fear of strangers—also called *stranger anxiety*—is normal. Most infants develop it. Stranger anxiety appears at about 6 to 9 months of age. By 4 or 5 months of age, infants may compare the faces of strangers and their mothers, looking back and forth. Somewhat older infants show distress by crying, whimpering, gazing fearfully, and crawling away. Fear of strangers often peaks at 9–12 months and declines in the second year.

> **T** (F) Fear of strangers is abnormal among infants.
> False; the majority of infants are likely to develop fear of strangers at around 6 to 9 months of age.

Children with fear of strangers show less anxiety when their mothers are present (Thompson & Limber, 1990). Children also are less fearful when they are in familiar surroundings, such as their homes, rather than in the laboratory (Sroufe et al., 1974).

SOCIAL REFERENCING: WHAT SHOULD I DO NOW?

Social referencing is the seeking out of another person's reaction to a situation to help us form our own view of it (Hertenstein & Campos, 2004). Leslie Carver and Brenda Vaccaro (2007) suggest that social referencing requires three components: (1) looking at another, usually older, individual in a novel, ambiguous situation; (2) associating that individual's emotional response with the unfamiliar situation; and (3) regulating one's own emotional response in accord with the response of the older individual.

Infants display social referencing as early as 6 months of age. They use caregivers' facial expressions or tone of voice as clues on how to respond (Hertenstein & Campos, 2004). In one study, 8-month-old infants were friendlier to strangers when their mothers exhibited friendly facial expressions in the strangers' presence than when the mothers looked worried (Boccia & Campos, 1989).

EMOTIONAL REGULATION: KEEPING ON AN EVEN KEEL

Emotional regulation refers to the ways in which young children control their own emotions. Even infants display certain behaviors to control unpleasant emotional states. They may look away from a disturbing event or suck their thumb (Rothbart & Sheese, 2007). Caregivers help infants learn to regulate their emotions. A two-way communication system develops in which the infant signals the caregiver that help is needed and the caregiver responds. Claire Kopp (1989, p. 347) provides an example of such a system:

A 13-month-old, playing with a large plastic bottle, attempted to unscrew the cover, but could not. Fretting for a short time, she initiated eye contact with her mother and held out the jar. As her mother took it to unscrew the cover, the infant ceased fretting.

© Markus Guhl/iStockphoto.com

Research evidence suggests that the children of secure mothers are not only likely to be securely attached themselves but also are likely to regulate their own emotions in a positive manner (Grolnick et al., 2006; Thompson & Meyer, 2007). A German longitudinal study (Zimmermann et al., 2001) related emotional regulation in adolescence with patterns of attachment during infancy, as assessed using the strange-situation method. Forty-one adolescents, aged 16 and 17, were placed in complex problem-solving situations with friends. Those adolescents who were secure as infants were most capable of regulating their emotions to interact cooperatively with their friends.

emotional regulation
Techniques for controlling one's emotional states.

LO5 Personality Development

in this section, we look at the emergence of the self-concept. We then turn to a discussion of temperament. Finally, we consider sex differences in behavior.

THE SELF-CONCEPT

At birth, we may find the world to be a confusing blur of sights, sounds, and inner sensations—yet the "we" may be missing, at least for a while. When our hands first come into view, there is little evidence we realize that the hands "belong" to us and that we are separate and distinct from the world outside.

The self-concept appears to emerge gradually during infancy. At some point, infants understand that the hands they are moving in and out of sight are "their" hands. At some point, they understand that their own bodies extend only so far and then external objects and the bodies of others begin.

Development of the Self-Concept

Psychologists have devised ingenious methods to assess the development of the self-concept among infants. One of these is the *mirror technique,* which involves the use of a mirror and a dot of rouge. Before the experiment begins, the researcher observes the infant for baseline data on how frequently the infant touches his or her nose. Then the mother places rouge on the infant's nose, and the infant is placed before a mirror. Not until about the age of 18 months do infants begin to touch their nose upon looking in the mirror (Campbell et al., 2000; Keller et al., 2005).

Nose touching suggests that children recognize themselves and that they perceive that the dot of rouge is an abnormality. Most 2-year-olds can point to pictures of themselves, and they begin to use "I" or their own name spontaneously (Smiley & Johnson, 2006).

Self-awareness affects the infant's social and emotional development (Foley, 2006). Knowledge of the self permits the infant and child to develop notions of sharing and cooperation. In one study, 2-year-olds with a better developed sense of self were more likely to cooperate with other children (Brownell & Carriger, 1990).

Self-awareness also facilitates the development of so-called self-conscious emotions such as embarrassment, envy, empathy, pride, guilt, and shame (Foley, 2006). In one study, Deborah Stipek and her colleagues (1992) found that children older than 21 months often seek their mother's attention and approval when they have successfully completed a task, whereas younger toddlers do not.

Psychoanalytic Views of the Self-Concept

Margaret Mahler, a psychoanalyst, has proposed that development of the self-concept comes about through a process of **separation–individuation**, which lasts from about 5 months until 3 years of age (Mahler et al., 1975). Separation involves the child's growing perception that the mother is separate from him or her. Individuation refers to the child's increasing sense of independence and autonomy.

One of the ways toddlers demonstrate growing autonomy, much to the dismay of caregivers, is by refusing to comply with caregivers' requests.

separation–individuation The process of becoming separate from and independent of the mother.

temperament Individual style of reaction and adaptation that is present early in life and remains fairly stable.

Studies of toddlers and preschoolers between the ages of 1½ and 5 years have found that as children grow older, they adopt more skillful ways of expressing resistance to caregivers' requests (Smith et al., 2004; Stifter & Wiggins, 2004). For example, young toddlers are more likely to ignore a caregiver's request or defy it. Older toddlers and preschoolers are more likely to make excuses or negotiate.

TEMPERAMENT: EASY, DIFFICULT, OR SLOW TO WARM UP?

Each child has a characteristic **temperament**, a stable way of reacting and adapting to the world that is present early in life (Wachs, 2006). Many researchers believe that temperament involves a strong genetic component (Goldsmith et al., 2003; Wachs, 2006). The child's temperament includes many aspects of behavior, including activity level, smiling and laughter, regularity in eating and sleep habits, approach or withdrawal, adaptability to new situations, intensity of responsiveness, general cheerfulness or unpleasantness, distractibility or persistence, and soothability (Gartstein et al., 2003; Thomas & Chess, 1989).

Types of Temperament

Thomas and Chess (1989) found that from the first days of life, many of the children in their study (65%) could be classified into one of three types of temperament: *easy* (40% of their sample), *difficult* (10%), and *slow to warm up* (15%). Some of the differences among these three types of children are shown in Table 7.2. The easy child has regular sleep and feeding schedules, approaches new situations (such as a new food or a new school) with enthusiasm and adapts to them easily, and is generally cheerful. Some children are more inconsistent and show a mixture of temperament traits. For example, a toddler may have a pleasant disposition but be frightened of new situations.

The difficult child, on the other hand, has irregular sleep and feeding schedules, is slow to accept new people and situations, takes a long time to adjust to new routines, and responds to frustrations with tantrums and crying. The slow-to-warm-up child falls between the other two types.

TABLE 7.2
Types of Temperament

TEMPERAMENT CATEGORY	EASY	DIFFICULT	SLOW TO WARM UP
Regularity of biological functioning	Regular	Irregular	Somewhat irregular
Response to new stimuli	Positive approach	Negative withdrawal	Negative withdrawal
Adaptability to new situations	Adapts readily	Adapts slowly or not at all	Adapts slowly
Intensity of reaction	Mild or moderate	Intense	Mild
Quality of mood	Positive	Negative	Initially negative; gradually more positive

Sources: Chess & Thomas (1991) and Thomas & Chess (1989).

Stability of Temperament

There is at least moderate consistency in the development of temperament from infancy onward (Wachs, 2006). The infant who is highly active and cries in novel situations often becomes a fearful toddler. Difficult children in general are at greater risk for developing psychological disorders and adjustment problems later in life (Pauli-Pott et al., 2003; Rothbart et al., 2004). A longitudinal study tracked the progress of infants with a difficult temperament from 1½ through 12 years of age (Guerin et al., 1997). A difficult temperament correlated with parental reports of behavioral problems from ages 3 to 12, and teachers' reports of problems with attention span and aggression.

© Radius Images/Jupiterimages

Goodness of Fit: The Role of the Environment

Our daughter was a difficult infant, but we weathered the storm. At the age of 15, she was climbing out the second-story bedroom window at 2 A.M. to be with friends. When we discovered it, she sarcastically asked if we disapproved. "Yes," we said. "Use the front door; you're less likely to get hurt." She graduated college with honors. She has occasional outbursts, but that's her boyfriend's problem. And they love her on the job. She's a hard worker and the most creative thing they've ever seen.

The environment also affects the development of temperament. An initial biological predisposition to a certain temperament may be strengthened or weakened by the parents' reaction to the child. Parents may react to a difficult child by imposing rigid caregiving schedules, which in turn can cause the child to become even more difficult (Schoppe-Sullivan et al., 2007). This example illustrates a poor fit between the child's behavior style and the parents' response.

On the other hand, parents may modify a child's initial temperament in a more positive direction to achieve a **goodness of fit** between child and parent. Realizing that their youngster's problematic behavior does not mean that the child is deliberately disobedient or that they are bad parents helps parents modify their attitudes and behavior toward the child, whose behavior

goodness of fit Agreement between the parents' expectations of a child and the child's temperament.

may then improve (Bird et al., 2006; Schoppe-Sullivan et al., 2007).

> T F All children are born with the same temperament. Treatment by caregivers determines whether they are difficult or easygoing.
> False; it appears that genetic factors contribute to a child's temperament. There is also at least moderate consistency in the development of temperament from infancy onward.

SEX DIFFERENCES

All cultures distinguish between females and males and have expectations about how they ought to behave. For this reason, a child's sex is a key factor in society's efforts to shape the child's personality and behavior.

Behavior of Infant Girls and Boys

Girls tend to advance more rapidly in their motor development in infancy: They sit, crawl, and walk earlier than boys (Matlin, 2008). Although a few studies have found that infant boys are more active and irritable than girls, others have not (Matlin, 2008). Girls and boys are similar in their social behaviors. They are equally likely to smile at people's faces, for example, and they do not differ in their dependency on adults (Maccoby & Jacklin, 1974). Girls and boys do begin to differ early in their preferences for certain toys and play activities. By 12 to 18 months of age, girls prefer to play with dolls, doll furniture, dishes, and toy animals; boys prefer transportation toys (trucks, cars, airplanes, and the like), tools, and sports equipment as early as 9 to 18 month of age (Campbell et al., 2000; Serbin et al., 2001). Sex differences that show up later, such as differences in spatial relations skills, are not necessarily evident in infancy (Örnkloo & von Hofsten, 2007). By 24 months, both girls and boys appear to be aware of which behaviors are considered appropriate or inappropriate for their sex, according to cultural stereotypes (Hill & Flom, 2007).

> T F Girls prefer dolls and toy animals, and boys prefer toy trucks and sports equipment only after they have become aware of the gender roles assigned to them by society.
> False; girls and boys may show a preference for gender stereotypical toys before they have been socialized and possibly before they understand their own sex.

Adults' Behavior toward Infants

Adults interact differently with girls and boys. Researchers have presented American adults with an unfamiliar infant who is dressed in boy's clothes and has a boy's name or an infant who is dressed in girl's clothing and has a girl's name. (In reality, it is the same baby who simply is given different names and clothing.) When adults believe they are playing with a girl, they are more likely to offer "her" a doll; when they think the child is a boy, they are more likely to offer a football or a hammer. "Boys" also are encouraged to engage in more physical activity than "girls" (Worell & Goodheart, 2006).

Parents, especially fathers, are more likely to encourage rough-and-tumble play in sons than in daughters (Eccles et al., 2000; Fagot et al., 2000). On the other hand, parents talk more to infant daughters than to infant sons. They smile more at daughters and are more emotionally expressive toward them (Powlishta et al., 2001).

Infant girls are likely to be decked out in a pink or yellow dress and embellished with ruffles and lace, whereas infant boys wear blue or red (Eccles et al., 2000; Powlishta et al., 2001). Parents provide baby girls and boys with different bedroom decorations and toys. Examination of the contents of rooms of children from 5 months to 6 years of age found that boys' rooms were often decorated with animal themes and with blue bedding and curtains. Girls' rooms featured flowers, lace, ruffles, and pastels. Girls owned more dolls; boys had more vehicles, military toys, and sports equipment.

Parents react favorably when their infant daughters play with "girls' toys" and their sons play with "boys' toys." Adults, especially fathers, show more negative reactions when girls play with boys' toys and boys play with girls' toys (Martin et al., 2002; Worell & Goodheart, 2006). Parents thus try to shape their children's behavior during infancy and lay the foundation for development in early childhood.

Test coming up? Now what?

With CDEV you have a multitude of study aids at your fingertips. After reading the chapters, check out these ideas for further help.

Chapter in Review cards include all learning outcomes, definitions, and summaries for each chapter.

Printable flash cards give you three additional ways to check your comprehension of key childhood and adolescent development concepts.

Other great ways to help you study include **interactive flashcards**, downloadable **study aids, games, quizzes with feedback**, and **PowerVisuals** to test your knowledge of key concepts.

You can find it all at **4ltrpress.cengage.com/cdev.**

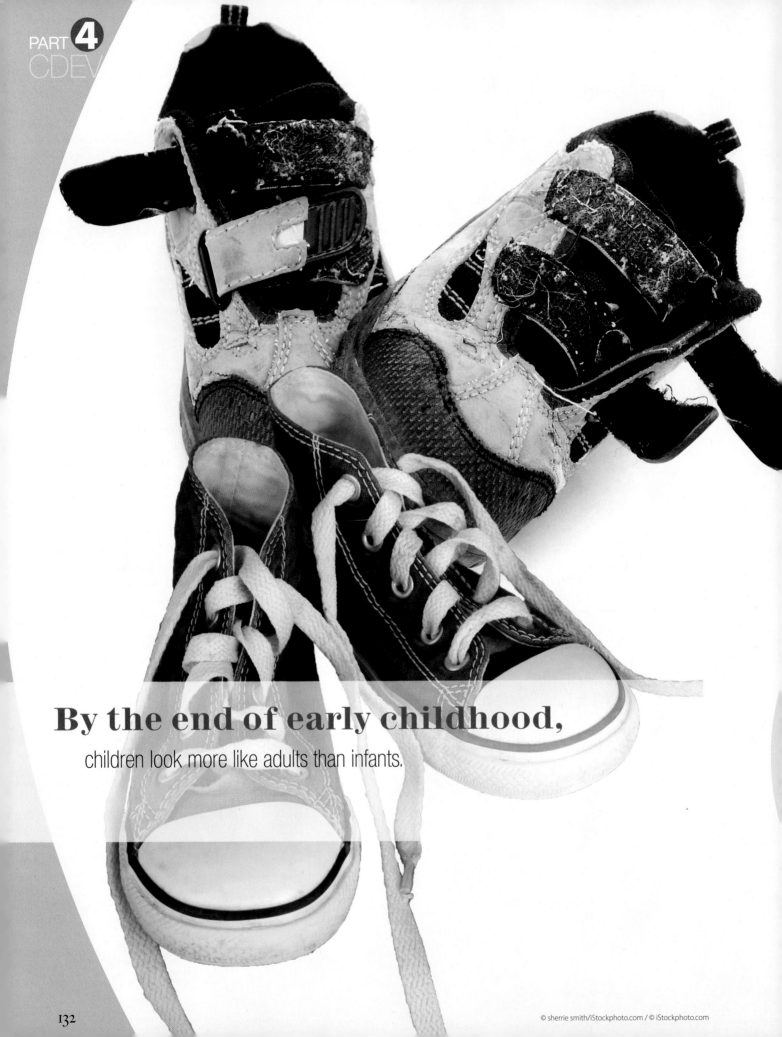

By the end of early childhood,
children look more like adults than infants.

8

Early Childhood: Physical Development

TRUTH OR FICTION?

T F Some children are left-brained, and others are right-brained.

T F A disproportionately high percentage of math whizzes are left-handed.

T F Some diseases are normal.

T F It is dangerous to awaken a sleepwalker.

T F Competent parents toilet train their child by the second birthday.

The years from 2 to 6 are referred to as *early childhood* or the *preschool years*. During early childhood, physical growth is slower than in infancy. Children become taller and leaner, and by the end of early childhood they look more like adults than infants. Motor skills develop. Children become stronger, faster, and better coordinated.

Language improves enormously, and children come to carry on conversations with others. As cognitive skills develop, a new world of make believe or "pretend" play emerges. Most preschoolers are curious and eager to learn. Increased physical and cognitive capabilities enable children to emerge from total dependence on caregivers to become part of the broader world outside the family. Peers take on an increasingly important role in the life of the preschooler. Children begin to acquire a sense of their abilities and shortcomings.

We learn about these developments of early childhood—physical, cognitive, social, and emotional—in Chapters 8, 9, and 10.

Learning Outcomes

LO1 Describe patterns of growth in early childhood.

LO2 Describe development of motor skills in early childhood, including drawing and handedness.

LO3 Describe nutritional needs in early childhood.

LO4 Describe health problems in early childhood, focusing on minor and major illness and on accidents.

LO5 Describe sleep patterns and sleep disorders of early childhood.

LO6 Describe elimination disorders, including their origins and possible treatment.

LO1 Growth Patterns

During the preschool years, physical and motor development proceeds, literally, by leaps and bounds.

HEIGHT AND WEIGHT

Following the dramatic gains in height in a child's first 2 years, the growth rate slows during the preschool years (Kuczmarski et al., 2000). Girls and boys tend to gain about 2 to 3 inches in height per year, and weight gains remain fairly even at about 4 to 6 pounds per year (see Figure 8.1). Children become increasingly slender as they gain in height and shed some "baby fat." Boys as a group become slightly taller and heavier than girls (Figure 8.1). Noticeable variations in growth occur from child to child.

DEVELOPMENT OF THE BRAIN

The brain develops more quickly than any other organ in early childhood. At 2 years of age, the brain already has attained 75% of its adult weight. By the age of 5, the brain has reached 90% of its adult weight, even though the body weight of the 5-year-old is barely one-third of what it will be as an adult (Tanner, 1989).

The increase in brain size is due in part to the continuing myelination of nerve fibers. Completion of myelination of the neural pathways that link the cerebellum to the cerebral cortex facilitates development of fine motor skills, balance, and coordination (Nelson & Luciana, 2001; Paus et al., 1999). Myelination of the cerebellum also enhances the child's balance and coordination.

FIGURE 8.1
Growth Curves for Height and Weight, Ages 2 to 6 Years

The numbers on the curves indicate the percentiles for height and weight at different ages. The growth rate slows down during early childhood. As in infancy, boys are slightly taller and heavier than girls.

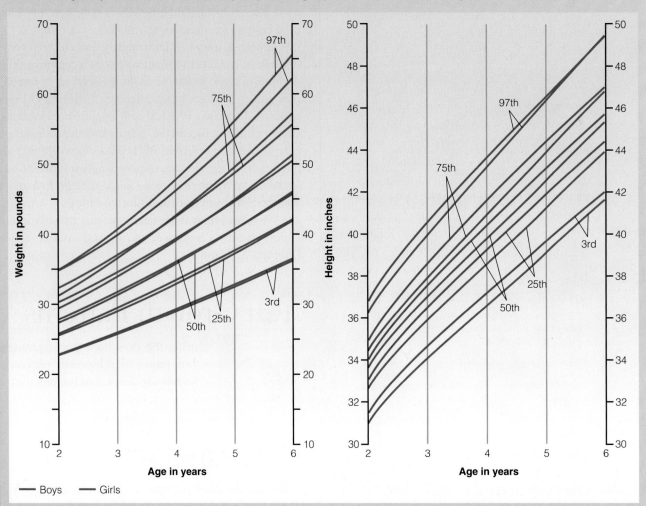

Source: Kuczmarski et al. (2000, Figures 9–12).

Completion of the mylination process helps facilitate development of balance and coordination.

Brain Development and Visual Skills

Brain development also improves processing of visual information (Yamada et al., 2000), facilitating learning to read. The parts of the brain that enable the child to sustain attention and screen out distractions become increasingly myelinated between the ages of about 4 and 7 (Nelson & Luciana, 2001), enabling most children to focus on schoolwork. The speed of processing of visual information improves throughout childhood, reaching adult levels at the onset of adolescence (Chou et al., 2006; Paus et al., 1999).

Right Brain, Left Brain?

We often hear of people being "right-brained" or "left-brained." The notion is that the hemispheres of the brain are involved in different kinds of intellectual and emotional activities. Research does suggest that in right-handed individuals, the left hemisphere is relatively more involved in intellectual undertakings that require logi-cal analysis and problem solving, language, and computation (Grindrod & Baum, 2005; O'Shea & Corballis, 2005). The other hemisphere (the right hemisphere) is usually superior in visual–spatial functions (such as piecing puzzles together), aesthetic and emotional responses, and understanding metaphors.

But it is not true that some children are left-brained and others are right-brained. Brain functions are not split completely. The functions of the left and right hemispheres overlap, and the hemispheres respond simultaneously when we focus on one thing or another. They are aided in "cooperation" by the myelination of the **corpus callosum**, a thick bundle of nerve fibers that connects the hemispheres (Kinsbourne, 2003). This process is largely complete by the age of 8, enabling the integration of logical and emotional functioning.

corpus callosum The thick bundle of nerve fibers that connects the left and right hemispheres of the brain.

plasticity The tendency of other parts of the brain to take up the functions of injured parts.

T   F   Some children are left-brained, and others are right-brained.
False; many functions of the two brain hemispheres overlap.

Plasticity of the Brain

Many parts of the brain have specialized functions, allowing our behavior to be more complex. But this specialization also means that injuries to certain parts of the brain can result in loss of these functions. However, the brain also shows **plasticity**, or the ability to compensate for injuries to particular areas. Plasticity is greatest at about 1 to 2 years of age and then gradually declines (Kolb & Gibb, 2007; Nelson et al., 2006). When adults suffer damage to the areas of the brain that control language, they may lose the ability to speak or understand language. However, other areas of the brain may assume these functions in preschoolers who suffer such damage. As a result, the youngsters may regain the ability to speak or comprehend language (Nelson et al., 2006).

Various factors are involved in the brain's plasticity (Nelson et al., 2006; Szaflarski et al., 2006). One is *sprouting,* or the growth of new dendrites, which can allow for the rearrangement of neural circuits. Another factor is the redundancy of neural connections, so that if one site of functioning is damaged, another may be able to develop to perform the function.

© Workbook Stock/Jupiterimages

LO2 Motor Development

the preschool years witness an explosion of motor skills, as children's nervous systems mature and their movements become more precise and coordinated.

GROSS MOTOR SKILLS

Gross motor skills involve the large muscles used in locomotion (see Table 8.1). At about the age of 3, children can balance on one foot. By age 3 or 4, they can walk up stairs as adults do, by placing a foot on each step. By age 4 or 5, they can skip and pedal a tricycle (McDevitt & Ormrod, 2002). Older preschoolers are better able to coordinate two tasks, such as singing and running at the same time.

gross motor skills Skills employing the large muscles used in locomotion.

In general, preschoolers appear to acquire motor skills by teaching themselves and observing other children. Imitating other children seems more important than adult instruction at this age.

Throughout early childhood, girls and boys are similar in motor skills. Girls are somewhat better at balance and precision. Boys show some advantage in throwing and kicking (McDevitt & Ormrod, 2002).

Individual differences are larger than sex differences throughout early and middle childhood. Some children are genetically predisposed to developing better coordination or more strength. Motivation and practice also are important. Motor experiences in infancy may affect the development of motor skills in early childhood. For example, children with early crawling experience perform better than those who lack such experience on tests of motor skills (McEwan et al., 1991).

PHYSICAL ACTIVITY

Preschoolers spend an average of more than 25 hours a week in large muscle activity (D. W. Campbell et al.,

TABLE 8.1
Development of Gross Motor Skills in Early Childhood

2 YEARS (24–35 MONTHS)	3 YEARS (36–47 MONTHS)	4 YEARS (48–59 MONTHS)	5 YEARS (60–71 MONTHS)
• Runs well straight ahead	• Goes around obstacles while running	• Turns sharp corners while running	• Runs lightly on toes
• Walks up stairs, two feet to a step	• Walks up stairs, one foot to a step	• Walks down stairs, one foot to a step	• Jumps a distance of 3 feet
• Kicks a large ball	• Kicks a large ball easily	• Jumps from a height of 12 inches	• Catches a small ball, using hands only
• Jumps a distance of 4–14 inches	• Jumps from the bottom step	• Throws a ball overhand	• Hops 2 to 3 yards forward on each foot
• Throws a small ball without falling	• Catches a bounced ball, using torso and arms to form a basket	• Turns sharp corners while pushing and pulling toys	• Stands on one foot for 8–10 seconds
• Pushes and pulls large toys	• Goes around obstacles while pushing and pulling toys	• Hops on one foot, four to six hops	• Climbs actively and skillfully
• Hops on one foot, two or more hops	• Hops on one foot, up to three hops	• Stands on one foot for 3–8 seconds	• Skips on alternate feet
• Tries to stand on one foot	• Stands on one foot	• Climbs ladders	• Rides a bicycle with training wheels
• Climbs on furniture to look out of window	• Climbs nursery-school apparatus	• Skips on one foot	
		• Rides a tricycle well	

Note: The ages are averages; there are individual variations.

Rough-and-tumble play is not the same as aggressive behavior.

2002). Younger preschoolers are more likely than older preschoolers to engage in physically oriented play, such as grasping, banging, and mouthing objects (D. W. Campbell et al., 2002).

Motor activity level begins to decline after 2 or 3 years of age. Children become less restless and are able to sit still longer. Between the ages of 2 and 4, children show an increase in sustained, focused attention.

Rough-and-Tumble Play

Rough-and-tumble play consists of running, chasing, fleeing, wrestling, hitting with an open hand, laughing, and making faces. Rough-and-tumble play is not the same as aggressive behavior, which involves hitting, pushing, taking, grabbing, and angry looks. Rough-and-tumble play helps develop physical and social skills (Fry, 2005; Smith, 2005).

Individual Differences in Activity Level

Physically active parents are likely to have physically active children. In a study of 4- to 7-year-olds, children

of active mothers were twice as likely to be active as children of inactive mothers (Moore et al., 1991). Children of active fathers were 3 1/2 times as likely to be active as children of inactive fathers.

Several factors may underlie this relationship. First, active parents may serve as role models for activity. Second, sharing of activities by family members may be responsible. Parents who are avid tennis players may involve their children in games of tennis from an early age. Active parents may also encourage their child's participation in physical activity. Also, twin studies suggest that there is a genetic tendency for activity level (Saudino & Eaton, 1993; Stevenson, 1992).

> **fine motor skills** Skills employing the small muscles used in manipulation and coordination, such as those in the fingers.

FINE MOTOR SKILLS

Fine motor skills develop gradually and lag gross motor skills. Fine motor skills involve the small muscles used in manipulation and coordination. Control over the wrists and fingers enables children to hold a pencil properly, dress themselves, and stack blocks (see Table 8.2). Preschoolers can labor endlessly in attempting to tie their shoelaces and get their jackets zipped.

CHILDREN'S DRAWINGS

The development of drawing is linked to the development of motor and cognitive skills. Children first begin to scribble during the second year of life. Initially, they seem to make marks for the sheer joy of it (Eisner, 1990).

TABLE 8.2
Development of Fine Motor Skills in Early Childhood

2 YEARS (24–35 MONTHS)	3 YEARS (36–47 MONTHS)	4 YEARS (48–59 MONTHS)	5 YEARS (60–71 MONTHS)
• Builds tower of 6 cubes • Copies vertical and horizontal lines • Imitates folding of paper • Paints on easel with a brush • Places simple shapes in correct holes	• Builds tower of 9 cubes • Copies circle and cross • Copies letters • Holds crayons with fingers, not fist • Strings four beads using a large needle	• Builds tower of 10 or more cubes • Copies square • Prints simple words • Imitates folding paper three times • Uses pencil with correct hand grip • Strings 10 beads	• Builds 3 steps from 6 blocks, using a model • Copies triangle and star • Prints first name and numbers • Imitates folding of piece of square paper into a triangle • Traces around a diamond drawn on paper • Laces shoes

Note: The ages are averages; there are individual variations.

Rhoda Kellogg (1959, 1970) found a meaningful pattern in the scribbles. She identified 20 basic scribbles that she considered the building blocks of art: vertical, horizontal, diagonal, circular, curving, waving or zigzagging lines, and dots (see Figure 8.2).

Children progress through four stages from making scribbles to drawing pictures: the *placement, shape, design,* and *pictorial* stages (see Figure 8.3). Two-year-olds scribble in various locations on the page (e.g., in the middle of the page or near one of the borders). By age 3, children are starting to draw basic shapes: circles, squares, triangles,

crosses, Xs, and odd shapes. As soon as they can draw shapes, children begin to combine them in the design stage. Between ages 4 and 5, children reach the pictorial stage, in which designs begin to resemble recognizable objects.

Children's early drawings tend to be symbolic of broad categories rather than specific. A child might draw the same simple building whether asked to draw a school or a house (Tallandini & Valentini, 1991). Children between 3 and 5 usually do not set out to draw a particular thing. They are more likely to see what they have drawn, then name it. As motor and cognitive skills develop beyond the age of 5, children become able to draw an object they have in mind (Matthews, 1990). They also improve at copying figures (Karapetsas & Kantas, 1991; Pemberton, 1990).

HANDEDNESS

Handedness emerges during infancy. By the age of 2 to 3 months, most infants will hold a rattle placed in their hands longer in the right hand than the left (Fitzgerald et al., 1991). By 4 months of age, most infants show a clear-cut right-hand preference in exploring objects with their hands (Streri, 2002). Preference for grasping with one hand or the other increases markedly between 7 and 11 months (Hinojosa et al., 2003). Handedness becomes more strongly established during early childhood (McManus et al., 1988). Most people are right-handed, although studies vary as to how many are left-handed.

FIGURE 8.2
The Twenty Basic Scribbles

By the age of 2, children can scribble. Rhoda Kellogg has identified these 20 basic scribbles as the building blocks of the young child's drawings.

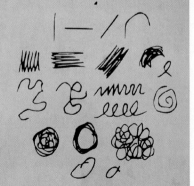

© Catherine dée Auvil/iStockphoto.com

Source: Kellogg (1970).

FIGURE 8.3
Four Stages in Children's Drawings

Children go through four stages in drawing pictures. (a) They first place their scribbles in various locations on the page. They then (b) draw basic shapes and (c, d) combine shapes into designs. Finally, (e) they draw recognizable objects.

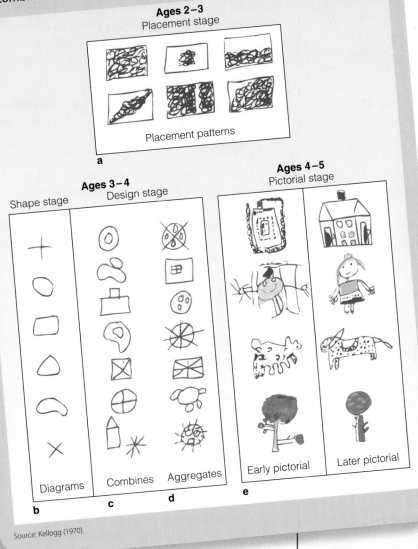

Ages 2–3
Placement stage

Placement patterns

a

Ages 3–4
Design stage

Ages 4–5
Pictorial stage

Shape stage

Diagrams   Combines   Aggregates

Early pictorial   Later pictorial

b   c   d   e

Source: Kellogg (1970).

Left-Handedness

Being a "lefty" was once seen as a deficiency. The language still swarms with slurs on lefties. We speak of "left-handed compliments," of having "two left feet," or of strange events as "coming out of left field." Being left-handed may matter because it appears to be correlated with language problems, such as dyslexia and stuttering, and with health problems, such as high blood pressure

and epilepsy (Andreou et al., 2002; Bryden et al., 2005). Left-handedness is also apparently correlated with psychological disorders, including schizophrenia and depression (Annett & Moran, 2006; Dollfus et al., 2005).

Even so, there may be advantages to being left-handed. A disproportionately high percentage of math whizzes (12- and 13-year-olds who aced the math part of the SAT) are left-handed (O'Boyle & Benbow, 1990).

Left-handedness (as well as use of both hands) has also been associated with success in athletic activities such as handball, fencing, boxing, basketball, and baseball (Coren, 1992; Dane & Erzurumluoglu, 2003). Higher frequencies of left-handedness are found among musicians, architects, and artists (Natsopoulos et al., 1992).

The origins of handedness apparently have a genetic component (Geschwind, 2000; McManus, 2003). In the English royal family, the Queen Mother, Queen Elizabeth II, Prince Charles, and Prince William are all left-handed (Rosenbaum, 2000). If both of your parents are right-handed, your chances of being right-handed are about 92%. If both of your parents are left-handed, your chances of also being left-handed are about 50% (Annett, 1999; Clode, 2006).

T F A disproportionately high percentage of math whizzes are left-handed.
True; in a survey reported by O'Boyle and Benbow (1990), 20% of the highest-scoring group on the math SATs was left-handed, whereas only 10% of the general population is left-handed.

CHAPTER 8: EARLY CHILDHOOD: PHYSICAL DEVELOPMENT   **139**

LO3 Nutrition

The average 4- to 6-year-old needs about 1,400 calories, compared with about 1,000 to 1,300 calories for the average 1- to 3-year-old (American Academy of Family Physicians, 2006). During the second and third years, a child's appetite typically becomes erratic, but because the child is growing more slowly than in infancy, he or she needs fewer calories. Children who eat little at one meal may compensate by eating more at another (Cooke et al., 2003).

Many children eat too much sugar and salt, which can be harmful to their health. Infants seem to be born liking the taste of sugar, although they are fairly indifferent to salt. But preference for sweet and salty foods increases if children are repeatedly exposed to them. Parents also serve as role models in the development of food preferences (Hannon et al., 2003).

What is the best way to get children to eat their green peas or spinach or other healthful foods they may dislike? Encourage the child to taste tiny amounts of the food 8 or 10 times within a period of a few weeks so that it becomes familiar.

LO4 Health and Illness

Almost all children become ill now and then. Some seem to be ill every other week or so. Most illnesses are minor, and children seem to eventually outgrow many of them. Fortunately, we can prevent or cure many others.

MINOR ILLNESSES

Minor illnesses refer to respiratory infections, such as colds, and to gastrointestinal upsets, such as nausea, vomiting, and diarrhea. These diseases are normal in that most children come down with them. They typically last a few days or less and are not life threatening. Although diarrheal illness in the United States is usually mild, it is a leading killer of children in developing countries (United Nations Children's Fund [UNICEF], 2007).

T F Some diseases are normal.
True; minor illnesses are generally normal, insofar as most children get them.

American children between the ages of 1 and 3 average eight to nine minor illnesses a year. Between the ages of 4 and 10, the average drops to four to six. Childhood illnesses can lead to the creation of antibodies that may prevent children from coming down with the same illnesses in adulthood when they can do more harm.

MAJOR ILLNESSES

Advances in immunization along with the development of antibiotics and other medications have dramatically reduced the incidence and effects of serious childhood diseases. Because most preschoolers and schoolchildren have been inoculated against major childhood illnesses such as rubella (German measles), measles, tetanus, mumps, whooping cough, diphtheria, and polio, these diseases no longer pose the threat they once did. The recommended immunization schedule is given in Figure 8.4.

Nearly one-third of the children in the United States younger than 18 years of age—about 20 million—suffer from a chronic illness (Agency for Healthcare Research and Quality, 2004). These illnesses include such major disorders as arthritis, diabetes, cerebral palsy, and cystic fibrosis.

Although many major childhood diseases have been largely eradicated in the United States and other industrialized nations, they remain fearsome killers of children in developing countries. Around the world, 8–9 million children die each year of just six diseases: pneumonia, diarrhea, measles, tetanus, whooping cough, and tuberculosis (UNICEF, 2007). Air pollution from the combustion of fossil fuels for heating and cooking causes many respiratory infections, which are responsible for nearly one death in five among children who are younger than 5 years of age (UNICEF, 2007). Diarrhea kills nearly 2 million children

FIGURE 8.4
Recommended Immunization Schedule for Persons Aged 0–6 Years: United States, 2009

Vaccine ▼ Age ▶	Birth	1 month	2 months	4 months	6 months	12 months	15 months	18 months	19–23 months	2–3 years	4–6 years
Hepatitis B	HepB	HepB			HepB						
Rotavirus			RV	RV	RV						
Diphtheria, Tetanus, Pertussis			DTaP	DTaP	DTaP		DTaP				DTaP
Haemophilus influenzae Type b			Hib	Hib	Hib	Hib					
Pneumococcal			PCV	PCV	PCV	PCV				PPSV	PPSV
Inactivated Poliovirus			IPV	IPV	IPV						IPV
Influenza					Influenza (Yearly)						
Measles, Mumps, Rubella						MMR					MMR
Varicella						Varicella					Varicella
Hepatitis A						HepA (2 doses)				HepA Series	
Meningococcal										MCV	MCV

Range of recommended ages

Certain high-risk groups

Source: Centers for Disease Control and Prevention (2009).

under the age of 5 each year. Diarrheal diseases are mostly related to unsafe drinking water and poor sanitation and hygiene (UNICEF, 2007).

Many youngsters are exposed to lead in early childhood, usually through eating chips of lead paint in their homes or breathing in dust from the paint. Infants fed formula made with tap water also are at risk of lead poisoning, because water pipes sometimes contain lead. Lead causes neurological damage and may result in lowered cognitive functioning and other delays in development during early childhood.

ACCIDENTS

Accidents cause more deaths in early childhood than the next six most frequent causes combined (National Center for Injury Prevention and Control, 2007a). The single most common cause of death in early childhood is motor vehicle accidents. Boys are more likely than girls to incur accidental injuries at all ages and in all socioeconomic groups. Poor children are five times as likely to die from fires and more than twice as likely to die in motor vehicle accidents than other children (National Center for Injury Prevention and Control, 2007a). The high accident rate among low-income children may result partly from living in dangerous housing and neighborhoods.

LO5 Sleep

Preschoolers do not need as much sleep as infants. Most preschoolers sleep 10 to 11 hours in a 24-hour period (National Sleep Foundation, 2007) (see Table 8.3). A common pattern includes 9 to 10 hours at night and a nap of 1 to 2 hours.

In the United States, the young child's bedtime routine typically includes putting on pajamas, brushing teeth, and being read a story. Many young children take a so-called "transitional object"—such as a favored blanket or a stuffed animal—to bed with them (Morelli et al., 1992).

TABLE 8.3
Sleep Obtained by Children during a 24-Hour Period

	INFANCY	PRESCHOOLERS	YOUNGER SCHOOL-AGE CHILDREN	OLDER SCHOOL-AGE CHILDREN
Bottom 25%	11 hours or less	9.9 hours or less	9 hours or less	8.9 hours or less
Middle 50%	11.1–14.9 hours	10–11 hours	9.1–10 hours	9–9.9 hours
Upper 25%	15 hours or more	11.1 hours or more	10.1 hours or more	10 hours or more

Source: National Sleep Foundation (2009).

Many children resist going to bed or going to sleep (National Sleep Foundation, 2009). Getting to sleep late can be a problem, because preschoolers tend not to make up fully for lost sleep (Kohyama et al., 2002).

SLEEP DISORDERS

In this section, we focus on the sleep disorders of sleep terrors, nightmares, and sleep walking.

Sleep Terrors and Nightmares

Sleep terrors are more severe than the anxiety dreams we refer to as nightmares. Sleep terrors usually occur during deep sleep. Nightmares take place during lighter rapid-eye-movement (REM) sleep, when about 80% of normal dreams occur.

Sleep terrors usually begin in childhood or early adolescence and are outgrown by late adolescence. They are sometimes associated with stress due to such things as moving to a new neighborhood, beginning school, adjusting to parental divorce, or being in a war zone. Children with sleep terrors may wake suddenly with a surge in heart and respiration rates, talk incoherently, and thrash about. Children may then fall back into more restful sleep. The incidence of

sleep terrors wanes as children develop, and they are all but absent among adults.

Children who have frequent nightmares or sleep terrors may come to fear going to sleep. They may show distress at bedtime, refuse to get into their pajamas, and insist that the lights be kept on. As a result, they can develop insomnia. Children with frequent nightmares or sleep terrors need caregivers' understanding and affection. They also profit from a regular routine in which they are expected to get to sleep at the same time each night (National Sleep Foundation, 2009).

Sleep Walking

Sleep walking, or **somnambulism**, is more common among children than adults. As with sleep terrors, sleep walking tends to occur during deep sleep (Stores & Wiggs, 2001). Onset is usually between the ages of 3 and 8.

While sleep walking, children may rearrange toys, go to the bathroom, or go to the refrigerator and have a glass of milk. Then they return to their rooms and go back to bed. There are several myths about sleep walking: that sleepwalkers' eyes are closed, that they will avoid harm, and that they will become violently agitated if they are awakened during an episode. All these notions are false.

Sleep walking in children is assumed to reflect immaturity of the nervous system. As with sleep terrors, the incidence of sleep walking drops as children develop. It may help to discuss a child's per-

sleep terrors Frightening dreamlike experiences that occur during the deepest stage of non-REM sleep, shortly after the child has gone to sleep.

somnambulism Sleep walking.

© Guy Cali/Corbis

sistent sleep terrors or sleep walking with a health professional.

> ⊤ Ⓕ It is dangerous to awaken a sleepwalker.
> *False; children may be difficult to rouse when they are sleep walking, but if they are awakened, they are more likely to be confused than violent.*

LO6 Elimination Disorders

The elimination of waste products occurs reflexively in neonates. As children develop, they learn to inhibit the reflexes that govern urination and bowel movements. The process by which parents teach their children to inhibit these reflexes is referred to as *toilet training*. The inhibition of eliminatory reflexes makes polite conversation possible.

In toilet training, maturation plays a crucial role. During the first year, only an exceptional child can be toilet trained.

> ⊤ Ⓕ Competent parents toilet train their child by the second birthday.
> *False; most American children are toilet trained between the ages of 3 and 4 (Scheres & Castellanos, 2003). They may have nighttime "accidents" for another year or so.*

© Fancy/Veer/Corbis

Caregivers are often motivated to toilet train early because of pressure from relatives and friends who tell them that you-know-whose children were toilet trained at a ridiculously young age. Caregivers, in turn, may pressure young children to become trained, and toilet training can become an arena for conflict. Children who do not become toilet trained within reasonable time frames may be diagnosed with enuresis, encopresis, or both.

> **enuresis** Failure to control the bladder once the normal age for control has been reached.
>
> **bed-wetting** Failure to control the bladder during the night.

ENURESIS

Enuresis is failure to control the bladder once the "normal" age for achieving bladder control has been reached. The American Psychiatric Association (2000) places the cutoff age at 5 years and does not consider "accidents" to represent enuresis unless they occur at least twice a month for 5- and 6-year-olds.

A nighttime "accident" is termed **bed-wetting**. Nighttime control is more difficult to achieve than daytime control. At night, children must first wake up when their bladders are full. Only then can they go to the bathroom. Overall, 8% to 10% of American children wet their beds (Mellon & Houts, 2006), and the problem is about twice as common among boys. Bed-wetting tends to occur during the deepest stage of sleep. That is also the stage when sleep terrors and sleep walking take place.

It is believed that enuresis might have organic causes, most often immaturity of the motor cortex of the brain (von Gontard et al., 2006). Thus, as with sleep walking (von Gontard, 2006), no treatment might be called for. Just as children outgrow sleep terrors and sleep walking, they tend to outgrow bed-wetting, almost always by adolescence, and usually by age 8 (Mellon & Houts, 2006).

Caregivers may pressure young children to become trained, and **toilet training can become an arena for conflict.**

encopresis Failure to control the bowels once the normal age for bowel control has been reached; also called *soiling*.

What to Do about Bed-Wetting

Parents are understandably disturbed when their children continue to wet their beds long after most children are dry through the night. Cleaning up is a hassle, and parents also often wonder what their child's bed-wetting means about the child and about their own adequacy as parents.

Bed-wetting may only "mean" that the child is slower than most children to keep his or her bed dry through the night. Bed-wetting may mean nothing at all about the child's intelligence or personality or about the parents' capabilities (von Gontard et al., 2006). Certainly a number of devices (alarms) can be used to teach the child to awaken in response to bladder pressure (Ikeda et al., 2006). Medications also can be used to help the child retain fluids through the night (Sumner et al., 2006). Before turning to these methods, however, parents can try the following simple measures.

Limit fluid intake late in the day. Less pressure on the bladder makes it easier to control urinating, but it is important not to risk depriving the child of liquids. On the other hand, it makes sense to limit fluid intake in the evening, especially at bedtime. Drinks with caffeine, such as colas, coffee, and tea, act as diuretics, making it more difficult to control urination.

Wake the child during the night. Waking the child at midnight or 1:00 in the morning may make it possible for him or her to go to the bathroom and urinate. Children may complain and say that they don't have to go, but often they will. Praise the child for making the effort.

Try a night-light. Many children fear getting up in the dark and trying to find their way to the bathroom. A night-light can make the difference.

Maintain a consistent sleep schedule. Having a regular bedtime not only helps ensure that a child gets enough sleep but also enables the child to get into a routine of urinating before going to bed and keeps the child's internal clock in sync with the clock on the wall.

Use a "sandwich" bed. This is a plastic sheet, covered with a cloth sheet, covered with yet another plastic sheet, and finally another cloth sheet. If the child wets his or her bed, the top wet sheet and plastic sheet can be pulled off, and the child can get back into a comfortable dry bed. In this way, the child develops the habit of sleeping in a dry bed. Moreover, the child learns how to handle his or her "own mess" by removing the wet sheets.

Have the child help clean up. The child can throw the sheets into the wash and, perhaps, operate the washing machine. The child can make the bed, or at least participate. These behaviors are not punishments; they help connect the child to the reality of what is going on.

Reward the child's successes. Parents risk becoming overly punitive when they pay attention only to the child's failures. Ignoring successes also allows those positive steps to go unreinforced. When the child has a dry night, or half of a dry night, make a note of it. Track successes on a calendar. Connect them with small treats, such as more TV time or time with you. Consider rewarding partial successes, such as the child's getting up after beginning to urinate so that there is less urine in the bed.

Show a positive attitude. ("Accentuate the positive.") Talk with your child about "staying dry" rather than "not wetting." Communicate the idea that you have confidence that things will get better. (They almost always do.)

ENCOPRESIS

Soiling, or **encopresis**, is lack of control over the bowels. Soiling, like enuresis, is more common among boys. About 1% to 2% of children at the ages of 7 and 8 have continuing problems controlling their bowels (Mellon, 2006; von Gontard, 2006). Soiling, in contrast to enuresis, is more likely to occur during the day. Thus, it can be embarrassing to the child, especially in school.

Encopresis stems from both physical causes, such as chronic constipation, and psychological factors (Mellon, 2006; von Gontard, 2006). Soiling may follow harsh punishment for toileting accidents, especially in children who are already anxious or under stress. Punishment may cause the child to tense up on the toilet, when moving one's bowels requires that one relax the anal sphincter muscles. Soiling, punishment, and anxiety can become a vicious cycle.

© Nick White & Carrie Beecroft/Getty Images

Speak Up!

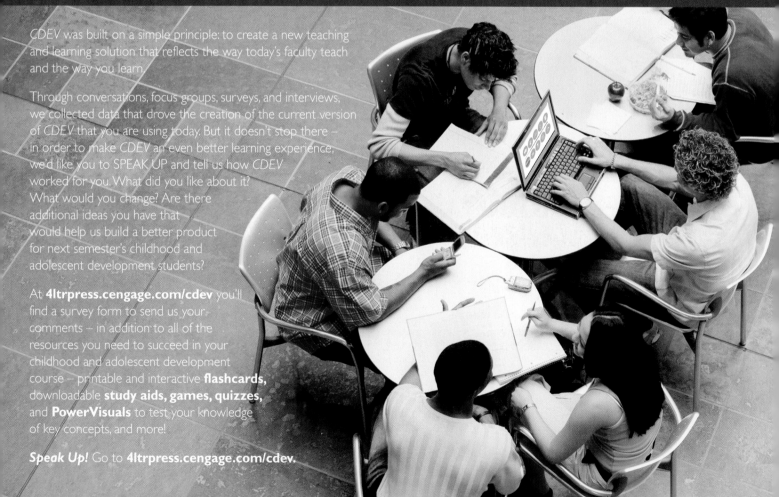

CDEV was built on a simple principle: to create a new teaching and learning solution that reflects the way today's faculty teach and the way you learn.

Through conversations, focus groups, surveys, and interviews, we collected data that drove the creation of the current version of *CDEV* that you are using today. But it doesn't stop there — in order to make *CDEV* an even better learning experience, we'd like you to SPEAK UP and tell us how *CDEV* worked for you. What did you like about it? What would you change? Are there additional ideas you have that would help us build a better product for next semester's childhood and adolescent development students?

At **4ltrpress.cengage.com/cdev** you'll find a survey form to send us your comments — in addition to all of the resources you need to succeed in your childhood and adolescent development course — printable and interactive **flashcards**, downloadable **study aids, games, quizzes,** and **PowerVisuals** to test your knowledge of key concepts, and more!

Speak Up! Go to **4ltrpress.cengage.com/cdev.**

Preoperational thought
is characterized by the use of symbols to represent objects and relationships among them.

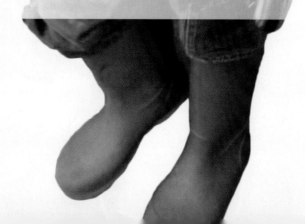

9

Early Childhood: Cognitive Development

TRUTH OR FICTION?

T F A preschooler's having imaginary play-mates is a sign of loneliness or psychological problems.

T F Two-year-olds tend to assume that their parents are aware of everything that is happening to them, even when their parents are not present.

T F "Because Mommy wants me to" may be a perfectly good explanation for a 3-year-old.

T F Children's levels of intelligence—not just their knowledge—are influenced by early learning experiences.

T F Three-year-olds are likely to say "Daddy goed away" instead of "Daddy went away" because they *do* understand rules of grammar.

Learning Outcomes

LO1 Outline the cognitive developments of Piaget's preoperational stage.

LO2 Discuss factors in cognitive development, focusing on Vygotsky's views and the effects of the home environment, early childhood education, and television.

LO3 Discuss the development of theory of mind, including false memories, origins of knowledge, and the appearance–reality distinction.

LO4 Discuss memory development during early childhood, including strategies for remembering.

LO5 Outline language development during early childhood and explain the interactions between language and cognition.

I was confused when my daughter Allyn, at the age of 2 1/2, insisted that I continue to play "Billy Joel" on the stereo. Put aside the question of her taste in music. My problem was that when Allyn asked for Billy Joel, the name of the singer, she could only be satisfied when I played the song "Moving Out." When "Moving Out" had ended and the next song, "The Stranger," had begun to play, she would insist that I play "Billy Joel" again. "That is Billy Joel," I would protest. "No, no," she would insist, "I want Billy Joel!"

Finally, it dawned on me that, for her, "Billy Joel" symbolized the song "Moving Out," not the name of the singer. Of course my insistence that the second song was also "Billy Joel" could not satisfy her! She was conceptualizing "Billy Joel" as a property of a particular song, not as the name of a person who could sing many songs.

Children between the ages of 2 and 4 tend to show confusion between symbols and the objects they represent. They do not yet recognize that words are arbitrary symbols for objects and events and that people can use words in various ways. They tend to think of words as inherent properties of objects and events.

In this chapter, we discuss cognitive development during early childhood. First, we examine Jean Piaget's preoperational stage of cognitive development. Piaget largely viewed cognitive development in terms of maturation; however, in the section on factors in cognitive development, we will see that social and other factors foster cognitive development by placing children in "the zone," as Lev Vygotsky might have put it. Next, we consider other aspects of cognitive development, such as how children acquire a theory of mind and develop memory. Finally, we continue our exploration of language development.

LO1 Jean Piaget's Preoperational Stage

according to Piaget, the **preoperational stage** of cognitive development lasts from about age 2 to age 7. Be warned: Any resemblance between the logic of a preschooler and your own may be purely coincidental.

In this section, we will see that young children's logic is at best "under construction." The preoperational stage is characterized by egocentrism, immature notions about what causes what, confusion between mental and physical events, and the ability to focus on only one dimension at a time.

SYMBOLIC THOUGHT

Preoperational thought is characterized by the use of symbols to represent objects and relationships among them. Perhaps the most important kind of symbolic activity of young children is language, but children's early use of language leaves something to be desired in the realm of logic. According to Piaget, preschoolers' drawings are symbols of objects, people, and events in their own lives. Symbolism is also expressed as symbolic or pretend play.

SYMBOLIC OR PRETEND PLAY

Children's **symbolic play**—the "let's pretend" type of play—may seem immature to busy adults meeting the realistic demands of the business world, but it requires cognitive sophistication (Feldman & Masalha, 2007; Keen et al., 2007).

Symbolic play, such as dress-up or make-believe, requires the development of sophisticated cognitive processes.

© Tammy Bryngelson/iStockphoto.com

Piaget (1946/1962) wrote that pretend play usually begins in the second year, when the child begins to symbolize objects. The ability to engage in pretend play is based on the use and recollection of symbols, that is, on mental representations of things children have experienced or heard about.

Children first engage in pretend play at about 12 or 13 months. They make believe that they are performing familiar activities, such as sleeping or feeding themselves. By 15 to 20 months, they can shift their focus from themselves to others. A child may thus pretend to feed her doll. By 30 months, she or he can make believe that the other object takes an active role. The child may pretend that the doll is feeding itself (Paavola et al., 2006).

The quality of preschoolers' pretend play has implications for subsequent development. For example, preschoolers who engage in violent pretend play are less empathic, less likely to help other children, and more likely to engage in antisocial behavior later on (Dunn & Hughes, 2001). The quality of pretend play is connected with preschoolers' academic performance later on, their creativity, and their social skills (Russ, 2006; Stagnitti et al., 2000).

Imaginary friends are an example of pretend play. As many as 65% of preschoolers have imaginary friends; they are most common among firstborn and only children (Gleason et al., 2003). Children with imaginary friends are less aggressive, more cooperative, and more creative than children without them (Gleason, 2002). Children with imaginary friends have more real friends, show greater ability to concentrate, and are more advanced in language development (Taylor, 1999).

EGOCENTRISM: IT'S ALL ABOUT ME

Sometimes the attitude "it's all about me" is a sign of early childhood, not of selfishness. One consequence of one-dimensional thinking is egocentrism. **Egocentrism**, in Piaget's use of the term, means that preoperational children do not understand that other people may have different perspectives on the world. When I asked my daughter, aged 2 1/2, to tell me about a trip to the store with her mother, she answered, "You tell me." It did not occur to her that I could not see the world through her eyes.

Piaget used the *three-mountains test* (see Figure 9.1) to show that egocentrism prevents young children from taking the viewpoints of others. In this demonstration, the child sits at a table before a model of three mountains, which differ in color. One has a house on it, and another has a cross at the summit. A doll, such as the teddy bear shown in Figure 9.1, is then placed elsewhere on the table, and the child is asked what the doll sees. The language abilities of very young children do not permit them to provide verbal descriptions of what can be seen from where the doll is situated, so they can answer in one of two ways. They can either select a photograph taken from the proper vantage point or construct another model of the mountains as they would be seen by the doll. The results of a classic experiment with the three-mountains test suggest that 5- and 6-year-olds usually select photos or build models that correspond to their own viewpoints (Laurendeau & Pinard, 1970).

egocentrism Putting oneself at the center of things such that one is unable to perceive the world from another person's point of view.

precausal A type of thought in which natural cause-and-effect relationships are attributed to will and other preoperational concepts.

FIGURE 9.1
The Three-Mountains Test

Piaget used the three-mountains test to learn whether children at certain ages are egocentric or can take the viewpoints of others.

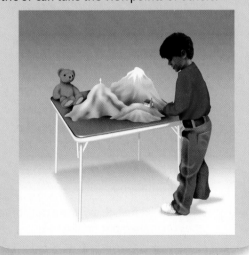

CAUSALITY: WHY? BECAUSE.

Preoperational children's responses to questions such as "Why does the sun shine?" show other facets of egocentrism. At the age of 2 or so, they may answer that they do not know or change the subject. Three-year-olds may report themselves as doing things because they want to do them or "because Mommy wants me to." In egocentric fashion, this explanation of behavior is extended to inanimate objects. The sun may be thought of as shining because it wants to shine or someone wants it to shine. In this case, the sun's behavior is thought of as being caused by will, perhaps the sun's wish to bathe the child in its rays or the child's wish to remain warm.

Piaget labeled this structuring of cause and effect **precausal**. Unless preoperational children know the natural causes of an event, their reasons are likely to have an egocentric flavor and not be based on science. Consider the question "Why does it get dark outside?" The preoperational child usually does not have knowledge of Earth's rotation and is likely to answer something like "So I can go to sleep" (see Table 9.1).

transductive reasoning
Reasoning from one specific isolated event to another specific isolated event

animism The attribution of life and intentionality to inanimate objects.

artificialism The belief that environmental features were made by people.

In **transductive reasoning**, children reason by going from one specific isolated event to another. For example, a 3-year-old may argue that she should go on her swings in the backyard *because* it is light outside or that she should go to sleep *because* it is dark outside. That is, separate events, daylight and going on the swings (or being awake), are thought of as having cause-and-effect relationships.

Preoperational children also show **animism** and **artificialism** in their attributions of causality. In animistic thinking, they attribute life and intentions to inanimate objects, such as the sun and the moon. ("Why is the moon gone during the day?" "It is afraid of the sun.") Artificialism assumes that environmental features such as rain and thunder have been designed and made by people.

T   F   "Because Mommy wants me to" may be a perfectly good explanation for a 3-year-old.

True; this belief about causality is common in a preoperational child.

CONFUSION OF MENTAL AND PHYSICAL EVENTS

What would you do if someone asked you to pretend you were a galaprock? Chances are, you might inquire what a galaprock is and how it behaves. So might a 5-year-old child. But a 3-year-old might not think that such information is necessary (Gottfried et al., 2003).

According to Piaget, the preoperational child has difficulty making distinctions between mental and physical events. Children between the ages of 2 and 4 show confusion between symbols and the things they represent. Egocentrism contributes to these children's

TABLE 9.1
Highlights of Preoperational Thought

TYPE OF THOUGHT	SAMPLE QUESTIONS	TYPICAL ANSWERS
Egocentrism (placing oneself at the center of things so one is unable to perceive the world from another's point of view)	Why does it get dark out?	So I can go to sleep.
	Why does the sun shine?	To keep me warm.
	Why is there snow?	For me to play in.
	Why is grass green?	Because that's my favorite color.
	What are TV sets for?	To watch my favorite shows and cartoons.
Animism (attributing life and intentionality to physical objects)	Why do trees have leaves?	To keep them warm.
	Why do stars twinkle?	Because they're happy and cheerful.
	Why does the sun move in the sky?	To follow children and hear what they say.
	Where do boats go at night?	They sleep like we do.
Artificialism (assuming that environmental events are human inventions)	What makes it rain?	Someone emptying a watering can.
	Why is the sky blue?	Somebody painted it.
	What is the wind?	A man blowing.
	What causes thunder?	A man grumbling.
	How does a baby get in Mommy's tummy?	Just make it first. (How?) You put some eyes on it, then put on the head.

FIGURE 9.2
Conservation

(a) The boy in this illustration agreed that the amount of water in two identical containers is equal. (b) He then watched as water from one container was poured into a tall, thin container. (c) When asked whether the amounts of water in the two containers are now the same, he says no.

(a) (b) (c)

assumption that their thoughts exactly reflect external reality. They do not recognize that words are arbitrary and that people can use different words to refer to things. In *Play, Dreams, and Imitation in Childhood,* Piaget (1946/1962) asked a 4-year-old child, "Could you call this table a cup and that cup a table?" "No," the child responded. "Why not?" "Because," explained the child, "you can't drink out of a table!" Another example of the preoperational child's confusion of the mental and the physical is the tendency of many 4-year-olds to believe that dreams are real (Meyer & Shore, 2001).

FOCUS ON ONE DIMENSION AT A TIME

To gain further insight into preoperational thinking, consider these two problems. First, imagine that you pour water from a low, wide container into a tall, thin one, as in Figure 9.2(b). Now, does the tall, thin container have more than, less than, or the same amount of water as in the low, wide one? We won't keep you in suspense. If you said the same amount (with possible minor exceptions for spillage and evaporation), you were correct.

Now that you're on a roll, here's another problem. If you flatten a ball of clay into a pancake, do you wind up with more, less, or the same amount of clay? If you said the same amount, you are correct once more.

To arrive at the correct answers to these questions, you must understand the law of **conservation**. The law of conservation holds that properties of substances such

as volume, mass, and number remain the same—or are conserved—even if you change their shape or arrangement.

Now, preoperational children tend to focus on only one aspect of a problem at a time, a characteristic of thought that Piaget called *centration*. Conservation requires the ability to focus on two aspects of a situation at once, such as height and width. The preoperational boy in Figure 9.2(c) focuses or centers on only one dimension at a time. First, the boy is shown two tall, thin containers of water and agrees that they have the same amount of water. Then, as he watches, water is poured from one tall container into a squat one. Asked which container has more water, he points to the tall one. Why? When he looks at the containers, he is swayed by the fact that the thinner one is taller.

The preoperational child's failure to understand conservation also comes about because of *irreversibility*. In the case of the water, the child does not realize that pouring water from the wide container to the tall container can be reversed, restoring things to their original condition.

You can show the demonstration with the water to a child and then try this one on conservation of number. Make two rows with four equally spaced pennies in each. As the 3-year-old child watches, move the pennies in the second row farther apart, as in Figure 9.3. Then ask the child which row has more pennies. What do you think the child will say? Why?

Class Inclusion

Class inclusion, as we are using it here, means including new objects or categories in broader mental classes or categories. Class inclusion also requires children to focus on two aspects of a situation at once. In one of Piaget's class-inclusion tasks, the child is shown several pictures from two subclasses of a larger class, for example, four cats and six dogs. She is asked whether

FIGURE 9.3

Conservation of Number

In this demonstration, we begin with two rows of pennies that are spread out equally, as shown in the left-hand part of the drawing. Then one row of pennies is spread out more, as shown in the drawing on the right-hand side. We then ask the child, "Do the two rows still have the same number of pennies?" Do you think that a preoperational child will conserve the number of pennies or focus on the length of the longer row in arriving at an answer?

Child is shown two rows of pennies.

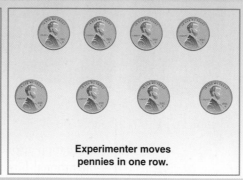

Experimenter moves pennies in one row.

there are more dogs or more animals. Now, she knows what dogs and cats are. She also knows that they are both animals. What do you think she will say? Preoperational children typically answer that there are more dogs than animals (Piaget, 1936/1963).

Why do preoperational children make this error? According to

Is this a dog or an animal? The anwer is both, but the preoperational child will have trouble making this connection.

scaffolding Vygotsky's term for temporary cognitive structures or methods of solving problems that help the child as he or she learns to function independently.

zone of proximal development (ZPD) Vygotsky's term for the range of tasks a child can carry out with the help of someone who is more skilled.

Piaget, they cannot think about the two subclasses and the larger class at the same time. Therefore, they cannot easily compare them. Children view dogs as dogs or as animals, but find it difficult to see them as both dogs and animals at once (Branco & Lourenço, 2004).

LO2 Factors in Cognitive Development

two factors that influence cognitive development in early childhood are Vygotsky's concepts of scaffolding and the zone of proximal development. Others include the home environment, preschool education, and television.

SCAFFOLDING AND THE ZONE OF PROXIMAL DEVELOPMENT

Parents' responsiveness to and interaction with children are key ingredients in children's cognitive development. One component of this interaction is **scaffolding** (see Chapter 1). Cognitive scaffolding refers to temporary support provided by a more skilled person to assist learning in children. The guidance provided by adults decreases as children become capable of carrying out the task on their own (Lengua et al., 2007; Sylva et al., 2007).

A related concept is Vygotsky's **zone of proximal development (ZPD)**. The zone refers to the gap between what children are capable of doing now and what they could do with help from others. Adults or older children can best guide children through this zone by gearing their assistance to children's capabilities, according to Lantolf and Thorne (2007) and Wennergren and Ronnerman (2006). These researchers argue that the key forms of children's cognitive activities develop through interaction with older, more experienced individuals who teach and guide them.

In a related study, K. Alison Clarke-Stewart and Robert Beck (1999) had 31 5-year-olds observe a videotaped film segment with their mothers, talk about it with their mothers, and then retell the story to an experimenter. Children whose mothers focused the children's attention on the tape, asked their children to talk about it, and discussed the feelings of the characters told better stories than children whose mothers did not use such scaffolding strategies and children in a control group who did not discuss the story at all.

TABLE 9.2
Scales of the HOME Inventory

SCALE	SAMPLE ITEMS
Parental emotional and verbal responsiveness	• The parent spontaneously vocalizes to the child during the visit. • The parent responds to the child's vocalizations with vocal or other verbal responses.
Avoidance of restriction and punishment	• The parent does not shout at the child. • The parent does not interfere with the child's actions or restrict the child's movements more than three times during the visit.
Organization of the physical environment	• The child's play environment seems to be safe and free from hazards.
Provision of appropriate play materials	• The child has a push or a pull toy. • The child has one or more toys or pieces of equipment that promote muscle activity. • The family provides appropriate equipment to foster learning.
Parental involvement with child	• The parent structures the child's play periods. • The parent tends to keep the child within her or his visual range and looks at the child frequently.
Opportunities for variety in daily stimulation	• The child gets out of the house at least four times a week. • The parent reads stories to the child at least three times a week.

© Nigel Carse/Shutterstock

THE HOME ENVIRONMENT

Bettye Caldwell and her colleagues (e.g., Bradley, Caldwell, & Corwyn, 2003) developed a measure for evaluating children's home environments labeled, appropriately enough, HOME, an acronym for Home Observation for the Measurement of the Environment. With this inventory, researchers directly observe parent–child interaction in the home. The HOME inventory contains six subscales, as shown in Table 9.2. The HOME inventory items are better predictors of young children's later IQ scores than social class, mother's IQ, or infant IQ scores (Bradley, 2006). Longitudinal research also shows that the home environment is connected with occupational success as an adult (Huesmann et al., 2006).

Early learning experiences affect children's levels of intellectual functioning. Being responsive to preschoolers, stimulating them, and encouraging independence is connected with higher IQ scores and greater school achievement later on (Bradley, 2006; Bradley & Corwyn, 2006; Molfese et al., 1997). Victoria Molfese and her colleagues (1997) found that the home environment is the single most important predictor of scores on IQ tests among children aged 3 to 8.

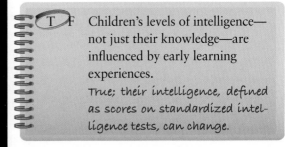

T F   Children's levels of intelligence—not just their knowledge—are influenced by early learning experiences.
True; their intelligence, defined as scores on standardized intelligence tests, can change.

EFFECTS OF EARLY CHILDHOOD EDUCATION

How important are academic experiences in early childhood? Do they facilitate cognitive development? Research suggests

Part of a Balanced Breakfast!

© Foodpix/Jupiterimages

theory of mind A commonsense understanding of how the mind works.

that preschool education enables children to get an early start on achievement in school.

Children reared in poverty generally perform less well on standardized intelligence tests than children of higher socioeconomic status, and they are at greater risk for school failure (Stipek & Hakuta, 2007; Whitehouse, 2006). As a result, preschool programs were begun in the 1960s to enhance those children's cognitive development and readiness for elementary school. Some, such as the federally funded Head Start program, also provide health care to children and social services to their families. Children in these programs typically are exposed to letters and words, numbers, books, exercises in drawing, pegs and pegboards, puzzles, and toy animals and dolls—materials and activities that middle-class children usually take for granted.

Studies of Head Start and other intervention programs show that environmental enrichment can enhance the cognitive development of economically disadvantaged children (Stipek & Hakuta, 2007; P. Wilson, 2004). In the Milwaukee Project, poor children of low-IQ mothers were provided with enriched day care from the age of 6 months. By the late preschool years, the children's IQ scores averaged about 121, compared with an average of 95 for peers who did not receive day care (Garber, 1988). Head Start and similar programs also lead to gains in school readiness tests and achievement tests (Stipek & Hakuta, 2007). Programs that involve and educate parents are particularly beneficial (Stipek & Hakuta, 2007).

TELEVISION

American children spend more time watching television than they do in school. By the time he or she turns 3, the average child already watches 2 to 3 hours of television a day (Palmer, 2003). Television has great potential for teaching a variety of cognitive skills, social behaviors, and attitudes. The Children's Television Act requires that networks devote a number of hours per week to educational television. Many but not all the resultant programs have been shown to have mild to moderate positive effects on preschoolers' cognitive development, more so with girls than with boys (Calvert & Kotler, 2003).

Sesame Street is the most successful children's educational TV program. The goal of *Sesame Street* is to promote the intellectual growth of preschoolers, particularly those of lower socioeconomic status. Large-scale evaluations of the effects of the program have concluded that regular viewing increases children's learning of numbers, letters, and cognitive skills such as sorting and classification (Fisch, 2004). These effects are found for African American and European American children, girls and boys, and urban, suburban, and rural children.

Preschoolers often are unable to tell the difference between TV commercials and program content (Kundanis & Massaro, 2004). Commercials that encourage children to choose nutritionally inadequate foods—such as sugared breakfast cereals, candy, and fast foods—are harmful to children's nutritional beliefs and diets (Pine & Nash, 2002).

LO3 Theory of Mind

adults appear to have a commonsense understanding of how the mind works—that is, a **theory of mind**. We understand that we can gain knowledge through our senses or through hearsay. We know the distinction between actual and mental events and between how things appear and how they really are. We can infer the perceptions, thoughts, and feelings of others. We understand that mental states affect behavior.

Piaget might have predicted that preoperational children are too egocentric and too focused on misleading external appearances to have a theory of mind, but research has shown that even preschoolers can accurately predict and explain human action and emotion in terms of mental states (Wellman et al., 2006).

FALSE BELIEFS: WHERE ARE THOSE CRAYONS?

One indication of preschoolers' understanding that mental states affect behavior is the ability to recognize false beliefs. This concept involves children's ability to separate their beliefs from those of another person who has false knowledge of a situation. It is illustrated in a study of 3-year-olds by Louis Moses and John Flavell (1990). The children were shown a videotape in which a girl named Cathy found some crayons in a bag. When Cathy left the room briefly, a clown entered the room. The clown removed the crayons from the bag, hid them in a drawer, and put rocks in the bag instead. When Cathy returned, the children were asked whether Cathy thought there would be rocks or crayons in the bag. Most of the 3-year-olds incorrectly answered "rocks," demonstrating their difficulty in understanding that the other person's belief would be different from their own (see Figure 9.4). But by the age of 4 to 5 years, children do not have trouble with this concept and correctly answer "crayons" (Flavell, 1993).

appearance–reality distinction The difference between real events on the one hand and mental events, fantasies, and misleading appearances on the other hand.

ORIGINS OF KNOWLEDGE

Another aspect of theory of mind is how we acquire knowledge. By age 3, most children begin to realize that people gain knowledge about something by looking at it (Pratt & Bryant, 1990). By age 4, children understand that particular senses provide information about only certain qualities of an object; for example, we come to know an object's color through our eyes, but we learn about its weight by feeling it (O'Neill & Chong, 2001). In a study by Daniela O'Neill and Alison Gopnik (1991), 3-, 4-, and 5-year-olds learned about the contents of a toy tunnel in one of three ways: They saw the contents, were told about them, or felt them. The children were then asked to state what was in the tunnel and how they knew. Although 4- and 5-year-olds had no trouble identifying the sources of their knowledge, the 3-year-olds did. For example, after feeling but not seeing a ball in the tunnel, a number of 3-year-olds told the experimenter that they could tell it was a blue ball. The children did not realize they could not learn the ball's color by feeling it.

THE APPEARANCE–REALITY DISTINCTION

Children must acquire an understanding of the difference between real events, on the one hand, and mental events, fantasies, and misleading appearances, on the other hand (Bialystock & Senman, 2004; Flavell et al., 2002). This understanding is known as the **appearance–reality distinction**.

Piaget's view was that children do not differentiate reality from appearances or mental events until the age

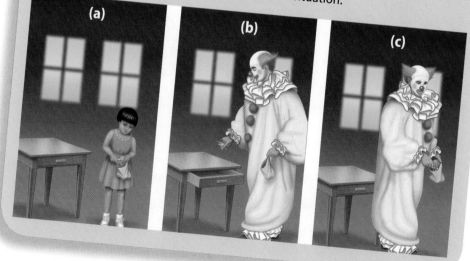

FIGURE 9.4
False Beliefs

Flavell and his colleagues showed preschoolers a videotape in which a girl named Cathy found crayons in a bag (a). When Cathy left the room, a clown entered, removed the crayons from the bag, hid them in a drawer (b), and filled the bag with rocks (c). When asked whether Cathy thought there would be rocks or crayons in the bag, most 3-year-olds said "rocks." Most 4-year-olds correctly answered "crayons," showing the ability to separate their own beliefs from those of someone who has erroneous knowledge of a situation.

of 7 or 8. In a study by Marjorie Taylor and Barbara Hort (1990), children age 3 to 5 were shown objects that had misleading appearances, such as an eraser that looked like a cookie. The children initially reported that the eraser looked like a cookie. However, once they learned that it was actually an eraser, they tended to report that it looked like an eraser. Apparently, the children could not mentally represent the eraser as both being an eraser and looking like a cookie.

Three-year-olds also apparently cannot understand changes in their mental states. In one study (Gopnik & Slaughter, 1991), 3-year-olds were shown a crayon box with candles inside. Before it was opened, they consistently said that they thought crayons were inside. After the box was opened, the children were asked what they had thought was in the box before it was opened; the children said "candles."

LO4 Development of Memory

Children, like adults, often remember what they *want* to remember (Ghetti & Alexander, 2004; Sales et al., 2003). By the age of 4 years, children can remember events that occurred at least 1 1/2 years earlier (Fivush & Hammond, 1990). Katherine Nelson (1990, 1993) interviewed children aged 2 to 5 to study their memory for recurring events in their lives, such as having dinner, playing with friends, and going to birthday parties. She found that 3-year-olds can present coherent, orderly accounts of familiar events. Furthermore, young children seem to form **scripts**, which are abstract, generalized accounts of these repeated events. For example, in describing what happens during a birthday party, a child might say, "You play games,

open presents, and eat cake" (Fivush, 2002). However, an unusual experience, such as a hurricane, may be remembered in detail for years (Fivush et al., 2004).

Young children begin forming scripts after experiencing an event only once. The script becomes more elaborate with repeated experiences. Older preschoolers form detailed scripts more quickly than younger preschoolers (Fivush, 2002).

Even though children as young as 1 and 2 years of age can remember events, these memories seldom last into adulthood. The memory of specific events—known as **autobiographical memory**, or *episodic memory*—is facilitated when children talk about the events with others (Nelson & Fivush, 2004).

FACTORS INFLUENCING MEMORY

Factors that affect memory include what the child is asked to remember, the interest level of the child, the availability of retrieval cues (reminders), and what memory measure we are using. First, children find it easier to remember events that follow a fixed and logical order than events that do not. For instance, 3- and 5-year-olds have a better memory for the activities involved in making pretend cookies out of Play-Doh (you put the ingredients in the bowl, then mix the ingredients, then roll out the dough, and so on) than they do for the activities involved in sand play, which can occur in any order (Fivush et al., 1992). Furthermore, children's interest level affects their memory. Research

WHAT TO DO AT A BIRTHDAY PARTY

STEP 1 · STEP 2 · STEP 3

consistently shows that (most) preschool boys are more interested in playing with toys such as cars and weapons, whereas (most) preschool girls are more interested in playing with dolls, dishes, and teddy bears. Later, the children typically show better recognition and recall for the toys in which they were interested (Martin & Ruble, 2004).

Retrieval Cues

To retrieve information (a file) from your computer's storage, you have to remember its name or some part of it. Then you can use a Search routine. The name is the retrieval cue. Although young children can remember a great deal, they depend more than older children do on cues provided by adults to help them retrieve their memories. Consider the following interchange between a mother and her 2-year-old child (Hudson, 1990, p. 186):

> Mother: What did we look for in the grass and in the bushes?
>
> Child: Easter bunny.
>
> Mother: Did we hide candy eggs outside in the grass?
>
> Child: (nods)
>
> Mother: Remember looking for them? Who found two? Your brother?
>
> Child: Yes, brother.

Elaborating on the child's experiences and asking questions that encourage the child to contribute information to the narrative generally help a child remember an episode (Nelson & Fivush, 2004).

rehearsal Mental repetition.

Types of Measurement

What we find is in part determined by how we measure it. Children's memory can often be measured or assessed by asking them to say what they remember. But verbal reports, especially from preschoolers, appear to underestimate children's memory (Mandler, 1990). In one longitudinal study, children's memory for certain events was tested at age 2 1/2 and again at age 4. Most of the information recalled at age 4 had not been mentioned at age 2 1/2, indicating that when they were younger, the children remembered more than they reported (Fivush & Hammond, 1990). One study found that when young children were allowed to use dolls to reenact an event, their recall was better than when they gave a verbal report (Goodman et al., 1990).

MEMORY STRATEGIES: REMEMBERING TO REMEMBER

Adults and older children use strategies to help them remember things. One strategy is mental repetition, or **rehearsal**. If you are trying to remember a new friend's phone number, for example, you might repeat it several times. Another strategy is to organize things to be remembered into categories. Most preschoolers do not engage in rehearsal until about 5 years of age (Labrell & Ubersfeld, 2004). They also rarely group objects into related categories to help them remember. By about age 5, many children have learned to verbalize information silently to themselves by counting mentally, for example, rather than aloud.

Having preschoolers sort objects into categories enhances

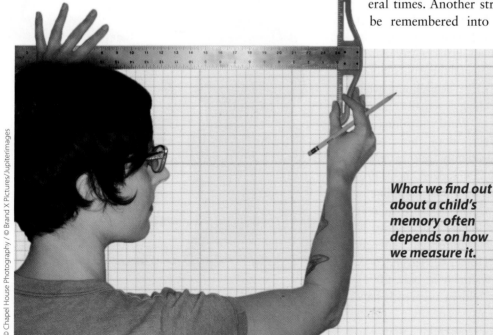

What we find out about a child's memory often depends on how we measure it.

© Chapel House Photography / © Brand X Pictures/Jupiterimages

memory (Howe, 2006; Lange & Pierce, 1992). Even 3- and 4-year-olds will use rehearsal and labeling if they are asked to try to remember something.

The preschooler's use of memory strategies is not nearly as sophisticated as that of the school-age child. Children's use of strategies and understanding of how memory works advance greatly in middle childhood.

LO5 Language Development: Why "Daddy Goed Away"

Children's language skills mushroom during the preschool years. By the fourth year, children are asking adults and each other questions, taking turns talking, and engaging in lengthy conversations.

DEVELOPMENT OF VOCABULARY

The development of vocabulary proceeds at an extraordinary pace. Preschoolers learn an average of nine new words per day (Tamis-LeMonda et al., 2006). But how can that be possible when each new word has so many potential meanings? Consider the following example. A toddler observes a small, black dog running through the park. His older sister points to the animal and says, "doggy." The word *doggy* could mean this particular dog, or all dogs, or all animals. It could refer to one part of the dog (e.g., its tail) or to its behavior (running, barking) or to its characteristics (small, black) (Waxman & Lidz, 2006). Does the child consider all these possibilities before determining what "doggy" actually means?

Word learning, in fact, does not occur gradually but is better characterized as a process of **fast mapping** in which the child quickly attaches a new word to its appropriate concept (Homer & Nelson, 2005; Waxman & Lidz, 2006). Children apparently have early cognitive biases or constraints that lead them to prefer certain meanings over others (Waxman & Lidz, 2006).

Children also assume that words refer to whole objects and not to their component parts or their characteristics, such as color, size, or texture (Bloom, 2002). This bias is called the **whole-object assumption**. Therefore, the young child would assume that the word *doggy* refers to the dog rather than to its tail, its color, or its barking.

Children also seem to assume that objects have only one label. Therefore, novel terms must refer to unfamiliar objects and not to familiar objects that already have labels. This concept is the **contrast assumption**, which is also known as the *mutual exclusivity assumption* (Bloom, 2002; Waxman & Lidz, 2006). Suppose that a child is shown two objects, one of which has a known label ("doggy") and one of which is unknown. Let us further suppose that an adult now says, "Look at the lemur." If the child assumes that "doggy" and "lemur" each can refer to only one object, the child will correctly figure out that "lemur" refers to the other object and is not just another name for "doggy" (Homer & Nelson, 2005; Waxman & Lidz, 2006).

fast mapping A process of quickly determining a word's meaning, which facilitates children's vocabulary development.

whole-object assumption The assumption that words refer to whole objects and not to their component parts or characteristics.

contrast assumption The assumption that objects have only one label; also known as the *mutual exclusivity assumption*.

THIS IS A DOG

THIS IS A LEMUR

Through contrast assumption, the child can determine that "lemur" is not just another name for "dog."

DEVELOPMENT OF GRAMMAR

There is a "grammar explosion" during the third year (Tamis-LeMonda et al., 2006). Children's sentence structure expands to include the words missing in telegraphic speech. Children usually add to their vocabulary an impressive array of articles (*a, an, the*), conjunctions (*and, but, or*), possessive adjectives (*your, her*), pronouns (*she, him, one*), and prepositions (*in, on, over, around, under, through*). Usually between the ages of 3 and 4, children show knowledge of rules for combining phrases and clauses into complex sentences, as in "You goed and Mommy goed, too."

Overregularization

The apparent basis of one of the more intriguing language developments—**overregularization**—is that children acquire grammatical rules as they learn language. At young ages, they tend to apply these rules rather strictly, even in cases that call for exceptions (Jacobson & Schwartz, 2005; Stemberger, 2004). Consider the formation of the past tense and plurals in English. We add *-d* or *-ed* to regular verbs and *-s* to regular nouns. Thus, *walk* becomes *walked* and *toy* becomes *toys*. But then there are irregular verbs and irregular nouns. For example, *sit* becomes *sat* and *go* becomes *went*. *Sheep* remains *sheep* (plural) and *child* becomes *children*.

At first, children learn a small number of these irregular constructions by imitating their parents. Two-year-olds tend to form them correctly for a while. Then as children become aware of the syntactic rules for forming the past tense and plurals in English, they often misapply them to irregular words. As a result, they tend to make charming errors (Stemberger, 2004). Some 3- to 5-year-olds are more likely to say "Mommy sitted down" than "Mommy sat down" or talk about the "sheeps" they "seed" on the farm and about all the "childs" they ran into at the playground.

> T F Three-year-olds are likely to say "Daddy goed away" instead of "Daddy went away" because they *do* understand rules of grammar.
> True; they are applying a rule for forming the past tense of regular verbs to an irregular verb.

Some parents recognize that their children at first were forming the past tense of irregular verbs correctly but that they then began to make errors. Some of these parents become concerned that their children are "slipping" in their language development and attempt to correct them. However, overregularization reflects accurate knowledge of grammar, not faulty language development. In another year or two, *mouses* will be boringly transformed into *mice*, and Mommy will no longer have *sitted* down. Parents might as well enjoy overregularization while they can.

Asking Questions

Children's first questions are telegraphic and characterized by a rising pitch (which signifies a question mark in English) at the end. Depending on the context, "More milky?" can be translated into "May I have more milk?" or "Would you like more milk?" or "Is there more milk?" It is usually toward the latter part of the third year that the *wh-* questions appear. Consistent with the child's general cognitive development, certain *wh-* questions (*what, who,* and *where*) appear earlier than others (*why, when, which,* and *how*) (Tamis-LeMonda et al., 2006). *Why* is usually too philosophical for a 2-year-old, and *how* is too involved. Two-year-olds are also likely to be now-oriented, so *when* is of little concern. By the fourth year, most children are spontaneously producing *why, when,* and *how* questions. These *wh-* words are initially tacked on to the beginnings of sentences. "Where Mommy go?" can stand for "Where is Mommy going?" or "Where did Mommy go?" or "Where will Mommy go?"; its meaning must be derived from context. Later on, the child will add the auxiliary verbs *is, did,* and *will* to indicate whether the question concerns the present, past, or future.

How can the dogfood be eaten by the dog? Passive sentences are often difficult for 2- and 3-year-olds to understand.

© Chapell House Photography

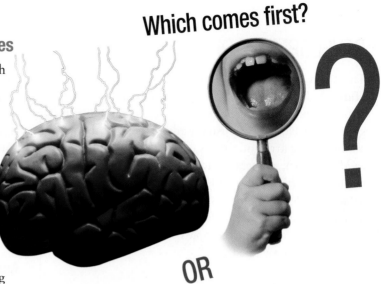

pragmatics The practical aspects of communication, such as adaptation of language to fit the social situation.

Passive Sentences

Passive sentences, such as "The dog food is eaten by the dog," are difficult for 2- and 3-year-olds to understand, and so young preschoolers almost never produce them. In a study of children's comprehension (Strohner & Nelson, 1974), 2- to 5-year-olds used puppets and toys to act out sentences that were read to them. Two- and 3-year-olds made errors in acting out passive sentences (e.g., "The car was hit by the truck") 70% of the time. Older children had less difficulty interpreting the meanings of passive sentences correctly. However, most children usually do not produce passive sentences spontaneously even at the ages of 5 and 6.

PRAGMATICS

Pragmatics refers to the practical aspects of communication. Children show pragmatism when they adjust their speech to fit the social situation (Nelson, 2006). For example, children show greater formality in their choice of words and syntax when they are role-playing high-status figures, such as teachers or physicians, in their games. They say "please" more often when making requests of high-status people or when they use Motherese in talking to an infant.

Preschoolers tend to be egocentric; therefore, a 2-year-old who tells another child "Gimme my book," without specifying which book, may assume that the other child knows what she herself knows. Once children can perceive the world through the eyes of others, they advance in their abilities to make themselves understood. A more mature child recognizes that the other child will require a description of the book or of its location to carry out the request.

LANGUAGE AND COGNITION

Language and cognitive development are interwoven (Homer & Nelson, 2005; Waxman & Lidz, 2006). For example, the child gradually gains the capacity to discriminate between animals on the basis of distinct features, such as size, patterns of movement, and the sounds they make. At the same time, the child also is acquiring words that represent broader categories, such as *mammal* and *animal*.

But which comes first? Does the child first develop concepts and then acquire the language to describe them, or does the child's increasing language ability lead to the development of new concepts?

Does Cognitive Development Precede Language Development?

Piaget (1976) believed that cognitive development precedes language development. He argued that children must understand concepts before they use words to describe them. From Piaget's perspective, children learn words to describe classes or categories that they have already created (Nelson, 2005). Children can learn the word *doggy* because they have perceived the characteristics that distinguish dogs from other things.

Some studies support the notion that cognitive concepts may precede language. For example, the vocabulary explosion that occurs at about 18 months of age is related to the child's ability to group a set of objects into two categories, such as "dolls" and "cars" (Gopnik & Meltzoff, 1992). Other research suggests that young children need to experience an action themselves or by observation to learn the meaning of a verb (Pulverman et al., 2006).

Children show greater formality in their choice of words and syntax when they are role-playing high-status figures, such as teachers or physicians, in their games.

In the early stages of language development, concepts often precede words, and many of the infant's words describe classes that have already developed. But later language influences thought.

Does Language Development Precede Cognitive Development?

Although many theorists argue that cognitive development precedes language development, others reverse the causal relationship and claim that children create cognitive classes to understand things that are labeled by words (Clark, 1983). When children hear the word *dog*, they try to understand it by searching for characteristics that separate dogs from other things.

The Interactionist View: Outer Speech and Inner Speech

Today, most developmentalists find something of value in each of these views (Waxman & Lidz, 2006). In the early stages of language development, concepts often precede words, and many of the infant's words describe classes that have already developed. But later language influences thought.

Vygotsky believed that during most of the first year, vocalizations and thought are separate. But during the second year, thought and speech combine forces. Children discover that objects have labels. Learning labels becomes more self-directed. Children ask what new words mean. Learning new words fosters creation of new categories, and new categories become filled with labels for new things.

Vygotsky's concept of **inner speech** is a key feature of his position. At first children's thoughts are spoken aloud. You can hear the 3-year-old instructing herself as she plays with toys. At this age, her vocalizations serve to regulate her behavior, but they gradually become internalized. What was spoken aloud at 4 and 5 becomes an internal dialogue by 6 or 7. Inner speech is the ultimate binding of language and thought. It is involved in the development of planning and self-regulation, and it facilitates learning.

inner speech Vygotsky's concept of the ultimate binding of language and thought. Inner speech originates in vocalizations that may regulate the child's behavior and become internalized by age 6 or 7.

12 months < time at which children begin to engage in pretend play

65% < percentage of preschoolers with imaginary friends

6 < number of subscales in the HOME inventory

121 < average IQ score of late preschoolers who participated in Head Start programs

95 < average IQ score of late preschoolers who did not participate in Head Start programs

2–3 hours < average amount of TV watched by a three-year-old child per day

70% < rate at which 2- and 3-year-olds fail in acting out passive sentences

18 months < age at which the vocabulary explosion occurs

Preschoolers usually

spend most of their time with the family.

10

Early Childhood: Social and Emotional Development

TRUTH OR FICTION?

T F Parents who are restrictive and demand mature behavior wind up with rebellious children, not mature children.

T F Firstborn children are more highly motivated to achieve than later-born children are.

T F Children who are physically punished are more likely to be aggressive than children who are not.

T F Children who watch 2 to 4 hours of TV a day will see 8,000 murders and another 100,000 acts of violence by the time they have finished elementary school.

T F Children mechanically imitate the aggressive behavior they view in the media.

T F The most common fear among preschoolers is fear of social disapproval.

Learning Outcomes

LO1 Describe the dimensions of child rearing and the styles of parenting.

LO2 Explain how siblings, birth order, peers, and other factors affect social development during early childhood.

LO3 Discuss personality and emotional development during early childhood, focusing on the self, Erikson's views, and fears.

LO4 Discuss the development of gender roles and sex differences.

Preschoolers usually spend most of their time with the family. Most parents want preschoolers to develop a sense of responsibility and develop into well-adjusted individuals. They want them to acquire social skills. How do parents try to achieve these goals? What role do siblings play? How do children's peers influence social and emotional development?

LO1 Dimensions of Child Rearing

Parents have different approaches to rearing their children. Investigators of parental patterns of child rearing have found it useful to classify them according to two broad dimensions: warmth–coldness and restrictiveness–permissiveness (Baumrind, 1989, 2005).

Warm parents are affectionate toward their children. They tend to hug and kiss them and smile at them frequently. Warm parents are caring and supportive. They communicate their enjoyment in being with their children. Warm parents are less likely than cold parents to use physical discipline (Bender et al., 2007).

inductive Characteristic of disciplinary methods, such as reasoning, that attempt to foster understanding of the principles behind parental demands.

How would you reason with this child to encourage desirable behavior?

© Rhienna Cutler/iStockphoto.com

Cold parents may not enjoy their children and may have few feelings of affection for them. They are likely to complain about their children's behavior, saying they are naughty or have "minds of their own."

It requires no stretch of the imagination to conclude that it is better to be warm than cold toward children. The children of parents who are warm and accepting are more likely to develop internal standards of conduct and a moral sense or conscience (Bender et al., 2007; Lau et al., 2006). Parental warmth also is related to a child's social and emotional well-being (Lau et al., 2006; Leung et al., 2004).

Where does parental warmth come from? Some of it reflects parental beliefs about how to best rear children, and some reflects parents' tendencies to imitate the behavior of their own parents. But research by Hetherington and her colleagues (Feinberg et al., 2001) suggests that genetic factors may be involved as well.

Parents decide how restrictive they will be. How will they respond when children make excessive noise, play with dangerous objects, damage property, mess up their rooms, hurt others, or masturbate? Parents who are restrictive tend to impose rules and to watch their children closely.

Consistent control and firm enforcement of rules can have positive consequences for the child, particularly when combined with strong support and affection (Grusec, 2006). This parenting style is termed the *authoritative style*. On the other hand, if "restrictiveness" means physical punishment, interference, or intrusiveness, it can give rise to disobedience, rebelliousness, and lower levels of cognitive development (Paulussen-Hoogeboom et al., 2007; Rudy & Grusec, 2006).

T F Parents who are restrictive and demand mature behavior wind up with rebellious children, not mature children.

False; authoritarianism is more likely than restrictiveness to lead to rebelliousness in children.

Permissive parents supervise their children less closely than restrictive parents do. Permissive parents allow their children to do what is "natural," such as make noise, treat toys carelessly, and experiment with their bodies. They may also allow their children to show some aggression, intervening only when another child is in danger.

HOW PARENTS ENFORCE RESTRICTIONS

Regardless of their general approaches to child rearing, most parents are restrictive now and then, even if only when they are teaching their children not to run into the street or to touch a hot stove. Parents tend to use the methods of induction, power assertion, and withdrawal of love.

Inductive methods aim to give knowledge that will enable children to generate desirable behavior on their own. The main inductive technique is *reasoning*, or explaining why one kind of behavior is good and another is not. Reasoning with a 1- or 2-year-old can be basic. "Don't do that—it hurts!" qualifies as reasoning with toddlers. "It hurts!" is an explanation, though brief. The inductive approach helps the child understand moral behavior and fosters prosocial behavior such as helping and sharing (Paulussen-Hoogeboom et al., 2007).

Power-assertive methods include physical punishment and denial of privileges. Parents often justify physical punishment with sayings such as "Spare the rod, spoil the child." Parents may insist that power assertion is necessary because their children are noncompliant. However, use of power assertion is related to parental authoritarianism as well as children's behavior (Roopnarine et al., 2006; Rudy & Grusec, 2006). Parental power assertion is associated with lower acceptance by peers, poorer grades, and more antisocial behavior in children. The more parents use power-assertive techniques, the less children appear to develop internal standards of conduct. Parental punishment and rejection are often linked with aggression and delinquency.

Some parents control children by threatening withdrawal of love. They isolate or ignore misbehaving children. Because most children need parental approval and contact, loss of love can be more threatening than physical punishment. Withdrawal of love may foster compliance but also instill guilt and anxiety (Grusec, 2002).

Preschoolers more readily comply when asked to do something than when asked to *stop* doing something (Kochanska et al., 2001). One way to manage children who are doing something wrong or bad is to involve them in something else.

PARENTING STYLES: HOW PARENTS TRANSMIT VALUES AND STANDARDS

Diana Baumrind (1989, 1991b) focused on the relationship between parenting styles and the development of competent behavior in young children. She used the dimensions of warmth–coldness and restrictiveness–permissiveness to develop a grid of four parenting styles based on whether parents are high or low in each dimension (see Table 10.1).

The parents of the most capable children are rated high in both dimensions (see Table 10.1). They are highly restrictive and make strong demands for maturity. However, they also reason with their children and show strong support and feelings of love. Baumrind applies the label **authoritative** to these parents; they know what they want their children to do but also respect their children and are warm toward them.

TABLE 10.1
Baumrind's Patterns of Parenting

PARENTAL STYLE	PARENTAL BEHAVIOR PATTERNS	
	RESTRICTIVENESS AND CONTROL	WARMTH AND RESPONSIVENESS
Authoritative	High	High
Authoritarian	High	Low
Permissive–Indulgent	Low	High
Rejecting–Neglecting	Low	Low

Compared with other children, the children of authoritative parents tend to show self-reliance and independence, high self-esteem, high levels of activity and exploratory behavior, and social competence. They are highly motivated to achieve and do well in school (Baumrind, 1989, 1991b; Grusec, 2006).

"Because I say so" could be the motto of parents that Baumrind labels **authoritarian**. Authoritarians value obedience for its own sake. They have strict guidelines for right and wrong and demand that their children accept them without question. Like authoritative parents, they are controlling. But unlike authoritative parents, their enforcement methods rely on force. Moreover, authoritarian parents do not communicate well with their children or respect their children's viewpoints. Most researchers find them to be generally cold and rejecting (Grusec, 2002).

Baumrind found the sons of authoritarian parents to be relatively hostile and defiant and the daughters to be low in independence and dominance (Baumrind, 1989). Other researchers have found that the children of authoritarian parents are less competent socially and academically than those of authoritative parents. They are anxious, irritable, and restrained in their social interactions (Grusec, 2002). As adolescents, they may be conforming and obedient but have low self-reliance and self-esteem.

authoritative A child-rearing style in which parents are restrictive and demanding yet communicative and warm.

authoritarian A child-rearing style in which parents demand submission and obedience.

© Andrew Johnson/iStockphoto.com

Baumrind found two types of parents who are permissive as opposed to restrictive. One is permissive–indulgent and the other rejecting–neglecting. **Permissive-indulgent** parents rate low in their attempts to control their children and in their demands for mature behavior. They are easygoing and unconventional. Their brand of permissiveness is accompanied by high nurturance (warmth and support).

Rejecting–neglecting parents also rate low in their demands for mature behavior and attempts to control their children. Unlike indulgent parents, they are low in support and responsiveness. The children of neglectful parents are the least competent, responsible, and mature. The children of permissive–indulgent parents, like those of neglectful parents, are less competent in school and show more misconduct and substance abuse than children of more restrictive, controlling parents. But children from permissive–indulgent homes, unlike those from neglectful homes, are fairly high in social competence and self-confidence (Baumrind, 1991a).

EFFECTS OF THE SITUATION AND THE CHILD ON PARENTING STYLES

Parenting styles are not merely a one-way street, from parent to child. Parenting styles also depend partly on the situation and partly on the characteristics of the child (Grusec, 2006). For example, parents are most likely to use power-assertive techniques when dealing with aggressive behavior (Casas et al., 2006; Lipman et al., 2006). Parents prefer power assertion to induction when they believe that children understand the rules they have violated and are capable of acting appropriately. Stress also contributes to use of power.

TABLE 10.2
Advice for Parents in Guiding Young Children's Behavior

DO …	DON'T …
• Reward good behavior with praises, smiles, and hugs.	• Pay attention only to a child's misbehavior.
• Give clear, simple, realistic rules appropriate to the child's age.	• Issue too many rules or enforce them haphazardly.
• Enforce rules with reasonable consequences.	• Try to control behavior solely in the child's domain, such as thumb sucking, which can lead to frustrating power struggles.
• Ignore annoying behavior such as whining and tantrums.	• Nag, lecture, shame, or induce guilt.
• Childproof the house, putting dangerous and breakable items out of reach. Then establish limits.	• Yell or spank.
• Be consistent.	• Be overly permissive.

Baumrind's research suggests that we can make an effort to avoid some of the pitfalls of being authoritarian or overly permissive. Some recommended techniques that parents can use to help control and guide their children's behavior are listed in Table 10.2.

LO2 Social Behaviors

during early childhood, children make tremendous advances in social skills and behavior. Their play increasingly involves other children. They learn how to share, cooperate, and comfort others. But young children, like adults, can be aggressive as well as loving and helpful.

INFLUENCE OF SIBLINGS

Siblings serve many functions, including giving physical care, providing emotional support and nurturance, offering advice, serving as role models, providing social interaction that helps develop social skills, making demands, and imposing restrictions (McHale et al., 2006; Parke & Buriel, 2006).

Siblings make a unique contribution to each other's social, emotional, and cognitive development.

© stocklight/Shutterstock

In early childhood, siblings' interactions have positive aspects (cooperation, teaching, nurturance) and negative aspects (conflict, control, competition) (Parke & Buriel, 2006). Older siblings tend to be more caring but also more dominating than younger siblings. Younger siblings are more likely to imitate older siblings and accept their direction.

In many cultures, older girls care for younger siblings (Clark, 2005). Parents often urge their children to stop fighting among themselves, and there are times when these conflicts look deadly (and occasionally they are). But garden-variety sibling conflict can enhance children's social competence, their development of self-identity (who they are and what they stand for), and their ability to rear their own children (Ross et al., 2006).

There is more conflict between siblings when the parents play favorites (Scharf et al., 2005). Conflict between siblings is also greater when the relationships between the parents or between the parents and children are troubled (Kim et al., 2006).

Adjusting to the Birth of a Sibling

The birth of a sister or brother is often a source of stress for preschoolers because of changes in family relationships (Volling, 2003). When a new baby comes into the home, the mother pays relatively more attention to that child and spends less time with the older child, so the older child may feel displaced and resentful.

Children show a mixture of negative and positive reactions to the birth of a sibling. These reactions include **regression** to baby-like behaviors, such as increased clinging, crying, and toilet accidents. Anger and naughtiness may increase. But the same children may also show increased independence and maturity, insisting on feeding or dressing themselves and helping to care for the baby (Volling, 2003). Parents can help a young child cope with the arrival of a baby by explaining in advance what is to come (Kavcic & Zupancic, 2005).

regression A return to behavior characteristic of earlier stages of development.

BIRTH ORDER

Differences in personality and achievement have been linked to birth order. Firstborn children, as a group, are more highly motivated to achieve than later-born children are (Latham & Budworth, 2007). Firstborn and only children perform better academically and are more cooperative (Healy & Ellis, 2007). They are more adult-oriented and less aggressive than later-born children (Beck et al., 2006; Zajonc, 2001). They obtain higher standardized test scores, including IQ and SAT scores (Kristensen & Bjerkedal, 2007; Sulloway, 2007). On the negative side, firstborn and only children show greater anxiety and are less self-reliant than later-born children.

T F Firstborn children are more highly motivated to achieve than later-born children are.
True, but the reasons are not fully clear.

Later-born children may learn to act aggressively to compete for the attention of their parents and older siblings (Carey, 2007b). Their self-concepts tend to be lower than those of firstborn or only children, but the social skills later-born children acquire from dealing with their family position seem to translate into greater popularity with peers (Carey, 2007b). They also tend to be more rebellious and liberal than firstborn children (Beck et al., 2006; Zweigenhaft & Von Ammon, 2000).

By and large, parents are more relaxed and flexible with later-born children. Many parents see that the firstborn child is turning out well and perhaps they assume that later-born children will also turn out well.

PEER RELATIONSHIPS

Peer interactions foster social skills—sharing, helping, taking turns, and dealing with conflict. Groups teach children how to lead and how to follow. Physical and cognitive skills develop through peer interactions. Peers also provide emotional support (Dishion & Stormshak, 2007b; Grusec, 2006).

By about 2 years of age, children imitate one another's play and engage in social games such as follow the leader (Fontaine, 2005; Kavanaugh, 2006). By the age of 2, children show preferences for particular playmates—an early sign of friendship (Sherwin-White, 2006). Friendship is characterized by shared positive experiences and feelings of attachment (Grusec, 2002). Even early friendships can be fairly stable (Rubin et al., 2006).

When preschoolers are asked what they like about their friends, they typically mention the toys and activities they share (Gleason & Hohmann, 2006). Primary school-children usually report that their friends are the children with whom they do things and have fun (Gleason & Hohmann, 2006). Not until late childhood and adolescence do friends' traits and the perception of trust, communication, and intimacy between friends become important.

PLAY—CHILD'S PLAY, THAT IS

Play is more than fun; it is also meaningful, voluntary, and internally motivated (Elkind, 2007). Play helps children develop motor skills and coordination. It contributes to social development, because children learn to share play materials, take turns, and, through **dramatic play**, try on new roles (Elkind, 2007). It supports the development of such cognitive qualities as curiosity, exploration, symbolic thinking, and

FUNCTIONAL PLAY

SYMBOLIC PLAY

CONSTRUCTIVE PLAY

FORMAL GAMES

problem solving. Play may even help children learn to control impulses (Elkind, 2007).

Play and Cognitive Development

Play contributes to and expresses milestones in cognitive development. Jean Piaget (1946/1962) identified several kinds of play, each characterized by increasing cognitive complexity:

- *Functional play*. Beginning in the sensorimotor stage, the first kind of play involves repetitive motor activity, such as rolling a ball or running and laughing.

- *Symbolic play*. Also called *pretend play, imaginative play,* or *dramatic play,* symbolic play emerges toward the end of the sensorimotor stage and increases during early childhood. In symbolic play, children create settings, characters, and scripts (Kavanaugh, 2006).

- *Constructive play*. Children use objects or materials to draw something or make something, such as a tower of blocks.

- *Formal games*. Games with rules include board games, which are sometimes enhanced or invented by children, and games involving motor skills, such as marbles and hopscotch, ball games involving sides or teams, and video games. Such games may involve social interaction as well as physical activity and rules. People play such games for a lifetime.

Mildred Parten focused on the social dimensions of play.

Parten's Types of Play

In classic research on children's play, Mildred Parten (1932) observed the development of six types of play among 2- to 5-year-old nursery school children: unoccupied play, solitary play, onlooker play, parallel play, associative play, and cooperative play (see Table 10.3). Solitary play and onlooker play are considered **nonsocial play**, that is, play in which

TABLE 10.3
Parten's Categories of Play

CATEGORY	NONSOCIAL OR SOCIAL?	DESCRIPTION
Unoccupied play	Nonsocial	Children do not appear to be playing. They may engage in random movements that seem to be without a goal. Unoccupied play appears to be the least frequent kind of play in nursery schools.
Solitary play	Nonsocial	Children play with toys by themselves, independently of the children around them. Solitary players do not appear to be influenced by children around them. They make no effort to approach them.
Onlooker play	Nonsocial	Children observe other children who are at play. Onlookers frequently talk to the children they are observing and may make suggestions, but they do not overtly join in.
Parallel play	Social	Children play with toys similar to those of surrounding children. However, they treat the toys as they choose and do not directly interact with other children.
Associative play	Social	Children interact and share toys. However, they do not seem to share group goals. Although they interact, individuals still treat toys as they choose. The association with the other children appears to be more important than the nature of the activity. They seem to enjoy each other's company.
Cooperative play	Social	Children interact to achieve common, group goals. The play of each child is subordinated to the purposes of the group. One or two group members direct the activities of others. There is also a division of labor, with different children taking different roles. Children may pretend to be members of a family, animals, space monsters, or other sorts of creatures.

children do not interact socially. Nonsocial play occurs more often in 2- and 3-year-olds than in older preschoolers. Parallel play, associative play, and cooperative play are considered **social play**. In each case, children are influenced by other children as they play. Parten found that associative play and cooperative play become common by age 5. They are more likely to be found among older and more experienced preschoolers (Dyer & Moneta, 2006). Girls are somewhat more likely than boys to engage in social play (Zheng & Colombo, 1989).

But there are exceptions. Nonsocial play can involve educational activities that foster cognitive development. In fact, many 4- and 5- year-olds spend a good deal of time in parallel constructive play. For instance, they may work on puzzles or build with blocks near other children. Parallel constructive players are frequently perceived by teachers to be socially skillful and are popular with their peers (Coplan et al., 1994). Two-year-olds with older siblings or with group experience may engage in advanced social play.

Lisa Serbin and her colleagues (2001) explored infants' visual preferences for gender-stereotyped toys using the assumption that infants spend more time looking at objects that are of greater interest. They found that both

social play Play in which children interact with and are influenced by others.

girls and boys showed significant preferences for gender-stereotyped toys by 18 months of age. Although preferences for gender-stereotyped toys are well developed by the ages of 15 to 36 months, girls are more likely to stray from the stereotypes (Bussey & Bandura, 1999). Girls ask for and play with "boys' toys" such as cars and trucks more often than boys choose dolls and other "girls' toys."

Sex Differences in Play

Girls and boys differ not only in toy preferences but also in their choice of play environments and activities. During the preschool and early elementary school years, boys prefer vigorous physical outdoor activities such as climbing, playing with large vehicles, and rough-and-tumble play (Else-Quest et al., 2006). In middle childhood, boys spend more time than girls in play groups of five or more children and in competitive play (Crombie & Desjardins, 1993; Else-Quest et al., 2006). Girls are more likely than boys to engage in arts and crafts and domestic play. Girls' activities are more closely directed and structured by adults (A. Campbell et al., 2002). Girls spend more time than boys playing with one other child or a small group (Crombie & Desjardins, 1993).

Why do children show these early preferences for gender-stereotyped toys and activities? Biological factors may play a role, for example, boys' slightly greater strength and activity levels and girls' slightly greater physical maturity and coordination. But adults treat girls and boys differently. They provide gender-stereotyped toys and room furnishings and encourage gender typing in play and household chores (Leaper, 2002). Children, moreover, tend to seek out information on which kinds of toys and play are "masculine" or "feminine" and then to conform to the label (Martin & Ruble, 2004).

Some studies find that children who "cross the line" by showing interest in toys or activities considered appropriate for the other sex are often teased, ridiculed, rejected, or ignored by their parents, teachers, other adults, and peers. Boys are more likely than girls to be criticized (Fagot & Hagan, 1991; Garvey, 1990).

Another well-documented finding is that children begin to prefer playmates of the same sex by the age of 2. Girls develop this preference somewhat earlier than boys (Fagot, 1990; Hay et al., 2004). The tendency strengthens during middle childhood.

Eleanor Maccoby (1990) believes that two factors are involved in the choice of the sex of playmates in early childhood. One is that boys' play is more oriented toward dominance, aggression, and rough play. The second is that boys are not very responsive to girls' polite suggestions. Boys may avoid girls because they see them as inferior (Caplan & Larkin, 1991).

PROSOCIAL BEHAVIOR

Prosocial behavior, also known as *altruism,* is intended to benefit another without expectation of reward. Prosocial behavior includes sharing, cooperating, and helping and comforting others in distress (Strayer & Roberts, 2004). It is shown by the preschool and early school years (Knafo & Plomin, 2006b) and is linked to the development of empathy and perspective taking.

Empathy

Empathy is sensitivity to the feelings of others and is connected with sharing and cooperation. Infants frequently begin to cry when they hear other children crying, although this early agitated response may be largely reflexive (Strayer & Roberts, 2004). Empathy promotes prosocial behavior and decreases aggressive behavior, and these effects are evident by the second year (Hastings et al., 2000). During the second year, many children approach other children and adults who are in distress and try to help them. They may hug a crying child or tell the child not to cry. Toddlers who are rated as emotionally unresponsive to the feelings of others are more likely to behave aggressively throughout the school years (Olson et al., 2000).

© Ulrik Tofte/Getty Images

Girls show more empathy than boys (Strayer & Roberts, 2004). It is unclear whether this sex difference reflects genetic factors or socialization of girls to be attuned to the emotions of others.

Perspective Taking

According to Piaget, preoperational children tend to be egocentric. They tend not to be able to see things from the vantage points of others. It turns out that various cognitive abilities, such as being able to take another person's perspective, are related to knowing when someone is in need or distress. Perspective-taking skills improve with age, and so do prosocial skills. Among children of the same age, those with better developed perspective-taking ability also show more prosocial behavior and less aggressive behavior (Hastings et al., 2000).

Influences on Prosocial Behavior

Although altruistic behavior is defined as prosocial behavior that occurs in the absence of rewards or the expectations of rewards, it is influenced by rewards and punishments. The peers of nursery school children who are cooperative, friendly, and generous respond more positively to them than they do to children whose behavior is self-centered (Hartup, 1983). Children who are rewarded for acting prosocially are likely to continue these behaviors (Knafo & Plomin, 2006a).

Parents foster prosocial behavior when they use inductive techniques such as explaining how behavior affects others ("You made Josh cry. It's not nice to hit"). Parents of prosocial children are more likely to expect mature behavior from their children. They are less likely to use power-assertive techniques of discipline (Strayer & Roberts, 2004).

DEVELOPMENT OF AGGRESSION

Children, like adults, can not only be loving and altruistic, they can also be aggressive. Some children, of course, are more aggressive than others. *Aggression* refers to behavior intended to hurt or injure another person.

Aggressive behavior, like other social behavior, seems to follow developmental patterns. The aggression of preschoolers is frequently instrumental or possession oriented (Persson, 2005). Younger preschoolers tend to use aggression to obtain the toys and situations they want, such as a favored seat at the table or in the car. Older preschoolers are more likely to resolve conflicts over toys by sharing rather than fighting (Caplan et al., 1991). Anger and aggression in preschoolers usually

> By age 6 or 7, aggression becomes hostile and person oriented.

cause other preschoolers to reject them (Henry et al., 2000; Walter & LaFreniere, 2000).

By age 6 or 7, aggression becomes hostile and person oriented. Children taunt and criticize one another and call one another names; they also attack one another physically.

Aggressive behavior appears to be generally stable and predictive of social and emotional problems later on, especially among boys (Nagin & Tremblay, 2001; Tapper & Boulton, 2004). Toddlers who are perceived as difficult and defiant are more likely to behave aggressively throughout the school years (Olson et al., 2000). A longitudinal study of more than 600 children found that aggressive 8-year-olds tended to remain more aggressive than their peers 22 years later, at age 30 (Eron et al., 1991). Aggressive children of both sexes are more likely to have criminal convictions as adults, to abuse their spouses, and to drive while drunk.

THEORIES OF AGGRESSION

What causes some children to be more aggressive than others? Aggression in childhood appears to result from a complex interplay of biological factors and environmental factors such as reinforcement and modeling.

Evidence suggests that genetic factors may be involved in aggressive behavior, including criminal and antisocial behavior (Hicks et al., 2007; Lykken, 2006a; E. O. Wilson, 2004). There is a greater concordance (agreement) rate for criminal behavior between monozygotic (MZ) twins, who fully share their genetic code, than between dizygotic (DZ) twins, who, like other brothers and sisters, share only half of their genetic code (Tehrani & Mednick, 2000). If genetics is involved in aggression, genes may do their work at least in part through the male sex hormone testosterone. Testosterone is apparently connected with feelings of self-confidence, high activity levels, and—the negative side—aggressiveness (Archer, 2006; Cunningham &

disinhibit To stimulate a response that has been suppressed by showing a model engaging in that response.

McGinnis, 2007; Popma et al., 2007).

Cognitive research with primary schoolchildren finds that children who believe in the legitimacy of aggression are more likely to behave aggressively when they are presented with social provocations (Tapper & Boulton, 2004). Aggressive children are also often found to be lacking in empathy and the ability to see things from the perspective of other people (Hastings et al., 2000). They fail to conceptualize the experiences of their victims and are thus less likely to inhibit aggressive impulses.

Social cognitive explanations of aggression focus on environmental factors such as reinforcement and observational learning. When children repeatedly push, shove, and hit to grab toys or break into line, other children usually let them have their way (Kempes et al., 2005). Children who are thus rewarded for acting aggressively are likely to continue to use aggressive means, especially if they do not have alternative means to achieve their ends. Aggressive children may also associate with peers who value and encourage aggression (Stauffacher & DeHart, 2006).

T F Children who are physically punished are more likely to be aggressive than children who are not.
True; children who are physically punished are more likely to be aggressive themselves than children who are not physically punished (Patterson, 2005). Physically aggressive parents serve as models for aggression and also stoke their children's anger.

Media Influences

Real people are not the only models of aggressive behavior in children's lives. A classic study by Albert Bandura and his colleagues (1963) suggested that televised models had a powerful influence on children's aggressive behavior. One group of preschoolers observed a film of an adult model hitting and kicking an inflated Bobo doll, whereas a control group saw an aggression-free film. The experimental and control children were then left alone in a room with the same doll as hidden observers recorded their behavior. The children who had observed the aggressive model showed significantly more aggressive behavior toward the doll than did the

children who did not see the aggressive model (see Figure 10.1). Many children imitated bizarre attack behaviors devised for the model in this experiment, behaviors they would not have thought up themselves.

Television is a fertile source of aggressive models (Villani, 2001). Children are routinely exposed to TV scenes of murder, beating, and sexual assault. Children who watch 2 to 4 hours of TV a day will see 8,000 murders and another 100,000 acts of violence by the time they have finished elementary school (Eron, 1993).

T F Children who watch 2 to 4 hours of TV a day will see 8,000 murders and another 100,000 acts of violence by the time they have finished elementary school.
True.

Consider a number of ways in which depictions of violence contribute to violence:

- *Observational learning.* Children learn from observation (Holland, 2000). TV violence supplies models of aggressive "skills," which children may acquire.

- *Disinhibition.* Punishment inhibits behavior. Conversely, media violence may **disinhibit** aggressive behavior, especially when characters "get away" with it.

- *Increased arousal.* Media violence and aggressive video games increase viewers' level of arousal. We are more likely to be aggressive under high levels of arousal.

- *Priming of aggressive thoughts and memories.* Media violence "primes" or arouses aggressive ideas and memories (Bushman, 1998; Meier et al., 2006).

- *Habituation.* We become used to repeated stimuli. Children exposed to violence are more likely to assume that violence is acceptable or normal and become desensitized to it (Holland, 2000)

Though exposure to violence in the media increases the probability of violence by viewers, there is no simple one-to-one connection between media violence and violence in real life. According to social cognitive theory, children also choose whether to imitate the behavior they observe.

T F Children mechanically imitate the aggressive behavior they view in the media.
False; children frequently weigh the pros and cons of imitating the behavior they observe.

FIGURE 10.1
Photos from Albert Bandura's Classic Experiment in the Imitation of Aggressive Models

LO3 Personality and Emotional Development

In early childhood, children's sense of self—who they are and how they feel about themselves—develops and grows more complex. They begin to acquire a sense of their own abilities and their increasing mastery of the environment. As they move out into the world, they also face new experiences that may cause them to feel fearful and anxious.

THE SELF

The sense of self, or the self-concept, emerges gradually during infancy. Infants and toddlers visually begin to recognize themselves and differentiate from other individuals such as their parents.

In the preschool years, children continue to develop their sense of self. Almost as soon as they begin to speak, they describe themselves in terms of certain categories, such as age groupings (baby, child, adult) and sex (girl, boy). Self-definitions that refer to concrete external traits have been called the **categorical self**.

Children as young as 3 years are able to describe themselves in terms of behaviors and internal states that occur often and are fairly stable over time (Eder, 1989, 1990). For example, in response to the question "How do you feel when you're scared?" young children frequently respond, "Usually like running away" (Eder, 1989). In answer to the question "How do you usually act around grown-ups?" a typical response might be, "I mostly been good with grown-ups."

One aspect of the self-concept is self-esteem. Children with high self-esteem are more likely to be securely attached and have parents who are attentive to their needs (Booth-LaForce et al., 2006; Patterson & Bigler, 2006). They also are more likely to show prosocial behavior (Salmivalli et al., 2005).

Preschool children begin to make evaluative judgments about two different aspects of themselves by the age of 4 (Harter & Pike, 1984). One is their cognitive and physical competence (e.g., being good at puzzles, counting, swinging, tying shoes), and the second is their social acceptance by peers and parents (e.g., having lots of friends,

categorical self Definitions of the self that refer to external traits.

being read to by Mom). But preschoolers do not yet clearly distinguish between different areas of competence. A preschooler is not likely to report being good in school but poor in physical skills. One is either "good at doing things" or one is not (Clark & Symons, 2000; Piek et al., 2006).

INITIATIVE VERSUS GUILT

As preschoolers continue to develop a separate sense of themselves, they increasingly move out into the world and take the initiative in learning new skills. Erik Erikson (1963) refers to these early childhood years as the *stage of initiative versus guilt.*

Children in this stage strive to achieve independence from their parents and master adult behaviors. They are curious, try new things, and test themselves. Children learn that not all their plans, dreams, and fantasies can be realized. Adults prohibit children from doing certain things, and children begin to internalize adult rules. Fear of violating the rules may cause the child to feel guilty and may curtail efforts to master new skills. Parents can help children develop and maintain a healthy sense of initiative by encouraging their attempts to learn and explore and by not being unduly critical and punitive.

FEARS: THE HORRORS OF EARLY CHILDHOOD

In Erikson's view, fear of violating parental prohibitions can be a powerful force in the life of a young child. Children's fears change as they move from infancy into the preschool years. The number of fears seems to peak between 2½ and 4 years and then taper off (Miller et al., 1990). The preschool period is marked by a decline in fears of loud noises, falling, sudden movement, and strangers. Preschoolers are most likely to fear animals, imaginary creatures, the dark, and personal danger (Field, 2006; Muris et al., 2003). The fantasies of young children frequently involve stories they are told and media imagery. Frightening images of imaginary creatures can persist. Many preschoolers are reluctant to have the lights turned off at night for fear that such creatures may assault them. Real objects and situations also cause many preschoolers to fear for their personal safety—lightning, thunder and other loud noises, high places, sharp objects and being cut, blood, unfamiliar people, strange people, and stinging and crawling insects.

Children's **fears** change as they move from infancy into the preschool years. The number of fears seems to **peak between 2 1/2 and 4 years** and then taper off.

T͟ F͟ The most common fear among preschoolers is fear of social disapproval.

False; preschoolers are most likely to fear animals, imaginary creatures, and the dark.

During middle childhood, children become less fearful of imaginary creatures, but fears of bodily harm and injury remain common. Children grow more fearful of failure and criticism in school and in social relationships (Ollendick & King, 1991). Girls report more fears and higher levels of anxiety than boys (Weems et al., 1999).

LO4 Development of Gender Roles and Sex Differences

I am woman, hear me roar … I am strong

I am invincible

I am woman

These lyrics are from the song "I Am Woman" by Helen Reddy and Ray Burton. They caught attention because they counter the **stereotype** of vulnerable woman who needs the protection of a man. The stereotype of the vulnerable woman is a fixed, oversimplified, and conventional idea. So is the stereotype of the chivalrous, protective man. Unfortunately, these stereotypes create demands on and limit opportunities for both sexes.

Cultural stereotypes of males and females are broad expectations of traits and behaviors that we call **gender roles**. In our culture, the feminine gender-role stereotype includes such traits as dependence, gentleness, helpfulness, warmth, emotionality, submissiveness, and a home orientation. The masculine gender-role stereotype includes aggressiveness, self-confidence, independence, competitiveness, and competence in business, math, and science (Miller et al., 2006).

Gender-role stereotypes develop in stages. First, children learn to label the sexes. At about 2 to 2 1/2 years of age, they can identify pictures of girls and boys (Fagot & Leinbach, 1993). By age 3, they display knowledge of gender stereotypes for toys, clothing, work, and activities (Campbell et al., 2004). Children of this age generally agree that boys play with cars and trucks, help their fathers, and tend to hit others. They agree that girls play with dolls, help their mothers, and do not hit others (Cherney et al., 2006). One study found that preschool boys but not girls were rejected by their peers when they showed distress (Walter & LaFreniere, 2000).

Children become increasingly traditional in their stereotyping of activities, jobs, and personality traits between the ages of 3 and 9 or 10 (Miller et al., 2006).

stereotype A fixed, over-simplified, conventional idea about a group.

gender role A cluster of traits and behaviors that a culture expects females or males to exhibit.

Children become increasingly traditional in their stereotypes of personality traits between 3 and 9 or 10. Gender stereotypes, however, can limit opportunities for both sexes.

© Erik Dreyer/Getty Images

For example, traits such as "cruel" and "repairs broken things" are viewed as masculine, and traits such as "often is afraid" and "cooks and bakes" are seen as feminine.

Children and adolescents perceive their own sex in a somewhat better light. For example, girls perceive other girls as nicer, more hardworking, and less selfish than boys. Boys, on the other hand, think that they are nicer, more hardworking, and less selfish than girls (Matlin, 2008; Miller et al., 2006).

SEX DIFFERENCES

Clearly, females and males are anatomically different. And according to gender-role stereotypes, people believe that females and males also differ in their behaviors, personality characteristics, and abilities. Sex differences in infancy are small and rather inconsistent. Preschoolers display some differences in their choices of toys and play activities. Boys engage in more rough-and-tumble play and are more aggressive. Girls tend to show more empathy and to report more fears. Girls show somewhat greater verbal ability than boys, whereas boys show somewhat greater visual–spatial ability than girls.

THEORIES OF THE DEVELOPMENT OF SEX DIFFERENCES

Why is it that little girls (often) grow up to behave according to the cultural stereotypes of what it means to be female? Why is it that little boys (often) grow up to behave like male stereotypes?

The Roles of Evolution and Heredity

According to evolutionary psychologists, sex differences were fashioned by natural selection in response to problems in adaptation that were repeatedly encountered by humans over thousands of generations (Buss & Duntley, 2006; Geary, 2006). The story of the survival of our ancient ancestors is etched in our genes. Genes that bestow attributes that increase an organism's chances of surviving to produce viable offspring are most likely to be transmitted to future generations. We thus possess the genetic codes for traits that helped our ancestors survive and reproduce. These traits include structural sex differences, such as those found in the brain, and differences in body chemistry, such as hormones.

The question is whether evolution has also etched social and psychological sex differences into our genes.

Consider a sex difference. Males tend to place relatively more emphasis on physical appearance in mate selection than females do, whereas females tend to place relatively more emphasis on personal factors such as financial status and reliability (Brase, 2006).

Organization of the Brain

The organization of the brain is largely genetically determined (Collins et al., 2000; Maccoby, 2000). The hemispheres of the brain are specialized to perform certain functions, as noted in Chapter 6. Both males and females have a left hemisphere and a right hemisphere, but the question is whether they use them in quite the same way. Consider the hippocampus, a brain structure that is involved in the formation of memories and the relay of incoming sensory information to other parts of the brain (Ohnishi et al., 2006). Matthias Riepe and his colleagues (Grön et al., 2000) have studied the ways in which humans and rats use the hippocampus when they are navigating mazes. Males use the hippocampus in both hemispheres when they are navigating (Grön et al., 2000). Women, however, rely on the hippocampus in the right hemisphere along with the right prefrontal cortex, an area of the brain that evaluates information and makes plans. Riepe and his colleagues wonder whether different patterns of brain activity might contribute to preference for using landmarks or maps.

What psychological factors contribute to the acquisition of gender roles? Psychoanalytic theory focuses on the concept of identification. Social cognitive theory focuses on imitation of the behavior patterns of the same-sex adults and reinforcement by parents and peers.

Sex Hormones

Sex hormones and other chemical substances stoke the prenatal differentiation of sex organs. Toward the end of the embryonic stage, androgens—male sex hormones—are sculpting male genital organs. These chemicals may also "masculinize" or "feminize" the brain; that is, give rise to behavioral tendencies that are in some ways consistent with gender-role stereotypes (Cohen-Bendahan et al., 2004; Pei et al., 2006).

Social Cognitive Theory

Social cognitive theorists consider both the roles of rewards and punishments (reinforcement) in gender typing and the ways in which children learn from observing others and decide which behaviors are appropriate for them. Children learn much about what society considers "masculine" or "feminine" by observing and imitating models of the same sex. These models may be their parents, other adults, other children, even characters in electronic media such as TV and video games.

Socialization also plays a role. Parents, teachers, other adults—even other children—provide children with information about the gender-typed behaviors expected of them (Sabattini & Leaper, 2004). Children are rewarded with smiles and respect and companionship when they display "gender-appropriate" behavior. Children are punished with frowns and loss of friends when they display "inappropriate" behavior.

Boys are encouraged to be independent, whereas girls are more likely to be restricted. Boys are allowed to roam farther from home at an earlier age and are more likely to be left unsupervised after school (Miller et al., 2006).

Primary schoolchildren show less stereotyping if their mothers frequently engage in traditionally "masculine" tasks such as washing the car, taking children to ball games, or assembling toys (Powlishta, 2004). Maternal employment is associated with less polarized gender-role concepts for girls and boys (Sabattini & Leaper, 2004; Powlishta, 2004).

Cognitive-Developmental Theory

Lawrence Kohlberg (1966) proposed a cognitive-developmental view of gender typing. According to this perspective, children form concepts about gender and then fit their behavior to the concepts (Martin & Ruble, 2004). These developments occur in stages and are entwined with general cognitive development.

According to Kohlberg, gender typing involves the emergence of three concepts: gender identity, gender stability, and gender constancy. The first step in gender typing is attaining **gender identity**. Gender identity is the knowledge that one is male or female. At 2 years, most children can say whether they are boys or girls. By the age of 3, many children can discriminate anatomic sex differences (Campbell et al., 2004; Ruble et al., 2006).

At around age 4 or 5, most children develop the concept of **gender stability**, according to Kohlberg. They recognize that people retain their sexes for a lifetime. Girls no longer believe that they can grow up to be daddies, and boys no longer think that they can become mommies.

By the age of 5 to 7 years, Kohlberg believes that most children develop the more sophisticated concept of **gender constancy** and recognize that people's sex does not change, even if they change their dress or behavior. A woman who cuts her hair short remains a woman. A man who dons an apron and cooks remains a man. Once children have established concepts of gender stability and constancy, they seek to behave in ways that are consistent with their sex (Martin & Ruble, 2004).

Cross-cultural studies in the United States, Samoa, Nepal, Belize, and Kenya have found that the concepts of gender identity, gender stability, and gender constancy emerge in the order predicted by Kohlberg (Leonard & Archer, 1989; Munroe et al., 1984). However, gender constancy and gender-typed play emerge earlier than predicted by Kohlberg. Girls show preferences for dolls and soft toys and boys for hard transportation toys by the age of 1 1/2 to 3 (Alexander, 2003; Campbell et al., 2004; Powlishta, 2004). At this age, children may have a sense of gender identity, but gender stability and gender constancy remain a year or two away.

Gender-Schema Theory

Gender-schema theory proposes that children use sex as one way of organizing their perceptions of the world (Campbell et al., 2004; Martin & Ruble, 2004). A *gender schema* is a cluster of concepts about male and female physical traits, behaviors, and personality traits. For example, consider the dimension of strength–weakness. Children learn that strength is linked to the male gender-role stereotype and weakness to the female stereotype.

> **gender identity** Knowledge that one is female or male.
>
> **gender stability** The concept that one's sex is unchanging.
>
> **gender constancy** The concept that one's sex remains the same despite changes in appearance or behavior.
>
> **gender-schema theory** The view that one's knowledge of the gender schema in one's society guides one's assumption of gender-stereotyped preferences and behavior patterns.

They also learn that some dimensions, such as strength–weakness, are more relevant to one gender than the other—in this case, to males.

From the viewpoint of gender-schema theory, gender identity alone can inspire "gender-appropriate" behavior (Ruble et al., 2006). As soon as children understand the labels "girl" and "boy," they seek information concerning gender-typed traits and try to live up to them. A boy may fight back when provoked because boys are expected to do so. A girl may be gentle and kind because that is expected of girls. Both boys' and girls' self-esteem will depend on how they measure up to the gender schema.

Studies indicate that children organize information according to a gender schema. For example, boys show better memory for "masculine" toys, activities, and occupations, whereas girls show better memory for "feminine" toys, activities, and occupations (Martin & Ruble, 2004). However, gender-schema theory does not address the issue of whether biological forces also play a role in gender typing.

PSYCHOLOGICAL ANDROGYNY

Cultural stereotypes tend to polarize females and males. They tend to push females and males to the imagined far ends of a continuum of gender-role traits (Rathus et al., 2008). It is common to label people as masculine or feminine. It is also common to assume that the more feminine people are, the less masculine they are, and vice versa. That is, the female U.S. Marine helicopter pilot usually is not conceptualized as wearing lipstick or baking. The tough male business executive is not usually conceptualized as changing diapers and playing peek-a-boo. An "emotional" boy who also shows the "feminine" traits of nurturance and tenderness is probably thought of as less masculine than other boys. Outspoken, competitive girls are likely to be seen as not only masculine but also as unfeminine.

However, the traits that supposedly characterize masculinity and femininity can be found within the same individual. That is, people (male or female) who obtain high scores on measures of masculine traits on personality tests can also score high on feminine traits. People with both stereotypical feminine and stereotypical masculine traits are termed **psychologically androgynous**. People who are high in stereotypical masculine traits only are typed as masculine. People who are high in stereotypical feminine traits only are typed as feminine (Bem, 1993).

Some psychologists suggest that it is worthwhile to promote psychological androgyny in children because they will be able to summon up a wider range of traits to meet the challenges in their lives (Lefkowitz & Zeldow, 2006). For example, compared with their masculine or feminine peers, androgynous children and adolescents have better social relations, superior adjustment, greater creativity (Norlander et al., 2000), and more willingness to pursue occupations stereotyped as "belonging" to the other sex (Hebert, 2000).

© Emmanuel Faure/Getty Images

Learning Your Way

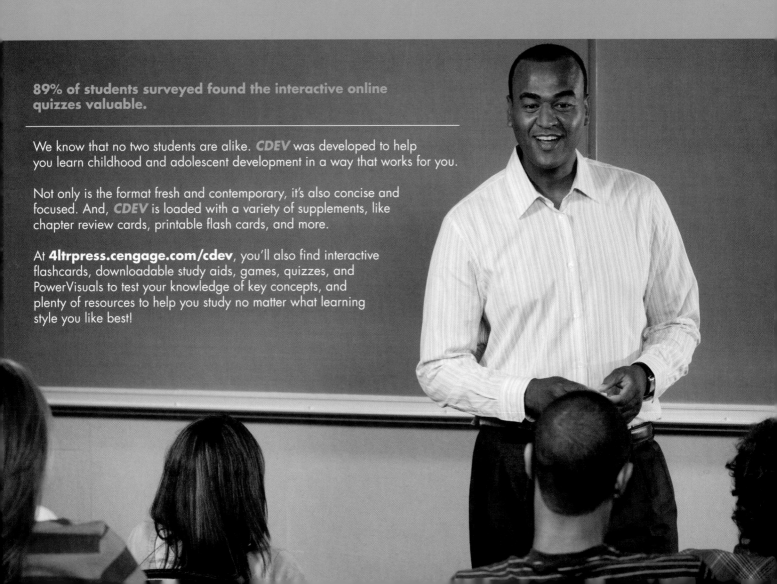

89% of students surveyed found the interactive online quizzes valuable.

We know that no two students are alike. *CDEV* was developed to help you learn childhood and adolescent development in a way that works for you.

Not only is the format fresh and contemporary, it's also concise and focused. And, *CDEV* is loaded with a variety of supplements, like chapter review cards, printable flash cards, and more.

At **4ltrpress.cengage.com/cdev**, you'll also find interactive flashcards, downloadable study aids, games, quizzes, and PowerVisuals to test your knowledge of key concepts, and plenty of resources to help you study no matter what learning style you like best!

Competence in motor skills

enhances self-esteem and acceptance by peers.

11

Middle Childhood: Physical Development

TRUTH OR FICTION?

T F Children outgrow "baby fat."

T F The typical American child is exposed to about 10,000 food commercials each year.

T F Most American children are physically fit.

T F Hyperactivity is caused by chemical food additives.

T F Stimulants are often used to treat children who are already hyperactive.

T F Some children who are intelligent and provided with enriched home environments cannot learn how to read or do simple math problems.

Learning Outcomes

LO1 Describe growth patterns in middle childhood.

LO2 Discuss nutrition and overweight in childhood, focusing on incidence, origins, and treatment of the problem.

LO3 Describe motor development in middle childhood, focusing on sex differences, exercise, and fitness.

LO4 Discuss the symptoms, possible origins, and treatment of attention-deficit/hyperactivity disorder (ADHD).

LO5 Discuss the various kinds of learning disorders and their possible origins.

It is 6-year-old Jessica's first day of school. During recess, she runs to the climbing apparatus in the school-yard and climbs to the top. As she reaches the top, she announces to the other children, "I'm coming down." She then walks to the parallel bars, goes halfway across, lets go, and tries again.

Steve and Mike are 8-year-olds. They are riding their bikes up and down the street. Steve tries riding with no hands on the handlebars. Mike starts riding fast, standing up on the pedals. Steve shouts, "Boy, you're going to break your neck!" (adapted from Rowen, 1973).

Middle childhood is a time for learning many new motor skills. Success in both gross and fine motor skills reflects children's increasing physical maturity, their opportunities to learn, and personality factors such as their persistence and self-confidence. Competence in motor skills enhances children's self-esteem and their acceptance by their peers.

In this chapter, we examine physical and motor development during middle childhood. We also discuss children with certain disorders.

LO1 Growth Patterns

gains in height and weight are fairly steady throughout middle childhood. But notable variations in growth patterns also occur from child to child. Following the growth trends begun in early childhood, boys and girls continue to gain a little

growth spurt A period during which growth advances at a dramatically rapid rate compared with other periods.

over 2 inches in height per year during the middle childhood years. This pattern of gradual gains does not vary significantly until children reach the adolescent **growth spurt** (see Figure 11.1). The average gain in weight between the ages of 6 and 12 is about 5 to 7 pounds a year. During these years, children continue to become less stocky and more slender (Kuczmarski et al., 2000).

Most deviations from these average height and weight figures are quite normal. Individual differences are more marked in middle childhood than they were earlier. For example, most 3-year-olds are within 8 to 10 pounds and 4 inches of each other. But by the age of 10, children's weights may vary by as much as 30 to 35 pounds, and their heights may vary by as much as 6 inches.

NUTRITION AND GROWTH

In middle childhood, average body weight doubles. Children also expend a good deal of energy as they engage in physical activity and play. To fuel this growth and activity, children need to eat more than they did in the preschool years. The average 4- to 6-year-old needs 1,400 to 1,800 calories per day. But the average 7- to 10-year-old requires 2,000 calories a day (Gidding et al., 2006).

Nutrition involves much more than calories, as we will see in the section on childhood overweight. The federal government has a food pyramid that suggests that it is healthful to eat fruits and vegetables, fish, poultry (without skin), and whole grains and to limit intake of fats, sugar, and starches. However, the food offered to children in school and elsewhere tends to be heavy on sugar, animal fats, and salt (Bauer et al., 2004; Watson, 2008). In addition, food portions have grown over the past couple of decades, particularly for salty snacks, desserts, soft drinks,

FIGURE 11.1
Growth Curves for Height and Weight

Gains in height and weight are fairly steady during middle childhood.

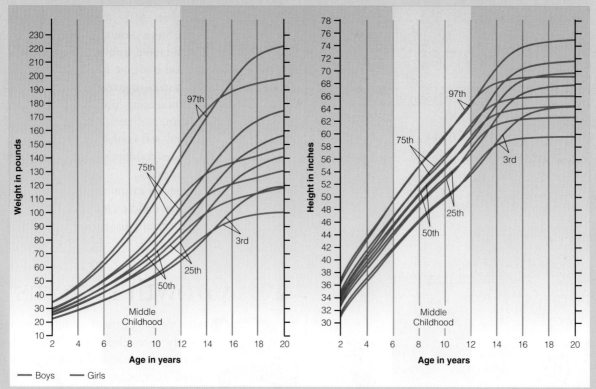

Source: Kuczmarski et al. (2000, Figures 9–12).

© Joe Raedle/Getty Images

fruit drinks, french fries, hamburgers, cheeseburgers, and Mexican food (Nielsen & Popkin, 2003).

The largest portions and most fattening foods are eaten at fast-food restaurants. The National Bureau of Economic Research (NBER) found that for 9th graders, having a fast-food restaurant within a tenth of a mile of their school is connected with a 5.2% increase in their obesity rate (Currie et al., 2009). The NBER found no association between the obesity rate and the presence of a fast-food restaurant when the restaurant was a quarter or a half mile away.

Nutrition and social class are also connected. Consider two studies with African American mothers and daughters. Daughters living at the poverty line were likely to be fed diets high in fats and fast foods (Miklos et al., 2004). Middle-class mothers, however, were concerned about the weight of their daughters and encouraged physical activity as a means of weight control. The mothers also tended to limit consumption of snack foods and sugar-laden carbonated beverages. Instead, they encouraged their daughters to drink water (V. J. Thompson et al., 2003).

> Only about 40% of normal-weight boys and 20% of normal-weight girls become overweight adults.

SEX SIMILARITIES AND DIFFERENCES IN PHYSICAL GROWTH

Figure 11.1 also reveals that boys continue to be slightly heavier and taller than girls through the age of 9 or 10. Girls then begin their adolescent growth spurt and surpass boys in height and weight until about age 13 or 14. At that time, boys are approaching the peak of their adolescent growth spurt, and they become taller and heavier than girls (Högler et al., 2008; Wehkalampi et al., 2008).

The steady gain in height and weight during middle childhood is paralleled by an increase in muscular strength for both girls and boys (Högler et al., 2008; Wehkalampi et al., 2008). The relative proportion of muscle and fatty tissue is about the same for boys and girls in early middle childhood. But this begins to change at about age 11, as males develop relatively more muscle tissue and females develop more fatty tissue.

LO2 Overweight in Children

the American Heart Association (AHA, 2007) defines being overweight not only in terms of weight, but also in terms of body composition—that is, the amount of muscle and fatty tissue. As you can see in Figure 11.2, research including the three largest ethnic groups in the United States reveals that from one in six (16% to 17%) to one in four (about 25%) children and adolescents in the United States are overweight. The AHA (2007) compared all groups of American children combined from the 1970s with all groups of children combined of the early 2000s. It found that for 6- to 11-year-olds, the percentage of overweight children has increased from 4.0% to 17.5%. For 12- to 19-year-olds, the percentage of overweight adolescents has increased from 6% to 17%.

Although parents often assume that heavy children will outgrow "baby fat"—especially once they hit the growth spurt of adolescence—it is not so. In the United States, most overweight children become overweight adults (AHA, 2007; Daniels, 2006; Tercyak & Tyc, 2006). By contrast, only about 40% of normal-weight boys and 20% of normal-weight girls become overweight adults. However, in samples of overweight Japanese and Swiss children, most did not become overweight adults (Funatogawa et al., 2008; Junod, 2008). Perhaps there is greater social pressure in those cultures to slim down as one develops.

T F Children outgrow "baby fat."
False; most overweight children become overweight adults.

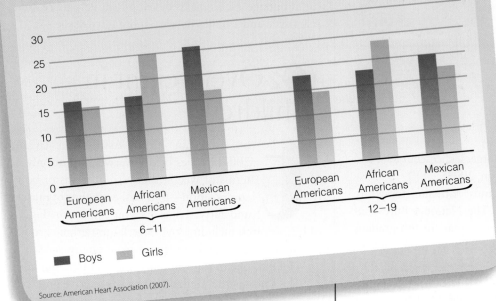

FIGURE 11.2
Overweight Children in America

Percent of children (ages 6–11) and adolescents (ages 12–19) who are overweight, according to the American Heart Association (AHA).

Boys ■ Girls ■

Source: American Heart Association (2007).

Overweight children, despite the stereotype, are usually far from jolly. Research suggests that heavy children are often rejected or derided by their peers (Storch et al., 2007; Zeller et al., 2008). They usually perform poorly in sports, which can provide a source of prestige for slimmer children (Salvy et al., 2008). As overweight children approach adolescence, they become even less popular, because they are less likely to be found sexually attractive. It is no surprise, then, that overweight children have poorer body images than children of normal weight (Storch et al., 2007). Moreover, overweight adolescents are more likely to be depressed and anxious than peers who are normal in weight (Kirkcaldy et al., 2002).

Children who are overweight are also at greater risk of encountering a number of physical health problems, both in childhood and later in life (Roden, 2009). Among these are high blood pressure, hardening of the arteries (atherosclerosis), type 2 diabetes, fatty liver disease, ovary disorders, and abnormal breathing patterns during sleep (Stabouli & Kotsis, 2009). Being overweight in childhood can accelerate the development of heart disease, which can lead to heart attacks or stroke in adulthood. The dramatically increased prevalence of overweight in childhood might even reverse the contemporary increase in

adipose tissue Fat cells.

life expectancy; that is, overweight youth might lead less healthy and shorter lives than their parents, which as Daniels (2006) notes, would be the first reversal in lifespan in modern life.

CAUSES OF OVERWEIGHT

Being overweight runs in families (Hebebrand & Hinney, 2009). Research provides convincing evidence that heredity plays a role (Casper et al., 2008). Some people, for example, apparently inherit a tendency to burn up extra calories, whereas others inherit a tendency to turn their extra calories into fat (Kolata, 2007). Research shows that identical twins have a similar body weight in adulthood whether they had been reared together or apart (Bogardus, 2009). Childhood experiences apparently have less effect on adult weight.

Weight has also been related to the amount of fat cells, or **adipose tissue**, that we have, and we may have some tendency to inherit different numbers of fat cells. The hunger drive is connected with the quantity of fat accumulated in these cells. The blood-sugar level is relatively high after one has eaten; then it drops as time elapses. As the blood-sugar level declines, the well of fat in fat cells is tapped to nourish the person, and the cells shrivel up. Eventually—and in some cases, "eventually" happens sooner than we might like—the hypothalamus (a

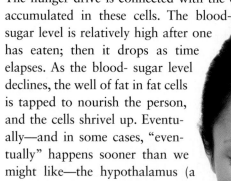

Once blood sugar runs low and the body starts using fat cells to nourish itself, the hypothalamus starts working and kicks the hunger drive back in. Sometimes this happens sooner than we'd like.

structure of the brain) learns of the deficit and stirs the hunger drive (Woods & Seeley, 2002).

Children who have more fat cells than other children feel hungry sooner, even if they are the same in weight. Perhaps the possession of more fat cells means that more signals are being transmitted to the hypothalamus. Children (and adults) who are overweight and those who were once overweight usually have more fat cells than individuals who have weighed less. This abundance is no blessing. Being overweight in childhood may cause adolescent or adult dieters to feel persistent hunger, even after they have leveled off at a weight they prefer (Guerdjikova et al., 2007).

Evidence that genetic and physiological factors are involved in weight does not mean that the environment is without influence. Family, peers, and other environmental factors also play roles in children's eating habits (Bauer et al., 2004; Moens et al., 2007). Overweight parents, for example, may be models of poor exercise habits, may encourage overeating, and may keep the wrong kinds of food in the house (Treuth et al., 2004).

Watching television also affects children's weight (Schumacher & Queen, 2007). Children who watch television extensively during the middle childhood years are more likely to become overweight as adolescents (Schumacher & Queen, 2007). The influence of TV watching is at least threefold (Stephenson & Banet-Weiser, 2007). First, children tend to consume snacks while watching. Second, television bombards children with commercials for fattening foods, such as candy and potato chips. Third, watching television is a sedentary activity. We burn fewer calories sitting than engaging in physical activity. Children who are heavy TV viewers are less physically active overall.

> **T** F The typical American child is exposed to about 10,000 food commercials each year. *True, and these commercials contribute to overeating or eating unhealthful foods. The bulk of them are for fast foods (such as Burger King and Pizza Hut), highly sweetened cereals, soft drinks, and candy bars (Goossens et al., 2007; Theim et al., 2007).*

Stressors and emotional reactions also play roles in prompting children to eat (Schumacher & Queen, 2007). Overeating may occur in response to severe stresses, such as bickering in the home, parental divorce, or the birth of a sibling. Family celebrations and arguments are quite different, but both can lead to overeating or

breaking a diet. Efforts to curb food intake also may be hampered by negative feeling states, such as anxiety and depression (Goossens et al., 2007; Guerdjikova et al., 2007). The rule of thumb here seems to be something like this: If life is awful, try chocolate (or french fries, or pizza, or whatever).

Helping Overweight Children Manage Their Weight

Health-conscious parents not only want to be slimmer themselves but are also more aware of the health benefits their children gain by avoiding being overweight. However, losing weight is a difficult problem in self-control for children and adults alike. Nevertheless, childhood is the optimal time to prevent or reverse being overweight because it is easiest to promote a lifetime pattern of healthful behaviors during childhood (Blom-Hoffman et al., 2006; Schumacher & Queen, 2007).

Cognitive behavioral methods show promise in helping children lose weight (AHA, 2007; Johnston & Steele, 2007; Wadden & Stunkard, 2002) by (1) improving nutritional knowledge, (2) reducing calories, (3) introducing exercise, and (4) modifying behavior. Behavioral methods involve tracking the child's calorie intake and weight, keeping the child away from temptations, setting a good example, and systematically using praise and other rewards. The most successful weight-loss programs for children combine exercise, decreased caloric intake, behavior modification, and emotional support from parents. Here are some suggestions from researchers:

- Teach children about nutrition: calories, protein, vitamins, minerals, fiber, food groups, and so on. Indicate which foods may be eaten in nearly unlimited quantities (e.g., green vegetables) and which foods should be eaten only sparingly (cakes, cookies, soft drinks sweetened with sugar, and so on). Check out the Traffic Light Diet (Figure 11.3).

- Do not insist that the entire family sit down at the same time for a large meal. Allow your child to eat only when hungry.

- Substitute low-calorie foods for high-calorie foods.

- Allow children to stop eating when they feel full.

- Prepare low-calorie snacks for your child to eat throughout the day. Children who feel deprived of food may go on a binge.

- Do not cook, eat, or display fattening foods at home. Their sight and aroma can be tantalizing.

- If you take your child food shopping, avoid the aisles with ice cream, cake, and candy.

FIGURE 11.3
The Traffic Light Diet

Johnston and Steele (2007) have shown that the Traffic Light Diet can help children manage their weight. Children (or adults using the diet) may eat unlimited quantities of green foods, which consist mainly of vegetables (without butter or salad dressing) and fruit. They may use reasonable amounts of low-fat (preferably nonfat) milk, roasted or baked poultry (but not the skin), fish, pasta, whole-grain cereals and baked goods (without the butter or margarine), beans, nuts, and small quantities of relatively low-fat cuts of meat (pork is lower in fat than beef). Vegetable oils (such as olive oil) are amber foods whose fat content is high in calories but not otherwise harmful to the cardiovascular system. Red foods are to be eaten in relatively small quantities by children, and adolescents and adults who are trying to lose weight should eat them rarely or in very small amounts; they consist of animal fats, cream, full-fat cheeses, butter, margarine, mayonnaise, and the like.

- Ask relatives and friends not to offer fattening treats when you visit.
- Do not allow snacking in front of the TV set or while playing, reading, or engaging in any other activity.
- Involve the child in calorie-burning exercise, such as swimming or prolonged bicycle riding. Exercise will burn calories, increase the child's feelings of competence and self-esteem, improve cardiovascular condition, and, possibly, promote lifetime exercise habits.
- Reward the child for steps in the right direction, such as eating less or exercising more.

Do not assume that it is a catastrophe if the child slips and goes on a binge. Talk over what triggered the binge with the child to avert similar problems in the future.

LO3 Motor Development

the school years are marked by increases in the child's speed, strength, agility, and balance (Abdelaziz et al., 2001; Loovis & Butterfield, 2000). These developments, in turn, lead to more skillful performance of motor activities, such as skipping.

GROSS MOTOR SKILLS

Throughout middle childhood, children show steady improvement in their ability to perform various gross motor skills (Abdelaziz et al., 2001; Karatekin et al., 2007). School-age children are usually eager to participate in group games and athletic activities that require the movement of large muscles, such as catching and throwing balls. Children are hopping, jumping, and climbing by age 6 or so; and by age 6 or 7, they are usually capable of pedaling and balancing on a bicycle. By the age of 8 to 10, children are showing the balance, coordination, and strength that allow them to engage in gymnastics and team sports.

During these years, the muscles are growing stronger, and the pathways that connect the cerebellum to the cortex are becoming increasingly myelinated. Experience also plays an indispensable role in refining many sensorimotor abilities, especially at championship levels, but individual differences that seem inborn are also present. Some people, for example, have better visual acuity or better depth perception than others. For reasons such as these, they will have an edge in playing the outfield or hitting a golf ball.

One of the most important factors in athletic performance is **reaction time**, or the amount of time required to respond to a stimulus. Reaction time is basic to the child's timing of a swing of the bat to meet the ball. Reaction time is basic to adjusting to a fly ball or hitting a tennis ball. Reaction time is also involved in children's responses to cars and other (sometimes deadly) obstacles when they are riding their bicycles or running down the street.

Reaction time gradually improves (i.e., decreases) from early childhood to about age 18 (Abdelaziz et al., 2001; Karatekin et al., 2007). However, individual differences can be large (Largo et al., 2001). Reaction time begins to increase again in the adult years. Even so, 75-year-olds still outperform children. Baseball and volleyball may be "child's play," but, everything else being equal, adults will respond to the ball more quickly.

FINE MOTOR SKILLS

By the age of 6 to 7 years, children can usually tie their shoelaces and hold their pencils as adults do. Their abilities to fasten buttons, zip zippers, brush teeth, wash themselves, and coordinate a knife and fork or use chopsticks all develop during the early school years and improve during childhood (Abdelaziz et al., 2001; Beilei et al., 2002).

SEX SIMILARITIES AND DIFFERENCES IN MOTOR DEVELOPMENT

reaction time The amount of time required to respond to a stimulus.

Throughout the middle childhood years, boys and girls perform similarly in most motor activities. Boys show slightly greater overall strength and, in particular, more forearm strength, which aids them in swinging a bat or throwing a ball (Butterfield & Loovis, 1993).

Girls, on the other hand, show somewhat greater limb coordination and overall flexibility, which is valuable in dancing, balancing, and gymnastics (Abdelaziz et al., 2001; Cratty, 1986). Girls with a certain type of physique seem particularly well suited to gymnastics. Those who are short, lean, and small boned make the best gymnasts, according to Olympic coaches, because they displace gravity most effectively. This may explain why female gymnasts are considered old for the sport by the time they reach their late teens. By then, they have often grown taller and their body contours have filled out.

At puberty, sex differences in motor performance that favor boys become progressively greater (Smoll & Schultz, 1990). What factors might account for the development of sex differences in physical performance? In their review of research studies on this topic, Thomas and French (1985) concluded that the slight sex differences in motor performance before puberty are not large enough to be attributed to biological variables. (The one exception may be throwing, a skill in which boys excel from an early age.) Boys are more likely than girls to receive encouragement, support, and opportunities for participation in sports (Geary, 1998). Even during the preschool years, parents emphasize physical activity in boys more than in girls. By middle childhood, boys are more involved in competitive games and in games of longer duration than girls are. They also engage in more vigorous activity on average than girls do (A. M. Thompson et al., 2003).

At puberty, when boys begin to excel in such areas as running, the long jump, sit-ups, and grip strength, boys' greater size and strength confer a biological advantage. But some environmental factors that operated in middle childhood may exert even greater importance in puberty. "Tomboy" behavior in girls is less socially accepted in adolescence than it was in middle childhood. Therefore, girls may become less interested in participating in athletic activities and may be less motivated to do well in the ones in which they do engage (Geary, 1998; Vu et al., 2006). By the ages of 12 and 13, girls are less likely than boys to perceive themselves as competent (Whitehead & Corbin, 1991), and self-perception of competence predicts participation in sports (Papaioannou et al., 2006).

Physical activity decreases with age between middle childhood and adolescence in both sexes (A. M. Thompson et al., 2003). Physical activities become increasingly stereotyped by children as being masculine (e.g., football) or feminine (e.g., dance) (Meaney et al., 2002).

EXERCISE AND FITNESS

The health benefits of exercise for both adults and children are well known. Exercise reduces the risk of heart disease, stroke, diabetes, and certain forms of cancer (Atkinson & Davenne, 2007; Daubenmier et al., 2007). Exercise confers psychological benefits as well. Physically active adolescents have a better self-image and better coping skills than those who are inactive (Kirkcaldy et al., 2002).

T F Most American children are physically fit.
False; most children in the United States are not physically fit (Schumacher & Queen, 2007).

What are some possible reasons for the lack of fitness? Again, one obvious culprit is watching television. Students who watch relatively little television have less body fat and are more physically fit than those who watch for several hours per day (Schumacher & Queen, 2007).

Cardiac and muscular fitness, in both childhood and adulthood, is developed by participation in continuous exercise such as running, walking quickly, swimming laps, bicycling, or jumping rope for intervals of several minutes at a time. However, schools and parents tend to focus on sports such as baseball and football, which are less apt to promote fitness (Schumacher & Queen, 2007).

Children with high levels of physical activity are more likely to have school officials and parents who encourage children to exercise and who actively exercise themselves (Schumacher & Queen, 2007).

Organized sports for children are enormously popular, but many children lose their enthusiasm and drop out. Participation in sports declines as middle childhood progresses (Schumacher & Queen, 2007).

Tips for Encouraging Physical Activity

How, then, can more children be motivated to engage in regular physical activity? Here are some ideas for parents:

- Engage in family outdoor activities that promote fitness: walking, swimming, bicycling, skating.
- Reduce the amount of time spent watching television.
- Encourage outdoor play during daylight hours after school.
- Do not assume that your child gets sufficient exercise by participating in a team sport. Many team sports involve long periods of inactivity.

Why? Sometimes children are pushed too hard, too early, or too quickly by parents or coaches. If competition is stressed, children may feel frustrated or inferior; they are sometimes injured. Hence, parents are advised not to place excessive demands for performance on their children. Let them progress at their own pace. Encourage them to focus on the fun and health benefits of physical activity and sports, not on winning.

Children with Disorders

Certain disorders of childhood are most apt to be noticed in the middle childhood years, when the child enters school. The school setting requires that a child sit still, pay attention, and master a number of academic skills. But some children have difficulty with one or more of these demands. In the following sections, we focus on children with various disorders. Table 11.1 highlights the types of disorders that can affect a child's functioning, especially in school. Let us consider attention-deficit/hyperactivity disorder and learning disorders in greater depth.

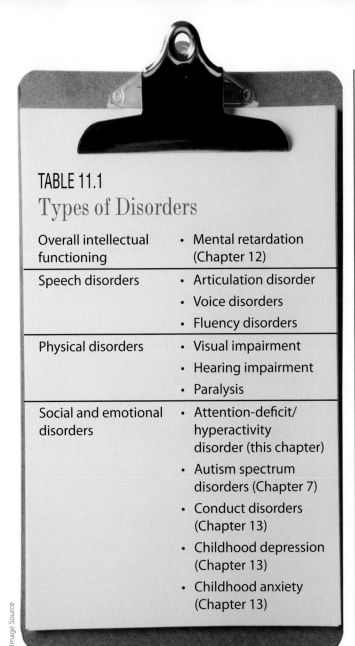

TABLE 11.1
Types of Disorders

Overall intellectual functioning	• Mental retardation (Chapter 12)
Speech disorders	• Articulation disorder • Voice disorders • Fluency disorders
Physical disorders	• Visual impairment • Hearing impairment • Paralysis
Social and emotional disorders	• Attention-deficit/ hyperactivity disorder (this chapter) • Autism spectrum disorders (Chapter 7) • Conduct disorders (Chapter 13) • Childhood depression (Chapter 13) • Childhood anxiety (Chapter 13)

© Image Source

LO4 Attention-Deficit/ Hyperactivity Disorder (ADHD)

many parents think that their children do not pay enough attention to them—that they tend to run around as the whim strikes and to do things in their own way. Some inattention, especially at early ages, is to be expected. In **attention-deficit/hyperactivity disorder (ADHD)**, the child shows developmentally inappropriate or excessive inattention, impulsivity, and **hyperactivity**

THE CASE OF EDDIE

Nine-year-old Eddie is a problem in class. His teacher complains that he is so restless and fidgety that the rest of the class cannot concentrate on their work. He hardly ever sits still. He is in constant motion, roaming the classroom, talking to other children while they are working. He has been suspended repeatedly for outrageous behavior, most recently for swinging from a fluorescent light fixture and unable to get himself down. His mother reports that Eddie has been a problem since he was a toddler. By the age of 3, he had become unbearably restless and demanding. He has never needed much sleep and always awakens before anyone else in the family, making his way downstairs and wrecking things in the living room and kitchen. Once, at the age of 4, he unlocked the front door and wandered into traffic, but was rescued by a passerby.

Psychological testing shows Eddie to be average in academic ability, but to have a "virtually nonexistent" attention span. He shows no interest in television or in games or toys that require some concentration. He is unpopular with peers and prefers to ride his bike alone or to play with his dog. He has become disobedient at home and at school and has stolen small amounts of money from his parents and classmates.

Eddie has been treated with methylphenidate (Ritalin), but it was discontinued because it had no effect on his disobedience and stealing. However, it did seem to reduce his restlessness and increase his attention span at school.

—Adapted from Spitzer et al., 2002

(Nigg et al., 2006; Weisler & Sussman, 2007). A list of specific behaviors associated with this disorder is shown in Table 11.2. The degree of hyperactive behavior is crucial, because many normal children are labeled overactive and fidgety from

attention-deficit/ hyperactivity disorder (ADHD) A behavior disorder characterized by developmentally inappropriate or excessive inattention, impulsiveness, and hyperactivity.

hyperactivity Excessive restlessness and overactivity; one of the primary problems in attention deficit/hyperactivity disorder (ADHD).

TABLE 11.2
Symtoms of Attention-Deficit/Hyperactivity Disorder (ADHD)

KIND OF PROBLEM	SPECIFIC PATTERNS OF BEHAVIOR
Lack of attention	• Fails to attend to details or makes careless errors in schoolwork, and so on • Has difficulty sustaining attention in schoolwork or play activities • Does not appear to pay attention to what is being said • Fails to follow through on instructions or to finish work • Has trouble organizing work and other activities • Avoids work or activities that require sustained attention • Loses work tools (e.g., pencils, books, assignments) or toys • Becomes readily distracted • Is forgetful in daily activities
Hyperactivity	• Fidgets with hands or feet or squirms in his or her seat • Leaves seat in situations such as the classroom in which remaining seated is required • Constantly runs around or climbs on things; "running like a motor" • Has difficulty playing quietly • Shows excessive motor activity when asleep • Talks excessively
Impulsivity	• Often acts without thinking • Shifts from activity to activity • Cannot organize tasks or work • Requires constant supervision • Often "calls out" in class • Does not wait in line, to take a turn in games, and so on

Source: Adapted from American Psychiatric Association (2000).

time to time. In fact, if talking too much were the sole criterion for ADHD, the label would have applied to many of us.

The onset of ADHD occurs by age 7. According to the American Psychiatric Association (2000), the behavior pattern must have persisted for at least 6 months for the diagnosis to be made. The hyperactivity and restlessness of children with ADHD impair their ability to function in school. They simply cannot sit still. They also have difficulty getting along with others. Their disruptive and noncompliant behavior often elicits punishment from parents. ADHD is quite common. It is diagnosed in about 1% to 5% of school-age children and is one of the most common causes of childhood referrals to mental health clinics. ADHD is many times more common in boys than in girls.

Some psychologists and educators argue that ADHD is often overdiagnosed (Weisler & Sussman, 2007). That is, many children who do not toe the line in school tend to be diagnosed with ADHD and are medicated to encourage more acceptable behavior. Research does suggest that those who diagnose children with ADHD tend to be "suggestible." That is, they are more likely to diagnose children with the disorder when they are given other sources of information—for example, from teachers and parents—to the effect that the children do not adequately control their behavior (Reddy & De Thomas, 2007; Wiesler & Sussman, 2007).

CAUSES OF ADHD

Because ADHD is in part characterized by excessive motor activity, many theorists focus on possible physical causes. For one thing, ADHD tends to run in families, for both girls and boys with the disorder (Faraone et al., 2000). Some researchers suggest there may be a genetic component to the disorder (Thapar et al., 2007; Walitza et al., 2006). If so, such a genetic component might involve the manner in which the brain processes the neurotransmitter (brain chemical) dopamine (Mazei-Robison et al., 2005; Walitza et al., 2006). Brain-imaging studies support the probability that many genes are involved and that they affect the regulation of dopamine (Walitza et al., 2006).

ADHD is also found to coexist with other psychological disorders and problems, ranging most commonly from oppositional defiant disorder and anxiety disorders to mood disorders and tics (Biederman et al., 2007; Hasler et al., 2007). Studies using brain imaging have found differences in the brain chemistry of children with ADHD and those with ADHD plus other disorders such as serious mood disorders, leading to the prospect that different causes and treatments will be discovered for various groups of children with ADHD.

In the 1970s, it was widely believed—because of the arguments and anecdotes of Benjamin Feingold—that artificial food colorings and food preservatives (benzoate) were largely responsible for hyperactivity. Feingold then introduced what became dubbed the "Feingold diet," which proscribed foods containing such chemicals and, according to Feingold and a few researchers, reduced hyperactivity in children who followed it.

> T ~~F~~ Hyperactivity is caused by chemical food additives.
> False; studies in the use of the Feingold diet yielded conflicting results, and researchers now generally agree that food coloring and preservatives do not cause ADHD (Cruz & Bahna, 2006).

Joel T. Nigg (2001; Nigg et al., 2006) notes that ADHD is widely thought to be caused by inhibitory processes that do not work efficiently. That is, children with ADHD do not inhibit, or control, impulses that most children are capable of controlling. But Nigg argues that "inhibition" is defined in somewhat different ways by different theorists. Nigg (2001, Nigg et al., 2006) distinguishes between inhibition that is under the executive control of the brain—a sort of cognitive–neurological inhibition—and inhibition that is normally motivated by emotions such as anxiety and fear (e.g., anxiety about disappointing a teacher or fear of earning poor grades). Nigg argues that ADHD is unlikely to reflect failure to respond to feelings of anxiety or fear. He believes that the disorder is more likely due to a lack of executive control but admits that the precise nature of this control—the specific neurological basis—remains poorly understood.

stimulants Drugs that increase the activity of the nervous system.

TREATMENT AND OUTCOME

Stimulants such as Ritalin are the most widespread treatment for ADHD. It may seem ironic that stimulants are used with children who are already overly active. However, the stimulants promote the activity of the neurotransmitters dopamine and noradrenaline which stimulate the "executive center" of the brain to control more primitive areas of the brain. The rationale is that the activity of the hyperactive child stems from an inability of the cerebral cortex to inhibit more primitive areas of the brain (Hazell, 2007; Reiff & Mansoor, 2007). The drugs block the reuptake (reabsorption) of dopamine and noradrenaline. Keeping more of these neurotransmitters active has the effect of stimulating the cerebral cortex and facilitating its control of primitive areas of the brain. This interpretation is supported by evidence that caffeine—the stimulant found in coffee, tea, colas, and chocolate (yes, chocolate)—also helps children control hyperactivity (Leon, 2000; Rezvani & Levin, 2001).

Children with ADHD who are given stimulants show increased attention span, improved cognitive and academic performance, and a reduction in disruptive, annoying, and aggressive behaviors (Posey et al., 2007). The use of stimulants is controversial, however. Some critics argue that stimulants suppress gains in height and weight, do not contribute to academic gains, and lose effectiveness over time. Another concern is that stimulants are overused or misused in an attempt to control normal high-activity levels of children at home or in the classroom.

Cognitive behavioral therapy also shows some promise in treating children with ADHD. This approach attempts to increase the child's self-control and problem-solving abilities through modeling, role playing, and self-instruction. A Spanish study found that it was possible to teach many children with ADHD to "stop and think" before giving in to angry impulses and behaving in an aggressive manner (Miranda & Presentacion, 2000). However, the Multimodal Treatment Study sponsored by the National Institute of Mental Health found that

dyslexia A reading disorder characterized by problems such as letter reversals, mirror reading, slow reading, and reduced comprehension.

learning disorders A group of disorders characterized by inadequate development of specific academic, language, and speech skills.

stimulant medication was more effective than cognitive behavioral therapy (Greene & Ablon, 2001; Whalen, 2001). Hinshaw (2006) argues that cognitive behavioral programs for children should use clear rewards and behavioral contingencies and should involve parents and teachers. Waxmonsky (2005) suggests that children may fare better with medication, whereas adolescents and adults with ADHD may be able to profit better from cognitive behavioral therapy.

Many but not all children "outgrow" ADHD. Longitudinal studies have found that at least two-thirds of children with ADHD continue to exhibit one or more of the core symptoms in adolescence and adulthood (Barkley, 2004; Nigg et al., 2004). Problems in attention, conduct, hyperactivity, and learning frequently continue.

T F Stimulants are often used to treat children who are already hyperactive.
True; although it may seem counterintuitive, stimulants increase children's attention span, improve their academic performance, and reduce their disruptive behavior (Posey et al., 2007).

LO5 Learning Disorders

elson Rockefeller served as vice president of the United States under Gerald Ford. He was intelligent and well educated. Yet despite the best of tutors, he could never master reading. Rockefeller suffered from **dyslexia**.

Dyslexia is one type of **learning disorder**. The term *learning disorders* refers to a group of disorders characterized by inadequate development of specific academic, language, and speech skills. Children with learning disorders may show problems in math, writing, or reading. Some have difficulties in articulating sounds of speech or in understanding spoken language. Others have problems in motor coordination. Children are usually considered to have a learning disorder when they are performing below the level expected for their age and level of intelligence and when there is no evidence of other handicaps such as vision or hearing problems,

intellectual deficiency, or socioeconomic disadvantage (Joshi, 2003; Lyon et al., 2003). However, some psychologists and educators, such as Frank Vellutino (Vellutino et al., 2004), argue that too much emphasis is placed on the discrepancy between intelligence and reading achievement.

T F Some children who are intelligent and provided with enriched home environments cannot learn how to read or do simple math problems.
True; they are said to have learning disorders.

Children with learning disorders frequently display other problems as well. They are more likely than other children to have ADHD (Schulte-Körne et al., 2006), and, as they mature, they are more likely than other adolescents or adults to develop schizophrenia (Maneschi et al., 2006). They do not communicate as well with their peers, have poorer social skills, show more behavior problems in the classroom, and are more likely to experience emotional problems (Frith, 2001; Lyon et al., 2003).

For most children with a learning disorder, the disorder persists through life. But with early recognition and appropriate remediation, many individuals can learn to overcome or compensate for their disorder (Vellutino et al., 2004).

It has been estimated that dyslexia affects anywhere from 5% to 17.5% of American children (Shaywitz, 1998). Most studies show that dyslexia is much more common in boys than in girls. Figure 11.4 is a writing sample from a dyslexic child.

In childhood, treatment of dyslexia focuses on remediation (Bakker, 2006; Tijms, 2007). Children are given highly structured exercises to help them become aware of how to blend sounds to form words, such as identifying word pairs that rhyme and those that do not rhyme. Later in life, the focus tends to be on accommodation rather than on remediation. For example, college students with dyslexia may be given extra time to do the reading involved in taking tests. Interestingly, college students with dyslexia are frequently excellent at word recognition. Even so, they continue to show problems in decoding new words.

ORIGINS OF DYSLEXIA

Current ideas about the origins of dyslexia focus on the ways in which sensory and neurological problems may contribute to the reading problems of dyslexic individuals, but genetic factors do appear to be involved in dys-

FIGURE 11.4
Writing Sample of a Dyslexic Child

Dyslexic children may perceive letters as upside down (confusing *w* with *m*) or reversed (confusing *b* with *d*), leading to rotations or reversals in writing, as shown here.

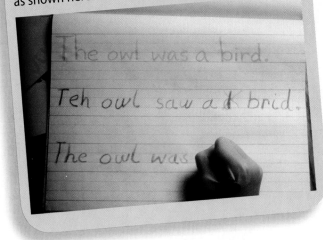

© Will and Deni McIntyre/Science Source/Photo Researchers

© Andrew Lambert Photography/Photo Researchers, Inc.

lexia. Dyslexia runs in families. It has been estimated that 25% to 65% of children who have one dyslexic parent are dyslexic themselves (Fernandez & State, 2004; Plomin & Walker, 2003). About 40% of the siblings of children with dyslexia are also dyslexic.

Genetic factors may give rise to neurological problems. The problems can involve "faulty wiring" or circulation problems in the left hemisphere of the brain, which is usually involved in language functions (Arduini et al., 2006). Such circulation problems result in less oxygen than is desirable. A part of the brain called the *angular gyrus* lies in the left hemisphere between the visual cortex and Wernicke's area. The angular gyrus "translates" visual information, such as written words, into auditory information (sounds) and sends it on to Wernicke's area. Problems in the angular gyrus may give rise to reading problems by making it difficult for the reader to associate letters with sounds (Grigorenko, 2007; S. E. Shaywitz et al., 2006). Other researchers find evidence that brain abnormalities that pose a risk for schizophrenia also pose a

> Genetic factors may give rise to neurological problems.

risk for dyslexia, suggesting an overall vulnerability to cognitive deficits (Leonard et al., 2008; Steinbrink et al., 2008).

Some researchers report evidence that dyslexic children have difficulty controlling their eye movements (Boden & Giaschi, 2007), but most researchers today focus on dyslexic individuals' *phonological processing*—that is, the ways in which they make, or do not make, sense of sounds. It was once thought that dyslexic children hear as well as other children do, but now it seems that they may not discriminate sounds as accurately as other children do (Bergmann & Wimmer, 2008; Halliday & Bishop, 2006). As a result, *b*'s and *d*'s and *p*'s, for example, may have been hard to tell apart at times, creating confusion that impaired reading ability (Boada & Pennington, 2006; B. A. Shaywitz et al., 2006).

Another view is the **double-deficit hypothesis** of dyslexia, which suggests that dyslexic children have neurologically based deficits both in *phonological processing* and in *naming speed* (Sawyer, 2006; Vukovic & Siegel, 2006). Therefore, not only do they have difficulty sounding out a *b* as a *b*; it also takes them longer than other children to name or identify a *b* when they attempt to do so.

double-deficit hypothesis The theory of dyslexia which suggests that dyslexic children have biological deficits in *phonological processing* (interpreting sounds) and in *naming speed* (identifying letters—such as *b* versus *d*, or *w* versus *m*).

mainstreaming Placing disabled children in classrooms with nondisabled children.

EDUCATING CHILDREN WITH DISORDERS

Special educational programs have been created to meet the needs of schoolchildren with mild to moderate disorders. These disorders include learning disorders, emotional disturbance, mild intellectual deficiency, and physical disabilities such as blindness, deafness, or paralysis. Evidence is mixed on whether placing disordered children in separate classes can also stigmatize them and segregate them from other children. In **mainstreaming**, disordered children are placed in regular classrooms that have been adapted to their needs. Most students with mild learning disorders spend most of their school day in regular classrooms (Fergusson, 2007; Soan & Tod, 2006).

Children make enormous strides

in their cognitive development during middle childhood.

12

Middle Childhood: Cognitive Development

TRUTH OR FICTION?

T F Don't try the "Yes, but..." defense with a 5-year-old. If you did it, you're guilty, even if it was an accident.

T F Memorizing the alphabet requires that children keep 26 bits of information in mind at once.

T F An IQ is a score on a test.

T F Two children can answer exactly the same items on an intelligence test correctly, yet one can be above average in intelligence and the other below average.

T F Highly intelligent children are creative.

T F Adopted children are more similar in intelligence to their adoptive parents than to their biological parents.

T F Bilingual children do not encounter more academic problems than children who speak only one language.

Did you hear the one about the judge who pounded her gavel and yelled, "Order! Order in the court!"? "A hamburger and french fries, Your Honor," responded the defendant. Such children's jokes are based on ambiguities in the meanings of words and phrases. Most 7-year-olds will find the joke about order in the court funny because they recognize that the word *order* has more than one meaning. At about the age of 11, children can understand ambiguities in grammatical structure. Children make enormous strides in their cognitive development during middle childhood as their thought processes and language become more logical and complex.

Learning Outcomes

LO1 Describe the developments in Piaget's concrete-operational stage, focusing on examples of decentration, such as conservation and seriation.

LO2 Discuss the theories of moral development of Piaget and Kohlberg.

LO3 Discuss information processing in middle childhood, focusing on developments in selective attention and memory.

LO4 Discuss theories, measurement, and determinants of intelligence, and the relationship of intelligence to achievement and creativity.

LO5 Discuss language development in middle childhood, emphasizing vocabulary, grammar, reading, and bilingualism.

LO1 Piaget: The Concrete-Operational Stage

according to Jean Piaget, the typical child is entering the stage of **concrete operations** by the age of 7. In this stage, which lasts until about the age of 12, children show the beginnings of

> **concrete operations** The third stage in Piaget's model of development, characterized by flexible, reversible thought concerning tangible objects and events.

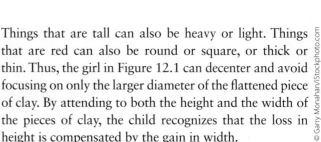

Things that are tall can also be heavy or light. Things that are red can also be round or square, or thick or thin. Thus, the girl in Figure 12.1 can decenter and avoid focusing on only the larger diameter of the flattened piece of clay. By attending to both the height and the width of the pieces of clay, the child recognizes that the loss in height is compensated by the gain in width.

TRANSITIVITY

If your parents are older than you are and you are older than your children, are your parents older than your children? The answer, of course, is yes. But how did you arrive at this answer? If you said yes simply on the basis of knowing that your parents are older than your children (e.g., 58 and 56 compared with 5 and 3), your answer did not require concrete-operations thought. One aspect of concrete-operations is the principle of **transitivity**: If A exceeds B in some property (say, age or height) and if B exceeds C, then A must also exceed C.

Researchers can assess whether children understand the principle of transitivity by asking them to place objects in a series, or in order, according to some property, such as lining up one's family members according

decentration Simultaneous focusing on more than one aspect or dimension of a problem or situation.

transitivity The principle that if A > B and B > C, then A > C.

adult logic but generally focus on tangible objects rather than abstract ideas, which is why they are "concrete."

Concrete-operational thought is reversible and flexible. Adding the numbers 2 and 3 to get 5 is an operation. Subtracting 2 from 5 to get 3 reverses the operation. Subtracting 3 from 5 to get 2 demonstrates flexibility.

Concrete-operational children are less egocentric than preoperational children. They recognize that people see things in different ways because of different situations and values. Concrete-operational children also engage in **decentration**. They can focus on multiple parts of a problem or situation at once.

CONSERVATION

Concrete-operational children show understanding of the laws of conservation. The 7-year-old girl in Figure 12.1 would say that the flattened ball of clay still has the same amount of clay as the round one. If asked why, she might reply, "Because you can roll it up again like the other one." This answer shows reversibility.

The concrete-operational child knows that objects can have several properties or dimensions.

FIGURE 12.1
Conservation of Mass

This girl is in the concrete-operational stage of cognitive development. She has rolled two clay balls. In the photo on the left, she agrees that both have the same amount (mass) of clay. In the photo on the right, she (gleefully) flattens one clay ball. When asked whether the two pieces still have the same amount of clay, she says yes.

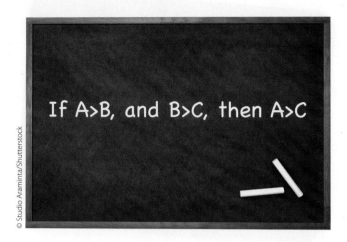

If A>B, and B>C, then A>C

to age, height, or weight. Placing objects in such a way is termed **seriation**. Consider some examples with preoperational and concrete-operational children.

Piaget assessed the development of seriation by asking children to place 10 sticks in order of size. Children who are 4 to 5 years old usually place the sticks in

seriation Placing objects in an order or series according to a property or trait.

a random sequence, or in small groups, as in small, medium, or large. But consider the approach of 7- and 8-year-olds who are capable of concrete operations. They look over the array of sticks, then select either the longest or shortest and place it at the point from which they will begin. Then they select the next longest (or shortest) and continue until the task is complete.

Concrete-operational children also have the decentration capacity to allow them to seriate in two dimensions at once, unlike preoperational children. Consider a seriation task used by Piaget and Inhelder. In this test, children are given 49 leaves and asked to classify them according to size and brightness (from small to large and from dark to light) (see Figure 12.2). As the grid is completed from left to right, the leaves become lighter. As it is filled in from top to bottom, the leaves become larger. Preoperational 6-year-olds can usually order the leaves according to size or brightness, but not both at once. Concrete-operational children of age 7 or 8 can work with both dimensions at once and fill in the grid properly.

CLASS INCLUSION

In one Piagetian task, described in Chapter 9, a 4-year-old was shown pictures of four cats and six dogs. When asked whether there were more dogs or more animals, she said more dogs. This preoperational child apparently could not focus on the two subclasses (dogs, cats) and the larger subclass (animals) at the same time. But concrete-operational children can do so. Therefore, they are more likely to answer the question about the dogs and the animals correctly (Chapman & McBride, 1992).

APPLICATIONS OF PIAGET'S THEORY TO EDUCATION

Piaget believed that learning involves active discovery. Therefore, teachers should not simply try to impose knowledge on the child but instead should find interesting and stimulating materials.

FIGURE 12.2
A Grid for Demonstrating the Development of Seriation

To classify these leaves, children must focus on two dimensions at once: size and lightness. They must also understand the principle of *transitivity*—that if A > B and B > C, then A > C.

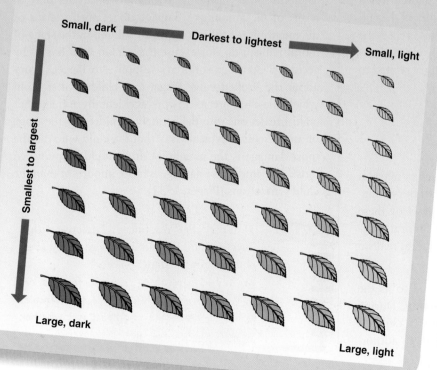

Small, dark — Darkest to lightest → Small, light

Smallest to largest

Large, dark

Large, light

moral realism The judgment of acts as moral when they conform to authority or to the rules of the game.

objective morality The perception of morality as objective, that is, as existing outside the cognitive functioning of people.

immanent justice The view that retribution for wrongdoing is a direct consequence of the wrongdoing.

Second, instruction should be geared to the child's level of development. When teaching a concrete-operational child about fractions, for example, the teacher should not only lecture but should also allow the child to divide concrete objects into parts. Third, Piaget believed that learning to take into account the perspectives of others is a key ingredient in the development of both cognition and morality. Accordingly, he thought that teachers should promote group discussions and interactions among their students.

LO2 Moral Development: The Child as Judge

On a cognitive level, moral development concerns the basis on which children make judgments that an act is right or wrong. Jean Piaget and Lawrence Kohlberg believed that moral reasoning undergoes the same cognitive-developmental pattern around the world. The moral considerations that children weigh at a given age may be influenced by the values of the cultural settings in which they are reared, but also reflect the orderly unfolding of cognitive processes (Krebs & Denton, 2006; Lapsley, 2006). Moral reasoning is related to the child's overall cognitive development.

PIAGET'S THEORY OF MORAL DEVELOPMENT

Piaget observed children playing games such as marbles and making judgments on the seriousness of the wrongdoing of characters in stories. On the basis of these observations, he concluded that children's moral judgments develop in two overlapping stages: moral realism and autonomous morality (Piaget, 1932).

STAGE 1 The first stage is usually referred to as the stage of **moral realism**, or **objective morality**. During this stage, which emerges at about the age of 5, children consider behavior correct when it conforms to author-

Children in the moral realism stage generally do not factor in motives when considering whether someone deserves punishment.

© Ryan McVay/Getty Images

ity or to the rules of the game. When asked why something should be done in a certain way, the 5-year-old may answer "Because that's the way to do it" or "Because my Mommy says so." Five-year-olds perceive rules as embedded in the structure of things. Rules, to them, reflect ultimate reality, hence the term *moral realism*. Rules and right and wrong are seen as absolute, not as deriving from people to meet social needs.

Another consequence of viewing rules as embedded in the fabric of the world is **immanent justice**, or automatic retribution. This involves thinking that negative experiences are punishment for prior misdeeds, even when realistic causal links are absent (Callan et al., 2006).

You are most likely guilty in the eyes of a 5-year-old even if your error was an accident. Preoperational children tend to focus on only one dimension at a time. Therefore, they judge the wrongness of an act only in terms of the amount of damage done, not in terms of the intentions of the wrongdoer. Children in the stage of moral realism do not excuse the person who harms by accident. Consider children's response to Piaget's story about the broken cups. Piaget told children a story in which one child breaks 15 cups accidentally and another child breaks one cup deliberately. Children in the stage of moral realism typically say that the child who did the most damage is the naughtiest and should be punished most. The amount of damage is more important than the child's intentions (Piaget, 1932).

T **F** Don't try the "Yes, but . . ." defense with a 5-year-old. If you did it, you're guilty, even if it was an accident.

True; the typical 5-year-old focuses on only one dimension at a time, for example, the amount of damage done, not whether the act was accidental or purposeful.

STAGE 2 Piaget found that when children reach the ages of 9 to 11, they begin to show **autonomous morality**. Their moral judgments tend to become more self-governed, as children come to view social rules as social agreements that can be changed. Children realize that circumstances can warrant breaking rules. Children who show autonomous morality can focus simultaneously on multiple dimensions, so they consider social rules and the motives of the wrongdoer.

Children in this stage also show a greater capacity to take the point of view of others, to empathize with them. Decentration and increased empathy prompt children to weigh the intentions of the wrongdoer more heavily than the amount of damage done. The child who broke one cup deliberately may be seen as deserving of more punishment than the child who broke 15 cups accidentally. Accidents are less likely to be considered crimes.

KOHLBERG'S THEORY OF MORAL DEVELOPMENT

Kohlberg (1981, 1985) proposed a cognitive-developmental theory of moral development that elaborated on the kinds of information children use and on the complexities of moral reasoning. Before we discuss Kohlberg's views, read "The Case of Heinz," the tale that Kohlberg used in his research.

THE CASE OF HEINZ

In Europe, a woman was near death from a special kind of cancer. There was one drug that the doctors thought might save her. It was a form of radium that a druggist in the same town had recently discovered. The drug was expensive to make, but the druggist was charging 10 times what the drug cost him to make. He paid $200 for the radium and charged $2,000 for a small dose of the drug. The sick woman's husband, Heinz, went to everyone he knew to borrow the money, but he could only get together about $1,000, which was half of what it cost. He told the druggist that his wife was dying and asked him to sell it cheaper or let him pay later. But the druggist said: "No, I discovered the drug and I'm going to make money from it." So Heinz got desperate and broke into the man's store to steal the drug for his wife.

—Kohlberg (1969)

Kohlberg emphasized the importance of being able to view the moral world from the perspective of another person (Krebs & Denton, 2005). Look at this situation from Heinz's perspective. What do you think? Should Heinz have tried to steal the drug? Was he right or wrong? As you can see from Table 12.1, the question requires more than a simple yes or no answer. Heinz is caught in a moral dilemma in which legal or social rules (in this case, laws against stealing) are pitted against a strong human need (Heinz's desire to save his wife). According to Kohlberg's theory, children and adults arrive at their answers for different reasons. These reasons can be classified according to the level of moral development they reflect.

Children (and adults) are faced with many moral dilemmas. Consider cheating in school. When children fear failing a test, they may be tempted to cheat. Different children may decide not to cheat for different reasons. One child may fear getting caught. Another may decide that it is more important to live up to her moral principles than to get the highest possible grade. In each case, the child's decision is to not cheat. However, the decisions reflect different levels of reasoning.

Kohlberg argued that the developmental stages of moral reasoning follow the same sequence in all children. Children progress at different rates, and not everyone reaches the highest stage. But children must experience Stage 1 before Stage 2, and so on. Kohlberg theorizes three levels of moral development and two stages within each level.

The Preconventional Level

STAGE 1 In the **preconventional level**, children base their moral judgments on the consequences of their behavior. Stage 1 is oriented toward obedience and punishment.

> **autonomous morality**
> The second stage in Piaget's cognitive-developmental theory of moral development, in which children base moral judgments on the intentions of the wrongdoer and on the amount of damage done.
>
> **preconventional level**
> According to Kohlberg, a period during which moral judgments are based largely on expectations of rewards or punishments.

TABLE 12.1
Kohlberg's Levels and Stages of Moral Development

STAGE OF DEVELOPMENT	EXAMPLES OF MORAL REASONING THAT SUPPORT HEINZ'S STEALING THE DRUG	EXAMPLES OF MORAL REASONING THAT OPPOSE HEINZ'S STEALING THE DRUG
LEVEL I: PRECONVENTIONAL—TYPICALLY BEGINS IN EARLY CHILDHOOD[a]		
Stage 1: Judgments guided by obedience and the prospect of punishment (the consequences of the behavior)	It is not wrong to steal the drug. Heinz did try to pay the druggist for it, and it is only worth $200, not $2,000.	Taking things without paying is wrong because it is against the law. Heinz will get caught and go to jail.
Stage 2: Naively egoistic, instrumental orientation (things are right when they satisfy people's needs)	Heinz ought to steal the drug because his wife really needs it. He can always pay the druggist back.	Heinz should not steal the drug. If he gets caught and winds up in jail, it won't do his wife any good.
LEVEL II: CONVENTIONAL—TYPICALLY BEGINS IN MIDDLE CHILDHOOD		
Stage 3: Good-boy/good-girl orientation (moral behavior helps others and is socially approved)	Stealing is a crime, so it is bad, but Heinz should steal the drug to save his wife or else people would blame him for letting her die.	Stealing is a crime. Heinz should not steal the drug because his family will be dishonored and they will blame him.
Stage 4: Law-and-order orientation (moral behavior is doing one's duty and showing respect for authority)	Heinz must steal the drug to do his duty to save his wife. Eventually, he has to pay the druggist for it, however.	If we all took the law into our own hands, civilization would fall apart, so Heinz should not steal the drug.
LEVEL III: POSTCONVENTIONAL—TYPICALLY BEGINS IN ADOLESCENCE[b]		
Stage 5: Contractual, legalistic orientation (one must weigh pressing human needs against society's need to maintain social order)	This thing is complicated because society has a right to maintain law and order, but Heinz has to steal the drug to save his wife.	I can see why Heinz feels he has to steal the drug, but laws exist for the benefit of society as a whole and cannot simply be cast aside.
Stage 6: Universal ethical principles orientation (people must follow universal ethical principles and their own conscience, even if it means breaking the law)	In this case, the law comes into conflict with the principle of the sanctity of human life. Heinz must steal the drug because his wife's life is more important than the law.	If Heinz truly believes that stealing the drug is worse than letting his wife die, he should not steal it. People have to make sacrifices to do what they think is right.

[a]Tends to be used less often in middle childhood.
[b]May not develop at all.

Good behavior means being obedient so one can avoid punishment. According to Stage 1 reasoning, Heinz could be urged to steal the drug because he did ask to pay for it first. But he could also be urged not to steal the drug so that he will not be sent to jail (see Table 12.1).

STAGE 2 In Stage 2, good behavior allows people to satisfy their own needs and, perhaps, the needs of others. A Stage 2 reason for stealing the drug is that Heinz's wife needs it. Therefore, stealing the drug is not wrong. A Stage 2 reason for not stealing the drug would be that Heinz's wife might die even if he does so. Thus, he might wind up in jail needlessly.

In a study of American children aged 7 through 16, Kohlberg (1963) found that Stage 1 and 2 types of moral judgments were offered most frequently by 7- and 10-year-olds. Stage 1 and 2 judgments fell off steeply after age 10.

The Conventional Level

STAGE 3 In the **conventional level** of moral reasoning, right and wrong are judged by conformity to conventional (family, religious, societal) standards of right and wrong. According to the Stage 3 *good-boy/good-girl orientation*, it is good to meet the needs and expectations of others. Moral behavior is what is "normal," what the majority does. From the Stage 3 perspective, Heinz should steal the drug because that is what a "good husband" would do. It is "natural" or "normal" to try to help one's wife. Or Heinz should not steal the drug because "good people do not steal."

STAGE 4 In Stage 4, moral judgments are based on rules that maintain the social order. Showing respect for authority and duty is valued highly. From this perspective, one could argue that Heinz must steal the drug, because it is his duty to save his wife. He would pay the druggist when he could. Or one could argue that Heinz should not steal the drug, because he would be breaking the law. He might also be contributing to the breakdown of the social order. Many people do not develop beyond the conventional level. Kohlberg (1963) found that Stage 3 and 4 types of judgments emerge during middle childhood. They are all but absent among 7-year-olds. However, they are reported by about 20% of 10-year-olds and by higher percentages of adolescents.

LO3 Information Processing

Key elements in children's information processing include the following (Pressley & Hilden, 2006):

- Development of selective attention
- Development of memory capacity and of understanding of the processes of memory
- Development of ability to solve problems, for example, by finding the correct formula and applying it

DEVELOPMENT OF SELECTIVE ATTENTION

The ability to focus one's attention and screen out distractions advances steadily through middle childhood (Rubia et al., 2006). Preoperational children engaged in problem solving tend to focus (or center) their attention on one element of the problem at a time, which is a major reason they lack conservation. Concrete-operational children can attend to multiple aspects of the problem at once, permitting them to conserve number and volume.

An experiment illustrates how selective attention and the ability to ignore distraction develop during middle childhood. The researchers (Strutt et al., 1975) asked children between 6 and 12 years of age to sort a deck of cards as quickly as possible on the basis of the figures depicted on each card (e.g., circle versus square). In one condition, only the relevant dimension (i.e., form) was shown on each card. In another condition, a dimension not relevant to the sorting also was present (e.g., a horizontal or vertical line in the figure). In a third condition, two irrelevant dimensions were present (e.g., a star above or below the figure, in addition to a horizontal or vertical line in the figure). As seen in Figure 12.3 on the next page, the irrelevant information interfered with sorting ability for all age groups, but older children were much less affected than younger children.

DEVELOPMENTS IN THE STORAGE AND RETRIEVAL OF INFORMATION

Psychologists use the term *memory* to refer to the processes of storing and retrieving information. Many psychologists divide memory functioning into three major processes or structures: sensory memory, working memory, and long-term memory (see Figure 12.4 on p. 203).

Sensory Memory

When we look at an object and then blink our eyes, the visual impression of the object lasts for a fraction of a second in what is called **sensory memory**, or the **sensory register**. Then the "trace" of the stimulus decays. The concept of sensory memory applies to all the senses. For

conventional level According to Kohlberg, a period during which moral judgments largely reflect social rules and conventions.

sensory memory (sensory register) The structure of memory first encountered by sensory input. Information is maintained in sensory memory for only a fraction of a second.

FIGURE 12.3

Development of the Ability to Ignore Distractions

Irrelevant information interfered with sorting ability for all age groups, but older children are less affected than younger ones.

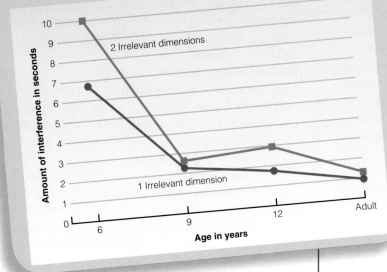

Source: Strutt et al. (1975).

example, when we are introduced to somebody, the trace of the sound of the name immediatly starts to decay, but we can remember the name by focusing on it.

Working Memory (Short-Term Memory)

When children focus on a stimulus in the sensory register, it tends to be retained in **working memory** (also called *short-term memory*) for up to 30 seconds after the trace of the stimulus decays. Ability to maintain information in short-term memory depends on cognitive strategies and on capacity to continue to perceive a vanished stimulus. Memory function in middle childhood seems largely adult-like in organization and strategies and shows only quantitative improvement through early adolescence (Alloway et al., 2004; Archibald & Gathercole, 2006).

Auditory stimuli can be maintained longer in short-term memory than visual stimuli. For this reason, one strategy for promoting memory is to **encode** visual stimuli as sounds. Then the sounds can be repeated out loud

working memory The structure of memory that can hold a sensory stimulus for up to 30 seconds after the trace decays.

encode To transform sensory input into a form that is more readily processed.

rehearse Repeat mentally.

or mentally. In Figure 12.4, mentally repeating, or **rehearsing**, the sound of Linda's name helps the other young woman remember it.

The capacity of short-term memory can be described in terms of the number of bits of information that can be kept in memory at once. To remember a new phone number, for example, one must keep seven bits of information in short-term memory simultaneously; that is, one must rehearse them consecutively. The typical adult can keep about seven bits of information—plus or minus two—in short-term memory at a time; such a group of bits is called a *chunk* (Miller, 1956). As measured by the ability to recall digits, the typical 5- to 6-year-old can work on two bits of information at a time. The ability to recall a series of digits improves throughout middle childhood, and adolescents can keep about seven bits of information in short-term memory at the same time (Towse & Cowan, 2005; Gathercole et al., 2004b).

The information-processing view focuses on children's memory capacity and their use of cognitive strategies, such as the way in which they focus their attention (Gathercole et al., 2004a, 2004b). Certain Piagetian tasks require several cognitive strategies instead of one. Young children frequently fail at such tasks

FIGURE 12.4
The Structure of Memory

rote learning Simple associative learning based on repetition.

long-term memory The memory structure capable of relatively permanent storage of information.

Many psychologists divide memory into three processes or structures. Sensory information enters sensory memory, where memory traces are held briefly before decaying. If we attend to the information, much of it is transferred to working memory (also called short-term memory), where it may decay or be displaced if it is not transferred to long-term memory. We may use rehearsal (repetition) or elaborative strategies to transfer information to long-term memory, from which memories can be retrieved with the proper cues.

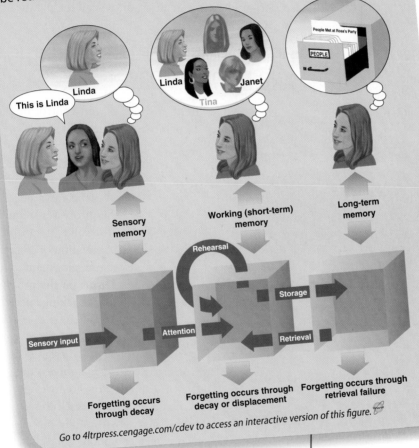

Go to 4ltrpress.cengage.com/cdev to access an interactive version of this figure.

the alphabet by rote will not be able to answer the question "What letter comes after N?" However, if you recite "H, I, J, K, L, M, N" to the child and then pause, the child is likely to say, "O." The 3-year-old probably will not realize that he or she can find the answer by using the cognitive strategy of reciting the alphabet, but many 5- or 6-year-olds will.

T (F) Memorizing the alphabet requires that children keep 26 bits of information in mind at once.

False; children tend to learn the alphabet by rote—that is, through extensive repetition.

Long-Term Memory

Think of **long-term memory** as a vast storehouse of information containing names, dates, places, what Johnny did to you in second grade, what Alyssa said about you when you were 12, and so on. Long-term memories may last days, years, or even most of a lifetime.

There is no known limit to the amount of information that can be stored in long-term memory. From time to time, it may seem that we have forgotten, or lost, a long-term memory, such as the name of an elementary or high school classmate. But it is more likely that we cannot find the right cues to retrieve it. It is "lost" in the same way as a misplaced object that we know is still in the house.

Older children are more likely than younger children to use rote rehearsal, or repetition, to try to remember information (Saito & Miyake, 2004; Towse

because they cannot simultaneously hold many pieces of information in their short-term memories. Put another way, preschoolers can solve problems with one or two steps, whereas older children can retain information from earlier steps as they proceed to subsequent steps.

But how do young children remember the alphabet, which is 26 bits of information? Children usually learn the alphabet by **rote learning**, simple associative learning based on repetition. After the alphabet is repeated many, many times, M triggers the letter N, N triggers O, and so on. The typical 3-year-old who has learned

elaborative strategy
A method for increasing retention of new information by relating it to well-known information.

metacognition Awareness of and control of one's cognitive abilities.

metamemory Awareness of the functions and processes involved in one's storage and retrieval of information.

& Cowan, 2005). A more effective method than rote rehearsal is to purposefully relate new material to well-known information, making it meaningful. Relating new material to known material is called an **elaborative strategy**. English teachers use an elaborative strategy when they have children use new words in sentences to help remember them.

Organization in Long-Term Memory

As children's knowledge of concepts advances, the storehouse of their long-term memory becomes organized according to categories. Preschoolers tend to organize their memories by grouping objects that share the same function (Lucariello et al., 2004; Towse, 2003). "Toast" may be grouped with "peanut butter sandwich," because both are edible. In middle childhood, "toast" and "peanut butter" are likely to be joined as foods.

When items are correctly categorized in long-term memory, children are more likely to recall accurate information about them. For instance, do you "remember" whether whales breathe underwater? If you did not know that whales are mammals or if you knew nothing about mammals, a correct answer might depend on an instance of rote learning. If children have incorrectly classified whales as fish, they might search their memories and construct the wrong answer.

Knowledge in a particular area increases the capacity to store and retrieve related information. For example, chess experts were found to be superior to amateurs at remembering where chess pieces had been placed on the board (Gobet & Simon, 2000). In this study, the experts were 8- to 12-year-old children and the amateurs were adults!

DEVELOPMENT OF RECALL MEMORY

Children's memory is a good overall indicator of their cognitive ability (Gathercole et al., 2004a, 2004b; Towse & Cowan, 2005). In an experiment on categorization and memory, researchers placed objects that fell into four categories (furniture, clothing, tools, fruit) on a table before second- and fourth-graders (Hasselhorn, 1992). The children were allowed 3 minutes to arrange the pictures as they wished and to remember as many as they could. Fourth-graders were more likely than second-graders to categorize and recall the pictures.

DEVELOPMENT OF METACOGNITION AND METAMEMORY

Children's awareness and control of their cognitive abilities is termed **metacognition**. The development of metacognition is shown by the ability to formulate problems, awareness of the processes required to solve a problem, activation of cognitive strategies, maintaining focus on the problem, and checking answers.

When a sixth-grader decides which homework assignments to do first, memorizes the state capitals for tomorrow's test, and then tests herself to see which ones she needs to study more, she is displaying metacognition (Flavell et al., 2002). **Metamemory** is an aspect of metacognition that refers to children's awareness of the functioning of their memory. Older children show greater insight into how memory works. For example, young elementary school students often announce that they have memorized educational materials before they have actually done so. Older students are more likely to accurately assess their knowledge. As a result, older children store and retrieve information more effectively (Towse & Cowan, 2005).

Older children also show more knowledge of strategies that can be used to facilitate memory. Preschoolers will usually use rehearsal if someone suggests they do, but not until about the age of 6 or 7 do children

Jean Piaget distinctly "remembered" an attempt to kidnap him from his baby carriage as he was being wheeled along the Champs Élysées. He recalled the excited throng, the abrasions on the face of the nurse who rescued him, the police officer's white baton, and the flight of the assailant. Although they were graphic, Piaget's memories were false. Years later, the nurse admitted that she had made up the tale.

A child witness is typically asked questions to prompt information. But such questions may be leading; that is, they may suggest an answer. For example, "What happened at school?" is not a leading question, but "Did your teacher touch you?" is. Can children's testimony be distorted by leading questions? It appears that by the age of 10 or 11, children are no more suggestible than adults, but younger children are more likely to be misled (Bruck et al., 2006; Krackow & Lynn, 2003). Research also indicates that repeated questioning may lead children to make up events that never happened to them (Roebers et al., 2001).

What, then, are investigators to do when the only witnesses to criminal events are children? Maggie Bruck and her colleagues (2006) recommend that interviewers avoid leading or suggestive questions to minimize influencing children's responses.

use it on their own (Flavell et al., 2002). As children develop, they are more likely to use selective rehearsal to remember important information.

If you are trying to remember a new phone number, you would know to rehearse it several times or to write it down before setting out to do math problems. However, 5-year-olds, asked whether it would make a difference if they jotted the number down before or after doing the math problems, do not reliably report that doing the problems first would matter. But 10-year-olds know that new mental activities (math problems) can interfere with previous ones (memorizing the telephone number) and usually suggest jotting the number down before doing the math problems.

LO4 Intellectual Development, Creativity, and Achievement

at an early age, we gain impressions of how intelligent we are compared with other family members and schoolmates. We associate intelligence with academic success, advancement on the job, and appropriate social behavior. Despite our sense of familiarity with the concept of intelligence, intelligence cannot be seen, touched, or measured physically. For this reason, intelligence is subject to various interpretations.

Intelligence is usually perceived as a child's underlying competence, or *learning ability*, whereas **achievement** involves a child's acquired competencies, or *performance*. Most psychologists also would agree that many of the competencies underlying intelligence are first exhibited during middle childhood, when most children are first exposed to formal schooling.

THEORIES OF INTELLIGENCE

Let's consider some theoretical approaches to intelligence. Then we will see how researchers and practitioners assess intellectual functioning.

Factor Theories

Many investigators view intelligence as consisting of one or more major mental abilities, or *factors*. In 1904, Charles Spearman suggested that the behaviors we consider

intelligence Defined by Wechsler as the "capacity … to understand the world [and the] resourcefulness to cope with its challenges."

achievement That which is attained by one's efforts and presumed to be made possible by one's abilities.

© Nicholas Belton/iStockphoto.com / © iStockphoto.com / ©Glow Images/Alamy / © U.P. Images/iStockphoto.com

intelligent have a common underlying factor *g*, or general intelligence, which represents broad reasoning and problem-solving abilities. He also noted that people seem more capable in some areas—perhaps in music or business or poetry—than in others. For this reason, he suggested that specific capacities, or *s* factors, account for certain individual abilities (Lubinski, 2004).

Psychologist Louis Thurstone (1938) believed that intelligence consists of several specific factors, or *primary mental abilities*, including visual–spatial abilities, perceptual speed, numerical ability, the ability to learn the meanings of words, ability to bring to mind the right word rapidly, and ability to reason. Thurstone's research suggested that these factors were somewhat independent; therefore, someone might be able to easily develop lists of words that rhyme but have difficulty solving math problems.

Sternberg's Theory of Intelligence

Psychologist Robert Sternberg (Sternberg, 2000) constructed a three-part, or triarchic, theory of intelligence. The parts are *analytical intelligence, creative intelligence,* and *practical intelligence* (see Figure 12.5).

Analytical intelligence is academic ability. It enables us to solve problems and acquire new knowledge. Creative intelligence is defined by the abilities to cope with novel situations and to profit from experience. Creativity allows us to relate novel situations to familiar situations (i.e., to perceive similarities and differences) and fosters adaptation. Practical intelligence means "street smarts." Practical intelligence enables people to adapt to the demands of their environment, including the social environment. Psychologists who believe that creativity is separate from analytical intelligence (academic ability) find only small to moderate relationships between academic ability and creativity (Kim, 2005). But to Sternberg, creativity is a basic part of intelligence.

Gardner's Theory of Multiple Intelligences

Psychologist Howard Gardner (1983, 2006), like Sternberg, believes that intelligence reflects more than academic ability. Gardner theorizes that there are various kinds of intelligences, which differ in quality (see Figure 12.6).

Three of Gardner's intelligences are linguistic intelligence, logical–mathematical intelligence, and spatial intelligence (visual–spatial skills). Others include bodily–kinesthetic intelligence (as shown by dancers and gymnasts), musical intelligence, interpersonal intelligence (as shown by empathy and the ability to relate to others), and intrapersonal intelligence (self-insight). Individuals may show great "intelligence" in one area—such as the genius of the young Mozart with the piano or that of a Pacific Islands girl who can navigate her small boat to hundreds of islands by observing the changing patterns of the stars—without having notable abilities in others. Critics of Gardner's theory agree that many people have special talents, as in music, but they question whether such talents are "intelligences" (Neisser et al., 1996).

MEASUREMENT OF INTELLECTUAL DEVELOPMENT

There may be disagreements about the nature of intelligence, but thousands of intelligence tests are administered by psychologists and educators every day.

FIGURE 12.5
Sternberg's Triarchic Theory of Intelligence

Robert Sternberg views intelligence as three-pronged: as having analytical, creative, and practical aspects.

Analytical intelligence
(academic ability)
Abilities to solve problems, compare and contrast, judge, evaluate, and criticize

Creative intelligence
(creativity and insight)
Abilities to invent, discover, suppose, and theorize

Practical intelligence
("street smarts")
Abilities to adapt to the demands of one's environment and apply knowledge in practical situations

FIGURE 12.6
Gardner's Theory of Multiple Intelligences

Gardner argues that there are many intelligences and that each has its neurological bases in certain parts of the brain.

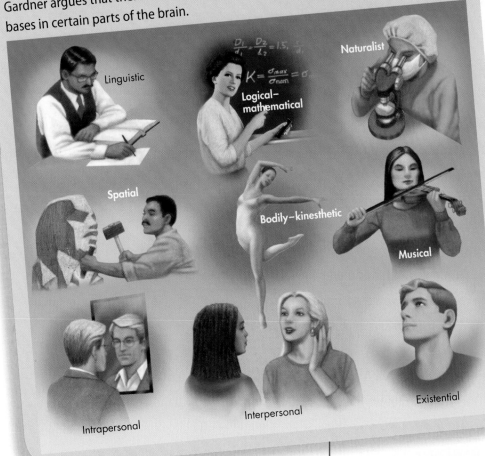

Linguistic

Logical–mathematical

Naturalist

Spatial

Bodily–kinesthetic

Musical

Intrapersonal

Interpersonal

Existential

The Stanford–Binet Intelligence Scale

The SBIS originated in the work of Frenchmen Alfred Binet and Theodore Simon about a century ago for the French public school system. Binet assumed that intelligence increased with age. Therefore, older children should get more items right. Thus, Binet arranged a series of questions in order of difficulty, from easier to harder. The Binet–Simon scale came into use in 1905. Since then, it has undergone revision and refinement. The Binet–Simon scale yielded a score called a **mental age (MA)**. The MA shows

The Stanford–Binet Intelligence Scale (SBIS) and the Wechsler scales for children and adults are the most widely used and well-respected intelligence tests. The SBIS and the Wechsler scales yield scores called **intelligence quotients (IQs)**. Both scales have been carefully developed and revised over the years. Each of them has been used to make vital educational decisions about children. In many cases, children whose test scores fall below or above certain scores are placed in special classes for intellectually deficient or gifted children.

In 1905, Alfred Binet and Theodore Simon in France introduced the idea of measuring intelligence. This version of the test was produced in 1937 by Lewis Terman and Maude Merrill in the United States and was specifically designed for younger children.

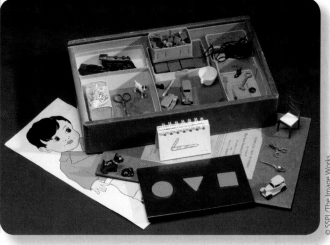

© SSPL/The Image Works

T F   An IQ is a score on a test.
True; intelligence is measured by tests which yield scores called intelligence quotients, or IQs.

TABLE 12.2
Items Similar to Those on the Stanford–Binet Intelligence Scale

AGE	ITEM
2 years	1. Children show knowledge of basic vocabulary words by identifying parts of a doll, such as the mouth, ears, and hair.
	2. Children show counting and spatial skills along with visual–motor coordination by building a tower of four blocks to match a model.
4 years	1. Children show word fluency and categorical thinking by filling in the missing words in sentences such as "Father is a man; mother is a _____" and "Hamburgers are hot; ice cream is _____."
	2. Children show comprehension by answering correctly when they are asked questions such as "Why do people have automobiles?" and "Why do people have medicine?"
9 years	1. Children can point out verbal absurdities, as in this question: "In an old cemetery, scientists unearthed a skull which they think was that of George Washington when he was only 5 years of age. What is silly about that?"
	2. Children display fluency with words, as shown by answering questions such as "Can you tell me a number that rhymes with snore?" and "Can you tell me a color that rhymes with glue?"
Adult	1. Adults show knowledge of the meanings of words and conceptual thinking by correctly explaining the differences between pairs of words such as "sickness and misery," "house and home," and "integrity and prestige."
	2. Adults show spatial skills by correctly answering questions such as "If a car turned to the right to head north, in what direction was it heading before it turned?"

chronological age (CA)
A person's actual age.

the intellectual level at which a child is functioning. A child with an MA of 6 is functioning, intellectually, like the average 6-year-old child. An MA of 8 is an above-average score for a 6-year-old but a below-average score for a 10-year-old.

Louis Terman adapted the Binet–Simon scale for use with American children in 1916. Because Terman carried out his work at Stanford University, it is now named the Stanford–Binet Intelligence Scale. The SBIS yields an intelligence quotient, or IQ, rather than an MA. Today, the SBIS can be used with children aged 2 or older and with adults. Table 12.2 shows the kinds of items used with individuals of various ages.

The IQ states the relationship between a child's mental age and his or her actual or **chronological age (CA)**. The IQ is computed by the formula

$$IQ = \frac{Mental\ Age\ (MA)}{Chronological\ Age\ (CA)} \times 100$$

According to this formula, a child with an MA of 6 and a CA of 6 would have an IQ of 100. Two children can answer exactly the same items on an intelligence test correctly, yet one can be above average in intelligence and the other below average. Children who can handle intellectual problems and older children will have IQs above 100. An 8-year-old who does as well on the SBIS as the average 10-year-old will attain an IQ of 125. Children who do not answer as many items correctly as other children of their age will attain MAs that are lower than their CAs. Their IQ scores will be below 100.

T F Two children can answer exactly the same items on an intelligence test correctly, yet one can be above average in intelligence and the other below average.
True; the younger of the two children would obtain a higher IQ score.

Today, IQ scores on the SBIS are derived by comparing children's and adults' performances with those of other people of the same age. People who get more items correct than average attain IQ scores above 100, and people who answer fewer items correctly attain scores below 100.

The Wechsler Scales

David Wechsler (1975) developed a series of scales for use with school-age children (Wechsler Intelligence Scale for Children or WISC), younger children (Wechsler Preschool and Primary Scale of Intelligence or WPPSI), and adults (Wechsler Adult Intelligence Scale or WAIS). These tests have been repeatedly updated.

The Wechsler scales group test questions into subtests (such as those shown in Table 12.3), which measure different intellectual tasks. For this reason, subtests compare a person's level of competence on one type of task (such as defining words) with that on another (such as using blocks to construct geometric designs). The Wechsler scales thus suggest children's strengths and weaknesses as well as provide overall measures of intellectual functioning.

TABLE 12.3
Kinds of Items Found on Wechsler's Intelligence Scales

VERBAL ITEMS

Information: "What is the capital of the United States?" "Who was Shakespeare?"

Comprehension: "Why do we have ZIP codes?" "What does 'A stitch in time saves 9' mean?"

Arithmetic: "If 3 candy bars cost 25 cents, how much will 18 candy bars cost?"

Similarities: "How are good and bad alike?" "How are peanut butter and jelly alike?"

Vocabulary: "What does 'canal' mean?"

Digit span: Repeating a series of numbers, presented by the examiner, forward and backward.

PERFORMANCE ITEMS

Picture completion: Pointing to the missing part of a picture.

Picture arrangement: Arranging cartoon pictures in sequence so that they tell a meaningful story.

Block design: Copying pictures of geometric designs using multicolored blocks.

Object assembly: Putting pieces of a puzzle together so that they form a meaningful object.

Coding: Rapid scanning and drawing of symbols that are associated with numbers.

Mazes: Using a pencil to trace the correct route from a starting point to home.

Note: Items for verbal subtests are similar but not identical to actual test items on the Wechsler intelligence scales.

© Stefanie Timmermann/iStockphoto.com

Wechsler described some subtests as measuring verbal tasks and others as assessing performance tasks. In general, verbal subtests require knowledge of verbal concepts, whereas performance subtests (see Figure 12.7) require familiarity with spatial-relations concepts. Wechsler's scales permit the computation of verbal and performance IQs.

Figure 12.8 indicates the labels that Wechsler assigned to various IQ scores and the approximate percentages of the population who attain IQ scores at those levels. Most children's IQ scores cluster around the average. Only about 5% of the population have IQ scores above 130 or below 70.

The Testing Controversy

Most psychologists and educational specialists consider intelligence tests to be at least somewhat biased against African Americans and members of lower social classes (Snyderman & Rothman, 1990). If scoring well on intelligence tests requires a certain type of cultural experience, the tests are said to have a **cultural bias**. Children reared in African American neighborhoods could be at a disadvantage because of cultural differences (Helms, 2006). Latino and Latina American children's performance might be compromised by differences in motivation and lack of self-confidence (Stevens et al., 2006). For such reasons, psychologists have tried to construct **culture-free** or culture-fair intelligence tests.

Some tests do not rely on expressive language at all. For example, Raymond Cattell's (1949) Culture-Fair Intelligence Test evaluates reasoning ability through the child's comprehension of the rules that govern a progression of geometric designs, as shown in Figure 12.9.

But culture-free tests have not lived up to their promise. First, middle-class children still outperform lower-class children on them (Rushton et al., 2003). Middle-class children, for example, are more likely to have basic familiarity with materials such as blocks and pencils and paper. They are more likely to have played with blocks (a practice relevant to the Cattell test). Second, culture-free tests do not predict academic success as well as other intelligence tests, and scholastic aptitude remains the central concern of educators (Keogh & Whyte, 2006).

PATTERNS OF INTELLECTUAL DEVELOPMENT

Intellectual growth seems to occur in at least two major spurts. The first occurs at about the age of 6. It coincides with entry into school and also with the shift from preoperational to concrete-operational thought. School may help crystallize intellectual functioning at this time. The second spurt occurs at about age 10 or 11.

But once they reach middle childhood, children appear to undergo relatively more stable patterns of gains in intellectual functioning,

FIGURE 12.7
Performance Items on an Intelligence Test

The items below resemble those found on the Wechsler Intelligence Scale for Children.

Picture arrangement

These pictures tell a story, but they are in the wrong order. Put them in the right order so that they tell a story.

Picture completion

What part is missing from this picture?

Block design

Put the blocks together to make this picture.

Object assembly

Put the pieces together as quickly as you can.

Go to 4ltrpress.cengage.com/cdev to access an interactive version of this figure.

FIGURE 12.8

Variations in IQ Scores

IQ scores generally vary according to a bell-shaped, or normal, curve.

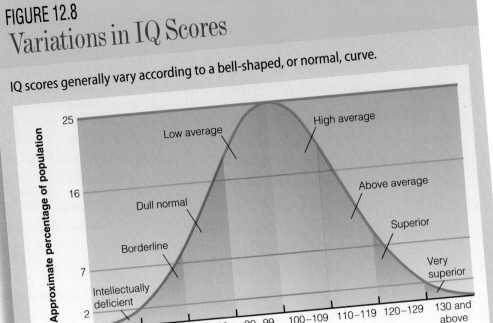

et al., 1973). Many factors influence changes in IQ scores, including changes in the home, socioeconomic circumstances, and education (Deary et al., 2004).

DIFFERENCES IN INTELLECTUAL DEVELOPMENT

The average IQ score in the United States is close to 100. About half the children in the United States attain IQ scores in the broad average range from 90 to 110 (see Figure 12.8). Nearly 95% attain scores between 70 and 130. Children who attain IQ scores below 70 are generally labeled "intellectually deficient." Children who attain scores of 130 or above are usually labeled "gifted."

Intellectual Disability

According to the American Association on Intellectual and Developmental Disabilities (AAIDD, 2009), "mental retardation is a disability characterized by significant

although there are still spurts (Deary et al., 2004). As a result, intelligence tests gain greater predictive power. In a classic study by Marjorie Honzik and her colleagues (1948), intelligence test scores taken at the age of 9 correlated strongly (+0.90) with scores at the age of 10 and more moderately (+0.76) with scores at the age of 18. Testing at age 11 even shows a moderate to high relationship with scores at the age of 77 (Deary et al., 2004).

Despite the increased predictive power of intelligence tests during middle childhood, individual differences exist. In the classic Fels Longitudinal Study (see Figure 12.10), two groups of children (Groups 1 and 3) made reasonably consistent gains in intelligence test scores between the ages of 10 and 17, whereas three groups declined. Group 4, children who had shown the most intellectual promise at age 10, went on to show the most precipitous decline, although they still wound up in the highest 2% to 3% of the population (McCall

FIGURE 12.9

Sample Items from Cattell's Culture-Fair Intelligence Test

Culture-fair tests attempt to exclude items that discriminate on the basis of cultural background rather than intelligence.

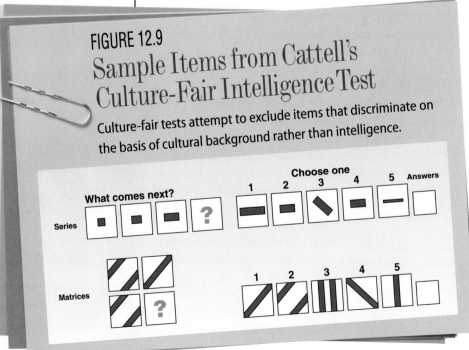

FIGURE 12.10
Five Patterns of Change in IQ Scores for Children in the Fels Longitudinal Study

In the Fels Longitudinal Study, IQ scores remained stable between the ages of 2½ and 17 for only one of five groups, Group 1.

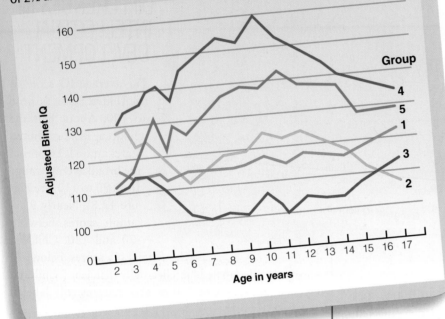

Source: McCall et al. (1973).

Some causes of intellectual disability are biological. Intellectual disability can stem from chromosomal abnormalities such as Down syndrome, genetic disorders such as phenylketonuria (PKU), and brain damage (AAIDD, 2007). Brain damage can have many origins, including childhood accidents and problems during pregnancy. For example, maternal alcohol abuse, malnutrition, or disease can damage the fetus. In **cultural–familial intellectual disability**, children are biologically normal but do not develop age-appropriate behavior at the normal pace because of an impoverished home environment. They may have little opportunity to interact with adults or play with stimulating toys.

Giftedness

Giftedness involves higher than excellent scores on standard intelligence tests. In determining who is gifted, most educators include children who have outstanding abilities; are capable of high performance in a specific academic area, such as language or mathematics; or who show creativ-

limitations both in intellectual functioning and in adaptive behavior as expressed in conceptual, social, and practical adaptive skills." Mental retardation involves an IQ score of no more than 70 to 75.

Most of the children (more than 80%) who are intellectually disabled are mildly so. Mildly intellectually disabled children are the most capable of adjusting to the demands of educational institutions and to society at large. Many mildly intellectually disabled children are mainstreamed in regular classrooms rather than placed in special-needs classes.

Children with Down syndrome are most likely to be moderately intellectually disabled. They can learn to speak, dress, feed, clean themselves, and engage in useful work under supportive conditions, as in a sheltered workshop, but they usually do not acquire skills in reading and math. Severely and profoundly intellectually disabled children may not acquire speech and self-help skills and may remain dependent on others for survival.

cultural–familial intellectual disability
Substandard intellectual performance stemming from lack of opportunity to acquire knowledge and skills.

Depending on the extent of their disabilities, many individuals, such as those with Down syndrome, can still engage in productive work activities under the right conditions. The Parkview Café, in Cardiff, England, helps people with learning disabilities gain vocational skills in catering and customer service.

© Matt Faber/PA Wire URN:7170655 (Press Association via AP Images)

ity, leadership, distinction in the visual or performing arts, or bodily talents, as in gymnastics and dancing. Sternberg (2007) presents a WICS model of giftedness, whose name is a play on the letters in WISC. Sternberg describes giftedness as involving wisdom, intelligence, and creativity.

Socioeconomic and Ethnic Differences in IQ

Research has found differences in IQ scores for various socioeconomic and ethnic groups. Lower-class American children attain IQ scores some 10 to 15 points lower than those obtained by middle- and upper-class children. African American children, Latino and Latina American children, and Native American children all tend to score below the norms for European Americans (Neisser et al., 1996). Youth of Asian descent frequently outscore youth of European backgrounds on achievement tests in math and science, including the math portion of the SAT (Dandy & Nettelbeck, 2002; Stevenson et al., 1993).

Asian students and their mothers tend to attribute academic success to hard work (Randel et al., 2000), whereas American mothers are more likely to attribute academic success to natural ability (Basic Behavioral Science Task Force, 1996). Thus, Asian students may work harder.

CREATIVITY AND INTELLECTUAL DEVELOPMENT

Creativity is the ability to do things that are novel and useful (Sternberg, 2007). Creative children and adults can solve problems for which there are no preexisting solutions, no tried and tested formulas (Simonton, 2006b). Creative children take chances (Milgram & Livne, 2006; Sternberg, 2006): They refuse to accept limitations. They appreciate art and music. They challenge social norms. They examine ideas that other people accept at face value.

The relationship between creativity and intelligence depends on how one defines intelligence. If one accepts Sternberg's model, creativity is one of the three parts of intelligence (along with analytical intelligence and practical intelligence).

T F Highly intelligent children are creative.
False; although this statement would be generally true according to Sternberg's theory, which considers creativity to be an aspect of intelligence, children with average IQ scores may excel in creative activities such as art and music.

Some scientists argue that creativity and innovation require high levels of general intelligence (Heilman et al., 2003), but the tests we use to measure intelligence and creativity tend to show only a moderate relationship between IQ scores and measures of creativity (Sternberg & Williams, 1997). Some children who obtain average IQ scores excel in creative areas such as music or art.

Children mainly use convergent thinking to arrive at the correct answers on intelligence tests. In **convergent thinking**, thought is limited to present facts; the problem solver narrows his or her thinking to find the best solution. A child uses convergent thinking to arrive at the right answer to a multiple-choice question or to a question on an intelligence test.

Creative thinking tends to be divergent rather than convergent (Vartanian et al., 2003). In **divergent thinking**, the child associates freely to the elements of the problem. (We use divergent thinking when we are trying to generate ideas to answer an essay question or to find keywords to search on the Internet.) Tests of creativity determine how flexible, fluent, and original a person's thinking is. A measure of creativity might ask you how many ways you can classify the following group of names:

Martha   Paul   Jeffrey   Sally   Pablo   Joan

> **creativity** A trait characterized by flexibility, ingenuity, and originality.
>
> **convergent thinking** A thought process that attempts to focus in on the single best solution to a problem.
>
> **divergent thinking** Free and fluent association to the elements of a problem.

Creative thinking tends to be divergent. In divergent thinking, the child associates freely to the elements of the problem.

© iStockphoto.com

Other measures of creativity include suggesting improvements or unusual uses for a familiar toy or object, naming things that belong in the same class, producing words similar in meaning, and writing different endings for a story.

DETERMINANTS OF INTELLECTUAL DEVELOPMENT

If heredity is involved in human intelligence, closely related people ought to have more similar IQs than distantly related or unrelated people, even when the closely related individuals are reared separately. Figure 12.11 shows the averaged results of more than 100 studies of IQ and heredity (Bouchard et al., 1990). The IQ scores of identical (MZ) twins are more alike than the scores for any other pairs of individuals, even when the twins have been reared apart. The average correlation for identical twins reared together is +0.85; for those reared apart, it is +0.67. Correlations between the IQ scores of fraternal (DZ) twins, siblings, and parents and children are generally comparable, as is their degree of genetic relationship. The correlations tend to vary from about +0.40 to +0.59.

Overall, studies suggest that the **heritability** of intelligence is between 40% and 60% (Bouchard et al., 1990; Neisser et al., 1996). About half of the difference between your IQ score and those of other people can be explained in terms of genetic factors.

In Figure 12.11, also note that genetic pairs (identical twins and siblings) reared together show higher correlations between IQ scores than similar genetic pairs who were reared apart. This finding also holds for MZ twins, siblings, parents, children, and unrelated people. For this reason, the same group of studies that suggests that heredity plays a role in determining IQ scores also suggests that the environment plays a role.

When children are separated from their biological parents at early ages, one can argue that strong relationships between their IQ scores and those of their natural parents reflect genetic influences. Strong relationships between their IQs and those of their adoptive parents, on the other hand, might reflect environmental influences. Classic projects involving adopted children in Colorado, Texas, and Minnesota (Iacono et al., 2006; Johnson et al., 2007) have found a stronger relationship between the IQ scores of adopted children and their biological parents than between the IQ scores of adopted children and their adoptive parents.

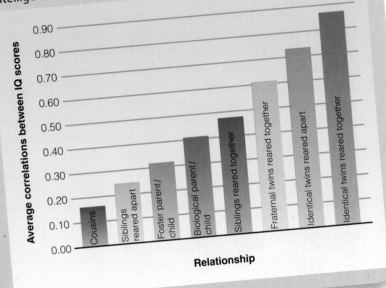

FIGURE 12.11
Findings of Studies of the Relationship Between IQ Scores and Heredity

Correlations are stronger for persons who are more closely related and for persons who are reared together or living together, thus supporting both genetic and environmental hypotheses of the origins of intelligence.

Source: Bouchard, et al. (1990).

T (F) Adopted children are more similar in intelligence to their adoptive parents than to their biological parents.

False; the average correlation between the IQ scores of children and their natural parents (+0.48) is higher than that between children and adoptive parents (+0.18), suggestive of the role of genetic factors in intellectual functioning.

Studies of environmental influences on IQ use several research strategies, including discovering situational factors that affect IQ scores, exploring children's abilities to rebound from early deprivation, and exploring the effects of positive early environments. Children whose parents are responsive and provide appropriate play materials and varied experiences during the early years attain higher IQ and achievement test scores (Bradley, 2006). Graduates of Head Start and other preschool programs also show significant gains in IQ and other test scores (Phillips & Styfco, 2007).

Many psychologists believe that heredity and environment interact to influence intelligence (Lubinski & Benbow, 2000; Winner, 2000). An impoverished environment may prevent some children from living up to their potential. An enriched environment may encourage others to realize their potential.

LO5 Language Development and Literacy

Children's language ability grows more sophisticated in middle childhood. Children learn to read as well. Many children are exposed to a variety of linguistic experiences, and these experiences affect their cognitive development.

VOCABULARY AND GRAMMAR

By the age of 6, the average child's vocabulary has expanded to nearly 10,000 words. By 7 to 9 years of age, most children realize that words can have different meanings, and they become entertained by riddles and jokes that require semantic sophistication. (Remember the joke at the beginning of this chapter.) By the age of 8 or 9, children are able to form *tag questions*, in which a question is tagged onto the end of a declarative sentence, as in "You want more ice cream, don't you?" and "You're sick, aren't you?" (Weckerly et al., 2004).

Children make subtle advances in articulation and in the capacity to use complex grammar. Preschoolers have difficulty understanding passive sentences such as "The truck was hit by the car," but children in the middle years have less difficulty interpreting them (Aschermann et al., 2004).

During these years, children develop the ability to use connectives, as illustrated by the sentence "I'll eat my spinach, but I don't want to." They also learn to form indirect object–direct object constructions (e.g., "She showed her sister the toy").

READING SKILLS AND LITERACY

Table 12.4 reveals that millions of people around the world are not literate and therefore cannot access contemporary knowledge. Even in the United States, some people cannot read or write, and the problem is most severe among recent immigrants.

Reading involves perceptual, cognitive, and linguistic processes (Smolka & Eviatar, 2006). It relies on the integration of visual and auditory information. Children must accurately perceive the sounds in their language and make basic visual discriminations (Levinthal & Lleras, 2007). Children must perceive the visual differences between letters such as *b* and *d* and *p* and *q*.

TABLE 12.4
Literacy Rates of 15- to 24-Year-Olds, 2000–2004

REGION/NATION	TOTAL	MEN	WOMEN
Europe	99.4	99.4	99.3
Northern Africa	78.5	84.1	72.5
Sub-Saharan Africa	76.6	81.0	72.3
Latin America and the Caribbean	94.7	94.2	95.2
Eastern Asia	98.9	99.2	98.6
Southern Asia	72.3	81.5	62.5
Southeastern Asia	95.4	96.0	94.9
United States	97.0	97.0	97.0
Western Asia	85.6	84.4	78.1

Sources: Central Intelligence Agency (2004) and United Nations Statistics Division (2004).

© Image Source

word-recognition method A method for learning to read in which children come to recognize words through repeated exposure to them.

phonetic method A method for learning to read in which children decode the sounds of words based on their knowledge of the sounds of letters and letter combinations.

sight vocabulary Words that are immediately recognized on the basis of familiarity with their overall shapes, rather than decoded.

bilingual Using or capable of using two languages with nearly equal or equal facility.

How do children become familiar with their own written languages? More and more American children are being exposed to TV programs such as *Sesame Street*. Children are exposed to books, street signs, names of stores and restaurants, and the writing on packages. Children from homes where books and other sources of stimulation are plentiful learn to read more readily. Reading storybooks with parents in the preschool years helps prepare a child for learning to read (Dockett et al., 2006; Raikes et al., 2006).

METHODS OF TEACHING READING

Children read by integrating visual and auditory information (they associate what they see with sounds), whether they use the word-recognition method or the phonetic method. The **word-recognition method** associates visual stimuli such as *cat* and *Robert* with the sound combinations that produce the spoken words. This capacity is usually acquired by rote learning, or extensive repetition.

In the **phonetic method**, children learn to associate written letters and letter combinations (such as *ph* or *sh*) with the sounds they indicate. Then they sound out words. The phonetic method provides skills children can use to decode new words, but some children learn more rapidly at early ages through the word-recognition method.

Research shows only some mixing of languages in bilingual children.

The phonetic method can slow their processing of familiar words. Most children and adults read familiar words by word recognition and make some effort to sound out new words.

Some English words can be read only by recognition, as with *one* and *two*. This method is useful when it comes to words such as *danger, stop, poison,* and a child's name, because it provides children with a basic **sight vocabulary**. But decoding skills help children read new words on their own.

BILINGUALISM: LINGUISTIC PERSPECTIVES ON THE WORLD

In 2000, approximately 47 million U.S. residents spoke a language other than English at home (Shin & Bruno, 2003; see Table 12.5). Spanish, Chinese, Korean, or Russian is spoken in many U.S. homes and neighborhoods.

Bilingual children do not encounter more academic problems than children who speak only one language. Nevertheless, a century ago it was widely believed that children reared in bilingual homes were deficient in their cognitive development. The theory was that mental capacity is limited, so people who store two linguistic systems are crowding their mental abilities. Despite these concerns, the evidence shows that although there is some "mixing" of languages by bilingual children (Gonzalez, 2005), they can generally separate the two languages from an early age. At least half the children in the United States who speak Spanish in the home are proficient in both Spanish and English (Shin & Bruno, 2003).

Today, most linguists consider it advantageous for children to be bilingual because knowledge of more than one language contributes to the complexity of the child's cognitive processes (Bialystok & Craik, 2007; Gort, 2006). For example, bilingual children are more likely to understand that the symbols used in language are arbitrary. Monolingual children are more likely to think erroneously that the word *dog* is somehow intertwined with the nature of the beast. Bilingual children therefore have somewhat more cognitive flexibility.

T F Bilingual children do not encounter more academic problems than children who speak only one language.

True, and bilingualism may very well contribute to children's cognitive flexibility.

© Rubberball/Jupiterimages

TABLE 12.5

Languages Most Often Spoken at Home According to English Ability for U.S. Residents 5 Years of Age and Above

LANGUAGE SPOKEN AT HOME	TOTAL	ENGLISH-SPEAKING ABILITY (PERCENTS)			
		VERY WELL	WELL	NOT WELL	NOT AT ALL
Spanish	28,101,052	51.1%	20.1%	18.0%	9.9%
Chinese	2,022,143	42.3%	29.4%	20.2%	8.0%
French	1,643,838	74.8%	16.4%	8.4%	0.5%
German	1,382,613	78.1%	15.9%	5.8%	0.3%
Tagalog	1,224,241	67.6%	25.4%	6.5%	0.4%
Vietnamese	1,009,627	33.9%	33.7%	26.8%	5.5%
Italian	1,008,370	69.5%	19.4%	9.8%	1.2%
Korean	894,063	40.4%	30.0%	25.5%	4.0%
Russian	706,242	43.2%	29.6%	21.2%	6.2%
Polish	667,414	58.1%	25.1%	14.2%	2.6%
Arabic	614,582	65.6%	22.8%	9.5%	2.0%
Portuguese	564,630	56.8%	22.2%	16.0%	5.0%
Japanese	477,997	50.6%	30.7%	17.6%	1.2%
French Creole	453,368	54.2%	26.9%	15.7%	3.2%
Greek	365,436	71.9%	17.8%	9.1%	1.2%
Hindi	317,057	77.3%	16.4%	5.3%	1.0%
Persian	312,085	63.5%	22.7%	10.6%	3.3%
Urdu	262,900	68.5%	21.6%	7.9%	2.0%

Source: Adapted from U.S. Census Bureau. (2007, July). Census 2000 Summary File 3. SF3/18 (RV). Technical documentation. Retrieved from www.census.gov/prod/cen2000/doc/sf3.pdf.

In the years between 6 and 12,

the child's social world expands.

13

Middle Childhood: Social and Emotional Development

TRUTH OR FICTION?

T F Children's self-esteem tends to rise in middle childhood.

T F The daughters of employed women are more achievement oriented and set higher career goals for themselves than the daughters of unemployed women do.

T F In middle childhood, popular children tend to be attractive and relatively mature for their age.

T F Some children blame themselves for all the problems in their lives, whether they deserve the blame or not.

T F It is better for children with school phobia to remain at home until the origins of the problem are uncovered and resolved.

In the years between the ages of 6 and 12, the child's social world expands. Peers take on greater importance and friendships deepen. Entry into school exposes the child to the influence of teachers. Relationships with parents change as children develop greater independence.

LO1 Theories of Social and Emotional Development in Middle Childhood

he major theories of personality have had less to say about this age group than about the other periods of childhood and adolescence. Nevertheless, common threads emerge.

PSYCHOANALYTIC THEORY

According to Freud, children in the middle years are in the **latency stage**. Freud believed that sexual feelings remain repressed (unconscious)

latency stage In psychoanalytic theory, the fourth stage of psychosexual development, characterized by repression of sexual impulses and development of skills.

Learning Outcomes

LO1 Explain theories of social and emotional development in middle childhood.

LO2 Discuss the influences of the family on social development in middle childhood.

LO3 Discuss the influences of peers on social development in middle childhood.

LO4 Discuss the influence of the school on development in middle childhood.

LO5 Discuss social and emotional problems that tend to develop in middle childhood.

during this period. Children use this period to focus on developing intellectual, social, and other culturally valued skills.

Erik Erikson, like Freud, sees the major developmental task of middle childhood as the acquisition of cognitive and social skills. Erikson labels this stage **industry versus inferiority**. Children who are able to master the challenges of the middle years develop a sense of industry or competence. Children who have difficulties in school or with peer relationships may develop a sense of inferiority.

SOCIAL COGNITIVE THEORY

Social cognitive theory focuses on the importance of rewards and modeling in middle childhood. During these years, children depend less on external rewards and punishments and increasingly regulate their own behavior. Children are exposed to an increasing variety of models. Not only parents but also teachers, other adults, peers, and symbolic models (such as TV characters or the heroine in a story) serve as influential models (Anderson et al., 2007; Oates & Messer, 2007).

COGNITIVE-DEVELOPMENTAL THEORY AND SOCIAL COGNITION

According to Piaget, middle childhood coincides with the stage of concrete operations and is partly characterized by a decline in egocentrism and an expansion of the capacity to view the world and oneself from other people's perspectives. This cognitive advance affects the child's social relationships (Mischo, 2004; Zan & Hildebrandt, 2003).

Social cognition refers to perception of the social world and the relationships between self and others, which requires the development of children's perspective-taking skills. Robert Selman and his colleagues (Selman, 1980; Selman & Dray, 2006) studied the development of these skills by presenting children with a social dilemma such as the one in "Holly's Dilemma."

HOLLY'S DILEMMA

Holly is an 8-year-old girl who likes to climb trees. She is the best tree climber in the neighborhood. One day while climbing down from a tall tree, she falls off the bottom branch but does not hurt herself. Her father sees her fall. He is upset and asks her to promise not to climb trees any more. Holly promises. Later that day, Holly and her friends meet Sean. Sean's kitten is caught up in a tree and can't get down. Something has to be done right away, or the kitten may fall. Holly is the only one who climbs trees well enough to reach the kitten and get it down, but she remembers her promise to her father.

—Selman (1980, p. 36)

The children then were asked questions such as "How will Holly's father feel if he finds out she climbed the tree?" Based on the children's responses, Selman (1976) described five levels of perspective-taking skills in childhood (see Table 13.1). Children with better perspective-taking skills tend to have better peer relationships (Selman & Dray, 2006).

DEVELOPMENT OF THE SELF-CONCEPT IN MIDDLE CHILDHOOD

In early childhood, children's self-concepts focus on concrete external traits, such as appearance, activities, and living situations. But as children undergo the cognitive developments of middle childhood, more abstract internal traits, or personality traits, begin to play a role. Social relationships and group memberships take on significance (Harter, 2006; Thompson, 2006).

An investigative method called the Twenty Statements Test bears out this progression. Children are given a sheet of paper with the question "Who am I?" and 20 spaces in which to write answers. Consider the answers of a 9-year-old boy and an 11-year-old girl:

The nine-year-old boy: My name is Bruce C. I have brown eyes. I have brown hair. I have brown eyebrows. I'm 9 years old. I LOVE? sports. I have 7 people in my family. I have great? eye site. I have lots! of friends. I live on 1923 Pinecrest Drive. I'm going on 10 in September. I'm a boy. I have an uncle that is almost

TABLE 13.1
Levels of Perspective Taking

LEVEL	APPROXIMATE AGE (YEARS)[a]	WHAT HAPPENS
0	3–6	Children are egocentric and do not realize that other people have perspectives different from their own. A child of this age will typically say that Holly will save the kitten because she likes kittens and that her father will be happy because he likes kittens too. The child assumes that everyone feels as she does.
1	5–9	Children understand that people in different situations may have different perspectives. The child still assumes that only one perspective is "right." A child might say that Holly's father would be angry if he did not know why she climbed the tree. But if she told him why, he would understand. The child recognizes that the father's perspective may differ from Holly's because of lack of information. But once he has the information, he will assume the "right" (i.e., Holly's) perspective.
2	7–12	The child understands that people may think or feel differently because they have different values or ideas. The child also recognizes that others are capable of understanding the child's own perspective. Therefore, the child is better able to anticipate reactions of others. The typical child of this age might say that Holly knows that her father will understand why she climbed the tree and that he therefore will not punish her.
3	10–15	The child finally realizes that both she and another person can consider each other's point of view at the same time. The child may say something similar to this reasoning: Holly's father will think that Holly shouldn't have climbed the tree. But when he has heard her side of the story, he will feel that she was doing what she thought was right. Holly realizes that her father will consider how she felt.
4	12 and above	The child realizes that mutual perspective taking does not always lead to agreement. The perspectives of the larger social group also must be considered. A child of this age might say that society expects children to obey their parents and therefore that Holly should realize why her father might punish her.

Source: Selman (1976).
[a]Note that age ranges overlap.

7 feet tall. My school is Pinecrest. My teacher is Mrs. V. I play hockey! I'm also the smartest boy in the class. I LOVE! food. I love fresh air. I LOVE school.

The eleven-year-old girl: My name is A. I'm a human being. I'm a girl. I'm a truthful person. I'm not pretty. I do so-so in my studies. I'm a very good cellist. I'm a very good pianist. I'm a little bit tall for my age. I like several boys. I like several girls. I'm old fashioned. I play tennis. I am a very good musician. I try to be helpful. I'm always ready to be friends with anybody. Mostly I'm good, but I lose my temper. I'm not well liked by some girls and boys. I don't know if boys like me or not.

—Montemayor & Eisen (1977, pp. 317–318)

Only the 9-year-old lists his age and address, discusses his family, and focuses on physical traits, such as eye color, in his self-definition. The 9-year-old mentions his likes, which can be considered rudimentary psychological

learned helplessness
An acquired (hence, learned) belief that one is unable to control one's environment.

traits, but they are tied to the concrete, as would be expected of a concrete-operational child. The 9- and 11-year-olds both list their competencies. The 11-year-old's struggle to bolster her self-esteem—her insistence on her musical abilities despite her qualms about her attractiveness—shows a greater concern with psychological traits and social relationships.

Self-Esteem

As children enter middle childhood, they evaluate their self-worth in many different areas (Tassi et al., 2001). Preschoolers tend to see themselves as generally "good at doing things" or not. But by 5 to 7 years of age, children are able to judge their performance in seven different areas: physical ability, physical appearance, peer relationships, parent relationships, reading, math, and general school performance. They also report a general self-concept (Harter, 2006).

Children's self-esteem declines throughout middle childhood, reaching a low ebb at 12 or 13. Then it increases during adolescence (Harter, 2006). What accounts for the decline? Because preschoolers are egocentric, their self-concepts may be unrealistic. By middle childhood, children can compare themselves with other children and arrive at a more honest and critical self-appraisal. Girls tend to have more positive self-concepts than boys do regarding reading, general academics, and helping others. Boys tend to have more positive self-concepts in math, physical ability, and physical appearance (Jacobs et al., 2005; Wang, 2005).

© Jim Kolaczko/iStockphoto.com

T **F** Children's self-esteem tends to rise in middle childhood.

False; self-esteem usually declines in middle childhood.

Authoritative parenting apparently contributes to children's self-esteem (Baumrind, 1991a, 1991b; Supple & Small, 2006). Children with a favorable self-image tend to have parents who are restrictive, involved, and loving. Children with low self-esteem are more likely to have authoritarian or rejecting–neglecting parents.

Social acceptance by peers is related to self-perceived competence in academic, social, and athletic domains (Nesdale & Lambert, 2007). Parents and classmates have an equally strong effect on children's self-esteem in middle childhood. Friends and teachers have relatively less influence but also matter (Harter, 2006).

Learned Helplessness

One outcome of low self-esteem about academics is known as **learned helplessness**. Learned helplessness is the acquired belief that one is unable to obtain the rewards that one seeks. "Helpless" children tend to quit after experiencing failure, whereas children who believe in their own ability tend to persist or change their strategies (Zimmerman, 2000). One reason for this difference is that helpless children believe that success is due more to ability than effort and that they have little ability in a particular area. Consequently, persistence seems futile (Bandura et al., 2001). Helpless children typically obtain lower grades and lower scores on IQ and achievement tests (Goldstein & Brooks, 2005).

A sex difference in mathematics emerges in middle childhood (Simpkins et al., 2006). Researchers have found that even when girls are performing as well as boys in math and science, they have less confidence in their abilities (Anderman et al., 2001). Why? Many parents hold the stereotype that girls have less math ability than boys despite their daughters' abilities.

LO2 The Family

n middle childhood, the family continues to play a key role in socializing the child, although peers, teachers, and other outsiders begin to play a greater role (Harter, 2006).

PARENT–CHILD RELATIONSHIPS

Parent–child interactions focus on some new concerns during middle childhood. These include school-related matters, assignment of chores, and peer activities (Collins et al., 2003). Parents do less monitoring of children's activities and provide less direct feedback than they did in the preschool years. Control is gradually transferred from parent to child in a process known as **coregulation** (Maccoby, 2002; Wahler et al., 2001). Children begin to internalize the standards of their parents.

Children and parents spend less time together in middle childhood than in the preschool years. Children spend more time with their mothers than with their fathers. Mothers' interactions with school-age children continue to revolve around caregiving; fathers are relatively more involved in recreation (Wolfenden & Holt, 2005).

Because of their developing cognitive ability, 10- to 12-year-olds evaluate their parents more harshly than they did in early childhood (Selman & Dray, 2006). But throughout middle childhood, children rate their parents as their best source of emotional support (Cowan & Cowan, 2005; Katz et al., 2005).

LESBIAN AND GAY PARENTS

"Where did you get that beautiful necklace?" I asked the little girl in the pediatrician's office. "From my Moms," she answered. It turned out that her family consisted of two women, each of whom had a biological child, one girl and one boy.

Research studies on lesbian and gay parenting fit into two general categories: those that focus on the general adjustment of children of lesbian and gay parents and those that explore whether these children are more likely than other children to be lesbian or gay themselves. Research by Charlotte Patterson (2006) has generally found that the psychological adjustment of children of lesbian and gay parents is comparable to that of children of heterosexual parents. Despite the stigma attached to homosexuality, many lesbians and gay men sustain positive family relationships (Wainright et al., 2004).

What of the sexual orientation of the children of lesbian and gay parents? Green (1978) observed

37 children and young adults, aged 3 to 20, who were being reared—or had been reared—by lesbians or **transsexuals**. All but one of the children reported or recalled preferences for toys, clothing, and friends (male or female) that were typical for their sex and age. All of the 13 older children who reported sexual fantasies or sexual behavior were heterosexually oriented.

> **coregulation** A gradual transferring of control from parent to child, beginning in middle childhood.
>
> **transsexual** A person who would prefer to be a person of the other sex and who may undergo hormone treatments, cosmetic surgery, or both to achieve the appearance of being a member of the other sex.

GENERATION X OR GENERATION EX? WHAT HAPPENS TO CHILDREN WHOSE PARENTS GET DIVORCED?

Is this the time of "Generation Ex"—a generation characterized by ex-wives and ex-husbands? More than 1 million American children each year experience the divorce of their parents. Nearly 40% of European American children and 75% of African American children in the United States who are born to married parents will spend at least part of their childhoods in single-parent families as a result of divorce (Marsiglio, 2004).

Divorce may be tough on parents; it can be even tougher on children (Amato, 2006). No longer do children eat with both parents. No longer do they go to ball games, movies, or Disneyland with both of them. The parents are now often supporting two households, resulting in fewer resources for the children (Tashiro et al., 2006). Many children who live with their mothers scrape by—or fail to scrape by—in poverty. The mother who was once always available may become inaccessible spending more time at work and placing the kids in day care for extended periods.

Most children live with their mothers after a divorce (Amato, 2006). Some fathers remain devoted to their children despite the split, but others tend to spend less time with their children as time

© U.P. Images/iStockphoto.com / © Mike Kemp/Rubberball/Jupiterimages

goes on. Not only does the drop-off in paternal attention deprive children of activities and social interactions, but it also saps their self-esteem: "Why doesn't Daddy love me anymore? What's wrong with me?"

The children of divorce are more likely to have conduct disorders, abuse drugs, and perform poorly in school (Amato, 2006). Their physical health may decline (Troxel & Matthews, 2004). By and large, the fallout for children is worst during the first year after the breakup. Children tend to rebound after a couple of years or so (Malone et al., 2004).

Life in Stepfamilies: His, Hers, Theirs, and …

Most divorced people remarry, usually while the children are young. More than one in three American children will spend part of his or her childhood in a stepfamily (U.S. Census Bureau, 2004).

The rule of thumb about the effects of living in stepfamilies is that there is no rule of thumb (Coleman et al., 2000). Stepparents may claim stepchildren as their own (Marsiglio, 2004). There are also some risks to living in stepfamilies, such as the greater risk of being physically abused by stepparents than by biological parents (Adler-Baeder, 2006). There is also a significantly higher incidence—by a factor of eight—of sexual abuse by stepparents than by natural parents.

Why do we find these risks in stepfamilies? According to evolutionary psychologists, people often behave as though they want their genes to flourish in the next generation. Thus, it could be that stepparents are less devoted to rearing other people's children.

Should We Remain Married "for the Sake of the Children?"

Many people believe—for moral reasons—that marriage and family life must be permanent, no matter what. We all have to consider the moral aspects of divorce in light of our own value systems. But—from a purely psychological perspective—what should bickering parents do? The answer seems to depend largely on how they behave in front of the children. Research shows that severe parental bickering is linked to the same kinds of problems that children experience when their parents get separated or divorced (Troxel & Matthews, 2004). When children are exposed to adult or marital conflict, they display a biological *alarm reaction*: their heart rate, blood pressure, and sweating rise sharply (El-Sheikh, 2007). Therefore, Hetherington and her colleagues suggest that divorce can be a posi-

When children are exposed to adult or marital conflict they display a biological alarm reaction.

© IFA Bilderteam/Jupiterimages

tive alternative to family conflict (Hetherington, 1989; Wallerstein et al., 2005).

THE EFFECTS OF MATERNAL EMPLOYMENT

Why is this section titled "The Effects of Maternal Employment"? Why not "Parental Employment" or "Paternal Employment"? Perhaps because of the traditional role of women as homemakers. A half-century ago, most women remained in the home, but today, nearly three out of four married mothers of children under age 18 are employed, as are four out of five divorced, separated, or widowed mothers (U.S. Census Bureau, 2007).

Many commentators have been concerned about the effects of maternal employment on children. In part, this concern has been based on more traditional values that call for the mother to remain in the home. But concern has also been based on research findings that suggest that maternal employment (and nonmaternal care) have some negative effects on children (Belsky, 2006b).

One common belief is that Mom's being in the workforce rather than in the home leads to delinquency. Researchers using data on 707 adolescents, aged 12 to 14, from the National Longitudinal Survey of Youth examined whether the occupational status of a mother was connected with delinquent behavior (Vander Ven & Cullen, 2004). They found that maternal employment in and of itself made no difference, but delinquency *was* connected with lack of supervision.

LO3 Peer Relationships

families exert the most powerful influences on a child during his or her first few years. But as children move into middle childhood, peers take on more importance.

PEERS AS SOCIALIZATION INFLUENCES

Parents can only provide children with experience relating to adults. Children profit from experience with peers because peers have interests and skills that are those of the same generation (Molinari & Corsaro, 2000).

Peers afford practice in cooperating, relating to leaders, and coping with aggressive impulses, both others' and one's own. Peers can be important confidants (Dunn et al., 2001; Hanlon et al., 2004). Peers, like parents, help children learn what types of impulses—affectionate, aggressive, and so on—they can safely express. Children who are at odds with their parents can turn to peers as sounding boards. They can compare feelings and experiences. When children share troubling ideas and experiences with peers, they realize they are normal and not alone (Barry & Wentzel, 2006).

PEER ACCEPTANCE AND REJECTION

Acceptance or rejection by peers is important in childhood because problems with peers affect adjustment later on (Wentzel et al., 2004). Popular children tend to be attractive, although attractiveness seems to be more important for girls than boys (Langlois et al., 2000). They also have high self-esteem.

Children who are aggressive and disrupt group activities are more likely to be rejected by peers (Boivin et al.,

2005; Wojslawowicz Bowker et al., 2006). Most rejected children do not learn to conform. Instead, they remain on the fringes of the group and may find aggressive friends (Digout Erhardt, 2005; Rose et al., 2004).

DEVELOPMENT OF FRIENDSHIPS

In the preschool years and early years of middle childhood, friendships are based on geographic closeness or proximity. Friendships are superficial: quickly formed, easily broken. What matters are shared activities and who has the swing set or sandbox (Berndt, 2004; Gleason et al., 2005).

Between the ages of 8 and 11, children recognize the importance of friends meeting each other's needs and possessing desirable traits (Zarbatany et al., 2004). They are more likely to say that friends are nice and share their interests. They increasingly pick friends who are similar in behavior and personality. Trustworthiness, mutual under-standing, and a willingness to disclose personal information characterize friendships in middle childhood and beyond (Rotenberg et al., 2004; Wojslawowicz Bowker et al., 2006). Girls tend to develop closer friendships than boys do and to seek confidants (Zarbatany et al., 2000).

Robert Selman (1980) described five stages in children's changing concepts of friendship (see Table 13.2). The stages correspond to the levels of perspective-taking skills discussed earlier.

Friends behave differently with each other than with other children. School-age friends are more verbal, attentive, relaxed, and responsive to each other during play than are mere acquaintances (Cleary et al., 2002). Conflicts can occur among friends, but when they do, they tend to be less intense and get resolved in positive ways (Wojslawowicz Bowker et al., 2006).

Children in middle childhood will typically say they have more than one "best" friend (Wojslawowicz Bowker, et al., 2006). Nine-year-olds report an average of four best friends (Lewis & Feiring, 1989). Best friends tend to be more like a child than his or her other friends are.

TABLE 13.2
Stages in Children's Concepts of Friendship

STAGE	NAME	APPROXIMATE AGE (YEARS)[a]	WHAT HAPPENS
0	Momentary physical interaction	3–6	Children remain egocentric. Their concept of a friend is someone who likes to play with the same things and lives nearby.
1	One-way assistance	5–9	Children are less egocentric but view a friend as someone who does what they want.
2	Fair-weather cooperation	7–12	Friends are viewed as doing things for one another, but the focus remains on self-interest.
3	Intimate and mutual sharing	10–15	The focus is on the relationship rather than on the individuals separately. Friendship is viewed as providing mutual support over a long period of time.
4	Autonomous interdependence	12 and above	Children (and adolescents and adults) understand that friendships grow and change as people change and that a person may need different friends to satisfy different needs.

Source: Selman (1980).
[a]Note that age ranges overlap.

In middle childhood, boys tend to play in larger groups than girls. Children's friendships are almost exclusively with others of the same sex, continuing the trend of sex segregation (Hartup, 1983).

LO4 The School

the school exerts a powerful influence on many aspects of a child's development. Schools, like parents, set limits on behavior, make demands for mature behavior, attempt to communicate, and are oriented toward nurturing positive physical, social, and cognitive development. Schools influence children's IQ scores, achievement motivation, and career aspirations (Aber et al., 2007; Woolfolk, 2008). Schools also influence social and moral development (Killen & Smetana, 2006).

Schools are also competitive environments, and children who do too well—and students who do not do well enough—may incur the resentment or ridicule of others.

ENTRY INTO SCHOOL

Children must master many new tasks when they start school—new academic challenges, new school and teacher expectations, fitting into a new peer group, coping with extended separation from parents, and developing increased self-control and self-help skills.

How well prepared are children to enter school? School readiness depends on at least three critical factors:

1. The diversity and inequity of children's early life experiences

2. Individual differences in young children's development and learning

3. The degree to which schools establish reasonable and appropriate expectations of children's capabilities when they enter school

Some children enter school less well prepared than others. Kindergarten teachers report that many students begin school unprepared to learn (Slavin, 2009; Woolfolk, 2008). Most teachers say that children often lack the language skills needed to succeed. Poor health care and nutrition, and lack of adequate parental stimulation and support place many children at risk for academic failure before they enter school.

THE SCHOOL ENVIRONMENT: SETTING THE STAGE FOR SUCCESS, OR ...

Research summaries (Slavin, 2009; Woolfolk, 2008) indicate that an effective school has the following characteristics:

- An active, energetic principal
- An orderly but not oppressive atmosphere
- Empowerment of teachers, that is, teachers' participation in decision making
- Teachers with high expectations that children will learn
- A curriculum that emphasizes academics
- Frequent assessment of student performance
- Empowerment of students, that is, students' participation in setting goals, making decisions, and engaging in cooperative learning activities

Other aspects of the school environment are important as well. One key factor is class size. Smaller classes permit students to receive more individual attention and are particularly useful in teaching the "basics"—reading, writing, and arithmetic—to students at risk for academic failure (Slavin, 2009; Woolfolk, 2008).

TEACHERS

Teachers, like parents, set limits, make demands, communicate values, and foster development. They are powerful role models and dispensers of reinforcement. After all, children spend several hours each weekday with teachers.

Bullying

Nine-year-old Stephanie appeared anxious at the thought of going to school, but this was not a case of separation anxiety. She had gotten into a disagreement with Susan, and Susan had shoved Stephanie across the hall and said she would beat Stephanie mercilessly if she came to school again. Stephanie was a victim of bullying. Susan was a bully. Stephanie did not know it, but Susan was also bullied by a couple of other girls.

Boys are more likely than girls to be bullies, but many girls engage in bullying (Perren & Alsaker, 2006). Children who speak another language in the home also tend to be picked on more often (Yu et al., 2003). It is estimated that 70% to 75% of students have been bullied (Li, 2007).

Bullying transforms the perception of school from a safe place into a violent place (Lazar, 2008). Bullying also impairs adjustment to middle school, where older children sometimes bully younger children (Scheithauer et al., 2006).

Many bullies have things in common. Their grades tend to be lower than average, so peer approval might be more important to them than academics (Perren & Alsaker, 2006). Bullies are more likely to come from homes of lower socioeconomic status, where there is violence between parents (Baldry, 2003; Pereira et al., 2004).

Pygmalion effect
The fulfillment of positive expectations due to the behavior of those who hold the expectations.

self-fulfilling prophecy
An event that occurs because of the behavior of those who expect it to occur.

sexism Discrimination or bias against people based on their sex.

Teacher Influences on Student Performance

Achievement is enhanced when teachers expect students to master the curriculum, allocate most of the available time to academic activities, and manage the classroom effectively. Students learn more in classes when they are actively instructed or supervised by teachers than when they are working on their own. The most effective teachers ask questions, give personalized feedback, and provide opportunities for drill and practice (Slavin, 2009).

Student achievement also is linked to the emotional climate of the classroom (Slavin, 2009; Woolfolk, 2008). Students do not do as well when teachers rely heavily on criticism, ridicule, threats, or punishment. Achievement is high in classrooms with a pleasant, friendly—but not overly warm—atmosphere.

Teacher Expectations

There is a saying that "you find what you're looking for." Consider the so-called **Pygmalion effect** in education. In Greek mythology, the amorous sculptor Pygmalion breathed life into a beautiful statue he had carved. Teachers also try to bring out positive traits they believe dwell within their students. A classic experiment by Robert Rosenthal and Lenore Jacobson (1968) suggested that teacher expectations can become **self-fulfilling prophecies**. Rosenthal and Jacobson first gave students a battery of psychological tests. Then they informed teachers that a handful of the students, although average in performance to date, were about to blossom forth intellectually in the current school year.

In fact, the tests indicated nothing about the "chosen" children. These children had been selected at random. The purpose of the experiment was to determine whether enhancing teacher expectations could affect student performance. It did; the identified children made significant gains in IQ scores.

In subsequent research, however, results have been mixed. Some studies have found support for the Pygmalion effect (Madon et al., 2001; Sarrazin et al., 2005a, 2005b). Others have not. But these findings have serious implications for children from ethnic minority and low-income families because there is some indication that teachers expect less from children in these groups (Slavin, 2009; Woolfolk, 2008). Teachers who expect less may spend less time encouraging and working with children.

What are some of the ways that teachers can help motivate all students to do their best? Anita Woolfolk (2008) suggests the following:

- Make the classroom and the lesson interesting and inviting.
- Ensure that students can profit from social interaction.
- Make the classroom a safe and pleasant place.
- Recognize that students' backgrounds can give rise to diverse patterns of needs.
- Help students take appropriate responsibility for their successes and failures.
- Encourage students to perceive the links between their own efforts and their achievements.
- Help students set attainable short-term goals.

Sexism in the Classroom

Although girls were systematically excluded from formal education for centuries, we do not expect to find **sexism** among teachers today. Teachers, after all, are generally well educated. They are also trained to be fair-minded and sensitive to the needs of their young charges in today's changing society.

However, we may not have heard the last of sexism in our schools. According to a classic review of more than 1,000 research publications about girls and education, girls are treated unequally by their teachers, their male peers, and the school curriculum (American Association of University Women [AAUW], 1992). The reviewers concluded:

- Many teachers pay less attention to girls than boys, especially in math, science, and technology classes.

- Many girls are subjected to **sexual harassment**—unwelcome verbal or physical conduct of a sexual nature—from male classmates, and many teachers ignore it.
- Some textbooks still stereotype or ignore women, portraying males as the shakers and movers in the world.

In a widely cited study, Myra Sadker and David Silber (2007) observed students in fourth-, sixth-, and eighth-grade classes in four states and in the District of Columbia. Teachers and students were European American and African American, urban, suburban, and rural. In almost all cases, the findings were depressingly similar. Boys generally dominated classroom communication, whether the subject was math (a traditionally "masculine" area) or language arts (a traditionally "feminine" area). Despite the stereotype that girls are more likely to talk or even chatter, boys were eight times more likely than girls to call out answers without raising their hands. So far, it could be said, we have evidence of a sex difference, but not of sexism. However, teachers were less than impartial in responding to boys and girls when they called out. Teachers, male and female, were more likely to accept calling out from boys. Girls were more likely to be reminded that they should raise their hands and wait to be called on. Boys, it appears, are expected to be impetuous, but girls are reprimanded for "unladylike behavior." Until they saw videotapes of themselves, the teachers were largely unaware they were treating girls and boys differently.

LO5 Social and Emotional Problems

millions of children in the United States suffer from emotional or behavioral problems that could profit from professional treatment, but most of them are unlikely to receive it. Here, we focus on conduct disorders, depression, and anxiety.

David is a 16-year-old high school dropout. He has just been arrested for the third time in 2 years for stealing video equipment and computers from people's homes. Acting alone, David was caught in each case when he tried to sell the stolen items. In describing his actions in each crime, David expressed defiance and showed a lack of remorse. In fact, he bragged about how often he had gotten away with similar crimes.

—Adapted from Halgin & Whitbourne (1993, p. 335)

CONDUCT DISORDERS

David has a **conduct disorder**. Children with conduct disorders persistently break rules or violate the rights of others. They exhibit behaviors such as lying, stealing, fire setting, truancy, cruelty to animals, and fighting (American Psychiatric Association, 2000). Conduct disorders typically emerge by 8 years of age and are much more common among boys than girls (Nock et al., 2006).

Children with conduct disorders are often involved in sexual activity before puberty and smoke,

sexual harassment Unwelcome verbal or physical conduct of a sexual nature.

conduct disorders Disorders marked by persistent breaking of rules and violations of the rights of others.

attributional style The way in which one is disposed to interpret outcomes (successes or failures), tending to place blame or responsibility on oneself or on external factors.

drink, and abuse other substances. They have a low tolerance for frustration and may have temper flare-ups. They tend to blame other people for their scrapes. Academic achievement is usually below grade level, but intelligence is usually at least average. Many children with conduct disorders also are diagnosed with ADHD (Chronis et al., 2007).

Origins of Conduct Disorders

Conduct disorders may have a genetic component (Scourfield et al., 2004). Other contributing factors include antisocial family members, deviant peers, inconsistent discipline, parental insensitivity to the child's behavior, physical punishment, and family stress (Black, 2007).

Treatment of Conduct Disorders

The treatment of conduct disorders is challenging, but it seems that cognitive-behavioral techniques involving parent training hold promise (Kazdin, 2000; Sukhodolsky et al., 2005). Children profit from interventions in which their behavior is monitored closely, there are consequences (such as time-outs) for unacceptable behavior, physical punishment is avoided, and positive social behavior is rewarded (Cavell, 2001).

CHILDHOOD DEPRESSION

KRISTIN'S DEPRESSION

Kristin, age 11, feels "nothing is working out for me." For the past year, she has been failing in school, although she previously had been a B student. She has trouble sleeping, feels tired all the time, and has started refusing to go to school. She cries easily and thinks her peers are making fun of her because she is "ugly and stupid." Her mother recently found a note written by Kristin that said she wanted to jump in front of a car "to end my misery."

—Adapted from Weller & Weller (1991, p. 655)

Many children, like Kristin, are depressed. Depressed children may feel sad, blue, or down in the dumps. They may show poor appetite, insomnia, lack of energy and inactivity, loss of self-esteem, difficulty concentrating, loss of interest in people and activities they usually enjoy, crying, feelings of hopelessness and helplessness, and thoughts of suicide (American Psychiatric Association, 2000).

But many children do not recognize depression in themselves until the age of 7 or so. When children cannot report their feelings, depression is inferred from behavior, such as withdrawal from social activity. In some cases, childhood depression is masked by conduct disorders, physical complaints, academic problems, and anxiety.

It has been estimated that between 5% and 9% of children are seriously depressed in any given year. Depression occurs equally often in girls and boys.

Origins of Depression

The origins of depression are complex and varied. Psychological and biological explanations have been proposed.

Some social cognitive theorists explain depression in terms of relationships between competencies (knowledge and skills) and feelings of self-esteem. Children who gain academic, social, and other competencies tend to be admired by peers, usually leading to high self-esteem. Perceived low levels of competence or rejection by peers are linked to low self-esteem and depression (Pedersen et al., 2007). Longitudinal studies have found that problems in academics, socializing, physical appearance, and sports can predict feelings of depression (Kistner, 2006). Some competent children might not give themselves enough credit because of excessive parental expectations. Or children may be perfectionistic themselves. Perfectionistic children may be depressed because they cannot meet their own standards.

A tendency to blame oneself (an internal attribution) or others (an external attribution) is called a child's **attributional style**. Certain attributional styles can contribute to helplessness and hopelessness and hence to depression (Kagan et al., 2004; Runyon & Kenny, 2002).

T F Some children blame themselves for all the problems in their lives, whether they deserve the blame or not.
True; such inappropriate self-blame is connected with feelings of depression.

Research shows that children who are depressed are more likely to attribute the causes of their failures to internal, stable, and global factors, factors they are relatively helpless to change (Lewinsohn et al., 2000). Helplessness triggers depression. Consider the case of two children who do poorly on a math test. John thinks, "I'm a jerk! I'm just no good in math! I'll never learn." Jim thinks, "That test was tougher than I thought it would be. I'll have to work harder next time." John is perceiving the problem as global (he's "a jerk") and stable (he'll "never learn"). Jim perceives the problem as specific rather than global (related to the type of math test the teacher makes up) and as unstable rather than stable (he can change the results by working harder). In effect, John thinks "It's me" (an internal attribution). By contrast, Jim thinks "It's the test" (an external attribution). Depressed children tend to explain negative events in terms of internal, stable, and global causes. As a result, they, like John, are more likely than Jim to be depressed.

There is also evidence of genetic factors in depression (Kendler et al., 2007). A Norwegian study of 2,794 twins estimated that the heritability of depression was 49% in females and 25% in males (Orstavik et al., 2007). On a neurological level, evidence suggests that the brains of depressed children (and adults) underutilize the neurotransmitter **serotonin** (Vitiello, 2006).

Treatment of Depression

Parents and teachers can do a good deal to alleviate relatively mild feelings of depression among children—involve them in enjoyable activities, encourage them to develop skills, praise them when appropriate, and point out when they are being too hard on themselves. But if feelings of depression persist, treatment is called for.

Psychotherapy for depression currently tends to be cognitive-behavioral. Children (and adolescents) are encouraged to do enjoyable things and build social skills. They are made aware of their tendencies to minimize their accomplishments, exaggerate their problems, and overly blame themselves for shortcomings (e.g., Ellis & Dryden, 1996).

Because the brains of depressed children may underutilize serotonin, drugs that increase the action of this neurotransmitter in the brain (selective serotonin reuptake inhibitors, or SSRIs, e.g., Luvox, Pro-

© Rubberball/Jupiterimages

zac, and Zoloft) are sometimes used to treat childhood depression. Although SSRIs are often effective, the Food and Drug Administration has warned that there may be a link between their use and suicidal thinking in children (Harris, 2004).

CHILDHOOD ANXIETY

Children show many kinds of anxiety disorders, and they are accompanied by depression in 50% to 60% of children (Kendler et al., 2007). Yet many children show anxiety disorders, such as **generalized anxiety disorder**, in the absence of depression (Kearney & Bensaheb, 2007). Other anxiety disorders shown by children include **phobias**, such as **separation anxiety disorder** and stage fright. (Beidel & Turner, 2007).

Separation Anxiety Disorder

It is normal for children to show anxiety when they are separated from their caregivers. Separation anxiety is normal and begins during the first year. But the sense of security that is usually provided by bonds of attachment encourages children to explore their environment and become progressively independent.

Separation anxiety disorder affects an estimated 4% to 5% of children and young adolescents (American Psychiatric Association, 2000; Shear et al., 2006). It occurs more often in girls and is often associated with school refusal. The disorder may persist into adulthood, leading to an exaggerated concern about the well-being of one's children and spouse and

serotonin A neurotransmitter that is involved in mood disorders such as depression.

generalized anxiety disorder An anxiety disorder in which anxiety appears to be present continuously and is unrelated to the situation.

phobia An irrational, excessive fear that interferes with one's functioning.

separation anxiety disorder An extreme form of otherwise normal separation anxiety that is characterized by anxiety about separating from parents; SAD often takes the form of refusal to go to school.

school phobia Fear of attending school, marked by extreme anxiety at leaving parents.

difficulty tolerating separation from them.

SAD is diagnosed when separation anxiety is persistent and excessive, when it is inappropriate for the child's developmental level, and when it interferes with activities or developmental tasks, such as attending school. Six-year-olds ought to be able to enter first grade without nausea and vomiting and without dread that they or their parents will come to harm. Children with SAD tend to cling to their parents and follow them around the house. They may voice concerns about death and dying and insist that someone stay with them at bedtime. They may complain of nightmares and have "stomachaches" on school days. They may throw tantrums or plead with their parents not to leave the house.

SAD may occur before middle childhood, preventing adjustment to day care or nursery school. SAD usually becomes a significant problem in middle childhood because that is when children are expected to adjust to school.

Separation Anxiety Disorder, School Phobia, and School Refusal

SAD is an extreme form of separation anxiety. It is characterized by anxiety about separating from parents and may be expressed as **school phobia**—fear of school—or as refusal to go to school (which can be based on fear or other factors). Separation anxiety is not behind all instances of school refusal. Some children refuse school because they perceive it as unpleasant, unsatisfying, or hostile, and it may be. Some children are concerned about doing poorly in school or being asked questions in class (in which case, they may have stage fright). High parental expectations may heighten concern, as may problems with classmates.

Treatment of School Phobia or School Refusal

T F It is better for children with school phobia to remain at home until the origins of the problem are uncovered and resolved.
False; most professionals agree that the first rule in the treatment of school phobia is: Get the child back into school.

There is nothing wrong with trying to understand why a child refuses to attend school. Knowledge of the reasons for refusal can help parents and educators devise strategies for assisting the child. But perhaps such understanding need not precede insistence that the child return to school. Here are things parents can do to get a child back into school:

- Do not accede to the child's demands to stay home.
- Secure the cooperation of the child's teacher, principal, and school nurse.
- If there is a specific school-related problem, such as an overly strict teacher, help the child—and teacher—find ways to handle the situation.
- Reward the child for attending school.

Antidepressant medication has been used successfully—often in conjunction with cognitive-behavioral methods—to treat school phobia (Brown et al., 2008). However, drugs do not teach children how to cope. Many health professionals suggest that the drugs are best used only when psychological treatments have proven to be ineffective (Masi et al., 2001).

It may be misleading to end the discussion of middle childhood with the topic of social and emotional problems. Most children in developed nations come through middle childhood quite well, in good shape for the challenges of adolescence.

© iStockphoto.com

Test coming up? Now what?

With CDEV you have a multitude of study aids at your fingertips.
After reading the chapters, check out these ideas for further help.

Chapter in Review cards include all learning outcomes,
definitions, and summaries for each chapter.

Printable flash cards give you three additional
ways to check your comprehension of key
child development concepts.

Other great ways to help you study include **interactive
flashcards**, downloadable **study aids, games, quizzes
with feedback**, and **PowerVisuals** to test your knowledge
of key concepts.

You can find it all at **4ltrpress.cengage.com/cdev.**

Adolescence is a transitional period

between childhood and adulthood, a coming of age.

14

Adolescence: Physical Development

TRUTH OR FICTION?

T F American adolescents are growing taller than their parents.

T F Girls are fertile immediately after their first menstrual period.

T F Most adolescents in the United States are unaware of the risks of HIV/AIDS.

T F You can never be too rich or too thin.

T F Some college women control their weight by going on cycles of binge eating followed by self-induced vomiting.

T F Substance abuse is on the rise among high school students.

"When will it happen?"

"Why is my voice acting so funny?"

"How tall will I be?"

"Why do I get pimples?"

"Why am I getting hairy?"

"Why is mine not like his?"

"What's happening to me?"

Perhaps no other period of life is as exciting—and as bewildering—as adolescence. Except for infancy, more changes occur during adolescence than during any other time of life.

In our society, adolescents are "neither fish nor fowl," as the saying goes, neither children nor adults. Adolescents may be old enough to reproduce and may be as large as their parents, yet they are required to remain in school through age 16, they may not be allowed to get drivers' licenses until they are 16 or 17, and they cannot attend R-rated films unless accompanied by an adult. Given the restrictions placed on adolescents, their growing yearning for independence, and a sex drive heightened by high levels of sex hormones, it is not surprising that adolescents occasionally are in conflict with their parents.

The capacity to think abstractly and hypothetically emerges during the teenage years. This ability gives rise to a stream of seemingly endless "Who am I?" questions, as adolescents search for a sense of identity and ponder the possible directions their adult lives may take.

Learning Outcomes

LO1 Describe the changes of puberty and its effects on adolescents.

LO2 Discuss emerging sexuality and the risks of sexually transmitted infections among adolescents.

LO3 Discuss adolescent health, including causes of death and nutritional issues.

LO4 Discuss substance abuse and dependence among adolescents.

genital stage In psychoanalytic theory, the fifth and final stage of psychosexual development in which gratification is attained through sex with a person of the other sex.

puberty The biological stage of development characterized by changes that lead to reproductive capacity. Puberty signals the beginning of adolescence.

primary sex characteristics The structures that make reproduction possible.

secondary sex characteristics Physical indicators of sexual maturation—such as voice change and bodily hair—that do not directly involve reproductive structures.

Adolescence is a transitional period between childhood and adulthood, a coming of age. A century ago, most children in the United States assumed adult responsibilities early. Adolescence began to emerge as a distinct stage of development between childhood and adulthood when the demands of an increasingly complex society required a longer period of education and delayed entry into the labor force. It is no longer easy for American adolescents to know when they have made the transition to adulthood. One legally becomes an adult at different ages, depending on whether one is enlisting in the armed services, buying a drink, driving a car, voting, or getting married.

G. Stanley Hall (1904), an early American psychologist, proposed that adolescence is an important and separate developmental stage. Hall believed that adolescence is marked by intense turmoil, and he used the German term *Sturm und Drang* ("storm and stress") to describe it. According to Hall, adolescents swing back and forth between happiness and sadness, overconfidence and self-doubt, dependence and independence. Hall believed that mood swings and conflicts with parents are a necessary part of growing up. He thought that children have to rebel against their parents to make the transition to adulthood.

According to Sigmund Freud (1933/1964), we enter the **genital stage** of psychosexual development at puberty. Sexual feelings are initially aimed at the parent of the other sex, but they become transferred, or displaced, onto other adults or adolescents of the other sex. Anna Freud (1969), Freud's daughter, saw adolescence as normally a turbulent period resulting from an increase in the sex drive. The adolescent tries to keep surging sexual impulses in check and redirects them from the parents to more acceptable outlets. The result is unpredictable behavior, defiance of parents, confusion, and mood swings.

But contemporary theorists no longer see storm and stress as inevitable in adolescence (Smetana, 2005; Susman & Rogol, 2004). Instead, they see adolescence as a period when biological, cognitive, and social and emotional functioning is reorganized.

Even if adolescence does not necessarily involve storm and stress, adolescents need to adapt to numerous biological, cognitive, and social and emotional changes. In this chapter, we focus on the biological and physical changes of adolescence. Let us begin—as adolescence begins—with puberty.

LO1 Puberty: The Biological Eruption

Puberty is a stage of development characterized by the attainment of sexual maturity and the ability to reproduce. The onset of adolescence coincides with the advent of puberty.

Puberty is controlled by a feedback loop involving the hypothalamus, pituitary gland, gonads—ovaries in females and testes in males—and hormones. The hypothalamus signals the pituitary gland, which, in turn, releases hormones that control physical growth and the functioning of the gonads. The gonads respond to pituitary hormones by increasing their production of sex hormones (androgens and estrogens). The sex hormones further stimulate the hypothalamus, thus perpetuating the feedback loop.

The sex hormones also trigger the development of primary and secondary sex characteristics. **Primary sex characteristics** are the structures that make reproduction possible. In girls, these structures are the ovaries, vagina, uterus, and fallopian tubes. In boys, they are the penis, testes, prostate gland, and seminal vesicles. **Secondary sex characteristics** are physical indicators of sexual maturation that do not involve the reproductive

© Gene Rhoden/Alamy

structures. They include the development of breasts, the deepening of the voice, and the appearance of facial, pubic, and underarm hair.

THE ADOLESCENT GROWTH SPURT

The stable growth patterns in height and weight that characterize early and middle childhood end abruptly with the adolescent growth spurt. Girls start to spurt in height sooner than boys, at an average age of a little over 10. Boys start to spurt about 2 years later, at about 12. Girls and boys reach their periods of peak growth in height about 2 years after the spurt begins, at about 12 and 14 years, respectively (see Figure 14.1). The spurt in height continues for about another 2 years at a gradually declining pace. Boys grow more than girls do during their spurt, averaging nearly 4 inches per year during the fastest year of the spurt compared with slightly more than 3 inches per year for girls. Overall, boys add an average of 14½ inches to their height during the spurt and girls add a little more than 13 inches (Tanner, 1991a).

A spurt in weight begins about half a year after the spurt in height. Peak growth in weight occurs about a year and a half after the onset of the spurt. As with height, the growth spurt in weight then continues for a little more than 2 years for both girls and boys. As you can see in Figure 14.2, girls are taller and heavier than boys from about age 9 or 10 until about age 13 or 14 because their growth spurt occurs earlier. Once boys begin to spurt, they catch up with girls and eventually become taller and heavier.

Because the spurt in weight lags the spurt in height, many adolescents are relatively slender compared with their preadolescent and postadolescent physique. However, adolescents tend to eat enormous quantities of food to fuel their growth spurts. Active 14- and 15-year-old boys may consume 3,000 to 4,000 calories a day without becoming obese. If they were to eat this much 20 years later, they might gain upward of 100 pounds per year.

Girls' and boys' body shapes begin to differ in adolescence. For one thing, boys' shoulders become broader than those of girls, whereas the hip dimensions of both sexes do not differ much. Girls' hips thus grow broader than their shoulders, whereas the opposite is true for boys. A girl's body shape is also more rounded because, during puberty, girls gain almost twice as much fatty tissue as boys do. Boys, on the other hand, gain twice as much muscle tissue as girls do.

Children who spurt earlier are likely to wind up with somewhat shorter legs and longer torsos; children who spurt late are longer legged. However, there are no significant differences between early and late spurters in height at maturity (Peeters et al., 2005; Tanner, 1991a). There is a moderate to high correlation between a child's height at the onset of adolescence and his or her height at maturity (Tanner, 1989). Despite exceptions, a tall child has a reasonable expectation of becoming a tall adult, and vice versa.

Adolescents are often awkward and gawky because of **asynchronous growth**;

> **asynchronous growth**
> Imbalanced growth, such as the growth that occurs during the early part of adolescence and causes many adolescents to appear gawky.

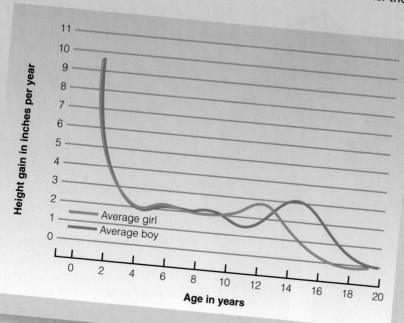

FIGURE 14.1
Spurts in Growth

Girls begin the adolescent growth spurt about 2 years earlier than boys. Girls and boys reach their periods of peak growth about 2 years after the spurt begins.

Average girl
Average boy

Height gain in inches per year

Age in years

FIGURE 14.2
Growth Curves for Height and Weight

Girls are taller and heavier than boys from about age 9 or 10 until about age 13 because their growth spurt occurs earlier. Once boys begin their spurt, they catch up with girls and eventually become taller and heavier.

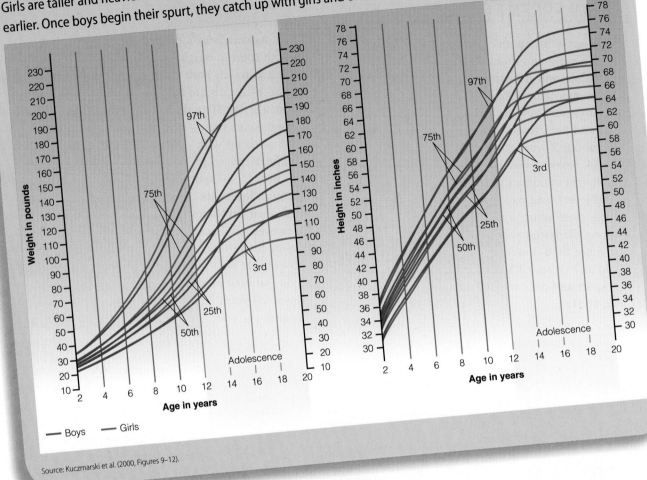

Source: Kuczmarski et al. (2000, Figures 9–12).

secular trend A historical trend toward increasing adult height and earlier puberty.

that is, different parts of the body grow at different rates. In an exception to the principle of proximodistal growth, the hands and feet mature before the arms and legs do. As a consequence, adolescent girls and boys may complain of big hands or feet. And, in an apparent reversal of cephalocaudal growth, legs reach peak growth before the shoulders and chest (Tanner, 1989).

The Secular Trend

During the past century, children in the Western world have grown dramatically more rapidly and have wound up taller than children from earlier times (Sun et al., 2005). This historical trend toward increasing adult height, which also has been accompanied by an earlier onset of puberty, is known as the **secular trend**. Figure 14.3 shows that Swedish boys and girls grew more rapidly in 1938 and 1968 than they did in 1883 and ended up several inches taller. At the age of 15, the boys were more than 6 inches taller and the girls were more than 3 inches taller, on average, than their counterparts from the previous century (Tanner, 1989). The occurrence of a secular trend in height and weight has been documented in most developed countries.

© Adrian Bischoff/Photolibrary

FIGURE 14.3
Are We Still Growing Taller than Our Parents?

Twentieth-century children grew taller than children in preceding centuries. Children from affluent families are no longer growing taller than their parents, but children from the lower part of the socioeconomic spectrum are still doing so.

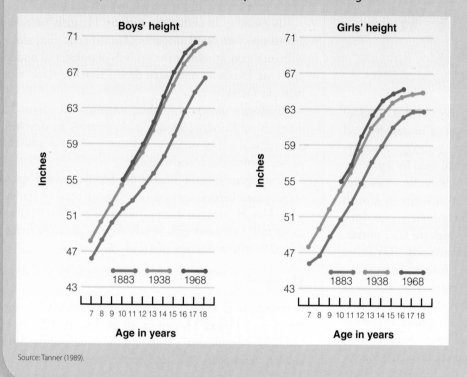

Source: Tanner (1989).

T (F) American adolescents are growing taller than their parents.

False; children from middle- and upper-class families in industrialized countries, including the United States, have stopped growing taller.

Although middle- and upper-income children are no longer growing taller than their parents, poorer children continue to make gains in height from generation to generation (Tanner, 1989). Why? Nutrition apparently plays a role. Children from middle- and upper-class families are taller and heavier than their age-mates from lower-class families. Perhaps Americans who have had nutritional and medical advantages have reached their full genetic potential in height. Continued gains among children of lower socioeconomic status suggest that those

PUBERTAL CHANGES IN BOYS

At puberty, the pituitary gland stimulates the testes to increase their output of testosterone, spurring further development of the male genitals. The first visible sign of puberty is accelerated growth of the testes, which begins at about 11 1/2, although any age from 9 1/2 to 13 1/2 is normal. Testicular growth further accelerates testosterone production and other pubertal changes. The penis begins a growth spurt about a year later, and pubic hair follows.

Underarm hair appears at about age 15. Facial hair is at first a fuzz on the upper lip. An actual beard does not develop for another 2 to 3 years. The beard and chest hair continue to develop past the age of 20.

At 14 or 15, the voice deepens because of growth of the voice box, or *larynx*, and the lengthening of the vocal cords. Because development is gradual, the voice of adolescent boys sometimes cracks embarrassingly.

Testosterone also triggers the development of acne, which afflicts up to 85% of 12- to 24-year-olds—females as well as males (Bauer et al., 2009). Severe acne is manifested by multiple pimples and blackheads on the face, chest, and back. Although boys are more prone to acne than girls, a smooth complexion has a higher value for girls, and girls who have acne that boys would consider mild may suffer terribly.

Males are capable of erection in early infancy (and some male babies are born with erections), but erections are not frequent until age 13 or 14. Many boys worry that they will be caught with unwanted erections when walking between classes or when asked to stand before the class.

semen The fluid that contains sperm and substances that nourish and transport sperm.

nocturnal emission Emission of seminal fluid while asleep.

gynecomastia Enlargement of breasts in males.

epiphyseal closure Turning to bone of the cartilage that separates the long end (epiphysis) of a bone from the main part of the bone.

mammary glands Glands that secrete milk.

menarche The onset of menstruation.

The organs that produce **semen** grow rapidly, and boys typically ejaculate seminal fluid by age 13 or 14—about 1½ years after the penis begins its growth spurt. About a year later, they begin to have **nocturnal emissions**, also called *wet dreams* because of the myth that emissions accompany erotic dreams. However, nocturnal emissions and erotic dreams need not coincide. Mature sperm are found in ejaculatory emissions by about the age of 15.

Nearly half of all boys experience enlargement of the breasts, or **gynecomastia**, which usually declines in a year or two. Gynecomastia stems from the small amount of female sex hormones secreted by the testes. When gynecomastia persists or becomes distressful, it can be treated with drugs, such as tamoxifen, or surgery (Derman et al., 2003).

At age 20 or 21, men stop growing taller because testosterone causes **epiphyseal closure**, which prevents the long bones from making further gains in length. Puberty for males draws to a close.

PUBERTAL CHANGES IN GIRLS

In girls, the pituitary gland signals the ovaries to vastly increase estrogen production at puberty. Estrogen may stimulate the growth of breast tissue (breast buds) as early as the age of 8 or 9, but the breasts usually begin to enlarge during the 10th year. The development of fatty tissue and ducts elevates the areas of the breasts surrounding the nipples and causes the nipples to protrude. Breasts typically reach full size in about 3 years, but **mammary glands** do not mature fully until a woman has a baby. Growth of the breasts varies considerably.

Estrogen also stokes the growth of the fatty and supporting tissue in the hips and buttocks, which, along with the widening of the pelvis, rounds the hips.

Beginning at about the age of 11, girls' adrenal glands produce small amounts of androgens that, along with estrogen, stimulate the growth of pubic and underarm hair. Excessive androgen production can darken or increase facial hair.

Estrogen causes the labia, vagina, and uterus to develop, and androgens cause the clitoris to develop. The vaginal lining varies in thickness with the amount of estrogen in the bloodstream.

Estrogen typically brakes the female growth spurt some years before testosterone brakes that of males. Girls low in estrogen during their late teens may grow quite tall, but most girls reach their genetically determined height by the age of 16 to 18.

Menarche

Menarche (first menstruation) commonly occurs between the ages of 11 and 14, plus or minus 2 years (Capron et al., 2007; Mendle et al., 2006). In the middle of the 19th century, European girls first menstruated at about the age of 16, as shown in Figure 14.4. During the next century, however, puberty occurred at earlier ages in Western nations. By the 1960s, the average age of menarche in the United States had plummeted to its current 12 1/2 (Tanner, 1991b). The average age of the advent of puberty for girls and boys has leveled off in recent years. The precipitous drop shown in Figure 14.4 seems to have come to an end.

T (F) Girls are fertile immediately after their first menstrual period.

False; girls usually begin to ovulate—that is, release egg cells that are capable of being fertilized—12 to 18 months after menarche.

What accounts for the earlier age of menarche? One hypothesis is that girls must accumulate a certain amount of body fat to trigger pubertal changes such as menarche, and girls now acquire more fat earlier than in

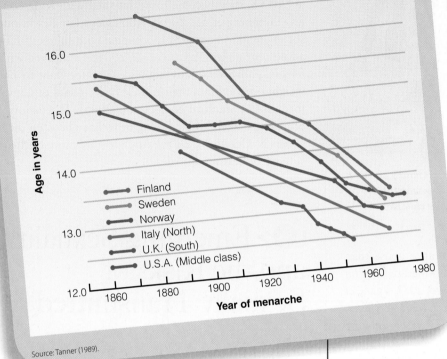

FIGURE 14.4
The Decline in Age at Menarche

The age at menarche has been declining since the mid-1800s among girls in Western nations, apparently because of improved nutrition and health care.

Finland
Sweden
Norway
Italy (North)
U.K. (South)
U.S.A. (Middle class)

Age in years
Year of menarche

Source: Tanner (1989).

Girls' cycles are often irregular for a few years after menarche but later tend to assume patterns that are reasonably regular.

EARLY VERSUS LATE MATURERS

Early-maturing boys tend to be more popular than their late-maturing peers and more likely to be leaders in school (Graber et al., 2004; Weichold et al., 2003). They are more poised, relaxed, and good-natured. Their edge in sports and the admiration of their peers heighten their sense of worth. On the negative side, early maturation is associated with greater risks of aggression and delinquency and abuse of alcohol and other drugs (Costello et al., 2007; Lynne et al., 2007). Coaches may expect too much of them in sports, and peers may want them to fight their battles for them (O'Sullivan et al., 2000). Sexual opportunities may create demands before they know how to respond (Lam et al., 2002).

Late maturers have the "advantage" of not being rushed into maturity. On the other hand, late-maturing boys often feel dominated by early-maturing boys. They have been found to be more dependent and insecure and may be more likely to get involved in disruptive behavior (Ge et al., 2003).

The benefits of early maturation appear to be greatest among lower-income adolescents, who often place more value on physical prowess. Middle- and upper-income adolescents are likely to value the types of achievements—academic and so on—available to late-maturing boys (Graber et al., 2004; Weichold et al., 2003).

Although boys who mature early usually have higher self-esteem than those who mature late, early-maturing girls may feel awkward, because they are among the first of their peers to begin the physical changes of puberty. They become conspicuous because of their height and their developing breasts. Boys may tease them. Tall girls of dating age frequently find that shorter boys are reluctant to approach them or be seen with them. All in all, early-maturing girls are at greater risk for a host of psychological problems and

the past. Fat cells secrete the protein leptin, which then signals the brain to secrete a cascade of hormones that raise estrogen levels. Menarche comes later to girls with less body fat, such as those with eating disorders or athletes (Bosi & de Oliveira, 2006; Angier, 2007).

Hormonal Regulation of the Menstrual Cycle

Testosterone levels remain fairly stable in adolescent girls, although they decline gradually in adulthood. However, estrogen and progesterone levels vary markedly and regulate the menstrual cycle. Following menstruation—the sloughing off of the endometrium—estrogen levels increase, leading once more to the growth of endometrial tissue. A ripe ovum is released by the ovary when estrogen reaches peak blood levels. Then the lining of the uterus thickens in response to the secretion of progesterone, enabling it to support an embryo. If the ovum is not fertilized, estrogen and progesterone levels drop suddenly, triggering menstruation once again.

The average menstrual cycle is 28 days, but variation between girls and in the same girl is common.

The effects of early maturation in boys are generally positive. Late-maturing boys may feel conspicuous because they are among the last of their peers to lose their childlike appearance.

HIV/AIDS Human immunodeficiency virus (HIV) is the cause of acquired immunodeficiency syndrome (AIDS), a condition that cripples the immune system.

for substance abuse than girls who mature later on (Hayward, 2003; Lynne et al., 2007). Many girls who mature early obtain lower grades in school and initiate sexual activity earlier (Lam et al., 2002). For reasons such as these, the parents of early-maturing girls may increase their vigilance and restrictiveness, leading to additional child–parent conflict.

Adolescent females in our society are much more preoccupied with appearance, body weight, and slimness than are adolescent males. Why?

Body Image

Adolescents are quite concerned about their physical appearance, particularly in early adolescence when the rapid physical changes of puberty are occurring (Jones & Crawford, 2006; Stanford & McCabe, 2005). By the age of 18, they become more satisfied with their bodies (Eisenberg et al., 2005). Adolescent females in our society tend to be more preoccupied with slimness than adolescent males (Paxton et al., 2005). Compared with females, however, many adolescent males want to put weight on and build their muscle mass (Jones & Crawford, 2006; Stanford & McCabe, 2005). The majority of girls are likely to be dieting or to have been on diets (Jones & Crawford, 2006). And girls are more likely to suffer from eating disorders.

LO2 Emerging Sexuality and the Risks of Sexually Transmitted Infections

i n an episode of the TV series *Growing Pains*, an adolescent was referred to as a "hormone with feet." Many or most adolescents are preoccupied with sex to some degree—a preoccupation fueled by a powerful sex drive. And many or most adolescents are not quite sure what to do about these pressing urges. Should they masturbate? Should they pet? Should they engage in sexual intercourse? Parents and sex educators often say "No," or "Wait." Yet it can seem that "Everyone's doing it." In Chapter 16, we discuss various sexual outlets. Here, we focus on sexually transmitted infections (STIs).

Given a body that is suddenly sexually mature, a high sex drive, vulnerability to peer pressure, and limited experience in handling temptation, teenagers are at particular risk for STIs. Sexually active adolescents have higher rates of STIs than any other age group. Each year, an estimated one of every six American adolescents contracts an STI (Centers for Disease Control and Prevention [CDC], 2006b). Chlamydia (a bacterial infection of the vagina or urinary tract that can result in sterility) is the most commonly occurring STI in adolescents, followed by gonorrhea, genital warts, genital herpes, syphilis, and **HIV/AIDS**. Because of its lethality, HIV/AIDS tends to capture most of the headlines.

TABLE 14.1

U.S. Adolescents and Adults with AIDS— Number of Cases by Exposure Category

	ESTIMATED NUMBER OF AIDS CASES, THROUGH 2006		
TRANSMISSION CATEGORY	ADULT AND ADOLESCENT MALES	ADULT AND ADOLESCENT FEMALES	TOTAL
Male-to-male sexual contact	465,965	—	465,965
Injection drug use	170,171	74,718	244,889
Male-to-male sexual contact and injection drug use	68,516	—	68,516
Male–female sexual contact	65,241	108,252	173,493
Other*	13,893	6,596	20,489

* Includes hemophilia, blood transfusion, perinatal exposure, and risk not reported or not identified.

Source: Centers for Disease Control and Prevention. (2008, August 3). AIDS cases by transmission category. Retrieved January 7, 2009, from http://www.cdc.gov/hiv/topics/surveillance/basic.htm

However, other STIs are more widespread, and some of them can also be deadly.

The incidence of chlamydia is especially high among teenagers and college students (CDC, 2006). Chlamydia is a major cause of pelvic inflammatory disease (PID), which can lead to infertility.

Infections with the human papilloma virus (HPV) cause genital warts and are associated with cervical cancer. A vaccine prevents most young women from being infected and is best administered before they become sexually active (Pichichero, 2006). It is estimated that more than half of the sexually active adolescent women in some cities in the United States are infected with HPV. Genital warts may appear in visible areas of the skin, but most appear in unseen areas, such as on the cervix in women or in the urethra in men. Women who initiate sexual intercourse before the age of 18 and who have many sex partners are particularly susceptible to infection. Fortunately, most healthy young women clear HPV infections on their own.

HIV/AIDS

HIV/AIDS is the most devastating of STIs; if left untreated, it is lethal. And the long-term prospects of those who do receive treatment remain unknown. HIV—the virus that causes AIDS—is spreading rapidly around the world, and, by the end of the 20th century, it had infected nearly 39 million people worldwide (Joint United Nations Programme on HIV/AIDS [UNAIDS],

2006). About 1,100,000 people in the United States are now living with HIV/AIDS (CDC, 2008a; Hall et al., 2008). Young gay males and homeless and runaway youths have elevated risk for HIV/AIDS. Anal intercourse is a likely route of transmission of HIV and is often practiced by gay males (see Table 14.1). Injecting drugs is another risk factor, because sharing infected needles can transmit HIV.

Women account for a minority of cases of HIV/AIDS in the United States but a United Nations study in Europe, Africa, and Southeast Asia found that sexually active teenage girls have higher rates of HIV infection than older women or young men (UNAIDS, 2006). It is erroneous to think that worldwide HIV/AIDS is primarily a disease of gay men and people who inject drugs. The primary mode of transmission worldwide is male–female intercourse. More than half of U.S. women with HIV/AIDS are infected by male–female intercourse (CDC, 2008a; see Table 14.1).

T (F) Most adolescents in the United States are unaware of the risks of HIV/AIDS.
False; studies regarding knowledge, attitudes, and beliefs about HIV/AIDS find that even children in the early school years are aware of HIV/AIDS.

Nearly all high school students know that HIV/AIDS is transmitted by sexual intercourse, but about half do not modify their sexual practices as a result of fear of

TABLE 14.2

Percentage of Adolescents Who Have Engaged in Sexual Intercourse, According to the National Survey of Family Growth

Age	15	16	17	18	19	20–21	22–24
Male	25	37	46	62	69	85	89
Female	26	40	49	70	77	81	92

Source: Mosher et al. (2005, figures 2 and 3).

the disease (Santelli et al., 2000). Adolescents often deny that HIV/AIDS could be a threat to them. As one high school girl said, "I can't believe that anyone I would have sex with would be infected." Some are, of course.

RISK FACTORS

Adolescents often take risks, with harmful consequences for their health and well-being. The most obvious risk factor for STIs is sexual activity itself. A U.S. government survey found that the percentage of adolescents who engage in sexual intercourse increases dramatically between the ages of 15 and 18 (Table 14.2). At the age of 15, about one adolescent in four has engaged in sexual intercourse, but the number surges to about two out of three by the age of 18.

A second risk factor for contracting STIs is sex with multiple partners. About 15% of high school students have had four or more sex partners (CDC, 2008b).

A third factor is failure to use condoms. In a recent survey by the Centers for Disease Control and Prevention, only about 62% of high school students used a condom the last time they had sexual intercourse (CDC, 2008b).

A fourth factor is drug abuse (UNAIDS, 2006). Adolescents who abuse drugs are also more likely to engage in other risky behaviors, such as sex without condoms (Abbey et al., 2006; Appel et al., 2006; Parkes et al., 2007).

The causes, methods of transmission, symptoms, and treatments for STIs are described in Table 14.3.

PREVENTION OF STIS

Prevention and education are the basic weapons against STIs (UNAIDS, 2006). Adolescents need to know about the transmission, symptoms, and consequences of STIs and about safer sex techniques, including abstinence and the use of condoms. Educating young people to

use condoms lowers levels of infection (Wingood et al., 2006).

But knowledge alone may not change behavior. For example, many female adolescents lack power in their relationships. Males are likely to pressure them into unwanted or unprotected sex (Wingood et al., 2006).

LO3 Health in Adolescence

adolescents are young and growing. Most seem sturdy. Injuries tend to heal quickly. Few are chronically ill or miss school. However, about 18% of the nation's adolescents have at least one serious health problem (Bloom et al., 2006).

Why do you think adolescents are so willing to engage in activities in which they might suffer serious injury or even death?

TABLE 14.3
Overview of Sexually Transmitted Infections (STIs)

STI AND CAUSE	TRANSMISSION	SYMPTOMS	DIAGNOSIS	TREATMENT
Gonorrhea ("clap," "drip"): Gonococcus bacterium (*Neisseria gonorrhoeae*)	Vaginal, oral, or anal sex. To newborns passing through the birth canal of an infected mother	In men, yellowish, thick discharge, burning urination. Women may be symptom-free or have vaginal discharge, burning urination, or irregular menstruation	Clinical inspection	Antibiotics
Syphilis: Treponemapallidum	Vaginal, oral, or anal sex. Touching an infectious chancre. Congenital	Hard, painless chancre appears at site of infection within 2–4 weeks. May progress through additional stages if untreated	Culture of discharge. Clinical inspection or examination of fluid from a chancre. Blood test	Antibiotics
Chlamydia and nongonococcal urethritis: caused by *Chlamydia trachomatous* bacterium in women	Vaginal, oral, or anal sex. To newborns passing through birth canal of infected mother	Women and men may be symptom-free or have frequent and painful urination and a discharge	Analysis of cervical smear in women. Analysis of penile fluid in men	Antibiotics
Genital herpes: caused by Herpes simplex virus-type 2 (HSV-2)	Vaginal, oral, or anal sex	Painful, reddish bumps around the genitals, thighs, or buttocks. Bumps become blisters that fill with pus and break, shedding viral particles. Fever, aches and pains possible	Clinical inspection of sores. Culture and examination of fluid drawn from sore	Antiviral drugs may provide relief and help with healing but are not cures
HIV/AIDS: Human immunodeficiency virus (HIV), the cause of acquired immunodeficiency syndrome (AIDS)	Vaginal or anal sex. Infusion of contaminated blood by needle sharing or from mother to baby during childbirth. Breast-feeding	Usually symptom-free for many years. Swollen lymph nodes, fever, weight loss, fatigue, diarrhea. Deadly opportunistic infections	Blood, saliva, or urine tests detect HIV antibodies. Other tests confirm the presence of HIV itself	There is no cure for HIV/AIDS. A "cocktail" of highly active antiviral therapy (HAART) prolongs life in many people living with HIV/AIDS
HPV/Genital warts: caused by human papilloma virus (HPV)	Sexual contact. Contact with infected towels or clothing	Painless warts resembling cauliflowers on the genitals or anus or in the rectum. Associated with cervical cancer	Clinical inspection	A vaccine can prevent infection in most young women. Warts removed by freezing, topical drugs, burning, and surgery
Pubic lice ("crabs"): *Pthirus pubis* (an insect, not a crab)	Sexual contact. Contact with an infested towel, sheet, or toilet seat	Intense itching in pubic area and other hairy regions to which lice can attach	Clinical inspection	Topical drugs containing pyrethrins or piperonal butoxide

RISK TAKING IN ADOLESCENCE

Adolescents are more likely than younger children to engage in risky behavior: excessive drinking, substance abuse, reckless driving, violence, disordered eating behavior, and unprotected sexual activity (Bloom et al., 2006). Let us consider the causes of death in adolescence and then turn to three major health problems faced by teens. We already discussed the first—STIs. The second and third are eating disorders and substance abuse.

Causes of Death

Death rates are low in adolescence, although they are higher for older adolescents than for younger ones. For example, each year about twice as many 15- to 17-year-olds as 12- to 14-year-olds die (National Center for Health Statistics [NCHS], 2008). Death rates are nearly twice as great for male adolescents as for female adolescents. A major reason for this discrepancy is that males are more likely to take risks that end in death by accident, suicide, or homicide (NCHS, 2008).

Seventy-five percent of adolescent deaths in the United States result from injuries (NCHS, 2008). Sixty percent are due to accidents, and most of these involve motor vehicles (NCHS, 2008). Alcohol is also often implicated in drowning and falling (NCHS, 2008).

Poor, urban adolescents have the greatest risk of death by homicide (CDC, 2008b). African American adolescents are more likely than European American adolescents to fit this description. Therefore, it is not surprising that the homicide rate among African American male adolescents, aged 15–19, is nearly 10 times as high as for European Americans (see Figure 14.5). African American females, aged 15 to 19, are more than five times as likely as their European American counterparts to be victims of homicide. The figures for Latino and Latina American adolescents are between those of African American and European American youth (Forum on Child and Family Statistics, 2005).

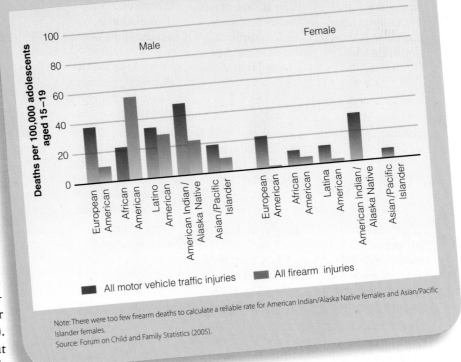

FIGURE 14.5

Injury Death Rates among Adolescents Ages 15–19 by Sex, Ethnicity, and Type of Injury

Note: There were too few firearm deaths to calculate a reliable rate for American Indian/Alaska Native females and Asian/Pacific Islander females.

Source: Forum on Child and Family Statistics (2005).

NUTRITION: AN ABUNDANCE OF FOOD

Physical growth occurs more rapidly in the adolescent years than at any other time after birth, with the exception of the first year of life. To fuel the adolescent growth spurt, the average girl, depending on activity level, needs to consume 1,800 to 2,400 calories per day, and the average boy needs 2,200 to 3,200 calories (U.S. Department of Agriculture [USDA], 2005). The nutritional needs of adolescents vary according to their stage of pubertal development. At the peak of their growth spurt, adolescents use twice as much calcium, iron, zinc, magnesium, and nitrogen as they do during the other years of adolescence (USDA, 2005). Calcium intake is particularly important for females to build up their bone density and help prevent *osteoporosis*—a progressive loss of bone, later in life. But most teenagers—both girls and boys—do not consume enough calcium. Adolescents also are likely to obtain less vitamin A, thiamine, and iron but more fat, sugar, protein, and sodium than recommended (USDA, 2005).

One reason for adolescents' nutritional deficits is irregular eating patterns. Breakfast is often skipped, especially by girls who are watching their weight (Niemeier et al., 2006). Teenagers are more likely to miss meals or eat away from home than they were in childhood (Thompson et al., 2004). They may consume large amounts of fast food and junk food, which are high in fat and calories but not very nutritious (Niemeier et al., 2006). Junk food is connected with being overweight, and heaviness in adolescence can lead to chronic illness and earlier death in adulthood, even for teens who later lose weight (Niemeier et al., 2006). Overweight adolescents are more likely to incur heart disease, strokes, and cancer as adults (USDA, 2005).

AN ABUNDANCE OF EATING DISORDERS

The American ideal has slimmed down to where most American females of average weight are dissatisfied with the size and shape of their bodies (Paxton et al., 2006; Striegel-Moore et al., 2003). The wealthier your family, the more unhappy you are likely to be with your body (Polivy et al., 2006). Perhaps, then, it is no surprise that dieting has become the normal way of eating for most U.S. adolescent females (Polivy et al., 2006)!

In Chapter 15, we will see that adolescents also tend to think that others are paying a great deal of attention to their appearance. Because of the cultural emphasis on slimness and the psychology of the adolescent, adolescents—especially girls—are highly vulnerable to eating disorders. The eating disorders *anorexia nervosa* and *bulimia nervosa* are characterized by gross disturbances in patterns of eating.

Anorexia Nervosa

More adolescent girls diet than not. But some, such as the girl in "Rachel's Case," go to extremes and develop anorexia nervosa. **Anorexia nervosa** is a life-threatening eating disorder characterized by extreme fear of being too heavy, dramatic weight loss, distorted body image, and resistance to eating enough to reach or maintain a healthy weight.

Adolescents with anorexia nervosa weigh less than 85% of the desirable body weight. Anorexia nervosa afflicts males as well as females, but most studies put the female-to-male ratio at 10 to 1 or greater, although some find a smaller sex difference (Kjelsås et al., 2004;

anorexia nervosa An eating disorder characterized by extreme fear of being too heavy, dramatic weight loss, distorted body image, and resistance to eating enough to reach or maintain a healthy weight.

RACHEL'S CASE: ANOREXIA NERVOSA

I wanted to be a runner. Runners were thin and I attributed this to dieting, not training. So I began restricting my diet: No butter, red meat, pork, dessert, candy, or snacking. If I ate any of the forbidden items, I obsessed about it and felt guilty for days.

As a high school freshman, I wanted to run with the fastest girls so I trained hard, really hard, and ate less. Lunch was lettuce sandwiches, carrots, and an apple. By my senior year, I was number three on the team and lunch was a bagel and an orange.

I maintained a rigid schedule—running cross country and track, having a seat on student council, volunteering, and maintaining a 3.9 GPA throughout high school—while starving myself (1,000 calories per day), trying to attain the impossible perfection I thought couldn't be far away if I only slimmed down a little bit more. . . .

I dropped 10 pounds my freshman year—from 125 to 115 pounds. I was five feet, eight inches tall and wore a size five. I hated my body so I starved myself and ran like a mad woman.

In quiet moments, I was sad and worried about what might be going on inside me.

I was already taking birth control to regain my menstrual cycle; my weight was 15% below what was recommended for my height; I was always cold; I had chest pains and an irregular heartbeat; my hair was limp and broke off; my skin was colorless.

It wasn't until I came to the University of Iowa and joined the varsity women's cross country team that I began to see what I was doing to myself. A teammate had an eating problem. Every time I saw her, I felt sick to my stomach. She had sunken cheeks, eyes so big they swallowed her face. She was an excellent student and a college-level varsity athlete. Many people wondered at her determination, but I understood. She used the same excuses I did.

Source: University of Iowa Hospitals and Clinics

bulimia nervosa An eating disorder characterized by cycles of binge eating and purging to prevent weight gain.

Striegel-Moore & Cachelin, 2001). By and large, anorexia nervosa afflicts women during adolescence and young adulthood (Polivy et al., 2005). The typical person with anorexia is a young European American female of higher socioeconomic status (Striegel-Moore et al, 2003). Affluent females have greater access to fitness centers and health clubs and are more likely to read the magazines that idealize slender bodies and shop in the boutiques that cater to females with svelte figures. All in all, they are regularly confronted with unrealistically high standards of slimness that make them dissatisfied with their own physiques (Forbush et al., 2007). The incidences of anorexia nervosa and bulimia nervosa have increased markedly in recent years.

Females with anorexia nervosa can drop 25% or more of their weight within a year. Severe weight loss triggers abnormalities in the endocrine system (i.e., with hormones) that prevent ovulation (Nielsen & Palmer, 2003). General health declines. Nearly every system in the body is affected. There are problems with the respiratory system (Forman-Hoffman et al., 2006) and with the cardiovascular system (Katzman, 2005). Females with anorexia are at risk for premature development of osteoporosis (Katzman, 2005). Given these problems, it is not surprising that the mortality rate for anorexic females is approximately 4% to 5%.

In one common pattern, the girl sees that she has gained some weight after menarche, and she resolves that she must lose it. But even after the weight is gone, she maintains her pattern of dieting and, in many cases, exercises at a fever pitch (Shroff et al., 2006). This pattern continues even after those who care about her tell her that she is becoming all skin and bones. However, anorexic girls deny any health problems, pointing to their feverish exercise routines as evidence. Distortion of the body image is a feature of the disorder. Others see anorexic females as skin and bones, whereas someone with the disorder looks in a mirror and sees a body that is too heavy.

 T (F) You can never be too rich or too thin.
Most teens are not worried about a fat bank account, but as in the case of Rachel, one can certainly be too skinny.

Bulimia Nervosa

Bulimia nervosa is sort of a companion disorder to anorexia nervosa, as we see in the case of Nicole:

NICOLE'S CASE: BULIMIA NERVOSA

Nicole awakens in her cold dark room and already wishes it was time to go back to bed. She dreads the thought of going through this day, which will be like so many others in her recent past. She asks herself the question every morning, "Will I be able to make it through the day without being totally obsessed by thoughts of food, or will I blow it again and spend the day [binge eating]?" She tells herself that today she will begin a new life, today she will start to live like a normal human being. However, she is not at all convinced that the choice is hers.

—Boskind-White & White (1983, p. 29)

So, does Nicole begin a new life today? No. Despite her pledge to herself, Nicole begins the day with eggs and toast, butter included. Then she downs cookies; bagels smothered with cream cheese, butter, and jelly; doughnuts; candy bars; bowlfuls of cereal and milk—all in less than an hour. When her body cries "No more!" she turns to the next step: purging. In the bathroom, she ties back her hair. She runs the shower to mask noise, drinks some water, and makes herself throw everything up. Afterward she makes another pledge to herself: "Starting tomorrow, I'm going to change." Will she change? In truth, she doubts it.

Bulimia nervosa, Nicole's eating disorder, is symptomized by recurrent cycles of binge eating and purging. Binge eating often follows on the heels of food restriction, or dieting (Williams, 2004). There are various methods of purging. Nicole vomited. Other avenues include strict dieting or fasting, laxatives, and demanding, prolonged exercise regimes. Individuals with eating disorders, such as Rachel and Nicole, tend to be perfectionistic about their bodies. They will not settle for less than their idealized body shape and weight (Kaye et al., 2004). Bulimia nervosa, like anorexia nervosa, tends to afflict women during adolescence and young adulthood (Nolen-Hoeksema et al., 2007).

 (T) F Some college women control their weight by going on cycles of binge eating followed by self-induced vomiting.
True; they are diagnosed with bulimia nervosa.

Perspectives on Eating Disorders

According to some psychoanalysts, anorexia nervosa may symbolize a young woman's efforts to cope with sexual fears, especially the possibility of becoming pregnant. Anorexia nervosa prevents some adolescents from separating from their families and assuming adult responsibilities. Their breasts and hips flatten once more because of the loss of fatty tissue. In the adolescent's fantasies, perhaps, she remains a sexually undifferentiated child.

Many parents are obsessed with encouraging their children—especially their infants—to eat adequately. Thus, some observers suggest that children may refuse to eat as a way of battling with their parents. ("You have to eat something!" "I'm not hungry!") Parents in such families are often unhappy and have their own issues with eating and dieting. They also "act out" against their daughter, letting her know that they consider her unattractive and, before the development of the eating disorder, letting her know that they think she should lose weight (Hanna & Bond, 2006).

Many individuals with eating disorders have a history of child abuse, particularly sexual abuse (Corstorphine et al., 2007). One study found a history of childhood sexual abuse in about half of women with bulimia nervosa, as opposed to a rate of about 7% among women without the disorder (Deep et al., 1999).

Certainly young women have a very slender social ideal set before them in women such as Paris Hilton. Miss America, the annually renewed American role model, has also been slenderizing across the years. Over the past 80 years, the winner has added only 2% in height but has lost 12 pounds in weight. In the early days of the 1920s, Miss America's weight relative to her height yielded a body mass index (BMI) of 20 to 25, which is considered normal by the World Health Organization (WHO). The WHO labels people as malnourished when their BMIs are lower than 18.5. However, recent Miss Americas have had BMIs near 17 (Rubinstein & Caballero, 2000). As the cultural ideal slenderizes, women with desirable body weights, according to the health charts, feel overweight, and overweight women feel gargantuan (Winzelberg et al., 2000).

You can calculate your body mass index as follows. Write down your weight in pounds. Multiply it by 703. Divide the product by your height in inches squared. For example, if you weigh 160 lbs and are 5 feet 8 inches tall, your BMI is $(160 \times 703)/68^2$, or 24.33. A BMI of more than 25 is defined as overweight.

Eating disorders tend to run in families, which raises the possibility of genetic involvement (Bellodi et al., 2001; Kaye et al., 2004; Speranza et al., 2001). Genetic factors may involve obsessionistic and perfectionistic personality traits (Kaye et al., 2004). In a society in which there is so much stress on slimness, these personality traits encourage dieting (Wade et al., 2000).

Treatment and Prevention

Treatment of eating disorders—particularly anorexia nervosa—is a great challenge. Because the low weight of individuals with anorexia is often life-threatening, some adolescent girls are admitted to the hospital for treatment against their will (Brunner et al., 2005). Many girls deny that they have a problem. When the girl does not—or cannot—eat adequately through the mouth, measures such as tube feeding may be used.

Antidepressants are frequently used in the treatment of eating disorders (Grilo et al., 2005; Walsh et al., 2006). Antidepressants such as Prozac and Zoloft enhance the activity of serotonin in the brain, often increasing food intake in anorexic individuals and decreasing binge eating in bulimic people.

Cognitive-behavioral therapy has been used to help anorexic and bulimic individuals challenge their

The World Health Organization labels people as malnourished when their BMIs are lower than 18.5. However, recent Miss Americas have had BMIs near 17.

© Nicholas Belton/iStockphoto.com / © iStockphoto.com

As the cultural ideal becomes slimmer, many normal weight women begin to feel overweight, especially those with obsessive or perfectionistic personality traits.

substance abuse A persistent pattern of use of a substance characterized by frequent intoxication and impairment of physical, social, or emotional well-being.

substance dependence A persistent pattern of use of a substance that is accompanied by physiological addiction.

perfectionism and distorted body images. It has also been used to systematically reinforce appropriate eating behavior. But let's remember that eating disorders are connected with cultural attitudes that idealize excessive

thinness. Preventive efforts will have to address cultural values as well as potential problems in individual adolescents.

LO4 Substance Abuse and Dependence

think of the United States as a cafeteria with brightly colored drugs glimmering on the shelves and in the trays. Adolescents who do not use drugs certainly deserve credit. They generally refuse them as a matter of choice, not because of lack of supply. The drugs are there, and some of the most harmful drugs are perfectly legal, at least for adults.

Adolescents use drugs not only to cope with medical problems but also to deal with daily tensions, run-of-the-mill depression, even boredom. Many adolescents use drugs because they are imitating peers or rebelling against parents who beg them not to (Costello, 2007). They use drugs to experience pleasure, to deaden pain, and to earn prestige among peers.

Adolescents frequently get involved with drugs that cripple their ability to attend school or to pay attention when they do. Alcohol and other drugs are also linked with reckless, sometimes deadly, behavior (CDC, 2008b). Alcohol is the BDOC—the Big Drug on Campus. It is the most widely used substance in high schools and on college campuses (Johnston et al., 2008a). Marijuana is no slacker either. Nearly half of high school students have tried it before they graduate (Johnston et al., 2008a).

When does the use of a drug or substance become substance abuse? According to the American Psychiatric Association (2000), **substance abuse** is the ongoing use of a substance despite the social, occupational, psychological, or physical problems it causes. When adolescents miss school or fail to complete assignments because they are intoxicated or "sleeping it off," they are abusing alcohol. The amount they drink is not the issue; the problem is the role that it plays in their lives.

Substance dependence is more serious. An adolescent who is dependent on a substance loses control and may organize his or her life around getting the substance and using it. Substance dependence also changes the body. Having it in the body becomes the norm, and so the adolescent may experience tolerance,

© Jan Tadeusz/Alamy

withdrawal symptoms, or both. **Tolerance** develops as the body becomes habituated to the substance; therefore, the adolescent has to use progressively higher doses to achieve the same effects. A number of substances are physically addictive; so when the addicted adolescent stops using such a substance or lowers the dosage, a set of withdrawal symptoms known as an **abstinence syndrome** occurs. When addicted individuals lower their intake of alcohol, they may experience symptoms such as tremors (shakes), high blood pressure, rapid heart and pulse rate, anxiety, restlessness, and weakness. Many adolescents who begin to use substances such as alcohol for pleasure wind up using them to escape the abstinence syndrome.

Why, you might wonder, are psychologists and educators so concerned about substance abuse? Drugs are not "bad" simply because they are illegal. Drugs can have serious harmful effects on health. Consider the effects of some depressants, stimulants, and hallucinogenics.

DEPRESSANTS

All depressants slow the activity of the nervous system. Beyond that, they have different cognitive and biological effects. Depressants include alcohol, narcotics derived from the opium poppy (heroin, morphine, and the like), and **sedatives** (such as barbiturates and methaqualone).

Alcohol lessens inhibitions, so drinkers may do things when drinking that they would otherwise resist (Bartholow et al., 2006; Donohue et al., 2007). Ingesting five or more drinks in a row—that is, *binge drinking*—is connected with bad grades and risky behavior, including risky (unprotected, promiscuous) sex, acts of aggression, and accidents (Birch et al., 2007; Keller et al.,

© Nicholas Belton/iStockphoto.com

2007). Small amounts of alcohol can be stimulating, but high doses have a sedative effect, which is why alcohol is labeled a depressant. Alcohol is also an intoxicant: It distorts perceptions, impairs concentration, hinders coordination, and slurs the speech. The media pay more attention to deaths resulting from heroin and cocaine overdoses, but hundreds of college students die each year from causes related to drinking, including accidents and overdoses (Forum on Child and Family Statistics, 2005). (Yes, a person can die from drinking too much at one time.)

tolerance Habituation to a drug creating a need to use increasingly higher doses to achieve similar effects.

abstinence syndrome A group of symptoms that results from a sudden decrease in the level of usage of a substance.

sedatives Drugs that soothe or quiet restlessness or agitation.

Do You Have a Problem With Alcohol?

How can you tell whether you may have a drinking problem? Answering the following four questions can help you find out (National Institute on Alcohol Abuse and Alcoholism [NIAAA], 2005):

Yes	No	Have you ever felt you should cut down on your drinking?
Yes	No	Have people annoyed you by criticizing your drinking?
Yes	No	Have you ever felt bad or guilty about your drinking?
Yes	No	Have you ever had a drink first thing in the morning (as an "eye opener") to steady your nerves or get rid of a hangover?

Just one "yes" answer suggests a possible alcohol problem. Two or more "yes" answers make it highly likely that a problem exists. In either case, it is advisable to discuss your answers with your doctor or another health care provider.

Adolescent drinking often leads to drinking as an adult, and chronic drinking can lead to serious physical disorders such as cirrhosis or cancer of the liver. Chronic heavy drinking has been linked to cardiovascular disorders. Heavy drinking increases the risk of breast cancer among women and may harm the embryo if she is pregnant (Rathus et al., 2008).

Heroin is a depressant that is derived from the opium poppy. Like morphine and other opioids, its major medical use is relief from pain. But it also can provide a euphoric "rush," which is why many experimenters are tempted to use it again. Heroin is addictive, and regular users develop tolerance.

Barbiturates are depressants with various legitimate medical uses, such as relief from pain, anxiety, and tension and treatment of insomnia, high blood pressure, and epilepsy; however, people can become rapidly dependent on them. These drugs are used illegally by adolescents because of their relaxing effects and their ability to produce a mild euphoria. Depressants have additive effects; therefore, mixing barbiturates and other depressants is risky.

STIMULANTS

Using stimulants is like stepping on the body's accelerator pedal. Stimulants speed up the heartbeat and other bodily functions. They can also keep people awake and alert, but at the expense of some wear and tear on the body. Nicotine, cocaine, and amphetamines are the most commonly used stimulants.

Nicotine is found in cigars, cigarettes, and chewing tobacco. Nicotine causes the release of the hormone adrenaline, which causes the heart rate to increase or changes its rhythm and causes the liver to pour sugar into the blood. Nicotine, like other stimulants, also raises the rate at which the body burns calories and lowers the appetite, so some adolescents smoke as a means of weight control (Anzengruber et al., 2006; Copeland et al., 2006). Nicotine is also the chemical that addicts people to tobacco (Nonnemaker & Homsi, 2007). The abstinence syndrome from nicotine includes symptoms such as drowsiness and loss of energy (the stimulant is gone, after all), palpitations of the heart (irregular heartbeats), sweating, tremors, lightheadedness and dizziness, insomnia, headaches, and digestive problems (irregular bowel movements and cramps). Nearly 450,000 Americans die from smoking-related problems each year (American Lung Association, 2007). Cigarette smoke contains carbon monoxide, which causes shortness of breath, and hydrocarbons ("tars"), which are responsible for most respiratory diseases and cases of lung cancer (American Lung Association, 2007). Pregnant smokers increase the risk of miscarriage, stillbirth, preterm birth, and low birth-weight (American Lung Association, 2007).

The stimulant cocaine produces feelings of euphoria, relieves pain, boosts self-confidence, and reduces the appetite. Cocaine has biological as well as psychological effects: It accelerates the heart rate, spikes the blood pressure, constricts the arteries of the heart, and thickens the blood, a combination of effects that can cause cardiovascular and respiratory collapse (Mitchell, 2006). Cocaine has caused the deaths of several young athletes who used it to boost performance and confidence. Because cocaine is a stimulant, overdoses can cause restlessness, insomnia, and tremors.

Amphetamines are widely known to students as enablers of all-night cram sessions. Many dieters rely on them to reduce their appetites. Tolerance for amphetamines develops rapidly, and adolescents can become dependent on them, especially when they use them to self-medicate themselves for depression. If used regularly, the powerful amphetamine called *methamphetamine* may be physically addictive (Jonkman, 2006; Shen et al., 2007), but the extent to which amphetamines cause physical addiction has been a subject of controversy. High doses of amphetamines, like high doses of cocaine, can cause restlessness and insomnia, irritability, and loss of appetite.

HALLUCINOGENICS

Hallucinogenics give rise to perceptual distortions called *hallucinations*. The hallucinator may believe that the hallucination cannot be real, yet it assaults the senses so strongly that it is confused with reality. Marijuana, Ecstasy, LSD, and PCP are examples of hallucinogenic drugs.

Marijuana is derived from the *Cannabis sativa* plant. It is typically smoked, although it can be eaten. Many adolescents report that marijuana helps them relax and elevates their mood. Adolescents who use marijuana report greater sensory awareness, self-insight, creativity, and empathy for other people's feelings. Smokers become highly attuned to bodily sensations, especially their heartbeat, which tends to accelerate. They experience hallucinations; for example, time may seem to slow down so much that a song goes on indefinitely.

Driving while using hallucinogenic drugs poses grave risks.

© Flickr/Getty Images

But strong intoxication can disorient and frighten some smokers.

Marijuana carries a number of health risks. For example, it impairs the perceptual–motor coordination used in driving. It impairs short-term memory and slows learning (Egerton et al., 2006; Lamers et al., 2006). Although it causes positive mood changes in many people, some experience anxiety and confusion (Bonn-Miller et al., 2007). Users can become psychologically dependent on marijuana, and research also suggests that regular users can experience withdrawal, which is a sign of physical addiction (Budney et al., 2007).

Ecstasy—also known as MDMA (an abbreviation for its chemical formula)—is a popular "party drug" or "club drug." Its chemical formula has similarities to those of both amphetamines and mescaline, another hallucinogenic drug (Lamers et al., 2006). As a result, Ecstasy gives users the boost of a stimulant, making them somewhat more alert and suffusing them with feelings of elation and self-confidence. As a mild hallucinogenic, it also removes users a bit from reality. The combined effect appears to free them to some degree from inhibitions and cognitive awareness of the possible consequences of risky behavior, such as unprotected sex. Ecstasy can also impair working memory (not helpful for studying), increase anxiety, and lead to depression (Lamers et al., 2006).

LSD is the acronym for lysergic acid diethylamide, another hallucinogenic drug. Regular use of hallucinogenics can cause psychological dependence and tolerance, but people are not known to become physically

Regular use of **hallucinogenics** can cause **psychological dependence** and tolerance, but people are not known to become physically addicted to them. High doses can impair coordination and judgment, change mood, and cause hallucinations and paranoid delusions.

addicted to them. High doses can impair coordination and judgment (driving while using hallucinogenic drugs poses grave risks), change mood, and cause hallucinations and paranoid delusions (belief that one is in danger or being observed or followed).

PREVALENCE OF SUBSTANCE ABUSE

Table 14.4 on the next page compares self-reported substance abuse in 1991 with that in 2008 for eighth-, tenth-, and twelfth-graders. The incidence of use of some drugs was relatively high: alcohol, cigarettes (nicotine is actually the drug in cigarettes), and marijuana. Some drugs have been used by fewer than 10% of students: MDMA, cocaine, LSD, steroids, and heroin. Only one-fifth of eighth-graders now report that they have ever used cigarettes (Johnston et al., 2008b). Perhaps warnings about the dangers of cigarettes have gotten through.

Less than 2% of high school students report they have used steroids. Steroids, which build muscle mass, are typically used by boys to improve athletic performance.

T (F) Substance abuse is on the rise among high school students.

False; ongoing surveys of high school students by the Institute of Social Research at the University of Michigan find that use of illicit drugs by eighth- through twelfth-graders has generally declined over the past few decades (Johnston et al., 2008a).

TABLE 14.4

Trends in Lifetime Use of Various Substances for Eighth-, Tenth-, and Twelfth-Graders, 1991 versus 2008 (Percents)

SUBSTANCE	GRADE	1991	2008
Alcohol	Eighth	70.1%	38.9%
	Tenth	83.8	58.3
	Twelfth	88.0	71.9
Cigarettes	Eighth	44.0	20.5
	Tenth	51.1	31.7
	Twelfth	63.1	44.7
Marijuana	Eighth	10.2	14.6
	Tenth	23.4	29.9
	Twelfth	36.7	42.6
Amphetamines	Eighth	10.5	6.8
	Tenth	13.2	9.0
	Twelfth	15.4	10.5
Inhalants	Eighth	17.6	15.7
	Tenth	15.7	12.8
	Twelfth	17.6	9.9
Barbiturates	Eighth	—	—
	Tenth	—	—
	Twelfth	6.2	8.5
MDMA (Ecstasy)	Eighth	—	2.4
	Tenth	—	2.3
	Twelfth	—	6.2
Cocaine	Eighth	2.3	3.0
	Tenth	4.1	4.5
	Twelfth	7.8	7.2
LSD	Eighth	2.7	1.9
	Tenth	5.6	2.6
	Twelfth	8.8	4.0
Steroids	Eighth	1.9	1.4
	Tenth	1.8	1.4
	Twelfth	2.1	2.2
Heroin	Eighth	1.2	1.4
	Tenth	1.2	1.2
	Twelfth	0.9	1.3

Source: Johnston et al. (2008a, Table 1).

STUDENTS' ATTITUDES TOWARD DRUGS

The University of Michigan researchers have also tracked the extent to which high school students disapproved of drug use over the past generation (Johnston et al., 2008a). Table 14.5 shows the percentage of high school seniors who disapproved of various kinds of drug use in the year 1978 and 30 years later in 2008. Students in both groups were more likely to disapprove of regular drug use than experimental drug use. For example, one-third to one-half of students disapproved of use of marijuana on an experimental basis (33.4% in 1978 and 55.5% in 2008), but the disapproval rate for regular smoking of marijuana was 43.5% in 1978 and 79.6% in 2008. Only a minority of high school seniors (15.6% in 1978 and 29.8% in 2008) disapproved of trying a drink or two. However, most seniors in both eras disapproved of regular drinking. Overall, disapproval ratings were somewhat higher in 2008 than in 1978.

FACTORS IN SUBSTANCE ABUSE AND DEPENDENCE

Adolescents often become involved with substance abuse and dependence through experimental use (Commission on Adolescent Substance and Alcohol Abuse, 2005; Costello, 2007). Some are conforming to peer pressure (Costello, 2007). Some are rebelling against moral or social constraints. Others are trying to escape from boredom or from the pressures of school or the neighborhood. Some are imitating their parents. A drug can be reinforcing by enhancing the user's mood or by reducing unpleasant emotions such as anxiety and tension. For individuals who are addicted, the prevention of the abstinence syndrome is reinforcing.

Open lines of communication with a parent helps inhibit drug use. The authoritative pattern of child rearing appears to protect children from substance abuse (Dorius et al., 2004; Patock-Peckham & Morgan-Lopez, 2006). Heavy drug use is most likely to occur in families where the parenting style is permissive or neglecting–rejecting.

Adolescent drug users often do poorly in school (Dunn & Mezzich, 2007). Psychological characteristics associated with drug use include anxiety and depression, antisocial behavior, and low self-esteem (Donohue et al., 2006; Gau et al., 2007).

Children may also inherit genetic predispositions toward abuse of specific drugs, including depressants, stimulants, and hallucinogenics (Lynskey et al., 2007; Redgrave et al., 2007; Slutske et al., 2008). For example,

TABLE 14.5
Disapproval of Drug Use by Twelfth-Graders, 1978 versus 2008

DO YOU DISAPPROVE OF PEOPLE (WHO ARE 18 OR OLDER) DOING EACH OF THE FOLLOWING?	PERCENT DISAPPROVING, CLASS OF 1978	PERCENT DISAPPROVING, CLASS OF 2008
Try marijuana once or twice	33.4%	55.5%
Smoke marijuana regularly	43.5	79.6
Try LSD once or twice	85.4	85.5
Take LSD regularly	96.4	93.5
Try MDMA (Ecstasy) one or twice	—	88.2
Try cocaine once or twice	77.0	89.2
Take cocaine regularly	91.9	94.8
Try heroin once or twice	92.0	93.3
Take heroin regularly	97.8	95.9
Try amphetamines once or twice	74.8	87.2
Take amphetamines regularly	93.5	94.2
Try barbiturates once or twice	82.4	86.1
Take barbiturates regularly	94.3	94.3
Try one or two drinks of an alcoholic beverage (beer, wine, liquor)	15.6	29.8
Take one or two drinks nearly every day	67.7	74.5
Take four or five drinks nearly every day	90.2	89.8
Have five or more drinks once or twice each weekend	56.2	68.9
Smoke one or more packs of cigarettes per day	67.0	80.5
Take steroids	—	90.9

Source: Johnston et al. (2008a, Table 10). Retrieved from http://www.monitoringthefuture.org/data/08data/pr08t10.pdf.

children who are born of alcoholic biological parents and reared by non-alcoholic adoptive parents are more likely to abuse alcohol than are the biological children of the adoptive parents.

TREATMENT AND PREVENTION

Health professionals, educators, law enforcement officials, and laypeople have devised many approaches to the prevention and treatment of substance abuse and dependence among adolescents. However, treatment has been a frustrating endeavor, and it is not clear which approaches are most effective. In many cases, adolescents with drug dependence really do not want to discontinue the substances they are abusing. Many are referred to treatment by parents or school systems, but they deny the negative effect of drugs on their lives. Their peer group may frown on prevention or treatment (Lochman et al., 2007). Helping adolescents through withdrawal may be straightforward, but once their bodies no longer require the substance, they may return to the social milieu that fosters abuse (Anderson et al., 2007; Lochman et al., 2007).

The ability of teenagers to deal with the physical changes of adolescence and to engage in health-promoting behaviors depends in part on their growing cognitive abilities. We examine development in that area in Chapter 15.

The adolescent, like the adult,

can ponder abstract ideas and see the world as it could be.

15

Adolescence: Cognitive Development

I am a college student of extremely modest means. Some crazy psychologist interested in something called "formal operational thought" has just promised to pay me $20 if I can make a coherent logical argument for the proposition that the federal government should under no circumstances ever give or lend more to needy college students. Now what could people who believe that possibly say by way of supporting that argument? Well, I suppose they could offer this line of reasoning ...

—Flavell et al. (2002)

This "college student of extremely modest means" is thinking like an adolescent, quite differently from an elementary school child and differently from most middle-school children. Children in the concrete-operational stage are bound by the facts as they are. They are not given to hypothetical thinking, to speculation about what might be. They are mainly stuck in what is. But the adolescent, like the adult, can ponder abstract ideas and see the world as it could be. The "college student of extremely modest means" recognizes that a person can find arguments for causes in which he or she does not believe.

In this chapter, we learn about cognitive development in adolescence.

Learning Outcomes

LO1 Describe the cognitive advances that define adolescent thinking.

LO2 Describe and evaluate Kohlberg's view of the kinds of moral judgments made by many adolescents (and adults).

LO3 Discuss the transition to high school and factors associated with dropping out.

LO4 Discuss career development and the pluses and minuses of part-time work for high school students.

LO1 The Adolescent in Thought: My, My, How "Formal"

the growing intellectual capabilities of adolescents change the way they approach the world. The cognitive changes of adolescence influence how adolescents view themselves and their families and friends and how they deal with broader social and moral questions.

PIAGET'S STAGE OF FORMAL OPERATIONS

The stage of **formal operations** is the top level in Jean Piaget's theory. Children or adolescents in this stage have reached cognitive maturity, even if some rough edges remain. Yet for many children in developed nations, the stage of formal operations can begin at about the time of puberty, 11 or 12 years old. But some adolescents reach this stage later, others not at all. Piaget describes the stage of formal operations in terms of the individual's increased ability to classify objects and ideas, engage in logical thought, and hypothesize, just as researchers make hypotheses in their investigations. The adolescent can group and classify symbols, statements, and theories, just as psychologists classify certain views of child development as psychoanalytic theories, learning theories, or sociocultural theories, even if they differ in their particulars. Formal operations are flexible and reversible. Adolescents can formulate and follow arguments from their premises to their conclusions and back again, even if they do not believe in them. Hypothetical thinking, the use of symbols to represent other symbols, and deductive reasoning allow the adolescent to better comprehend the real world and to play with the world that dwells within the mind alone.

Hypothetical Thinking

In formal-operational thought, adolescents discover the concept of "what might be" in addition to "what is." Adolescents can project themselves into situations that transcend their immediate experience, and, for this reason, they may become wrapped up in lengthy fantasies. Many adolescents can explore endless corridors of the mind, perceiving what would happen as one decision leads to a point where a choice presents itself—and then still another decision is made. Adolescents become aware that situations can have different outcomes. They can think ahead, systematically trying out various possibilities in their minds.

You may think of scientists as people in white lab coats and with advanced degrees. And some are like that, of course. But many more wear blue jeans and experiment with their hair and ways of relating to people whom they find attractive. Many adolescents in the stage of formal operations conduct research daily to see whether their hypotheses about themselves and their friends and teachers are correct. Adolescents explore uncharted territory by trying on different clothes and attitudes to see which work best for them.

Adolescents may also see many possibilities for themselves. Some recognize that they can, to a large extent, fashion themselves according to their own images of what they are capable of becoming. The wealth of possible directions leads some adolescents to experience anxiety about whether they will pick the careers that best suit them and to experience a sense of loss because they may be able to choose only one.

This capacity to look ahead, to fashion futures, also frequently leads to **utopian** thinking. Just as adolescents

Adolescents are able to consider "what might be," dreaming up ideas about what they want to be.

© Suzanne Tucker/iStockphoto.com

---

formal operations
The fourth stage in Piaget's cognitive-developmental theory, characterized by the capacity for flexible, reversible operations concerning abstract ideas and concepts, such as symbols and theories.

utopian Referring to an ideal vision of society.

can foresee many possibilities for themselves, they can also imagine different outcomes for suffering humanity. "What if" thinking enables adolescents to fashion schemes for putting an end to hunger, disease, and international strife.

Sophisticated Use of Symbols

Children in elementary school can understand what is meant by abstract symbols such as 1 and 2. They can also perform operations in which numbers are manipulated—added, subtracted, and so on. But consider *x,* that unknown (and sometimes elusive) quantity in algebra. This *x* may be a familiar letter of the alphabet, but its designation as a symbol for an unknown quantity is a formal abstract operation. One symbol (*x*) is being made to stand for something just as abstract (the unknown). Children up to the age of 11 or 12 or so usually cannot fully understand this concept, even if they can be taught the mechanics of solving for *x* in simple equations. But older, formal-operational children show a sophisticated grasp of the nature of symbols.

These symbols include those used in geometry. Adolescents work with points that have no dimensions, lines that have no width and that are infinite in length, and circles that are perfectly round, even though they may never find them in nature. The ability to manipulate these symbols will eventually permit them to do work in theoretical physics or math or to design machines and buildings.

Formal-operational individuals can also understand, appreciate, and sometimes produce metaphors. *Metaphors* are figures of speech in which words or phrases that ordinarily signify one thing are applied to another. We find metaphors in literature, but consider how everyday figures of speech enhance our experience: *squeezing* out a living, *basking in the sunshine* of fame or glory, *hanging by a thread, jumping* to conclusions, and so on.

The moral judgments of many adolescents and adults are based on formal-operational thought. That is, they derive their judgments about what is right and wrong in specific situations by reasoning deductively from general moral principles. Their capacity for decentration allows them to focus on many aspects of a situation at once in making judgments and solving moral dilemmas.

Enhanced cognitive abilities can backfire when adolescents adamantly advance their religious, political, and social ideas without recognition of the subtleties and practical issues that might give pause to adults. For example, let's begin with the

premise, "Industries should not be allowed to pollute the environment." We then discover that Industry A pollutes the environment. An adolescent may argue to shut down Industry A, at least until it stops polluting. The logic is reasonable and the goal is noble enough, but Industry A may be indispensable to the nation at large, or many thousands of people may be put out of work if it is shut down. Many adults might prefer to seek a compromise.

Adolescents' new intellectual powers often present them with what seem to be crystal-clear solutions to the world's problems, and they may become intolerant of the relative stodginess of their parents. Their utopian images of how to reform the world make them unsympathetic to their parents' earthbound pursuit of a livelihood and other mundane matters.

Reevaluation of Piaget's Theory

Piaget's account of formal operations has received quite a bit of support. There appears to be little question that unique changes do occur in the nature of reasoning between preadolescence and adolescence (U. Mueller et al., 1999, 2001). For example, research strongly supports Piaget's view that the capacity to reason deductively does not emerge until adolescence (U. Mueller et al., 1999, 2001).

But formal-operational thought is not a universal step in cognitive development. The ability to solve abstract problems, such as those found in algebra, is most likely to be developed in technologically oriented Western societies or in major cities (Flavell et al., 2002; Siegler & Alibali, 2005). Moreover, formal-operational thought may occur later than Piaget thought, if at all. Reviews of research findings suggest that formal-operational thought is found among only 40% to 60% of first-year college students (Flavell et al., 2002; Siegler & Alibali, 2005). Also, the same individual may do well on one type of formal-operational task and poorly on another. We are more likely to use formal-operational thought in our own academic specialties. Piaget (1972) recognized that adolescents may not demonstrate formal-operational thought when they are unfamiliar with a particular task.

imaginary audience The belief that others around us are as concerned with our thoughts and behaviors as we are; one aspect of adolescent egocentrism.

personal fable The belief that our feelings and ideas are special and unique and that we are invulnerable; one aspect of adolescent egocentrism.

ADOLESCENT EGOCENTRISM: CENTER STAGE

Did you think that egocentrism was limited to the thought of preschool children, who show difficulty taking the perspective of other people in the three-mountains test? Wrong. Yes, teenagers are capable of hypothetical thinking, and they can argue for causes in which they do not believe (if you pay them enough to do so). However, they also can show a new brand of egocentrism. Adolescents comprehend the ideas of other people, but have difficulty sorting out those things that concern other people from the things that concern themselves.

The Imaginary Audience

Many adolescents fantasize about becoming rock stars or movie stars who are adored by millions. The concept of the **imaginary audience** achieves part of that fantasy, in a sense. It places the adolescent on stage, but more surrounded by critics than admirers. Adolescents assume that other people are concerned with their appearance and behavior, more so than those others really are (Elkind, 1967, 1985; Kuterbach, 2007).

T F Many adolescents see themselves as being on stage.
True; adolescents behave as though an imaginary audience is peering at them.

The imaginary audience may account for the intense desire for privacy that is common among adolescents and for their preoccupation with their appearance. It helps explain why the mirror is the constant companion of the teenager, who grooms endlessly, searches out every facial blemish, and agonizes over every zit. Being caught up with the mirror seems to peak sometime during eighth grade and declines over the remainder of adolescence.

Whereas some researchers view the emergence of the imaginary audience purely in cognitive-developmental terms, others believe that many adolescents are responding to increased social scrutiny (Bell & Brom-nick, 2003; Kelly et al., 2002). One research group attributes the imaginary audience more to social anxiety than to cognitive development (Kelly et al., 2002).

The Personal Fable

Spider-Man and the Fantastic Four: Stand aside! Because of the personal fable, many adolescents become action heroes, at least in their own minds. If the imaginary audience puts adolescents on stage, the personal fable justifies being there. The **personal fable**, another aspect of adolescent egocentrism, is the belief that one's thoughts and emotions are special and unique (Aalsma et al., 2006). It also refers to the common adolescent belief that one is all but invulnerable, like Superman or Superwoman.

T F It is normal for male adolescents to think of themselves as action heroes and to act as though they are made of steel.
True; according to one aspect of the personal fable, male adolescents tend to think of themselves as invulnerable and take significant risks.

The personal fable is connected with such behaviors as showing off and risk taking (Omori & Ingersoll, 2005). Many adolescents assume that they can smoke with impunity. Cancer? "It can't happen to me." They drive recklessly. They engage in spontaneous unprotected sexual activity, assuming that sexually transmitted infections (STIs) and unwanted pregnancies happen to other people, not to them. Ronald King (2000), of the HIV Community Coalition of Washington DC, put it this way: "All youth—rich, poor, black, white—have this sense of invincibility, invulnerability." Adolescents are more likely than their parents to minimize their assessment of risks (Berger et al., 2005; Nowinski, 2007).

Many adolescents believe that adults and sometimes peers can never feel what they are feeling or know the depth of their passions. "You just don't understand

© Martin Barraud/Getty Images

me!" claims the adolescent. But, at least often enough, we do.

SEX DIFFERENCES IN COGNITIVE ABILITIES

Although females and males do not differ noticeably in overall intelligence, sex differences appear in certain cognitive abilities beginning in childhood (Johnson & Bouchard, 2007). Females are somewhat superior to males in verbal ability. Males, on the other hand, seem somewhat superior in visual–spatial skills. The picture for mathematics ability is more complex, with females excelling in some areas and males excelling in others. Let's take a closer look at these sex differences.

Verbal Ability

Verbal ability includes a large number of language skills, such as reading, spelling, grammar, oral comprehension, and word fluency. As a group, females surpass males in verbal ability (Halpern, 2003, 2004). These differences show up early. Girls seem to acquire language faster than boys. They make more prelinguistic vocalizations, utter their first word sooner, and develop larger vocabularies. Boys in the United States are more likely than girls to be dyslexic (Halpern, 2003, 2004). They also are more likely to have other reading problems, such as reading below grade level.

Why do females excel in verbal ability? For one thing, parents talk more to their infant daughters than to their infant sons (see Chapter 6). This encouragement of verbal interaction may be connected with girls' relative verbal precocity. Because of this early language advantage, girls may rely more on verbal skills to interact with people, thus furthering their abilities in this area (Halpern & LaMay, 2000). How do we account for sex differences in reading? Biological factors such as the organization of the brain may play a role, but do not discount cultural factors. One factor is whether a culture stamps reading as a gender-neutral, masculine, or feminine activity (Goldstein, 2005). Consider Nigeria and England. Reading is looked on as a masculine activity in these nations, and boys traditionally surpass girls in reading ability (and other academic skills). In the United States and Canada, however, reading tends to be stereotyped as feminine, and girls tend to excel in reading in these nations. People of all ages and all cultures tend to apply themselves more diligently to pursuits that they believe are "meant" for them, whether it is the life of the nomad, ballet, ice hockey, or reading.

Visual–Spatial Ability

Visual–spatial ability refers to the ability to visualize objects or shapes and to mentally manipulate and rotate them. As you can imagine, this ability is important in such fields as art, architecture, and engineering. Boys begin to outperform girls on many types of visual–spatial tasks starting at age 8 or 9, and the difference persists into adulthood (Ecuyer-Dab & Robert, 2004; Johnson & Bouchard, 2007; Parsons et al., 2004). The sex difference is particularly notable on mental rotation tasks (see Figure 15.1), which require imagining how objects will look if they are rotated in space (Delgado & Prieto, 2004).

What is the basis for the sex difference in visual–spatial skills? A number of biological and environmental explanations have been offered. One biological theory that has received some attention is that visual–spatial ability is influenced by sex-linked recessive genes on the X sex chromosome. But this theory has not been supported by research (Halpern & LaMay, 2000).

Some researchers link visual–spatial performance to evolutionary theory and sex hormones. For example, male humans, like many other male mammals, have a larger "home range." Visual-spatial ability may be related to a genetic tendency to create and defend a territory; and the size of the home range is connected with spatial ability (Ecuyer-Dab & Robert, 2004). Also, high levels of prenatal androgens have been linked to better performance on visual–spatial and arithmetic tasks among 4- and 6-year-old girls (Finegan et al., 1992; Jacklin et al., 1988). One study (Kimura & Hampson, 1992) found that women performed better on visual–spatial tasks when their estrogen levels were low than when their estrogen levels were high. (By contrast, they were better at tasks involving verbal skills when estrogen levels were high.)

One environmental theory is that gender stereotypes influence the spatial experiences of children. Gender-stereotyped "boys' toys," such as blocks, Legos, and Erector sets, provide more practice with spatial skills than gender-stereotyped "girls' toys." Boys are also more likely to engage in sports, which involve moving balls and other objects through space. Boys are allowed to travel farther from home than girls are, providing greater opportunities for exploration and a larger home range (Halpern, 2004). It is no secret that participation in spatially related activities is associated with better performance on visual–spatial tasks.

Mathematical Ability

For decades, it has been believed that male adolescents generally outperform females in mathematics (Collaer &

FIGURE 15.1
Examples of Tests Used to Measure Visual–Spatial Ability

No sex differences are found on the spatial visualization tasks in part (a). Boys do somewhat better than girls on the tasks measuring spatial perception in part (b). The sex difference is greatest on the mental rotation tasks in part (c). What are some possible reasons for these differences?

a. Spatial visualization
Embedded-figure test. Study the figure on the left. Then cover it up and try to find where it is hidden in the figure on the right. The left-hand figure may need to be shifted in order to locate it in the right-hand figure.

b. Spatial perception
Water-level test. Examine the glass of water on the left. Now imagine that it is slightly tilted, as on the right. Draw in a line to indicate the location of the water level.

c. Mental rotation
Mental-rotation test. If you mentally rotate the figure on the left, which of the five figures on the right would you obtain?

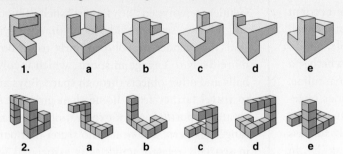

Answers: **a.** 1: Orient the pattern as if it were a tilted capital M, with the left portion along the top of the white triangle. 2: This pattern fits along the right sides of the two black triangles on the left. 3: Rotate this figure about 100° to the right, so that it forms a Z, with the top line coinciding with the top line of the top white triangle. **b.** The line should be horizontal, not tilted. **c.** 1: c; 2: d.

Go to 4ltrpress.cengage.com/cdev to access an interactive version of this figure.

Hill, 2006; Halpern, 2004). On the other hand, reviewers of the research on sex differences in math concluded that sex differences appear in adolescence, but in a review of 100 studies involving more than 3 million individuals, Janet Hyde and her colleagues (1990) found a slight superiority for girls in computational skills in the elementary and middle-school years. Boys began to perform better in word problems in high school and college. There were no sex differences in understanding math concepts at any age. Among groups of more highly selected individuals, such as college students or mathematically precocious youth, differences were larger and favored males.

However, a more recent study by Hyde and her colleagues (2008) of some 7 million second through eleventh graders found no sex differences for performance in mathematics on standardized tests. The complexity of the test items apparently made no difference. Nevertheless, most Americans have different expectations for boys and girls, and these expectations may still dissuade girls from entering fields in science and math (Hyde et al., 2008). The researchers did find that overall "There is evidence of slightly greater male variability in scores, although the causes remain unexplained" (p. 495). That is, males tended to have higher and lower scores, although the average scores did not differ between males and females. This finding is consistent with findings of other researchers that show more males obtaining high scores on the quantitative scale of the SATs. Even so, the Hyde group (2008) noted that differences in math scores among high scorers were not large enough to explain why females were less likely than males to pursue some

careers in science, technology, engineering, and mathematics. We can note that many or most Americans quite unfairly have different expectations for boys and girls, and that these expectations may affect performance in mathematics (Ceci & Williams, 2007; Eccles, 2007; Halpern, 2006).

T̶ F̲ Adolescent boys outperform adolescent girls in mathematics.
False; this wideheld belief is too broad to be accurate. Recent research, for example, shows no group differences in performance in math among second through eleventh graders.

What, then, shall we conclude about sex differences in cognitive abilities? First, it appears that girls show greater verbal ability than boys do but that boys show greater visual–spatial ability (Bailey, 2003; Halpern 2004). The debate about possible differences in math skills remains open. However, sex differences in cognitive skills are group differences, not individual differences. That is, the difference in, say, reading skills between a male who reads well and a male who is dyslexic is greater than the average group sex difference in reading ability. Moreover, despite group differences, millions of females exceed the average American male in math and visual–spatial skills. Similarly, despite group differences, millions of males exceed the average American female in writing, spelling, and articulation. Millions of women perform well in domains that had once been considered masculine, such as medicine and law.

While scholars sit around and debate sex differences in intellectual functioning, women have been voting on

the issue by flooding many fields once populated almost exclusively by men (Eccles, 2007; Halpern, 2006, 2007). Table 15.1 and Figure 15.2 show that women are tossing these stereotypes out the window by entering the sciences and professional fields ranging from business to law to medicine in increasing numbers.

TABLE 15.1

Women as a Percentage of College Students Receiving Bachelor's Degrees in the Sciences and Engineering

FIELD	1971	2005–2006
Biology	29%	63%
Chemistry	18	51
Computer science	14	21
Engineering	1	19
Geology	11	42
Mathematics	38	46
Physics	7	21

Sources: Cox & Alm (2005); National Center for Educational Statistics (NCES, 2007b)..

LO2 The Adolescent in Judgment: Moral Development

moral development in adolescence is a complex issue with cognitive and behavioral aspects. Children in early childhood tend to view right and wrong in terms of rewards and punishments. Lawrence Kohlberg referred to such judgments as *preconventional*. In middle childhood, *conventional* thought tends to emerge, and children usually begin to judge right and wrong in terms of social conventions, rules, and

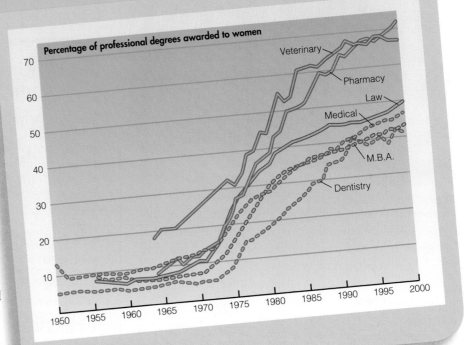

postconventional level
According to Kohlberg, a period during which moral judgments are derived from moral principles and people look to themselves to set moral standards.

laws (see Table 12.1 on page 200, reproduced in part in Table 15.2 below). In adolescence, many—not all—individuals become capable of formal-operational thinking, which allows them to derive conclusions about what they should do in various situations by reasoning from ethical principles. And many of these individuals engage in *post-conventional* moral reasoning. They *deduce* proper behavior just as they might deduce that a platypus is a mammal because platypuses feed their young with breast milk.

THE POSTCONVENTIONAL LEVEL

In the **postconventional level**, moral reasoning is based on the person's own moral standards. Moral judgments are derived from personal values, not from conven-

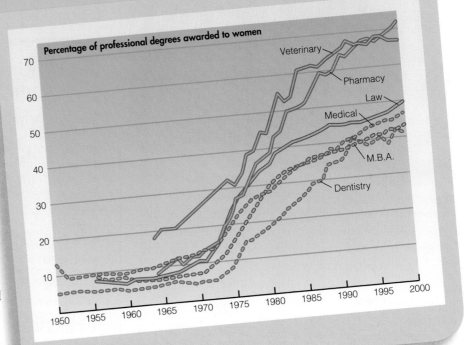

FIGURE 15.2

Women Flood Professions Once Populated Almost Exclusively by Men

Percentage of professional degrees awarded to women

tional standards or authority figures. In the contractual, legalistic orientation of Stage 5, it is recognized that laws stem from agreed-on procedures and that many rights have great value and should not be violated. But

TABLE 15.2

Kohlberg's Postconventional Level of Moral Development

STAGE	EXAMPLES OF MORAL REASONING THAT SUPPORT HEINZ'S STEALING THE DRUG	EXAMPLES OF MORAL REASONING THAT OPPOSE HEINZ'S STEALING THE DRUG
Stage 5: *Contractual, legalistic orientation:* One must weigh pressing human needs against society's need to maintain social order.	This thing is complicated because society has a right to maintain law and order, but Heinz has to steal the drug to save his wife.	I can see why Heinz feels he has to steal the drug, but laws exist for the benefit of society as a whole and cannot simply be cast aside.
Stage 6: *Universal ethical principles orientation:* People must follow universal ethical principles and their own conscience, even if it means breaking the law.	In this case, the law comes into conflict with the principle of the sanctity of human life. Heinz must steal the drug because his wife's life is more important than the law.	If Heinz truly believes that stealing the drug is worse than letting his wife die, he should not steal it. People have to make sacrifices to do what they think is right.

under exceptional circumstances, such as in the case of Heinz, laws cannot bind the individual. A Stage 5 reason why Heinz should steal the drug might be that it is the right thing to do, even though it is illegal. Conversely, it could be argued that if everyone in need broke the law, the legal system and the social contract would be destroyed.

Stage 6 thinking relies on supposed universal ethical principles, such as the sanctity of human life, individual dignity, justice, and **reciprocity**. Behavior that is consistent with these principles is considered right. If a law is seen as unjust or contradicts the right of the individual, it is wrong to obey it.

In the case of Heinz, it could be argued from the perspective of Stage 6 that the principle of preserving life takes precedence over laws prohibiting stealing. Therefore, it is morally necessary for Heinz to steal the drug, even if he must go to jail. Note that it could also be asserted, from the universal ethical principles orientation, that if Heinz finds the social contract or the law to be the highest principle, he must remain within the law, despite the consequences.

reciprocity The principle that actions have mutual effects and that people depend on one another to treat each other morally.

Stage 5 and 6 moral judgments were virtually absent among the 7- and 10-year-olds in Kohlberg's (1963) sample of American children. They increased in frequency during the early and middle teens. By age 16, Stage 5 reasoning was shown by about 20% of adolescents and Stage 6 reasoning was demonstrated by about 5% of adolescents. However, Stage 3 and 4 judgments were made more frequently at all ages—7 through 16—studied by Kohlberg and other investigators (Colby et al., 1983; Commons et al., 2006; Rest, 1983) (see Figure 15.3).

T F Most adolescents make moral decisions based on their own ethical principles and may choose to disobey laws that conflict with their principles. *False; postconventional moral reasoning appears in adolescence if it appears at all, but most adolescents reason at lower levels.*

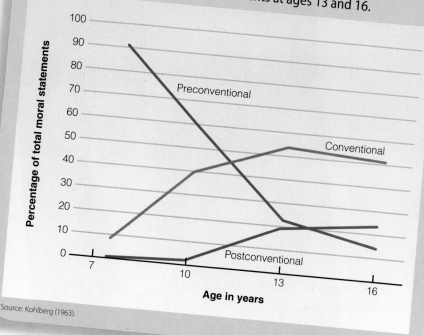

FIGURE 15.3
Age and Type of Moral Judgment

The incidence of preconventional reasoning declines from more than 90% of moral statements at age 7 to less than 20% of statements at age 16. Conventional moral statements increase with age between the ages of 7 and 13 but then level off to account for 50% to 60% of statements at ages 13 and 16. Postconventional moral statements are all but absent at ages 7 and 10 but account for about 20% to 25% of statements at ages 13 and 16.

Percentage of total moral statements

Preconventional
Conventional
Postconventional

Age in years

Source: Kohlberg (1963).

MORAL BEHAVIOR AND MORAL REASONING

Is there a relationship between moral cognitive development and moral behavior? Are individuals whose moral judgments are more mature more likely to engage in moral behavior? The answer seems to be yes; many studies have found positive relationships between a person's level of moral development and his or her behavior (Cheung et al., 2001; Emler et al., 2007; Greenberg, 2002).

Individuals whose moral reasoning is at Stage 2 cheat, steal, and engage in other problem behaviors more often than peers whose moral reasoning is at higher stages (Greenberg, 2002; Richards et al., 1992). Adolescents with higher levels of moral reasoning are more likely to exhibit moral behavior, including altruistic behavior (Hart et al., 2003; Maclean et al., 2004).

Experiments also have been conducted in the hope of advancing moral reasoning as a way of decreasing immoral behavior (Palmer, 2005). A number of studies have found that group discussion of moral dilemmas elevates delinquents' level of moral reasoning (Smetana, 1990). Is moral behavior affected as well? In one study, discussions of moral dilemmas improved moral reasoning and reduced incidents of, for example, school tardiness, behavior referrals, and police and court contacts among adolescents with behavioral problems (Arbuthnot & Gordon, 1988).

CROSS-CULTURAL DIFFERENCES IN MORAL DEVELOPMENT

Cultural background is a powerful shaper of moral reasoning. Kohlberg found postconventional thinking among a minority of American adolescents, and it was all but absent among adolescents in villages in Mexico, Taiwan, Turkey (Kohlberg, 1969), and the Bahamas (White et al., 1978). Reviews of research findings conclude that postconventional reasoning is more likely to be found in urban cultural groups and in middle-class populations but that it is rarely seen in traditional folk cultures (Boom et al., 2007; Dawson, 2002; Snarey, 1994).

A similar pattern has been found in comparisons of middle-class American and Hindu Indian children and adults. Hindu Indians are more likely to show a caring orientation in making moral judgments, whereas Americans more often demonstrate a justice orientation. These findings are consistent with the greater emphasis that Hindu Indian culture puts on taking responsibility for others (Miller, 1994; Miller & Bersoff, 1992).

> Postconventional reasoning is more likely to be found in urban cultural groups and in middle-class populations.

SEX DIFFERENCES IN MORAL DEVELOPMENT

Some researchers claim that males reason at higher levels of moral development than females in terms of responses to Heinz's dilemma. For example, Kohlberg and Kramer (1969) reported that the average stage of moral development for men was Stage 4, which emphasizes justice, law, and order. The average stage for women was reported to be Stage 3, which emphasizes caring and concern for others.

Carol Gilligan (Gilligan, 1977, 1982; Gilligan & Attanucci, 1988) argues that this sex difference reflects patterns of socialization. Gilligan provides two examples of responses to Heinz's dilemma. Eleven-year-old Jake views the dilemma as a math problem. He sets up an equation showing that life has greater value than property. Heinz should thus steal the drug. Eleven-year-old Amy, on the other hand, notes that stealing the drug and letting Heinz's wife die would both be wrong. Amy searches for alternatives, such as getting a loan, stating that it would profit Heinz's wife little if he went to jail and was no longer around to help her.

In Gilligan's illustration, eleven-year-old Jake looks at Heinz's decision based on a scale of comparative values, while eleven-year-old Amy views both options as wrong and looks for alternatives. According to Kohlberg, however, Amy's reasoning reflects a lower stage of moral development.

© Zia Soleil/Getty Images

Although Gilligan sees Amy's pattern of reasoning as being as sophisticated as Jake's, it would be rated as showing a lower level of moral development in Kohlberg's system. Gilligan asserts that Amy, like other girls, has been socialized into focusing on the needs of others and foregoing simplistic judgments of right and wrong. Jake, by contrast, has been socialized into making judgments based on logic. To him, clear-cut conclusions are to be derived from a set of premises. Amy was aware of the logical considerations that struck Jake, but she processed them as one source of information, not as the sole source. It is ironic that Amy's empathy, a trait that has "defined the 'goodness' of women," marks Amy "as deficient in moral development" (Gilligan, 1982, p. 18).

Kohlberg, Gilligan, and other researchers tend to agree that in making moral judgments, females are more likely to show a caring orientation, whereas males are more likely to assume a justice orientation (Jorgensen, 2006). But there remains a dispute as to whether this difference means that girls reason at a lower level than boys do (Jorgensen, 2006; Knox et al., 2004). Kohlberg, by the way, viewed Gilligan's ideas as an extension of his own views, not as a repudiation of them, and Gilligan largely supported Kohlberg's stage theory and his claim of its universality (Jorgensen, 2006).

Evaluation of Kohlberg's Theory

Evidence supports Kohlberg's view that the moral judgments of children develop in the sequence he suggested (Boom et al., 2007), even though most people do not reach postconventional thought. Formal-operational thinking appears to be a prerequisite for postconventional reasoning, and education is also likely to play a role (Boom et al., 2007; Patenaude et al., 2003). Parents are also important. Inductive disciplinary methods, including discussions of the feelings of others, advance moral reasoning (Dawson, 2002; Palmer & Hollin, 2001).

Postconventional reasoning appears to require the capacities to understand abstract moral principles and to empathize with the views and feelings of others. However, neither formal-operational thought nor education guarantees the development of postconventional reasoning.

Kohlberg believed that the stages of moral development are universal, but he may have underestimated the influence of social, cultural, and educational institutions (Dawson, 2002; Nucci, 2002). Postconventional thinking is all but absent in developing societies and uncommon in the United States (Commons et al., 2006; Snarey, 1994). Perhaps postconventional reasoning reflects Kohlberg's personal ideals and not a natural,

universal stage of development (Helwig, 2006). Stage 6 reasoning is based on the acceptance of supposedly universal ethical principles. The principles of freedom, justice, equality, tolerance, integrity, and reverence for human life have high appeal for most American adolescents who are reared to idealize these principles.

As we look around the world—and at many of the events unfolding in the 21st century—we find that principles such as freedom and tolerance of differences are not universally admired. They may reflect Western cultural influences more than the cognitive development of the child. In his later years, Kohlberg (1985) dropped Stage 6 reasoning from his theory in recognition of these problems.

LO3 The Adolescent in School

It's clear that school is very important to the development of the adolescent. Adolescents are highly influenced by the opinions of their peers and their teachers. Their self-esteem rises or falls consistently with their acquisition of skills.

MAKING THE TRANSITION FROM ELEMENTARY SCHOOL

Students make at least one and sometimes two transitions to a new school before they complete high school. Think back to your own school days. Did you spend the years from kindergarten to eighth grade in one building and then move on to high school? Did you instead attend elementary school through sixth grade and then go to junior high for grades 7–9 before starting high school? Or did you complete kindergarten through grade 4 or 5 in one school, then attend a middle school for grades 5 or 6 to 8, and then move on to high school for grades 9–12?

The transition to middle, junior high, or high school generally involves a shift from a smaller neighborhood elementary school with self-contained classrooms to a larger, more impersonal setting with many more students and with different teachers for different classes. These changes may not fit very well with the developmental needs of early adolescents. For example, adolescents express a desire for increased autonomy, yet teachers in junior high typically allow less student input and exert

© Design Pics/Jupiterimages

more behavioral control than teachers in elementary school (Tobbell, 2003). Moreover, in the shift to the new school, students move from being the "top dog" (i.e., the oldest and most experienced students) to being the "bottom dog." These changes are not the only ones facing the early adolescent. Many youngsters also are going through the early stages of pubertal development at about the same time they move to a new school.

How well do students adjust to the transition to a new school? Much of the research has examined children's experiences as they move from elementary school to junior high school. The transition to the new school setting often is accompanied by a decline in grades and in participation in school activities. Students may also experience a drop in self-esteem and an increase in psychological distress (Rudolph & Flynn, 2007; Tobbell, 2003). A German study found a connection between the adolescent's psychological adjustment and his or her grades by the end of the first year in high school (Ball et al., 2006).

The transition from elementary school appears to be more difficult for girls than for boys. In one study, girls who switched to a junior high for seventh grade showed a decrease in self-esteem, whereas girls who stayed in their kindergarten through eighth-grade school did not. Boys' self-esteem did not change when they switched to junior high (Simmons &

Blyth, 1987). The difference may reflect that fact that girls are more likely to be undergoing puberty at about this time. Girls at this age are also likely to earn the attention of boys in higher grades, whereas younger boys are not likely to be of much interest to older girls. Girls experience major life changes, and children who experience several life changes at once find it more difficult to adjust to a new school (Tobbell, 2003).

T F The transition from elementary school is more difficult for boys than for girls.
False; the transition is more difficult for girls.

But the school transition need not be that stressful. Students who are in greater control of their lives tend to do better with the transition (Rudolph et al., 2001). Elementary and middle schools can help ease the transition to high school. For example, one longitudinal study followed the progress of students who received a 2-year social decision-making and problem-solving program in elementary school. When followed in high school 4 to 6 years later, these students showed higher levels of prosocial behavior and fewer conduct problems than students who had not been in the program (Elias et al., 1991). Some middle schools create a more intimate, caring atmosphere by, for instance, establishing smaller schools within the school building. Others have "bridge programs" during the summer between middle school and high school. The programs introduce students to the new school culture and strengthen their academic skills.

DROPPING OUT

School is a key path to success in our society, but not all adolescents complete high school. The consequences of dropping out can be grim indeed. High school dropouts are more likely to be unemployed (Wald & Losen, 2007). They make lower salaries. Research suggests that each year of education, from grade school through graduate school, adds about 16% to an individual's lifetime earnings (Passell, 1992). (This finding is a good incentive for you not only to complete college but also to consider graduate work!)

© Peeter Viisimaa/iStockphoto.com

Dropouts are also more likely to show problem behaviors, including delinquency, criminal behavior, and substance abuse (Donovan & Wells, 2007; Wald & Losen, 2007). However, it is sometimes difficult to disentangle the consequences of dropping out from its causes. A pattern of delinquent behavior, for example, might precede as well as follow dropping out.

Who Drops Out?

It is difficult to estimate the magnitude of the school dropout problem, because states use different reporting systems and most do not track those who quit after eighth grade. Overall, about 15% of males, aged 18 to 24, and 12% of females in the same age group have dropped out of high school (NCES, 2007a). However, dropout rates vary considerably between ethnic groups (see Table 15.3). The dropout rate was highest for African Americans, at 7.3%. That rate was followed by Latino and Latina Americans, at 5%. European Americans dropped out at a reported rate of 2.8%. Students from lower-income backgrounds and older students were more likely to drop out. The higher dropout rates for children from African

TABLE 15.3

Dropout Rates and Distribution of 15- through 24-Year-Olds Who Dropped Out of Grades 10–12, According to Various Background Characteristics

CHARACTERISTIC	DROPOUT RATE (PERCENT)	NUMBER OF DROPOUTS (THOUSANDS)	POPULATION ENROLLED (THOUSANDS)	PERCENT OF ALL DROPOUTS
Total	3.8	414	10,870	100.0
Sex				
Male	4.2	233	5,515	56.3
Female	3.4	181	5,355	43.7
Race/ethnicity				
European American	2.8	196	6,897	47.3
African American	7.3	112	1,538	27.2
Latino and Latina American	5.0	86	1,717	20.8
Asian/Pacific Islander	1.6	6	411	1.5
More than one race	4.9	12	241	2.9
Family income				
Low income	8.9	137	1,544	33.1
Middle income	3.8	228	5,990	55.2
High income	1.5	49	3,326	11.7
Age				
15–16	2.1	72	3,347	17.4
17	2.4	93	3,797	22.5
18	3.9	105	2,693	25.3
19	9.1	64	702	15.4
20–24	24.4	81	331	19.5

Source: NCES (2007a, Table 1).

American and Latino and Latina American minority groups are linked to the lower socioeconomic status of their families (Suh et al., 2007). When income levels are held constant, racial and ethnic differences in school dropout rates are reduced (NCES, 2007a).

Excessive school absence and reading below grade level are two of the earliest and strongest predictors of dropping out (Lever et al., 2004). Other risk factors include low grades, poor problem-solving ability, low self-esteem, problems with teachers, dissatisfaction with school, substance abuse, being old for one's grade level, and being male (Christenson & Thurlow, 2004; South et al., 2007). Adolescents who adopt adult roles early, especially marrying at a young age or becoming a parent, are also more likely to drop out (Bohon et al., 2007). Students from low-income households, large urban areas, and the West and South are at greater risk (NCES, 2007a). But not all dropouts come from low-income families. Middle-class youth who feel bored with school, alienated, or strongly pressured to succeed also are at risk (Battin-Pearson et al., 2000; Lee & Burkam, 2003).

Preventing Dropping Out

Many programs have been developed to prevent dropping out. Successful programs have some common characteristics (Bost & Riccomini, 2006; Reschly & Christenson, 2006):

- Early preschool intervention (as with Head Start)
- Identification and monitoring of high-risk students throughout the school years
- Small class size, individualized instruction, and counseling
- Vocational components that link learning and community work experiences
- Involvement of families or community organizations
- Positive school climate
- Clear and reasonable educational goals (if you don't know where you're going, how you get there isn't very important), student accountability for behavior, and motivational systems that involve penalties and rewards

Most intervention efforts are usually not introduced until students are on the verge of dropping out—when it is usually too late.

LO4 The Adolescent at Work: Career Development and Work Experience

deciding what job or career we will pursue after completion of school is one of the most important choices we make.

CAREER DEVELOPMENT

Children's career aspirations may not be practical at first. They become increasingly realistic—and often more conventional—as children mature and gain experience. In adolescence, ideas about the kind of work one wants to do tend to become more firmly established, or crystallized, but a particular occupation may not be chosen until the college years or afterward (Rottinghaus et al., 2003; Sullivan & Hansen, 2004).

Holland's Career Typology

Psychologists have devised approaches to matching personality traits with careers to predict adjustment in a given career. John Holland's (1997) RIASEC method, as used in his Vocational Preference Inventory, matches six personality types to various kinds of careers: realistic, investigative, artistic, social, enterprising, and conventional. Within each "type" of career, some are more sophisticated than others and require more education and training.

- Realistic people, according to Holland, are concrete in thinking. They are mechanically oriented. They tend to be best adjusted in occupations that involve motor activity. Examples of such occupations include unskilled labor, such as attending gas stations; farming; and the skilled trades, such as auto repair, electrical work, plumbing, or construction work.

- Investigative people are abstract in their thinking. They are creative and tend to be introverted but open to new experiences. They tend to do well in college and university teaching and in research positions.

- Artistic people also tend to be creative and open to new experiences. As a group, they are emotional, interested in the emotional life, and intuitive. They tend to be happiest in the visual and the performing arts.

- Socially oriented people tend to be outgoing (extraverted) and concerned for social welfare. They often are agreeable and have a need for affiliation. They gravitate toward occupations in teaching (kindergarten through high school), counseling, and social work.

- Enterprising people tend to be adventurous. They tend to be outgoing and dominant. They gravitate toward industrial roles that involve leadership and planning. They climb the ladder in government and social organizations.

- Conventional people thrive on routine. They are not particularly imaginative. They have needs for order, self-control, and social approval. They gravitate toward occupations in banking, accounting, clerical work, and the military.

Many people combine several of these vocational types (Darcy & Tracey, 2007; Nauta, 2007). A copywriter in an advertising agency might be both artistic and enterprising. Clinical and counseling psychologists tend to be investigative, artistic, and socially oriented. Military people and beauticians tend to be realistic and conventional. But military leaders who plan major operations and form governments are also enterprising; and individuals who create new hair styles and fashions are also artistic. Holland's Vocational Preference Inventory assesses these personality types, as do various vocational tests that are used in high schools and colleges.

All in all, more than 20,000 occupations are found in *The Dictionary of Occupational Titles*, which is compiled by the U.S. Department of Labor. But most young people choose from a relatively small range of occupations on the basis of their personalities, experiences, and opportunities (Arbona, 2005; Laplan, 2004). Many fall into jobs that are offered to them or follow career paths that are blazed by parents or role models in the community (Laplan, 2004; Nauta, 2007).

> Most young people choose from a relatively small range of occupations on the basis of their personalities, experiences, and opportunities.

ADOLESCENTS IN THE WORKFORCE

Kimberly, age 16, has a job at a fast-food restaurant located in the suburb of a midwestern city. She has already saved $1,000 toward a car and a stereo by working at the restaurant after school and on weekends. Kimberly is worried because her state legislature is considering regulations that would cut back the number of hours she is allowed to work.

Life experiences help shape vocational development. One life experience that is common among American teenagers is holding a job.

Prevalence of Adolescent Employment

Chances are that you did hold a job. About half of all high school sophomores, two-thirds of juniors, and almost three-fourths of seniors have a job during the school year (Bachman et al., 2003). Girls and boys are equally likely to be employed, but boys work more hours (Staff et al., 2004).

Millions of adolescents between the ages of 14 and 18 are legally employed. But perhaps another 2 to 3 million are working illegally (Bachman et al., 2003; Holloway, 2004). Some of these teenagers are paid in cash so that their employers can avoid paying taxes or minimum wages. Others work too many hours, work late hours on school nights, or work at hazardous jobs. Some are younger than 14 and are too young to be legally employed except on farms.

Adolescent employment rates show ethnic and social-class differences (Bachman et al., 2003). European American teenagers are twice as likely to be employed as teenagers from ethnic minority groups, for example. In past years, teenagers from poorer households were more likely to work to help support the family. Nowadays, adolescent employment is more common among middle-class youth. This change may be partly because middle-class families are more likely to live near locations, such as suburban shopping malls, that are fertile sources of jobs for teenagers. But employed lower-income adolescents work longer hours than working middle-class teens do (Bachman et al., 2003).

Pros and Cons of Adolescent Employment

The potential benefits of adolescent employment include developing a sense of responsibility, self-reliance, and discipline; learning to appreciate the value of money and education; acquiring positive work habits and values; and enhancing occupational aspirations (Porfeli, 2007). On the other hand, the meaning of work for adolescents—at least for middle-class adolescents—seems to have changed. Most adolescents who work do not do so to help support their families or to put money away for college. Although adolescents of lower socioeconomic status work mainly to supplement the family income (Woodland, 2008), most middle-class adolescents use their income for personal purchases, such as clothing, iPods, CDs, gear, and car payments (Bachman et al., 2003). The proportion of earnings devoted to family expenses or put away for college is small.

Then, too, most working adolescents are in jobs with low pay, high turnover, little authority, and little chance for advancement. They typically perform simple, repetitive tasks requiring no special skills (Staff et al., 2004). Some question the benefits of such jobs, especially since envisioning a future career is apparently a stronger contributor to vocational development than work experience is (Porfeli, 2008).

Students who work lengthy hours—more than 11 to 13 hours per week—report lower grades, higher rates of drug and alcohol use, more delinquent behavior, lower self-esteem, and higher levels of psychological problems than students who do not work or who work only a few hours (Holloway, 2004; Long, 2008). Grades and time spent on homework drop for students who work long hours. Adolescents who work longer hours also spend less time in family activities, are monitored less by their parents, and are granted more freedom with day-to-day decisions (Oettinger, 1999; Singh & Ozturk, 2000).

T F Adolescents who work after school obtain lower grades.
This is true, especially among adolescents who work many hours.

Perhaps the most prudent course is for parents and educators to limit the number of hours adolescents work. Some are tightening their regulations on the number of hours teenagers can work during the school year.

40-60% < percentage of first-year college students exhibiting formal operational thought.

stages in Kohlberg's theory of moral development > **6**

20% < percentage of 16-year-olds exhibiting Stage 5 reasoning (based on Kohlberg's sample)

percentage of 16-year-olds exhibiting Stage 6 reasoning (based on Kohlberg's sample) > **5%**

16% < amount that each year of elementary through graduate school adds to an individual's lifetime earnings

percentage of 18–24-year-old males who have dropped out of high school > **15%**

12% < percentage of 18–24-year-old females who have dropped out of high school

number of 14–18-year-olds working illegally > **2–3 million**

Speak Up!

CDEV was built on a simple principle: to create a new teaching and learning solution that reflects the way today's faculty teach and the way you learn.

Through conversations, focus groups, surveys, and interviews, we collected data that drove the creation of the current version of CDEV that you are using today. But it doesn't stop there – in order to make CDEV an even better learning experience, we'd like you to SPEAK UP and tell us how CDEV worked for you. What did you like about it? What would you change? Are there additional ideas you have that would help us build a better product for next semester's childhood and adolescent development students?

At **4ltrpress.cengage.com/cdev** you'll find a survey form to send us your comments – in addition to all of the resources you need to succeed in your childhood and adolescent development course – printable and interactive **flashcards,** downloadable **study aids, games, quizzes,** and **PowerVisuals** to test your knowledge of key concepts, and more!

Speak Up! Go to **4ltrpress.cengage.com/cdev.**

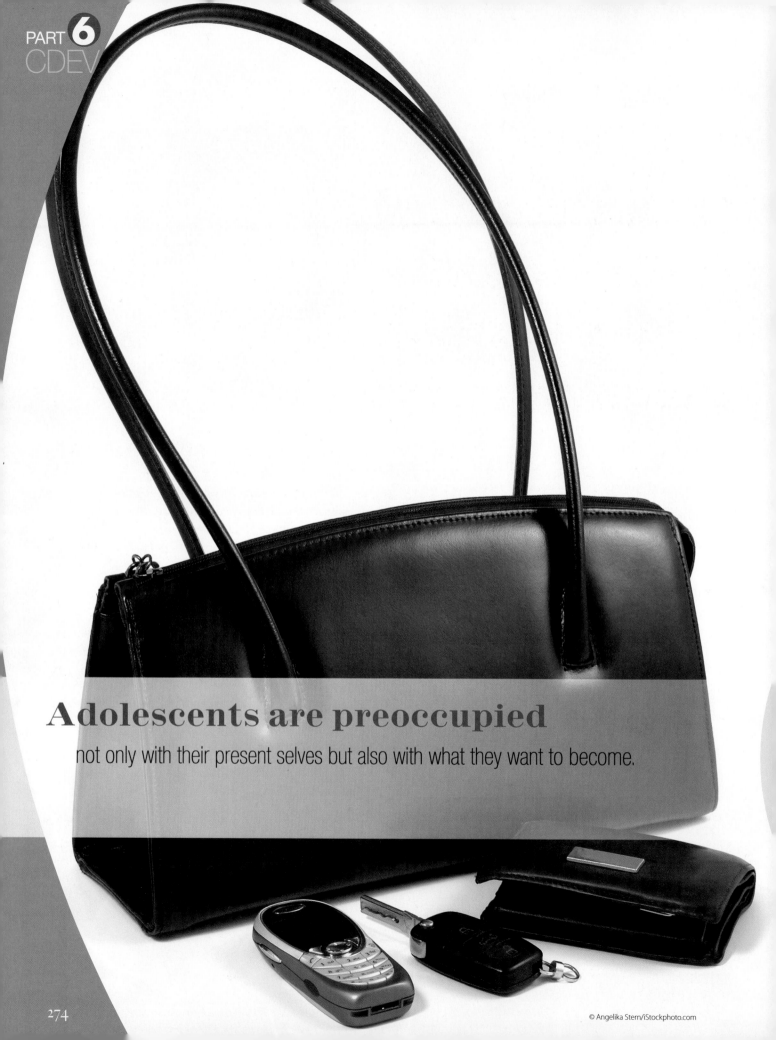

Adolescents are preoccupied

not only with their present selves but also with what they want to become.

16

Adolescence: Social and Emotional Development

Learning Outcomes

LO1 Discuss the formation of identity in adolescence.

LO2 Discuss relationships with parents and peers during adolescence.

LO3 Discuss sexuality during adolescence, focusing on sexual identity and teenage pregnancy.

LO4 Discuss the characteristics of juvenile delinquents.

LO5 Discuss risk factors for adolescent suicide.

LO6 Discuss the (theoretical) stage of emerging adulthood.

TRUTH OR FICTION?

T F American adolescent males are more concerned about occupational choices than American adolescent females are.

T F Adolescents are in a constant state of rebellion against their parents.

T F Most adolescents' friends are "bad influences."

T F About 800,000 American teenagers become pregnant each year.

T F Suicide is the leading cause of death among American adolescents.

T F Adolescents become adults at age 21.

What am I like as a person? Complicated! I'm sensitive, friendly and outgoing, though I can also be shy, self-conscious, and even obnoxious. . . . I'm responsible, even studious every now and then, but on the other hand I'm a goof-off too, because if you're too studious, you won't be popular. . . . Sometimes I feel phony, especially around boys. . . . I'll be flirtatious and fun-loving. And then everybody else is looking at me . . . Then I get self-conscious and embarrassed and become radically introverted, and I don't know who I really am! I can be my true self with my close friends. I can't be my real self with my parents. They don't understand me. They treat me like I'm still a kid. That gets confusing, though. I mean, which am I, a kid or an adult?

—Adapted from Harter (1990, pp. 352–353)

These thoughts of a 15-year-old girl illustrate a key aspect of adolescence: the search for an answer to the question "Who am I?" She is struggling to reconcile contradictory traits and behaviors to determine her "real self." Adolescents are preoccupied not only with their present selves but also with what they want to become.

LO1 Development of Identity: "Who Am I?"

in this chapter, we explore social and emotional development in adolescence. We begin with the formation of identity.

ERIKSON AND IDENTITY DEVELOPMENT

Erik Erikson's fifth stage of psychosocial development is called *identity versus identity diffusion*. The primary task is for adolescents to develop **ego identity**: a sense of who they are and what they stand for. They are faced with choices about their future occupations, political and religious beliefs, and gender roles. Because of formal-operational thinking, adolescents can weigh options they have not directly experienced (Roeser et al., 2006).

> **ego identity** According to Erikson, one's sense of who one is and what one stands for.
>
> **psychological moratorium** A time-out period when adolescents experiment with different roles, values, beliefs, and relationships.
>
> **identity crisis** A turning point in development during which one examines one's values and makes decisions about life roles.

One aspect of identity development is a **psychological moratorium** during which adolescents experiment with different roles, values, beliefs, and relationships (Erikson, 1968). During this time, adolescents undergo an **identity crisis** in which they examine their values and make decisions about their life roles. Should they attend college? What career should they pursue? Should they become sexually active? With whom?

Adolescents in developed nations may feel overwhelmed by their options. But inner-city adolescent girls of color are unlikely to have the choices that Erikson considered (Pastor et al., 2007). They may become sexually active at early ages due to local custom and peer pressure. College may be out of the question and occupational choices limited.

In their search for identity, many—not all—adolescents join "in" groups, slavishly imitating their peers' clothing, speech, hairstyles, and ideals (Erikson, 1963). Those who successfully resolve their identity crisis develop a strong sense of who they are and what they stand for. Those who do not may be intolerant of people who are different and blindly adhere to convention.

IDENTITY STATUSES

Building on Erikson's approach, James Marcia (1991) theorized four *identity statuses* that represent the four possible combinations of the dimensions of exploration and commitment that Erikson believed were critical to the development of identity (Schwartz, 2001) (see Table 16.1). *Exploration* involves active questioning and searching among alternatives to establish goals, values, or beliefs. *Commitment* is a stable investment in one's goals, values, or beliefs.

Exploration *involves active questioning to establish goals and values.*

> Because of formal-operational thinking, **adolescents** can **weigh options** they have not directly experienced.

TABLE 16.1
The Four Identity Statuses of James Marcia

COMMITMENT	EXPLORATION	
	Yes	**No**
Yes	**Identity Achievement** • Most developed in terms of identity • Has experienced a period of exploration • Has developed commitments • Has a sense of personal well-being, high self-esteem, and self-acceptance • Cognitively flexible • Sets goals and works toward achieving them	**Foreclosure** • Has commitments without considering alternatives • Commitments based on identification with parents, teachers, or other authority figures • Often authoritarian and inflexible
No	**Moratorium** • Actively exploring alternatives • Attempting to make choices with regard to occupation, ideological beliefs, and so on • Often anxious and intense • Ambivalent feelings toward parents and authority figures	**Identity Diffusion** • Least developed in terms of identity • Lacks commitments • Not trying to form commitments • May be carefree and uninvolved or unhappy and lonely • May be angry, alienated, rebellious

identity diffusion An identity status that characterizes those who have no commitments and who are not in the process of exploring alternatives.

foreclosure An identity status that characterizes those who have made commitments without considering alternatives.

moratorium An identity status that characterizes those who are actively exploring alternatives in an attempt to form an identity.

identity achievement An identity status that characterizes those who have explored alternatives and have developed commitments.

Identity diffusion is the least advanced status and characterizes adolescents who neither have commitments nor are trying to form them (Berzonsky, 2005). This stage is characteristic of younger adolescents and of older adolescents who drift through life or become alienated and rebellious (Snarey & Bell, 2003).

In the **foreclosure** status, individuals make commitments without considering alternatives. These commitments are usually established early in life and often based on identification with parents, teachers, or religious leaders who have made strong impressions (Saroglou & Galand, 2004).

The **moratorium** status refers to a person who is actively exploring alternatives in an attempt to make choices (Akman, 2007). Such individuals are often anxious and intense.

Identity achievement refers to those who have explored alternatives and developed relatively firm commitments. They generally have high self-esteem and self-acceptance (Adams et al., 2006).

Development of Identity Statuses

Before high school, children show little interest in questions of identity. Most have the identity status of identity diffusion or foreclosure. During the high school and college years, adolescents increasingly move from the statuses of diffusion and foreclosure to moratorium and achievement (Snarey & Bell, 2003). The greatest gains in identity formation occur in college (Berzonsky & Kuk, 2005). College students are exposed to a variety of lifestyles, beliefs, and career choices, which spur consideration of identity issues. Are you a student who has changed majors once or twice (or more)? If so, you have most likely experienced the moratorium identity status, which is common among college students. College seniors have a stronger sense of identity than first-year students as a result of having resolved their identity crises (Lewis, 2003).

ETHNICITY AND DEVELOPMENT OF IDENTITY

The development of self-identity is a key task for all adolescents. The task is more complex for adolescents who are members of ethnic minority groups (Phinney

ethnic identity A sense of belonging to an ethnic group.

unexamined ethnic identity The first stage of ethnic identity development; similar to the identity status of diffusion or foreclosure.

ethnic identity search The second stage of ethnic identity development; similar to the identity status of moratorium.

achieved ethnic identity The final stage of ethnic identity development; similar to identity achievement.

& Ong, 2007). Adolescents who belong to the dominant culture—in this country, European Americans—are usually faced with assimilating one set of cultural values into their identities. However, adolescents who belong to ethnic minority groups, such as African Americans and Latino and Latina Americans, confront two sets of cultural values: the values of the dominant culture and those of their particular ethnic group (Phinney & Alipuria, 2006). If the cultural values conflict, the adolescent needs to sort out the values that are most meaningful to him or her and incorporate them into his or her identity. Some adolescents do it cafeteria style; they take a little bit of this and a little bit of that. For example, a young Latina Catholic woman may decide to use artificial means of birth control even though doing so conflicts with her religion's teachings.

Adolescents from ethnic minority groups also often experience prejudice and discrimination. Their cultural heroes may be ignored. A relative scarcity of successful role models can be a problem, particularly for youth who live in poverty. Identifying too strongly with the dominant culture may also lead to rejection by the minority group. On the other hand, rejecting the dominant culture's values for those of the minority group may limit opportunities for advancement in the larger society.

Some researchers hypothesize three stages in the development of **ethnic identity** (Phinney, 2006). The first is **unexamined ethnic identity**. It is similar to Marcia's identity status of diffusion or foreclosure. In the second stage, the adolescent embarks on an **ethnic identity search**. This second stage, similar to Marcia's moratorium status, may be based on some incident that makes the adolescent aware of his or her ethnicity. During this stage, the adolescent may explore the ethnic culture, participating in cultural events, reading, and discussion. In the third stage, individuals have an **achieved ethnic identity** that involves self-acceptance as a member of the ethnic group and is similar to Marcia's identity achievement.

SEX AND DEVELOPMENT OF IDENTITY

Erikson believed that there were sex differences in the development of identity, and his views reflected the times in which he wrote. Identity development relates both to relationships and occupational choice, among other matters. Erikson (1968, 1975) assumed that relationships were more important to women's development of identity, whereas occupational and ideological matters were relatively more important to men's. He believed that a young woman's identity was intimately bound up with her roles as wife and mother. Studies today show that adolescent females and males are both concerned about occupational choices, even though females remain more likely to integrate occupational and family plans (Berzonsky, 2004). This sex difference may persist because females continue to assume primary responsibility for child rearing, even though most women are employed outside the home (Anthis et al., 2004).

T (F) American adolescent males are more concerned about occupational choices than American adolescent females are. *Though females remain more likely to integrate occupational and family plans, studies show this to be untrue.*

DEVELOPMENT OF THE SELF-CONCEPT

Before adolescence, children describe themselves primarily in terms of their physical characteristics and their actions. As they approach adolescence, children

begin to incorporate psychological characteristics and social relationships into their self-descriptions (Damon, 1991).

The self-concept becomes more differentiated in adolescence; adolescents add more categories to their self-description. Also, social roles begin to enter self-descriptions. Adolescents may describe themselves as anxious or sarcastic with parents but as talkative and cheerful with friends. Such contradictions and conflicts in self-description reach their peak at about age 14 and then decline (Harter & Monsour, 1992). The advanced formal-operational skills of older adolescents allow them to integrate contradictory aspects of the self. The older adolescent might say: "I'm very adaptable. When I'm around my friends, who think that what I say is important, I'm very talkative; but around my family, I'm quiet because they're not interested enough to really listen to me" (Damon, 1991, p. 988).

SELF-ESTEEM

Self-esteem tends to decline as the child progresses from middle childhood to about the age of 12 or 13 (Harter & Whitesell, 2003). The growing cognitive maturity of young adolescents makes them increasingly aware of the disparity between their ideal self and their real self, especially in terms of physical appearance (Durkin et al., 2007; Seidah & Bouffard, 2007). Boys might fantasize they would like to have the physiques of the warriors they see in video games or in the media (Konijn et al., 2007). Most girls want to be thin, thin, thin (O'Dea, 2006).

After hitting a low point at about age 12 or 13, self-esteem gradually improves (Harter & Whitesell, 2003). Perhaps adolescents adjust their ideal selves to better reflect reality. Also, as adolescents develop academic, physical, and social skills, they may grow less self-critical (Shirk et al., 2003).

> Teenagers have more **conflicts** with their mothers, but they also view their mothers as being **more supportive** and knowing them better.

For most adolescents, low self-esteem produces temporary discomfort (Harter & Whitesell, 2003). For others, low self-esteem has serious consequences. For example, low self-esteem is often found in teenagers who are depressed or suicidal (Shirk et al., 2003).

Emotional support from parents and peers is important to self-esteem. Adolescents who feel highly regarded by family and friends are more likely to feel positive about themselves (Costigan et al., 2007). In early adolescence, support from parents is as important as peer support. By late adolescence, peer support carries more weight.

LO2 Relationships with Parents and Peers

adolescents coping with the task of establishing a sense of identity and direction in their lives are heavily influenced by both parents and peers.

RELATIONSHIPS WITH PARENTS

During adolescence, children spend much less time with their parents than they did in childhood (Larson & Richards, 1991). Adolescents continue to interact more with their mothers than their fathers. Teenagers have more conflicts with their mothers, but they also view their mothers as being more supportive and knowing them better (Costigan et al., 2007). Adverse relationships with fathers are often associated with depression in adolescents (Sheeber et al., 2007), but good relationships with fathers contribute to psychological well-being (Flouri & Buchanan, 2003).

The decrease in time spent with the family may reflect adolescents' striving for independence. A certain degree of distancing from parents may be adaptive as adolescents form relationships outside the family. However, adolescents continue to maintain love, loyalty, and respect for their parents (Collins & Laursen, 2006). And adolescents who feel close to their parents have more self-reliance and self-esteem, better school performance, and fewer adjustment problems (Costigan et al., 2007).

The relationship between parents and teens is not always rosy. Early adolescence, in particular, is characterized by increased bickering and a decrease in shared activities and expressions of affection (Smetana et al.,

Early on, parents may try to retain control over many areas of adolescents' lives; as time goes on, they often learn to compromise and begin to grant adolescents greater responsibility.

2006). Conflicts typically center on the everyday details of family life, such as chores, homework, curfews, personal appearance, finances, and dating—often because adolescents believe that they should manage matters that were previously controlled by parents (Costigan et al., 2007). But parents, especially mothers, continue to believe that they should retain control in many areas, such as encouraging adolescents to do their homework and clean their rooms. As adolescents get older, they and their parents are more likely to compromise (Smetana et al., 2006). On the other hand, parents and adolescents are usually quite similar in their values and beliefs regarding social, political, religious, and economic issues (Collins & Laursen, 2006). Even though the notion of a generation gap between adolescents and their parents may persist as a stereotype, there is little evidence of one.

As adolescents grow older, parents are more likely to relax controls and less likely to use punishment (Smetana et al., 2006). Although parent–child relationships change, most adolescents feel that they are close to and get along with their parents, even though they may develop a less idealized view of them (Collins & Laursen, 2006).

T (F) Adolescents are in a constant state of rebellion against their parents.
False; parents and adolescents are usually quite similar in their values and beliefs regarding social, political, religious, and economic issues (Collins & Laursen, 2006).

Parenting Styles

Differences in parenting styles continue to influence the development of adolescents (Costigan et al., 2007). Adolescents from authoritative homes—whose parents are willing to exert control and explain the reasons for doing so—show the most competent behavior. They are more self-reliant, do better in school, have better mental health, and show the lowest incidence of psychological problems and misconduct, including drug use.

RELATIONSHIPS WITH PEERS

The transition from childhood to adolescence is accompanied by a shift in the relative importance of parents and peers. Although relationships with parents generally remain positive, the role of peers as a source of activities, influence, and support increases. Parents are perceived as the most frequent providers of social and emotional support by fourth-graders, but by seventh grade, friends of the same sex are seen to be as supportive as parents. By tenth grade, same-sex friends are viewed as providing more support than parents (Furman & Buhrmester, 1992).

Friendships in Adolescence

Adolescents have more friends than younger children do (Feiring & Lewis, 1991). Most adolescents have one or two "best friends" and several good friends. Teenagers see their friends frequently, usually several hours a day (Hartup, 1983). And when teenagers are not with their friends, they can often be found talking on the phone, texting, or instant messaging.

Friendships in adolescence differ from the friendships of childhood. Adolescents are more likely to stress acceptance, intimate self-disclosure, and mutual understanding (González et al., 2004). One eighth-grade girl described her best friend this way: "I can tell her things and she helps me talk. And she doesn't laugh at me if I do something weird—she accepts me for who I am" (Berndt & Perry, 1990, p. 269). Second, adolescents stress loyalty

and trustworthiness (Rotenberg et al., 2004). They may say that a friend will "stick up for you in a fight" and will not "talk about you behind your back." Finally, adolescents are more likely than younger children to share with friends and less likely to compete with them.

Adolescents and their friends are similar in many respects. They typically are the same age and the same race. They almost always are the same sex. Even though romantic attachments increase during the teen years, most adolescents still choose members of their own sex as best friends (Hartup, 1993). Friends are often alike in school attitudes, educational aspirations, and grades. Friends also tend to have similar attitudes about drinking, drug use, and sexual activity (Youniss & Haynie, 1992).

Friendship contributes to a positive self-concept and psychological adjustment. Adolescents who have a close friend have higher self-esteem than adolescents who do not (Berndt, 1992).

Intimacy and closeness appear to be more central to the friendships of girls than of boys (Schraf & Hertz-Lazarowitz, 2003). Adolescent and adult females also are generally more likely than males to disclose secrets, personal problems, thoughts, and feelings to their friends (Dindia & Allen, 1992).

Girls' friendship networks are smaller and more exclusive than boys' (Schraf & Hertz-Lazarowitz, 2003). Girls tend to have one or two close friends; boys tend to congregate in larger, less intimate groups. Girls' and boys' activities differ as well. Girls are more likely to engage in unstructured activities such as talking and listening to music. Boys are more likely to engage in organized activities, games, and sports.

Peer Groups

Most adolescents belong to one or more peer groups: *cliques* and *crowds* (Henzi et al., 2007). **Cliques** consist

of five to ten individuals who hang around together and share activities and confidences. **Crowds** are larger groups that may or may not spend much time together and are identified by their activities or attitudes. Crowds are usually labeled by other adolescents, for example, "jocks," "brains," "druggies," or "nerds." The most negatively labeled groups ("druggies," "rejects") show higher levels of alcohol and drug abuse, delinquency, and depression.

clique A group of five to ten individuals who hang around together and who share activities and confidences.

crowd A large, loosely organized group of people who may or may not spend much time together and who are identified by the activities of the group.

Adolescent peer groups function with less adult guidance or control than childhood peer groups (Staff et al., 2004). Adolescent groups may include members of the other sex; this inclusion sharply contrasts with the sex segregation of childhood groups. These connections may lead to dating and romantic relationships.

Dating and Romantic Relationships

Romantic relationships usually begin during early and middle adolescence, and most adolescents start dating or going out by the time they graduate from high school (Florsheim, 2003). For heterosexuals, the development of dating typically takes the following sequence: putting oneself in situations where peers of the other sex probably will be present (e.g., hanging out at the mall), group activities including peers of the other sex (e.g., school dances or parties), group dating (e.g., joining a mixed-sex group at the movies), and then traditional two-person dating (Connolly et al., 2004).

Adolescents usually develop friendships with people similar to themselves, often with respect to age, race, sex, and activities.

Dating serves a number of functions. First and foremost, people date to have fun. Dating, especially in early adolescence, enhances prestige with peers. Dating gives adolescents more experience in learning to relate to others. Finally, dating prepares adolescents for adult courtship (Florsheim, 2003).

Dating relationships tend to be casual and short-lived in early adolescence. In late adolescence, relationships tend to become more stable and committed (Connolly et al., 2000). Eighteen-year-olds are more likely than 15-year-olds to mention love, trust, and commitment when describing romantic relationships (Feiring, 1993).

Peer Influence

Peer pressure is fairly weak in early adolescence. It peaks during middle adolescence and declines after about age 17 (Reis & Youniss, 2004). Peer influence may increase during adolescence because peers provide a standard by which adolescents measure their own behavior as they develop independence from the family (Foster-Clark & Blyth, 1991). Peers also provide support in times of trouble (Kirchler et al., 1991).

Parents often worry that their teenage children will fall in with the wrong crowd and follow peers in self-destructive or immoral behavior. Despite the widespread assumption that peer influences and parental influences will be in conflict, parents and peers are usually complementary rather than competing influences (Reis & Youniss, 2004).

Parents and peers also seem to exert influence in different domains. Adolescents are more likely to conform to peer standards in matters pertaining to style and taste, such as clothing, hairstyles, speech patterns, and music (Camarena, 1991). They are more likely to agree with their parents on moral principles and future educational and career goals (Savin-Williams & Berndt, 1990).

Adolescents influence each other positively and negatively. In many cases, peer pressure to finish high school and achieve academically can be stronger than pressure to engage in misconduct (Brown et al., 1993; Steinberg, 1996). Yet many times adolescents discourage one another from doing well or at least *too* well in school. Adolescents who smoke, drink, use drugs, and engage in sexual activity also often have friends who engage in these behaviors, but adolescents tend to choose friends and peers who are like them to begin with.

Adolescents who smoke, drink, use drugs, and engage in sexual activity also often have friends who engage in these behaviors, but adolescents tend to **choose friends** and peers who are like them to begin with.

T F Most adolescents' friends are "bad influences."

Parents and peers are usually complementary rather than competing influences (Reis & Youniss, 2004).

LO3 Sexuality

My first sexual experience occurred in a car after the high school junior prom. We were both virgins, very uncertain but very much in love. We had been going together since eighth grade. The experience was somewhat painful. I remember wondering if I would look different to my mother the next day. I guess I didn't because nothing was said.

Because of the flood of sex hormones, adolescents tend to experience a powerful sex drive. In addition, they are bombarded with sexual messages in the media, including scantily clad hip-grinding, crotch-grabbing pop stars; print ads for barely-there underwear; and countless articles with titles like "How to tell if your boyfriend has been (whatever)" and "The 10 things that will drive your girlfriend wild." Teenagers are strongly motivated to follow the crowd, yet they are also influenced by the views of their parents and teachers. So what is a teen to do?

Sexual activity in adolescence can take many forms. In this section, we consider sexual identity, sexual behavior, and teenage pregnancy.

SEXUAL IDENTITY

Most people, including the great majority of adolescents, have a heterosexual sexual identity. They are sexually attracted to and interested in forming romantic relationships with people of the other sex. However, some people have a **homosexual** identity or orientation. They are attracted to and interested in forming romantic relationships with people of their own sex. Males with a homosexual orientation are referred to as *gay males*. Females with a homosexual orientation are referred to as *lesbians*. However, males and females with a homosexual orientation are sometimes categorized together as "gay people," or "gays." *Bisexual* people are attracted to both females and males.

According to Ritch Savin-Williams and Lisa Diamond (2004; Savin-Williams, 2007), the development of sexual identity in gay males and lesbians involves several steps: attraction to members of the same sex, self-labeling as gay or lesbian, sexual contact with members of the same sex, and eventual disclosure of one's sexual orientation to other people. There was generally about a 10-year gap between initial attraction to members of the same sex, which tended to occur at about the age of 8 or 9, and disclosure of one's orientation to other people, which usually occurred at about age 18. But some gay males and lesbians never disclose their sexual orientations to anyone or to certain people, such as their parents.

The process of "coming out"—that is, accepting one's homosexual orientation and declaring it to others—may be a long and painful struggle (Martell, 2008). Gay adolescents may be ostracized and rejected by family and friends (Savin-Williams, 2008). Depression and suicide rates are higher among gay youth than among heterosexual adolescents (Hershberger & D'Augelli, 2000). Homosexual adolescents often engage in substance abuse, run away from home, and do poorly in school (Russell, 2006).

"Coming out to others" sometimes means an open declaration to the world. More often, an adolescent feels more comfortable telling a couple of close friends. Before they inform family members, gay adolescents often anticipate their relatives' negative reactions, including denial, anger, and rejection (Bagley & D'Augelli, 2000). Yet some families are more accepting.

MASTURBATION

Masturbation, or sexual self-stimulation, is the most common sexual outlet in adolescence. Surveys indicate that most adolescents masturbate at some time. The Kinsey studies, published in the mid-20th century (Kinsey et al., 1948, 1953), suggested that masturbation was nearly universal among adolescent males but less common among adolescent females. This sex difference is confirmed in nearly every survey (Oliver & Hyde, 1993). Boys who masturbate do so more often than girls who masturbate. It is unclear whether this sex difference reflects a stronger sex drive in boys (Peplau, 2003), greater social constraints on girls (Pinkerton et al., 2002), or both. Beliefs that masturbation is harmful and guilt associated with it lessen the incidence of masturbation (Ortega et al., 2005), although it has not been shown to be physically harmful.

homosexual Referring to an erotic orientation toward members of one's own sex.

masturbation Sexual self-stimulation.

MALE–FEMALE SEXUAL BEHAVIOR

Adolescents today start dating and going out earlier than in past generations. Teens who date earlier are more likely to engage in sexual activity during high school

© Steve Niedorf Photography/Getty Images

(Guttmacher Institute, 2007). Teens who initiate sexual activity earlier are also less likely to use contraception and more likely to become pregnant. But early dating does not always lead to early sex, and early sex does not always lead to unwanted pregnancy.

Petting is practically universal among American adolescents and has been for many generations. Adolescents use petting to express affection, satisfy their curiosities, heighten their sexual arousal, and reach orgasm while avoiding pregnancy and maintaining virginity. Many adolescents do not see themselves as having sex if they stop short of vaginal intercourse (Guttmacher Institute, 2007). Girls are more likely than boys to be coerced into petting and to feel guilty about it (Larsson & Svedin, 2002).

Surveys show that since the early 1990s, the percentage of high school students who have engaged in sexual intercourse has been gradually declining (see Figure 16.1). Nevertheless, between 40% and 50% of high school students have had sexual intercourse. The incidences of kissing, petting, oral sex, and sexual intercourse all increase with age. For example, according to a survey by the Centers for Disease Control and Prevention (CDC), 42% of girls aged 15 to 17 reported engaging in oral sex, compared with 72% of girls aged 18 to 19 (Mosher et al., 2005).

The hormonal changes of puberty probably are partly responsible for the onset of sexual activity. In boys, levels of testosterone are associated with sexual behavior. In girls, however, testosterone levels are linked to sexual interests but not to sexual behavior. Social factors may therefore play a greater role in regulating sexual behavior in girls than boys (Browning et al., 2000; O'Donnell et al., 2003).

The physical changes associated with puberty also may trigger the onset of sexual activity. For example,

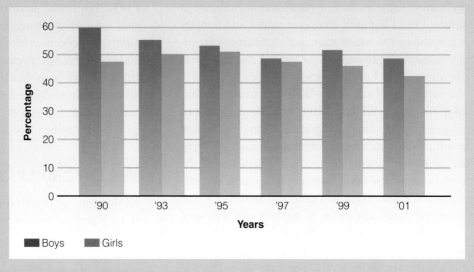

FIGURE 16.1
Percentage of Students in Grades 9–12 Who Report Having Had Sexual Intercourse

Despite a gradual decline in the incidence of sexual intercourse since the early 1990s, the incidence of high school students who have engaged in sexual intercourse remains between 40% and 50%.

Source: Centers for Disease Control and Prevention, the Alan Guttmacher Institute, and the Child Trends Databank.

the development of secondary sex characteristics such as breasts in girls and muscles and deep voices in boys may make them more sexually attractive. Early-maturing girls are more likely to have older friends, who may draw them into sexual relationships.

Teenagers who have close relationships with their parents are less likely to initiate sexual activity at an early age (Bynum, 2007). Adolescents who communicate well with their parents also delay the onset of sexual activity (Aspy et al., 2007). If these youngsters do have sexual intercourse, they are more likely to use birth control and have fewer partners.

A good predictor of sexual activity for adolescents is the sexual activity of their best friends (Dishion & Stormshak, 2007a). When teenagers are asked why they do not wait to have sex until they are older, the main reason reported is usually peer pressure (O'Donnell et al., 2003). Peers, especially those of the same sex, also serve as a key source of sex education for adolescents. Adolescents report that they are somewhat more likely to receive information about sex from friends and media sources—TV shows, films, magazines, and the

Internet—than from sex education classes or their parents (Kaiser Family Foundation et al., 2003).

Finally, achieving good grades in school is associated with delayed transition from virgin to non-virgin status (Laflin et al., 2008). Good grades, of course, reflect a combination of an internal desire to succeed and, often, external factors such as good communication with parents and positive peer pressure.

TEENAGE PREGNANCY

In the United States today, the great majority of adolescents who become pregnant do so accidentally and without committed partners (Forum on Child and Family Statistics, 2007). Most young women in developed nations defer pregnancy until after they have completed some or all of their education. Many do so until they are well into their careers and in their late 20s, their 30s, even their 40s. Why do adolescents get pregnant? For one thing, adolescent girls typically get little advice in school or at home about how to deal with boys' sexual advances. Another reason is failure to use contraception. Some adolescent girls initiate sex at very early ages, when they are least likely to use contraception (Buston et al., 2007). Many, especially younger adolescents, do not have access to contraceptive devices. Among those who do, fewer than half use them reliably (Buston et al., 2007). Some teenage girls purposefully get pregnant to try to force their partners to make a commitment to them. Some are rebelling against their parents

Students in this sex education program at High Park High School in New Jersey were given dolls that they had to care for over the course of a weekend like real babies.

© MIA SONG/Newhouse News Service/Landov

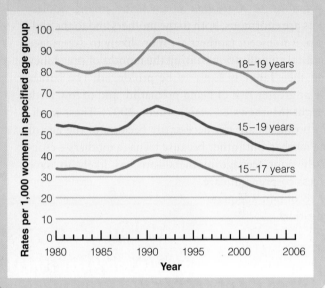

FIGURE 16.2
Birth Rates for Teenagers by Age, United States, 1980–2006

The birth rate for U.S. teenagers 15–19 years of age rose 3 percent from 2005 to 41.9 births per 1,000 females in 2006, the first increase since 1991. Even so, teenage birth rates are down markedly from the early 1990s.

Source: Hamilton et al. (2007).

or the moral standards of their communities. But most girls are impregnated because they and their partners miscalculate the odds of getting pregnant (Buston et al., 2007).

For all these reasons, about 800,000 teenage girls in the United States are impregnated each year. The pregnancies result in about half a million births. That number declined markedly from the peak in the early to middle 1990s, when about 1 million girls were getting pregnant each year. However, there has been an uptick in the incidence of teenage pregnancy (Hamilton et al., 2007; see Figure 16.2). Still, researchers at the CDC attribute the general drop-off in careless sex since the 1990s to educational efforts by schools, the media, religious institutions, and communities (Forum on Child and Family Statistics, 2007). Nearly half of pregnant teenagers will have an abortion (Guttmacher Institute, 2007). Most others will become single mothers.

Consequences of Teenage Pregnancy

Actually, the outcome of teenage pregnancy for young women who want their babies and have the resources to nurture them are generally good (Rathus et al., 2008). Females tend to be healthy in late adolescence. However, the medical, social, and economic costs of *unplanned* or *unwanted* pregnancies among adolescents are enormous, both to the mothers and to the children. Adolescent mothers are more likely to experience medical complications during the months of pregnancy and their labor is likely to be prolonged. The babies are at greater risk of being premature and of low birth weight (Mathews & MacDorman, 2007). These medical problems are not necessarily because of the age of the mother, but rather because teenage mothers—especially poor teenage mothers—are less likely to have access to prenatal care or to obtain adequate nutrition.

The teenage mother is less likely than her peers to graduate from high school or move on to post-secondary education. Therefore, she will earn less and be in greater need of public assistance. Few teenage mothers obtain assistance from the babies' fathers. The fathers typically cannot support themselves, much less a family.

Preventing Teenage Pregnancy

The past several decades have seen a dramatic increase in programs to help prevent teenage pregnancies. Prevention efforts include educating teenagers about sexuality and contraception and providing family planning services (Santelli et al., 2003). An overwhelming majority of American parents want their children to have sex education in school.

How successful are sex education programs? The better programs increase students' knowledge about sexuality. Despite fears that sex education will increase sexual activity in teenagers, some programs seem to delay the onset of sexual activity (Bennett & Assefi, 2005; Santelli et al., 2003). Among teenagers who already

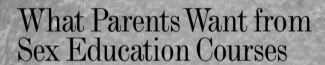

What Parents Want from Sex Education Courses

A survey conducted in 2004 by National Public Radio, the Kaiser Family Foundation, and Harvard University found that the overwhelming majority of parents want schools to provide sex education. Ninety-nine percent of parents want their children to be taught about sexually transmitted infections, and 96% want their adolescents to understand "how babies are made." Most parents (95%) would like their children to be encouraged to wait to have sex until they are older. And a majority want discussions to cover birth control (94%), abortion (85%), and even sexual orientation (73%). Smaller majorities— but majorities nonetheless—think that school discussions of oral sex (72%) and of how to get birth control pills without parental permission (71%) are appropriate.

Source: Sex Education in America. General Public/Parents Survey. A National Public Radio/ Kaiser Family Foundation/Harvard University John F. Kennedy School of Government Poll. (2004). Retrieved from http://www.npr.org/ templates/story/story.php?storyId=1622610

are sexually active, sex education is associated with the increased use of effective contraception.

LO4 Juvenile Delinquency

t he term **juvenile delinquency** refers to conduct in children or adolescents that is characterized by illegal activities and brings the individuals into contact with the criminal justice system. At the most extreme end, juvenile delinquency includes serious behaviors such as homicide, rape, and robbery. Less serious offenses, such as truancy, underage drinking, running away from home, and sexual promiscuity, are considered illegal only when performed by minors. Hence, these activities are termed *status offenses*.

Antisocial and criminal behaviors show a dramatic increase in many societies during adolescence and then taper off during adulthood. For example, about four in ten serious crimes in the United States are committed by individuals under the age of 21, and about three in ten are committed by adolescents under 18 (Snyder & Sickmund, 2006).

Many delinquent acts do not result in arrest or conviction. And when adolescents are arrested, their cases may be disposed of informally, as by referral to a mental health agency (Snyder & Sickmund, 2006).

ETHNICITY, SEX, AND JUVENILE DELINQUENCY

African American adolescents are more likely to be arrested than European American adolescents. For example, African American youths constitute about 13% of the adolescent population in the United States but account for about one-fourth of the juvenile arrests and about one-half of the arrests for violent crimes (Snyder & Sickmund, 2006). Figure 16.3 shows that the delinquency case rate for African American youngsters has been more than twice that for European American youngsters.

Criminologist Donna Bishop (2005) notes a couple of possible explanations for the difference between

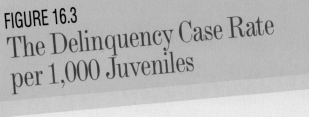

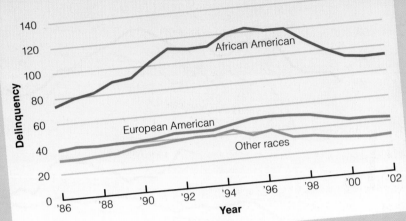

FIGURE 16.3

The Delinquency Case Rate per 1,000 Juveniles

European American and African American delinquency case rates. The *differential offending hypothesis* suggests that there are actual racial differences in the incidence and seriousness of delinquent behavior. The *differential treatment hypothesis* suggests that African American and European American youth probably do not behave differently but are treated differently—intentionally or accidentally—by the juvenile justice system. That is, "the system" expects worse behavior from African American youngsters, so it polices them more actively and cracks down on them more harshly. One result of differential treatment is that African American adolescents have more interaction with the juvenile justice system and are more likely to think of themselves as criminals.

Economic and family factors are also connected with racial and ethnic differences in juvenile offending. As you see in Figure 16.4 on the next page, African American (and Latino and Latina American) children and adolescents are three times as likely as European American youth to be living in poverty (Snyder & Sickmund, 2006). Moreover, African American children are less likely than European American (or Latino and Latina American) children to be living with both of their biological parents, regardless of whether or not

juvenile delinquency
Conduct in a child or adolescent characterized by illegal activities.

FIGURE 16.4
Percentage of Americans under the Age of 18 Who Are Living in Poverty

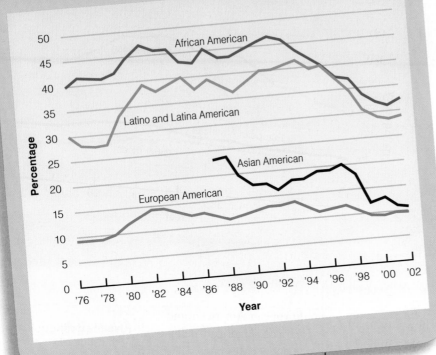

Graph showing Percentage (y-axis, 0 to 50) versus Year (x-axis, '76 to '02) for:
- African American
- Latino and Latina American
- Asian American
- European American

(Baron et al., 2007). Delinquency also is associated with having a lower verbal IQ, immature moral reasoning, low self-esteem, feelings of alienation, and impulsivity (Lynam et al., 2007). Other personal factors include little interest in school, early substance abuse, early sexuality, and delinquent friends (Ruchkin & Vermeiren, 2006).

The families of juvenile delinquents are often characterized by lax and ineffective discipline, low levels of affection, and high levels of family conflict, physical abuse, severe parental punishment, and neglect (Vermeiren et al., 2004). The parents and siblings of juvenile delinquents frequently have engaged in antisocial, deviant, or criminal behavior themselves (Snyder & Sickmund, 2006). Delinquents are also more likely to live in neighborhoods in which they themselves are likely to have been victimized, giving rise to the belief that crime is "normal" in a statistical sense and to feelings of anger (Hay & Evans, 2006).

their parents are married (Snyder & Sickmund, 2006). We cannot say that poverty *causes* delinquency or that a broken family *causes* delinquency, but poverty and broken families appear to be risk factors.

Boys are much more likely than girls to engage in delinquent behavior, especially crimes of violence. On the other hand, girls are more likely to commit status offenses such as truancy or running away (Snyder & Sickmund, 2006).

WHO ARE THE DELINQUENTS?

Even if the causal paths are less than clear, a number of factors are associated with delinquency. Children who show aggressive, antisocial, and hyperactive behavior at an early age are more likely to show delinquent behavior in adolescence

LO5 Suicide: When the Adolescent Has Nothing—Except Everything—to Lose

a dolescence is such an exciting time of life. For many, the future is filled with promise. Many count the days until they graduate high school, until they enter college. Many enjoy thrilling fantasies of what might be. And then there are those who take their own

© Maxim Lysenko/iStockphoto.com

lives. Suicide is the third leading cause of death among adolescents (NCHS, 2008). Since 1960, the suicide rate has more than tripled for young people aged 15 to 24. About 1 to 2 American adolescents in 10,000 commit suicide each year. About 1 in 10 has attempted suicide at least once.

> T (F) Suicide is the leading cause of death among American adolescents.
>
> *False; suicide is the third leading cause of death among adolescents, behind accidents and homicide (NCHS, 2008).*

RISK FACTORS IN SUICIDE

Most suicides among adolescents and adults are linked to feelings of depression and hopelessness (Cheng & Chan, 2007). Jill Rathus and her colleagues (Rathus & Miller, 2002) have found that suicidal adolescents experience four areas of psychological problems: (1) confusion about the self, (2) impulsiveness, (3) emotional instability, and (4) interpersonal problems. Some suicidal teenagers are highly achieving, rigid perfectionists who have set impossibly high expectations for themselves (Miller et al., 2007). Many teenagers throw themselves into feelings of depression and hopelessness by comparing themselves negatively with others, even when the comparisons are inappropriate. ("Yes, you didn't get into Harvard, but you did get into the University of California at Irvine, and it's a great school.")

Adolescent suicide attempts are more common after stressful life events, especially events that entail loss of social support, as in the death of a parent or friend, breaking up with a boyfriend or girlfriend, or a family member's leaving home (Cooper et al., 2002). Other contributors to suicidal behavior include concerns over sexuality, school grades, problems at home, substance abuse, and extreme body dissatisfaction (Crow et al., 2008; Cuellar & Curry, 2007). It is not always a stressful event itself that precipitates suicide but the adolescent's anxiety or fear of being "found out" for something, such as failing a course or getting arrested.

Suicide tends to run in families (National Center for Injury Prevention and Control, 2007b). Do genetic factors play a role, possibly leading to psychological disorders, such as depression, that are connected with suicide? Could it be that a socially impoverished family environment infuses several family members with feelings of hopelessness? Or does the suicide of one family member simply give others the idea that suicide is the way to manage problems?

Researchers have found the following factors associated with suicide among adolescents:

- Belief that it is acceptable to kill oneself (Joe et al., 2007)
- Drug abuse and other kinds of delinquency (Thompson et al., 2007)
- Victimization by bullying (Klomek et al., 2007)
- Extensive body piercing (Suris et al., 2007)
- Stress (Cheng & Chan, 2007)
- Hostility (Dervic et al., 2007)
- Depression and other psychological disorders (Smarty & Findling, 2007)
- Heavy smoking (Riala et al., 2007)
- Low self-esteem (Wong et al., 2007)
- Increasing age from 11 to 21 (Conner & Goldston, 2007)

© Bulent Ince/iStockphoto.com

ETHNICITY, SEX, AND SUICIDE

In 2007, 6.9% of American high school students attempted suicide (see Figure 16.5 on the next page). Rates of suicide and suicide attempts vary among different ethnic groups. Latino and Latina high school students have the highest rate (10.2%) of suicide attempts, in part because of the stresses to which they are exposed (Duarté-Vélez & Bernal, 2007; see Figure 16.5). African Americans (7.7%) are next. European American high school students (5.6%) are least likely to attempt suicide.

About twice as many female high school students (9.3%) as males (4.6%) attempt suicide, but males are more likely to "succeed" at an attempt (National Center for Injury Prevention and Control, 2007b). Males are more likely to use more rapid and lethal methods such as shooting themselves, whereas females are more likely to overdose on drugs like tranquilizers or sleeping pills (National Center for Injury Prevention & Control, 2007b). Females often do not take enough of these chemicals to kill themselves. It also takes time for them to work, providing other people the chance to intervene before the young woman dies.

FIGURE 16.5

Percentage of High School Students Who Attempted Suicide within 12 Months Prior to This Survey

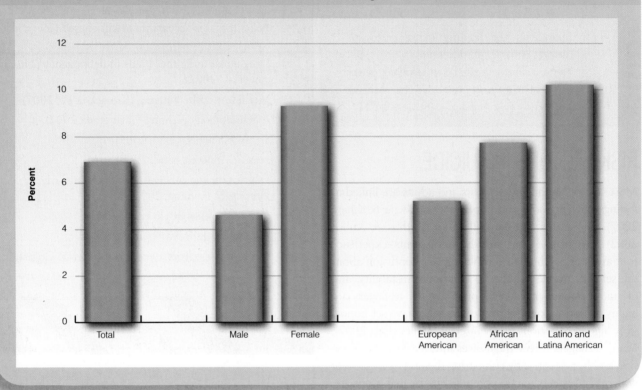

Source: USDHHS (2008, June 6). Youth risk behavior surveillance—United States, 2007. *Morbidity & Mortality Weekly Report 2008,* 57(SS-4). Retrieved June 26, 2009, from http://www.cdc.gov/HealthyYouth/yrbs/index.htm.

LO6 Epilogue: Emerging Adulthood— Bridging Adolescence and the Life Beyond

When our mothers were our age, they were engaged. They at least had some idea what they were going to do with their lives. I, on the other hand, will have a dual degree in majors that are ambiguous at best and impractical at worst (English and political science), no ring on my finger and no idea who I am, much less what I want to do. Under duress, I will admit that this is a pretty exciting time. Sometimes, when I look out across the wide expanse that is my future, I can see beyond the void. I realize that having nothing ahead to count on means I now

have to count on myself; that having no direction means forging one of my own.

—Kristen, age 22 (Page, 1999, pp. 18, 20)

Well, Kristen has some work to do: She needs to forge her own direction. Just think: What if Kristen had been born into the feudal system of old England or the caste system of India, into a traditional Islamic society, or into the United States of the 1950s, where the TV sitcom *Father Knows Best* was perennially in the top 10? Kristen would have had a sense of direction, that's certain. But, of course, it would have been the sense of direction society or tradition created for her, not her own.

But Kristen was not born into any of these societies. She was born into the open and challenging United States of the current generation. She has the freedom to become whatever the interaction of her genetic heritage and her educational and social opportunities will enable her to become—and the opportunities are many. With freedom comes the need to make choices. When

© Stock Image/Jupiterimages

we need to make choices, we profit from information. Kristen is in the process of accumulating information about herself and about the world outside. According to psychologist Jeffrey Arnett (2007), she is in emerging adulthood. In earlier days, adolescents made a transition, for better or worse, directly into adulthood. Now many of them—especially those in affluent nations with abundant opportunities—spend time in what some theorists think of as a new period of development roughly spanning the ages from 18 to 25.

Legally speaking, adulthood begins at many ages, depending on what you want to do. The age of consent to marry varies from state to state, but in general, marriage is permitted at 18 years of age. The age for drinking legally is 21. The age for driving varies. By and large, however, adulthood is usually defined in terms of what people do rather than how old they are. Over the years, marriage has been a key criterion for people who write about human development (Carroll et al., 2007). Other criteria include holding a full-time job and living independently (not with one's parents). Today, the transition to adulthood is mainly marked by adjustment issues, such as deciding on one's values and beliefs, accepting self-responsibility, becoming financially independent, and establishing an equal relationship with one's parents (Arnett, 2007; Gottlieb et al., 2007). Marriage is no longer necessarily a crucial marker for entering adulthood (Gottlieb et al., 2007).

T F Adolescents become adults at age 21.
The answer depends on how you define adulthood. Legally, adolescents do become adults at 21, but many remain in a transitional stage termed emerging adulthood.

Adulthood itself has been divided into stages, and the first of these, early adulthood, has been largely seen as the period of life when people focus on establishing their careers or pathways in life. It has been acknowledged that the transition to adulthood can be slow or piecemeal, with many individuals in their late teens and early 20s remaining dependent on their parents and reluctant or unable to make enduring commitments, in terms of either identity formation or the development of intimate relationships. The question is whether we can speak of the existence of another stage of development, one that bridges adolescence and young adulthood. A number of developmental theorists, including Arnett (2007), believe that we can.

Emerging adulthood is theorized to be a distinct period of development that is found in societies that allow young people an extended opportunity to explore their roles in life. These tend to be affluent societies, such as those found in developed nations, our own among them. Parents in the United States are often affluent enough to continue to support their children throughout college and in graduate school. When parents cannot do the job, the government often steps in to help, for example, through student loans. These supports allow young people the luxury of sorting out identity issues and creating meaningful life plans—even if some still do not know where they are going after they graduate from college. Should they know who they are and what they are doing by the age of 21 or 22? Are they spoiled? These questions call for value judgments. However, note that many adults change their careers several times, partly because they did not sort out who they were and where they were going at an early age. On the other hand, even in the United States, many people cannot obtain the support necessary for sojourning in emerging adulthood.

Arnett (2007) summarizes the kinds of social and technological influences that have spurred the rise of emerging adulthood:

- The change from a manufacturing-based economy to an information-based economy increased the need for advanced education and training.

- The advent of the birth control pill made it possible for late adolescents to become sexually active without becoming parents.

- Increased social acceptance of premarital sex and cohabitation weakened the traditional connection between marriage and the onset of sexual activity; therefore, the median ages for beginning marriage and parenthood rose to the middle to late 20s.

- The period of life from the late teens through the mid-20s became, for many in the developed world, a period of advanced self-development and of gradually laying a foundation for "adulthood."

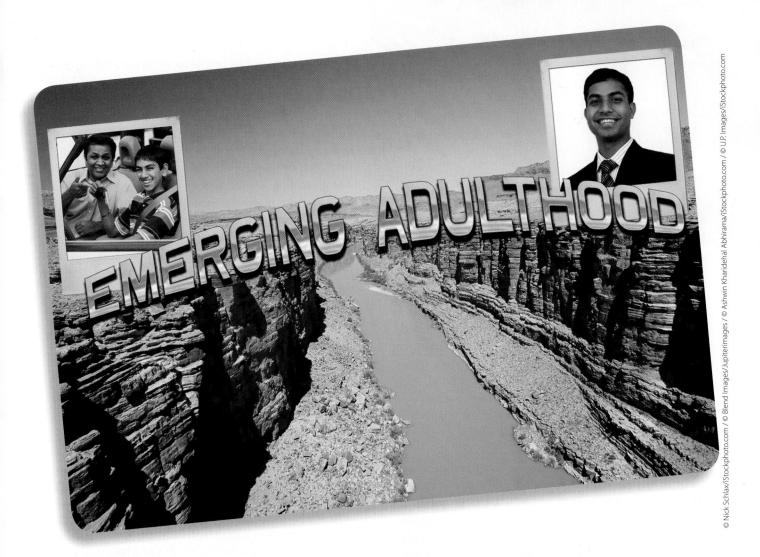

© Nick Schlax/iStockphoto.com / © Blend Images/Jupiterimages / © Ashwin Kharidehal Abhirama/iStockphoto.com / © U.P. Images/iStockphoto.com

Erik Erikson (1968) did not use the term *emerging adulthood*, but he did recognize that developed nations tend to elongate the period of adolescence. Erikson used the term *moratorium* to describe the extended quest for identity among people who dwell in adolescence. Erikson and other theorists also believed that it was more meaningful for the individual to take the voyage to identity rather than foreclose it by adopting the viewpoints of other people. Although there are advantages to taking time to formulate one's identity, there are downsides. For example, remaining dependent on parents can compromise an individual's self-esteem. Taking out loans for graduate school means that there is more to pay back; many individuals mortgage their own lives as they invest in their futures. Women who focus on their educations and their careers may marry and bear children later. Although many people appreciate chil-

dren more when they bear them later in life, people also become less fertile as the years pass, and they may find themselves in a race with their "biological clock."

Young people in the United States seem to be generally aware of the issues involved in defining the transition from adolescence to adulthood (Luyckx et al., 2008). Arnett (2000) reported what individuals in their late teens and early 20s say when they are asked whether they think they have become adults. About three in five say something like, "In some respects yes and in other respects no." Many think that they have developed beyond the conflicts and exploratory voyages of adolescence but may have not yet obtained the ability to assume the financial and interpersonal responsibilities they associate with adulthood (Luyckx et al., 2008).

And then, of course, there are those who remain adolescents forever.

Aalsma, M. C., Lapsley, D. K., & Flannery, D. J. (2006). Personal fables, narcissism, and adolescent adjustment. *Psychology in the Schools, 43*(4), 481–491.

Abbey, A., Saenz, C., Buck, P. O., Parkhill, M. R., & Hayman, L. W. Jr. (2006). The effects of acute alcohol consumption, cognitive reserve, partner risk, and gender on sexual decision making. *Journal of Studies on Alcohol, 67*(1), 113–121.

Abdelaziz, Y. E., Harb, A. H., & Hisham, N. (2001). *Textbook of clinical pediatrics.* Philadelphia: Lippincott Williams & Wilkins.

Aber, J. L., Bishop-Josef, S. J., Jones, S. M., McLearn, K. T., & Phillips, D. A. (Eds.). (2007). *Child development and social policy: Knowledge for action. APA Decade of Behavior volumes.* Washington, DC: American Psychological Association.

Abravanel, E., & DeYong, N. G. (1991). Does object modeling elicit imitative-like gestures from young infants? *Journal of Experimental Child Psychology, 52,* 22–40.

Adams, G. R., Berzonsky, M. D., & Keating, L. (2006). Psychosocial resources in first-year university students: The role of identity processes and social relationships. *Journal of Youth and Adolescence, 35*(1), 81–91.

Adler-Baeder, F. (2006). What do we know about the physical abuse of stepchildren? A review of the literature. *Journal of Divorce & Remarriage, 44*(3–4), 67–81.

Adolph, K. E., & Berger, S. E. (2005). Physical and motor development. In M. H. Bornstein & M. E. Lamb (Eds.), *Developmental science: An advanced textbook* (5th ed., pp. 223–281). Hillsdale, NJ: Erlbaum.

Agency for Healthcare Research and Quality. (2004, April). Chronic illnesses. In *Child Health Research Findings,* Program Brief, AHRQ Publication 04-P011. Rockville, MD: Agency for Healthcare Research and Quality. Retrieved from http://www.ahrq.gov/research/childfind/chfchrn.htm

Aguiar, A., & Baillargeon, R. (2002). Developments in young infants' reasoning about occluded objects. *Cognitive Psychology, 45*(2), 267–336.

Ainsworth, M. D. S. (1967). *Infancy in Uganda: Infant care and the growth of love.* Baltimore: Johns Hopkins University Press.

Ainsworth, M. D. S. (1989). Attachments beyond infancy. *American Psychologist, 44,* 709–716.

Ainsworth, M. D. S., Blehar, M. C., Waters, E., & Wall, S. (1978). *Patterns of attachment: A psychological study of the Strange Situation.* Hillsdale, NJ: Erlbaum.

Ainsworth, M. D. S., & Bowlby, J. (1991). An ethological approach to personality development. *American Psychologist, 46*(4), 333–341.

Akman, Y. (2007). Identity status of Turkish university students in relation to their evaluation of family problems. *Social Behavior and Personality, 35*(1), 79–88.

Alexander, G. M. (2003). An evolutionary perspective of sex-typed toy preferences: Pink, blue, and the brain. *Archives of Sexual Behavior, 32*(1), 7–14.

Alfirevic, Z., Sundberg, K., & Brigham, S. (2003). Amniocentesis and chorionic villus sampling for prenatal diagnosis. *Cochrane Database of Systematic Reviews.* doi: 10.1002/14651858.CD003252

Alloway, T. P., Gathercole, S. E., Willis, C., & Adams, A. (2004). A structural analysis of working memory and related cognitive skills in young children. *Journal of Experimental Child Psychology, 87*(2), 85–106.

Amato, P. R. (2006). Marital discord, divorce, and children's well-being: Results from a 20-year longitudinal study of two generations. In A. Clarke-Stewart & J. Dunn (Eds.), *Families count: Effects on child and adolescent development* (pp. 179–202). New York: Cambridge University Press.

American Academy of Family Physicians. (2006). Nutrition in toddlers. *American Family Physician, 74*(9). Retrieved from http://www.aafp.org/afp/20061101/1527.html

American Academy of Pediatrics. (2007). *A woman's guide to breastfeeding.* Retrieved from http://www.aap.org

American Association of University Women. (1992). *How schools shortchange women: The AAUW report.* Washington, DC: AAUW Educational Foundation.

American Association on Intellectual and Developmental Disabilities. (2009). "Frequently Asked Questions on Intellectual Disability and the AAIDD Definition," American Association of Intellectual and Development Disabilities (http://www.aamr.org/content_185.cfm) Accessed July 30, 2009.

American Fertility Association. (2007). Available at http://www.theafa.org/fertility/malefactor/index.html. Accessed February 6, 2007.

American Heart Association. (2007). *Overweight in children.* Retrieved May 18, 2007, from http://www.americanheart.org/presenter.jhtml?identifier=4670

American Lung Association. (2007). Various fact sheets. Retrieved June 24–July 5, 2007, from http://www.lungusa.org/

American Psychiatric Association. (2000). *Diagnostic and statistical manual of mental disorders* (4th ed., text revision). Washington, DC: Author.

Ammaniti, M., Speranza, A. M., & Fedele, S. (2005). Attachment in infancy and in early and late childhood: A longitudinal study. In K. A. Kerns & R. A. Richardson (Eds.), *Attachment in middle childhood* (pp. 115–136). New York: Guilford.

Ances, B. M. (2002). New concerns about thalidomide. *Obstetrics & Gynecology, 99,* 125–128.

Anderman, E. M., et al. (2001). Learning to value mathematics and reading: Relations to mastery and performance-oriented instructional practices. *Contemporary Educational Psychology, 26*(1), 76–95.

Anderson, K. G., Ramo, D. E., Schulte, M. T., Cummins, K., & Brown, S. A. (2007). Substance use treatment outcomes for youth: Integrating personal and environmental predictors. *Drug and Alcohol Dependence, 88*(1), 42–48.

Andreou, G., Krommydas, G., Gourgoulianis, K. I., Karapetsas, A., & Molyvdas, P. A. (2002). Handedness, asthma, and allergic disorders: Is there an association? *Psychology, Health, and Medicine, 7*(1), 53–60.

Angier, N., (1997, January 7) Chemical tied to fat control could help trigger puberty. *The New York Times,* pp. C1, C3.

Angier, N. (2007, June 12). Sleek, fast, and focused: The cells that make dad dad. *The New York Times,* pp. F1, F6.

Annett, M. (1999). Left-handedness as a function of sex, maternal versus paternal inheritance, and report bias. *Behavior Genetics, 29*(2), 103–114.

Annett, M., & Moran, P. (2006). Schizotypy is increased in mixed-handers, especially right-handed writers who use the left hand for primary actions. *Schizophrenia Research, 81*(2–3), 239–246.

Anthis, K. S., Dunkel, C. S., & Anderson, B. (2004). Gender and identity status differences in late adolescents' possible selves. *Journal of Adolescence, 27*(2), 147–152.

Anzengruber, D., et al. (2006). Smoking in eating disorders. *Eating Behaviors, 7*(4), 291–299.

Appel, P. W., Piculell, R., Jansky, H. K., & Griffy, K. (2006). Assessing alcohol and other drug problems (AOD) among sexually transmitted disease (STD) clinic patients with a modified CAGE-A: Implications for AOD intervention services and STD prevention. *American Journal of Drug and Alcohol Abuse, 32*(2), 225–236.

Arbona, C. (2005). Promoting the career development and academic achievement of at-risk youth: College access programs. In S. D. Brown & R. W. Lent (Eds.), *Career development and counseling: Putting theory and research to work* (pp. 525–550). Hoboken, NJ: Wiley.

Arbuthnot, J., & Gordon, D. A. (1988). Crime and cognition: Community applications of sociomoral reasoning development. *Criminal Justice and Behavior, 15*(3), 379–393.

Archer, J. (2006). Testosterone and human aggression: An evaluation of the challenge hypothesis. *Neuroscience & Biobehavioral Reviews, 30*(3), 319–345.

Archibald, L. M. D., & Gathercole, S. E. (2006). Short-term memory and working memory in specific language impairment. In T. P. Alloway & S. E. Gathercole (Eds.), *Working memory and neurodevelopmental disorders* (pp. 139–160). New York: Psychology Press.

Arduini, R. G., Capellini, S. A., & Ciasca, S. M. (2006). Comparative study of the neuropsychological and neuroimaging evaluations in children with dyslexia. *Arquivos de Neuro-Psiquiatría, 64*(2-B), 369–375.

Arija, V., et al. (2006). Nutritional status and performance in test of verbal and non-verbal intelligence in 6-year-old children. *Intelligence, 34*(2), 141–149.

Arnett, J. J. (2000). Emerging adulthood. *American Psychologist, 55*(5), 469–480.

Arnett, J. J. (2007). Socialization in emerging adulthood: From the family to the wider world, from socialization to self-socialization. In J. E. Grusec & P. D. Hastings (Eds.), *Handbook of socialization: Theory and research* (pp. 208–231). New York: Guilford.

Arnon, S., et al. (2006). Live music is beneficial to preterm infants in the neonatal intensive care unit environment. *Birth: Issues in Perinatal Care, 33*(2), 131–136.

Aschermann, E., Gülzow, I., & Wendt, D. (2004). Differences in the comprehension of passive voice in German- and English-speaking children. *Swiss Journal of Psychology, 63*(4), 235–245.

Ash, D. (2004). Reflective scientific sense-making dialogue in two languages: The science in the dialogue and the dialogue in the science. *Science Education, 88*(6), 855–884.

Aslin, R. N., & Schlaggar, B. L. (2006). Is myelination the precipitating neural event for language development in infants and toddlers? *Neurology, 66*(3), 304–305.

Aspy, C. B., et al. (2007). Parental communication and youth sexual behaviour. *Journal of Adolescence, 30*(3), 449–466.

Atkinson, G., & Davenne, D. (2007). Relationships between sleep, physical activity and human health. *Physiology & Behavior, 90*(2–3), 229–235.

August, D., Carlo, M., Dressler, C., & Snow, C. (2005). The critical role of vocabulary development for English language learners. *Learning Disabilities Research & Practice, 20*(1), 50–57.

Bachman, J. G., Safron, D. J., Sy, S. R., & Schulenberg, J. E. (2003). Wishing to work: New perspectives on how adolescents' part-time work intensity is linked to educational disengagement, substance use, and other problem behaviours. *International Journal of Behavioral Development, 27*(4), 301–315.

Bagley, C., & D'Augelli, A. R. (2000). Suicidal behaviour in gay, lesbian, and bisexual youth. *British Medical Journal, 320*, 1617–1618.

Bailey, J. M. (2003). *The man who would be queen: The science of gender-bending and transsexualism.* Washington, DC: Joseph Henry.

Bakker, D. J. (2006). Treatment of developmental dyslexia: A review. *Pediatric Rehabilitation, 9*(1), 3–13.

Baldry, A. C. (2003). Bullying in schools and exposure to domestic violence. *Child Abuse and Neglect, 27*(7), 713–732.

Ball, J., Lohaus, A., & Miebach, C. (2006). Psychological adjustment and school achievement during transition from elementary to secondary school. *Zeitschrift für Entwicklungspsychologie und Pädagogische Psychologie, 38*(3), 101–109.

Bandura, A. (1986). *Social foundations of thought and action: A social-cognitive theory.* Englewood Cliffs, NJ: Prentice Hall.

Bandura, A. (2006a). Going global with social cognitive theory: From prospect to paydirt. In S. I. Donaldson, D. E. Berger, & K. Pezdek (Eds.), *Applied psychology: New frontiers and rewarding careers* (pp. 53–79). Hillsdale, NJ: Erlbaum.

Bandura, A. (2006b). Toward a psychology of human agency. *Perspectives on Psychological Science, 1*(2), 164–180.

Bandura, A., Barbaranelli, C., Vittorio Caprara, G., & Pastorelli, C. (2001). Self-efficacy beliefs as shapers of children's aspirations and career trajectories. *Child Development, 72*(1), 187–206.

Bandura, A., Ross, S. A., & Ross, D. (1963). Imitation of film-mediated aggressive models. *Journal of Abnormal and Social Psychology, 66*, 3–11.

Barkley, R. A. (2004). Adolescents with attention-deficit/hyperactivity disorder: An overview of empirically based treatments. *Journal of Psychiatric Practice, 10*(1), 39–56.

Baron, S. W., Forde, D. R., & Kay, F. M. (2007). Self-control, risky lifestyles, and situation: The role of opportunity and context in the general theory. *Journal of Criminal Justice, 35*(2), 119–136.

Barr, R. G., Paterson, J. A., MacMartin, L. M., Lehtonen, L., & Young, S. N. (2005). Prolonged and unsoothable crying bouts in infants with and without colic. *Journal of Developmental & Behavioral Pediatrics, 26*(1), 14–23.

Barr, R., Rovee-Collier, C., & Campanella, J. (2005). Retrieval protracts deferred imitation by 6-month-olds. *Infancy, 7*(3), 263–283.

Barry, C. M., & Wentzel, K. R. (2006). Friend influence on prosocial behavior: The role of motivational factors and friendship characteristics. *Developmental Psychology, 42*(1), 153–163.

Bartholow, B. D., Dickter, C. L., & Sestir, M. A. (2006). Stereotype activation and control of race bias: Cognitive control of inhibition and its impairment by alcohol. *Journal of Personality and Social Psychology, 90*(2), 272–287.

Basic Behavioral Science Task Force, National Advisory Mental Health Council. (1996). Basic behavioral science research for mental health: Sociocultural and environmental practices. *American Psychologist, 51*, 722–731.

Bateson, P., & Mameli, M. (2007). The innate and the acquired: Useful clusters or a residual distinction from folk biology? *Developmental Psychobiology, 49*(8), 818–831.

Battin-Pearson, S., et al. (2000). Predictors of early high school dropout: A test of five theories. *Journal of Educational Psychology. 92*(3), 568–582.

Bauer, K. A. et al. (2009). Acne vulgaris and steroid acne. In R. Fife, S. Schrager, & S. B. Schrager (Eds.), *The ACP handbook of women's health.* (pp. 337ff.). Philadelphia: ACP Press.

Bauer, K. W., Yang, Y. W., & Austin, S. B. (2004). "How can we stay healthy when you're throwing all of this in front of us?" Findings from focus groups and interviews in middle schools on environmental influences on nutrition and physical activity. *Health Education and Behavior, 31*(1), 33–46.

Bauman, M. L., Anderson, G., Perry, E., & Ray, M. (2006). Neuroanatomical and neurochemical studies of the autistic brain: Current thought and future directions. In S. O. Moldin & J. L. R. Rubenstein (Eds.), *Understanding autism: From basic neuroscience to treatment* (pp. 303–322). Boca Raton, FL: CRC.

Baumrind, D. (1989). Rearing competent children. In W. Damon (Ed.), *Child development today and tomorrow.* San Francisco: Jossey-Bass.

Baumrind, D. (1991a). The influence of parenting style on adolescent competence and substance use. *Journal of Early Adolescence, 11*, 56–95.

Baumrind, D. (1991b). Parenting styles and adolescent development. In J. Brooks-Gunn, R. Lerner, & A. C. Petersen (Eds.), *Encyclopedia of adolescence.* New York: Garland.

Baumrind, D. (2005). Taking a stand in a morally pluralistic society: Constructive obedience and responsible dissent in moral/character education. In L. Nucci (Ed.), *Conflict, contradiction, and contrarian elements in moral development and education* (pp. 21–50). Mahwah, NJ: Erlbaum.

Bearce, K. H., & Rovee-Collier, C. (2006). Repeated priming increases memory accessibility in infants. *Journal of Experimental Child Psychology, 93*(4), 357–376.

Beck, E., Burnet, K. L., & Vosper, J. (2006). Birth-order effects on facets of extraversion. *Personality and Individual Differences, 40*(5), 953–959.

Behrman, R. E., Kliegman, R. M., & Jenson, H. B. (2000). *Nelson review of pediatrics* (2nd ed.). Philadelphia: Saunders.

Beidel, D. C., & Turner, S. M. (2007). Clinical presentation of social anxiety disorder in children and adolescents. In D. C. Beidel & S. M. Turner (Eds.), *Shy children, phobic adults: Nature and treatment of social anxiety disorders* (2nd ed., pp. 47–80). Washington, DC: American Psychological Association.

Beilei, L., Lei, L., Qi, D., & von Hofsten, C. (2002). The development of fine motor skills and their relations to children's academic achievement. *Acta Psychologica Sinica, 34*(5), 494–499.

Belkin, L. (2009, April 5). Your old man. *The New York Times Magazine.* Retrieved from http://www.nytimes.com/pages/magazine.

Bell, J. H., & Bromnick, R. D. (2003). The social reality of the imaginary audience: A ground theory approach. *Adolescence, 38*(150), 205–219.

Bellodi, L., et al. (2001). Morbidity risk for obsessive-compulsive spectrum disorders in first-degree relatives of patients with eating disorders. *American Journal of Psychiatry, 158*, 563–569.

Belmonte, M. K., & Carper, R. A. (2006). Monozygotic twins with Asperger syndrome: Differences in behaviour reflect variations in brain structure and function. *Brain and Cognition, 61*(1), 110–121.

Belsky, J. (2006a). Determinants and consequences of infant–parent attachment. In L. Balter & C. S. Tamis-LeMonda (Eds.), *Child psychology: A handbook of contemporary issues* (2nd ed., pp. 53–77). New York: Psychology Press.

Belsky, J. (2006b). Early child care and early child development: Major findings of the NICHD Study of Early Child Care. *European Journal of Developmental Psychology, 3*(1), 95–110.

Belsky, J., et al. (2007). Are there long-term effects of early child care? *Child Development, 78*(2), 681–701.

Bem, S. L. (1993). *The lenses of gender.* New Haven, CT: Yale University Press.

Bender, H. L., et al. (2007). Use of harsh physical discipline and developmental outcomes in adolescence. *Development and Psychopathology, 19*(1) 227–242.

Bennett, S. E., & Assefi, N. P. (2005). School-based teenage pregnancy prevention programs: A systematic review of randomized controlled trials. *Journal of Adolescent Health, 36*(1), 72–81.

Berg, C. J., Chang, J., Callaghan, W. M., & Whitehead, S. J. (2003). Pregnancy-related mortality in the United States, 1991–1997. *Obstetrics and Gynecology, 101*, 289–296.

Berger, L. E., Jodl, K. M., Allen, J. P., McElhaney, K. B., & Kuperminc, G. P. (2005). When adolescents disagree with others about their symptoms: Differences in attachment organization as an explanation of discrepancies between adolescent, parent, and peer reports of behavior problems. *Development and Psychopathology, 17*(2), 509–528.

Bergmann, J., & Wimmer, H. (2008). A dual-route perspective on poor reading in a regular orthography: Evidence from phonological and orthographic lexical decisions. *Cognitive Neuropsychology, 25*(5), 653–676.

Berndt, T. J. (1992). Friendship and friends' influence in adolescence. *Current Directions in Psychological Science, 1,* 156–159.

Berndt, T. J. (2004). Friendship and three A's (aggression, adjustment, and attachment). *Journal of Experimental Child Psychology, 88*(1), 1–4.

Berndt, T. J., & Perry, T. B. (1990). Distinctive features and effects of early adolescent friendships. In R. Montemayor, G. R. Adams, & T. P. Gullotta (Eds.), *From childhood to adolescence: A transitional period?* Newbury Park, CA: Sage.

Bernstein, I. M., et al. (2005). Maternal smoking and its association with birth weight. *Obstetrics & Gynecology, 106,* 986–991.

Berzonsky, M. D. (2004). Identity style, parental authority, and identity commitment. *Journal of Youth and Adolescence, 33*(3), 213–220.

Berzonsky, M. D. (2005). Ego identity: A personal standpoint in a postmodern world. *Identity, 5*(2), 125–136.

Berzonsky, M. D., & Kuk, L. S. (2005). Identity style, psychosocial maturity, and academic performance. *Personality and Individual Differences, 39*(1), 235–247.

Bialystok, E. K., & Craik, F. I. M. (2007). Bilingualism and naming: Implications for cognitive assessment. *Journal of the International Neuropsychological Society, 13*(2), 209–211.

Bialystok, E. K., & Senman, L. (2004). Executive processes in appearance–reality tasks: The role of inhibition of attention and symbolic representation. *Child Development, 75*(2), 562–579.

Biederman, J., et al. (2007). Effect of comorbid symptoms of oppositional defiant disorder on responses to atomoxetine in children with ADHD: A meta-analysis of controlled clinical trial data. *Psychopharmacology, 190*(1), 31–41.

Birch, C. D., Stewart, S. H., & Brown, C. G. (2007). Exploring differential patterns of situational risk for binge eating and heavy drinking. *Addictive Behaviors, 32*(3), 433–448.

Bird, A., Reese, E., & Tripp, G. (2006). Parent–child talk about past emotional events: Associations with child temperament and goodness-of-fit. *Journal of Cognition and Development, 7*(2), 189–210.

Bishop, D. M. (2005). The role of race and ethnicity in juvenile justice processing. In D. F. Hawkins & K. Kempf-Leonard (Eds.), *Our children, their children: Confronting racial and ethnic differences in American juvenile justice* (pp. 23–82). The John D. and Catherine T. MacArthur Foundation series on mental health and development. Chicago: University of Chicago Press.

Black, D. W. (2007). Antisocial personality disorder, conduct disorder, and psychopathy. In J. E. Grant & M. N. Potenza (Eds.), *Textbook of men's mental health* (pp. 143–170). Washington, DC: American Psychiatric Publishing.

Blakeslee, S. (1998, August 4), Re-evaluating significance of baby's bond with mother, *The New York Times,* pp. F1, F2.

Blass, E. M., & Camp, C. A. (2003). Changing determinants in 6- to 12-week-old human infants. *Developmental Psychobiology, 42*(3), 312–316.

Bloch, M., Rotenberg, N., Koren, D., & Ehud, K. (2006). Risk factors for early postpartum depressive symptoms. *General Hospital Psychiatry, 28*(1), 3–8.

Blom-Hoffman, J., George, J. B., & Franko, D. L. (2006). Childhood overweight. In G. G. Bear & K. M. Minke (Eds.), *Children's needs III: Development, prevention, and intervention* (pp. 989–1000). Washington, DC: National Association of School Psychologists.

Bloom, B., Dey, A. N., & Freeman, G. (2006). Summary health statistics for U.S. children: National Health Interview Survey, 2005. *National Center for Health Statistics, Vital Health Stat, 10*(231).

Bloom, L. (1998). Language acquisition in its developmental context. In W. Damon (Ed.), *Handbook of child psychology* (5th ed.), Vol. 2. New York: Wiley.

Bloom, P. (2002). Mind reading, communication, and the learning of names for things. *Mind and Language, 17*(1–2), 37–54.

Boada, R., & Pennington, B. F. (2006). Deficient implicit phonological representations in children with dyslexia. *Journal of Experimental Child Psychology, 95*(3), 153–193.

Boccia, M., & Campos, J. J. (1989). Maternal emotional signals, social referencing, and infants' reactions to strangers. In N. Eisenberg (Ed.), *New directions for child development: No. 44, Empathy and related emotional responses.* San Francisco: Jossey-Bass.

Boden, C., & Giaschi, D. (2007). M-stream deficits and reading-related visual processes in developmental dyslexia. *Psychological Bulletin, 133*(2), 346–366.

Bogardus, C. (2009). Missing heritability and GWAS utility. *Obesity, 17*(2), 209–210.

Bohon, C., Garber, J., & Horowitz, J. L. (2007). Predicting school dropout and adolescent sexual behavior in offspring of depressed and nondepressed mothers. *Journal of the American Academy of Child & Adolescent Psychiatry, 46*(1), 15–24.

Boivin, M., Vitaro, F., & Poulin, F. (2005). Peer relationships and the development of aggressive behavior in early childhood. In R. E. Tremblay, W. W. Hartup, & J. Archer (Eds.), *Developmental origins of aggression* (pp. 376–397). New York: Guilford.

Bonn-Miller, M. O., Zvolensky, M. J., & Bernstein, A. (2007). Marijuana use motives: Concurrent relations to frequency of past 30-day use and anxiety sensitivity among young adult marijuana smokers. *Addictive Behaviors, 32*(1) 49–62.

Boom, J., Wouters, H., & Keller, M. (2007). A cross-cultural validation of stage development: A Rasch re-analysis of longitudinal socio-moral reasoning data. *Cognitive Development, 22*(2), 213–229.

Booth-LaForce, C., et al. (2006). Attachment, self-worth, and peer-group functioning in middle childhood. *Attachment & Human Development, 8*(4), 309–325.

Bosi, M,. L. & de Oliveira, F. P. (2006). Bulimic behavior in adolescent athletes. In P. I. Swain (Ed.), *New developments in eating disorders research* (pp. 123–133). Hauppauge, NY: Nova Science.

Boskind-White, M., & White, W. C. (1983). *Bulimarexia: The binge/purge cycle.* New York: Norton.

Bost, L. W., & Riccomini, P. J. (2006). Effective instruction: An inconspicuous strategy for dropout prevention. *Remedial and Special Education, 27*(5), 301–311.

Bouchard, T. J., Jr., & Loehlin, J. C. (2001). Genes, evolution, and personality. *Behavior Genetics, 31*(3), 243–273.

Bouchard, T. J., Jr., Lykken, D. T., McGue, M., Segal, N. L., & Tellegen, A. (1990). Sources of human psychological differences: The Minnesota study of twins reared apart. *Science, 250,* 223–228.

Bower, T. G. R. (1974). *Development in infancy.* San Francisco: W. H. Freeman.

Bowlby, J. (1988). *A secure base.* New York: Basic Books.

Bradley, R. H. (2006). The home environment. In N. F. Watt et al. (Eds.), *The crisis in youth mental health: Critical issues and effective programs: Vol. 4. Early intervention programs and policies, child psychology and mental health* (pp. 89–120). Westport, CT: Praeger/Greenwood.

Bradley, R. H., Caldwell, B. M., & Corwyn, R. F. (2003). The child care HOME inventories: Assessing the quality of family child care homes. *Early Childhood Research Quarterly, 18*(3), 294–309.

Bradley, R. H., & Corwyn, R. F. (2006). The family environment. In L. Balter & C. S. Tamis-LeMonda (Eds.), *Child psychology: A handbook of contemporary issues* (2nd ed., pp. 493–520). New York: Psychology Press.

Branco, J. C., & Lourenço, O. (2004). Cognitive and linguistic aspects in 5- to 6-year-olds' class-inclusion reasoning. *Psicologia Educação Cultura, 8*(2), 427–445.

Brandtjen, H., & Verny, T. (2001). Short and long term effects on infants and toddlers in full time daycare centers. *Journal of Prenatal & Perinatal Psychology & Health, 15*(4), 239–286.

Brase, G. L. (2006). Cues of parental investment as a factor in attractiveness. *Evolution and Human Behavior, 27*(2), 145–157.

Brazier, A., & Rowlands, C. (2006). PKU in the family: Working together. *Clinical Child Psychology and Psychiatry, 11*(3), 483–488.

Bremner, A., & Bryant, P. (2001). The effect of spatial cues on infants' responses in the AB task, with and without a hidden object. *Developmental Science, 4*(4), 408–415.

Briones, T. L., Klintsova, A. Y., & Greenough, W. T. (2004). Stability of synaptic plasticity in the adult rat visual cortex induced by complex environment exposure. *Brain Research, 1018*(1), 130–135.

Brody, L. R., Zelazo, P. R., & Chaika, H. (1984). Habituation–dishabituation to speech in the neonate. *Developmental Psychology, 20,* 114–119.

Bronfenbrenner, U., & Morris, P. A. (2006). The bioecological model of human development. In R. M. Lerner & W. Damon (Eds.), *Handbook of child psychology Vol. 1. Theoretical models of human development* (6th ed., pp. 793–828). Hoboken, NJ: Wiley.

Bronson, G. W. (1990). Changes in infants' visual scanning across the 2- to 14-week age period. *Journal of Experimental Child Psychology, 49*, 101–125.

Bronson, G. W. (1991). Infant differences in rate of visual encoding. *Child Development, 62*, 44–54.

Bronson, G. W. (1997). The growth of visual capacity: Evidence from infant scanning patterns. *Advances in Infancy Research, 11*, 109–141.

Brown, B. B., Mounts, N., Lamborn, S. D., & Steinberg, L. (1993). Parenting practices and peer group affiliation in adolescence. *Child Development, 64*, 467–482.

Brown, R. (1973). *A first language: The early stages.* Cambridge, MA: Harvard University Press.

Brown, R. T., et al. (2008). Anxiety disorders. In R. T. Brown et al. (Eds.), *Childhood mental health disorders: Evidence base and contextual factors for psychosocial, psychopharmacological, and combined interventions* (pp. 59–67). Washington, DC: American Psychological Association.

Brownell, C. A., & Carriger, M. S. (1990). Changes in cooperation and self-other differentiation during the second year. *Child Development, 61*, 1164–1174.

Browning, J. R., Hatfield, E., Kessler, D., & Levine, T. (2000). Sexual motives, gender, and sexual behavior. *Archives of Sexual Behavior, 29*(2), 135–153.

Bruck, M., Ceci, S. J., & Principe, G. F. (2006). The child and the law. In K. Renninger, I. E. Sigel, W. Damon, & R. M. Lerner (Eds.), *Handbook of child psychology: Vol. 4. Child psychology in practice* (6th ed., pp. 776–816). Hoboken, NJ: Wiley.

Bruckner, T. A. (2008). Economic antecedents of parenting behavior and infant mortality. *Dissertation Abstracts International B: The Sciences and Engineering, 68*(8-B), pp. 5108.

Brunner, R., Parzer, P., & Resch, F. (2005). Involuntary hospitalization of patients with anorexia nervosa: Clinical issues and empirical findings. *Fortschritte der Neurologie, Psychiatrie, 73*(1), 9–15.

Bryden, P. J., Bruyn, J., & Fletcher, P. (2005). Handedness and health: An examination of the association between different handedness classifications and health disorders. *Laterality: Asymmetries of Body, Brain and Cognition, 10*(5), 429–440.

Budney, A. J., Vandrey, R. G., Hughes, J. R., Moore, B. A., & Bahrenburg, B. (2007). Oral delta-9-tetrahydrocannabinol suppresses cannabis withdrawal symptoms. *Drug and Alcohol Dependence, 86*(1), 22–29.

Bugental, D. B., & Happaney, K. (2004). Predicting infant maltreatment in low-income families: The interactive effects of maternal attributions and child status at birth. *Developmental Psychology, 40*(2), 234–243.

Bunikowski, R., et al. (1998). Neuro-developmental outcome after prenatal exposure to opiates. *European Journal of Pediatrics, 157*(9), 724–730.

Bushman, B. J. (1998). Priming effects of media violence on the accessibility of aggressive constructs in memory. *Personality and Social Psychology Bulletin, 24*(5), 537–545.

Bushnell, E. W. (1993, June). *A dual-processing approach to cross-modal matching: Implications for development.* Paper presented at the meeting of the Society for Research in Child Development, New Orleans.

Bushnell, I. W. R. (2001). Mother's face recognition in newborn infants: Learning and memory. *Infant and Child Development, 10*(1–2), 67–74.

Buss, D. M., & Duntley, J. D. (2006). The evolution of aggression. In M. Schaller, J. A. Simpson, & D. T. Kenrick (Eds.), *Evolution and social psychology: Frontiers of social psychology* (pp. 263–285). Madison, CT: Psychosocial Press.

Bussey, K., & Bandura, A. (1999). Social cognitive theory of gender development and differentiation. *Psychological Review, 106*(4), 676–713.

Buston, K., Williamson, L., & Hart, G. (2007). Young women under 16 years with experience of sexual intercourse: Who becomes pregnant? *Journal of Epidemiology & Community Health, 61*(3) 221–225.

Butterfield, S. A., & Loovis, E. M. (1993). Influence of age, sex, balance, and sport participation on development of throwing by children in grades K–8. *Perceptual and Motor Skills, 76*, 459–464.

Bynum, M. S. (2007). African American mother–daughter communication about sex and daughters' sexual behavior: Does college racial composition make a difference? *Cultural Diversity & Ethnic Minority Psychology, 13*(2), 151–160.

Callan, M. J., Ellard, J. H., & Nicol, J. E. (2006). The belief in a just world and immanent justice reasoning in adults. *Personality and Social Psychology Bulletin, 32*(12), 1646–1658.

Calvert, S. L., & Kotler, J. A. (2003). Lessons from children's television: The impact of the Children's Television Act on children's learning. *Journal of Applied Developmental Psychology, 24*(3), 275–335.

Camarena, P. M. (1991). Conformity in adolescence. In R. M. Lerner, A. C. Petersen, & J. Brooks-Gunn (Eds.), *Encyclopedia of adolescence.* New York: Garland.

Campanella, J., & Rovee-Collier, C. (2005). Latent learning and deferred imitation at 3 months. *Infancy, 7*(3), 243–262.

Campbell, A., Shirley, L., & Caygill, L. (2002). Sex-typed preferences in three domains: Do two-year-olds need cognitive variables? *British Journal of Psychology, 93*(2), 203–217.

Campbell, A., Shirley, L., Heywood, C., & Crook, C. (2000). Infants' visual preference for sex-congruent babies, children, toys and activities: A longitudinal study. *British Journal of Developmental Psychology, 18*(4), 479–498.

Campbell, D. A., Lake, M. F. Falk, M., & Backstrand, J. R. (2006). A randomized control trial of continuous support in labor by a lay doula. *Journal of Obstetric, Gynecologic, and Neonatal Nursing, 35*(4), 456–464.

Campbell, D. W., Eaton, W. O., & McKeen, N. A. (2002). Motor activity level and behavioural control in young children. *International Journal of Behavioral Development, 26*(4), 289–296.

Campbell, S. B., et al. (2004). The course of maternal depressive symptoms and maternal sensitivity as predictors of attachment security at 36 months. *Development and Psychopathology, 16*(2), 231–252.

Campos, J. J., Hiatt, S., Ramsey, D., Henderson, C., & Svejda, M. (1978). The emergence of fear on the visual cliff. In M. Lewis & L. Rosenblum (Eds.), *The origins of affect.* New York: Plenum.

Campos, J. J., Langer, A., & Krowitz, A. (1970). Cardiac responses on the visual cliff in prelocomotor human infants. *Science, 170*, 196–197.

Camras, L. A., et al. (2007). Do infants show distinct negative facial expressions for fear and anger? Emotional expression in 11-month-old European American, Chinese, and Japanese infants. *Infancy, 11*(2), 131–155.

Candy, T. R., Crowell, J. A., & Banks, M. S. (1998). Optical, receptoral, and retinal constraints on foveal and peripheral vision in the human neonate. *Vision Research, 38*(24), 3857–3870.

Canitano, R. (2007). Epilepsy in autism spectrum disorders. *European Child & Adolescent Psychiatry, 16*(1), 61–66.

Caplan, M., Vespo, J., Pedersen, J., & Hale, D. F. (1991). Conflict and its resolution in small groups of one and two-year-olds. *Child Development, 62*, 1513–1524.

Caplan, P. J., & Larkin, J. (1991). The anatomy of dominance and self-protection. *American Psychologist, 46*, 536.

Capron, C., Thérond, C., & Duyme, M. (2007). Brief report: Effect of menarcheal status and family structure on depressive symptoms and emotional/behavioural problems in young adolescent girls. *Journal of Adolescence, 30*(1), 175–179.

Carey, B. (2007a, March 26). Poor behavior is linked to time in day care. *The New York Times.* Retrieved from http://www.nytimes.com

Carey, B. (2007b, June 22). Research finds firstborns gain the higher I.Q. *The New York Times.* Retrieved from http://www.nytimes.com

Carroll, J. S., et al. (2007). So close, yet so far away: The impact of varying marital horizons on emerging adulthood. *Journal of Adolescent Research, 22*(3), 219–247.

Carver, L. J., & Vaccaro, B. G. (2007). 12-month-old infants allocate increased neural resources to stimuli associated with negative adult emotion. *Developmental Psychology, 43*(1), 54–69.

Casas, J. F., et al. (2006). Early parenting and children's relational and physical aggression in the preschool and home contexts. *Journal of Applied Developmental Psychology, 27*(3), 209–227.

Casper, R. C., Sullivan, E. L., & Tecott, L. (2008). Relevance of animal models to human eating disorders and obesity. *Psychopharmacology, 199*(3), 313–329.

Cassia, V. M., Simion, F., & Umilta, C. (2001). Face preference at birth: The role of an orienting mechanism. *Developmental Science, 4*(1), 101–108.

Caton, D., et al. (2002). Anesthesia for childbirth: Controversy and change. *American Journal of Obstetrics & Gynecology, 186*(5), S25–S30.

Cattell, R. B. (1949). *The culture-fair intelligence test.* Champaign, IL: Institute for Personality and Ability Testing.

Caulfield, R. (2000). Beneficial effects of tactile stimulation on early development. *Early Childhood Education Journal, 27*(4), 255–257.

Cavallini, A., et al. (2002). Visual acuity in the first two years of life in healthy term newborns: An experience with the Teller Acuity Cards. *Functional Neurology: New*

Trends in Adaptive and Behavioral Disorders, 17(2), 87–92.

Cavell, T. A. (2001). Updating our approach to parent training. I. The case against targeting noncompliance. *Clinical Psychology: Science and Practice,* 8(3), 299–318.

Ceci, S. J., & Williams, W. M. (Eds.). (2007). *Why aren't more women in science?: Top researchers debate the evidence.* Washington, DC: American Psychological Association.

Centers for Disease Control and Prevention. (2005). National Center for Health Statistics. *America's children, 2005. America's children: Key national indicators of well-being 2005.* Childstats.gov. Retrieved from http://www.childstats.gov/amchildren05/hea8.asp

Centers for Disease Control and Prevention. (2006a). Breastfeeding: Frequently asked questions (FAQs). Retrieved July 16, 2007, from http://www.cdc.gov/breastfeeding/faq/index.htm

Centers for Disease Control and Prevention. (2006b). *HIV/AIDS surveillance report,* 2005, Vol. 17. Atlanta: U.S. Department of Health and Human Services, Centers for Disease Control and Prevention. Retrieved from http://www.cdc.gov/hiv/topics/surveillance/resources/reports

Centers for Disease Control and Prevention. (2008a). *HIV/AIDS statistics and surveillance.* Retrieved from http://www.cdc.gov/hiv/topics/surveillance/

Centers for Disease Control and Prevention. (2008b, June 6). Youth risk behavior surveillance—United States, 2007. *Morbidity & Mortality Weekly Report,* 57(SS-4), 1–131. Retrieved from http://www.cdc.gov/healthyyouth/yrbs/pdf/yrbss07_mmwr.pdf

Centers for Disease Control and Prevention. (2009). Recommended immunization schedule for persons aged 0 through 6 years—United States 2009. Department of Health and Human Services. Available at www.cdc.gov/vaccines/recs/schedules/downloads/child/2009/09_0-6yrs_schedule_pr.pdf. Accessed July 30, 2009.

Central Intelligence Agency. (2004, September 17). *The World Factbook.* Retrieved from http://www.cia.gov/cia/publications/factbook/geos/us.html#People

Cernoch, J., & Porter, R. (1985). Recognition of maternal axillary odors by infants. *Child Development,* 56, 1593–1598.

Chapman, M., & McBride, M. C. (1992). Beyond competence and performance: Children's class inclusion strategies, superordinate class cues, and verbal justifications. *Developmental Psychology,* 28, 319–327.

Cheng, S. T., & Chan, A. C. M. (2007). Multiple pathways from stress to suicidality and the protective effect of social support in Hong Kong adolescents. *Suicide and Life-Threatening Behavior,* 37(2), 187–196.

Cherney, I. D., Harper, H. J., & Winter, J. A. (2006). Nouveaux jouets: Ce que les enfants identifient comme "jouets de garcons" et "jouets de filles." *Enfance,* 58(3), 266–282.

Chess, S., & Thomas, A. (1991). Temperament. In M. Lewis (Ed.), *Child and adolescent psychiatry: A comprehensive textbook.* Baltimore: Williams & Wilkins.

Cheung, C., Chan, W., Lee, T., Liu, S., & Leung, K. (2001). Structure of moral consciousness and moral intentions among youth in Hong Kong. *International Journal of Adolescence and Youth,* 9(2–3), 83–116.

Chomsky, N. (1988). *Language and problems of knowledge.* Cambridge, MA: MIT Press.

Chomsky, N. (1990). On the nature, use, and acquisition of language. In W. G. Lycan (Ed.), *Mind and cognition.* Oxford: Blackwell.

Chou, T. L., et al. (2006). Developmental and skill effects on the neural correlates of semantic processing to visually presented words. *Human Brain Mapping,* 27(11), 915–924.

Christenson, S. L., & Thurlow, M. L. (2004). School dropouts: Prevention considerations, interventions, and challenges. *Current Directions in Psychological Science,* 13(1), 36–39.

Christian, P., et al. (2003). Effects of alternative maternal micronutrient supplements on low birth weight in rural Nepal: Double blind randomised community trial. *British Medical Journal,* 326, 571.

Chronis, A. M., et al. (2007). Maternal depression and early positive parenting predict future conduct problems in young children with attention-deficit/hyperactivity disorder. *Developmental Psychology,* 43(1), 70–82.

Cicchetti, D., Rogosch, F. A., & Toth, S. L. (2006). Fostering secure attachment in infants in maltreating families through preventive interventions. *Development and Psychopathology,* 18(3), 623–649.

Clancy, B., & Finlay, B. (2001). Neural correlates of early language learning. In M. Tomasello & E. Bates (Eds.), *Language development: The essential readings.* Malden, MA: Blackwell.

Clark, E. V. (1973). What's in a word? On the child's acquisition of semantics in his first language. In E. Moore (Ed.), *Cognitive development and the acquisition of language.* New York: Academic.

Clark, E. V. (1975). Knowledge, context, and strategy in the acquisition of meaning. In D. P. Date (Ed.), *Georgetown University roundtable on language and linguistics.* Washington, DC: Georgetown University Press.

Clark, J. (2005). Sibling relationships: Theory and issues for practice. *Child & Family Social Work,* 10(1), 90–91.

Clark, R. (1983). *Family life and school achievement: Why poor black children succeed or fail.* Chicago: University of Chicago Press.

Clark, S. E., & Symons, D. K. (2000). A longitudinal study of Q-sort attachment security and self-processes at age 5. *Infant and Child Development,* 9(2), 91–104.

Clarke-Stewart, K. A., & Beck, R. J. (1999). Maternal scaffolding and children's narrative retelling of a movie story. *Early Childhood Research Quarterly,* 14(3), 409–434.

Clayton, R., & Crosby, R. A. (2006) Measurement in health promotion. In R. A. Crosby, R. J. DiClemente, & L. F. Salazar (Eds.), *Research methods in health promotion* (pp. 229–259). San Francisco: Jossey-Bass.

Cleary, D. J., Ray, G. E., LoBello, S. G., & Zachar, P. (2002). Children's perceptions of close peer relationships: Quality, congruence and meta-perceptions. *Child Study Journal,* 32(3), 179–192.

Clode, D. (2006). [Review of *A left-hand turn around the world: Chasing the mystery and meaning of all things southpaw*]. *Laterality: Asymmetries of Body, Brain and Cognition,* 11(6), 580–581.

Cnattingius, S. (2004). The epidemiology of smoking during pregnancy: Smoking prevalence, maternal characteristics, and pregnancy outcomes. *Nicotine & Tobacco Research,* 6(Supp. l2), S125–S140.

Cohen, L. S., et al. (2006). Relapse of major depression during pregnancy in women who maintain or discontinue antidepressant treatment. *Journal of the American Medical Association,* 295(5), 499–507.

Cohen-Bendahan, C. C. C., Buitelaar, J. K., van Goozen, S. H. M., & Cohen-Kettenis, P. T. (2004). Prenatal exposure to testosterone and functional cerebral lateralization: A study in same-sex and opposite-sex twin girls. *Psychoneuroendocrinology,* 29(7), 911–916.

Colby, A., Kohlberg, L. G., J., & Lieberman, M. (1983). A longitudinal study of moral judgment. *Monographs of the Society for Research in Child Development,* 48(4, Serial No. 200).

Coleman, M., Ganong, L. H., & Fine, M. (2000). Reinvestigating remarriage: Another decade of progress. *Journal of Marriage & the Family,* 62(4) 1288–1307.

Coleman, P. K. (2003). Perceptions of parent–child attachment, social self-efficacy, and peer relationships in middle childhood. *Infant and Child Development,* 12(4), 351–368.

Collaer, M. L., & Hill, E. M. (2006). Large sex difference in adolescents on a timed line judgment task: Attentional contributors and task relationship to mathematics. *Perception,* 35(4), 561–572.

Collins, W. A., & Laursen, B. (2006). Parent–adolescent relationships. In P. Noller & J. A. Feeney (Eds.), *Close relationships: Functions, forms and processes* (pp. 111–125). Hove, England: Psychology Press/Taylor & Francis.

Collins, W. A., Maccoby, E. E., Steinberg, L., Hetherington, E. M., & Bornstein, M. H. (2000). Contemporary research on parenting: The case for nature and nurture. *American Psychologist,* 55(2), 218–232.

Collins, W. A., Maccoby, E. E., Steinberg, L., Hetherington, E. M., & Bornstein, M. H. (2003). Contemporary research on parenting: The case for nature and nurture. In M. E. Hertzig & E. A. Farber (Eds.), *Annual progress in child psychiatry and child development: 2000–2001* (pp. 125–153). New York: Brunner-Routledge.

Colombo, J. (1993). *Infant cognition.* Newbury Park, CA: Sage.

Commission on Adolescent Substance and Alcohol Abuse. (2005). Prevention of substance use disorders. In D. L. Evans et al. (Eds.), *Treating and preventing adolescent mental health disorders: What we know and what we don't know: A research agenda for improving the mental health of our youth* (pp. 411–426). New York: Oxford University Press.

Commons, M. L., Galaz-Fontes, J. F., & Morse, S. J. (2006). Leadership, cross-cultural contact, socio-economic status, and formal operational reasoning about moral dilemmas among Mexican non-literate adults and high school students. *Journal of Moral Education,* 35(2), 247–267.

Conel, J. L. (1959). *The postnatal development of the human cerebral cortex: Vol. 5. The cortex of the 15-month infant.* Cambridge, MA: Harvard University Press.

Conner, K. R., & Goldston, D. B. (2007). Rates of suicide among males increase steadily from age 11 to 21: Developmental framework and outline for prevention. *Aggression and Violent Behavior, 12*(2), 193–207.

Connolly, J., Craig, W., Goldberg, A., & Pepler, D. (2004). Mixed-gender groups, dating, and romantic relationships in early adolescence. *Journal of Research on Adolescence, 14*(2), 185–207.

Connolly, J., Furman, W., & Konarski, R. (2000). The role of peers in the emergence of heterosexual romantic relationships in adolescence. *Child Development, 71*(5), 1395–1408.

Connor, P. D., Sampson, P. D., Streissguth, A. P., Bookstein, F. L., & Barr, H. M. (2006). Effects of prenatal alcohol exposure on fine motor coordination and balance: A study of two adult samples. *Neuropsychologia, 44*(5), 744–751.

Constantino, J. N., et al. (2006). Autistic social impairment in the siblings of children with pervasive developmental disorders. *American Journal of Psychiatry, 163*(2), 294–296.

Cooke, B. M., Breedlove, S. M., & Jordan, C. L. (2003). Both estrogen receptors and androgen receptors contribute to testosterone-induced changes in the morphology of the medial amygdala and sexual arousal in male rats. *Hormones & Behavior, 43*(2), 336–346.

Cooper, J., Appleby, L., & Amos, T. (2002). Life events preceding suicide by young people. *Social Psychiatry and Psychiatric Epidemiology, 37*(6), 271–275.

Coovadia, H. (2004). Antiretroviral agents: How best to protect infants from HIV and save their mothers from AIDS. *New England Journal of Medicine, 351*(3), 289–292.

Copeland, A. L., Martin, P. D., Geiselman, P. J., Rash, C. J., & Kendzor, D. E. (2006). Smoking cessation for weight-concerned women: Group vs. individually tailored, dietary, and weight-control follow-up sessions. *Addictive Behaviors, 31*(1), 115–127.

Coplan, R. J., Rubin, K. H., Fox, N. A., Calkins, S. D., & Stewart, S. L. (1994). Being alone, playing alone, and acting alone: Distinguishing among reticence and passive and active solitude in young children. *Child Development, 65,* 129–137.

Coren, S. (1992). *The left-hander syndrome.* New York: Free Press.

Cornwell, A. A. C., & Feigenbaum, P. (2006). Sleep biological rhythms in normal infants and those at high risk for SIDS. *Chronobiology International, 23*(5), 935–961.

Corstorphine, E., Waller, G., Lawson, R., & Ganis, C. (2007). Trauma and multi-impulsivity in the eating disorders. *Eating Behaviors, 8*(1), 23–30.

Costello, E. J. (2007). Psychiatric predictors of adolescent and young adult drug use and abuse. *Drug and Alcohol Dependence, 88,* S1–S3.

Costello, E. J., Sung, M., Worthman, C., & Angold, A. (2007). Pubertal maturation and the development of alcohol use and abuse. *Drug and Alcohol Dependence, 88,* S50–S59.

Costigan, C. L., Cauce, A. M., & Etchison, K. (2007). Changes in African American mother–daughter relationships during adolescence: Conflict, autonomy, and warmth. In B. J. R. Leadbeater & N. Way (Eds.), *Urban girls revisited: Building strengths* (pp. 177–201). New York: New York University Press.

Courage, M. L., Howe, M. L., & Squires, S. E. (2004). Individual differences in 3.5-month

olds' visual attention: What do they predict at 1 year? *Infant Behavior and Development, 27*(1), 19–30.

Cowan, P. A., & Cowan, C. P. (2005). Five-domain models: Putting it all together. In P. A. Cowan, C. P. Cowan, J. C. Ablow, V. K. Johnson, & J. R. Measelle (Eds.), *The family context of parenting in children's adaptation to elementary school* [Monograph] (pp. 315–333). Mahwah, NJ: Erlbaum.

Cox, W. M., & Alm, R. (2005, February 25). Scientists are made, not born. *The New York Times.* Retrieved from http://www.nytimes.com

Cratty, B. (1986). *Perceptual and motor development in infants and children* (3rd ed.). Englewood Cliffs, NJ: Prentice Hall.

Crombie, G., & Desjardins, M. J. (1993, March). *Predictors of gender: The relative importance of children's play, games, and personality characteristics.* Paper presented at the meeting of the Society for Research in Child Development, New Orleans.

Crook, C. K., & Lipsitt, L. P. (1976). Neonatal nutritive sucking: Effects of taste stimulation upon sucking rhythm and heart rate. *Child Development, 47,* 518–522.

Crow, S., Eisenberg, M. E., Story, M., & Neumark-Sztainer, D. (2008). Are body dissatisfaction, eating disturbance, and body mass index predictors of suicidal behavior in adolescents? A longitudinal study. *Journal of Consulting and Clinical Psychology, 76*(5), 887–892.

Crowther, C., et al. (2006). Neonatal respiratory distress syndrome after repeat exposure to antenatal corticosteroids: A randomised control trial. *Lancet, 367*(9526), 1913–1919.

Crusio, W. E. (2006). Inheritance of behavioral and neuroanatomical phenotypical variance. *Behavior Genetics, 36*(5), 723-731.

Cruz, N. V., & Bahna, S. L. (2006). Do foods or additives cause behavior disorders? *Psychiatric Annals, 36*(10), 724–732.

Cuellar, J., & Curry, T. R. (2007). The prevalence and comorbidity between delinquency, drug abuse, suicide attempts, physical and sexual abuse, and self-mutilation among delinquent Hispanic females. *Hispanic Journal of Behavioral Sciences, 29*(1), 68–82.

Cunningham, R. L., & McGinnis, M. Y. (2007). Factors influencing aggression toward females by male rats exposed to anabolic androgenic steroids during puberty. *Hormones and Behavior, 51*(1), 135–141.

Currie, J., DellaVigna, S., Moretti, E., & Pathania, V. (2009). The effect of fast food restaurants on obesity. National Bureau of Economic Research (NBER). NBER Working Paper No. W14721.

Cystic Fibrosis Foundation. (2007). Available at www.cff.org. Accessed February 23, 2007.

Daman-Wasserman, M., Brennan, B., Radcliffe, F., Prigot, J., & Fagen, J. (2006). Auditory-visual context and memory retrieval in 3-month-old infants. *Infancy, 10*(3) 201–220.

Damon, W. (1991). Adolescent self-concept. In R. M. Lerner, A. C. Petersen, & J. Brooks-Gunn (Eds.), *Encyclopedia of adolescence.* New York: Garland.

Dandy, J., & Nettelbeck, T. (2002). The relationship between IQ, homework, aspirations and academic achievement for Chinese, Vietnamese and Anglo-Celtic Australian school children. *Educational Psychology, 22*(3), 267–276.

Dane, S., & Erzurumluoglu, A. (2003). Sex and handedness differences in eye–hand visual reaction times in handball players. *International Journal of Neuroscience, 113*(7), 923–929.

Dang-Vu, T. T., Desseilles, M., Peigneux, P., & Maquet, P. (2006). A role for sleep in brain plasticity. *Pediatric Rehabilitation, 19*(2) 98–118.

Daniels, S. R. (2006). The consequences of childhood overweight and obesity. *The Future of Children, 16*(1), 47–67.

Darcy, M. U. A., & Tracey, T. J. G. (2007). Circumplex structure of Holland's RIASEC interests across gender and time. *Journal of Counseling Psychology, 54*(1), 17–31.

Daubenmier, J. J., et al. (2007). The contribution of changes in diet, exercise, and stress management to changes in coronary risk in women and men in the Multisite Cardiac Lifestyle Intervention Program. *Annals of Behavioral Medicine, 33*(1), 57–68.

Davis, A. (1991). Piaget, teachers and education: Into the 1990s. In P. Light, S. Sheldon, & M. Woodhead (Eds.), *Learning to think.* New York: Routledge.

Davis, L., Edwards, H., Mohay, H., & Wollin, J. (2003). The impact of very premature birth on the psychological health of mothers. *Early Human Development, 73*(1–2), 61–70.

Davis, S. R., Davison, S. L., Donath, S., & Bell, R. J. (2005). Circulating androgen levels and self-reported sexual function in women. *Journal of the American Medical Association, 294*(1), 91–96.

Dawson, T. L. (2002). New tools, new insights: Kohlberg's moral judgement stages revisited. *International Journal of Behavioral Development, 26*(2), 154–166.

de Haan, M., & Groen, M. (2006). Neural bases of infants' processing of social information in faces. In P. J. Marshall & N. A. Fox (Eds.), *The development of social engagement: Neurobiological perspectives* (pp. 46–80). New York: Oxford University Press.

de Villiers, J. G., & de Villiers, P. A. (1999). Language development. In M. H. Bornstein & M. E. Lamb (Eds.), *Developmental psychology: An advanced textbook* (4th ed., pp. 313–373). Mahwah, NJ: Erlbaum.

de Vries, J. I. P., & Hopkins, B. (2005). Fetal movements and postures: What do they mean for postnatal development? In B. Hopkins & S. P. Johnson (Eds.), *Prenatal development of postnatal functions: Advances in infancy research* (pp. 177–219). Westport, CT: Praeger/Greenwood.

Deary, I. J., Whiteman, M. C., Starr, J. M., Whalley, L. J., & Fox, H. C. (2004). The impact of childhood intelligence on later life: Following up the Scottish mental surveys of 1932 and 1947. *Journal of Personality and Social Psychology, 86*(1), 130–147.

DeCasper, A. J., & Fifer, W. P. (1980). Of human bonding: Newborns prefer their mothers' voices. *Science, 208,* 1174–1176.

DeCasper, A. J., & Prescott, P. A. (1984). Human newborns' perception of male voices: Preference, discrimination, and reinforcing value. *Developmental Psychobiology, 17,* 481–491.

DeCasper, A. J., & Spence, M. J. (1991). Auditorily mediated behavior during the perinatal period: A cognitive view. In M. J. Weiss & P. R. Zelazo (Eds.), *Infant attention* (pp. 142–176). Norwood, NJ: Ablex.

Deep, A. L., et al. (1999). Sexual abuse in eating disorder subtypes and control women: The role of comorbid substance dependence in bulimia nervosa. *International Journal of Eating Disorders, 25*(1), 1–10.

Dehaene-Lambertz, G., Pena, M., Christophe, A., & Landrieu, P. (2004). Phoneme perception in a neonate with a left sylvian infarct. *Brain and Language, 88*(1), 26–38.

Del Giudice, M., Manera, V., & Keysers, C. (2009). Programmed to learn? The ontogeny of mirror neurons. *Developmental Science, 12*(2), 50-363.

Delgado, A. R., & Prieto, G. (2004). Cognitive mediators and sex-related differences in mathematics. *Intelligence, 32*(1), 25–32.

Dennis, W. (1960). Causes of retardation among institutional children: Iran. *Journal of Genetic Psychology, 96*, 47–59.

Dennis, W., & Dennis, M. G. (1940). The effect of cradling practices upon the onset of walking in Hopi children. *Journal of Genetic Psychology, 56*, 77–86.

Dennis, W., & Saygh, Y. (1965). The effect of supplementary experiences upon the behavioral development of infants in institutions. *Child Development, 36*, 81ff.

Derman, O., Kanbur, N. O., & Kutluk, T. (2003). Tamoxifen treatment for pubertal gynecomastia. *International Journal of Adolescent Medicine and Health, 15*(4), 359–363.

Dervic, K., Grunebaum, M. F., Burke, A. K., Mann, J. J., & Oquendo, M. A. (2007). Cluster C personality disorders in major depressive episodes: The relationship between hostility and suicidal behavior. *Archives of Suicide Research, 11*(1), 83–90.

Dezoete, J. A., MacArthur, B. A., & Tuck, B. (2003). Prediction of Bayley and Stanford–Binet scores with a group of very low birthweight children. *Child: Care, Health and Development, 29*(5), 367–372.

Dieterich, S. E., Hebert, H. M., Landry, S. H., Swank, P. R., & Smith, K. E. (2004). Maternal and child characteristics that influence the growth of daily living skills from infancy to school age in preterm and term children. *Early Education and Development, 15*(3), 283–303.

Digout Erhardt, A. R. (2005). Friendship processes in childhood and adolescence: Homophily, selection, and socialization of aggressive behaviours and depressive symptoms. *Dissertation Abstracts International, 66* (2-B), pp. 12–18.

DiLalla, D. L., Gottesman, I. I., Carey, G., & Bouchard, T. J., Jr. (1999). Heritability of MMPI Harris–Lingoes and Subtle–Obvious subscales in twins reared apart. *Assessment, 6*(4), 353–366.

Dindia, K., & Allen, M. (1992). Sex differences in self-disclosure: A meta-analysis. *Psychological Bulletin, 112*, 106–124.

Dishion, T. J., & Stormshak, E. A. (2007a). Child and adolescent intervention groups. In T. J. Dishion & E. A. Stormshak (Eds.), *Intervening in children's lives: An ecological, family-centered approach to mental health care* (pp. 201–215). Washington, DC: American Psychological Association.

Dishion, T. J., & Stormshak, E. A. (2007b). Family and peer social interaction. In T. J. Dishion & E. A. Stormshak. (Eds.), *Intervening in children's lives: An ecological, family-centered approach to mental health care* (pp. 31–48). Washington, DC: American Psychological Association.

Dockett, S., Perry, B., & Whitton, D. (2006). Picture storybooks and starting school. *Early Child Development and Care, 76*(8), 835–848.

Dollfus, S., et al. (2005). Atypical hemispheric specialization for language in right-handed schizophrenia patients. *Biological Psychiatry, 57*(9), 1020–1028.

Dombrowski, M. A. S., et al. (2000). Kangaroo skin-to-skin care for premature twins and their adolescent parents. *American Journal of Maternal/Child Nursing, 25*(2), 92–94.

Donohue, B. C., Karmely, J., & Strada, M. J. (2006). Alcohol and drug abuse. In M. Hersen (Ed.), *Clinician's handbook of child behavioral assessment* (pp. 337–375). San Diego, CA: Elsevier Academic.

Donohue, K. F., Curtin, J. J., Patrick, C. J., & Lang, A. R. (2007). Intoxication level and emotional response. *Emotion, 7*(1), 103–112.

Donovan, D. M., & Wells, E. A. (2007). "Tweaking 12-step": The potential role of 12-step self-help group involvement in methamphetamine recovery. *Addiction, 102*(Suppl. 1), 121–129.

Dorius, C. J., Bahr, S. J., Hoffmann, J. P., & Harmon, E. L. (2004). Parenting practices as moderators of the relationship between peers and adolescent marijuana use. *Journal of Marriage and Family, 66*(1), 163–178.

Dorling, J., et al. (2006). Data collection from very low birthweight infants in a geographical region: Methods, costs, and trends in mortality, admission rates, and resource utilization over a five-year period. *Early Human Development, 82*(2), 117–124.

Drasgow, E., Halle, J. W., & Phillips, B. (2001). Effects of different social partners on the discriminated requesting of a young child with autism and severe language delays. *Research in Developmental Disabilities, 22*(2), 125–139.

Drewett, R., Blair, P., Emmett, P., Emond, A., & The ALSPAC Study Team. (2004). Failure to thrive in the term and preterm infants of mothers depressed in the postnatal period: A population-based birth cohort study. *Journal of Child Psychology and Psychiatry and Allied Disciplines, 45*(2), 359–366.

Duarté-Vélez, Y. M., & Bernal, G. (2007). Suicide behavior among Latino and Latina adolescents: Conceptual and methodological issues. *Death Studies, 31*(5) 425–455.

Duggan, A., et al. (2004). Evaluating a statewide home visiting program to prevent child abuse in at-risk families of newborns: Fathers' participation and outcomes. *Child Maltreatment: Journal of the American Professional Society on the Abuse of Children, 9*(1), 3–17.

Dunn, J., & Hughes, C. (2001). "I got some swords and you're dead!": Violent fantasy, antisocial behavior, friendship, and moral sensibility in young children. *Child Development, 72*(2), 491–505.

Dunn, J., Davies, L. C., O'Connor, T. G., & Sturgess, W. (2001). Family lives and friendships: The perspectives of children in step-, single-parent, and nonstep families. *Journal of Family Psychology, 15*(2), 272–287.

Dunn, M. G., & Mezzich, A. C. (2007). Development in childhood and adolescence: Implications for prevention research and practice. In P. Tolan, J. Szapocznik, & S. Sambrano (Eds.), *Preventing youth substance abuse: Science-based programs for children and adolescents* (pp. 21–40). Washington, DC: American Psychological Association.

Durkin, S. J., Paxton, S. J., & Sorbello, M. (2007). An integrative model of the impact of exposure to idealized female images on adolescent girls' body satisfaction. *Journal of Applied Social Psychology, 37*(5), 1092–1117.

Dyer, S., & Moneta, G. B. (2006). Frequency of parallel, associative, and cooperative play in British children of different socioeconomic status. *Social Behavior and Personality, 34*(5), 587–592.

Dykman, R. A., Casey, P. H., Ackerman, P. T., & McPherson, W. B. (2001). Behavioral and cognitive status in school-aged children with a history of failure to thrive during early childhood. *Clinical Pediatrics, 40*(2), 63–70.

Eccles, J. S. (2007). Where are all the women? Gender differences in participation in physical science and engineering. In S. J. Ceci & W. M. Williams (Eds.), *Why aren't more women in science: Top researchers debate the evidence* (pp. 199–210). Washington, DC: American Psychological Association.

Eccles, J. S., et al. (2000). Gender-role socialization in the family: A longitudinal approach. In T. Eckes & H. M. Trautner (Eds.), *The developmental social psychology of gender* (pp. 333–360). Mahwah, NJ: Erlbaum.

Eckerman, C. O., Hsu, H.-C., Molitor, A., Leung, E. H. L., & Goldstein, R. F. (1999). Infant arousal in an en-face exchange with a new partner: Effects of prematurity and perinatal biological risk. *Developmental Psychology, 35*(1), 282–293.

Ecuyer-Dab, I., & Robert, M. (2004). Spatial ability and home-range size: Examining the relationship in Western men and women (*Homo sapiens*). *Journal of Comparative Psychology, 118*(2), 217–231.

Eder, R. A. (1989). The emergent personologist: The structure and content of 3 1/2-, 5 1/2-, and 7 1/2-year-olds' concepts of themselves and other persons. *Child Development, 60,* 1218–1228.

Eder, R. A. (1990). Uncovering young children's psychological selves: Individual and developmental differences. *Child Development, 61,* 849–863.

Edwards, V. J., Holden, G. W., Felitti, V. J., & Anda, R. F. (2003). Relationship between multiple forms of childhood maltreatment and adult mental health in community respondents: Results from the Adverse Childhood Experiences Study. *American Journal of Psychiatry, 160*(8), 1453–1460.

Egeland, B., & Sroufe, L. A. (1981). Attachment and early maltreatment. *Child Development, 52,* 44–52.

Egerton, A., Allison, C., Brett, R. R., & Pratt, J. A. (2006). Cannabinoids and prefrontal cortical function: Insights from preclinical studies. *Neuroscience & Biobehavioral Reviews, 30*(5), 680–695.

Eimas, P. D., Siqueland, E. R., Juscyk, P., & Vigorito, J. (1971). Speech perception in infants. *Science, 171,* 303–306.

Eisenberg, M. E., Neumark-Sztainer, D., & Paxton, S. J. (2006). Five-year change in body satisfaction among adolescents. *Journal of Psychosomatic Research, 61*(4), 521–527.

Eisner, E. W. (1990). The role of art and play in children's cognitive development. In E. Klugman & S. Smilansky (Eds.), *Children's play and learning: Perspectives and policy implications.* New York: Teachers College Press.

Elias, M. J., Gara, M. A., Schuyler, T. F., Brandon-Muller, L. R., & Sayette, M. A. (1991). The promotion of social competence: Longitudinal study of a preventative school-based program. *American Journal of Orthopsychiatry, 61,* 409–417.

Elkind, D. (1967). Egocentrism in adolescence. *Child Development, 38,* 1025–1034.

Elkind, D. (1985). Egocentrism redux. *Developmental Review, 5,* 218–226.

Elkind, D. (2007). *The power of play: How spontaneous imaginative activities lead to happier, healthier children.* Cambridge, MA: Da Capo.

Ellis, A., & Dryden, W. (1996). *The practice of rational emotive behavior therapy.* New York: Springer.

Else-Quest, N. M., Hyde, J. S., Goldsmith, H. H., & Van Hulle, C. A. (2006). Gender differences in temperament: A meta-analysis. *Psychological Bulletin, 132*(1), 33–72.

El-Sheikh, M. (2007). Children's skin conductance level and reactivity: Are these measures stable over time and across tasks? *Developmental Psychobiology, 49*(2), 180–186.

Eltzschig, H., Lieberman, E., & Camann, W. (2003). Regional anesthesia and analgesia for labor and delivery. *New England Journal of Medicine, 348*(4), 319–332.

Emler, N., Tarry, H., & St. James, A. (2007). Postconventional moral reasoning and reputation. *Journal of Research in Personality, 41*(1), 76–89.

Erikson, E. H. (1963). *Childhood and society.* New York: Norton.

Erikson, E. H. (1968). *Identity: Youth and crisis.* New York: Norton.

Erikson, E. H. (1975). *Life history and the historical moment.* New York: Norton.

Eron, L. D. (1993). No doubt about it—media violence affects behavior. *Media & Values, 63,* 14.

Eron, L. D., Huesmann, L. R., & Zelli, A. (1991). The role of parental variables in the learning of aggression. In D. J. Pepler & K. H. Rubin (Eds.), *The development and treatment of childhood aggression.* Hillsdale, NJ: Erlbaum.

Fagot, B. I. (1990). A longitudinal study of gender segregation: Infancy to preschool. In F. F. Strayer (Ed.), *Social interaction and behavioral development during early childhood.* Montreal: La Maison D'Ethologie de Montreal.

Fagot, B. I., & Hagan, R. (1991). Observations of parent reactions to sex-stereotyped behaviors: Age and sex effects. *Child Development, 62,* 617–628.

Fagot, B. I., & Leinbach, M. D. (1993). Gender-role development in young children: From discrimination to labeling. *Developmental Review, 13,* 205–224.

Fagot, B. I., Rodgers, C. S., & Leinbach, M. D. (2000). Theories of gender socialization. In T. Eckes & H. M. Trautner (Eds.), *The developmental social psychology of gender* (pp. 65–89). Mahwah, NJ: Erlbaum.

Fantz, R. L. (1961). The origin of form perception. *Scientific American, 204,* 66–72.

Fantz, R. L., Fagan, J. F., III, & Miranda, S. B. (1975). Early visual selectivity. In L. B. Cohen & P. Salapatek (Eds.), *Infant perception: Vol. 1. From sensation to cognition.* New York: Academic.

Faraone, S. V., et al. (2000). Family study of girls with attention deficit hyperactivity disorder.

American Journal of Psychiatry, 157(7), 1077–1083.

Farmer, A., Elkin, A., & McGuffin, P. (2007). The genetics of bipolar affective disorder. *Current Opinion in Psychiatry, 20*(1), 8–12.

Feijó, L., et al. (2006). Mothers' depressed mood and anxiety levels are reduced after massaging their preterm infants. *Infant Behavior & Development, 29*(3), 476–480.

Feinberg, M. E., Reiss, D., Neiderhiser, J. M., & Hetherington, E. M. (2005). Differential association of family subsystem negativity on siblings' maladjustment: Using behavior genetic methods to test process theory. *Journal of Family Psychology, 19*(4), 601–610.

Feinberg, M. E., Neiderhiser, J. M., Howe, G., & Hetherington, E. M. (2001). Adolescent, parent, and observer perceptions of parenting: Genetic and environmental influences on shared and distinct perceptions. *Child Development, 72*(4), 1266–1284.

Feiring, C. (1993, March). *Developing concepts of romance from 15 to 18 years.* Paper presented at the meeting of the Society for Research in Child Development, New Orleans.

Feiring, C., & Lewis, M. (1991). The transition from middle to early adolescence: Sex differences in the social network and perceived self-competence. *Sex Roles, 24,* 489–509.

Feldman, R., & Masalha, S. (2007). The role of culture in moderating the links between early ecological risk and young children's adaptation. *Development and Psychopathology, 19*(1), 1–21.

Fergusson, A. (2007). What successful teachers do in inclusive classrooms: Research-based teaching strategies that help special learners succeed. *European Journal of Special Needs Education, 22*(1), 108–110.

Fernandez, T., & State, M. (2004). Genetics and genomics of neurobehavioral disorders. *Journal of the American Academy of Child Psychiatry, 43*(3), 370–371.

Fernandez-Twinn, D. S., & Ozanne, S. E. (2006). Mechanisms by which poor early growth programs type-2 diabetes, obesity and the metabolic syndrome. *Physiology & Behavior, 88*(3), 234–243.

Féron, J., Gentaz, E., & Streri, A. (2006). Evidence of amodal representation of small numbers across visuo-tactile modalities in 5-month-old infants. *Cognitive Development, 21*(2), 81–92.

Field, A. P. (2006). The behavioral inhibition system and the verbal information pathway to children's fears. *Journal of Abnormal Psychology, 115*(4), 742–752.

Field, T. (1999). Sucking and massage therapy reduce stress during infancy. In M. Lewis & D. Ramsay (Eds.), *Soothing and stress* (pp. 157–169). Hillsdale, NJ: Erlbaum.

Field, T., Hernandez-Reif, M., Feijo, L., & Freedman, J. (2006). Prenatal, perinatal and neonatal stimulation: A survey of neonatal nurseries. *Infant Behavior & Development, 29*(1), 24–31.

Finegan, J. K., Niccols, G. A., & Sitarenios, G. (1992). Relations between prenatal testosterone levels and cognitive abilities at 4 years. *Developmental Psychology, 28,* 1075–1089.

Fisch, S. M. (2004). *Children's learning from educational television: Sesame Street and beyond.* Mahwah, NJ: Erlbaum.

Fitzgerald, H. E., et al. (1991). The organization of lateralized behavior during infancy. In H. E. Fitzgerald, B. M. Lester, & M. W. Yogman (Eds.), *Theory and research in behavioral pediatrics.* New York: Plenum.

Fivush, R. (2002). Scripts, schemas, and memory of trauma. In N. L. Stein et al. (Eds.), *Representation, memory, and development: Essays in honor of Jean Mandler* (pp. 53–74). Mahwah, NJ: Erlbaum.

Fivush, R., & Hammond, N. R. (1990). Autobiographical memory across the preschool years: Toward reconceptualizing childhood amnesia. In R. Fivush & J. A. Hudson (Eds.), *Knowing and remembering in young children.* Cambridge: Cambridge University Press.

Fivush, R., Kuebli, J., & Clubb, P. A. (1992). The structure of events and event representations: A developmental analysis. *Child Development, 63,* 188–201.

Fivush, R., Sales, J, M., Goldberg, A., Bahrick, L., & Parker, J. (2004). Weathering the storm: Children's long-term recall of Hurricane Andrew. *Memory, 12*(1), 104–118.

Flavell, J. H. (1993). Young children's understanding of thinking and consciousness. *Current Directions in Psychological Science, 2,* 40–43.

Flavell, J. H., Miller, P. H., & Miller, S. A. (2002). *Cognitive development* (4th ed.). Upper Saddle River, NJ: Prentice Hall.

Florsheim, P. (Ed.). (2003). *Adolescent romantic relations and sexual behavior: Theory, research, and practical implications.* Mahwah, NJ: Erlbaum.

Flouri, E., & Buchanan, A. (2003). The role of father involvement and mother involvement in adolescents' psychological well-being. *British Journal of Social Work, 33*(3), 399–406.

Focus on Child and Family Statistics. (2007). Birth rates for females ages 15–17 by race and Hispanic origin, 1980–2005. *America's children: Key national indicators of well-being, 2007.* Washington, DC: National Center for Health Statistics. Retrieved from http://www.childstats.gov/pdf/ac2007/ac_07.pdf

Foley, G. M. (2006). Self and social–emotional development in infancy: A descriptive synthesis. In G. M. Foley & J. D. Hochman (Eds.), *Mental health in early intervention: Achieving unity in principles and practice* (pp. 139–173). Baltimore: Brookes.

Fontaine, A-M. (2005). Écologie développementale des premières interactions entre enfants: Effet des matériels de jeu. *Enfance, 57*(2), 137–154.

Forbush, K., Heatherton, T. F., & Keel, P. K. (2007). Relationships between perfectionism and specific disordered eating behaviors. *International Journal of Eating Disorders, 40*(1), 37–41.

Forman-Hoffman, V. L., Ruffin, T., & Schultz, S. K. (2006). Basal metabolic rate in anorexia nervosa patients: Using appropriate predictive equations during the refeeding process. *Annals of Clinical Psychiatry, 18*(2), 123–127.

Forum on Child and Family Statistics. National Center for Health Statistics. (2005). *America's children: Key national indicators of well-being 2005.* Retrieved from http://www.childstats.gov/

Foster-Clark, F. S., & Blyth, D. A. (1991). Peer relations and influences. In R. M. Lerner, A. C. Petersen, & J. Brooks-Gunn (Eds.),

Encyclopedia of adolescence. New York: Garland.

Fouad, N. A., & Arredondo, P. (2007). Implications for psychologists as researchers. In N. A. Fouad & P. Arredondo (Eds.), *Becoming culturally oriented: Practical advice for psychologists and educators* (pp. 81–93). Washington, DC: American Psychological Association.

Franklin, A., Pilling, M., & Davies, I. (2005). The nature of infant color categorization: Evidence from eye movements on a target detection task. *Journal of Experimental Child Psychology, 91*(3), 227–248.

Freeman, M. S., Spence, M. J., & Oliphant, C. M. (1993, June). *Newborns prefer their mothers' low-pass filtered voices over other female filtered voices.* Paper presented at the meeting of the American Psychological Society, Chicago.

Frerichs, L., Andsager, J. L., Campo, S., Aquilino, M., & Dyer, C. S. (2006). Framing breastfeeding and formula-feeding messages in popular U.S. magazines. *Women & Health, 44*(1), 95–118.

Freud, A. (1969). Adolescence as a developmental disturbance. In G. Caplan, & S. Lebovici (Eds.), *Adolescence: Psychosocial perspectives.* (pp. 5-10). New York: Basic Books.

Freud, S. (1964 [1933]). *New introductory lectures on psycho-analysis.* Standard Edition 22: 3-182 London: Hogarth Press.

Fried, P. A., & Smith, A. M. (2001). A literature review of the consequences of prenatal marijuana exposure: An emerging theme of a deficiency in aspects of executive function. *Neurotoxicology and Teratology, 23*(1), 1–11.

Frith, U. (2001). What framework should we use for understanding developmental disorders? *Developmental Neuropsychology, 20*(2), 555–563.

Frodi, A. M. (1985). When empathy fails: Infant crying and child abuse. In B. M. Lester & C. F. Z. Boukydis (Eds.), *Infant crying.* New York: Plenum.

Fromkin, V., et al. (2004). *The development of language in Genie: A case of language acquisition beyond the "critical period."* New York: Psychology Press.

Fry, D. P. (2005). Rough-and-tumble social play in humans. In A. D. Pellegrini & P. K. Smith (Eds.), *The nature of play: Great apes and humans* (pp. 54–85). New York: Guilford.

Funatogawa, K., Funatogawa, T., & Yano, E. (2008). Do overweight children necessarily make overweight adults? Repeated cross sectional annual nationwide survey of Japanese girls and women over nearly six decades. *British Medical Journal, 337,* a802. doi:10.1136/bmj.a802

Furman, W., & Buhrmester, D. (1992). Age and sex differences in perceptions of networks of personal relationships. *Child Development, 63,* 103–115.

Furman, W., Rahe, D., & Hartup, W. W. (1979). Social rehabilitation of low-interactive preschool children by peer intervention. *Child Development, 50,* 915–922.

Ganesh, M. P., & Magdalin, S. (2007). Perceived problems and academic stress in children of disrupted and non-disrupted families. *Journal of the Indian Academy of Applied Psychology, 33*(1), 53–59.

Garber, H. L. (1988). *The Milwaukee Project: Preventing mental retardation in children at risk.* Washington, DC: American Association on Mental Retardation.

Gardner, H. (1983). *Frames of mind: The theory of multiple intelligences.* New York: Basic Books.

Gardner, H. (2006). *The development and education of the mind: The selected works of Howard Gardner.* Philadelphia: Routledge/Taylor & Francis.

Gartstein, M. A., Slobodskaya, H. R., & Kinsht, I. A. (2003). Cross-cultural differences in temperament in the first year of life: United States of America (U.S.) and Russia. *International Journal of Behavioral Development, 27*(4), 316–328.

Garvey, C. (1990). *Developing child.* Cambridge, MA: Harvard University Press.

Gathercole, S. E., Pickering, S. J., Ambridge, B., & Wearing, H. (2004a). The structure of working memory from 4 to 15 years of age. *Developmental Psychology, 40*(2), 177–190.

Gathercole, S. E., Pickering, S. J., Knight, C., & Stegmann, Z. (2004b). Working memory skills and educational attainment: Evidence from national curriculum assessments at 7 and 14 years of age. *Applied Cognitive Psychology, 18*(1), 1–16.

Gau, S. S. F., et al. (2007). Psychiatric and psychosocial predictors of substance use disorders among adolescents. Longitudinal study. *British Journal of Psychiatry, 190*(1), 42–48.

Gavin, N. I., et al. (2005). Perinatal depression: A systematic review of prevalence and incidence. *Obstetrics & Gynecology, 106,* 1071–1083.

Ge, X., et al. (2003). It's about timing and change: Pubertal transition effects on symptoms of major depression among African American youths. *Developmental Psychology, 39*(3), 430–439.

Geary, D. C. (1998). *Male, female: The evolution of human sex differences.* Washington, DC: American Psychological Association.

Geary, D. C. (2006). Sex differences in social behavior and cognition: Utility of sexual selection for hypothesis generation. *Hormones and Behavior, 49*(3), 273–275.

Geller, P. A., Kerns, D., & Klier, C. M. (2004). Anxiety following miscarriage and the subsequent pregnancy: A review of the literature and future directions. *Journal of Psychosomatic Research, 56*(1), 35–45.

Georgiades, S., et al. (2007). Structure of the autism symptom phenotype: A proposed multidimensional model. *Journal of the American Academy of Child & Adolescent Psychiatry, 46*(2), 188–196.

Geschwind, D. H. (2000). Interview reported by D. E. Rosenbaum, On left-handedness, its causes and costs, *The New York Times* (May 16, 2000), pp. F1, F6.

Gesell, A. (1928). *Infancy and human growth.* New York: Macmillan.

Gesell, A. (1929). Maturation and infant behavior patterns. *Psychological Review, 36,* 307–319.

Ghetti, S., & Alexander, K. W. (2004). "If it happened, I would remember it": Strategic use of event memorability in the rejection of false autobiographical events. *Child Development, 75*(2), 542–561.

Gibson, E. J. (1969). *Principles of perceptual learning and development.* New York: Appleton-Century-Crofts.

Gibson, E. J. (1991). *An odyssey in learning and perception.* Cambridge, MA: MIT Press.

Gibson, E. J., & Walk, R. D. (1960). The visual cliff. *Scientific American, 202,* 64–71.

Gidding, S. S., et al. (2006). Dietary recommendations for children and adolescents: A guide for practitioners. *Pediatrics, 117*(2), 544–559. doi:10.1542/peds.2005-2374

Gilligan, C. (1977). In a different voice: Women's conceptions of self and morality. *Harvard Educational Review, 47,* 481–517.

Gilligan, C. (1982). *In a different voice.* Cambridge, MA: Harvard University Press.

Gilligan, C., & Attanucci, J. (1988). Two moral orientations: Gender differences and similarities. *Merrill–Palmer Quarterly, 34,* 223–237.

Gleason, T. R. (2002). Social provisions of real and imaginary relationships in early childhood. *Developmental Psychology, 38*(6), 979–992.

Gleason, T. R. (2004). Imaginary companions and peer acceptance. *International Journal of Behavioral Development, 28*(3), 204–209.

Gleason, T. R., & Hohmann, L. M. (2006). Concepts of real and imaginary friendships in early childhood. *Social Development, 15*(1), 128–144.

Gleason, T. R., Gower, A. L., Hohmann, L. M., & Gleason, T. C. (2005). Temperament and friendship in preschool-aged children. *International Journal of Behavioral Development, 29*(4), 336–344.

Gleason, T. R., Sebanc, A. M., & Hartup, W. W. (2003). Imaginary companions of preschool children. In M. E. Hertzig & E. A. Farber (Eds.), *Annual progress in child psychiatry and child development: 2000–2001* (pp. 101–121). New York: Brunner-Routledge.

Gobet, F., & Simon, H. A. (2000). Five seconds or sixty? Presentation time in expert memory. *Cognitive Science, 24*(4), 651–682.

Goel, P., Radotra, A., Singh, I., Aggarwal, A., & Dua, D. (2004). Effects of passive smoking on outcome in pregnancy. *Journal of Postgraduate Medicine, 50*(1), 12–16.

Golan, H., & Huleihel, M. (2006). The effect of prenatal hypoxia on brain development: Short- and long-term consequences demonstrated in rodent models. *Developmental Science, 9*(4), 338–349.

Goldberg, J., Holtz, D., Hyslop, T., & Tolosa, J. E. (2002). Has the use of routine episiotomy decreased? Examination of episiotomy rates from 1983 to 2000. *Obstetrics and Gynecology, 99*(3), 395–400.

Goldschmidt, L., Day, N. L., & Richardson, G. A. (2000). Effects of prenatal marijuana exposure on child behavior problems at age 10. *Neurotoxicology and Teratology, 22*(3), 325–336.

Goldsmith, H. H., et al. (2003). Part III: Genetics and development. In R. J. Davidson et al. (Eds.), *Handbook of affective sciences.* London: Oxford University Press.

Goldstein, E. B. (2005). *Cognitive psychology: Connecting mind, research, and everyday experience.* Belmont, CA: Wadsworth.

Goldstein, S., & Brooks, R. B. (2005). *Handbook of resilience in children.* New York: Kluwer Academic/Plenum.

Gonzalez, V. (2005). Cultural, linguistic, and socioeconomic factors influencing monolingual and bilingual children's cognitive development. In V. Gonzalez & J. Tinajero (Eds.), *Review of research and practice* (Vol. 3, pp. 67–104). Mahwah, NJ: Erlbaum.

González, Y. S., Moreno, D. S., & Schneider, B. H. (2004). Friendship expectations of early adolescents in Cuba and Canada. *Journal of Cross-Cultural Psychology, 35*(4), 436–445.

Goodman, G. S., Rudy, L., Bottoms, B. L., & Aman, C. (1990). Children's concerns and memory: Issues of ecological validity in the study of children's eyewitness testimony. In R. Fivush & J. A. Hudson (Eds.), *Knowing and remembering in young children.* Cambridge: Cambridge University Press.

Goossens, L., Braet, C., & Decaluwé, V. (2007). Loss of control over eating in obese youngsters. *Behaviour Research and Therapy, 45*(1), 1–9.

Gopnik, A., & Meltzoff, A. N. (1992). Categorization and naming: Basic-level sorting in 18-month-olds and its relation to language. *Child Development, 63,* 1091–1103.

Gopnik, A., & Slaughter, V. (1991). Young children's understanding of changes in their mental states. *Child Development, 62,* 98–110.

Gormally, S., et al. (2001). Contact and nutrient caregiving effects on newborn infant pain responses. *Developmental Medicine and Child Neurology, 43*(1), 28–38.

Gort, M. (2006). Strategic code-switching, inter-literacy, and other phenomena of emergent bilingual writing: Lessons from first grade dual language classrooms. *Journal of Early Childhood Literacy, 6*(3), 323–354.

Gottfried, G. M., Hickling, A. K., Totten, L. R., Mkroyan, A., & Reisz, A. (2003). To be or not to be a galaprock: Preschoolers' intuitions about the importance of knowledge and action for pretending. *British Journal of Developmental Psychology, 21*(3), 397–414.

Gottlieb, B. H., Still, E., & Newby-Clark, I. R. (2007). Types and precipitants of growth and decline in emerging adulthood. *Journal of Adolescent Research, 22*(2), 132–155.

Gottlieb, G. (2007). Developmental neurobehavioral genetics: Development as explanation. In B. C. Jones & P. Mormède (Eds.), *Neurobehavioral genetics: Methods and applications* (2nd ed., pp. 17–27). Boca Raton, FL: CRC.

Graber, J. A., Seeley, J. R., Brooks-Gunn, J., & Lewinsohn, P. M. (2004). Is pubertal timing associated with psychopathology in young adulthood? *Journal of the American Academy of Child and Adolescent Psychiatry, 43*(6), 718–726.

Greco, C., Rovee-Collier, C., Hayne, H., Griesler, P., & Early, L. (1986). Ontogeny of early event memory: II. Encoding and retrieval by 2- and 3-month-olds. *Infant Behavior and Development, 9,* 461–472.

Green, R. (1978). Sexual identity of 37 children raised by homosexual or transsexual parents. *American Journal of Psychiatry, 135,* 692–697.

Greenberg, J. (2002). Who stole the money, and when? Individual and situational determinants of employee theft. *Organizational Behavior and Human Decision Processes, 89*(1), 985–1003.

Greene, R. W., & Ablon, J. S. (2001). What does the MTA study tell us about effective psychosocial treatment for ADHD? *Journal of Clinical Child Psychology, 30*(1), 114–121.

Greene, S. M., Anderson, E. R., Doyle, E. A., Riedelbach, H., & Bear, G. G. (2006). Divorce. In K. M. Minke (Ed.), *Children's needs III: Development, prevention, and intervention* (pp. 745–757). Bethesda, MD: National Association of School Psychologists.

Greenough, W. T., Black, J. E., & Wallace, C. S. (2002). Experience and brain development. In M. H. Johnson, Y. Munakata, & R. O. Gilmore (Eds.), *Brain development and cognition: A reader* (2nd ed., pp. 186–216). Malden, MA: Blackwell.

Grigorenko, E. L. (2007). Triangulating developmental dyslexia: Behavior, brain, and genes. In D. Coch, G. Dawson, & K. W. Fischer (Eds.), *Human behavior, learning, and the developing brain: Atypical development* (pp. 117–144). New York: Guilford.

Grilo, C. M., Masheb, R. M., & Wilson, G. T. (2005). Efficacy of cognitive behavioral therapy and fluoxetine for the treatment of binge eating disorder: A randomized double-blind placebo-controlled comparison. *Biological Psychiatry, 57*(3), 301–309.

Grindrod, C. M., & Baum, S. R. (2005). Hemispheric contributions to lexical ambiguity resolution in a discourse context: Evidence from individuals with unilateral left and right hemisphere lesions. *Brain and Cognition, 57*(1), 70–83.

Grolnick, W. S., McMenamy, J. M., & Kurowski, C. O. (2006). Emotional self-regulation in infancy and toddlerhood. In L. Balter & C. S. Tamis-LeMonda (Eds.), *Child psychology: A handbook of contemporary issues* (2nd ed., pp. 3–25). New York: Psychology Press.

Grön, G., Wunderlich, A. P., Spitzer, M., Tomczak, R., & Riepe, M. W. (2000). Brain activation during human navigation: Gender-different neural networks as substrate of performance. *Nature Neuroscience, 3*(4), 404–408.

Grossmann, K., et al. (2002). The uniqueness of the child–father attachment relationship: Fathers' sensitive and challenging play as a pivotal variable in a 16-year longitudinal study. *Social Development, 11*(3), 307–331.

Grusec, J. E. (2002). Parenting socialization and children's acquisition of values. In M. H. Bornstein (Ed.), *Handbook of parenting:* Vol. 5. *Practical issues in parenting* (5th ed., pp. 143–167). Mahwah, NJ: Erlbaum.

Grusec, J. E. (2006). The development of moral behavior and conscience from a socialization perspective. In M. Killen & J. G. Smetana (Eds.), *Handbook of moral development* (pp. 243–265). Mahwah, NJ: Erlbaum.

Guerdjikova, A. I., McElroy, S. L., Kotwal, R., Stanford, K., & Keck, P. E., Jr. (2007). Psychiatric and metabolic characteristics of childhood versus adult-onset obesity in patients seeking weight management. *Eating Behaviors, 8*(2), 266–276.

Guerin, D. W., Gottfried, A. W., & Thomas, C. W. (1997). Difficult temperament and behavior problems: A longitudinal study from 1.5 to 12 years. *International Journal of Behavioral Development, 21*(1), 71–90.

Guerrini, I., Thomson, A. D., & Gurling, H. D. (2007). The importance of alcohol misuse, malnutrition and genetic susceptibility on brain growth and plasticity. *Neuroscience & Biobehavioral Reviews, 31*(2), 212–220.

Güntürkün, O. (2006). Letters on nature and nurture. In P. B. Baltes et al. (Eds.), *Life span development and the brain: The perspective of biocultural co-constructivism* (pp. 379–397). New York: Cambridge University Press.

Gutknecht, L. (2001). Full-genome scans with autistic disorder: A review. *Behavior Genetics, 31*(1), 113–123.

Guttmacher Institute. (2007, June 8). Available at http://www.guttmacher.org/

Guzikowski, W. (2006). Doula—a new model of delivery (continuous, nonprofessional care during the delivery). *Ceska Gynekologie, 71*(2), 103–105.

Haapasalo, J., & Moilanen, J. (2004). Official and self-reported childhood abuse and adult crime of young offenders. *Criminal Justice and Behavior, 31*(2), 127–149.

Haith, M. M. (1966). The response of the human newborn to visual movement. *Journal of Experimental Child Psychology, 3,* 235–243.

Haith, M. M. (1979). Visual cognition in early infancy. In R. B. Kearsly & I. E. Sigel (Eds.), *Infants at risk: Assessment of cognitive functioning.* Hillsdale, NJ: Erlbaum.

Haith, M. M. (1990). Progress in the understanding of sensory and perceptual processes in early infancy. *Merrill–Palmer Quarterly, 36,* 1–26.

Halgin, R. P., & Whitbourne, S. K. (1993). *Abnormal psychology.* Fort Worth, TX: Harcourt.

Hall, G. S. (1904). *Adolescence: Its psychology and its relations to physiology, anthropology, sociology sex, crime, religion and education, Vol. II.* New York: Appleton.

Hall, H. I., et al. (2008). Estimation of HIV incidence in the United States. *Journal of the American Medical Association, 300*(5), 520–529.

Halliday, L. F., & Bishop, D. V. M. (2006). Auditory frequency discrimination in children with dyslexia. *Journal of Research in Reading, 29*(2), 213–228.

Halpern, D. F. (2003). Sex differences in cognitive abilities. *Applied Cognitive Psychology, 17*(3), 375–376.

Halpern, D. F. (2004). A cognitive-process taxonomy for sex differences in cognitive abilities. *Current Directions in Psychological Science, 13*(4), 135–139.

Halpern, D. F. (2006). Girls and academic success: Changing patterns of academic achievement. In J. Worell & C. D. Goodheart (Eds.), *Handbook of girls' and women's psychological health: Gender and well-being across the lifespan* (pp. 272–282). Oxford series in clinical psychology. New York: Oxford University Press.

Halpern, D. F. (2007). Science, sex, and good sense: Why women are underrepresented in some areas of science and math. In S. J. Ceci & W. M. Williams (Eds.), *Why aren't more women in science: Top researchers debate the evidence* (pp. 121–130). Washington, DC: American Psychological Association.

Halpern, D. F., & LaMay, M. L. (2000). The smarter sex: A critical review of sex differences in intelligence. *Educational Psychology Review, 12*(2), 229–246.

Hamilton, B. E., et al. (2007). Births: Preliminary data for 2006. *National Vital Statistics Reports, 56*(7). Retrieved December 25, 2008, from http://www.cdc.gov/nchs/data/nvsr/nvsr56/nvsr56_07.pdf

Hamilton, B. E., Martin, J. A., & Ventura, S. J. (2009, March 18). Births: Preliminary data for 2007. *National Vital Statistics Reports, 5*(12). Retrieved July, 28, 2009, from http://www.cdc.gov/nchs/data/nvsr/nvsr57/nvsr57_12.pdf

Hangal, S., & Aminabhavi, V. A. (2007). Self-concept, emotional maturity, and achievement motivation of the adolescent children of employed mothers and homemakers. *Journal of the Indian Academy of Applied Psychology, 33*(1), 103–110.

Hanlon, T. E., Bateman, R. W., Simon, B. D., O'Grady, K. E., & Carswell, S. B. (2004). Antecedents and correlates of deviant activity in urban youth manifesting behavioral problems. *Journal of Primary Prevention, 24*(3), 285–309.

Hanna, A. C., & Bond, M. J. (2006). Relationships between family conflict, perceived maternal verbal messages, and daughters' disturbed eating symptomatology. *Appetite, 47*(2), 205–211.

Hannon, P., Bowen, D. J., Moinpour, C. M., & McLerran, D. F. (2003). Correlations in perceived food use between the family food preparer and their spouses and children. *Appetite, 40*(1), 77–83.

Harel, J., & Scher, A. (2003). Insufficient responsiveness in ambivalent mother–infant relationships: Contextual and affective aspects. *Infant Behavior and Development, 26*(3), 371–383.

Harlow, H. F., & Harlow, M. K. (1966). Learning to love. *American Scientist, 54,* 244–272.

Harlow, H. F., Harlow, M. K., & Suomi, S. J. (1971). From thought to therapy: Lessons from a primate laboratory. *American Scientist, 59,* 538–549.

Harris, G. (2004, September 14). FDA links drugs to being suicidal. *The New York Times.* Retrieved from http://www.nytimes.com

Harris, J. R. (2007, March 26). Day care and a child's behavior [Letter to the Editor]. *The New York Times.* Retrieved from http://www.nytimes.com

Harris, S. R., Megens, A. M., Backman, C. L., & Hayes, V. E. (2005). Stability of the Bayley II Scales of Infant Development in a sample of low-risk and high-risk infants. *Developmental Medicine & Child Neurology, 47*(12), 820–823.

Hart, D., Burock, D., London, B., & Atkins, R. (2003). Prosocial tendencies, antisocial behavior, and moral development. In A. Slater & G. Bremner (Eds.), *An introduction to developmental psychology* (pp. 334–356). Malden, MA: Blackwell.

Hart, S. J., Davenport, M. L., Hooper, S. R., & Belger, A. (2006). Visuospatial executive function in Turner syndrome: Functional MRI and neurocognitive findings. *Brain: A Journal of Neurology, 129*(5), May, 1125–1136.

Harter, S. (1990). Self and identity development. In S. S. Feldman & G. R. Elliott (Eds.), *At the threshold: The developing adolescent.* Cambridge, MA: Harvard University Press.

Harter, S. (2006). The self. In K. A. Renninger, I. E. Sigel, W. Damon, & R. M. Lerner (Eds.), *Handbook of child psychology: Vol. 4. Child psychology in practice* (6th ed., pp. 505–570). Hoboken, NJ: Wiley.

Harter, S., & Monsour, A. (1992). Developmental analysis of conflict caused by opposing attributes in the adolescent self-portrait. *Developmental Psychology, 28,* 251–260.

Harter, S., & Pike, R. (1984). The pictorial scale of perceived competence and social acceptance for young children. *Child Development, 55,* 1969–1982.

Harter, S., & Whitesell, N. R. (2003). Beyond the debate: Why some adolescents report stable self-worth over time and situation, whereas others report changes in self-worth. *Journal of Personality, 71*(6), 1027–1058.

Hartup, W. W. (1983). The peer system. In P. H. Mussen (Ed.), *Handbook of child psychology: Vol. 4. Socialization, personality, and social development.* New York: Wiley.

Hasler, G., et al. (2007). Familiality of factor analysis-derived YBOCS dimensions in OCD-affected sibling pairs from the OCD Collaborative Genetics Study. *Biological Psychiatry, 61*(5), 617–625.

Hasselhorn, M. (1992). Task dependency and the role of typicality and metamemory in the development of an organizational strategy. *Child Development, 63,* 202–214.

Hastings, P. D., Zahn-Waxler, C., Robinson, J., Usher, B., & Bridges, D. (2000). The development of concern for others in children with behavior problems. *Developmental Psychology, 36*(5), 531–546.

Hatcher, R. A., et al. (Eds.). (2007). *Contraceptive technologies* (18th rev. ed.). New York: Ardent Media.

Hay, C., & Evans, M. M. (2006). Violent victimization and involvement in delinquency: Examining predictions from general strain theory. *Journal of Criminal Justice, 34*(3), 261–274.

Hay, D. F., Payne, A., & Chadwick, A. (2004). Peer relations in childhood. *Journal of Child Psychology and Psychiatry, 45*(1), 84–108.

Hayne, H., & Fagen, J. W. (Eds.). (2003). *Progress in infancy research: Vol. 3.* Mahwah, NJ: Erlbaum.

Hayward, C. (Ed.). (2003). *Gender differences at puberty.* New York: Cambridge University Press.

Hazell, P. (2007). Drug therapy for attention-deficit/hyperactivity disorder-like symptoms in autistic disorder. *Journal of Paediatrics and Child Health, 43*(1–2), 19–24.

Healy, M. D., & Ellis, B. J. (2007). Birth order, conscientiousness, and openness to experience tests of the family-niche model of personality using a within-family methodology. *Evolution and Human Behavior, 28*(1), 55–59.

Hebebrand, J., & Hinney, A. (2009). Environmental and genetic risk factors in obesity. *Child and Adolescent Psychiatric Clinics of North America, 18*(1), 83–94.

Hebert, T. P. (2000). Gifted males pursuing careers in elementary education: Factors that influence a belief in self. *Journal for the Education of the Gifted, 24*(1), 7–45.

Heilman, K. M., Nadeau, S. E., & Beversdorf, D. O. (2003). Creative innovation: Possible brain mechanisms. *Neurocase, 9*(5), 369–379.

Heimann, M., et al. (2006). Exploring the relation between memory, gestural communication, and the emergence of language in infancy: A longitudinal study. *Infant and Child Development, 15*(3), 233–249.

Heindel, J. J., & Lawler, C. (2006). Role of exposure to environmental chemicals in developmental origins of health and disease. In P. Gluckman & M. Hanson (Eds.), *Developmental origins of health and disease* (pp. 82–97). New York: Cambridge University Press.

Helms, J. E. (2006). Fairness is not validity or cultural bias in racial-group assessment: A quantitative perspective. *American Psychologist, 61*(8), 845–859.

Helwig, C. C. (2006). Rights, civil liberties, and democracy across cultures. In M. Killen & J. G. Smetana (Eds.), *Handbook of moral development* (pp. 185–210). Mahwah, NJ: Erlbaum.

Henry, D., et al. (2000). Normative influences on aggression in urban elementary school classrooms. *American Journal of Community Psychology, 28*(1) 59–81.

Henzi, S. P., et al. (2007). Look who's talking: developmental trends in the size of conversational cliques. *Evolution and Human Behavior, 28*(1), 66–74.

Hershberger, S. L., & D'Augelli, A. R. (2000). Issues in counseling lesbian, gay, and bisexual adolescents. In R. M. Perez, K. A. De-Bord, & K. J. Bieschke (Eds.), *Handbook of counseling and psychotherapy with lesbian, gay, and bisexual clients* (pp. 225–247). Washington, DC: American Psychological Association.

Hertenstein, M. J., & Campos, J. J. (2004). The retention effects of an adult's emotional displays on infant behavior. *Child Development, 75*(2), 595–613.

Hetherington, E. M. (1989). Coping with family transition: Winners, losers, and survivors. *Child Development, 60,* 1–14.

Hetherington, E. M. (2006). The influence of conflict, marital problem solving and parenting on children's adjustment in nondivorced, divorced and remarried families. In A. Clarke-Stewart & J. Dunn (Eds.), *Families count: Effects on child and adolescent development. The Jacobs Foundation series on adolescence* (pp. 203–237). Cambridge, UK: Cambridge University Press.

Hetherington, E. M., et al. (1992). Coping with marital transitions. *Monographs of the Society for Research in Child Development, 57*(2–3, Serial No. 227).

Hicks, B. M., et al. (2007). Genes mediate the association between P3 amplitude and externalizing disorders. *Psychophysiology, 44*(1), 98–105.

Hill, S. E., & Flom, R. (2007). 18- and 24-month-olds' discrimination of gender-consistent and inconsistent activities. *Infant Behavior & Development, 30*(1) 168–173.

Hill, S. Y., et al. (2007). Cerebellar volume in offspring from multiplex alcohol dependence families. *Biological Psychiatry, 61*(1), 41–47.

Hindmarsh, G. J., O'Callaghan, M. J., Mohay, H. A., & Rogers, Y. M. (2000). Gender differences in cognitive abilities at 2 years in ELBW infants. *Early Human Development, 60*(2), 115–122.

Hines, D. A., & Finkelhor, D. (2007). Statutory sex crime relationships between juveniles and adults: A review of social scientific research. *Aggression and Violent Behavior, 12*(3), 300–314.

Hinojosa, T., Sheu, C., & Michel, G. F. (2003). Infant hand-use preferences for grasping objects contributes to the development of a hand-use preference for manipulating objects. *Developmental Psychobiology, 43*(4), 328–334.

Hinshaw, S. P. (2006). Treatment for children and adolescents with attention-deficit/hyperactivity disorder. In P. C. Kendall (Ed.), *Child and adolescent therapy: Cognitive-behavioral procedures* (3rd ed., pp. 82–113). New York: Guilford.

Hoegh, D. G., & Bourgeois, M. J. (2002). Prelude and postlude to the self: Correlates of achieved identity. *Youth and Society, 33*(4), 573–594.

Hoff, E. (2006). Language experience and language milestones during early childhood. In K. McCartney & D. Phillips (Eds.),

Blackwell handbook of early childhood development (pp. 233–251). Malden, MA: Blackwell.

Hoff, E. V. (2005). A friend living inside me—the forms and functions of imaginary companions. *Imagination, Cognition and Personality, 24*(2), 151–189.

Hogan, A. M., de Haan, M., Datta, A., & Kirkham, F. J. (2006). Hypoxia: An acute, intermittent and chronic challenge to cognitive development. *Developmental Science, 9*(4), 335–337.

Högler, W., et al. (2008). Sex-specific developmental changes in muscle size and bone geometry at the femoral shaft. *Bone, 42*(5), 982–989.

Holland, J. J. (2000, July 25). Groups link media to child violence. Retrieved from http://www.ap.org/

Holland, J. L. (1997). *Making vocational choices: A theory of vocational personalities and work environments* (3rd ed.). Odessa, FL: Psychological Assessment Resources.

Holloway, J. H. (2004). *Part-time work and student achievement.* Alexandria VA: Association for Supervision and Curriculum Development. Retrieved from http://www.ascd.org/publications/ed_lead/200104/holloway.html

Homer, B. D., & Nelson, K. (2005). Seeing objects as symbols and symbols as objects: Language and the development of dual representation. In B. D. Homer & C. S. Tamis-LeMonda (Eds.), *The development of social cognition and communication* (pp. 29–52). Mahwah, NJ: Erlbaum.

Honzik, M. P., Macfarlane, J. W., & Allen, L. (1948). The stability of mental test performance between 2 and 18 years. *Journal of Experimental Education, 17,* 309–324.

Hossain, M., Chetana, M., & Devi, P. U. (2005). Late effect of prenatal irradiation on the hippocampal histology and brain weight in adult mice. *International Journal of Developmental Neuroscience, 23*(4), 307–313.

Howe, M. L. (2006). Developmentally invariant dissociations in children's true and false memories: Not all relatedness is created equal. *Child Development, 77*(4), 1112–1123.

Hudson, J. A. (1990). The emergence of autobiographical memory in mother–child conversation. In R. Fivush & J. A. Hudson (Eds.), *Knowing and remembering in young children.* Cambridge: Cambridge University Press.

Huesmann, L. R., Dubow, E. F., Eron, L. D., & Boxer, P. (2006). Middle childhood family contextual factors as predictors of adult outcomes. In A. C. Huston & M. N. Ripke (Eds.), *Middle childhood: Contexts of development.* Cambridge, UK: Cambridge University Press.

Huestis, M. A., et al. (2002). Drug abuse's smallest victims: in utero drug exposure. *Forensic Science International, 128*(2), 20.

Huizink, A. C., & Mulder, E. J. H. (2006). Maternal smoking, drinking or cannabis use during pregnancy and neurobehavioral and cognitive functioning in human offspring. *Neuroscience & Biobehavioral Reviews, 30*(1), 24–41.

Hunt, C. E., & Hauck, F. R. (2006). Sudden infant death syndrome. *Canadian Medical Association Journal, 174*(13), 1861–1869.

Hunter, B. C., & Sahler, O. J. Z. (2006). Music for very young ears. *Birth: Issues in Perinatal Care, 33*(2), 137–138.

Hur, Y. (2005). Genetic and environmental influences on self-concept in female pre-adolescent twins: Comparison of Minnesota and Seoul data. *Twin Research and Human Genetics, 8*(4), 291–299.

Hurd, Y. L., et al. (2005). Marijuana impairs growth in mid-gestation fetuses. *Neurotoxicology and Teratology, 27*(2), 221–229.

Hyde, J. S., Fennema, E., & Lamon, S. J. (1990). Gender differences in mathematics performance: A meta-analysis. *Psychological Bulletin, 107,* 139–155.

Hyde, J. S., Lindberg, S. M., Linn, M. C., Ellis, A. B., & Williams, C. C. (2008). Gender similarities characterize math performance. *Science, 321,* 494–495.

Hynes, M., Sheik, M., Wilson, H. G., & Spiegel, P. (2002). Reproductive health indicators and outcomes among refugee and internally displaced persons in postemergency phase camps. *Journal of the American Medical Association, 288,* 595–603.

Iacono, W. G., McGue, M., & Krueger, R. F. (2006). Minnesota Center for Twin and Family Research. *Twin Research and Human Genetics, 9*(6), 978-984.

Ikeda, K., Koga, A., & Minami, S. (2006). Evaluation of a cure process during alarm treatment for nocturnal enuresis. *Journal of Clinical Psychology, 62*(10), 1245–1257.

International Human Genome Sequencing Consortium. (2006). A global map of p53 transcription-factor binding sites in the human genome. *Cell, 124*(1), 207–219.

Jacklin, C. N., Wilcox, K. T., & Maccoby, E. E. (1988). Neonatal sex-steroid hormones and cognitive abilities at 6 years. *Developmental Psychobiology, 21,* 567–574.

Jacobs, D. M., Levy, G., & Marder, K. (2006). Dementia in Parkinson's disease, Huntington's disease, and related disorders. In M. J. Farah & T. E. Feinberg (Eds.), *Patient-based approaches to cognitive neuroscience* (2nd ed., pp. 381–395). Cambridge, MA: MIT Press.

Jacobs, J. E., Davis-Kean, P., Bleeker, M., Eccles, J. S., & Malanchuk, O. (2005). "I can, but I don't want to": The impact of parents, interests, and activities on gender differences in math. In A. M. Gallagher & J. C. Kaufman (Eds.), *Gender differences in mathematics: An integrative psychological approach* (pp. 246–263). New York: Cambridge University Press.

Jacobson, J. L., Jacobson, S. W., Padgett, R. J., Brumitt, G. A., & Billings, R. L. (1992). Effects of prenatal PCB exposure on cognitive processing efficiency and sustained attention. *Developmental Psychology, 28,* 297–306.

Jacobson, P. F., & Schwartz, R. G. (2005). English past tense use in bilingual children with language impairment. *American Journal of Speech-Language Pathology, 14*(4), 313–323.

Jeng, S.-F., Yau, K.-I. T., Liao, H.-F., Chen, L.-C., & Chen, P.-S. (2000). Prognostic factors for walking attainment in very low birthweight preterm infants. *Early Human Development, 59*(3), 159–173.

Joe, S., Romer, D., & Jamieson, P. (2007). Suicide acceptability is related to suicide planning in U.S. adolescents and young adults. *Suicide and Life-Threatening Behavior, 37*(2), 165–178.

Johnson, W., & Bouchard, T. J., Jr. (2007). Sex differences in mental abilities: g masks the dimensions on which they lie. *Intelligence, 35*(1), 23–39.

Johnson, W., & Krueger, R. F. (2006). How money buys happiness: Genetic and environmental processes linking finances and life satisfaction. *Journal of Personality and Social Psychology, 90*(4), 680–691.

Johnson, W., McGue, M., & Iacono, W. G. (2007). Socioeconomic status and school grades: Placing their association in broader context in a sample of biological and adoptive families. *Intelligence, 35*(6), 526-541.

Johnson, W., McGue, M., Krueger, R. F., & Bouchard, T. J., Jr. (2004). Marriage and personality: A genetic analysis. *Journal of Personality and Social Psychology, 86*(2), 285–294.

Johnston, C. A., & Steele, R. G. (2007). Treatment of pediatric overweight: An examination of feasibility and effectiveness in an applied clinical setting. *Journal of Pediatric Psychology, 32*(1), 106–110.

Johnston, L. D., O'Malley, P. M., Bachman, J. G., & Schulenberg, J. E. (2008a). Various stimulant drugs show continuing gradual declines among teens in 2008, most illicit drugs hold steady. University of Michigan News Service: Ann Arbor, MI. Retrieved February 6, 2009, from http://www.monitoringthefuture.org

Johnston, L. D., O'Malley, P. M., Bachman, J. G., & Schulenberg, J. E. (2008b). More good news on teen smoking: Rates at or near record lows. University of Michigan News Service: Ann Arbor, MI. Retrieved February 6, 2009, from http://www.monitoringthefuture.org

Joint United Nations Programme on HIV/AIDS. (2006). *Report on the global AIDS epidemic: Executive summary.* Geneva, Switzerland: UNAIDS.

Jones, D. C., & Crawford, J. K. (2006). The peer appearance culture during adolescence: Gender and body mass variations. *Journal of Youth and Adolescence, 35*(2), 257–269.

Jones, S. S., & Hong, H-W. (2005). How some infant smiles get made. *Infant Behavior & Development, 28*(2), 194–205.

Jonkman, S. (2006). Sensitization facilitates habit formation: Implications for addiction. *Journal of Neuroscience, 26*(28), 7319–7320.

Jorgensen, G. (2006). Kohlberg and Gilligan: Duet or duel? *Journal of Moral Education, 35*(2), 179–196.

Joshi, P. T., Salpekar, J. A., & Daniolos, P. T. (2006). Physical and sexual abuse of children. In M. K. Dulcan & J. M. Wiener (Eds.), *Essentials of child and adolescent psychiatry* (pp. 595–620). Washington, DC: American Psychiatric Publishing.

Joshi, R. M. (2003). Misconceptions about the assessment and diagnosis of reading disability. *Reading Psychology, 24*(3–4), 247–266.

Junod, A. F. (2008). Overweight children do not necessarily become overweight adults. *Swiss Medical Review, 4*(174), 2175.

Kagan, J., & Klein, R. E. (1973). Cross-cultural perspectives on early development. *American Psychologist, 28,* 947–961.

Kagan, L. J., MacLeod, A. K., & Pote, H. L. (2004). Accessibility of causal explanations for future positive and negative events in adolescents with anxiety and depression. *Clinical Psychology and Psychotherapy, 11*(3), 177–186.

Kaiser Family Foundation, Holt, T., Greene, L., & Davis, J. (2003). *National survey of adolescents and young adults: Sexual health knowledge, attitudes, and experiences.* Menlo Park, CA: Henry J. Kaiser Family Foundation.

Kaminski, R. A., & Stormshak, E. A. (2007). Project STAR: Early intervention with preschool children and families for the prevention of substance abuse. In P. Tolan, J. Szapocznik, & S. Sambrano (Eds.), *Preventing youth substance abuse: Science-based programs for children and adolescents* (pp. 89–109). Washington, DC: American Psychological Association.

Kanevsky, L., & Geake, J. (2004). Inside the zone of proximal development: Validating a multifactor model of learning potential with gifted students and their peers. *Journal for the Education of the Gifted, 28*(2), 182–217.

Karapetsas, A., & Kantas, A. (1991). Visuomotor organization in the child: A neuropsychological approach. *Perceptual and Motor Skills, 72,* 211–217.

Karatekin, C., Marcus, D. J., & White, T. (2007). Oculomotor and manual indexes of incidental and intentional spatial sequence learning during middle childhood and adolescence. *Journal of Experimental Child Psychology, 96*(2), 107–130.

Karavasilis, L., Doyle, A. B., & Markiewicz, D. (2003). Associations between parenting style and attachment to mother in middle childhood and adolescence. *International Journal of Behavioral Development, 27*(2), 153–164.

Katz, R., Lowenstein, A., Phillips, J., & Daatland, S. O. (2005). Theorizing inter-generational family relations: Solidarity, conflict, and ambivalence in cross-national contexts. In V. L. Bengtson et al. (Eds.), *Sourcebook of family theory and research* (pp. 393–420). Thousand Oaks, CA: Sage.

Katzman, D. K. (2005). Medical complications in adolescents with anorexia nervosa: A review of the literature. *International Journal of Eating Disorders, 37*(Suppl.), S52–S59.

Kavanaugh, R. D. (2006). Pretend play. In B. Spodek & O. N. Saracho (Eds.), *Handbook of research on the education of young children* (2nd ed., pp. 269–278). Mahwah, NJ: Erlbaum.

Kavcic, T., & Zupancic, M. (2005). Sibling relationship in early/middle childhood: Trait- and dyad-centered approach. *Studia Psychologica, 47*(3), 179–197.

Kaye, W. H., et al. (2004). Genetic analysis of bulimia nervosa: Methods and sample description. *International Journal of Eating Disorders, 35*(4), 556–570.

Kazdin, A. E. (2000). Treatments for aggressive and antisocial children. *Child and Adolescent Psychiatric Clinics of North America, 9*(4), 841–858.

Kazui, M., Endo, T., Tanaka, A., Sakagami, H., & Suganuma, M. (2000). Intergenerational transmission of attachment: Japanese mother–child dyads. *Japanese Journal of Educational Psychology, 48*(3), 323–332.

Kearney, C. A., & Bensaheb, A. (2007). Assessing anxiety disorders in children and adolescents. In S. R. Smith & L. Handler (Eds.), *The clinical assessment of children and adolescents: A practitioner's handbook* (pp. 467–483). Mahwah, NJ: Erlbaum.

Keen, D., Rodger, S., Doussin, K., & Braithwaite, M. (2007). A pilot study of the effects of a social-pragmatic intervention on the communication and symbolic play of children with autism. *Autism, 11*(1), 63–71.

Keller, H., Kärtner, J., Borke, J., Yovsi, R., & Kleis, A. (2005). Parenting styles and the development of the categorical self: A longitudinal study on mirror self-recognition in Cameroonian Nso and German families. *International Journal of Behavioral Development, 29*(6), 496–504.

Keller, S., Maddock, J. E., Laforge, R. G., Velicer, W. F., & Basler, H-D. (2007). Binge drinking and health behavior in medical students. *Addictive Behaviors, 32*(3), 505–515.

Kellman, P. J., & Arterberry, M. E. (2006). Infant visual perception. In D. Kuhn et al. (Eds.), *Handbook of child psychology: Vol. 2. Cognition, perception, and language* (6th ed., pp. 109–160). Hoboken, NJ: Wiley.

Kellogg, R. (1959). *What children scribble and why.* Oxford: National Press.

Kellogg, R. (1970). Understanding children's art. In P. Cramer (Ed.), *Readings in developmental psychology today.* Del Mar, CA: CRM.

Kelly, K. M., Jones, W. H., & Adams, J. M. (2002). Using the Imaginary Audience Scale as a measure of social anxiety in young adults. *Educational and Psychological Measurement, 62*(5), 896–914.

Kempes, M., Matthys, W., de Vries, H., & van Engeland, H. (2005). Reactive and proactive aggression in children: A review of theory, findings and the relevance for child and adolescent psychiatry. *European Child & Adolescent Psychiatry, 14*(1), 11–19.

Kendler, K. S., Gardner, C. O., Gatz, M., & Pedersen, N. L. (2007). The sources of comorbidity between major depression and generalized anxiety disorder in a Swedish national twin sample. *Psychological Medicine, 37*(3), 453–462.

Keogh, A. F., & Whyte, J. (2006). Exploring children's concepts of intelligence through ethnographic methods. *Irish Journal of Psychology, 27*(1–2), 69–78.

Kerns, K. A., Abraham, M. M., Schlegelmilch, A., & Morgan, T. A. (2007). Mother–child attachment in later middle childhood: Assessment approaches and associations with mood and emotion regulation. *Attachment & Human Development, 9*(1), 33–53.

Kidd, E., & Bavin, E. L. (2007). Lexical and referential influences on on-line spoken language comprehension: A comparison of adults and primary-school-age children. *First Language, 27*(1), 29–52.

Killen, M., & Smetana, J. G. (Eds.). (2006). *Handbook of moral development.* Mahwah, NJ: Erlbaum.

Kim, J-Y., McHale, S. M., Osgood, D. W., & Crouter, A. C. (2006). Longitudinal course and family correlates of sibling relationships from childhood through adolescence. *Child Development, 77*(6), 1746–1761.

Kim, K. H. (2005). Can only intelligent people be creative? A meta-analysis. *Journal of Secondary Gifted Education, 16*(2–3), 57–66.

Kimura, D., & Hampson, E. (1992). Neural and hormonal mechanisms mediating sex differences in cognition. In P. A. Vernon (Ed.), *Biological approaches to the study of human intelligence.* Norwood, NJ: Ablex.

King, R. (2000). Interview reported in L. Frazier, The new face of HIV is young, black, *The Washington Post* (July 16, 2000), p. C01.

Kinsbourne, M. (2003). The corpus callosum equilibrates the cerebral hemispheres. In E. Zaidel & M. Iacoboni (Eds.), *The parallel brain: The cognitive neuroscience of the corpus callosum* (pp. 271–281). Cambridge, MA: MIT Press.

Kinsey, A. C., Pomeroy, W. B., & Martin, C. E. (1948). *Sexual behavior in the human male.* Philadelphia: W. B. Saunders.

Kinsey, A. C., Pomeroy, W. B., Martin, C. E., & Gebhard, P. H. (1953). *Sexual behavior in the human female.* Philadelphia: W. B. Saunders.

Kirchler, E., Pombeni, M. L., & Palmonari, A. (1991). Sweet sixteen . . . adolescents' problems and the peer group as source of support. *European Journal of Psychology of Education, 6,* 393–410.

Kirkcaldy, B. D., Shephard, R. J., & Siefen, R. G. (2002). The relationship between physical activity and self-image and problem behavior among adolescents. *Social Psychiatry and Psychiatric Epidemiology, 37*(11), 544–550.

Kistner, J. (2006). Children's peer acceptance, perceived acceptance, and risk for depression. In T. E. Joiner, J. S. Brown, & J. Kistner (Eds.), *The interpersonal, cognitive, and social nature of depression* (pp. 1–21). Mahwah, NJ: Erlbaum.

Kjelsås, E., Bjornstrom, C., & Götestam, K. G. (2004). Prevalence of eating disorders in female and male adolescents (14–15 years). *Eating Behaviors, 5*(1), 13–25.

Klaus, M. H., & Kennell, J. H. (1978). Parent-to-infant attachment. In J. H. Stevens, Jr., & M. Mathews (Eds.), *Mother/child, father/child relationships.* Washington, DC: National Association for the Education of Young Children.

Klein, P. J., & Meltzoff, A. N. (1999). Long-term memory, forgetting and deferred imitation in 12-month-old infants. *Developmental Science, 2*(1), 102–113.

Klier, C. M. (2006). Mother–infant bonding disorders in patients with postnatal depression: The Postpartum Bonding Questionnaire in clinical practice. *Archives of Women's Mental Health, 9*(5), 289–291.

Klintsova, A. Y., & Greenough, W. T. (1999). Synaptic plasticity in cortical systems. *Current Opinion in Neurobiology, 9*(2), 203–208.

Klomek, A. B., et al. (2007). Bullying, depression, and suicidality in adolescents. *Journal of the American Academy of Child & Adolescent Psychiatry, 46*(1), 40–49.

Knaak, S. (2005). Breast-feeding, bottle-feeding and Dr. Spock: The shifting context of choice. *Canadian Review of Sociology and Anthropology, 42*(2), 197–216.

Knafo, A., & Plomin, R. (2006a). Parental discipline and affection and children's prosocial behavior: Genetic and environmental links. *Journal of Personality and Social Psychology, 90*(1), 147–164.

Knafo, A., & Plomin, R. (2006b). Prosocial behavior from early to middle childhood: Genetic and environmental influences on stability and change. *Developmental Psychology, 42*(5), 771–786.

Knox, P. L., Fagley, N. S., & Miller, P. M. (2004). Care and justice moral orientation among African American college students. *Journal of Adult Development, 11*(1), 41–45.

Kochanska, G. (2001). Emotional development in children with different attachment histories: The first three years. *Child Development, 72*(2), 474–490.

Kochanska, G., Coy, K. C., & Murray, K. T. (2001). The development of self-regulation in the first four years of life. *Child Development, 72*(4), 1091–1111.

Kogan, M. D., et al. (2000). Trends in twin birth outcomes and prenatal care utilization in the United States, 1981–1997. *Journal of the American Medical Association, 284*(3), 335–341.

Kohl, C. (2004). Postpartum psychoses: Closer to schizophrenia or the affective spectrum? *Current Opinion in Psychiatry, 17*(2), 87–90.

Kohlberg, L. (1963). Moral development and identification. In H. W. Stevenson (Ed.), *Child psychology: 62nd yearbook of the National Society for the Study of Education.* Chicago: University of Chicago Press.

Kohlberg, L. (1966). Cognitive stages and preschool education. *Human Development, 9,* 5–17.

Kohlberg, L. (1969). Stage and sequence: The cognitive-developmental approach to socialization. In D. A. Goslin (Ed.), *Handbook of socialization theory and research.* Chicago: Rand McNally.

Kohlberg, L. (1981). *The meaning and measurement of moral development.* Worcester, MA: Clark University Press.

Kohlberg, L. (1985). *The psychology of moral development.* San Francisco: Harper.

Kohlberg, L., & Kramer, R. (1969). Continuities and discontinuities in childhood and adult moral development. *Human Development, 12,* 93–120.

Kohyama, J., Shiiki, T., Ohinata-Sugimoto, J., & Hasegawa, T. (2002). Potentially harmful sleep habits of 3-year-old children in Japan. *Journal of Developmental and Behavioral Pediatrics, 23*(2), 67–70.

Kolata, G. (2007, May 8). Genes take charge, and diets fall by the wayside. *The New York Times.* Retrieved from http://www.nytimes.com

Kolb, B., & Gibb, R. (2007). Brain plasticity and recovery from early cortical injury. *Developmental Psychobiology, 49*(2), 107–118.

Konijn, E. A., Bijvank, M. N., & Bushman, B. J. (2007). I wish I were a warrior: The role of wishful identification in the effects of violent video games on aggression in adolescent boys. *Developmental Psychology, 43*(4), 1038–1044.

Kopp, C. B. (1989). Regulation of distress and negative emotions: A developmental view. *Developmental Psychology, 25,* 343–354.

Krackow, E., & Lynn, S. J. (2003). Is there touch in the game of Twister? The effects of innocuous touch and suggestive questions on children's eyewitness memory. *Law and Human Behavior, 27*(6), 589–604.

Krebs, D. L., & Denton, K. (2005). Toward a more pragmatic approach to morality: A critical evaluation of Kohlberg's model. *Psychological Review, 112*(3), 629–649.

Krebs, D. L., & Denton, K. (2006). Explanatory limitations of cognitive-developmental approaches to morality. *Psychological Review, 113*(3), 672–675.

Kristensen, P., & Bjerkedal, T. (2007). Explaining the relation between birth order and intelligence. *Science, 313*(5832), 1717.

Kroeger, K. A., & Nelson, W. M., III. (2006). A language programme to increase the verbal production of a child dually diagnosed with Down syndrome and autism. *Journal of Intellectual Disability Research, 50*(2), 101–108.

Krojgaard, P. (2005). Continuity and discontinuity in developmental psychology. *Psyke & Logos, 26*(2), 377–394.

Krueger, C., Holditch-Davis, D., Quint, S., & De-Casper, A. (2004). Recurring auditory experience in the 28- to 34-week-old fetus. *Infant Behavior & Development, 27*(4), 537–543.

Kuczaj, S. A., II (1982). On the nature of syntactic development. In S. A. Kuczaj II (Ed.), *Language development: Vol. 1. Syntax and semantics.* Hillsdale, NJ: Erlbaum.

Kuczmarski, R. J., et al. (2000, December 4). CDC growth charts: United States. *Advance Data from Vital and Health Statistics, No. 314.* Hyattsville, MD: National Center for Health Statistics.

Kuhl, P. K., et al. (1997). Cross-language analysis of phonetic units in language addressed to infants. *Science, 277*(5326), 684–686.

Kuhl, P. K., et al. (2006). Infants show a facilitation effect for native language phonetic perception between 6 and 12 months. *Developmental Science, 9*(2), F13–F21.

Kuhn, D. (2007). Editorial. *Cognitive Development, 22*(1), 1–2.

Kulp, J. (2007, March 27). Day care and a child's behavior [Letter to the editor]. *The New York Times.* Retrieved from http://www.nytimes.com

Kundanis, R., & Massaro, D. W. (2004). Televisual media for children are more interactive. *American Journal of Psychology, 117*(4), 643–648.

Kuterbach, J. M. (2007). Factor structure of the New Imaginary Audience Scale in a sample of female college students. *College Student Journal, 41*(4, Part A), 813–822.

Kwok, H. W. M. (2003). Psychopharmacology in autism spectrum disorders. *Current Opinion in Psychiatry, 16*(5), 529–534.

Labrell, F., & Ubersfeld, G. (2004). Parental verbal strategies and children's capacities at 3 and 5 years during a memory task. *European Journal of Psychology of Education, 19*(2), 189–202.

Laflamme, D., Pomerleau, A., & Malcuit, G. (2002). A comparison of fathers' and mothers' involvement in childcare and stimulation behaviors during free-play with their infants at 9 and 15 months. *Sex Roles, 47*(11–12), 507–518.

Laflin, M. T., Wang, J., & Barry, M. (2008). A longitudinal study of adolescent transition from virgin to nonvirgin status. *Journal of Adolescent Health, 42*(3), 228–236.

Lai, H-L., et al. (2006). Randomized controlled trial of music during kangaroo care on maternal state anxiety and preterm infants' responses. *International Journal of Nursing Studies, 43*(2), 139–146.

Lam, K. S. L., Aman, M. G., & Arnold, L. E. (2006). Neurochemical correlates of autistic disorder: A review of the literature. *Research in Developmental Disabilities, 27*(3), 254–289.

Lam, T. H., Shi, H. J., Ho, L. M., Stewart, S. M., & Fan, S. (2002). Timing of pubertal maturation and heterosexual behavior among Hong Kong Chinese adolescents. *Archives of Sexual Behavior, 31*(4), 359–366.

Lamb, M. E., & Ahnert, L. (2006). Nonparental child care: Context, concepts, correlates, and consequences. In K. A. Renninger, I. E. Sigel, W. Damon, & R. M. Lerner (Eds.), *Handbook of child psychology: Vol. 4. Child psychology in practice* (6th ed., pp. 950–1016). Hoboken, NJ: Wiley.

Lamers, C. T. J., Bechara, A., Rizzo, M., & Ramaekers, J. G. (2006). Cognitive function and mood in MDMA/THC users, THC users and non-drug using controls. *Journal of Psychopharmacology, 20*(2), 302–311.

Lampl, M., Veldhuis, J. D., & Johnson, M. L. (1992). Saltation and stasis: A model of human growth. *Science, 258,* 801–803.

Lange, G., & Pierce, S. H. (1992). Memory-strategy learning and maintenance in preschool children. *Developmental Psychology, 28,* 453–462.

Langlois, J. H., et al. (2000). Maxims or myths of beauty? A meta-analytic and theoretical review. *Psychological Bulletin, 126*(3), 390–423.

Langlois, J. H., Ritter, J. M., Casey, R. J., & Sawin, D. B. (1995). Infant attractiveness predicts maternal behaviors and attitudes. *Developmental Psychology, 31*(3), 464–472.

Lansford, J. E., Malone, P. S., Castellino, D. R., Dodge, K. A., Pettit, G. S., & Bates, J. E. (2006). Trajectories of internalizing, externalizing, and grades for children who have and have not experienced their parents' divorce or separation. *Journal of Family Psychology, 20*(2), 292–301.

Lantolf, J. P., & Thorne, S. L. (2007). Sociocultural theory and second language learning. In B. VanPatten & J. Williams (Eds.), *Theories in second language acquisition: An introduction* (pp. 201–224). Mahwah, NJ: Erlbaum.

Laplan, R. T. (2004). *Career development across the K-16 years: Bridging the present to satisfying and successful futures.* Alexandria, VA: American Counseling Association.

LaPointe, L. L. (Ed.). (2005). Feral children. *Journal of Medical Speech-Language Pathology, 13*(1), vii–ix.

Lapsley, D. K. (2006). Moral stage theory. In K. Killen & J. G. Smetana (Eds.), *Handbook of moral development* (pp. 37–66). Mahwah, NJ: Erlbaum.

Largo, R. H., et al. (2001). Neuromotor development from 5 to 18 years. Part 1: Timed performance. *Developmental Medicine and Child Neurology, 43*(7), 436–443.

Larroque, B., et al. (2005). Temperament at 9 months of very preterm infants born at less than 29 weeks' gestation: The Epipage study. *Journal of Developmental & Behavioral Pediatrics, 26*(1), 48–55.

Larson, R., & Richards, M. H. (1991). Daily companionship in late childhood and early adolescence: Changing developmental contexts. *Child Development, 62,* 284–300.

Larsson, I., & Svedin, C. (2002). Experiences in childhood: Young adults' recollections. *Archives of Sexual Behavior, 31*(3), 263–273.

Latham, G. P., & Budworth, M.-H. (2007). The study of work motivation in the 20th century. In L. L. Koppes (Ed.), *Historical perspectives in industrial and organizational psychology* (pp. 353–381). Mahwah, NJ: Erlbaum.

Lau, A. S., Litrownik, A. J., Newton, R. R., Black, M. M., & Everson, M. D. (2006). Factors affecting the link between physical discipline and child externalizing problems in Black and White families. *Journal of Community Psychology, 34*(1), 89–103.

Laurendeau, M., & Pinard, A. (1970). *The development of the concept of space in the child.* New York: International Universities Press.

Lawson, K., & Ruff, H. A. (2004). Early focused attention predicts outcome for children born prematurely. *Journal of Developmental & Behavioral Pediatrics, 25*(6), 399–406.

Lazar, R. E. (2008). Beat the bully: An evaluation of the effectiveness of the anti-bully efforts implemented in a Southeastern Michigan suburban school district. *Dissertation Abstracts International, 68* (8-A), pp. 32–34.

Leaper, C. (2002). Parenting girls and boys. In M. H. Bornstein (Ed.), *Handbook of parenting: Vol. 1. Children and parenting* (2nd ed., pp. 189–225). Mahwah, NJ: Erlbaum.

Lecanuet, J. P., Granier-Deferre, C., & DeCasper, A. (2005). Are we expecting too much from prenatal sensory experiences? In B. Hopkins & S. P Johnson (Eds.), *Prenatal development of postnatal functions: Advances in infancy research* (pp. 31–49). Westport, CT: Praeger/ Greenwood.

Lecanuet, J. P., Graniere-Deferre, C., Jacquet, A.-Y., & DeCasper, A. J. (2000). Fetal discrimination of low-pitched musical notes. *Developmental Psychobiology, 36*(1), 29–39.

Lee, V. E., & Burkam, D. T. (2003). Dropping out of high school: The role of school organization and structure. *American Educational Research Journal, 40*(2), 353–393.

Leerkes, E. M., & Crockenberg, S. C. (2006). Antecedents of mothers' emotional and cognitive responses to infant distress: The role of family, mother, and infant characteristics. *Infant Mental Health Journal, 27*(4), 405–428.

Lefkowitz, E. S., & Zeldow, P. B. (2006). Masculinity and femininity predict optimal mental health: A belated test of the androgyny hypothesis. *Journal of Personality Assessment, 87*(1), 95–101.

Legro, R. S., et al. (2007). Clomiphene, metformin, or both for infertility in the polycystic ovary syndrome. *New England Journal of Medicine, 356*(6), 551–566.

Lejeune, C., et al. (2006). Prospective multicenter observational study of 260 infants born to 259 opiate-dependent mothers on methadone or high-dose buprenophine substitution. *Drug and Alcohol Dependence, 82*(3), 250–257.

Lengua, L. J., Honorado, E., & Bush, N. R. (2007). Contextual risk and parenting as predictors of effortful control and social competence in preschool children. *Journal of Applied Developmental Psychology, 28*(1), 40–55.

Lenneberg, E. H. (1967). *Biological foundations of language.* New York: Wiley.

Leon, M. R. (2000). Effects of caffeine on cognitive, psychomotor, and affective performance of children with attention-deficit/hyperactivity disorder. *Journal of Attention Disorders, 4*(1) 27–47.

Leonard, C. M., et al. (2008). Identical neural risk factors predict cognitive deficit in dyslexia and schizophrenia. *Neuropsychology, 22*(2), 147–158.

Leonard, S. P., & Archer, J. (1989). A naturalistic investigation of gender constancy in three- to four-year-old children. *British Journal of Developmental Psychology, 7,* 341–346.

Leonardo, E. D., & Hen, R. (2006). Genetics of affective and anxiety disorders. *Annual Review of Psychology, 57,* 117–137.

Letourneau, E. J., Schoenwald, S. K., & Sheidow, A. J. (2004). Children and adolescents with sexual behavior problems. *Child Maltreatment: Journal of the American Professional Society on the Abuse of Children, 9*(1), 49–61.

Leung, C., McBride-Chang, C., & Lai, B. (2004). Relations among maternal parenting style,

academic competence, and life satisfaction in Chinese early adolescents. *Journal of Early Adolescence, 24*(2), 113–143.

Lever, N., et al. (2004). A drop-out prevention program for high-risk inner-city youth. *Behavior Modification, 28*(4), 513–527.

Levinthal, B. R., & Lleras, A. (2007). The unique contributions of retinal size and perceived size on change detection. *Visual Cognition, 15*(1), 101–105.

Lewinsohn, P. M., Rohde, P., Seeley, J. R., Klein, D. N., & Gotlib, I. H. (2000). Natural course of adolescent major depressive disorder in a community sample: Predictors of recurrence in young adults. *American Journal of Psychiatry, 157,* 1584–1591.

Lewis, B. A., et al. (2004). Four-year language outcomes of children exposed to cocaine in utero. *Neurotoxicology and Teratology, 26*(5), 617–627.

Lewis, H. L. (2003). Differences in ego identity among college students across age, ethnicity, and gender. *Identity, 3*(2), 159–189.

Lewis, M., & Feiring, C. (1989). Early predictors of childhood friendship. In T. J. Berndt & G. W. Ladd (Eds.), *Peer relationships in child development.* New York: Wiley.

Li, Q. (2007). New bottle but old wine: A research of cyberbullying in schools. *Computers in Human Behavior, 23*(4), 1777–1791.

Lickliter, R. (2001). The dynamics of language development: From perception to comprehension. *Developmental Science, 4*(1), 21–23.

Lickliter, R., & Logan, C. (2007). Developmental psychobiology special issue: "Gilbert Gottlieb's legacy: Probabilistic epigenesist and the development of individuals and species." *Developmental Psychobiology, 49*(8), 747–748.

Lipman, E. L., et al. (2006). Testing effectiveness of a community-based aggression management program for children 7 to 11 years old and their families. *Journal of the American Academy of Child & Adolescent Psychiatry, 45*(9), 1085–1093.

Lipsitt, L. P. (2002). Early experience and behavior in the baby of the 21st century. In J. Gomes-Pedro et al. (Eds.), *The infant and family in the twenty-first century* (pp. 55–78). London: Brunner-Routledge.

Lipsitt, L. P. (2003). Crib death: A biobehavioral phenomenon? *Current Directions in Psychological Science, 12*(5), 164–170.

Lochman, J. E., Wells, K. C., & Murray, M. (2007). The Coping Power Program: Preventive intervention at the middle school transition. In P. Tolan, J. Szapocznik, & S. Sambrano (Eds.), *Preventing youth substance abuse: Science-based programs for children and adolescents* (pp. 185–210). Washington, DC: American Psychological Association.

Long, L. H. (2008). Relationship between extent of extracurricular participation, employment, and substance use among middle and high school students. *Dissertation Abstracts International, 68* (11-A), p. 4620.

Loovis, E. M., & Butterfield, S. A. (2000). Influence of age, sex, and balance on mature skipping by children in grades K–8. *Perceptual and Motor Skills, 90*(3), 974–978.

Lorenz, K. (1962). *King Solomon's ring.* London: Methuen.

Lorenz, K. (1981). *The foundations of ethology.* New York: Springer-Verlag.

Lovaas, O. I. (1977). *The autistic child: Language development through behavior modification.* New York: Halstead.

Lovaas, O. I., Smith, T., & McEachin, J. J. (1989). Clarifying comments on the young autism study: Reply to Schapler, Short, and Mesibov. *Journal of Consulting and Clinical Psychology, 57,* 165–167.

Lubinski, D. (2004). Introduction to the special section on cognitive abilities: 100 years after Spearman's (1904) "'General intelligence,' objectively determined and measured." *Journal of Personality and Social Psychology, 86*(1), 96–111.

Lubinski, D., & Benbow, C. P. (2000). States of excellence. *American Psychologist, 55,* 137–150.

Lucariello, J. M., Hudson, J. A., Fivush, R., & Bauer, P. J. (Eds.). (2004). *The development of the mediated mind: Sociocultural context and cognitive development.* Mahwah, NJ: Erlbaum.

Luciano, M., Kirk, K. M., Heath, A. C., & Martin, N. G. (2005). The genetics of tea and coffee drinking and preference for source of caffeine in a large community sample of Australian twins. *Addiction, 100*(10), 1510–1517.

Luyckx, K., Schwartz, S. J., Goossens, L., & Pollock, S. (2008). Employment, sense of coherence, and identity formation: Contextual and psychological processes on the pathway to sense of adulthood. *Journal of Adolescent Research, 23*(5), 566–591.

Lykken, D. T. (2006a). In C. J. Patrick (Ed.), *Psychopathic personality: The scope of the problem* (pp. 3–13). New York: Guilford.

Lykken, D. T. (2006b). The mechanism of emergenesis. *Genes, Brain & Behavior, 5*(4), 306–310.

Lynam, D. R., Caspi, A., Moffitt, T. E., Loeber, R., & Stouthamer-Loeber, M. (2007). Longitudinal evidence that psychopathy scores in early adolescence predict adult psychopathy. *Journal of Abnormal Psychology, 116*(1), 155–165.

Lynne, S. D., Graber, J. A., Nichols, T. R., Brooks-Gunn, J., & Botvin, G. J. (2007). Links between pubertal timing, peer influences, and externalizing behaviors among urban students followed through middle school. *Journal of Adolescent Health, 40*(2), 181.e7–181.e13.

Lynskey, M. T., et al. (2007). Stimulant use and symptoms of abuse/dependence: Epidemiology and associations with cannabis use—a twin study. *Drug and Alcohol Dependence, 86*(2–3) 147–153.

Lyon, G. R., Shaywitz, S. E., & Shaywitz, B. A. (2003). A definition of dyslexia. *Annals of Dyslexia, 53,* 1–14.

Maccoby, E. E. (1990). The role of gender identity and gender constancy in sex-differentiated development. In D. Schrader (Ed.), *New directions for child development,* no. 47, *The legacy of Lawrence Kohlberg.* San Francisco: Jossey-Bass.

Maccoby, E. E. (2000). Perspectives on gender development. *International Journal of Behavioral Development, 24*(4), 398–406.

Maccoby, E. E. (2002). Parenting effects: Issues and controversies. In J. G. Borkowski et al. (Eds.), *Parenting and the child's world: Influences on academic, intellectual, and social-emotional development* (pp. 35–46). Mahwah, NJ: Erlbaum.

Maccoby, E. E., & Jacklin, C. N. (1974). *The psychology of sex differences.* Stanford, CA: Stanford University Press.

Macfarlane, A. (1975). Olfaction in the development of social preferences in the human neonate. In M. A. Hofer (Ed.), *Parent–infant interaction*. Amsterdam: Elsevier.

Macfarlane, A. (1977). *The psychology of childbirth*. Cambridge, MA: Harvard University Press.

Mackic-Magyar, J., & McCracken, J. (2004). Review of autism spectrum disorders: A research review for practitioners. *Journal of Child and Adolescent Psychopharmacology, 14*(1), 17–18.

Maclean, A. M., Walker, L. J., & Matsuba, M. K. (2004). Transcendence and the moral self: Identity integration, religion, and moral life. *Journal for the Scientific Study of Religion, 43*(3), 429–437.

Madon, S., et al. (2001). Am I as you see me or do you see me as I am? Self-fulfilling prophecies and self-verification. *Personality and Social Psychology Bulletin, 27*(9), 1214–1224.

Mahler, M. S., Pine, F., & Bergman, A. (1975). *The psychological birth of the human infant: Symbiosis and individuation*. New York: Basic Books.

Maimburg, R. D., & Væth, M. (2006). Perinatal risk factors and infantile autism. *Acta Psychiatrica Scandinavica, 114*(4), 257–264.

Malinosky-Rummell, R., & Hansen, D. H. (1993). Long-term consequences of childhood physical abuse. *Psychological Bulletin, 114*, 68–79.

Malone, P. S., et al. (2004). Divorce and child behavior problems: Applying latent change score models to life event data. *Structural Equation Modeling, 11*(3), 401–423.

Maluccio, A. N., & Ainsworth, F. (2003). Drug use by parents: A challenge for family reunification practice. *Children and Youth Services Review, 25*(7), 511–533.

Mandler, J. M. (1990). Recall and its verbal expression. In R. Fivush & J. A. Hudson (Eds.), *Knowing and remembering in young children*. Cambridge: Cambridge University Press.

Maneschi, M. L., Maddalena, F., & Bersani, G. (2006). The role of genetic factors in developmental dyslexia. Convergence between schizophrenia and other psychiatric disorders. *Rivista di Psichiatria, 41*(2), 81–92.

Maratsos, M. P. (2007). Commentary. *Monographs of the Society for Research in Child Development, 72*(1), 121–126.

Marcia, J. E. (1991). Identity and self-development. In R. M. Lerner, A. C. Petersen, & J. Brooks-Gunn (Eds.), *Encyclopedia of adolescence*. New York: Garland.

Marcovitch, S., & Zelazo, P. D. (2006). The influence of number of A trials on 2-year-olds' behavior in two A-not-B-type search tasks: A test of the hierarchical competing systems model. *Journal of Cognition and Development, 7*(4), 477–501.

Marean, G. C., Werner, L. A., & Kuhl, P. K. (1992). Vowel categorization by very young infants. *Developmental Psychology, 28*, 396–405.

Marsiglio, W. (2004). When stepfathers claim stepchildren: A conceptual analysis. *Journal of Marriage and Family, 66*(1), 22–39.

Martell, C. R. (2008). Lesbian, gay, and bisexual women and men. In M. A. Whisman (Ed.), *Adapting cognitive therapy for depression: Managing complexity and comorbidity* (pp. 373–393). New York: Guilford.

Martin, C. L., & Ruble, D. (2004). Children's search for gender cues: Cognitive perspectives on gender development. *Current Directions in Psychological Science, 13*(2), 67–70.

Martin, C. L., Ruble, D. N., & Szkrybalo, J. (2002). Cognitive theories of early gender development. *Psychological Bulletin, 128*(6), 903–933.

Masi, G., Mucci, M., & Millepiedi, S. (2001). Separation anxiety disorder in children and adolescents: Epidemiology, diagnosis, and management. *CNS Drugs, 15*(2), 93–104.

Maternity Center Association. (2004, April). *What every pregnant woman needs to know about cesarean section*. New York: MCA.

Mathews, T. J., & MacDorman, M. F. (2007). Infant mortality statistics from the 2004 period linked birth/infant death data set. *National Vital Statistics Reports, 55*(14). Hyattsville, MD: National Center for Health Statistics.

Matlin, M. W. (2008). *The psychology of women* (8th ed.). Belmont, CA: Thomson/Wadsworth.

Matthews, J. (1990). Drawing and individual development. In R. M. Thomas (Ed.), *The encyclopedia of human development and education: Theory, research, and studies*. Oxford: Pergamon.

Maurer, D. M., & Maurer, C. E., (1976, October). Newborn babies see better than you think. *Psychology Today*, pp. 85–88.

Mazei-Robison, M. S., Couch, R. S., Shelton, R. C., Stein, M. A., & Blakely, R. D. (2005). Sequence variation in the human dopamine transporter gene in children with attention deficit hyperactivity disorder. *Neuropharmacology, 49*(6), 724–736.

McCall, R. B., Applebaum, M. I., & Hogarty, P. S. (1973). Developmental changes in mental performance. *Monographs of the Society for Research in Child Development, 38*(3, Serial No. 150).

McCartney, K., Owen, M. T., Booth, C. L., Clarke-Stewart, K. A., & Vandell, D. L. (2004). Testing a maternal attachment model of behavior problems in early childhood. *Journal of Child Psychology and Psychiatry, 45*(4), 765–778.

McClellan, J. M., & Werry, J. S. (2003). Evidence-based treatments in child and adolescent psychiatry: An inventory. *Journal of the American Academy of Child and Adolescent Psychiatry, 42*(12), 1388–1400.

McCrae, R. R., et al. (2000). Nature over nurture: Temperament, personality, and life span development. *Journal of Personality and Social Psychology, 78*(1), 173–186.

McDevitt, T. M., & Ormrod, J. E. (2002). *Child development and education*. Upper Saddle River, NJ: Prentice Hall.

McDonough, L. (2002). Basic-level nouns: First learned but misunderstood. *Journal of Child Language, 29*(2), 357–377.

McEwan, M. H., Dihoff, R. E., & Brosvic, G. M. (1991). Early infant crawling experience is reflected in later motor skill development. *Perceptual and Motor Skills, 72*, 75–79.

McGlaughlin, A., & Grayson, A. (2001). Crying in the first year of infancy: Patterns and prevalence. *Journal of Reproductive and Infant Psychology, 19*(1), 47–59.

McGrath, M., et al. (2005). Early precursors of low attention and hyperactivity in a preterm sample at age four. *Issues in Comprehensive Pediatric Nursing, 28*(1), 1–15.

McHale, S. M., Kim, J.-Y., & Whiteman, S. D. (2006). Sibling relationships in childhood and adolescence. In P. Noller & J. A. Feeney (Eds.), *Close relationships: Functions, forms and processes* (pp. 127–149). New York: Psychology Press/Taylor & Francis.

McIlvane, W. J., & Dube, W. V. (2003). Stimulus control topography coherence theory: Foundations and extensions. *Behavior Analyst, 26*(2), 195–213.

McManus, C. (2003). Right hand, left hand: The origins of asymmetry in brains, bodies, atoms and cultures. *Cortex, 39*(2), 348–350.

McManus, I. C., et al. (1988). The development of handedness in children. *British Journal of Developmental Psychology, 6*, 257–273.

Meaney, K. S., Dornier, L. A., & Owens, M. S. (2002). Sex-role stereotyping for selected sport and physical activities across age groups. *Perceptual and Motor Skills, 94*(3), 743–749.

Meier, B. P., Robinson, M. D., & Wilkowski, B. M. (2006). Turning the other cheek: Agreeableness and the regulation of aggression-related primes. *Psychological Science, 17*(2), 136–142.

Meldrum, M. L. (2003). A capsule history of pain management. *Journal of the American Medical Association, 290*, 2470–2475.

Mellon, M. W. (2006). Enuresis and encopresis. In G. G. Bea & K. M. Minke (Eds.), *Children's needs III: Development, prevention, and intervention* (pp. 1041–1053). Washington, DC: National Association of School Psychologists.

Mellon, M. W., & Houts, A. C. (2006). Nocturnal enuresis. In J. E. Fisher & W. T. O'Donohue (Eds.), *Practitioner's guide to evidence-based psychotherapy* (pp. 432–441). New York: Springer Science + Business Media.

Meltzoff, A. N. (1988). Infant imitation after a 1-week delay: Long-term memory for novel acts and multiple stimuli. *Developmental Psychology, 24*(4), 470-476.

Meltzoff, A. N., & Prinz, W. (Eds.). (2002). *The imitative mind: Development, evolution, and brain bases*. New York: Cambridge University Press.

Mendle, J., et al. (2006). Family structure and age at menarche: A children-of-twins approach. *Developmental Psychology, 42*(3), 533–542.

Merrill, L. L., Crouch, J. L., Thomsen, C. J., & Guimond, J. M. (2004). Risk for intimate partner violence and child physical abuse: Psychosocial characteristics of multi-risk male and female Navy recruits. *Child Maltreatment: Journal of the American Professional Society on the Abuse of Children, 9*(1), 18–29.

Metcalfe, J. S., et al. (2005). Development of somatosensory-motor integration: An event-related analysis of infant posture in the first year of independent walking. *Developmental Psychobiology, 46*(1), 19–35.

Metzger, K. L., et al. (2007). Effects of nicotine vary across two auditory evoked potentials in the mouse. *Biological Psychiatry, 61*(1), 23–30.

Meyer, S., & Shore, C. (2001). Children's understanding of dreams as mental states. *Dreaming, 11*(4), 179–194.

Miklos, E. A., Brahler, C. J., Baer, J. T., & Dolan, P. (2004). Dietary deficiencies and excesses: A sample of African American mothers and daughters eligible for nutrition assistance programs. *Family and Community Health, 27*(2), 123–129.

Milgram, R. M., & Livne, N. L. (2006). Research on creativity in Israel: A chronicle of theoretical and empirical development. In J. C. Kaufman & R. J. Sternberg (Eds.), *The international handbook of creativity* (pp. 307–336). New York: Cambridge University Press.

Miller, A. L., Rathus, J. H., & Linehan, M. M. (2007). *Dialectical behavior therapy with suicidal adolescents.* New York: Guilford Press.

Miller, C. F., Trautner, H. M., & Ruble, D. N. (2006). The role of gender stereotypes in children's preferences and behavior. In L. Balter & C. S. Tamis-LeMonda (Eds.), *Child psychology: A handbook of contemporary issues* (2nd ed., pp. 293–323). New York: Psychology Press.

Miller, G. A. (1956). The magical number seven, plus or minus two: Some limits on our capacity to process information. *Psychological Review, 63,* 81–97.

Miller, J. G. (1994). Cultural diversity in the morality of caring: Individually-oriented versus duty-based interpersonal moral codes. *Cross-Cultural Research, 28,* 3–39.

Miller, J. G., & Bersoff, D. M. (1992). Culture and moral judgment: How are conflicts between justice and interpersonal responsibilities resolved? *Journal of Personality and Social Psychology, 62,* 541–554.

Miller, S. M., Boyer, B. A., & Rodoletz, M. (1990). Anxiety in children: Nature and development. In M. Lewis & S. M. Miller (Eds.), *Handbook of developmental psychopathology.* New York: Plenum.

Miranda, A., & Presentacion, M. J. (2000). Efectos de un tratamiento cognitivoconductual en ninos con trastorno por deficit de atencion con hiperactividad, agresivos y no agresivos: Cambio clinicamente significativo. *Infancia y Aprendizaje, 92,* 51–70.

Mischo, C. (2004). Fördert Gruppendiskussion die Perspektiven-Koordination? *Zeitschrift für Entwicklungspsychologie und Pädagogische Psychologie, 36*(1), 30–37.

Mitchell, A. L. (2006). Medical consequences of cocaine. *Journal of Addictions Nursing, 17*(4), 249.

Moens, E., Braet, C., & Soetens, B. (2007). Observation of family functioning at mealtime: A comparison between families of children with and without overweight. *Journal of Pediatric Psychology, 32*(1), 52–63.

Molfese, V. J., DiLalla, L. F., & Bunce, D. (1997). Prediction of the intelligence test scores of 3- to 8-year-old children by home environment, socioeconomic status, and biomedical risks. *Merrill–Palmer Quarterly, 43*(2), 219–234.

Molinari, L., & Corsaro, W. A. (2000). Le relazioni amicali nella scuola dell'infanzia e nella scuola elementare: Uno studio longitudinale. *Eta Evolutiva, 67,* 40–51.

Montemayor, R., & Eisen, M. (1977). The development of self-conceptions from childhood to adolescence. *Developmental Psychology, 13,* 314–319.

Moore, L. L. et al. (1991). Influence of parents' physical activity levels on activity levels of young children. *Journal of Pediatrics, 118,* 215-219.

Morelli, G. A., Oppenheim, D., Rogoff, B., & Goldsmith, D. (1992). Cultural variation in infants' sleeping arrangements: Questions of independence. *Developmental Psychology, 28,* 604–613.

Morley, J. E., & Perry, H. M., III (2003). Androgens and women at the menopause and beyond. *Journals of Gerontology, Biological Sciences and Medical Sciences, 58A*(5), 409–416.

Morrell, J., & Steele, H. (2003). The role of attachment security, temperament, maternal perception, and care-giving behavior in persistent infant sleeping problems. *Infant Mental Health Journal, 24*(5), 447–468.

Morton, S. M. B. (2006). Maternal nutrition and fetal growth and development. In P. Gluckman & M. Hanson (Eds.), *Developmental origins of health and disease* (pp. 98–129). New York: Cambridge University Press.

Moses, L. J., & Flavell, J. H. (1990). Inferring false beliefs from actions and reactions. *Child Development, 61,* 929–945.

Mosher, W. D., Chandra, A., & Jones, J. (2005). *Sexual behavior and selected health measures: men and women 1–B 44 years of age, United States, 2002. Advance data from vital and health statistics* (CDC Report No. 362, Figs. 2 and 3). Washington, DC: National Center for Health Statistics.

Mueller, R., Pierce, K., Ambrose, J. B., Allen, G., & Courchesne, E. (2001). Atypical patterns of cerebral motor activation in autism: A functional magnetic resonance study. *Biological Psychiatry, 49*(8) 665–676.

Mueller, U., Overton, W. F., & Reene, K. (2001). Development of conditional reasoning: A longitudinal study. *Journal of Cognition and Development, 2*(1), 27–49.

Mueller, U., Sokol, B., & Overton, W. F. (1999). Developmental sequences in class reasoning and propositional reasoning. *Journal of Experimental Child Psychology, 74*(2), 69–106.

Munroe, R. H., Shimmin, H. S., & Munroe, R. L. (1984). Gender role understanding and sex role preference in four cultures. *Developmental Psychology, 20,* 673–682.

Muris, P., Bodden, D., Merckelbach, H., Ollendick, T. H., & King, N. (2003). Fear of the beast: A prospective study on the effects of negative information on childhood fear. *Behaviour Research and Therapy, 41*(2), 195–208.

Nadeau, L., et al. (2003). Extremely premature and very low birthweight infants: A double hazard population? *Social Development, 12*(2), 235–248.

Nagin, D. S., & Tremblay, R. E. (2001). Parental and early childhood predictors of persistent physical aggression in boys from kindergarten to high school. *Archives of General Psychiatry, 58*(4), 389–394.

Narusyte, J., et al. (2008). Testing different types of genotype–environment correlation: An extended children-of-twins model. *Developmental Psychology, 44*(6), 1591–1603.

National Center for Children in Poverty. (2004). *Low-income children in the United States.* Retrieved from http://cpmcnet.columbia.edu/dept/nccp/

National Center for Education Statistics. (2007a, June). Dropout rates in the United States: 2005. Retrieved July 20, 2007, from http://nces.ed.gov/pubs2007/dropout05/

National Center for Education Statistics. (2007b). *2005–06 integrated postsecondary education data system (IPEDS).* Retrieved January 1, 2009, from http://nces.ed.gov/programs/digest/d07/tables/dt07_265.asp?referrer=list

National Center for Health Statistics. (2006). *Infant mortality statistics from the 2001 period linked birth/infant death data set. NVSR, 52*(2).

National Center for Health Statistics, Centers for Disease Prevention and Control. (2008). NCHS data on adolescent health. Retrieved January 6, 2009, from http://www.cdc.gov/nchs/data/infosheets/inforsheet_adoleshealth.pdf

National Center for Injury Prevention and Control, Office of Statistics and Programming, Centers for Disease Control and Prevention. (2007a, March 29). National Center for Health Statistics (NCHS), National Vital Statistics System. Retrieved May 7, 2007, from http://webappa.cdc.gov/cgi-bin/broker.exe

National Center for Injury Prevention and Control. (2007b, July 11). Suicide: Fact sheet. Retrieved from http://www.cdc.gov/ncipc/factsheets/suifacts.htm

National Guideline Clearinghouse. (2007). Use of clomiphene citrate in women. Retrieved February 6, 2007, from http://www.guideline.gov/summary/summary.aspx?ss=15&doc_id=4843&nbr=3484. Last updated January 29, 2007.

National Institute on Alcohol Abuse and Alcoholism [NIAAA]. (2005). Cage Questionnaire. Retrieved from http://pubs.niaaa.hih.gov/publications/Assessing%20Alcohol/InstrumentPDFs/16_CAGE.pdf

National Institute of Child Health and Human Development. (2006). Safe sleep for your baby: Ten ways to reduce the risk of sudden infant death syndrome (SIDS). Retrieved December 25, 2008, from http://www.nichd.nih.gov/publications/pubs/safe_sleep_gen.cfm#risk

National Institutes of Health. (2002). Available at http://cerhr.niehs.nih.gov/genpub/topics/vitamin-a-ccae.html

National Library of Medicine (2009, Feb 19). *Miscarriage.* Retrieved July, 1, 2009 from http://www.nlm.nih.gov/medlineplus/ency/article/001488.htm

National Library of Medicine. (2007, January 11). *Miscarriage.* Retrieved February 23, 2007, from http://www.nlm.nih.gov/medlineplus/ency/article/001488.htm

National Library of Medicine. National Institutes of Health. (2007). Infant and toddler nutrition. *MedlinePlus.* Retrieved April 10, 2007, from http://www.nlm.nih.gov/medlineplus/infantandtoddlernutrition.html

National Sleep Foundation. (2007). Children's sleep habits. Retrieved from http://www.sleepfoundation.org/site/c.huIXKjM0IxF/b.2453615/apps/nl/content3.asp?content_id={5239AA1B-DB37-42DA-B1ED-436FA086D3AC}&notoc=1

National Sleep Foundation. (2009). Children's sleep habits. Retrieved January 6, 2009, from http://www.sleepfoundation.org/site/c.huIXKjM0IxF/b.2419295/k.5AAB/Childrens_Sleep_Habits.htm

Natsopoulos, D., Kiosseoglou, G., & Xeromeritou, A. (1992). Handedness and spatial ability in children: Further support for Geschwind's hypothesis of "pathology of superiority" and for Annett's theory of intelligence. *Genetic, Social, and General Psychology Monographs, 118*(1) 103–126.

Nauta, M. M. (2007). Career interests, self-efficacy, and personality as antecedents of career exploration. *Journal of Career Assessment, 15*(2), 162–180.

Nduati, R., et al. (2000). Effect of breastfeeding and formula feeding on transmission of HIV-1. *Journal of the American Medical Association, 283,* 1167–1174.

Neisser, U., et al. (1996). Intelligence: Knowns and unknowns. *American Psychologist, 51,* 77–101.

Nelson, C. A., & Luciana, M. (Eds.). (2001). *Handbook of developmental cognitive neuroscience.* Cambridge, MA: MIT Press.

Nelson, C. A., & Ludemann, P. M. (1989). Past, current, and future trends in infant face perception research. *Canadian Journal of Psychology, 43,* 183–198.

Nelson, C. A., de Haan, M., & Thomas, K. M. (2006). *Neuroscience of cognitive development: The role of experience and the developing brain.* Hoboken, NJ: Wiley.

Nelson, K. (1973). Structure and strategy in learning to talk. *Monographs of the Society for Research in Child Development, 38*(1–2, Serial No, 149).

Nelson, K. (1981). Individual differences in language development: Implications for development of language. *Developmental Psychology, 17,* 170–187.

Nelson, K. (1990). Remembering, forgetting, and childhood amnesia. In R. Fivush & J. A. Hudson (Eds.), *Knowing and remembering in young children.* Cambridge: Cambridge University Press.

Nelson, K. (1993). Events, narratives, memory: What develops? In C. A. Nelson (Ed.), *Minnesota symposia on child psychology: Vol. 26. Memory and affect in development.* Hillsdale, NJ: Erlbaum.

Nelson, K. (2005). Cognitive functions of language in early childhood. In B. D. Homer & C. S. Tamis-LeMonda (Eds.), *The development of social cognition and communication* (pp. 7–28). Mahwah, NJ: Erlbaum.

Nelson, K. (2006). Advances in pragmatic developmental theory: The case of language acquisition. *Human Development, 49*(3), 184–188.

Nelson, K., & Fivush, R. (2004). The emergence of autobiographical memory: A social cultural developmental theory. *Psychological Review, 111*(2), 486–511.

Nesdale, D., & Lambert, A. (2007). Effects of experimentally manipulated peer rejection on children's negative affect, self-esteem, and maladaptive social behavior. *International Journal of Behavioral Development, 31*(2), 115–122.

Newburn-Cook, C. V., et al. (2002). Where and to what extent is prevention of low birth weight possible? *Western Journal of Nursing Research, 24*(8), 887–904.

Newman, R., Ratner, N. B., Jusczyk, A. M., Jusczyk, P. W., & Dow, K. A. (2006). Infants' early ability to segment the conversational speech signal predicts later language development: A retrospective analysis. *Developmental Psychology, 42*(4), 643–655.

Nielsen, S. J., & Popkin, B. M. (2003). Patterns and trends in food portion sizes, 1977–1998. *Journal of the American Medical Association, 289*(4), 450–453.

Nielsen, S., & Palmer, B. (2003). Diagnosing eating disorders: AN, BN, and the others. *Acta Psychiatrica Scandinavica, 108*(3), 161–162.

Niemeier, H. M., Raynor, H. A., Lloyd-Richardson, E. E., Rogers, M. L., & Wing, R. R. (2006). Fast food consumption and breakfast skipping: Predictors of weight gain from adolescence to adulthood in a nationally representative sample. *Journal of Adolescent Health, 39*(6), 842–849.

Nigg, J. T. (2001). Is ADHD a disinhibitory disorder? *Psychological Bulletin, 127*(5), 571–598.

Nigg, J. T., Goldsmith, H. H., & Sachek, J. (2004). Temperament and attention deficit hyperactivity disorder: The development of a multiple pathway model. *Journal of Clinical Child and Adolescent Psychology, 33*(1), 42–53.

Nigg, J. T., Hinshaw, S. P., & Huang-Pollock, C. (2006). Disorders of attention and impulse regulation. In D. Cicchetti & D. J. Cohen (Eds.), *Developmental psychopathology: Vol. 3. Risk, disorder, and adaptation* (2nd ed., pp. 358–403). Hoboken, NJ: Wiley.

Nock, M. K., Kazdin, A. E., Hiripi, E., & Kessler, R. C. (2006). Prevalence, subtypes, and correlates of DSM-IV conduct disorder in the National Comorbidity Survey Replication. *Psychological Medicine, 36,* 699–710.

Nolen-Hoeksema, S., Stice, E., Wade, E., & Bohon, C. (2007). Reciprocal relations between rumination and bulimic, substance abuse, and depressive symptoms in female adolescents. *Journal of Abnormal Psychology, 116*(1), 198–207.

Nomaguchi, K. M. (2006). Maternal employment, nonparental care, mother–child interactions, and child outcomes during preschool years. *Journal of Marriage and Family, 68*(5), 1341–1369.

Nonaka, A. M. (2004). The forgotten endangered languages: Lessons on the importance of remembering from Thailand's Ban Khor sign language. *Language in Society, 33*(5), 737–767.

Nonnemaker, J. M., & Homsi, G. (2007). Measurement properties of the Fagerström Test for nicotine dependence adapted for use in an adolescent sample. *Addictive Behaviors, 32*(1), 181–186.

Norlander, T., Erixon, A., & Archer, T. (2000). Psychological androgyny and creativity: Dynamics of gender-role and personality trait. *Social Behavior and Personality, 28*(5), 423–435.

Nowinski, J. (2007). *The identity trap: Saving our teens from themselves.* New York: AMACOM.

Nucci, L. P. (2002). The development of moral reasoning. In U. Goswami (Ed.), *Blackwell handbook of childhood cognitive development* (pp. 303–325). Malden, MA: Blackwell.

Nyunt, A., et al. (2005). Androgen status in healthy premenopausal women with loss of libido. *Journal of Sex & Marital Therapy, 31*(1), 73–80.

Oates, J., & Messer, D. (2007). Growing up with TV. *The Psychologist, 20*(1), 30–32.

O'Boyle, M. W., & Benbow, C. P. (1990). Handedness and its relationship to ability and talent. In S. Coren (Ed.), *Left-handedness: Behavior implications and anomalies.* Amsterdam: North-Holland.

O'Dea, J. A. (2006). Self-concept, self-esteem and body weight in adolescent females: A three-year longitudinal study. *Journal of Health Psychology, 11*(4), 599–611.

O'Donnell, L., et al. (2003). Long-term influence of sexual norms and attitudes on timing of sexual initiation among urban minority youth. *Journal of School Health, 23*(2), 68–75.

Oettinger, G. (1999). Does high school employment affect high school academic performance? *Industrial and Labor Relations Review, 53*(1), 136–151.

Office of National Statistics. (2006). Available at http://www.multiplebirths.org.uk/media.asp. Accessed February 6, 2007.

Ohnishi, T., Matsuda, H., Hirakata, M., & Ugawa, Y. (2006). Navigation ability dependent neural activation in the human brain: An fMRI study. *Neuroscience Research, 55*(4), 361–369.

O'Keeffe, M. J., O'Callaghan, M., Williams, G. M., Najman, J. M., & Bor, W. (2003). Learning, cognitive, and attentional problems in adolescents born small for gestational age. *Pediatrics, 112*(2), 301–307.

O'Neill, D. K., & Chong, S. C. F. (2001). Preschool children's difficulty understanding the types of information obtained through the five senses. *Child Development, 72*(3), 803–815.

O'Neill, D. K., & Gopnik, A. (1991). Young children's ability to identify the sources of their beliefs. *Developmental Psychology, 27,* 390–397.

Oliver, M. B., & Hyde, J. S. (1993). Gender differences in sexuality: A meta-analysis. *Psychological Bulletin, 114*(1), 29–51.

Ollendick, T. H., & King, N. J. (1991). Origins of childhood fears: An evaluation of Rachman's theory of teen-acquisition. *Behavior Research and Therapy, 29,* 117–123.

Olson, S. L., Bates, J. E., Sandy, J. M., & Lanthier, R. (2000). Early developmental precursors of externalizing behavior in middle childhood and adolescence. *Journal of Abnormal Child Psychology, 28*(2), 119–133.

Omori, M., & Ingersoll, G. M. (2005). Health-endangering behaviours among Japanese college students: A test of psychosocial model of risk-taking behaviours. *Journal of Adolescence, 28*(1), 17–33.

Örnkloo, H., & von Hofsten, C. (2007). Fitting objects into holes: On the development of spatial cognition skills. *Developmental Psychology, 43*(2), 404–416.

Orstavik, R. E., Kendler, K. S., Czajkowski, N., Tambs, K., & Reichborn-Kjennerud, T. (2007). Genetic and environmental contributions to depressive personality disorder in a population-based sample of Norwegian twins. *Journal of Affective Disorders, 99*(1–3), 181–189.

Ortega, V., Ojeda, P., Sutil, F., & Sierra, J. C. (2005). Culpabilidad sexual en adolescentes: Estudio de algunos factores relacionados. *Anales de Psicología, 21*(2), 268–275.

O'Shea, R. P., & Corballis, P. M. (2005). Binocular rivalry in the divided brain. In D. Alais & R. Blake (Eds.), *Binocular rivalry* (pp. 301–315). Cambridge, MA: MIT Press.

Oster, H. (2005). The repertoire of infant facial expressions: An ontogenetic perspective. In J. Nadel & D. Muir (Eds.), *Emotional development: Recent research advances* (pp. 261–292). New York: Oxford University Press.

O'Sullivan, L. F., Meyer-Bahlburg, H. F. L., & Watkins, B. X. (2000). Social cognitions associated with pubertal development in a sample of urban, low-income, African-American and Latina girls and mothers. *Journal of Adolescent Health, 27*(4), 227–235.

Ouellette, G. P. (2006). What's meaning got to do with it: The role of vocabulary in word reading and reading comprehension. *Journal of Educational Psychology, 98*(3), 554–566.

Oztop, E., Kawato, M., & Arbib, M. (2006). Mirror neurons and imitation: A computationally guided review. *Neural Networks, 19*(3), 254–271.

Paavola, L., Kemppinen, K., Kumpulainen, K., Moilanen, I., & Ebeling, H. (2006). Maternal sensitivity, infant co-operation and early linguistic development: Some predictive relations. *European Journal of Developmental Psychology, 3*(1), 13–30.

Page, K. (1999, May 16). The graduate. *The Washington Post Magazine, 152,* 18, 20.

Palmer, E. J. (2005). The relationship between moral reasoning and aggression, and the implications for practice. *Psychology, Crime & Law, 11*(4), 353–361.

Palmer, E. J., & Hollin, C. R. (2001). Sociomoral reasoning, perceptions of parenting and self-reported delinquency in adolescents. *Applied Cognitive Psychology, 15*(1), 85–100.

Palmer, E. L. (2003). Realities and challenges in the rapidly changing televisual media landscape. In E. L. Palmer & B. M. Young (Eds.), *The faces of televisual media: Teaching, violence, selling to children* (2nd ed., pp. 361–377). Mahwah, NJ: Erlbaum.

Papaioannou, A., Bebetsos, E., Theodorakis, Y., Christodoulidis, T., & Kouli, O. (2006). Causal relationships of sport and exercise involvement with goal orientations, perceived competence and intrinsic motivation in physical education: A longitudinal study. *Journal of Sports Sciences, 24*(4), 367–382.

Parke, R. D., & Buriel, R. (2006). Socialization in the family: Ethnic and ecological perspectives. In N. Eisenberg, W. Damon, & R. M. Lerner (Eds.), *Handbook of child psychology: Vol. 3. Social, emotional, and personality development* (6th ed., pp. 429–504). Hoboken, NJ: Wiley.

Parkes, A., Wight, D., Henderson, M., & Hart, G. (2007). Explaining associations between adolescent substance use and condom use. *Journal of Adolescent Health, 40*(2), 180. e1–180.e18.

Parsons, T. D., et al. (2004). Sex differences in mental rotation and spatial rotation in a virtual environment. *Neuropsychologia, 42*(4), 555–562.

Parten, M. B. (1932). Social participation among preschool children. *Journal of Abnormal and Social Psychology, 27,* 243–269.

Passell, P. (1992, August 9). Twins study shows school is a sound investment. *The New York Times,* p. A14.

Pastor, J., et al. (2007). Makin' homes: An urban girl thing. In B. J. R. Leadbeater & N. Way (Eds.), *Urban girls revisited: Building strengths* (pp. 75–96). New York: New York University Press.

Patenaude, J., Niyonsenga, T., & Fafard, D. (2003). Changes in students' moral development during medical school: A cohort study. *Canadian Medical Association Journal, 168*(7), 840–844.

Paterson, D. S., et al. (2006). Multiple serotonergic brainstem abnormalities in sudden infant death syndrome. *Journal of the American Medical Association, 296,* 2124–2132.

Patock-Peckham, J. A., & Morgan-Lopez, A. A. (2006). College drinking behaviors: Mediational links between parenting styles, impulse control, and alcohol-related outcomes. *Psychology of Addictive Behaviors, 20*(2), 117–125.

Patterson, C. J. (2006). Children of lesbian and gay parents. *Current Directions in Psychological Science, 15*(5), 241–244.

Patterson, G. R. (2005). The next generation of PMTO models. *The Behavior Therapist, 28*(2), 27–33.

Patterson, M. M., & Bigler, R. S. (2006). Preschool children's attention to environmental messages about groups: Social categorization and the origins of intergroup bias. *Child Development, 77*(4), 847–860.

Pauli-Pott, U., Mertesacker, B., & Beckmann, D. (2003). Ein Fragebogen zur Erfassung des frühkindlichen Temperaments im Elternurteil. *Zeitschrift für Kinder- und Jugendpsychiatrie und Psychotherapie, 31*(2), 99–110.

Paulussen-Hoogeboom, M. C., Stams, G. J. J. M., Hermanns, J. M. A., & Peetsma, T. T. D. (2007). Child negative emotionality and parenting from infancy to preschool: A meta-analytic review. *Developmental Psychology, 43*(2), 438–453.

Paus, T., et al. (1999). Structural maturation of neural pathways in children and adolescents: In vivo study. *Science, 283*(5409), 1908–1911.

Paxton, S. J., Neumark-Sztainer, D., Hannan, P. J., & Eisenberg, M. E. (2006). Body dissatisfaction prospectively predicts depressive mood and low self-esteem in adolescent girls and boys. *Journal of Clinical Child and Adolescent Psychology, 35*(4), 539–549.

Paxton, S. J., Norris, M., Wertheim, E. H., Durkin, S. J., & Anderson, J. (2005). Body dissatisfaction, dating, and importance of thinness to attractiveness in adolescent girls. *Sex Roles, 53*(9–10), 663–675.

Pedersen, S., Vitaro, F., Barker, E. D., & Borge, A. I. H. (2007). The timing of middle-childhood peer rejection and friendship: Linking early behavior to early-adolescent adjustment. *Child Development, 78*(4), 1037–1051.

Peeters, M. W., et al. (2005). Genetic and environmental causes of tracking in explosive strength during adolescence. *Behavior Genetics, 35*(5), 551–563.

Pei, M., Matsuda, K., Sakamoto, H., & Kawata, M. (2006). Intrauterine proximity to male fetuses affects the morphology of the sexually dimorphic nucleus of the preoptic area in the adult rat brain. *European Journal of Neuroscience, 23*(5), 1234–1240.

Pelphrey, K. A., et al. (2004). Development of visuospatial short-term memory in the second half of the first year. *Developmental Psychology, 40*(5), 836–851.

Pemberton, E. F. (1990). Systematic errors in children's drawings. *Cognitive Development, 5,* 395–404.

Penn, H. E. (2006). Neurobiological correlates of autism: A review of recent research. *Child Neuropsychology, 12*(1), 57–79.

Peplau, L. A. (2003). Human sexuality: How do men and women differ? *Current Directions in Psychological Science, 12*(2), 37–40.

Pereira, B., Mendonça, D., Neto, C., Valente, L., & Smith, P. K. (2004). Bullying in Portuguese schools. *School Psychology International, 25*(2), 241–254.

Perren, S., & Alsaker, F. D. (2006). Social behavior and peer relationships of victims, bullyvictims, and bullies in kindergarten. *Journal of Child Psychology and Psychiatry, 47*(1), 45–57.

Perrin, M. C., Brown, A. S., & Malaspina, D. (2007, August 21). Aberrant epigenetic regulation could explain the relationship of paternal age to schizophrenia. *Schizophrenia Bulletin online.* Retrieved from http:// schizophreniabulletin.oxfordjournals.org/cgi/content/abstract/sbm093v1

Persson, G. E. B. (2005). Developmental perspectives on prosocial and aggressive motives in preschoolers' peer interactions. *International Journal of Behavioral Development, 29*(1), 80–91.

Philip, J., et al. (2004). Late first-trimester invasive prenatal diagnostic results of an international randomized trial. *Obstetrics & Gynecology, 103*(6), 1164–1173.

Phillips, D. A., & Styfco, S. J. (2007). Child development research and public policy: Triumphs and setbacks on the way to maturity. In J. L. Aber et al. (Eds.), *Child development and social policy: Knowledge for action* (pp. 11–27). Washington, DC: American Psychological Association.

Phinney, J. S. (2006). Ethnic identity exploration in emerging adulthood. In J. J. Arnett & J. L. Tanner (Eds.), *Emerging adults in America: Coming of age in the 21st century* (pp. 117–134). Washington, DC: American Psychological Association.

Phinney, J. S., & Alipuria, L. L. (2006). Multiple social categorization and identity among multiracial, multiethnic, and multicultural individuals: Processes and implications. In R. J. Crisp & M. Hewstone (Eds.), *Multiple social categorization: Processes, models and applications* (pp. 211–238). New York: Psychology Press.

Phinney, J. S., & Ong, A. D. (2007). Conceptualization and measurement of ethnic identity: Current status and future directions. *Journal of Counseling Psychology, 54*(3), 271–281.

Phipps, M. G., Blume, J. D., & DeMonner, S. M. (2002). Young maternal age associated with increased risk of postneonatal death. *Obstetrics and Gynecology, 100,* 481–486.

Piaget, J. (1932). *The moral judgment of the child.* London: Kegan Paul.

Piaget, J. (1962). *Play, dreams, and imitation in childhood.* New York: Norton. (Original work published 1946).

Piaget, J. (1963). *The origins of intelligence in children.* New York: Norton. (Original work published 1936).

Piaget, J. (1972). Intellectual evolution from adolescence to adulthood. *Human Development, 15,* 1–12.

Piaget, J. (1976). *The grasp of consciousness: Action and concept in the young child.* Cambridge, MA: Harvard University Press.

Pichichero, M. E. (2006). Prevention of cervical cancer through vaccination of adolescents. *Clinical Pediatrics, 45*(5), 393–398.

Piek, J. P. (2006). *Infant motor development.* Champaign, IL: Human Kinetics.

Piek, J. P., Baynam, G. B., & Barrett, N. C. (2006). The relationship between fine and gross motor ability, self-perceptions and self-worth in children and adolescents. *Human Movement Science, 25*(1), 65–75.

Pierce, K. M., & Vandell, D. L. (2006). Child care. In G. G. Bear & K. M. Minke (Eds.), *Children's needs III: Development, prevention, and intervention* (pp. 721–732). Washington, DC: National Association of School Psychologists.

Pine, K. J., & Nash, A. (2002). Dear Santa: The effects of television advertising on young children. *International Journal of Behavioral Development, 26*(6), 529–539.

Pinker, S. (1994). *The language instinct*. New York: Morrow.

Pinker, S., & Jackendoff, R. (2005). The faculty of language: What's special about it? *Cognition, 95*(2), 201–236.

Pinkerton, S. D., Bogart, L. M., Cecil, H., & Abramson, P. R. (2002). Factors associated with masturbation in collegiate sample. *Journal of Psychology & Human Sexuality, 14*(2–3), 103–121.

Plomin, R. (Ed.). (2002). *Behavioral genetics in the postgenomic era*. Washington, DC: American Psychological Association.

Plomin, R., & Daniels, D. (1987). Why are children in the same family so different from one another? *Behavioral and Brain Sciences, 10*(1), 1-16.

Plomin, R., & Walker, S. O. (2003). Genetics and educational psychology. *British Journal of Educational Psychology, 73*(1), 3–14.

Plomin, R., Owen, M. J., & McGuffin, P. (1994). The genetic basis of complex human behaviors. *Science, 264*, 1733–1739.

Polivy, J., Herman, C. P., & Boivin, M. (2005). Eating disorders. In J. E. Maddux & B. A. Winstead (Eds.), *Psychopathology: Foundations for a contemporary understanding* (pp. 229–254). Mahwah, NJ: Erlbaum.

Popma, A., et al. (2007). Cortisol moderates the relationship between testosterone and aggression in delinquent male adolescents. *Biological Psychiatry, 61*(3), 405–411.

Porfeli, E. J. (2007). Work values system development during adolescence. *Journal of Vocational Behavior, 70*(1), 42–60.

Porfeli, E. J. (2008). The dynamic between work values and part-time work experiences across the high school years. *Journal of Vocational Behavior, 73*(1), 143–158.

Porter, R. H., Makin, J. W., Davis, L. B., & Christensen, K. M. (1992). Breast-fed infants respond to olfactory cues from their own mother and unfamiliar lactating females. *Infant Behavior and Development, 15*, 85–93.

Posey, D. J., et al. (2007). Positive effects of methylphenidate on inattention and hyperactivity in pervasive developmental disorders: An analysis of secondary measures. *Biological Psychiatry, 61*(4), 538–544.

Posner, M. I., & Rothbart, M. K. (2007). *Relating brain and mind. Educating the human brain*. Washington, DC: American Psychological Association.

Powlishta, K. K. (2004). Gender as a social category: Intergroup processes and gender-role development. In M. Bennett & F. Sani (Eds.), *The development of the social self* (pp. 103–133). New York: Psychology Press.

Powlishta, K. K., Sen, M. G., Serbin, L. A., Poulin-Dubois, D., & Eichstedt, J. A. (2001). From infancy through middle childhood: The role of cognitive and social factors in becoming gendered. In R. K. Unger (Ed.), *Handbook of the psychology of women and gender* (pp. 116–132). New York: Wiley.

Pratt, C., & Bryant, P. (1990). Young children understand that looking leads to knowing (so long as they are looking into a single barrel). *Child Development, 61*, 973–982.

Pressley, M., & Hilden, K. (2006). Cognitive strategies. In D. Kuhn, R. S. Siegler, W. Damon, & R. M. Lerner (Eds.), *Handbook of child psychology: Vol. 2. Cognition, perception, and language* (6th ed., pp. 511–556). Hoboken, NJ: Wiley.

Priner, R., Freeman, S., Perez, R., & Sohmer, H. (2003). The neonate has a temporary conductive hearing loss due to fluid in the middle ear. *Audiology & Neurotology, 8*(2), 100–110.

Provence, S., & Lipton, R. C. (1962). *Infants in institutions*. New York: International Universities Press.

Pugh, K. R., et al. (2000). The angular gyrus in developmental dyslexia: Task-specific differences in functional connectivity within posterior cortex. *Psychological Science, 11*(1), 51–56.

Pujol, J., et al. (2006). Myelination of language-related areas in the developing brain. *Neurology, 66*(3), 339–343.

Pulverman, R., Hirsh-Pasek, K., Golinkoff, R. M., Pruden, S., & Salkind, S. J. (2006). Conceptual foundations for verb learning: Celebrating the event. In K. Hirsh-Pasek & R. M. Golinkoff (Eds.), *Action meets word: How children learn verbs* (pp. 134–159). New York: Oxford University Press.

Raikes, H., et al. (2006). Mother–child book-reading in low-income families: Correlates and outcomes during the first three years of life. *Child Development, 77*(4), 924–953.

Ramey, C. T., Campbell, F. A., & Ramey, S. L. (1999). Early intervention: Successful pathways to improving intellectual development. *Developmental Neuropsychology, 16*(3) 385–392.

Randel, B., Stevenson, H. W., & Witruk, E. (2000). Attitudes, beliefs, and mathematics achievement of German and Japanese high school students. *International Journal of Behavioral Development, 24*(2), 190–198.

Rapin, I. (1997). Autism. *New England Journal of Medicine, 337*, 97–104.

Rathus, J. H., & Miller, A. L. (2002). Dialectical behavior therapy adapted for suicidal adolescents. *Suicide and Life-Threatening Behavior, 32*(2), 146–157.

Rathus, S. A., Nevid, J. S., & Fichner-Rathus, L. (2008). *Human sexuality in a world of diversity* (7th ed.). Boston: Allyn & Bacon.

Rebar, R. W., & DeCherney, A. H. (2004). Assisted reproductive technology in the United States. *New England Journal of Medicine, 350*(16), 1603–1604.

Reddy, L. A., & De Thomas, C. (2007). Assessment of attention-deficit/hyperactivity disorder with children. In S. R. Smith & L. Handler (Eds.), *The clinical assessment of children and adolescents: A practitioner's handbook* (pp. 365–387). Mahwah, NJ: Erlbaum.

Redgrave, G. W., Coughlin, J. W., Heinberg, L. J., & Guarda, A. S. (2007). First-degree relative history of alcoholism in eating disorder inpatients: Relationship to eating and substance use psychopathology. *Eating Behaviors, 8*(1), 15–22.

Reef, S., Zimmerman-Swain, L., & Coronado, V. (2004). *Disease description: Rubella is a viral illness caused by a toga virus of the genus* Rubivirus. Retrieved from http://www.cdc.gov/nip/diseases/rubella/default.htm

Rees, S., Harding, R., & Inder, T. (2006). The developmental environment and the origins of neurological disorders. In P. Gluckman & M. Hanson (Eds.), *Developmental origins of health and disease* (pp. 379–391). New York: Cambridge University Press.

Reichenberg, A., et al. (2006). Advancing paternal age and autism. *Archives of General Psychiatry, 63*(9), 1026–1032.

Reiff, M. I., & Mansoor, E. (2007). Journal article reviews: Attention-deficit/hyperactivity disorder. *Journal of Developmental & Behavioral Pediatrics, 28*(1), 71–72.

Reijneveld, S. A., et al. (2004). Infant crying and abuse. *Lancet, 364*(9442), 1340–1342.

Reis, O., & Youniss, J. (2004). Patterns in identity change and development in relationships with mothers and friends. *Journal of Adolescent Research, 19*(1), 31–44.

Reschly, A., & Christenson, S. L. (2006). School completion. In G. G. Bear & K. M. Minke (Eds.), *Children's needs, III: Development, prevention, and intervention* (pp. 103–113). Washington, DC: National Association of School Psychologists.

Rest, J. R. (1983). Morality. In P. H. Mussen (Ed.), *Handbook of child psychology: Vol. 3. Cognitive development*. New York: Wiley.

Rezvani, A. H., & Levin, E. D. (2001). Cognitive effects of nicotine. *Biological Psychiatry, 49*(3), 258–267.

Riala, K., et al. (2007). Heavy daily smoking among under 18-year-old psychiatric inpatients is associated with increased risk for suicide attempts. *European Psychiatry, 22*(4), 219–222.

Rice, C. E., et al. (2007). A public health collaboration for the surveillance of autism spectrum disorders. *Paediatric and Perinatal Epidemiology, 21*(2), 179–190.

Richards, H. C., Bear, G. G., Stewart, A. L., & Norman, A. D. (1992). Moral reasoning and classroom conduct: Evidence of a curvilinear relationship. *Merrill–Palmer Quarterly, 38*, 176–190.

Rizzolatti, G., Fadiga, L., Fogassi, L., & Gallese, V. (2002). From mirror neurons to imitation: Facts and speculations. In A. N. Meltzoff & W. Prinz (Eds.), *The imitative mind: Development, evolution, and brain bases*. New York: Cambridge University Press.

Robins Wahlin, T., Lundin, A., & Dear, K. (2007). Early cognitive deficits in Swedish gene carriers of Huntington's disease. *Neuropsychology, 21*(1), 31–44.

Roden, D. M. (2009). *Cardiovascular genetics and genomics*. Hoboken, NJ: Wiley-Blackwell.

Roebers, C. M., Moga, N., & Schneider, W. (2001). The role of accuracy motivation on children's and adults' event recall. *Journal of Experimental Child Psychology, 78*(4), 313–329.

Roeser, R. W., Peck, S. C., & Nasir, N. S. (2006). Self and identity processes in school motivation, learning, and achievement. In P. A. Alexander & P. H. Winne (Eds.), *Handbook of educational psychology* (pp. 391–424). Mahwah, NJ: Erlbaum.

Roffwarg, H. P., Muzio, J. N., & Dement, W. C. (1966). Ontogenetic development of the human sleep–dream cycle. *Science, 152*, 604–619.

Ronald, A., et al. (2006). Genetic heterogeneity between the three components of the autism spectrum: A twin study. *Journal of the American Academy of Child & Adolescent Psychiatry, 45*(6), 691–699.

Rondal, J. A., & Ling, L. (2006). Neurobehavioral specificity in Down's Syndrome. *Revista de Logopedia, Foniatría y Audiología, 26*(1), 12–19.

Roopnarine, J. L., Krishnakumar, A., Metindogan, A., & Evans, M. (2006). Links between parenting styles, parent–child academic interaction, parent–school interaction, and early academic skills and social behaviors in young children of English-speaking Caribbean immigrants. *Early Childhood Research Quarterly, 21*(2), 238–252.

Rose, A. J., Swenson, L. P., & Carlson, W. (2004). Friendships of aggressive youth: Considering the influences of being disliked and of being perceived as popular. *Journal of Experimental Child Psychology, 88*(1), 25–45.

Rose, S. A., Feldman, J. F., & Jankowski, J. J. (2001). Visual short-term memory in the first year of life: Capacity and recency effects. *Developmental Psychology, 37*(4), 539–549.

Rose, S. A., Feldman, J. F., & Jankowski, J. J. (2004). Infant visual recognition memory. *Developmental Review, 24*(1), 74–100.

Rose, S. A., Feldman, J. F., & Jankowski, J. J. (2005). The structure of infant cognition at 1 year. *Intelligence, 33*(3), 231–250.

Rose, S. A., Feldman, J. F., & Wallace, I. F. (1992). Infant information processing in relation to six-year cognitive outcomes. *Child Development, 63*, 1126–1141.

Rosenbaum, D. E. (2000, May 16). On left-handedness, its causes, and costs. *The New York Times*, pp. F1, F6.

Rosenblatt, J. S. (2007). Gilbert Gottlieb: Intermediator between psychology and evolutionary biology. *Developmental Psychobiology, 49*(8), 800-807.

Rosenstein, D., & Oster, H. (1988). Differential facial responses to four basic tastes. *Child Development, 59*, 1555–1568.

Rosenthal, R., & Jacobson, L. (1968). *Pygmalion in the classroom*. New York: Holt.

Ross, H., Ross, M., Stein, N., & Trabasso, T. (2006). How siblings resolve their conflicts: The importance of first offers, planning, and limited opposition. *Child Development, 77*(6), 1730–1745.

Rotenberg, K. J., et al. (2004). Cross-sectional and longitudinal relations among peer-reported trustworthiness, social relationships, and psychological adjustment in children and early adolescents from the United Kingdom and Canada. *Journal of Experimental Child Psychology, 88*(1), 46–67.

Rothbart, M. K., & Sheese, B. E. (2007). Temperament and emotion regulation. In J. J. Gross (Ed.), *Handbook of emotion regulation* (pp. 331–350). New York: Guilford.

Rothbart, M. K., Ellis, L. K., & Posner, M. I. (2004). Temperament and self-regulation. In R. F. Baumeister & K. D. Vohs (Eds.), *Handbook of self-regulation: Research, theory, and applications*. New York: Guilford.

Rottinghaus, P. J., Betz, N. E., & Borgen, F. H. (2003). Validity of parallel measures of vocational interests and confidence. *Journal of Career Assessment, 11*(4), 355–378.

Roulet-Perez, E., & Deonna, T. (2006). Autism, epilepsy, and EEG epileptiform activity. In R. Tuchman & I. Rapin (Eds.), *Autism: A neurological disorder of early brain development* (pp. 174–188). London: MacKeith Press.

Rovee-Collier, C. (1993). The capacity for long-term memory in infancy. *Current Directions in Psychological Science, 2*, 130–135.

Rowen, B. (1973). *The children we see*. New York: Holt, Rinehart & Winston.

Rubia, K., et al. (2006). Progressive increase of frontostriatal brain activation from childhood to adulthood during event- related tasks of cognitive control. *Human Brain Mapping, 27*(12), 973–993.

Rubin, K. H., Bukowski, W. M., & Parker, J. G. (2006). Peer interactions, relationships, and groups. In N. Eisenberg, W. Damon, & R. M. Lerner (Eds.), *Handbook of child psychology: Vol. 3. Social, emotional, and personality development* (pp. 571–645). Hoboken, NJ: Wiley.

Rubinstein, S., & Caballero, B. (2000). Is Miss America an undernourished role model? *Journal of the American Medical Association, 283*(12), 1569.

Ruble, D. N., Martin, C. L., & Berenbaum, S. A. (2006). Gender development. In N. Eisenberg, W. Damon, & R. M. Lerner (Eds.), *Handbook of child psychology: Vol. 3. Social, emotional, and personality development* (pp. 858–932). Hoboken, NJ: Wiley.

Ruchkin, V., & Vermeiren, R. (2006). Juvenile justice. *Child and Adolescent Psychiatric Clinics of North America, 15*(2), xix–xxii.

Rudolph, K. D., & Flynn, M. (2007). Childhood adversity and youth depression: Influence of gender and pubertal status. *Development and Psychopathology, 19*(2), 497–521.

Rudolph, K. D., Lambert, S. F., Clark, A. G., & Kurlakowsky, K. D. (2001). Negotiating the transition to middle school: The role of self-regulatory processes. *Child Development, 72*(3), 929–946.

Rudy, D., & Grusec, J. E. (2006). Authoritarian parenting in individualist and collectivist groups: Associations with maternal emotion and cognition and children's self-esteem. *Journal of Family Psychology, 20*(1), 68–78.

Rumbold, A. R., et al. (2006). Vitamins C and E and the risks of preeclampsia and perinatal complications. *New England Journal of Medicine, 354*, 1796–1806.

Runyon, M. K., & Kenny, M. C. (2002). Relationship of attributional style, depression, and posttrauma distress among children who suffered physical or sexual abuse. *Child Maltreatment: Journal of the American Professional Society on the Abuse of Children, 7*(3), 254–264.

Rushton, J. P., Skuy, M., & Fridjhon, P. (2003). Performance on Raven's Advanced Progressive Matrices by African, East Indian, and White engineering students in South Africa. *Intelligence, 31*(2), 123–137.

Russ, S. W. (2006). Pretend play, affect, and creativity. In P. Locher, C. Martindale, & L. Dorfman (Eds.), *New directions in aesthetics, creativity and the arts: Foundations and frontiers in aesthetics* (pp. 239–250). Amityville, NY: Baywood.

Russell, S. T. (2006). Substance use and abuse and mental health among sexual-minority youths: Evidence from add health. In A. M. Omoto & H. S. Kurtzman (Eds.), *Sexual orientation and mental health: Examining identity and development in lesbian, gay, and bisexual people* (pp. 13–35). Washington, DC: American Psychological Association.

Rutter, M. (2006). The psychological effects of early institutional rearing. In P. J. Marshall & N. A. Fox (Eds.), *The development of social engagement: Neurobiological perspectives* (pp. 355–391). New York: Oxford University Press.

Sabattini, L., & Leaper, C. (2004). The relation between mothers' and fathers' parenting styles and their division of labor in the home: Young adults' retrospective reports. *Sex Roles, 50*(3–4), 217–225.

Sadker, D. M., & Silber, E. S. (Eds.) (2007). *Gender in the classroom: Foundations, skills, methods, and strategies across the curriculum*. Mahwah, NJ: Erlbaum.

Sadler, T. W. (Ed.). (2005). Abstracts of papers presented at the 35th annual meeting of the Japanese Teratology Society, Tokyo, Japan. *Teratology, 52*(4), b1–b51.

Saffran, J. R., Werker, J. F., & Werner, L. A. (2006). The infant's auditory world: Hearing, speech, and the beginnings of language. In D. Kuhn, R. S. Siegler, W. Damon, & R. M. Lerner (Eds.), *Handbook of child psychology: Vol. 2. Cognition, perception, and language* (6th ed., pp. 58–108). Hoboken, NJ: Wiley.

Saigal, S., et al. (2006). Transition of extremely low-birth-weight infants from adolescence to young adulthood: Comparison with normal birth-weight controls. *Journal of the American Medical Association, 295*(6), 667–675.

Saiki, J., & Miyatsuji, H. (2007). Feature binding in visual working memory evaluated by type identification paradigm. *Cognition, 102*(1), 49–83.

Saito, S., & Miyake, A. (2004). On the nature of forgetting and the processing–storage relationship in reading span performance. *Journal of Memory and Language, 50*(4), 425–443.

Salapatek, P. (1975). Pattern perception in early infancy. In L. B. Cohen & P. Salapatek (Eds.), *Infant perception: From sensation to cognition*. New York: Academic.

Sales, J. M., Fivush, R., & Peterson, C. (2003). Parental reminiscing about positive and negative events. *Journal of Cognition and Development, 4*(2), 185–209.

Salmivalli, C., Ojanen, T., Haanpää, J., & Peets, K. (2005). "I'm OK but you're not" and other peer-relational schemas: Explaining individual differences in children's social goals. *Developmental Psychology, 41*(2), 363–375.

Salvy, S. J., et al. (2008). Peer influence on children's physical activity: An experience sampling study. *Journal of Pediatric Psychology, 33*(1), 39–49.

Salzarulo, P., & Ficca, G. (Eds.). (2002). *Awakening and sleep–wake cycle across development*. Amsterdam: John Benjamins.

Santelli, J. S., et al. (2003). Reproductive health in school-based health centers: Findings from the 1998–99 census of school-based health centers. *Journal of Adolescent Health, 32*(6), 443–451.

Santelli, J. S., Lindberg, J. D., Abma, J., McNeely, C. S., & Resnick, M. (2000). Adolescent sexual behavior: Estimates and trends from four nationally representative surveys. *Family Planning Perspectives, 32*(4), 156–165, 194.

Santos, D. C. C., Gabbard, C., & Goncalves, V. M. G. (2000). Motor development during the first 6 months: The case of Brazilian infants. *Infant and Child Development, 9*(3), 161–166.

Saroglou, V., & Galand, P. (2004). Identities, values, and religion: A study among Muslim, other immigrant, and native Belgian young adults after the 9/11 attacks. *Identity, 4*(2), 97–132.

Sarrazin, P., Trouilloud, D., & Bois, J. (2005a). Attentes du superviseur et performance sportive du pratiquant. Amplitude et fonctionnement de l'effet Pygmalion en context sportif. *Bulletin de Psychologie, 58*(1), 63–68.

Sarrazin, P., Trouilloud, D., Tessier, D., Chanal, J., & Bois, J. (2005b). Attentes de motivation et comportements différenciés de l'enseignant d'éducation physique et sportive à l'égard de ses élèves: Une étude en contexte naturel d'enseignement. *Revue Européenne de Psychologie Appliquée, 55*(2), 111–120.

Saudino, K. J., & Eaton, W. O. (1993, March). *Genetic influences on activity level. II. An analysis of continuity and change from infancy to early childhood.* Paper presented at the meeting of the Society for Research in Child Development, New Orleans.

Save the Children. (2008). *State of the world's mothers 2008.* Retrieved from http://www.savethechildren.org/publications/mothers/2008/SOWM-2008-full-report.pdf

Savin-Williams, R. C. (2007). Girl-on-girl sexuality. In B. J. R. Leadbeater & N. Way (Eds.), *Urban girls revisited: Building strengths* (pp. 301–318). New York: New York University Press.

Savin-Williams, R. C. (2008). Refusing and resisting sexual identity labels. In D. L. Browning (Ed.), *Adolescent identities* (pp. 67–91). New York: Analytic Press/Taylor & Francis.

Savin-Williams, R. C., & Berndt, T. (1990). Friendship and peer relations. In S. S. Feldman & G. R. Elliott (Eds.), *At the threshold: The developing adolescent.* Cambridge, MA: Harvard University Press.

Savin-Williams, R. C., & Diamond, L. M. (2004). Sex. In R. M. Lerner & L. Steinberg (Eds.), *Handbook of adolescent psychology* (2nd ed., pp. 189–231). Hoboken, NJ: Wiley.

Sawyer, D. J. (2006). Dyslexia: A generation of inquiry. *Topics in Language Disorders, 26*(2), 95–109.

Scarr, S. (1998). How do families affect intelligence? Social environmental and behavioral genetic predictions. In J. J. McArdle & R. W. Woodcock (Eds.), *Human cognitive abilities in theory and practice* (pp. 113–136). Mahwah, NJ: Erlbaum.

Schaffer, H. R., & Emerson, P. E. (1964). The development of social attachments in infancy. *Monographs of the Society for Research in Child Development, 29*(94).

Scharf, M., Shulman, S., & Avigad-Spitz, L. (2005). Sibling relationships in emerging adulthood and in adolescence. *Journal of Adolescent Research, 20*(1), 64–90.

Scheithauer, H., Hayer, T., Petermann, F., & Jugert, G. (2006). Physical, verbal, and relational forms of bullying among German students: Age trends, gender differences, and correlates. *Aggressive Behavior, 32*(3), 261–275.

Scheres, A., & Castellanos, F. X. (2003). Assessment and treatment of childhood problems, 2nd ed.: A clinician's guide. *Psychological Medicine, 33*(8), 1487–1488.

Schonfeld, A. M., Mattson, S. N., & Riley, E. P. (2005). Moral maturity and delinquency after prenatal alcohol exposure. *Journal of Studies on Alcohol, 66*(4), 545–554.

Schoppe-Sullivan, S. J., Mangelsdorf, S. C., Brown, G. L., & Sokolowski, M. S. (2007). Goodness-of-fit in family context: Infant temperament, marital quality, and early co-parenting behavior. *Infant Behavior & Development, 30*(1), 82–96.

Schraf, M., & Hertz-Lazarowitz, R. (2003). Social networks in the school context: Effects of culture and gender. *Journal of Social and Personal Relationships, 20*(6), 843–858.

Schuetze, P., Lawton, D., & Eiden, R. D. (2006). Prenatal cocaine exposure and infant sleep at 7 months of age: The influence of the caregiving environment. *Infant Mental Health Journal, 27*(4), 383–404.

Schuetze, P., Zeskind, P. S., & Eiden, R. D. (2003). The perceptions of infant distress signals varying in pitch by cocaine-using mothers. *Infancy, 4*(1), 65–83.

Schulte-Körne, G., Warnke, A., & Remschmidt, H. (2006). Genetics of dyslexia. *Zeitschrift für Kinder- und Jugendpsychiatrie und Psychotherapie, 34*(6), 435–444.

Schultz, D. P., & Schultz, S. E. (2008). *A history of modern psychology* (9th ed.). Belmont, CA: Thomson/Wadsworth.

Schumacher, D., & Queen, J. A. (2007). *Overcoming obesity in childhood and adolescence: A guide for school leaders.* Thousand Oaks, CA: Corwin.

Schwartz, S. J. (2001). The evolution of Eriksonian and neo-Eriksonian identity theory and research: A review and integration. *Identity, 1*(1), 7–58.

Scott, J. R. (2006). Preventing eclampsia. *Obstetrics & Gynecology, 108*, 824–825.

Scourfield, J., Van den Bree, M., Martin, N., & McGuffin, P. (2004). Conduct problems in children and adolescents: A twin study. *Archives of General Psychiatry, 61*, 489–496.

Secker-Walker, R. H., & Vacek, P. M. (2003). Relationships between cigarette smoking during pregnancy, gestational age, maternal weight gain, and infant birthweight. *Addictive Behaviors, 28*(1), 55–66.

Seidah, A., & Bouffard, T. (2007). Being proud of oneself as a person or being proud of one's physical appearance: What matters for feeling well in adolescence? *Social Behavior and Personality, 35*(2), 255–268.

Selman, R. L. (1976). Social-cognitive understanding. In T. Lickona (Ed.), *Moral development and behavior: Theory, research, and social issues.* New York: Holt.

Selman, R. L. (1980). *The growth of interpersonal understanding: Developmental and clinical analysis.* New York: Academic.

Selman, R. L., & Dray, A. J. (2006). Risk and prevention. In K. A. Renninger, I. E. Sigel, W. Damon, & R. M. Lerner (Eds.), *Handbook of child psychology: Vol. 4. Child psychology in practice* (6th ed., pp. 378–419). Hoboken, NJ: Wiley.

Serbin, L. A., Poulin-Dubois, D., Colburne, K. A., Sen, M. G., & Eichstedt, J. A. (2001). Gender stereotyping in infancy: Visual preferences for and knowledge of gender-stereotyped toys in the second year. *International Journal of Behavioral Development, 25*(1), 7–15.

Shaywitz, B. A., Lyon, G. R., & Shaywitz, S. E. (2006). The role of functional magnetic resonance imaging in understanding reading and dyslexia. *Developmental Neuropsychology, 30*(1), 613–632.

Shaywitz, S. E. (1998). Dyslexia. *New England Journal of Medicine, 338*, 307–312.

Shaywitz, S. E., Mody, M., & Shaywitz, B. A. (2006). Neural mechanisms in dyslexia. *Current Directions in Psychological Science, 15*(6), 278–281.

Shea, A. K., & Steiner, M. (2008). Cigarette smoking during pregnancy. *Nicotine & Tobacco Research, 10*(2), 267–278.

Shear, K., Jin, R., Ruscio, A. M., Walters, E. E., & Kessler, R. C. (2006). Prevalence and correlates of estimated DSM-IV child and adult separation anxiety disorder in the National Comorbidity Survey Replication. *American Journal of Psychiatry 163*, 1074–1083.

Sheeber, L. B., Davis, B., Leve, C., Hops, H., & Tildesley, E. (2007). Adolescents' relationships with their mothers and fathers: Associations with depressive disorder and subdiagnostic symptomatology. *Journal of Abnormal Psychology, 116*(1), 144–154.

Shen, R-Y, Choong, K-C, & Thompson, A. C. (2007). Long-term reduction in ventral tegmental area dopamine neuron population activity following repeated stimulant or ethanol treatment. *Biological Psychiatry, 61*(1), 93–100.

Sherwin-White, S. (2006). The social toddler: Promoting positive behaviour. *Infant Observation, 9*(1), 95–97.

Shin, H. B., & Bruno, R. (2003). *Language use and English speaking ability: 2000.* Washington, DC: U.S. Census Bureau.

Shirk, S., Burwell, R., & Harter, S. (2003). Strategies to modify low self-esteem in adolescents. In M. A. Reinecke et al. (Eds.), *Cognitive therapy with children and adolescents: A casebook for clinical practice* (2nd ed., pp. 189–213). New York: Guilford.

Shonk, S. M., & Cicchetti, D. (2001). Maltreatment, competency deficits, and risk for academic and behavioral maladjustment. *Developmental Psychology, 37*(1), 3–17.

Shroff, H., et al. (2006). Features associated with excessive exercise in women with eating disorders. *International Journal of Eating Disorders, 39*(6), 454–461.

Siegel, L. S. (1992). Infant motor, cognitive, and language behaviors as predictors of achievement at school age. In C. Rovee-Collier & L. P. Lipsitt (Eds.), *Advances in infancy research: Vol. 7.* Norwood, NJ: Ablex.

Siegler, R. S., & Alibali, M. W. (2005). *Children's thinking* (4th ed.). Upper Saddle River, NJ: Prentice Hall.

Signorello, L. B., & McLaughlin, J. K. (2004). Maternal caffeine consumption and spontaneous abortion: A review of the epidemiologic evidence. *Epidemiology, 15*(2), 229–239.

Silbereisen, R. K. (2006). Development and ecological context: History of the psychological science in a personal view and experience—an interview with Urie Bronfenbrenner. *Psychologie in Erziehung und Unterricht, 53*(1), 241–249.

Simion, F., Cassia, V. M., Turati, C., & Valenza, E. (2001). The origins of face perception: Specific versus nonspecific mechanisms. *Infant and Child Development, 10*(1–2), 59–65.

Simmons, R. G., & Blyth, D. A. (1987). *Moving into adolescence: The impact of pubertal change and school context.* Hawthorne, NY: Aldine deGruyter.

Simonelli, A., Monti, F., & Magalotti, D. (2005). The complex phenomenon of failure to thrive: Medical, psychological and relational-affective aspects. *Psicologia Clinica dello Sviluppo, 9*(2), 183–212.

Simonton, D. K. (2006a). Creative genius, knowledge, and reason: The lives and works of eminent creators. In J. C. Kaufman & J. Baer (Eds.), *Creativity and reason in cognitive development* (pp. 43–59). New York: Cambridge University Press.

Simonton, D. K. (2006b). Creativity around the world in 80 ways...but with one destination.

In J. C. Kaufman & R. Sternberg (Eds.), *The international handbook of creativity* (pp. 490–496). New York: Cambridge University Press.

Simpkins, S. D., Fredricks, J. A., Davis-Kean, P. E., & Eccles, J. S. (2006). Healthy mind, healthy habits: The influence of activity involvement in middle childhood. In A. C. Huston & M. N. Ripke (Eds.), *Developmental contexts in middle childhood: Bridges to adolescence and adulthood. Cambridge studies in social and emotional development* (pp. 283–302). New York: Cambridge University Press.

Singer, L. T., et al. (2005). Prenatal cocaine exposure and infant cognition. *Infant Behavior & Development, 28*(4), 431–444.

Singh, K., & Ozturk, M. (2000). Effect of part-time work on high school mathematics and science course taking. *Journal of Educational Research, 91*(2), 67–74.

Sirrs, S. M., et al. (2007). Normal-appearing white matter in patients with phenylketonuria: Water content, myelin water fraction, and metabolite concentrations. *Radiology, 242*, 236–243.

Skeels, H. M. (1966). Adult status of children with contrasting early life experiences: A follow-up study. *Monographs of the Society for Research in Child Development, 31*(3, Serial No. 105).

Skinner, B. F. (1957). *Verbal behavior.* New York: Appleton.

Skoczenski, A. M. (2002). Limitations on visual sensitivity during infancy: Contrast sensitivity, vernier acuity, and orientation processing. In J. W. Fagen & H. Hayne (Eds.), *Progress in infancy research: Vol. 2.* Mahwah, NJ: Erlbaum.

Slater, A. (2000). Visual perception in the young infant: Early organization and rapid learning. In D. Muir & A. Slater (Eds.), *Infant development: The essential readings.* Malden, MA: Blackwell.

Slater, A., Mattock, A., & Brown, E. (1990). Size constancy at birth: Newborn infants' responses to retinal and real size. *Journal of Experimental Child Psychology, 49*, 314–322.

Slavin, R. E. (2009). *Educational psychology: Theory and practice* (9th ed.). Upper Saddle River, NJ: Merrill.

Sloan, S., Sneddon, H., Stewart, M., & Iwaniec, D. (2006). Breast is best? Reasons why mothers decide to breastfeed or bottlefeed their babies and factors influencing the duration of breastfeeding. *Child Care in Practice, 12*(3), 283–297.

Slobin, D. I. (2001). Form/function relations: How do children find out what they are? In M. Tomasello & E. Bates (Eds.), *Language development: The essential readings.* Malden, MA: Blackwell.

Slutske, W. S., et al. (2008). Searching for an environmental effect of parental alcoholism on offspring alcohol use disorder: A genetically informed study of children of alcoholics. *Journal of Abnormal Psychology, 117*(3), 534–551.

Smarty, S., & Findling, R. L. (2007). Psychopharmacology of pediatric bipolar disorder: A review. *Psychopharmacology, 191*(1), 39–54.

Smetana, J. G. (1990). Morality and conduct disorders. In M. Lewis & S. M. Miller (Eds.), *Handbook of developmental psychopathology.* New York: Plenum.

Smetana, J. G. (2005). Adolescent–parent conflict: Resistance and subversion as developmental process. In L. Nucci (Ed.), *Conflict, contradiction, and contrarian elements in moral development and education* (pp. 69–91). Mahwah, NJ: Erlbaum.

Smetana, J. G., Campione-Barr, N., & Metzger, A. (2006). Adolescent development in interpersonal and societal contexts. *Annual Review of Psychology, 57*, 255–284.

Smiley, P. A., & Johnson, R. S. (2006). Self-referring terms, event transitivity and development of self. *Cognitive Development, 21*(3), 266–284.

Smith, C. L., Calkins, S. D., Keane, S. P., Anastopoulos, A. D., & Shelton, T. L. (2004). Predicting stability and change in toddler behavior problems: Contributions of maternal behavior and child gender. *Developmental Psychology, 40*(1), 29–42.

Smith, P. K. (2005). Play: Types and functions in human development. In B. J. Ellis & D. F. Bjorklund (Eds.), *Origins of the social mind: Evolutionary psychology and child development* (pp. 271–291). New York: Guilford.

Smolka, E., & Eviatar, Z. (2006). Phonological and orthographic visual word recognition in the two cerebral hemispheres: Evidence from Hebrew. Cognitive *Neuropsychology, 23*(6), 972–989.

Smoll, F. L., & Schultz, R. W. (1990). Quantifying gender differences in physical performance: A developmental perspective. *Developmental Psychology, 26*, 360–369.

Snarey, J. R. (1994). Cross-cultural universality of social-moral development: A critical review of Kohlbergian research. In B. Puka (Ed.), *New research in moral development* (pp. 268–298). New York: Garland.

Snarey, J. R., & Bell, D. (2003). Distinguishing structural and functional models of human development. *Identity, 3*(3), 221–230.

Snedeker, J., Geren, J., & Shafto, C. L. (2007). Starting over: International adoption as a natural experiment in language development. *Psychological Science, 18*(1), 79–87.

Snegovskikh, V., Park, J. S., & Norwitz, E. R. (2006). Endocrinology of parturition. *Endocrinology and Metabolism Clinics of North America, 35*(1), 173–191.

Snow, C. (2006). Cross-cutting themes and future research directions. In D. August & T. Shanahan (Eds.), *Developing literacy in second-language learners: Report of the National Literacy Panel on Language-Minority Children and Youth* (pp. 631–651). Mahwah, NJ: Erlbaum.

Snyder, H. M., & Sickmund, M. (2006). *Juvenile offenders and victims: 2006 national report.* Washington, DC: U.S. Department of Justice, Office of Justice Programs, Office of Juvenile Justice and Delinquency Prevention.

Snyderman, M., & Rothman, S. (1990). *The IQ controversy.* New Brunswick, NJ: Transaction.

Soan, S., & Tod, J. (2006). Review of dyslexia. *European Journal of Special Needs Education, 21*(3), 354–356.

Sontag, L. W., & Richards, T. W. (1938). Studies in fetal behavior: Fetal heart rate as a behavioral indicator. *Child Development Monographs, 3*(4).

Sorce, J., Emde, R. N., Campos, J. J., Klinnert, M. D. (2000). Maternal emotional signaling: Its effect on the visual cliff behavior of 1-year-olds. In D. Muir & A. Slater (Eds.), *Infant development: The essential readings* (pp. 282–292). Malden, MA: Blackwell.

Soussignan, R., & Schaal, B. (2005). Emotional processes in human newborns: A functionalist perspective. In J. Nadel & D. Muir (Eds.), *Emotional development: Recent research advances* (pp. 127–159). New York: Oxford University Press.

South, S. J., Haynie, D. L., & Bose, S. (2007). Student mobility and school dropout. *Social Science Research, 36*(1), 68–94.

Spelke, E. S., & Owsley, C. (1979). Inter-modal exploration and knowledge in infancy. *Infant Behavior and Development, 2*, 13–27.

Speranza, M., et al. (2001). Obsessive compulsive disorders in eating disorders. *Eating Behaviors, 2*(3), 193–207.

Spieker, S. J., et al. (2003). Joint influence of child care and infant attachment security for cognitive and language outcomes of low-income toddlers. *Infant Behavior and Development, 26*(3), 326–344.

Spitz, R. A. (1965). *The first year of life: A psychoanalytic study of normal and deviant object relations.* New York: International Universities Press.

Spitzer, R. L., Gibbon, M., Skodol, A. E., Williams, J. B. W., & First, M. B. (2002). *DSM–IV–TR casebook.* Washington, DC: American Psychiatric Press.

Sroufe, L. A., Waters, E., & Matas, L. (1974). Contextual determinants of infant affectional response. In M. Lewis & L. Rosenblum (Eds.), *The origins of fear.* New York: Wiley.

Stabouli, S., & Kotsis, V. (2009). Hypertension and target organ damage in obese children. *Pediatric Health, 3*(1), 3–6.

Staff, J., Mortimer, J. T., & Uggen, C. (2004). Work and leisure in adolescence. In L. Lerner & L. Steinberg (Eds.), *Handbook of adolescent psychology* (2nd ed., pp. 429–450). Hoboken, NJ: Wiley.

Stagnitti, K., Unsworth, C., & Rodger, S. (2000). Development of an assessment to identify play behaviours that discriminate between the play of typical preschoolers and preschoolers with pre-academic problems. *Canadian Journal of Occupational Therapy, 67*(5), 291–303.

Stahmer, A. C., Ingersoll, B., & Koegel, R. L. (2004). Inclusive programming for toddlers with autism spectrum disorders: Outcomes from the Children's Toddler School. *Journal of Positive Behavior Interventions, 6*(2), 67–82.

Stams, G. J. M., Juffer, F., & van IJzendoorn, M. H. (2002). Maternal sensitivity, infant attachment, and temperament in early childhood predict adjustment in middle childhood: The case of adopted children and their biologically unrelated parents. *Developmental Psychology, 38*(5), 806–821.

Stanford, J. N., & McCabe, M. P. (2005). Sociocultural influences on adolescent boys' body image and body change strategies. *Body Image, 2*(2), 105–113.

Stankoff, B., et al. (2006). Imaging of CNS myelin by positron-emission tomography. *Proceedings of the National Academy of Sciences, USA, 103*(24), 9304–9309.

Stauffacher, K., & DeHart, G. B. (2006). Crossing social contexts: Relational aggression between siblings and friends during early and middle childhood. *Journal of Applied Developmental Psychology, 27*(3), 228–240.

Steele, H. (2005a). Editorial. *Attachment & Human Development, 7*(4), 345.

Steele, H. (2005b). Editorial: Romance, marriage, adolescent motherhood, leaving for college, plus shyness and attachment in the preschool years. *Attachment & Human Development, 7*(2), 103–104.

Steinberg, L. (1996). *Beyond the classroom: Why school reform has failed and what parents need to do.* New York: Simon & Schuster.

Steinbrink, C., et al. (2008). The contribution of white and gray matter differences to developmental dyslexia: Insights from DTI and VBM at 3.0 T. *Neuropsychologia, 46*(13), 3170–3178.

Stemberger, J. P. (2004). Phonological priming and irregular past. *Journal of Memory and Language, 50*(1), 82–95.

Stephenson, R. H., & Banet-Weiser, S. (2007). Super-sized kids: Obesity, children, moral panic, and the media. In J. A. Bryant (Ed.), *The children's television community* (pp. 277–291). Mahwah, NJ: Erlbaum.

Sternberg, R. J. (2000). In search of the zipperump-a-zoo. *Psychologist, 13*(5), 250–255.

Sternberg, R. J. (2006). The nature of creativity. *Creativity Research Journal, 18*(1), 87–98.

Sternberg, R. J. (2007). A systems model of leadership: WICS. *American Psychologist, 62*(1), 34–42.

Sternberg, R. J., & Williams, W. M. (1997). Does the Graduate Record Examination predict meaningful success in the graduate training of psychologists? *American Psychologist, 52,* 630–641.

Stevens, B., et al. (2005). Consistent management of repeated procedural pain with sucrose in preterm neonates: Is it effective and safe for repeated use over time? *Clinical Journal of Pain, 21*(6), 543–548.

Stevens, T., Olivárez, Jr., A., & Hamman, D. (2006). The role of cognition, motivation, and emotion in explaining the mathematics achievement gap between Hispanic and White students. *Hispanic Journal of Behavioral Sciences, 28*(2), 161–186.

Stevenson, H. W., Chen, C., & Lee, S. (1993). Mathematics achievement of Chinese, Japanese, and American children: Ten years later. *Science, 259,* 53–58.

Stevenson, J. (1992). Evidence for a genetic etiology in hyperactivity in children. *Behavior Genetics, 22,* 337–344.

Stifter, C. A., & Wiggins, C. N. (2004). Assessment of disturbances in emotion regulation and temperament. In R. DelCarmen-Wiggins & A. Carter (Eds.), *Handbook of infant, toddler, and preschool mental health assessment* (pp. 79–103). New York: Oxford University Press.

Stipek, D., & Hakuta, K. (2007). Strategies to ensure that no child starts from behind. In J. L. Aber et al. (Eds.), *Child development and social policy: Knowledge for action* (pp. 129–145). Washington, DC: American Psychological Association.

Stipek, D., Recchia, S., & McClintic, S. (1992). Self-evaluation in young children. *Monographs of the Society for Research in Child Development, 57*(1, Serial No. 226).

Stoel-Gammon, C. (2002). Intervocalic consonants in the speech of typically developing children: Emergence and early use. *Clinical Linguistics and Phonetics, 16*(3), 155–168.

Storch, E. A., et al. (2007). Peer victimization, psychosocial adjustment, and physical activity in overweight and at-risk-for-overweight youth. *Journal of Pediatric Psychology, 32*(1), 80–89.

Stores, G., & Wiggs, L. (Eds.). (2001). *Sleep disturbance in children and adolescents with disorders of development: Its significance and management.* New York: Cambridge University Press.

Straus, M. A., & Field, C. J. (2003). Psychological aggression by American parents: National data on prevalence, chronicity, and severity. *Journal of Marriage and Family, 65*(4), 795–808.

Strayer, J., & Roberts, W. (2004). Children's anger, emotional expressiveness, and empathy: Relations with parents' empathy, emotional expressiveness, and parenting practices. *Social Development, 13*(2), 229–254.

Streri, A. (2002). Hand preference in 4-month-old infants: Global or local processing of objects in the haptic mode. *Current Psychology Letters: Behaviour, Brain and Cognition, 7,* 39–50.

Striegel-Moore, R. H., & Cachelin, F. M. (2001). Etiology of eating disorders in women. *Counseling Psychologist, 29*(5), 635–661.

Striegel-Moore, R. H., et al. (2003). Eating disorders in White and Black women. *American Journal of Psychiatry, 160*(7), 1326–1331.

Strock, M. (2004). *Autism spectrum disorders (pervasive developmental disorders)* (NIH Publication No. NIH-04–5511). Bethesda, MD: U.S. Department of Health and Human Services. Retrieved from http://www.nimh.nih.gov/publicat/autism.cfm

Strohner, H., & Nelson, K. E. (1974). The young child's development of sentence comprehension: Influence of event probability, nonverbal context, syntactic form, and strategies. *Child Development, 45,* 567–576.

Strutt, G. F., Anderson, D. R., & Well, A. D. (1975). A developmental study of the effects of irrelevant information on speeded classification. *Journal of Experimental Child Psychology, 20,* 127–135.

Suh, S., Suh, J., & Houston, I. (2007). Predictors of categorical at-risk high school dropouts. *Journal of Counseling & Development. 85*(2), 196–203.

Sukhodolsky, D. G., Golub, A., Stone, E. C., & Orban, L. (2005). Dismantling anger control training for children: A randomized pilot study of social problem-solving versus social skills training components. *Behavior Therapy, 36,* 15–23.

Sullivan, B. A., & Hansen, J. C. (2004). Mapping associations between interests and personality: Toward a conceptual understanding of individual differences in vocational behavior. *Journal of Counseling Psychology, 51*(3), 287–298.

Sulloway, F. J. (2007). Birth order and intelligence. *Science, 316*(5832), 1711–1712.

Sumner, C. R., Schuh, K. J., Sutton, V. K., Lipetz, R., & Kelsey, D. K. (2006). Placebo controlled study of the effects of atomoxetine on bladder control in children with nocturnal enuresis. *Journal of Child and Adolescent Psychopharmacology, 16*(6), 699–711.

Sun, S. S., et al. (2005). Is sexual maturity occurring earlier among U.S. children? *Journal of Adolescent Health, 37*(5), 345–355.

Suomi, S. J., Harlow, H. F., & McKinney, W. T. (1972). Monkey psychiatrists. *American Journal of Psychiatry, 128,* 927–932.

Supple, A. J., & Small, S. A. (2006). The influence of parental support, knowledge, and authoritative parenting on Hmong and European American adolescent development. *Journal of Family Issues, 27*(9), 1214–1232.

Suris, J. C., Jeannin, A., Chossis, I., & Michaud, P. A. (2007). Piercing among adolescents: Body art as risk marker—A population-based survey. *Journal of Family Practice, 56*(2), 126–130.

Susman, E. J., & Rogol, A. (2004). Puberty and psychological development. In R. M. Lerner & L. Steinberg (Eds.), *Handbook of adolescent psychology* (2nd ed.) (pp. 15–44). Hoboken, NJ: Wiley.

Sylva, K., et al. (2007). Curricular quality and day-to-day learning activities in pre-school. *International Journal of Early Years Education, 15*(1), 49–65.

Szaflarski, J. P., et al. (2006). A longitudinal functional magnetic resonance imaging study of language development in children 5 to 11 years old. *Annals of Neurology, 59*(5), 796–807.

Takahashi, M., & Sugiyama, M. (2003). Improvement and prevention of misbehavior in a junior high school student: An analysis of behavioral contingency and change of stimulus function in a social setting. *Japanese Journal of Counseling Science, 36*(2), 165–174.

Tallandini, M. A., & Valentini, P. (1991). Symbolic prototypes in children's drawings of schools. *Journal of Genetic Psychology, 152,* 179–190.

Tamis-LeMonda, C. S., Bornstein, M. H., & Baumwell, L. (2001). Maternal responsiveness and children's achievement of language milestones. *Child Development, 72*(3), 748–767.

Tamis-LeMonda, C. S., Cristofaro, T. N., Rodriguez, E. T., & Bornstein, M. H. (2006). Early language development: Social influences in the first years of life. In L. Balter & C. S. Tamis-LeMonda (Eds.), *Child psychology: A handbook of contemporary issues* (2nd ed., pp. 79–108). New York: Psychology Press.

Tanner, J. M. (1989). *Fetus into man: Physical growth from conception to maturity.* Cambridge, MA: Harvard University Press.

Tanner, J. M. (1991a). Adolescent growth spurt, I. In R. M. Lerner, A. C. Petersen, & J. Brooks-Gunn (Eds.), *Encyclopedia of adolescence.* New York: Garland.

Tanner, J. M. (1991b). Secular trend in age of menarche. In R. M. Lerner, A. C. Petersen, & J. Brooks-Gunn (Eds.), *Encyclopedia of adolescence.* New York: Garland.

Tapper, K., & Boulton, M. J. (2004). Sex differences in levels of physical, verbal, and indirect aggression amongst primary school children and their associations with beliefs about aggression. *Aggressive Behavior, 30*(2), 123–145.

Tashiro, T., Frazier, P., & Berman, M. (2006). Stress-related growth following divorce and relationship dissolution. In M. A. Fine & J. H. Harvey (Eds.), *Handbook of divorce and relationship dissolution* (pp. 361–384). Mahwah, NJ: Erlbaum.

Tassi, F., Schneider, B. H., & Richard, J. F. (2001). Competitive behavior at school in relation to social competence and incompetence in middle childhood. *Revue Internationale de Psychologie Sociale, 14*(2), 165–184.

Taylor, C. (2007). Day care and a child's behavior [Letter to the editor]. *The New York Times.* Retrieved from http://www.nytimes.com

Taylor, H. G., Minich, N. M., Klein, N., & Hack, M. (2004). Longitudinal outcomes of very low birth weight: Neuropsychological findings. *Journal of the International Neuropsychological Society, 10*(2), 149–163.

Taylor, M. (1999). *Imaginary companions and the children who create them.* London: Oxford University Press.

Taylor, M., & Hort, B. (1990). Can children be trained in making the distinction between appearance and reality. *Cognitive Development, 5*(1), 89-99.

Tehrani, J. A., & Mednick, S. A. (2000). Genetic factors and criminal behavior. *Federal Probation, 64*(2), 24–27.

Tercyak, K. P., & Tyc, V. L. (2006). Opportunities and challenges in the prevention and control of cancer and other chronic diseases: Children's diet and nutrition and weight and physical activity. *Journal of Pediatric Psychology, 31*(8), 750–763.

Thapar, A., Langley, K., Asherson, P., & Gill, M. (2007). Gene-environment interplay in attention-deficit hyperactivity disorder and the importance of a developmental perspective. *British Journal of Psychiatry, 190*(1), 1–3.

Theim, K. R., et al. (2007). Children's descriptions of the foods consumed during loss of control eating episodes. *Eating Behaviors, 8*(2), 258–265.

Thomas, A., & Chess, S. (1989). Temperament and personality. In G. A. Kohnstamm, J. E. Bates, & M. K. Rothbart (Eds.), *Temperament in childhood.* Chichester, England: Wiley.

Thomas, J. R., & French, K. E. (1985). Gender differences across age in motor performance: A meta-analysis. *Psychological Bulletin, 98,* 260–282.

Thompson, A. M., Baxter-Jones, A. D. G., Mirwald, R. L., & Bailey, D. A. (2003). Comparison of physical activity in male and female children: Does maturation matter? *Medicine and Science in Sports and Exercise. 35*(10), 1684–1690.

Thompson, M. P., Ho, C. H., & Kingree, J. B. (2007). Prospective associations between delinquency and suicidal behaviors in a nationally representative sample. *Journal of Adolescent Health, 40*(3), 232–237.

Thompson, O. M., et al. (2004). Food purchased away from home as a predictor of change in BMI *z*-score among girls. *International Journal of Obesity and Related Metabolic Disorders, 28*(2), 282–289.

Thompson, R. A. (2006). The development of the person: Social understanding, relationships, conscience, self. In N. Eisenberg, W. Damon, & R. M. Lerner (Eds.), *Handbook of child psychology: Vol. 3. Social, emotional, and personality development* (6th ed., pp. 24–98). Hoboken, NJ: Wiley.

Thompson, R. A., & Limber, S. P. (1990). "Social anxiety" in infancy: Stranger and separation reactions. In H. Leitenberg (Ed.), *Handbook of social and evaluation anxiety.* New York: Plenum.

Thompson, R. A., & Meyer, S. (2007). Socialization of emotion regulation in the family. In J. J. Gross (Ed.), *Handbook of emotion regulation* (pp. 249–268). New York: Guilford.

Thompson, R. A., Easterbrooks, M. A., & Padilla-Walker, L. M. (2003). Social and emotional development in infancy. In R. M. Lerner et al. (Eds.), *Handbook of psychology: Developmental psychology.* New York: Wiley.

Thompson, V. J., et al. (2003). Influences on diet and physical activity among middle-class African-American 8- to 10-year old girls at risk of becoming obese. *Journal of Nutrition Education and Behavior, 35*(3), 115–123.

Thurstone, L. L. (1938). Primary mental abilities. *Psychometric Monographs, 1.*

Tijms, J. (2007). The development of reading accuracy and reading rate during treatment of dyslexia. *Educational Psychology, 27*(2), 273–294.

Timmerman, L. M. (2006). Family care versus day care: Effects on children. In B. M. Gayle et al. (Eds.), *Classroom communication and instructional processes: Advances through meta-analysis* (pp. 245–260). Mahwah, NJ: Erlbaum.

Tobbell, J. (2003). Students' experiences of the transition from primary to secondary school. *Educational and Child Psychology, 20*(4), 4–14.

Towse, J. (2003). Lifespan development of human memory. *Quarterly Journal of Experimental Psychology: Human Experimental Psychology, 56A*(7), 1244–1246.

Towse, J., & Cowan, N. (2005). Working memory and its relevance for cognitive development. In W. Schneider, R. Schumann-Hengsteler, & B. Sodian (Eds.), *Young children's cognitive development: Interrelationships among executive functioning, working memory, verbal ability, and theory of mind* (pp. 9–37). Mahwah, NJ: Erlbaum.

Trainor, L. J., & Desjardins, R. N. (2002). Pitch characteristics of infant-directed speech affect infants' ability to discriminate vowels. *Psychonomic Bulletin & Review, 9*(2), 335–340.

Trehub, S. E., & Hannon, E. E. (2006). Infant music perception: Domain-general or domain-specific mechanisms? *Cognition, 100*(1), 73–99.

Treuth, M. S., Butte, N. F., Adolph, A. L., & Puyau, M. R. (2004). A longitudinal study of fitness and activity in girls predisposed to obesity. *Medicine and Science in Sports and Exercise, 36*(2), 198–204.

Trevarthen, C. (2003). Conversations with a two-month-old. In J. Raphael-Leff (Ed.), *Parent–infant psychodynamics: Wild things, mirrors, and ghosts.* London: Whurr.

Troxel, W. M., & Matthews, K. A. (2004). What are the costs of marital conflict and dissolution to children's physical health? *Clinical Child and Family Psychology Review, 7*(1), 29–57.

Tsuneishi, S., & Casaer, P. (2000). Effects of preterm extrauterine visual experience on the development of the human visual system: A flash VEP study. *Developmental Medicine and Child Neurology, 42*(10), 663–668.

U.S. Census Bureau. (2004). *Statistical abstract of the United States* (124th ed.). Washington, DC: U.S. Government Printing Office.

U.S. Census Bureau. (2006). *Statistical abstract of the United States* (126th ed.). Washington, DC: U.S. Government Printing Office.

U.S. Census Bureau. (2007). *Statistical abstract of the United States* (127th ed.). Washington, DC: U.S. Government Printing Office.

U.S. Census Bureau. (2008, December 15). *Historical estimates of world population.* Retrieved May 20, 2009, from http://www.census.gov/ipc/www/worldhis.html

U.S. Census Bureau. International Programs Center, International Data Base. (2004,

March 22). *Global population profile: 2002,* table A-12. Washington, DC: U.S. Government Printing Office.

U.S. Department of Agriculture. (2005). *Adequate nutrients within calorie needs. Dietary guidelines for Americans.* Retrieved from http://www.health.gov/dietaryguidelines/dga2005/document/html/chapter2.htm

U.S. Department of Health and Human Services. (2004). *Child abuse and neglect fatalities: Statistics and interventions—child maltreatment 2002.* Retrieved from http://nccanch.acf.hhs.gov/pubs/factsheets/fatality.cfm

U.S. Food and Drug Administration. (2004, July 20). *Decreasing the chance of birth defects.* Retrieved from http://www.fda.gov/fdac/features/996_bd.html

Umek, L. M., Podlesek, A., & Fekonja, U. (2005). Assessing the home literacy environment: Relationships to child language comprehension and expression. *European Journal of Psychological Assessment, 21*(4), 271–281.

United Nations Children's Fund (UNICEF). (2007). *The state of the world's children: 2007.* New York: United Nations.

United Nations Joint Programme on HIV/AIDS (UNAIDS). (2006). *Report on the global AIDS epidemic: Executive summary.* Geneva, Switzerland.

United Nations Statistics Division. (2004, March). *UNESCO: World and regional trends,* Table 8. Retrieved from http://millenniumindicators.un.org/unsd/mi/mi_worldregn.asp

University of Iowa Hospitals and Clinics (2006). Health reports: Can you be too rich or too thin? Accessed July 30, 2009. http://www.uihealthcare.com/reports/psychiatry/010716anorexia.html

Uylings, H. B. M. (2006). Development of the human cortex and the concept of "critical" or "sensitive" periods. *Language Learning, 56*(Suppl. 1), 59–90.

van IJzendoorn, M. H., & Hubbard, F. O. A. (2000). Are infant crying and maternal responsiveness during the first year related to infant–mother attachment at 15 months? *Attachment and Human Development, 2*(3), 371–391.

van IJzendoorn, M. H., & Juffer, F. (2006). The Emanuel Miller memorial lecture 2006. Adoption as intervention: Meta-analytic evidence for massive catch-up and plasticity in physical, socio-emotional, and cognitive development. *Journal of Child Psychology and Psychiatry, 47*(12), 1228–1245.

van IJzendoorn, M. H., Moran, G., Belsky, J., Pederson, D., Bakermans-Kranenburg, M. J., & Kneppers, K. (2000). The similarity of siblings' attachments to their mother. *Child Development, 71*(4), 1086–1098.

van Rijn, S., Swaab, H., Aleman, A., & Kahn, R. S. (2006). X chromosomal effects on social cognitive processing and emotion regulation: A study with Klinefelter men (47, XXY). *Schizophrenia Research, 84*(2–3), 194–203.

Vander Ven, T., & Cullen, F. T. (2004). The impact of maternal employment on serious youth crime: Does the quality of working conditions matter? *Crime & Delinquency, 50*(2), 272–291.

Vartanian, O., Martindale, C., & Kwiatkowski, J. (2003). Creativity and inductive reasoning: The relationship between divergent thinking and performance on Wason's 2-4-6 task. *Quarterly Journal of Experimental Psychology: Human Experimental Psychology. 56A*(4), 641–655.

Vellutino, F. R., Fletcher, J. M., Snowling, M. J., & Scanlon, D. M. (2004). Specific reading disability (dyslexia): What have we learned in the past four decades? *Journal of Child Psychology and Psychiatry, 45*(1), 2–40.

Verbeek, M. M. A., et al. (2008). Arousal and ventilatory responses to mild hypoxia in sleeping preterm infants. *Journal of Sleep Research, 17*(3), 344–353.

Veríssimo, M., & Salvaterra, F. (2006). Maternal secure-base scripts and children's attachment security in an adopted sample. *Attachment & Human Development, 8*(3), 261–273.

Vermeiren, R., Bogaerts, J., Ruchkin, V., Deboutte, D., & Schwab-Stone, M. (2004). Subtypes of self-esteem and self-concept in adolescent violent and property offenders. *Journal of Child Psychology and Psychiatry, 45*(2), 405–411.

Villani, S. (2001). Impact of media on children and adolescents: A 10-year review of the research. *Journal of the American Academy of Child and Adolescent Psychiatry, 40*(4), 392–401.

Virji-Babul, N., Kerns, K., Zhou, E., Kapur, A., & Shiffrar, M. (2006). Perceptual-motor deficits in children with Down syndrome: Implications for intervention. *Down Syndrome: Research & Practice, 10*(2), 74–82.

Visscher, W. A., Feder, M., Burns, A. M., Brady, T. M., & Bray, R. M. (2003). The impact of smoking and other substance use by urban women on the birthweight of their infants. *Substance Use and Misuse, 38*(8), 1063–1093.

Vitiello, B. (Ed.). (2006). Guest editorial: Selective serotonin reuptake inhibitors (SSRIs) in children and adolescents. *Journal of Child and Adolescent Psychopharmacology, 16*(1–2), 7–9.

Volkova, A., Trehub, S. E., & Schellenberg, E. G. (2006). Infants' memory for musical performances. *Developmental Science, 9*(6), 583–589.

Volling, B. L. (2003). Sibling relationships. In M. H. Bornstein et al. (Eds.), *Well-being: Positive development across the life course* (pp. 205–220). Mahwah, NJ: Erlbaum.

Volterra, M. C., Caselli, O., Capirci, E., & Pizzuto, E. (2004). Gesture and the emergence and development of language. In M. Tomasello & D. I. Slobin (Eds.), *Beyond nature–nurture*. Mahwah, NJ: Erlbaum.

von Gontard, A. (2006). Elimination disorders: Enuresis and encopresis. In C. Gillberg, R. Harrington, & H.-C. Steinhausen (Eds.), *A clinician's handbook of child and adolescent psychiatry* (pp. 625–654). New York: Cambridge University Press.

von Gontard, A., Freitag, C. M., Seifen, S., Pukrop, R., & Röhling, D. (2006). Neuromotor development in nocturnal enuresis. *Developmental Medicine & Child Neurology, 48*(9), 744–750.

Vu, M. B., Murrie, D., Gonzalez, V., & Jobe, J. B. (2006). Listening to girls and boys talk about girls' physical activity behaviors. *Health Education & Behavior, 33*(1), 81–96.

Vukovic, R. K., & Siegel, L. S. (2006). The double-deficit hypothesis: A comprehensive analysis of the evidence. *Journal of Learning Disabilities, 39*(1), 25–47.

Vygotsky, L. S. (1962). *Thought and language*. Cambridge, MA: MIT Press.

Vygotsky, L. S. (1978). *Mind in society: The development of higher psychological processes*. Cambridge, MA: Harvard University Press.

Wachs, T. D. (2006). The nature, etiology, and consequences of individual differences in temperament. In L. Balter & C. S. Tamis-LeMonda (Eds.), *Child psychology: A handbook of contemporary issues* (2nd ed., pp. 27–52). New York: Psychology Press.

Wadden, T. A., & Stunkard, A. J. (Eds.). (2002). *Handbook of obesity treatment*. New York: Guilford.

Wade, T. D., Bulik, C. M., Neale, M., & Kendler, K. S. (2000). Anorexia nervosa and major depression: Shared genetic and environmental risk factors. *American Journal of Psychiatry, 157,* 469–471.

Wahler, R. G., Herring, M., & Edwards, M. (2001). Coregulation of balance between children's prosocial approaches and acts of compliance: A pathway to mother–child cooperation? *Journal of Clinical Child Psychology, 30*(4), 473–478.

Wainright, J. L., Russell, S. T., & Patterson, C. J. (2004). Psychosocial adjustment, school outcomes, and romantic relationships of adolescents with same-sex parents. *Child Development, 75*(6), 1886–1898.

Wald, J., & Losen, D. J. (2007). Out of sight: The journey through the school-to-prison pipeline. In S. Books (Ed.), *Invisible children in the society and its schools* (3rd ed., pp. 23–37). Mahwah, NJ: Erlbaum.

Walitza, S., et al. (2006). Genetic and neuroimaging studies in attention deficit hyperactivity disorder. *Nervenheilkunde: Zeitschrift für interdisziplinaere Fortbildung, 25*(6), 421–429.

Wallerstein, J., Lewis, J., Blakeslee, S., Hetherington, E. M., & Kelly, J. (2005). Issue 17: Is divorce always detrimental to children? In R. P. Halgin (Ed.), *Taking sides: Clashing views on controversial issues in abnormal psychology* (3rd ed., pp. 298–321). New York: McGraw-Hill.

Walsh, B. T., et al. (2006). Fluoxetine after weight restoration in anorexia nervosa: A randomized controlled trial. *Journal of the American Medical Association, 295*(22), 2605–2612.

Walter, J. L., & LaFreniere, P. J. (2000). A naturalistic study of affective expression, social competence, and sociometric status in preschoolers. *Early Education and Development, 11*(1), 109–122.

Walther, F. J., den Ouden, A. L., & Verloove-Vanhorick, S. P. (2000). Looking back in time: Outcome of a national cohort of very preterm infants born in The Netherlands in 1983. *Early Human Development, 59*(3), 175–191.

Wang, L. (2005). Correlations between self-esteem and life satisfaction in elementary school students. *Chinese Mental Health Journal, 19*(11), 745–749.

Wang, S.-H., Baillargeon, R., & Paterson, S. (2005). Detecting continuity violations in infancy: A new account and new evidence from covering and tube events. *Cognition, 95*(2), 129–173.

Washburn, D. A. (Ed.). (2007). *Primate perspectives on behavior and cognition*. Washington, DC: American Psychological Association.

Watson, J. B. (1924). *Behaviorism*. New York: Norton.

Watson, S. (2008). *Fast food*. New York: Rosen.

Waxman, S. R., & Lidz, J. L. (2006). Early word learning. In D. Kuhn, R. S. Siegler, W. Damon, & R. M. Lerner (Eds.), *Handbook of child psychology: Vol. 2. Cognition, perception, and language* (6th ed., pp. 299–335). Hoboken, NJ: Wiley.

Waxmonsky, J. G. (2005). Nonstimulant therapies for attention-deficit hyperactivity disorder (ADHD) in children and adults. *Essential Psychopharmacology, 6*(5), 262–276.

Wechsler, D. (1975). Intelligence defined and undefined: A relativistic appraisal. *American Psychologist, 30,* 135–139.

Weckerly, J., Wulfeck, B., & Reilly, J. (2004). The development of morphosyntactic ability in atypical populations: The acquisition of tag questions in children with early focal lesions and children with specific-language impairment. *Brain and Language, 88*(2), 190–201.

Weems, C. F., Silverman, W. K., Saavedra, L. M., Pina, A. A., & Lumpkin, P. W. (1999). The discrimination of children's phobias using the Revised Fear Survey Schedule for Children. *Journal of Child Psychology and Psychiatry, 40*(6), 941–952.

Wehkalampi, K., et al. (2008). Genetic and environmental influences on pubertal timing assessed by height growth. *American Journal of Human Biology, 20*(4), 417–423.

Weichold, K., Silbereisen, R. K., & Schmitt-Rodermund, E. (2003). Short-term and long-term consequences of early versus late physical maturation in adolescents. In C. Hayward (Ed.), *Gender differences at puberty* (pp. 241–276). New York: Cambridge University Press.

Weinberg, R. A. (2004). The infant and the family in the 21st century. *Journal of the American Academy of Child and Adolescent Psychiatry, 43*(1), 115–116.

Weinberg, R. A., Waldman, I., van Dulmen, M. H. M., & Scarr, S. (2004). The Minnesota Transracial Adoption Study: Parent reports of psychosocial adjustment at late adolescence. *Adoption Quarterly, 8*(2), 27–44.

Weisler, R. H., & Sussman, N. (2007). Treatment of attention-deficit/hyperactivity disorder. *Primary Psychiatry, 14*(1), 39–42.

Weller, E. B., & Weller, R. A. (1991). Mood disorders. In M. Lewis (Ed.), *Child and adolescent psychiatry: A comprehensive textbook*. Baltimore: Williams & Wilkins.

Wellman, H. M., Cross, D., & Bartsch, K. (1986). Infant search and object permanence: A meta-analysis of the A-not-B error. *Monographs of the Society for Research in Child Development, 5*(3, Serial No. 214).

Wellman, H. M., Fang, F., Liu, D., Zhu, L., & Liu, G. (2006). Scaling of theory-of-mind understandings in Chinese children. *Psychological Science, 17*(12), 1075–1081.

Weng, X., Odouli, R., & Li, D-K. (2008). Maternal caffeine consumption during pregnancy and the risk of miscarriage: A prospective cohort study. *American Journal of Obstetrics and Gynecology,* available online.

Wennergren, A.-C., & Rönnerman, K. (2006). The relation between tools used in action research and the zone of proximal development. *Educational Action Research, 14*(4), 547–568.

Wentworth, N., Benson, J. B., & Haith, M. M. (2000). The development of infants' reaches for stationary and moving targets. *Child Development, 71*(3), 576–601.

Wentzel, K. R., Barry, C. M., & Caldwell, K. A. (2004). Friendships in middle school: Influences on motivation and school adjustment. *Journal of Educational Psychology, 96*(2), 195–203.

Werker, J. F. (1989). Becoming a native listener. *American Scientist, 77,* 54–59.

Werker, J. F., et al. (2007). Infant-directed speech supports phonetic category learning in English and Japanese. *Cognition, 103*(1), 147–162.

Werker, J. F., & Tees, R. C. (2005). Speech perception as a window for understanding plasticity and commitment in language systems of the brain. *Developmental Psychobiology, 46*(3), 233–234.

Werner, E. E. (1988). A cross-cultural perspective on infancy. *Journal of Cross-Cultural Psychology, 19,* 96–113.

Werner, L. A., & Bernstein, I. L. (2001). Development of the auditory, gustatory, olfactory, and somatosensory systems. In E. B. Goldstein (Ed.), *Blackwell handbook of perception* (pp. 669–708). Boston: Blackwell.

Whalen, C. K. (2001). ADHD treatment in the 21st century: Pushing the envelope. *Journal of Clinical Child Psychology, 30*(1), 136–140.

White, C. B., Bushnell, N., & Regnemer, J. L. (1978). Moral development in Bahamian school children: A three-year examination of Kohlberg's stages of moral development. *Developmental Psychology, 14,* 58–65.

Whitehead, J. R., & Corbin, C. B. (1991). Effects of fitness test type, teacher, and gender on exercise intrinsic motivation and physical self-worth. *Journal of School Health, 61,* 11–16.

Whitehouse, E. M. (2006). Poverty. In G. G. Bear & K. M. Minke (Eds.), *Children's needs III: Development, prevention, and intervention* (pp. 835–845). Washington, DC: National Association of School Psychologists.

Williams, M. S. (2004). The psychology of eating. *Psychology and Health, 19*(4), 541–542.

Wilson, E. O. (2004). *On human nature.* Cambridge, MA: Harvard University Press.

Wilson, P. (2004). A preliminary investigation of an early intervention program: Examining the intervention effectiveness of the Bracken Concept Development Program and the Bracken Basic Concept Scale–Revised with Head Start students. *Psychology in the Schools, 41*(3), 301–311.

Wingood, G. M., et al. (2006). Efficacy of an HIV prevention program among female adolescents experiencing gender-based violence. *American Journal of Public Health, 96*(6), 1085–1090.

Winner, E. (2000). The origins and ends of giftedness. *American Psychologist, 55,* 159–169.

Winzelberg, A. J., et al. (2000). Effectiveness of an Internet-based program for reducing risk factors for eating disorders. *Journal of Consulting and Clinical Psychology, 68,* 346–350.

Witherington, D. C., Campos, J. J., Anderson, D. I., Lejeune, L., & Seah, E. (2005). Avoidance of heights on the visual cliff in newly walking infants. *Infancy, 7*(3), 285–298.

Wocadlo, C., & Rieger, I. (2006). Educational and therapeutic resource dependency at early school-age in children who were born very preterm. *Early Human Development, 82*(1), 29–37.

Wodrich, D. L. (2006). Sex chromosome anomalies. In L. Phelps (Ed.), *Chronic health-related disorders in children: Collaborative medical and psychoeducational interventions* (pp. 253–270). Washington, DC: American Psychological Association.

Wojslawowicz Bowker, J. C., Rubin, K. H., Burgess, K. B., Booth-Laforce, C., & Rose-Krasnor, L. (2006). Behavioral characteristics associated with stable and fluid best friendship patterns in middle childhood. *Merrill-Palmer Quarterly, 52*(4), 671–693.

Wolfenden, L. E., & Holt, N. L. (2005). Talent development in elite junior tennis: Perceptions of players, parents, and coaches. *Journal of Applied Sport Psychology, 17*(2), 108–126.

Wong, S. S., Ang, R. P., & Huan, V. S. (2007). Externalizing problems, internalizing problems, and suicidal ideation in Singaporean adolescents: Sex differences. *Current Psychology: Developmental, Learning, Personality, Social, 25*(4), 231–244.

Woodland, M. H. (2008). Whatcha doin' after school?: A review of the literature on the influence of after-school programs on young Black males. *Urban Education, 43*(5), 537–560.

Woods, S. C., & Seeley, R. J. (2002). Hunger and energy homeostasis. In H. Pashler & R. Gallistel (Eds.), *Steven's handbook of experimental psychology: Vol. 3. Learning, motivation, and emotion* (3rd ed., pp. 633–668). Hoboken, NJ: Wiley.

Woolfolk, A. (2008). *Educational psychology* (10th ed.). Boston: Allyn & Bacon.

Worell, J., & Goodheart, C. D. (Eds.). (2006). *Handbook of girls' and women's psychological health: Gender and well-being across the lifespan.* New York: Oxford University Press.

Wozniak, J. R., & Lim, K. O. (2006). Advances in white matter imaging: A review of in vivo magnetic resonance methodologies and their applicability to the study of development and aging. *Neuroscience & Biobehavioral Reviews, 30*(6), 762–774.

Wright, C., & Birks, E. (2000). Risk factors for failure to thrive: A population-based survey. *Child: Care, Health, and Development, 26*(1), 5–16.

Wright, D. W., & Young, R. (1998). The effects of family structure and maternal employment on the development of gender-related attitudes among men and women. *Journal of Family Issues, 19*(3), 300–314.

Wulff, K., & Siegmund, R. (2001). Circadian and ultradian time patterns in human behaviour. Part 1: Activity monitoring of families from prepartum to postpartum. *Biological Rhythm Research, 31*(5), 581–602.

Xie, H. L., Yan, B., Signe M., Hutchins, B. C., & Cairns, B. D. (2006). What makes a girl (or a boy) popular (or unpopular)? African American Children's perceptions and developmental differences. *Developmental Psychology, 42*(4), 599–612.

Yamada, H., et al. (2000). A milestone for normal development of the infantile brain detected by functional MRI. *Neurology, 55*(2), 218–223.

Yarrow, L. J., & Goodwin, M. S. (1973). The immediate impact of separation: Reactions of infants to a change in mother figures. In L. J. Stone, H. T. Smith, & L. B. Murphy (Eds.), *The competent infant: Research and commentary.* New York: Basic Books.

Yarrow, L. J., Goodwin, M. S., Manheimer, H., & Milowe, I. D. (1971, March). *Infant experiences and cognitive and personality development at 10 years.* Paper presented at the meeting of the American Orthopsychiatric Association, Washington, DC.

Youniss, J., & Haynie, D. L. (1992). Friendship in adolescence. *Developmental and Behavioral Pediatrics, 13,* 59–66.

Yu, S., Huang, Z., Schwalberg, R., Overpeck, M., & Jogan, M. (2003). Acculturation and the health and well-being of U.S. immigrant adolescents. *Journal of Adolescent Health, 33*(6), 479–488.

Zajonc, R. B. (2001). The family dynamics of intellectual development. *American Psychologist, 56*(6/7), 490–496.

Zan, B., & Hildebrandt, C. (2003). First graders' interpersonal understanding during cooperative and competitive games. *Early Education and Development, 14*(4), 397–410.

Zarbatany, L., Conley, R., & Pepper, S. (2004). Personality and gender differences in friendship needs and experiences in preadolescence and young adulthood. *International Journal of Behavioral Development, 28*(4), 299–310.

Zarbatany, L., McDougall, P., & Hymel, S. (2000). Gender-differentiated experience in the peer culture: Links to intimacy in preadolescence. *Social Development, 9*(1), 62–79.

Zeifman, D. M. (2004). Acoustic features of infant crying related to intended caregiving intervention. *Infant and Child Development, 13*(2), 111–122.

Zelazo, P. R. (1998). McGraw and the development of unaided walking. *Developmental Review, 18*(4), 449–471.

Zeller, M. H., Reiter-Purtill, J., & Ramey, C. (2008). Negative peer perceptions of obese children in the classroom environment. *Obesity, 16*(4), 755–762.

Zheng, S., & Colombo, J. (1989). Sibling configuration and gender differences in preschool social participation. *Journal of Genetic Psychology, 150,* 45–50.

Zimmerman, B. J. (2000). Self-efficacy: An essential motive to learn. *Contemporary Educational Psychology, 25*(1), 82–91.

Zimmermann, P., Maier, M. A., Winter, M., & Grossmann, K. E. (2001). Attachment and adolescents' emotion regulation during a joint problem-solving task with a friend. *International Journal of Behavioral Development, 25*(4), 331–343.

Zweigenhaft, R. L., & Von Ammon, J. (2000). Birth order and civil disobedience: A test of Sulloway's "born to rebel" hypothesis. *Journal of Social Psychology, 140*(5), 624–627.

Log In!

CDEV was designed for students just like you—busy people who want choices, flexibility, and multiple learning options.

CDEV delivers concise, focused information in a fresh and contemporary format. And ... *CDEV* gives you a variety of online learning materials designed with you in mind.

At **4ltrpress.cengage.com/cdev**, you'll find electronic resources such as printable and interactive **flashcards,** downloadable **study aids, games, quizzes,** and **PowerVisuals** to test your knowledge of key concepts. These resources will help supplement your understanding of core childhood and adolescent development concepts in a format that fits your busy lifestyle.

Visit **4ltrpress.cengage.com/cdev** to learn more about the multiple *CDEV* resources available to help you succeed!

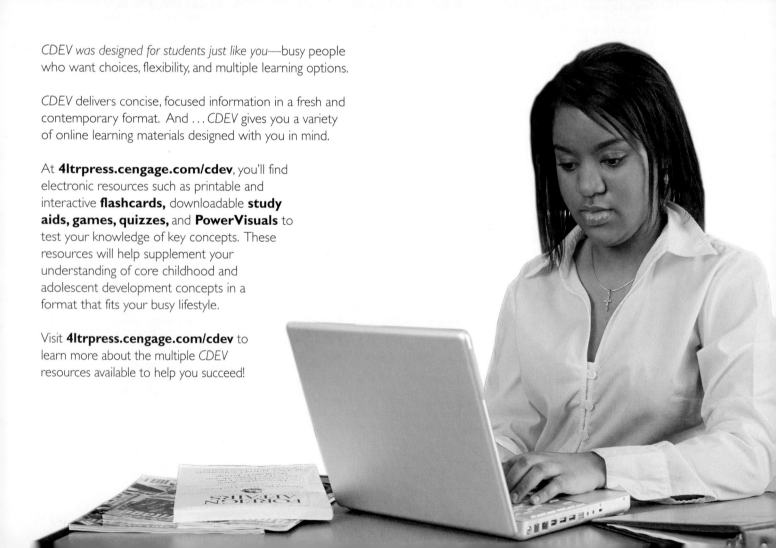

A

Aalsma, M. C., 260
Abbey, A., 244
Abdelaziz, Y. E., 186, 187
Aber, J. L., 226
Ablon, J. S., 192
Abravanel, E., 103
Adams, G. R., 277
Adler-Baeder, F., 224
Adolph, K. E., 46, 89, 90
Agency for Healthcare Research and Quality, 140
Aguiar, A., 100
Ahnert, L., 124
Ainsworth, F., 22
Ainsworth, M., 115, 116, 117, 119, 120
Akman, Y., 277
Alexander, G. M., 177
Alexander, K. W., 156
Alfirevic, Z., 31
Alibali, M. W., 11, 98, 101, 259
Alipuria, L. L., 278
Allen, M., 281
Alloway, T. P., 202
Alsaker, F. D., 227
Amato, P. R., 223, 224
American Academy of Family Physicians, 140
American Academy of Pediatrics, 82, 83
American Association of University Women (AAUW), 228
American Association on Intellectual and Developmental Disabilities (AAIDD), 211, 212
American Fertility Association, 27, 37
American Heart Association (AHA), 183, 184, 185
American Lung Association, 252
American Psychiatric Association, 66, 67, 143, 190, 229, 230, 231, 250
Aminabhavi, V. A., 225
Ammaniti, M., 117
Ances, B. M., 51
Anderman, E. M., 222
Anderson, K. G., 220, 255
Andreou, G., 139
Angier, N., 36, 241
Annett, M., 139
Anthis, K. S., 278
Anzengruber, D., 252
Appel, P. W., 244
Arbona, C., 271

Arbuthnot, J., 266
Archer, J., 12, 172, 177
Archibald, L. M. D., 202
Arduini, R. G., 193
Arija, V., 82
Arnett, J. J., 291, 292
Arnon, S., 66
Arredondo, P., 14
Arterberry, M. E., 69, 70
Aschermann, E., 215
Ash, D., 14
Aslin, R. N., 85
Aspy, C. B., 284
Assefi, N. P., 286
Atkinson, G., 188
Attanucci, J., 266
August, D., 110

B

Bachman, J. G., 271, 272
Bagley, C., 283
Bahna, S. L., 191
Bailey, J. M., 263
Baillargeon, R., 100
Bakker, D. J., 192
Baldry, A. C., 227
Ball, J., 268
Bandura, A., 9, 10, 170, 172, 173, 222
Banet-Weiser, S., 185
Barkley, R. A., 192
Baron, S. W., 288
Barr, R. G., 74, 102
Barry, C. M., 225
Bartholow, B. D., 251
Basic Behavioral Science Task Force, 213
Bateson, P., 33
Battin-Pearson, S., 270
Bauer, K. A., 239
Bauer, K. W., 182, 185
Baum, S. R., 135
Bauman, M. L., 123
Baumrind, D., 163, 165, 166, 222
Bavin, E. L., 111
Bayley, N., 103
Bearce, K. H., 102
Beck, E., 167
Beck, R. J., 153
Behrman, R. E., 54
Beidel, D. C., 231
Beilei, L., 187
Belkin, L., 53, 54
Bell, D., 277
Bell, J. H., 260
Bellodi, L., 249

Belmonte, M. K., 34
Belsky, J., 116, 117, 124, 125, 224
Bem, S. L., 178
Benbow, C. P., 139, 215
Bender, H. L., 163, 164
Bennett, S. F., 286
Bensaheb, A., 231
Berg, C. J., 54
Berger, L. E., 260
Berger, S. E., 46, 89, 90
Bergmann, J., 193
Bernal, G., 289
Berndt, T. J., 225, 280, 282
Bernstein, I. L., 71
Bernstein, I. M., 53
Bersoff, D. M., 266
Berzonsky, M. D., 277, 278
Bialystock, E. K., 155, 216
Biederman, J., 191
Bigler, R. S., 174
Binet, A., 4, 207
Birch, C. D., 251
Bird, A., 130
Birks, E., 82
Bishop, D. M., 287
Bishop, D. V. M., 193
Bjerkedal, T., 167
Black, D. W., 230
Blakeslee, S., 117
Blanton, M., 26
Blass, E. M., 71
Bloch, M., 66
Blom-Hoffman, J., 185
Bloom, B., 244, 246
Bloom, L., 112
Bloom, P., 158
Blyth, D. A., 268, 282
Boada, R., 193
Boccia, M., 127
Boden, C., 193
Bogardus, C., 184
Bohon, C., 270
Boivin, M., 225
Bond, M. J., 249
Bonn-Miller, M. O., 253
Boom, J., 266, 267
Booth-LaForce, C., 174
Bosi, M. L., 241
Boskind-White, M., 248
Bost, L. W., 270
Bouchard, T. J., Jr., 34, 214, 261
Bouffard, T., 279
Boulton, M. J., 171, 172
Bourgeois, M. J., 7
Bower, T. G. R., 93
Bowlby, J., 115–116, 119, 120
Bradley, R. H., 153, 215
Branco, J. C., 152

Brandtjen, H., 124
Brase, G. L., 176
Brazier, A., 29
Bremner, A., 101
Briones, T. L., 87
Brody, L. R., 71
Bromnick, R. D., 260
Bronfenbrenner, U., 12
Bronson, G. W., 92
Brooks, R. B., 222
Brown, B. B., 282
Brown, R. T., 232
Brown, R., 108, 110
Brownell, C. A., 128
Browning, J. R., 284
Bruck, M., 205
Bruckner, T.-A., 75
Brunner, R., 249
Bruno, R., 216
Bryant, P., 101, 155
Bryden, P. J., 139
Buchanan, A., 279
Budney, A. J., 253
Budworth, M.-H., 167
Bugental, D. B., 64, 122
Buhrmester, D., 280
Bunikowski, R., 51
Buriel, R., 166, 167
Burkam, D. T., 270
Burton, R., 175
Bushman, B. J., 172
Bushnell, E. W., 94
Bushnell, I. W. R., 91
Buss, D. M., 176
Bussey, K., 170
Buston, K., 285
Butterfield, S. A., 186, 187
Bynum, M. S., 284

C

Caballero, B., 249
Cachelin, F. M., 248
Caldwell, B. M., 153
Callan, M. J., 198
Calvert, S. L., 154
Camarena, P. M., 282
Camp, C. A., 71
Campanella, J., 102
Campbell, A., 127, 130, 170
Campbell, D. A., 62
Campbell, D. W., 136, 137
Campbell, S. B., 175, 177
Campos, J. J., 92, 126, 127
Camras, L. A., 125, 126
Candy, T. R., 69
Canitano, R., 123

Caplan, M., 171
Caplan, P. J., 170
Capron, C., 240
Carey, B., 124, 167
Carper, R. A., 34
Carriger, M. S., 128
Carroll, J. S., 291
Carver, L. J., 126
Casaer, P., 87
Casas, J. F., 166
Casper, R. C., 184
Cassia, V. M., 91
Castellanos, F. X., 143
Caton, D., 61
Cattell, R. B., 210
Caulfield, R., 66
Cavallini, A., 91
Cavell, T. A., 230
Ceci, S. J., 263
Centers for Disease Control and
    Prevention (CDC), 49, 50,
    51, 83, 141, 242, 243, 244,
    246, 250
Central Intelligence Agency, 215
Cernoch, J., 71
Chan, A. C. M., 289
Chapman, M., 197
Cheng, S. T., 289
Cherney, I. D., 175
Chess, S., 128, 129
Cheung, C., 265
Chomsky, N., 112
Chong, S. C. F., 155
Chou, T. L., 135
Christenson, S. L., 270
Christian, P., 48
Chronis, A. M., 230
Cicchetti, D., 117, 122
Clancy, B., 113
Clark, E. V., 108
Clark, J., 167
Clark, R., 161
Clark, S. E., 174
Clarke-Stewart, K. A., 153
Clayton, R., 67
Cleary, D. J., 225
Clode, D., 139
Cnattingius, S., 53
Cohen, L. S., 66
Cohen-Bendahan, C. C. C., 177
Colby, A., 265
Coleman, M., 224
Coleman, P. K., 117
Collaer, M. L., 261
Collins, W. A., 176, 223, 279, 280
Colombo, J., 104, 169
Commission on Adolescent
    Substance and Alcohol Abuse,
    254
Commons, M. L., 265, 267
Conel, J. L., 87
Conner, K. R., 289
Connolly, J., 281
Connor, P. D., 52
Constantino, J. N., 123
Cooke, B. M., 140

Cooper, J., 289
Coovadia, H., 49, 50
Copeland, A. L., 252
Coplan, R. J., 169
Corballis, P. M., 135
Corbin, C. B., 188
Coren, S., 139
Cornwell, A. A. C., 73
Corsaro, W. A., 225
Corwyn, R. F., 153
Costello, E. J., 241, 250, 254
Costigan, C. L., 279, 280
Courage, M. L., 105
Cowan, C. P., 223
Cowan, N., 202, 204
Cowan, P. A., 223
Craik, F. I. M., 216
Cratty, B., 187
Crawford, J. K., 242
Crockenberg, S. C., 67
Crombie, G., 170
Crook, C. K., 71
Crosby, R. A., 67
Crow, S., 289
Crowther, C., 64
Crusio, W. E., 32
Cruz, N. V., 191
Cuellar, J., 289
Cullen, F. T., 224
Cunningham, R. L., 172
Currie, J., 183
Curry, T. R., 289
Cystic Fibrosis Foundation, 30

Daman-Wasserman, M., 102
Damon, W., 279
Dandy, J., 213
Dane, S., 139
Dang-Vu, T. T., 74
Daniels, D., 33
Daniels, S. R., 183, 184
Darcy, M. U. A., 271
Darwin, C., 4, 11
Daubenmier, J. J., 188
D'Augelli, A. R., 283
Davenne, D., 188
Davis, A., 53
Davis, L., 64
Davis, S. R., 12
Dawson, T. L., 266, 267
Deary, I. J., 211
DeCasper, A. J., 45, 71, 72, 102
DeCherney, A. H., 36
Deep, A. L., 249
de Haan, M., 91
Dehaene-Lambertz, G., 71
DeHart, G. B., 172
Delgado, A. R., 261
Del Giudice, M., 32
Dennis, M., 90
Dennis, W., 90
Denton, K., 198, 199

de Oliveira, F. P., 241
Deonna, T., 123
Derman, O., 240
Dervic, K., 289
Desjardins, M. J., 170
Desjardins, R. N., 111
De Thomas, C., 190
de Villiers, J. G., 107
de Villiers, P. A., 107
de Vries, J. I. P., 46
DeYong, N. G., 103
Dezoete, J. A., 104
Diamond, L. M., 283
Dieterich, S. E., 64
Digout Erhardt, A. R., 225
DiLalla, D. L., 34
Dindia, K., 281
Dishion, T. J., 168, 284
Dockett, S., 216
Dollfus, S., 139
Dombrowski, M. A. S., 66
Donohue, B. C., 254
Donohue, K. F., 251
Donovan, D. M., 269
Dorius, C. J., 254
Dorling, J., 63
Drasgow, E., 124
Dray, A. J., 220, 223
Drewett, R., 64
Dryden, W., 231
Duarté-Veléz, Y. M., 289
Dube, W. V., 8
Duggan, A., 122
Dunn, J., 148, 225
Dunn, M. G., 254
Duntley, J. D., 176
Durkin, J. S., 279
Dyer, S., 169
Dykman, R. A., 82

Eaton, W. O., 137
Eccles, J. S., 130, 263
Eckerman, C. O., 64
Ecuyer-Dab, I., 261
Eder, R. A., 174
Edwards, V. J., 121
Egeland, B., 117
Egerton, A., 253
Eimas, P. D., 93
Eisen, M., 221
Eisenberg, M. E., 242
Eisner, E. W., 137
Elias, M. J., 268
Elkind, D., 107, 168, 260
Ellis, A., 231
Ellis, B. J., 167
Else-Quest, N. M., 170
El-Sheikh, M., 224
Eltzschig, H., 61
Emerson, P. E., 118
Emler, N., 265

Erikson, E., 5, 6–7, 119, 174,
    220, 276, 278, 292
Erikson, J., 6
Eron, L. D., 171, 172
Erzurumluoglu, A., 139
Evans, M. M., 288
Eviatar, Z., 215

F

Fagen, J. W., 102
Fagot, B. I., 130, 170, 175
Fantz, R., 70, 91
Faraone, S. V., 191
Farmer, A., 24
Feigenbaum, P., 73
Feijó, L., 64
Feinberg, M. E., 33, 164, 168
Feingold, B., 191
Feiring, C., 225, 280, 282
Feldman, R., 148
Fergusson, A., 193
Fernandez, T., 193
Fernandez-Twinn, D. S., 48
Féron, J., 94
Ferrell, M., 26
Ficca, G., 73
Field, A. P., 174
Field, C. J., 121
Field, T., 66, 75
Fifer, W. P., 45, 72, 102
Findling, R. L., 289
Finegan, J. K., 261
Finkelhor, D., 121
Finlay, B., 113
Fisch, S. M., 154
Fitzgerald, H. E., 138
Fivush, R., 156, 157
Flavell, J. H., 11, 98, 155, 204,
    205, 257, 259
Flom, R., 130
Florsheim, P., 281
Flynn, M., 268
Foley, G. M., 128
Fontaine, A. M., 168
Forbush, K., 248
Ford, G., 192
Forman-Hoffman, V. L., 248
Forum on Child and Family
    Statistics, 246, 251, 285
Foster-Clark, F. S., 282
Fouad, N. A., 14
Franklin, A., 70
Freeman, M. S., 71
French, K. E., 187
Frerichs, L., 83
Freud, A., 236
Freud, S., 4, 5, 6, 16, 119,
    219–220, 236
Fried, P. A., 52
Frith, U., 192
Frodi, A. M., 122

Fromkin, V., 113
Fry, D. P., 137
Funatogawa, K., 183
Furman, W., 120, 280

G

Galand, P., 277
Ganesh, M. P., 121
Garber, H. L., 154
Gardner, H., 206, 207
Gartstein, M. A., 128
Garvey, C., 170
Gathercole, S. E., 202, 204
Gau, S. S. F., 254
Ge, X., 241
Geake, J., 14
Geary, D. C., 12, 176, 187, 188
Geller, P. A., 43
Georgiades, S., 122, 123
Geschwind, D. H., 139
Gesell, A., 4, 5, 90
Ghetti, S., 156
Giaschi, D., 193
Gibb, R., 135
Gibson, E. J., 92, 95
Gidding, S. S., 182
Gilligan, C., 266, 267
Gleason, T. R., 148, 149, 168, 225
Gobet, F., 204
Goel, P., 53
Golan, H., 62
Goldberg, J., 60
Goldschmidt, L., 52
Goldsmith, H. H., 128
Goldstein, E. B., 261
Goldstein, S., 222
Goldston, D. B., 289
Gonzalez, V., 216
González, Y. S., 280
Goodheart, C. D., 130
Goodman, G. S., 157
Goodwin, M. S., 121
Goossens, L., 185
Gopnik, A., 155, 156, 160
Gordon, D. A., 266
Gormally, S., 74
Gort, M., 216
Gottfried, G. M., 150
Gottlieb, B. H., 291
Gottlieb, G., 32
Graber, J. A., 241
Grayson, A., 74
Greco, C., 102
Green, R., 223
Greenberg, J., 265
Greene, R. W., 192
Greene, S. M., 18
Greenough, W. T., 87, 95
Grigorenko, E. L., 193
Grilo, C. M., 249
Grindrod, C. M., 135

Groen, M., 91
Grolnick, W. S., 127
Grön, G., 176
Grossmann, K., 117
Grusec, J. E., 164, 165, 166
Guerdjikova, A. I., 185
Guerin, D. W., 129
Guerrini, I., 48, 52
Güntürkün, O., 87
Gutknecht, L., 123
Guttmacher Institute, 284, 285
Guzikowski, W., 62

H

Haapasalo, J., 122
Hagan, R., 170
Haith, M. M., 69, 91, 92
Hakuta, K., 154
Halgin, R. P., 229
Hall, G. S., 4, 236
Hall, H. I., 243
Halliday, L. F., 193
Halpern, D. F., 261, 262, 263
Hamilton, B. E., 62, 285
Hammond, N. R., 156, 157
Hampson, E., 261
Hangal, S., 225
Hanlon, T. E., 225
Hanna, A. C., 249
Hannon, E. E., 71
Hannon, P., 140
Hansen, D. H., 122
Hansen, J. C., 270
Happaney, K., 64, 122
Harel, J., 117
Harlow, H. F., 119, 120
Harlow, M. K., 119
Harris, G., 231
Harris, J. R., 125
Harris, S. R., 104
Hart, D., 266
Hart, S. J., 28
Harter, S., 174
Harter, S., 220, 222, 275, 279
Hartup, W. W., 171, 226, 280, 281
Hasler, G., 191
Hasselhorn, M., 204
Hastings, P. D., 170, 171, 172
Hatcher, R. A., 37
Hauck, F. R., 75
Hay, C., 288
Hay, D. F., 170
Hayne, H., 102
Haynie, D. L., 281
Hayward, C., 242
Hazell, P., 191
Healy, M. D., 167
Hebebrand, J., 184
Hebert, T. P., 178
Heilman, K. M., 213
Heimann, M., 105

Heindel, J. J., 53
Helms, J. E., 210
Helwig, C. C., 267
Hen, R., 24
Henry, D., 171
Henzi, S. P., 281
Hershberger, S. L., 283
Hertenstein, M. J., 126, 127
Hertz-Lazarowitz, R., 281
Hetherington, E. M., 18, 20, 164, 224
Hicks, B. M., 171
Hildebrandt, C., 220
Hilden, K., 201
Hill, E. M., 262
Hill, S. E., 130
Hill, S. Y., 24
Hindmarsh, G. J., 63
Hines, D. A., 121
Hinney, A., 184
Hinojosa, T., 138
Hinshaw, S. P., 192
Hoegh, D. G., 7
Hoff, E., 107, 108
Hoff, E. V., 149
Hogan, A. M., 62
Högler, W., 183
Hohmann, L. M., 168
Holland, J. J., 172
Holland, J. L., 270
Hollin, C. R., 267
Holloway, J. H., 271, 272
Holt, N. L., 223
Homer, B. D., 158, 160
Homsi, G., 252
Hong, H-W., 119
Honzik, M. P., 211
Hopkins, B., 46
Hort, B., 156
Hossain, M., 53
Houts, A. C., 143
Howe, M. L., 158
Hubbard, F. O. A., 74, 75
Hudson, J. A., 157
Huesmann, L. R., 153
Huestis, M. A., 51
Hughes, C., 148
Huizink, A. C., 52
Huleihel, M., 62
Hunt, C. E., 75
Hunter, B. C., 66
Hur, Y., 34
Hurd, Y. L., 51
Hyde, J. S., 262, 283
Hynes, M., 48

I

Iacono, W. G., 214
Ikeda, K., 144
Ingersoll, G. M., 260
Inhelder, 197
International Human Genome Sequencing Consortium, 24

J

Jackendoff, R., 110
Jacklin, C. N., 130, 261
Jacobs, D. M., 29
Jacobs, J. E., 222
Jacobson, J. L., 53
Jacobson, L., 228
Jacobson, P. F., 159
James, W., 69
Jeng, S.-F., 63
Joe, S., 289
Johnson, R. S., 127
Johnson, W., 24, 34, 214, 261
Johnston, C. A., 185, 186
Johnston, L. D., 250, 253, 254
Joint United Nations Programme on HIV/AIDS (UNAIDS), 84
Jones, D. C., 242
Jones, S. S., 119
Jonkman, S., 252
Jorgensen, G., 267
Joshi, P. T., 122
Joshi, R. M., 192
Juffer, F., 82
Junod, A. F., 183

K

Kagan, J., 121
Kagan, L. J., 230
Kaiser Family Foundation, 285
Kaminski, R. A., 12
Kanevsky, L., 14
Kantas, A., 138
Karapetsas, A., 138
Karatekin, C., 186, 187
Karavasilis, L., 117
Katz, R., 223
Katzman, D. K., 248
Kavanaugh, R. D., 168
Kavcic, T., 167
Kaye, W. H., 248, 249
Kazdin, A. E., 230
Kazui, M., 117
Kearney, C. A., 231
Keen, D., 148
Keller, H., 127
Keller, S., 251
Kellman, P. J., 69, 70
Kellogg, R., 138, 139
Kelly, K. M., 260
Kempes, M., 172
Kendler, K. S., 231
Kennell, J. H., 67
Kenny, M. C., 230
Keogh, A. F., 210
Kerns, K. A., 117
Kidd, E., 111
Killen, M., 226
Kim, J-Y., 167
Kim, K. H., 206

Kimura, D., 261
King, N. J., 175
King, R., 260
Kinsbourne, M., 135
Kinsey, A. C., 283
Kirchler, E., 282
Kirkcaldy, B. D., 184, 188
Kistner, J., 230
Kjelsås, E., 247
Klaus, M. H., 67
Klein, P. J., 102
Klein, R. E., 121
Klier, C. M., 67
Klintsova, A. Y., 87
Klomek, A. B., 289
Knaak, S., 83
Knafo, A., 24, 170, 171
Knox, P. L., 267
Kochanska, G., 126, 165
Kogan, M. D., 63
Kohl, C., 66
Kohlberg, L., 177, 198, 199, 200, 201, 265, 266, 267
Kohyama, J., 142
Kolata, G., 184
Kolb, B., 135
Konign, E. A., 279
Kopp, C. B., 127
Kotler, J. A., 154
Kotsis, V., 184
Krackow, E., 205
Kramer, R., 266
Krebs, D. L., 198, 199
Kristensen, P., 167
Kroeger, K. A., 110
Krojgaard, P., 101
Krueger, C., 46
Krueger, R. F., 24
Kuczaj, S. A., II, 109
Kuczmarski, R. J., 80, 81, 133, 134, 182
Kuhl, P. K., 93, 94
Kuhn, D., 101
Kuk, L. S., 277
Kulp, J., 125
Kundanis, R., 154
Kuterbach, J. M., 260
Kwok, H. W. M., 124

L

Labouvie-Vief, G., 11
Labrell, F., 157
Laflamme, D., 117
Laflin, M. T., 285
LaFreniere, P. J., 171, 175
Lai, H.-L., 66
Lam, K. S., 123
Lam, T. H., 242
LaMay, M. L., 261
Lamb, M. E., 124
Lambert, A., 222
Lamers, C. T. J., 253
Lampl, M., 81

Lange, G., 158
Langlois, J. H., 33, 225
Lansford, J. E., 18
Lantolf, J. P., 152
Laplan, R. T., 271
LaPointe, L. L., 113
Lapsley, D. K., 198
Largo, R. H., 187
Larkin, J., 170
Larroque, B., 64
Larson, R., 279
Larsson, I., 284
Latham, G. P., 167
Lau, 164
Laurendeau, M., 149
Laursen, B., 279, 280
Lawler, C., 53
Lawson, K., 64
Lazar, R. E., 227
Leaper, C., 170, 177
Lecanuet, J. P., 45, 46
Lee, V. E., 270
Leerkes, E. M., 67
Lefkowitz, E. S., 178
Legro, R. S., 37
Leinbach, M. D., 175
Lejeune, C., 51
Lengua, L. J., 152
Lenneberg, E. H., 106
Leon, M. R., 191
Leonard, C. M., 193
Leonard, S. P., 177
Leonardo, E. D., 24
Letourneau, E. J., 121, 122
Leung, 164
Lever, N., 270
Levin, E. D., 191
Levinthal, B. R., 215
Lewinsohn, P. M., 231
Lewis, B. A., 52
Lewis, H. L., 277
Lewis, M., 225, 280
Li, Q., 227
Lickliter, R., 34, 107
Lidz, J. L., 158, 160, 161
Lim, K. O., 87
Limber, S. P., 126
Ling, L., 28
Lipman, E. L., 166
Lipsitt, L. P., 71, 72
Lipton, R. C., 121
Livne, N. L., 213
Lleras, A., 215
Lochman, J. E., 255
Locke, J., 4, 16
Loehlin, J. C., 34
Logan, C., 24
Long, L. H., 272
Loovis, E. M., 186, 187
Lorenz, K., 11, 120
Losen, D. J., 268, 269
Lourenço, O., 152
Lovaas, O. I., 124
Lubinski, D., 206, 215
Lucariello, J. M., 204
Luciana, M., 34, 134, 135

Ludemann, P. M., 92
Luyckx, K., 292
Lykken, D. T., 34, 171
Lynam, D. R., 288
Lynn, S. J., 205
Lynne, S. D., 241, 242
Lynskey, M. T., 254
Lyon, G. R., 192

M

Maccoby, E. E., 130, 170, 176, 223
MacDorman, M. F., 286
Macfarlane, A., 71
Mackic-Magyar, J., 123
Maclean, A. M., 266
Madon, S., 228
Magdalin, S., 121
Mahler, M. S., 128
Maimburg, R. D., 123
Malinosky-Rummell, R., 122
Malone, P. S., 224
Maluccio, A. N., 122
Mameli, M., 33
Mandler, J. M., 157
Maneschi, M. L., 192
Mansoor, E., 191
Maratsos, M. P., 101
Marcia, J. E., 276
Marcovitch, S., 101
Marean, G. C., 94
Marsiglio, S., 224
Marsiglio, W., 223
Martell, C. R., 283
Martin, C. L., 130, 157, 170, 177, 178
Masalha, S., 148
Masi, G., 232
Massaro, D. W., 154
Maternity Center Association, 62
Mathews, T. J., 286
Matlin, M. W., 130, 176
Matthews, J., 138
Matthews, K. A., 224
Maurer, C. E., 70
Maurer, D. M., 70
Mazei-Robison, M. S., 191
McBride, M. C., 197
McCabe, M. P., 242
McCall, R. B., 211
McCartney, K., 116, 117
McClellan, J. M., 124
McCracken, J., 123
McCrae, R. R., 34
McDevitt, T. M., 136
McDonough, L., 108
McEwan, M. H., 136
McGinnis, M. Y., 172
McGlaughlin, A., 74
McGrath, M., 64
McHale, S. M., 166
McIlvane, W. J., 8
McLaughlin, J. K., 53
McManus, C., 139

McManus, I. C., 138
Meaney, K. S., 188
Mednick, S. A., 171
Meier, B. P., 172
Meldrum, M. L., 61
Mellon, M. W., 143, 144
Meltzoff, A. N., 101, 102, 103, 160
Mendle, J., 240
Merrill, L. L., 122
Merrill, M., 207
Messer, D., 220
Metcalfe, J. S., 89
Metzger, K. L., 24
Meyer, S., 127, 151
Mezzich, A. C., 254
Miklos, E. A., 183
Milgram, R. M., 213
Miller, A. L., 289
Miller, C. F., 175, 176, 177
Miller, G. A., 202
Miller, J. G., 266
Miller, S. M., 174
Miranda, A., 191
Mischo, C., 220
Mitchell, A. L., 252
Miyake, A., 203
Miyatsuji, H., 100
Moens, E., 185
Moilanen, J., 122
Molfese, V. J., 153
Molinari, L., 225
Moneta, G. B., 169
Monsour, A., 279
Montemayor, R., 221
Moore, L. L., 137
Moran, P., 139
Morelli, G. A., 141
Morgan-Lopez, A. A., 254
Morley, J. E., 44
Morrell, J., 117
Morris, P. A., 12
Morton, S. M. B., 48
Moses, L. J., 155
Mosher, W. D., 284
Mueller, R., 123
Mueller, U., 259
Mulder, E. J. H., 52
Munroe, R. H., 177
Muris, P., 174

N

Nadeau, L., 63
Nagin, D. S., 171
Narusyte, J., 32
Nash, A., 154
National Aids Hotline, 50
National Bureau of Economic Research (NBER), 183
National Center for Children in Poverty, 82
National Center for Education Statistics, 269, 270

National Center for Health Statistics (NCHS), 75, 246, 289
National Center for Injury Prevention and Control, 141, 289
National Guideline Clearinghouse, 26
National Institute of Child Health and Human Development (NICHD), 76, 77, 124
National Institutes of Health, 51
National Library of Medicine, 43, 83
National Sleep Foundation, 141, 142
Natsopoulos, D., 139
Nauta, M. M., 271
Nduati, R., 49
Neisser, U., 206, 213, 214
Nelson, C. A., 92, 134, 135
Nelson, K., 108, 110, 156, 157, 158, 160
Nelson, W. M., III, 110
Nesdale, D., 222
Nettelbeck, T., 213
Newburn-Cook, C. V., 53
Newman, R., 103, 107
Nielsen, S., 248
Nielsen, S. J., 183
Niemeier, H. M., 247
Nigg, J. T., 189, 191, 192
Nock, M. K., 229
Nolen-Hoeksema, S., 248
Nomaguchi, K. M., 225
Nonaka, A. M., 111
Nonnemaker, J. M., 252
Norlander, T., 178
Nowinski, J., 260
Nucci, L. P., 267
Nyunt, A., 44

O

Oates, J., 220
O'Boyle, M. W., 139
O'Dea, J. A., 279
O'Donnell, L., 284
Oettinger, G., 272
Office of National Statistics, 26
Ohnishi, T., 176
O'Keeffe, M. J., 63
Oliver, M. B., 283
Ollendick, T. H., 175
Olson, S. L., 170, 171
Omori, M., 260
O'Neill, D. K., 155
Ong, A. D., 278
Ormrod, J. E., 136
Örnkloo, H., 130
Orstavik, R. E., 231
Ortega, V., 283
O'Shea, R. P., 135
Oster, H., 71, 125

O'Sullivan, L. F., 241
Ouellette, G. P., 107
Owsley, C., 94
Ozanne, S. E., 48
Oztop, E., 103
Ozturk, M., 272

P

Paavola, L., 148
Page, K., 290
Palmer, B., 248
Palmer, E. J., 266, 267
Palmer, E. L., 154
Papaioannou, A., 188
Parke, R. D., 166, 167
Parkes, A., 244
Parsons, T. D., 261
Parten, M. B., 168, 169
Passell, P., 268
Pastor, J., 276
Patenaude, J., 267
Paterson, D. S., 75, 76
Patock-Peckham, J. A., 254
Patterson, C. J., 223
Patterson, G. R., 172
Patterson, M. M., 174
Pauli-Pott, U., 129
Paulussen-Hoogeboom, M. C., 164
Paus, T., 134, 135
Paxton, S. J., 242, 247
Pedersen, S., 230
Peeters, M. W., 237
Pei, M., 177
Pelphrey, K. A., 102
Pemberton, E. F., 138
Penn, H. E., 123
Pennington, B. F., 193
Peplau, L. A., 283
Pereira, B., 227
Perren, S., 227
Perrin, M. C., 54
Perry, H. M., III, 44
Perry, T. B., 280, 281
Perry, W., 11
Persson, G. E. B., 171
Philip, J., 31
Phillips, D. A., 215
Phinney, J. S., 277, 278
Phipps, M. G., 54
Piaget, J., 4, 9–11, 14, 16, 97, 98, 99, 100, 101, 147, 148, 149, 150, 151, 152, 154, 156, 160, 168, 171, 195, 197, 198, 199, 205, 220, 259
Pichichero, M. E., 243
Piek, J. P., 88, 174
Pierce, K. M., 124
Pierce, S. H., 158
Pike, R., 174
Pinard, A., 149
Pine, K. J., 154
Pinker, S., 109, 110, 112

Pinkerton, S. D., 283
Plomin, R., 24, 33, 34, 123, 170, 171, 193
Polivy, J., 247
Popkin, B. M., 183
Popma, A., 172
Porfeli, E. J., 272
Porter, R. H., 71
Posey, D. J., 191, 192
Posner, M. I., 87
Powlishta, K. K., 130, 177
Pratt, C., 155
Prescott, P. A., 71
Presentacion, M. J., 191
Pressley, M., 201
Prieto, G., 261
Priner, R., 71
Prinz, W., 102, 103
Provence, S., 121
Pugh, K. R., 113
Pujol, J., 85
Pulverman, R., 160

Q

Queen, J. A., 185, 188

R

Raikes, H., 216
Ramey, C. T., 48
Randel, B., 213
Rapin, I., 124
Rathus, J. H., 289
Rathus, S. A., 49, 178, 252, 286
Rebar, R. W., 36
Reddy, H., 175
Reddy, L. A., 190
Redgrave, G. W., 254
Reef, S., 50, 62
Reichenberg, A., 54
Reiff, M. I., 191
Reijneveld, S. A., 75
Reis, O., 282
Reschly, A., 270
Rest, J. R., 265
Rezvani, A. H., 191
Riala, K., 289
Riccomini, P. J., 270
Rice, C. E., 122
Richards, H. C., 265
Richards, M. H., 279
Richards, T. W., 45
Rieger, I., 63
Riepe, M. W., 176
Rizzolatti, G., 102, 103
Robert, M., 261
Roberts, W., 170, 171
Robins Wahlin, T., 29
Rockefeller, N., 192
Roden, D. M., 184
Roebers, C. M., 205

Roeser, R. W., 276
Roffwarg, H. P., 74
Rogol, A., 236
Ronald, A., 34
Rondal, J. A., 28
Rönnerman, K., 152
Roopnarine, J. L., 165
Rose, A. J., 225
Rose, S. A., 102, 103, 105
Rosenbaum, D. E., 139
Rosenblatt, J. S., 34
Rosenstein, D., 71
Rosenthal, R., 228
Ross, H., 167
Rotenberg, K. J., 225, 281
Rothbart, M. K., 87, 127, 129
Rothman, S., 210
Rottinghaus, P. J., 270
Roulet-Perez, E., 123
Rousseau, J.-J., 4
Rovee-Collier, C., 102
Rowen, B., 181
Rowlands, C., 29
Rubenstein, S., 249
Rubia, K., 201
Rubin, K. H., 168
Ruble, D. N., 157, 170, 177, 178
Ruchkin, V., 288
Rudolph, K. D., 268
Rudy, D., 164, 165
Ruff, H. A., 64
Rumbold, A. R., 50
Runyon, M. K., 230
Rushton, J. P., 210
Russ, S. W., 148
Russell, S. T., 283
Rutter, M., 121

S

Sabattini, L., 177
Sadker, D. M., 229
Sadler, T. W., 53
Saffran, J. R., 93
Sahler, O. J. Z., 66
Saigal, S., 64
Saiki, J., 100
Saito, S., 203
Salapatek, P., 92
Sales, J. M., 156
Salmivalli, C., 174
Salvaterra, F., 117, 120
Salvy, S-J., 184
Salzarulo, P., 73
Santelli, J. S., 244, 286
Santos, D. C. C., 88
Saroglou, V., 277
Sarrazin, P., 228
Saudino, K. J., 137
Save the Children, 54, 64, 65
Savin-Williams, R. C., 282, 283
Sawyer, D. J., 193
Sayegh, Y., 90
Scarr, S., 32

Schaal, B., 125
Schaffer, H. R., 118
Scharf, M., 167
Scheithauer, H., 227
Scher, A., 117
Scheres, 143
Schlaggar, B. L., 85
Schonfeld, A. M., 52
Schoppe-Sullivan, S. J., 129, 130
Schraf, M., 281
Schuetze, P., 52, 122
Schulte-Körne, G., 192
Schultz, D. P., 6
Schultz, R. W., 187
Schultz, S. E., 6
Schumacher, D., 185, 188
Schwartz, R. G., 159
Schwartz, S., 276
Scott, J. R., 50
Scourfield, J., 230
Secker-Walker, R. H., 53
Seeley, R. J., 185
Seidah, A., 279
Selman, R. L., 220, 221, 223, 225, 226
Senman, L., 155
Serbin, L. A., 130, 169
Shaywitz, B. A., 193
Shaywitz, S. E., 192, 193
Shea, A. K., 75
Shear, K., 231
Sheeber, L. B., 279
Sheese, B. E., 127
Shen, R-Y, 252
Sherwin-White, S., 168
Shin, H. B., 216
Shirk, S., 279
Shonk, S. M., 122
Shore, C., 151
Shroff, H., 248
Sickmund, M., 287, 288
Siegel, L. S., 104, 193
Siegler, R. S., 11, 98, 101, 259
Siegmund, R., 73
Signorello, L. B., 53
Silber, E. S., 229
Silbereisen, R. K., 12
Simion, F., 91
Simmons, R. G., 268
Simon, H. A., 204
Simon, T., 4, 207
Simonelli, A., 82
Simonton, D. K., 213
Simpkins, S. D., 222
Singer, L. T., 52
Singh, K., 272
Sirrs, S. M., 85
Skeels, H. M., 121
Skinner, B. F., 7, 8, 110
Skoczenski, A. M., 91
Slater, A., 93
Slaughter, V., 156
Slavin, R. E., 227, 228
Sloan, S., 83
Slobin, D. I., 109
Slutske, W. S., 254

Small, S. A., 222
Smarty, S., 289
Smetana, J. G., 226, 236, 279, 280, 266
Smiley, P. A., 127
Smith, A. M., 52
Smith, C. L., 128
Smith, P. K., 137
Smolka, E., 215
Smoll, F. L., 187
Snarey, J. R., 266, 267, 277
Snedeker, J., 111
Snegovskikh, V., 58
Snow, C., 113
Snyder, H. M., 287, 288
Snyderman, M., 210
Soan, S., 193
Sontag, L. W., 45
Sorce, J., 93
Soussignan, R., 125
Spearman, C., 205–206
Spelke, E. S., 94
Spence, M. J., 72, 102
Speranza, M., 249
Spieker, S. J., 117
Spitz, R. A., 121
Spitzer, R. L., 189
Sroufe, L. A., 126
Staff, J., 271, 272, 281
Stagnitti, K., 148
Stahmer, A. C., 124
Stams, G. J. M., 117
Stanford, J. N., 242
Stankoff, B., 85
State, M., 193
Stauffacher, K., 72
Steele, H., 117
Steele, R. G., 185, 186
Steinberg, L., 282
Steinbrink, C., 193
Steiner, M., 75
Stemberger, J. P., 159
Stephenson, R. H., 185
Sternberg, R. J., 206, 213
Stevens, B., 75
Stevens, T., 210
Stevenson, H. W., 213
Stevenson, J., 137
Stifter, C. A., 128
Stipek, D. 128, 154
Stoel-Gammon, C., 107
Storch, E. A., 184
Stores, G., 142
Stormshak, E. A., 12, 168, 284
Straus, M. A., 121
Strayer, J., 170, 171
Streri, A., 138
Striegel-Moore, R. H., 248
Strock, M., 123, 124
Strohner, H., 160
Strutt, G. F., 201, 202
Stunkard, A. J., 185
Styfco, S. J., 215
Sugiyama, M., 8
Suh, S., 270

Sukhodolsky, D. G., 230
Sullivan, B. A., 270
Sulloway, F. J., 167
Sumner, C. R., 144
Sun, S. S., 238
Suomi, S. J., 120
Supple, A. J., 222
Suris, J. C., 289
Susman, E. J., 236
Sussman, N., 189, 190
Svedin, C. 284
Sylva, K., 152
Symons, D. K., 174
Szaflarski, J. P., 135

T

Takahashi, M., 8
Tallandini, M. A., 138
Tamis-LeMonda, C. S., 107, 108, 109, 110, 111, 158, 159
Tanner, J. M., 82, 134, 237, 238, 239, 240
Tapper, K., 171, 172
Tashiro, T., 223
Tassi, F., 222
Taylor, C., 125
Taylor, H. G., 63
Taylor, M., 148, 156
Tees, R. C., 113
Tehrani, J. A., 171
Tercyak, K. P., 183
Terman, L., 207, 208
Theim, K. R., 185
Thomas, A., 128, 129
Thomas, J. R., 187
Thompson, A. M., 187, 188, 247
Thompson, M. P., 289
Thompson, R. A., 117, 126, 220
Thompson, V. J., 127, 183
Thorne, S. L., 152
Thurlow, M. L., 270
Thurmond, S., 53
Thurstone, L. L., 206
Tijms, J., 192
Timmerman, L. M., 124
Tinbergen, N., 11
Tobbell, J., 268
Tod, J., 193
Towse, J., 202, 203, 204
Tracey, T. J. G., 271
Trainor, L. J., 111
Trehub, S. E., 71
Tremblay, R. E., 171
Treuth, M. S., 185
Trevarthen, C., 111
Troxel, W. M., 224
Tsuneishi, S., 87
Turner, S. M., 231
Tyc, V. L., 183

U

Ubersfeld, G., 157
Umek, L. M., 14
United Nations Children's Fund (UNICEF), 140, 141
United Nations Department of Economic and Social Affairs, 47
United Nations Joint Programme on HIV/AIDS, 243, 244
United Nations Statistics Division, 215
University of Iowa Hospitals and Clinics, 247
U.S. Census Bureau, 14, 15, 46, 217, 224
U.S. Department of Agriculture, 246, 247
U.S. Department of Health and Human Services (USDHHS), 121
U.S. Food and Drug Administration, 50
Uylings, H. B. M., 113

V

Vaccaro, B. G., 126
Vacek, P. M., 53
Væth, M., 123
Valentini, P., 138
Vandell, D. L., 124
Vander Ven, T., 224
van IJzendoorn, M. H., 74, 75, 82, 117
van Rijn, S., 28
Vartanian, O., 213
Vellutino, F. R., 192
Verbeek, M. M. A., 75
Veríssimo, M., 117, 120
Vermeiren, R., 288
Verny, T., 124
Villani, S., 172
Virji-Babul, N., 28
Visscher, W. A., 51
Vitiello, B., 231
Volkova, A., 71
Volling, B. L., 167
Volterra, M. C., 107, 112
Von Ammon, J., 167
von Gontard, A., 143, 144
von Hofsten, C., 130
Vu, M. B., 188
Vukovic, R. K., 193
Vygotsky, L. S., 13–14, 148, 152, 161

W

Wachs, T. D., 128, 129
Wadden, T. A., 185

Wade, T. D., 249
Wahler, R. G., 223
Wainright, J. L., 223
Wald, J., 268, 269
Walitza, S., 191
Walk, R. D., 92
Walker, S. O., 193
Wallerstein, J., 224
Walsh, B. T., 249
Walter, J. L., 171, 175
Walther, F. J., 63
Wang, L., 222
Wang, S.-H., 101
Washburn, D. A., 11
Watson, J. B., 4–5, 7, 8
Watson, S., 182
Waxman, S. R., 158, 160, 161
Waxmonsky, J. G., 192
Wechsler, D., 205, 209, 210
Weckerly, J., 215
Weems, C. F., 175
Wehkalampi, K., 183
Weichold, J., 241
Weinberg, R. A., 32, 87
Weisler, R. H., 189, 190
Weller, E. B., 230

Weller, R. A., 230
Wellman, H. M., 101, 155
Wells, E. A., 269
Weng, X., 53
Wennergren, A.-C., 152
Wentworth, N., 88
Wentzel, K. R., 225
Werker, J. F., 94, 113
Werner, E. E., 101
Werner, L. A., 71
Werry, J. S., 124
Whalen, C. K., 192
Whitbourne, S. K., 229
White, C. B., 266
White, W. C., 248
Whitehead, J. R., 188
Whitehouse, E. M., 154
Whitesell, N. R., 279
Whyte, J., 210
Wiggins, C. N., 28
Wiggs, L., 142
Williams, M. S., 248
Williams, W. M., 213, 263
Wilson, E. O., 171
Wilson, P., 154
Wimmer, H., 193

Wingood, G. M., 244
Winner, E., 215
Winzelberg, A. J., 249
Witherington, D. C., 93
Wocadlo, C., 63
Wodrich, D. L., 28, 29
Wojslawowicz Bowker, J. C., 225
Wolfenden, L. E., 223
Wong, S. S., 289
Woodland, M. H., 272
Woods, S. C., 185
Woolfolk, A., 226, 227, 228
Worell, J., 130
Wozniak, J. R., 87
Wright, C., 82
Wright, D. W., 225
Wulff, K., 73

X
Xie, H. L., 225

Y
Yamada, H., 135
Yarrow, L. J., 121
Young, R., 225
Youniss, J., 281, 282
Yu, S., 227

Z
Zajonc, R. B., 167
Zan, B., 220
Zarbatany, L., 225
Zeifman, D. M., 74
Zelazo, P. R., 90, 101
Zeldow, P. B., 178
Zeller, M. H., 184
Zheng, S., 169
Zimmerman, B. J., 222
Zimmermann, P., 127
Zupancic, M., 167
Zweigenhaft, R. L., 167

Listen Up!

CDEV was designed for students just like you – busy people who want choices, flexibility, and multiple learning options.

CDEV delivers concise, focused information in a fresh and contemporary format. And... CDEV gives you a variety of online learning materials designed with you in mind.

At 4ltrpress.cengage.com/cdev, you'll find electronic resources such as printable and interactive flashcards, downloadable study aids, games, quizzes, and PowerVisuals. These resources will help supplement your understanding of childhood and adolescent development concepts in a format that fits your busy lifestyle.

Visit 4ltrpress.cengage.com/cdev to learn more about the multiple CDEV resources available to help you succeed!

SUBJECT INDEX

Note: Boldface terms and page numbers indicate key terms.

A

A not B error, 101
abortion, spontaneous, 35
abstinence syndrome, 251
abuse
    child, 121–122, 249
    sexual, 121, 249
    substance, 244, 250–255
accommodation
    in cognitive development,
    10, 98
    visual, 70
achieved ethnic identity, 278
achievement, 205
    identity, 277
acne, in puberty, 239
acquired immunodeficiency
  syndrome (AIDS), 40, 50, 84,
  242, 243–244, 245
active genetic–environmental
  correlation, 33
active–passive controversy, in
  perceptual development, 16,
  94–95
adaptation, 10
adenine with thymine (A with T),
  24
ADHD. *See* attention-deficit/
  hyperactivity disorder
adipose tissue, 184–185
adolescence
    body image in, 242, 247
    career development and work
      experience in, 270–272
    cognitive abilities in, 261–263
    dating in, 281–282
    death rates in, 246, 248
    delinquency in, 287–288
    early vs. late maturers in,
      241–242
    egocentrism in, 260–261
    emerging adulthood and,
      290–291
    formal operations stage and,
      258–259
    growth spurt in, 237–239
    health in, 242–244, 245,
      246–250
    identity in, 276–279, 281
    moral development in, 200,
      263–267
    peer relationships in, 280–282,
      284–285
    pubertal changes in, 236–242
    relationships with parents in,
      279–280
    school and, 267–270
    sex differences in cognitive
      abilities in, 261–263
    sexuality in, 282–287
    substance abuse in, 244,
      250–255

    suicide in, 288–289
adoption, 38
adoption studies, 34
adulthood, emerging, 290–292
AFP. *See* alpha-fetoprotein (AFP)
  assay
African Americans
    culture of, 14, 15
    death rates of adolescent, 246
    delinquency and, 287
    dropout rates and, 269–270
    identity development and, 278
    intelligence tests and, 210, 213
    nutrition and, 183, 184
    poverty and, 288
    sickle-cell anemia in, 29
    SIDS and, 75
    suicide and, 289, 290
afterbirth, 42, 44, 60
age
    chronological, 208–209
    dropout rates and, 269
    mental, 207–208
    moral judgment and, 265
    parental, 53–54
aggression, 18
    Bandura's experiment in, 172,
      173
    theories of, 171–173
AIDS. *See* HIV/AIDS
air pollution, 140
alarm reaction, 224
alcohol use
    in adolescence, 250, 251–252,
      254, 255
    during pregnancy, 52–53
    twins and, 34
allele, 26
alpha-fetoprotein (AFP) assay, 32
altruism, 170–171
Alzheimer's disease, 85
**ambivalent/resistant attachment,
  116, 126**
American Academy of Pediatrics,
  82
amniocentesis, 30–31
amniotic fluid, 44, 58
amniotic sac, 42, 44, 58
amphetamines, 252, 254, 255
amplitude, 71
anal-expulsive traits, 6
anal-retentive traits, 6
anal stage of psychosexual
  development, 5, 6
analytical intelligence, 206
androgens, 44, 240
androgyny, psychological, 178
anemia, sickle-cell, 29
anesthesia, general, 61
anesthetics, 61
angular gyrus, 113, 193
animism, 150
anorexia nervosa, 247–248

anoxia, 62
antidepressants, 231, 232, 249
anxiety
    disorders of, in middle child-
      hood, 231–232
    separation, 116
    stranger, 117, 118, 126
Apgar scale, 67
aphasia, 112
**appearance-reality distinction,
  155–156**
arousal, and media, 172, 173
artificial insemination, 37–38
artificialism, 150
ASDs. *See* autism spectrum
  disorders
Asian Americans, 15
    intelligence tests and, 213
    poverty and, 288
Asperger's disorder, 122
assay, AFP, 32
assimilation, 10, 97–98
associative play, 168, 169
assumption, contrast, 158
asynchronous growth, 237–238
attachment, 115
    ambivalent/resistant, 116, 126
    autism and, 122–124
    avoidant, 116, 126
    child abuse and, 121–122
    daycare and, 124–125
    disorganized-disoriented, 116
    emotional development and,
      126
    ethologist view of, 119–120
    fathers and, 117
    patterns of, 116–117, 126
    research with monkeys and, 19,
      119, 120
    secure, 116–117, 126
    social deprivation and, 120–121
    stability of, 117
    stages of, 117–118
    strange situation and, 116
    theories of, 118–120
**attachment-in-the-making phase,
  118**
attention, selective, 95, 201, 202
**attention-deficit/hyperactivity
  disorder (ADHD), 189–192**
attributional style, 230
audience, imaginary, 260
auditory stimuli, and short-term
  memory, 202
authoritarian (parenting style),
  165, 222
authoritative (parenting style), 164,
  165, 222, 254, 280
autism, 34, 122–124
    causes of, 123
    paternal age and, 54
    treatment of, 124
    twins and, 34

**autism spectrum disorders (ASDs),
  122**
    causes of, 123
    characteristics of, 123
    forms of, 122
    treatment of, 124
autobiographical memory, 156
automatic retribution, 198
autonomous morality, 199
autosomes, 25
    abnormalities in, 27
avoidant attachment, 116, 126
axon, 84, 85

B

babbling, 107
Babinski reflex, 69
baby biography, 4
baby blues, 66–67
Bandura, Albert, 9, 10
barbiturates, 252, 254, 255
bases (chemical compounds),
  24
Bayley Scales of Infant
  Development, 103, 104–105
bed-wetting, 7, 143–144
behavior(s)
    aggressive, 18, 171–173
    delinquent, 224, 287–288
    gender-appropriate, 9
    instinctive, 11–12
    moral, 265–266
    of neonates, 67–75
    prosocial, 170–171
    sexual, 282–287
    social, 166–173
behaviorism (Skinner), **4, 7–9**
    attachment and, 118
beliefs, false, 155
bell-and-pad method, 7
bias, cultural, 210
bilingualism, 216–217
Binet, Alfred, 4, 207, 208
Binet Institute, 9
Binet–Simon scale, 207
binge drinking, 251
binge eating, 248, 249–250
biography, baby, 4
biological perspective, 11–12
birth order, 167
birth rates, global, 46, 47
birth weight, 63, 80
bisexual, 283
blastocyst, 42
blood pressure, 50
blood tests, parental, 32
Bobo doll experiment (Bandura),
  172, 173
body image, in puberty, 242
bonding, 67
bottle feeding, 83–84

brain development
    in infancy, 84–87, 112–113
    in early childhood, 134–135,
        176
Braxton-Hicks contractions, 58
Brazelton Neonatal Behavioral
    Assessment Scale, 67, 103–104
breast milk, 82, 83–84
    HIV in, 49, 50, 84
bridge programs, 268
Broca's aphasia, 112
Bronfenbrenner, Urie, 12
bulimia nervosa, 248, 249–250
bullying, 227

C

CA. *See* chronological age
caffeine
    hyperactivity and, 191
    pregnancy and, 53
calcium intake, in adolescence, 246
canalization, 32, 82
Cannabis sativa. See marijuana
carbon monoxide, and pregnancy, 53
career development, 270–271
caring orientation, 266
carriers (of recessive gene), **26–27**
case study, 17
Cat in the Hat, The (Seuss), 45–46,
    72
categorical self, 174
Cattell, Raymond, 210
causality, 149–150
cell body, 84
cell firing, 44
Centers for Disease Control and
    Prevention (CDC), 284
cephalocaudal (development), **43**
    in infants, 80, 82, 87
    prenatal, 43
cerebellum, 85
cerebral cortex, 86, 112, 191
cerebral fissures, 86
cerebral palsy, 62
cerebrum, 86
cervix, dilation of, 58–59
cesarean section, 50, 62
child abuse, 121–122
child development
    biological perspective on, 11–12
    cognitive perspective on, 9–11
    controversies in, 15–16
    development of study of, 3–4
    ecological perspective on, 12
    how to study, 17–21
    learning perspective on, 7–9
    pioneers in study of, 4
    psychoanalytic perspective on,
        5–7
    sociocultural perspective on,
        12–15
    theories of, 4–15
child-directed speech, 111
child labor laws, 4
child rearing, 163–166
childbirth, 57–58
    anesthesia during, 61
    cesarean section and, 62

contractions and, 58–60
fetal monitoring during, 59
methods of, 61–62
oxygen deprivation during,
    62–63
premature, 50, 63–64, 66
prepared, 61
problems during, 62–66
stages of, 58–60
childhood disintegrative disorder,
    122
Children's Hospital Boston Study
    (of SIDS), 76
Children's Television Act, 154
chlamydia, 37, 242, 243, 245
chorion, 42
chorionic villus sampling (CVS), 31
chromosomes, 24
    abnormalities in, 27–29
    sex, 25–26, 27, 28–29, 44
chronological age (CA), 208–209
chronosystem, 12–13
chunk, of information, 202
cigarette smoking, 6
    in adolescence, 252, 254, 255
    during pregnancy, 53
cilia, 35
circular reactions, 98–99
class inclusion, 151–152, 197
class size, 227
classical conditioning, 7, 72
clear-cut-attachment phase, 118
cliques, 281
closure, epiphyseal, 240
cocaine use
    in adolescence, 252, 254, 255
    during pregnancy, 52
coefficient, correlation, 17–18
cognition, social, 9, 172, 176, 177,
    220, 230
cognitive behavioral methods
    ADHD and, 191–192
    conduct disorders and, 230
    eating disorders and, 249–250
    weight loss and, 185–186
cognitive development, 11
    attachment and, 118
    concrete operational stage of,
        195–198
    factors in, 152–154
    formal operational stage of,
        258–259
    language and, 158–161
    memory and, 156–158
    preoperational stage of, 147–152
    scaffolding and, 152–153
    sensorimotor stage of, 97–101
    television and, 154
    theory of mind and, 154–156
    zone of proximal development
        and, 152–153
cognitive-developmental theory,
    9–11, 220
    aggression and, 172
    attachment and, 118
    gender typing and, 177
cognitive harmony, 10
cognitive perspective. *See* cognitive-
    developmental theory
cohort effect, 20

colic, 74
comfort, contact, 119
commitment dimension of identity,
    276
conception, 34, 35–36
concrete-operational stage, 11,
    195–198
conditioned response, 7, 72
conditioned stimulus, 7, 72
conditioning
    classical, 7, 72
    operant, 7–9, 72–73
condom use, 244
conduct disorder, 229–230
congenital syphilis, 48–49
conservation, 151, 152, 196
constancy
    gender, 177
    shape, 93
    size, 93
constructive play, 168, 169
contact comfort, 119
continuity-discontinuity controversy,
    16
contraception use, and global
    fertility rates, 47
contractions, labor, 58–59
contractual, legalistic orientation,
    200, 264
contrast assumption, 158
control group, 19
conventional level (of moral
    reasoning), **200–201,** 263, 265
convergence, 70
convergent thinking, 213
cooing, 106–107
cooperative play, 168, 169
corpus callosum, 135
correlation, 17–18
    passive genetic–environmental,
        32–33
correlation coefficient, 17–18
counseling, genetic, 30–32
crawling, in infancy, 89
creative intelligence, 206
creativity, 213–214
creeping, in infancy, 89
crib death, 75–77
crisis
    identity, 7, 276
    life, 6
critical period, 119, 120
    in infant development, **119,** 120
    in prenatal development, **48,** 49
cross-cultural research
    on gender typing, 177
    on macrosystems, 12
    on motor behavior, 17
cross-sectional research, 19, 20–21
cross-sequential research, 21
crowds, 281
crowning, of baby's head, 59
crying
    empathic, 170
    of neonates, 74–75, 106, 107
C-section. *See* cesarean section
cues, retrieval, 157
cultural bias, 210
cultural-familial intellectual
    disability, 212

Culture-Fair Intelligence Test
    (Cattell), 210, 211
culture-free intelligence tests, 210
CVS. *See* chorionic villus sampling
Cyber Tipline, 122
cystic fibrosis, 27, 29–30
cytosine with guanine (C with G),
    24

D

Darwin, Charles, 4, 11
dates, small for, 63
dating, in adolescence, 281–282
day care, for infants, 124–125
deaths
    crib, 75–77
    rates of adolescent, 246, 248
    rates of global, 65
decentration, 196
deep structure (of language), **112**
deferred imitation, 101
delinquency
    in adolescence, 287–288
    in middle childhood, 224
dendrites, 84
Denver Developmental Screening
    Test, 104
deoxyribonucleic acid (DNA),
    24–25
dependence, substance, 250–251
dependent variables, 19
depressants, 251–252
depression
    heredity and, 231
    postpartum, 66–67
    in middle childhood, 230–231
    suicide and, 289
    twins and, 34, 231
depth perception, 92–93
DES, 51
design stage of children's drawings,
    138, 139
diabetes mellitus, 27
diarrhea, 140
Dictionary of Occupational Titles,
    The, 271
diethylstilbestrol. *See* DES
differential offending hypothesis, 287
differential treatment hypothesis,
    287
differentiation, 80
difficult temperament, 128–129
diffusion, identity, 277
dilate (cervix), **58**
disciplinary methods, 164–166. *See*
    also parenting styles
discontinuity-continuity controversy,
    16
disinhibit, 172
disk, embryonic, 42
disorganized-disoriented
    attachment, 116
divergent thinking, 213
diversity, 14–15. *See also* ethnicity;
    sex differences
divorce, 18, 223–224
dizygotic (DZ) twins, 26, 34
    aggressive behavior of, 171

autism in, 123
IQ scores of, 214
DNA. *See* deoxyribonucleic acid
dominant trait, 26–27
donor IVF, 38
dopamine, 191
double-deficit hypothesis (of dyslexia), **193**
Down syndrome, 27, 28, 31
dramatic play, 168–170
drawings, in early childhood, 137–138, 139
dropouts, 268–270
dropping (during pregnancy), 58
drugs, 244, 250–255
abuse of, 244, 250–255
for ADHD, 191–192
antidepressant, 231, 232, 249
depressant, 251–252, 254, 255
fertility, 37
hallucinogenic, 252–253, 254, 255
taken during pregnancy, 51–53
stimulant, 191–192, 252, 254, 255
for STIs, 245
students' attitudes toward, 254, 255
Duchenne muscular dystrophy, 30
dyslexia, 192–193
DZ twins. *See* dizygotic (DZ) twins

E

early amniocentesis, 30
early childhood
accidents in, 141
bed-wetting in, 143–144
brain development in, 134–135, 176
conservation in, 151–152
effects of education in, 153–154
egocentrism in, 149
elimination disorders in, 143–144
emotional development in, 174–175
gender role development in, 175–178
growth patterns in, 133–135
handedness in, 138–139
health and illness in, 140–141
home environment in, 153
language development in, 158–161
memory development in, 156–158
moral development in, 199–200
motor development in, 136–139
nutrition in, 140
parenting styles in, 163–166
personality development in, 174–175
physical activity in, 136–137
play in, 148, 168–170
precausal structuring in, 149–150
sleep in, 141–142
social behaviors in, 166–173

theory of mind and, 154–156
vision in, 135
zone of proximal development and, 152–153
easy temperament, 128
eating disorders, 247–250
echolalia, 107, 123
ecological systems theory, 12
ecology, 12
Ecstasy, 253, 254, 255
ectoderm, 43
education
in adolescence, 267–270, 286–287
in early childhood, 153–154
global fertility rates and, 47
in middle childhood, 197–198
sex, 286–287
efface (cervix), 58
effect, cognitive, 20
ego, 5
ego identity, 276
egocentrism, 149, 151, 260
elaborative strategy, 203, 204
electric shock treatment, for autism, 124
elimination disorders, in early childhood, 143–144
embedded-figure test, 262
embryonic disk, 42
embryonic stage, 43–44
emerging adulthood, 290–292
emissions, nocturnal, 240
emotional development
in early childhood, 174–175
in infancy, 125–127
in middle childhood, 219–222
emotional regulation, 127
empathy, 170–171
empirical, 16
encode, 202
encopresis, 144
endoderm, 43
endometriosis, 37
endometrium, 35
enuresis, 7, 143–144
environment
evaluating home, 153
heredity and, 32–34
intelligence and, 215
temperament and, 129–130
epidural block, 61
epigenesis, 33–34
epigenetic framework, 33–34
epilepsy, 27
epiphyseal closure, 240
episiotomy, 59–60
episodic memory, 156
equilibration, 10
erections, in puberty, 239–240
Erikson, Erik, 5, 6–7, 119, 220, 276, 278, 292
estrogen, 28
DES as, 51
menstruation and, 240–241
postpartum depression and, 66
visual–spatial tasks and, 261
ethical considerations, in research, 19, 21
ethnic identity, 278

ethnic identity search, 278
ethnicity, 14, 15
adolescent employment and, 271
death rates and, 246
delinquency and, 287
dropout rates and, 269–270
identity development and, 277–278
intelligence tests and, 210, 213
nutrition and, 183, 184
overweight children and, 183–184, 248
poverty and, 288
sickle-cell anemia and, 29
SIDS and, 75
suicide and, 289, 290
ethologists, 119–120
ethology, 11–12
European Americans
employment of, in adolescence, 271
body weight of, 183–184, 248
culture of, 14, 15
cystic fibrosis in, 29–30
death rates of adolescent, 246
delinquency and, 287
identity development and, 278
intelligence tests and, 213
poverty and, 288
suicide and, 289, 290
evocative genetic–environmental correlation, 33
evolution, and sex differences, 176
executive center, of brain, 191
exercise, 136–137, 188
exosystem, 12, 13
experimental group, 19
experiments, 18–19
exploration dimension of identity, 276
expressive language style, 108
expressive vocabulary, 107
extinction, 8, 110

F

fable, personal, 260–261
facial expressions
of caregivers, 127
of neonates, 72
factor theories of intelligence, 205–206
failure to thrive (FTT), 82
fallopian tubes, 35, 36, 38
false beliefs, 155
false labor contractions, 58
family(ies)
adolescents' relationships with, 279–280
divorce in, 223–224
early childhood and, 153, 163–166
income of, and adolescents, 269, 270, 271–272
during Industrial Revolution, 4
infancy and, 109–110, 126–127, 129, 130
middle childhood and, 222–225

prenatal development and, 48–54
preterm neonates and, 64
step-, 223–224
FAPs. *See* fixed action patterns
FAS. *See* fetal alcohol syndrome
fast mapping, 158
fat cells, 184–185
fathers
adolescents' relationships with, 279
attachment and, 117
divorced, 223–224
gay, 223
language development and, 109–110, 112
prenatal development and, 53–54
fear
in early childhood, 174
in middle childhood, 175
of strangers, 117, 118, 126
Feingold diet, 191
Fels Longitudinal Study, 211, 212
feminine traits, 175–176, 177–178
fertility
global rates of, 46, 47
sex and age differences in, 53–54
fertility drugs, 37
fetal alcohol effect, 52–53
fetal alcohol spectrum disorders, 52
fetal alcohol syndrome (FAS), 52–53
fetal hormones, 12, 58
fetal monitoring, 59
fetal stage, 45–47
field studies, 17
fine motor skills, 137
in early childhood, 136–137, 138
in middle childhood, 187
firstborn children, 167
fissures, cerebral, 86
fitness
in adolescence, 246–247
in early childhood, 140
in middle childhood, 188
fixation, 5–6
fixed action patterns (FAPs), 11–12
food coloring, artificial, 191
food portions, 182–183
food pyramid, 182
forceps, 59
foreclosure (as identity status), 277
formal games, 168
formal operations (Piaget), **11, 258–259**
framework, epigenetic, 33–34
fraternal twins. *See* dizygotic (DZ) twins
Freud, Sigmund, 5–6, 16, 119, 219–220
friends, imaginary, 148
friendships
in adolescence, 280–281
in early childhood, 168
in middle childhood, 225–226
FTT. *See* failure to thrive
functional play, 168

G

g, 206, 213
gay(s)
    as parents, 223
    as sexual identity, 283
gender, 15
gender-appropriate behaviors, 9
gender constancy, 177
gender identity, 177, 178
gender roles, 175–176, 177–178
gender-schema theory, 177–178
gender stability, 177
gender stereotyping, 169–170, 263, 264
    visual–spatial tasks and, 261
general anesthesia, 61
general intelligence (g), 206, 213
general nominals, 108
generalized anxiety disorder, 231
genes, 24, 26–27
    abnormalities of, 29–30
    carriers of recessive, 26–27
genetic counseling, 30–32
genetic–environmental correlation, 32–34
genetics, 23. See also heredity
genital herpes, 245
genital stage (of psychosexual development), 5–6, **236**
genital warts, 243, 245
genotype, 32
germinal stage, 41, 42–43
Gesell, Arnold, 5
giftedness, 212–213
gonorrhea, 37, 245
good-boy/good-girl orientation, 200, 201
goodness of fit, 129–130
grammar development
    in early childhood, 159–160
    in middle childhood, 215
grasping, 69, 88, 98
gross motor skills, 136, 186–187
growth
    in adolescence, 16, 182, 237–239
    asynchronous, 237–238
    in early childhood, 133–135
    in infancy, 79–84
    in middle childhood, 181–183
growth spurt, 16, 86, **182,** 237–239
    of brain, 86
guilt (versus initiative stage), 174
guanine (cytosine with), 24
gynecomastia, 28, 240

H

HAART. See highly active antiretroviral therapy
habituation, 93
    hearing and, 93
    to violence, 172
hair growth, in puberty, 239
Hall, G. Stanley, 4
hallucinogenics, 252–253
handedness, 138–139
harmony, cognitive, 10

harassment, sexual, 229
Harvard University, 286
HD. See Huntington's disease
Head Start, 154, 215, 270
health
    of adolescents, 242–244, 245, 246–250
    in early childhood, 140–141
    in middle childhood, 182–186
    of mother, 48–54, 84
hearing
    of infants, 93–94
    of neonates, 70–71
height gain
    in adolescence, 237–239
    in early childhood, 133–134
    in infancy, 80–82
    in middle childhood, 181–182, 183
Heinz, case of (Kohlberg), 199–201, 264–265, 266–267
helplessness, learned, 222
hemispheres, brain, 86, 135, 176
hemophilia, 30
heredity, 23–27
    aggression and, 171–172
    chromosomal abnormalities and, 27–29
    conduct disorders and, 230
    depression and, 231
    dyslexia and, 193
    eating disorders and, 249
    environment and, 32–34
    genetic abnormalities and, 29–30
    intelligence and, 214–215
    prenatal testing and, 30–32
    sex differences and, 176
    substance abuse and, 254–255
    suicide and, 289
    weight and, 184
heritability, 214
heroin, 51, 252, 254, 255
herpes, genital, 245
heterozygous, 26
high blood pressure, 50
highly active antiretroviral therapy (HAART), 50
Hindu Indians
    caring orientation of, 266
    discriminating the language of, 94
hippocampus
    sex differences and, 176
HIV/AIDS, 49
    in adolescence, 242, 243–244, 245
    in breast milk, 84
    prenatal development and, 49, 50
HIV Community Coalition, 260
Holly's dilemma (Selman), 220, 221
holophrases, 109
HOME inventory, 153
Home Observation for the Measurement of the Environment (HOME), 153
homosexual identity, 283
homozygous, 26
Hopi infants, motor development of, 90

hormones
    aggression and, 171–172
    fetal, 12, 58
    growth spurt and, 16
    postpartum depression and, 66–67
    in puberty, 236–237
    prescribed during pregnancy, 51
    sex differences and, 177
HPV. See human papilloma virus
human immunodeficiency virus/ acquired immunodeficiency syndrome. See HIV/AIDS
human papilloma virus (HPV), 243, 245
Huntington's disease (HD), 29
hyperactivity, 189–192
hypothalamus, 236
hypothesis, 18
    differential offending/treatment, 287
    double-deficit, 193
hypothetical thinking, 258–259
hypoxia, 62

I

id, 5
identical twins. See monozygotic (MZ) twins
identity
    ethnic, 278
    gender, 177, 178
    homosexual, 283
    versus identity diffusion, 276
    sexual, 283
identity achievement, 277
identity crisis, 7, 276
identity development
    in adolescence, 276–279, 281
    in early childhood, 174
    in infancy, 127–128
    in middle childhood, 220–222
identity diffusion, 277
identity statuses (Marcia), 276–277
imaginary audience, 260
imaginary friends, 148
imaginative play, 148, 168
imitation, in infancy, 101, 102–103, 109–110
immanent justice, 198
immunizations, 140, 141
imprinting, 119–120
impulsivity, in ADHD, 190, 191
in vitro fertilization (IVF), 38
inclusion, class, 151–152, 197
incubator, 64
independent variables, 19
indiscriminate attachment, 117–118
inductive methods of discipline, **164,** 171
Industrial Revolution, 4
industry versus inferiority, 220
infancy
    abuse/neglect in, 121–122
    attachment in, 115–120, 126
    autism spectrum disorders in, 122–124

    cephalocaudal development in, 80, 82, 87
    daycare in, 124–125
    emotional development in, 125–127
    feeding in, 49, 50, 82, 83–84
    imitation in, 101, 102–103, 109–110
    individual differences in intelligence in, 103–105
    information processing in, 101–103, 105
    language development in, 105–113
    motor development in, 80, 87–90
    nervous system/brain development in, 84–87, 112–113
    personality development of, 127–130
    physical growth in, 79–84
    Piaget's theory and, 97–101
    proximodistal development in, 80, 88
    sensory/perceptual development in, 90–95
    sex differences in, 130
    social deprivation in, 120–121
infant-directed speech, 111
infections
    infertility and, 37
    sexually transmitted, 242–244, 245
inferiority (versus industry stage), 220
infertility, 28, 29, 36–38
information gathering, 17
information processing
    in early childhood, 156–158
    in infancy, 101–103, 105
    in middle childhood, 201–205
    of neonates, 72–73
    theory of, 11
inhalants, 254
inhibition, in ADHD, 191
initial-preattachment phase, 118
initiative versus active guilt stage, 174
inner speech, 161
insemination, artificial, 37–38
instinctive behavior, 11–12
intellectual development
    creativity and, 213–214
    determinants of, 214–215
    differences in, 211–213
    patterns of, 210–211
intellectual disability, 211–212
intelligence, 205
    creative, 206
    environment and, 215
    general, 206, 213
    heredity and, 214–215
    individual differences in, among infants, 103–105
    measurement of, 206–210
    practical, 206
    theories of, 205–206
intelligence quotient (IQ), 207, 208–209
    instability of, in infancy, 104–105

longitudinal research and, 19–20
socioeconomic and ethnic differences in, 213
of twins, 213, 214
variations in, 211, 212
interactionist perspective, 161
internalization, 5
intonation, 107
inventory, HOME, 153
IQ. *See* intelligence quotient
irreversibility, 151
IVF. *See* in vitro fertilization

J

Jacobson, Lenore, 228
James, William, 69
Jewish Americans, and Tay-Sachs disease, 29
junk food, 247
justice, immanent, 198
justice orientation, 266
juvenile delinquency, 224, 287–288

K

Kaiser Family Foundation, 286
kangaroo care, 66
Kinsey studies, 283
kinship studies, 34
of autism, 123
Klinefelter syndrome, 28
Kohlberg, Lawrence, 198, 199–201, 263–265, 266–267

L

labor contractions, 58–59
Labouvie-Vief, Gisela, 11
LAD. *See* language acquisition device
Lamaze method, 61
language(s)
brain structures and, 112–113
discriminating the sounds of foreign, 94
styles of, 108
language acquisition device (LAD), 112
language development
in early childhood, 158–161
in infancy, 105–113
in middle childhood, 215–217
nature-nurture controversy and, 16, 109–111
theories of, 109–113
lanugo, 63
larynx, in puberty, 239
latency stage (of psychosexual development), 5, 6, **219–220**
Latino and Latina Americans
culture of, 14, 15
death rates of adolescent, 246
delinquency and, 287
dropout rates and, 269–270
identity development and, 278
intelligence tests and, 210, 213

poverty and, 287–288
sickle-cell anemia in, 29
suicide and, 289, 290
law-and-order orientation, 200
laws, child labor, 4
lead paint, 140
leading questions, 205
learned helplessness, 222
learning, 205
observational, 9
as perspective on child development, 7–9
rote, 203–204, 216
sociocultural theory and, 14
learning disorders, 192–193
learning perspective, 7–9
left-handedness, 139
leptin, 240–241
lesbian(s)
as parents, 223
as sexual identity, 283
lice, pubic, 245
life crises, 6
lightening (during pregnancy), 58
literacy
of adult females, and global mortality rates, 65
of 15- to 24-year-olds, global rates of, 215
global fertility rates and, 47
local anesthetics, 61
Locke, John, 4, 16
locomotion, 89–90
long-term memory, 11, 203–204
longitudinal research, 19–20, 224
looking chamber, 70
Lorenz, Konrad, 11
low birth weight, 63
LSD, 253, 254, 255

M

MA. *See* mental age
macrosystem, 12, 13
mainstreaming, 193
male–female sexual behavior, 283–285
mammary glands, 240
mapping, fast, 158
marijuana use
in adolescence, 250, 252–253
pregnancy and, 51–52
students' attitudes toward, 254, 255
masculine traits, 175–176, 177–178
masturbation, 6, 283
mathematical ability, sex differences in, 261–262
maturation, 5, 6, 16, 101, 241–242
MDMA, 253, 254, 255
media, and aggression, 172, 173
medulla, 76, 85
meiosis, 25
memory
autobiographical, 156
in early childhood, 156–158
in infancy, 101–103, 105
long-term, 11, 203–204
meta-, 204–205

in middle childhood, 201–205
recall, 204
sensory, 201–202, 203
short-term, 11, 202–203
visual recognition, 105
working, 202–203
menarche, 240–241
menstruation, 35, 240–241
mental age (MA), 207–209
mental exploration, in infancy, 100
mesoderm, 43
mesosystem, 12, 13
metacognition, 204–205
metamemory, 204–205
metaphors, 259
methadone use, in pregnancy, 51
methamphetamine, 252
Mexican Americans, body weight of, 184
microsystem, 12, 13
Middle Ages, 3
middle childhood
ADHD in, 189–192
anxiety in, 231–232
concrete-operational stage and, 195–198
conduct disorders in, 229–230
creativity in, 213–214
depression in, 230–231
family and, 222–225
growth patterns in, 181–183
information processing in, 201–205
intellectual development in, 205–215
language development in, 215–217
learned helplessness in, 222
learning disorders in, 192–193
moral development in, 198–201
motor development in, 186–188
nutrition in, 182–183
overweight in, 183–186
peer relationships in, 225–226
Piaget's theory and, 195–198, 219–220
school and, 226–229
self-conception in, 220–222
sex differences in play in, 170
midwife, 61
Milwaukee Project, 154
mind, theory of, 154–156
Minnesota Study of Twins Reared Apart, 34
mirror neurons, 103
mirror technique, 127
miscarriage
amniocentesis and, 31
in germinal stage, 42–43
hormones and, 51
mitosis, 24–25
models, 109
of aggressive behavior, 172, 173
parents as, 109
in social cognitive theory, 9
teachers as, 227
monozygotic (MZ) twins, 26, 34
aggressive behavior of, 171
autism in, 123
body weight of, 184

IQ scores of, 213, 214
moral behavior, and moral reasoning, 265–266
moral development
in adolescence, 259, 263–267
in early childhood, 199–200
in middle childhood, 198, 199–201
moral realism, 198
morality
autonomous, 199
objective, 198
moratorium, 276, 277, 292
Moro reflex, 69
mortality rates
in adolescence, 246, 248
global, 65
Motherese, 110, 111
mothers
adolescents' relationships with, 279
attachment and, 116–117, 118, 119, 120
divorced, 223–224
drugs taken by, 51–53
employment of, 224–225
fertility of, 37, 53–54
health of, 48–51
language development and, 109–112
lesbian, 223
postpartum depression of, 66–67
social referencing and, 127
motility (of sperm), **37**
motor development
in early childhood, 136–139
in infancy, 87–90
in middle childhood, 186–188
movement, in fetal stage, 46
multifactorial problems, 27
Multimodal Treatment Study, 191–192
multiple intelligences (Gardner), 206, 207
multiple partners, in adolescence, 244
multiple sclerosis, 85
muscular dystrophy, 30
mutations (generic), 25
mutism, 123
mutual exclusivity assumption, 158
myelin sheath, 84–85
myelination, 84–85, 86–87, 134
MZ twins. *See* monozygotic (MZ) twins

N

nail biting, 6
naively egoistic, instrumental orientation, 200
naming speed, 193
National Bureau of Economic Research (NBER), 183
National Institute of Mental Health, 192
National Institute of Child Health and Human Development (NICHD), 124–125

National Longitudinal Survey of Youth, 224
National Public Radio, 286
National Survey of Family Growth, 244
Native Americans
    intelligence tests and, 213
    motor development in (Hopi), 17, 90
natural childbirth, 61
naturalistic observation, 17
nature, 15
    brain development and, 87
    language development and, 110, 112
    motor development and, 89, 90
    perceptual development and, 95
nature–nurture controversy, 12, 15–16, 32, 34
NBER. *See* National Bureau of Economic Research
negative correlation, 18
negative reinforcers, 8, 9
neglect, 121, 165, 166, 222, 254
neonate(s), 41
    assessing health of, 67
    brain of, 85
    crying of, 74–75, 106, 107
    intervention for preterm, 64, 66
    learning and, 72–73
    parents and preterm, 64, 65
    reflexes of, 68–69
    sensory capabilities of, 69–72, 91
    SIDS and, 75–77
    sleep patterns of, 73–74
    weight of, 63, 80
nervous system development, 84–87, 112–113
neural tube, 43
neurons, 11, 84
    development of, 84–85
    mirror, 103
neurotransmitters, 84
NICHD. *See* National Institute of Child Health and Human Development
niche-picking, 33
nicotine
    adolescence and, 252, 254, 255
    pregnancy and, 53
nightmares, 142
nocturnal emissions, 240
NOFTT. *See* nonorganic failure to thrive
nominals, general/specific, 108
nongonococcal urethritis, 245
nonorganic failure to thrive (NOFTT), 82
non-rapid-eye-movement (non-REM) sleep, 73, 74
nonsocial play, 168–169
noradrenaline, 191
nose touching, 127–128
nurture, 15. *See also* nature–nurture controversy
    brain development and, 87
    language development and, 109–110, 111
    motor development and, 89, 90

perceptual development and, 95
nutrition
    in adolescence, 239, 246–247
    in early childhood, 140
    fetus and maternal, 48
    in infancy, 82–83
    in middle childhood, 182–186

O

object permanence, 100–101
objective morality, 198
observation, naturalistic, 17
observational learning, 9, 172
onlooker play, 168–169
only children, 167
operant conditioning, 7–9, 72–73
oral stage, of psychosexual development, 5–6
osteoporosis, 246
ova, 25, 35–36, 240–241
ovarian follicle, 35
overextension, 108
overregularization, 159
ovulation, 26, 37
oxygen deprivation, during childbirth, 62–63
oxytocin, 58

P

Pacific Islanders, 15
pacifier, 75
palmar reflex, 69
paradoxical sleep, 73–74
parallel play, 168, 169
parent–child relationships, 223–225, 279–280
parenting styles, 163–166, 171, 222, 254, 280
parents. *See also* fathers; mothers
    adolescents' relationships with, 279–280
    blood tests of, in genetic disorders, 32
    divorced, 223–224
    health of, 48–54, 84
    lesbian and gay, 223
    preterm neonates and, 64, 65
    selection of child's sex by, 38
passive-active controversy, 16
passive genetic–environmental correlation, 32–33
passive sentences, 160
pathogens, 48
PCBs. *See* polychlorinated biphenyls
peer relationships
    in adolescence, 280–282, 284–285
    in early childhood, 167–168
    in middle childhood, 225–226
pelvic inflammatory disease (PID), 37, 243
penis growth, in puberty, 239
peptic ulcers, 27
perception
    depth, in infancy, 92–93
    in fetal stage, 45–46

perceptual constancy, 93
perceptual development, in infants, 90–95
perfectionism
    depression and, 230
    eating disorders and, 248, 250
    suicide and, 289
performance, 205, 277
peripheral vision, of neonates, 91
permanence, object, 100–101
permissive-indulgent (parenting style), 164, 165, **166**
Perry, William, 11
personal fable, 260–261
personality development
    in early childhood, 174–175
    in infancy, 127–130
personality types, and careers, 270–271
perspective taking, 171, 220, 221
petting, 284
PGD. *See* preimplantation genetic diagnosis
phallic stage, of psychosexual development, 5, 6
phenotype, 32
phenylalanine, 29
phenylketonuria (PKU), 29, 85
phobia(s), 231
    school, 232
phonetic method, 216
phonological processing, 193
physical activity
    in early childhood, 136–137
    in middle childhood, 188
physical growth
    in adolescence, 237–239
    in early childhood, 133–135
    in infancy, 79–84
    in middle childhood, 181–186
Piaget, Jean, 9–11, 16, 97–101, 148–152, 168, 195–199, 205, 220, 258–259
Picasso, Pablo, 53
pictorial stage, of children's drawing, 138, 139
PID. *See* pelvic inflammatory disease
pincer grasp, 88
Pinker, Steven, 109
pitch, 71
pituitary gland, 236
PKU. *See* phenylketonuria
placement stage of children's drawings, 138, 139
placenta, 42, 44, 60
placental stage, 60
plasticity (of brain), **135**
play, in early childhood, 137, 148, 168–170
pollution, and pregnancy, 53
polychlorinated biphenyls (PCBs), and pregnancy, 53
polygenic (traits), **24**
positive correlation, 18
positive reinforcers, 8
postconventional level (of moral reasoning), 200, **264–265,** 266, 267
postpartum depression (PPD), 66–67

postpartum period, 66–67
poverty, and delinquency, 287–288
power-assertive methods of discipline, 165, 166
PPD. *See* postpartum depression
practical intelligence, 206
pragmatics, 160
precausal (thought), **149**
preconventional level (of moral reasoning), 199–200, 263, 265
pregnancy
    drugs taken during, 51–53
    teenage, 285–287
preimplantation genetic diagnosis (PGD), 38
prelinguistic (vocalizations), **105**
premature (birth), **50,** 63–64, 66
prenatal development, 30
    embryonic stage of, 43–44
    environmental influences on, 48–54
    fetal stage of, 45–47
    germinal stage of, 41–43
    sex hormones in, 12
    testing during, 30–32
preoperational stage of cognitive development, 148–152
prepared childbirth, 61
preschool years. *See* early childhood
preservation of sameness, 123
pretend play, 168
preterm (infant), **50,** 63–64, 66
primary circular reactions, 98
primary mental abilities, 206
primary sex characteristics, 236
priming, of aggressive thoughts, 172
prophecies, self-fulfilling, 228
progesterone, 241
progestin, 51
pronoun reversal, 123
prosocial behavior, 170–171
prostaglandins, 58
proximodistal (development), **43,** 80, 88
psychoanalytic perspective, 5–7
    on attachment in infancy, 118–119
    on gender roles, 176
    on identity development, 128, 174, 276, 278
    on middle childhood, 219–220
    on moratorium, 292
    on sexual feelings, 236
psycholinguistic theory, 112
psychological moratorium, 276
psychologically androgynous, 178
psychosexual development (Freud's theory of), 5–6, 16, 119, 219–220
psychosocial development (Erikson's theory of), 5, 6–7, 119, 220, 276, 278, 292
puberty, 236–237
    changes in boys in, 239–240
    changes in girls in, 240–241
    growth spurt in, 237–238
    hair growth in, 239
    motor development and, 187–188

pubic lice, 245
pudendal block, 61
punishment, 8–9, 165, 172
purging, 248, 249–250
Pygmalion effect, 228

Q

questions
    leading, 205
    wh-, 159

R

race, 14, 15
    dropout rates and, 269–270
radiation, and pregnancy, 53
random assignments, 19
rapid-eye-movement (REM) sleep,
    73–74
reaction range, 90
reaction time, 187
realism, moral, 198
reasoning
    as inductive technique, 164
    moral, 198–201, 259, 263–267
    transductive, 150
recall memory, 204
receptive vocabulary, 107
recessive trait, 26–27
reciprocity, 265
Reddy, Helen, 175
reduction division, 25
referencing, social, 126–127
reflexes, 10, 67, **68–69,** 88, 98
reflexive smiling, 125
refusal, school, 232
register, sensory, 201–202, 203
regression, 167
regulation, emotional, 127
rehearsal, 157, 202, 203–204, 205,
    216
reinforcement (Skinner), 7–9, 110
rejecting-neglecting (parenting
    style), 165, **166,** 222, 254
REM sleep. *See* rapid-eye-
    movement (REM) sleep
repetition, 157, 202, 203–204, 205,
    216
research
    cross-cultural, 12, 17, 177
    cross-sectional, 19, 20–21
    cross-sequential, 21
    ethics and, 19, 21
    longitudinal, 19–20, 224
respiratory distress syndrome, 64
response, conditioned, 7
restrictiveness–permissiveness
    dimension, 163–164, 165
retribution, automatic, 198
retrieval cues, 157
Rett's disorder, 122
Rh incompatibility, 32, 50–51
rhesus monkeys, experiments with,
    19, 119, 120
RIASEC method (Holland),
    270–271
risk taking, in adolescence, 244, 246

Ritalin, 189, 191
Rockefeller, Nelson, 192
roles, gender, 175–176, 177–178
rooting reflex, 68
Rosenthal, Robert, 228
rotation task, 261, 262
rote learning, 203–204, 216
rough-and-tumble play, 137
Rousseau, Jean-Jacques, 4
rubella, 49–50

S

s factors, 206
"Safe Sleep Top Ten, The," 76, 77
Salish language, 94
sameness, preservation of, 123
Save the Children, 64
SBIS. *See* Stanford–Binet
    Intelligence Scale
scaffolding, 14, 152–153
scheme, 10, 97, 99
schizophrenia, 62
    ADHD and, 192
    early-onset, 62
    twins and, 34
school
    adolescents in, 267–270
    environment of, 227
    impact of teachers at, 227–228
    phobias and, 232
    readiness for, 226–229
    sex differences and, 222, 229
    sexism in, 228–229
school phobia, 232
scribbles, 137–138, 139
scripts, 156
secondary circular reactions, 99
secondary sex characteristics,
    236–237, 284
secular trend (in height), **238–239**
secure attachment, 116–117, 126
sedatives, 251
selection factor, 18, 19
selective attention, 95, 201, 202
selective serotonin reuptake
    inhibitors (SSRIs), 231
self
    categorical, 174
    sense of, 6
self-concept, 127–128, 174
    in adolescence, 278–279
    in early childhood, 174
    in middle childhood, 220–222
self-consciousness, 128
self-esteem, 174
    in adolescence, 279, 281
    in early childhood, 174
    in middle childhood, 222, 268
self-fulfilling prophecies, 228
semen, 240
sensitive periods (in language
    learning), **113**
sensorimotor stage of cognitive
    development, 11, 98–100
sensory capabilities
    in early childhood, 136–139
    of infants, 90–95
    in middle childhood, 186–187

of neonates, 69–72
sensory memory, 201–202, 203
sensory register, 201–202, 203
sentences
    development of, 108–109
    passive, 160
    two-word, 109
separation anxiety, 116
separation anxiety disorder,
    231–232
separation-individuation, 128
seriation, 196–197
serotonin, 76, **231**
Sesame Street, 154
sex characteristics, 236–237, 284
sex chromosomes, 25–26, 44
    abnormalities in, 27, 28–29
sex differences
    in attempted suicide, 290
    in cognitive abilities, 261–263
    in dropout rates, 269
    in identity development, 278
    in infancy, 130
    in moral development, 266–267
    in motor development, 187–188
    in physical growth (in middle
        childhood), 183
    in play, 179
    pubertal changes and, 239–242
    in school (in middle childhood),
        222, 229
    theories of development of,
        176–178
sex education, 286–287
sex hormones
    aggression and, 171–172
    growth spurt and, 16
    in prenatal development, 12, 58
    in puberty, 236–237
    sex differences and, 177
sex-linked chromosomal
    abnormalities, 28
sex-linked genetic abnormalities, 30
sexism, 228–229
sexual abuse, 121, 249
sexual differentiation, of embryo,
    44
sexual gratification, psychosexual
    theory and, 6
sexual harassment, 229
sexual identity, 283
sexual intercourse, risk factors for,
    242–244
sexuality, adolescent, 282–287
    male–female behavior and,
        283–285
    masturbation and, 283
    sexual identity and, 283
    STIs and, 242–244, 245
    teenage pregnancy and,
        285–287
sexually transmitted infections
    (STIs), 242–244, 245
shape constancy, 93
shape stage of children's drawings,
    138, 139
shaping, 110
short-term memory, 11, 202–203
siblings, and social behaviors,
    166–167

sickle-cell anemia, 29
SIDS. *See* sudden infant death
    sydrome
sight vocabulary, 216
Simon, Theodore, 4, 207
size constancy, 93
Skinner, B. F., 7–8, 110
sleep
    in infancy, 73–75, 144
    in early childhood, 141–142,
        144
    in middle childhood, 144
sleep terrors, 142
sleep walking, 142
slow-to-warm-up temperament, 128
small for dates, 63
smell, and neonates, 71, 94
smiling
    reflexive, 125
    social, 119, 125
smoking, 6, 53, 252, 254, 255
social behaviors, 166–173
social class, and nutrition, 183
social cognition, 220
social cognitive theory, 9
    on aggression, 172
    on depression, 230
    on gender roles, 176, 177
    on rewards and modeling, 220
social deprivation, in infancy,
    120–121
social play, 169
social referencing, 126–127
social smile, 119, 125
socialization, 9
sociocultural perspective, 12–15
sociocultural theory (Vygotsky),
    13–14
socioeconomic differences
    in IQ, 213
    in maturation, 241
solitary play, 168–169
somnambulism, 142
sonogram, 31–32
sorting ability, 201, 202
Spearman, Charles, 205–206
specific capacities, 206
specific nominals, 108
speech
    child-directed, 111
    inner, 161
    telegraphic, 108–109
sperm, 25, 35–36, 37
spinal block, 61
spontaneous abortion, 35
sprouting, 135
SSRIs. *See* selective serotonin
    reuptake inhibitors
stability, gender, 177
stage theory, 5, 16
standardized tests, 17
Stanford–Binet Intelligence Scale
    (SBIS), 207–209
startle reflex, 69
status offenses, 287
statuses, identity, 276–277
stepfamilies, and middle childhood,
    224
stepping reflex, 69
stereotype, 175

stereotyping, gender, 169–170, 261, 263, 264
steroids, 253–254, 255
stillbirth, 48
stimulants, 191–192, 252
stimulus, conditioned, 7, 72
STIs. *See* sexually transmitted infections
strange-situation method, 116, 126
stranger anxiety, 117, 118, 126
strength–weakness dimension, 177–178
Sturm und Drang, 236. *See also* adolescence
substance abuse, 244, 250–255
substance dependence, 250–251
sucking reflex, 68–69, 75
sudden infant death syndrome (SIDS), 75–76, 77
suicide, adolescent, 288–290
superego, 5
surface structure (of language), **112**
surrogate mother, 38, 119, 120
symbol use
    in adolescence, 259
    in early childhood, 148
symbolic play, 148, 168
syntax, 109
syphilis, 48, 245
    congenital, 48–49

T

taste, neonates and, 71
Tay-Sachs disease, 29
telegraphic speech, 108–109
television watching
    aggressive behavior and, 172
    body weight and, 185, 188
    cognitive development and, 154
temperament, 128
    environment and, 129–130
    types of, 128–129
teratogens, 48, 49
term (time period), **58**
Terman Studies of Genius, 19–20
terrors, sleep, 142
tertiary circular reactions, 99
test-tube babies, 38
testes, 44, 239
testosterone, 28
    in adolescence, 239–240, 241, 284
    aggression and, 171–172

thalidomide, 51
theory of mind, 154–156
three-mountains test, 149
thymine (adenine with), 24
Thurmond, Strom, 53
time-lag comparison, 21
time out punishment, 8–9
Tinbergen, Niko, 11
tissue, adipose, 184–185
toddlers, 89
toilet training, 6, 142
tolerance, 251
tonic-neck reflex, 69
toxemia, 50
Traffic Light Diet, 186
traits
    anal-expulsive/retentive, 6
    dominant/recessive, 26–27
    environment and, 32–34
    feminine/masculine, 175–176, 177–178
    polygenic, 24
    transmission of, 24, 25, 26–27, 32–34
tranquilizers, 61
transductive reasoning, 150
transition (labor), **59**
transitional object, for sleeping, 141
transitivity, 196–197
transsexuals, 223
triarchic theory of intelligence (Sternberg), 206
Triple X syndrome, 29
trophoblast, 42
Turner syndrome, 28, 29
Twenty Statements Test, 220–221
twins, 26
    aggressive behavior of, 171
    autism in, 123
    body weight of, 184
    depression in, 231
    IQ scores of, 213, 214
    motor development in, 90
    studies of, 34
two-word sentences, 109

U

ulcers, peptic, 27
ulnar grasp, 88
ultrasound, 31–32
umbilical cord, 42, 60, 63
unconditioned response, 7, 72

unconditioned stimulus, 7, 72
unconscious, the, 5
unexamined ethnic identity, 278
universal ethical principles orientation, 200, 264
unoccupied play, 168, 169
urethritis, nongonoccal, 245
uterus, 31, 42
utopian, 258–259

V

vacuum extraction tube, 59
variables, independent/dependent, 19
verbal ability, sex differences in, 261
vernix, 63
very-low-birth-weight (VLBW) children, 63
vision
    in early childhood, 135
    in infancy, 90–93, 94
    of neonates, 69–70, 91
visual accommodation, 70
visual cliff, 92–93
visual recognition memory, 105
visual–spatial ability, sex differences in, 261, 262
visual stimuli, encoding, 202
visual tracking, 69, 98
vitamin K, 60
vitamins for pregnancy, 51
VLBW children. *See* very-low-birth-weight (VLBW) children
vocabulary, 107–108, 158, 160
    in early childhood, 158–160
    in middle childhood, 215, 216
    receptive, 107
vocalizations, prelinguistic, 105–107
Vocational Preference Inventory (Holland), 270–271
Vygotsky, Lev Semenovich, 13–14, 152–153, 161

W

WAIS. *See* Wechsler Adult Intelligence Scale
warmth–coldness dimension, 163–164, 165
warts, genital, 243, 245
water-level test, 262

Watson, John B., 4–5, 7, 8
Wechsler Adult Intelligence Scale (WAIS), 209–210
Wechsler Intelligence Scale for Children (WISC), 209–210
Wechsler Preschool and Primary Scale of Intelligence (WPPSI), 209–210
weight gain
    in adolescence, 237–238, 247–250
    in early childhood, 133–134
    in infancy, 80–82
    in middle childhood, 181–186
    in neonates, 63, 80
    in pregnancy, 48
Wernicke's aphasia, 112
wet dreams, 240
wh- questions, 159
WHO. *See* World Health Organization
whole-object assumption, 158
WICS model of giftedness (Sternberg), 213
WISC. *See* Wechsler Intelligence Scale for Children
withdrawal symptoms, 251
word-recognition method, 216
work experience, of adolescents, 271–272
working memory, 202–203
World Health Organization (WHO), 249
WPPSI. *See* Wechsler Preschool and Primary Scale of Intelligence

X

X sex chromosome, 25, 28–29
XXY syndrome, 29. *See also* Klinefelter syndrome
XYY syndrome, 27, 28, 29

Y

Y sex chromosome, 25, 28, 44

Z

zone of proximal development (ZPD), 14, 152–153
zygote, 24, 26, 41–43

To help you succeed, we've designed a review card for each chapter.

CHAPTER 4 IN REVIEW

Birth and the Newborn Baby: In the New World

Learning Outcomes

LO1 Identify the stages of childbirth.

The initiation of labor may be triggered by [...] fetus. Maternal hormones stimulate contractions strong en[...] rst stage of childbirth begins with the onset of regular [...] and dilating the cervix. During transition, the cervix is nearly [...] he fetus moves into the birth canal. The second stage begi[...] he opening of the birth canal. It ends with the birth of the bab[...] on its own, the umbilical cord is clamped and severed. Dur[...] a separates from the uterine wall and is expelled along with [...]

> In this column you'll find each chapter learning outcome with an accompanying summary to help you better understand important concepts.

LO2 Examine different methods of childbirth.

General anesthesia puts the woman to sleep; regional or local anesthetics deaden pain in parts of the body. The Lamaze method teaches women to dissociate uterine contractions from pain and fear by associating other responses, such as relaxation, with contractions. A coach aids the mother in the delivery room. A C-section delivers a baby surgically through the abdomen. Herpes and HIV infections in the birth canal can be bypassed by C-section.

LO3 Discuss potential problems with childbirth.

Prenatal oxygen deprivation can be fatal if prolonged; it can also impair development of the nervous system, leading to cognitive and motor problems. A baby is preterm when birth occurs at or before 37 weeks of gestation. A baby has a low birth weight when it weighs less than 5 1/2 pounds (about 2,500 grams). The risk of having preterm babies rises with multiple births. Risks include infant mortality and delayed neurological and motor development. Sucking and breathing reflexes may be weak. The walls of air sacs in the lungs may stick together, leading to respiratory distress. Preterm babies usually remain in incubators. Preterm infants profit from early stimulation.

LO4 Describe the postpartum period.

Women may encounter the baby blues, postpartum depression, and postpartum psychosis. These problems probably reflect hormonal changes following birth, although stress can play a role. Research by Klaus and Kennell suggested that the first few hours [...]n's hormone levels [...]e study confounded [...]h health professionals.

How to Use This Card

1. Look over the card to preview the new concepts you'll be introduced to in the chapter.
2. Read your chapter to fully understand the material.
3. Go to class (and pay attention).
4. Review the card one more time to make sure you've registered the key concepts.
5. Don't forget, this card is only one of many CDEV learning tools available to help you succeed in your childhood and adolescent development course.

Key Terms

full term The amount of time of a normal pregnancy: 266 days from the date of conception.

Braxton-Hicks contractions The first, usually painless, contractions of childbirth.

prostaglandins Hormones that stimulate labor contractions.

oxytocin A hormone that stimulates labor contractions.

efface Thin out.

dilate Widen or enlarge.

episiotomy An incision between the birth canal and anus that widens the vaginal opening to prevent random tearing during childbirth.

fetal mo[...] tronic sens[...] vital signs [...]

> Here you'll find key terms and definitions in the order in which they appear throughout the chapter.

forceps [...] the baby's [...] the birth ca[...]

vacuum [...] ment that u[...] through th[...]

transition Initial movement of the baby's head into the birth canal.

midwife A trained person who helps women in childbirth.

anesthetics Agents that lessen pain.

general anesthesia Putting a person to sleep to prevent her or him from feeling pain.

tranquilizer A drug that reduces feelings of anxiety and tension.

local anesthetic A method that reduces pain in an area of the body.

natural childbirth A method of childbirth in which women use no anesthesia but are educated about childbirth [...]th discomfort.

[...]dbirth meth[...] relax and [...] and lessen [...]g childbirth.

> When it's time to prepare for exams, use the review card and the technique to the left to ensure successful study sessions.

[...]ery of the [...]n in the

anoxia Lack of oxygen.

hypoxia Less oxygen than needed.

schizophrenia A psychological disorder characterized by disturbances in thought, perception and attention, motor activity, and mood.

breech presentation A position in which the fetus enters the birth canal buttocks first.

preterm Born at or before completion of 37 weeks of gestation.

small for dates Descriptive of full-term neonates who are unusually small for their age.

lanugo Fine, downy hair on the body of the neonate, especially preterm babies.

vernix An oily white substance that coats the skin of the neonate, especially preterm babies.

respiratory distress syndrome Breathing problems, including weak and irregular breathing, to which preterm babies are prone.

incubator A heated, protective container in which premature infants are kept.

postpartum period The period following childbirth.

postpartum depression (PPD) Severe, prolonged depression after delivery that is characterized by feelings of sadness, apathy, and worthlessness.

bonding The formation of feelings of attachment between caregiver and child.

Apgar scale A measure of a newborn's health that assesses appearance, pulse, grimace, activity level, and respiratory effort.

reflex An unlearned, stereotypical response to a stimulus.

visual accommodation The automatic adjustments made by the lenses of the eyes to focus on objects.

convergence The inward movement of the eyes to focus on a nearby object.

amplitude The height of sound waves; the greater the amplitude of sound waves, the louder the sound is.

pitch The highness or lowness of a

> Don't forget, you can find more study resources for CDEV online at 4ltrpress. cengage.com/cdev.

non-rapid-eye-movement (non-REM) sleep Periods of sleep during which no rapid eye movements occur.

LO5 Describe the characteristics of a neonate.

The neonate's health is usually evaluated according to the Apgar scale.

TABLE 4.2
The Apgar Scale

POINTS	0	1	2
Appearance: Color	Blue, pale	Body pink, extremities blue	Entirely pink
Pulse: Heart rate	Absent (not detectable)	Slow—below 100 beats/minute	Rapid—100–140 beats/minute
Grimace: Reflex irritability	No response	Grimace	Crying, coughing, sneezing
Activity level: Muscle tone	Completely flaccid, limp	Weak, inactive	Flexed arms and legs; resists extension
Respiratory effort: Breathing	Absent (infant is apneic)	Shallow, irregular, slow	Regular breathing; lusty crying

The Brazelton Neonatal Behavioral Assessment Scale screens for behavioral and neurological problems. The rooting and sucking reflexes are basic to survival. Neonates are nearsighted. Neonates visually detect movement, and many track movement. Fetuses respond to sound months before they are born. Neon[...] the sounds and rhythms of speech. The nasal and tast[...] to those of older children and adults. The sensations [...] and may contribute to formation of bonds of attachm[...] their time in sleep, and half of that in REM sleep (see F[...] of pain and discomfort. SIDS is a disorder of infancy th[...] baby is sleeping. SIDS is more common among babies who are put to sleep in the prone position, preterm and low-birth-weight infants, male infants, and infants whose mothers smoked during or after pregnancy.

> Important figures and tables from the chapter will accompany learning outcome summaries when relevant.

FIGURE 4.5
REM Sleep and Non-REM Sleep

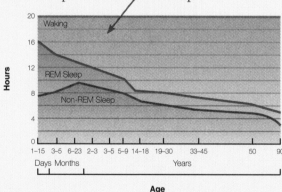

pacifier An artificial nipple, teething ring, or similar device that, when sucked, soothes babies.

sudden infant death syndrome (SIDS) The death, while sleeping, of apparently healthy babies who stop breathing for unknown reasons.

medulla A part of the brain stem that regulates vital and automatic functions such as breathing and the sleep-wake cycle.

Learning Outcomes

LO1 Outline the development of the field of child development.

The field of child development attempts to advance knowledge of the processes that govern the development of children's physical structures, traits, behaviors, and cognitions. Researchers study child development to gain insight into human nature, the origins of adult behavior, the origins of developmental problems, ways of optimizing development, and the effects of culture on development. Locke focused on the role of the environment or experience in development. Rousseau argued that children are good by nature, and if allowed to express their natural impulses, they would develop into moral and giving people. Darwin originated the modern theory of evolution and was one of the first observers to keep a baby biography.

LO2 Outline and evaluate the various theories of child development.

Freud viewed children as caught in conflict as sexual and aggressive impulses seek expression. He believed that they undergo oral, anal, phallic, latency, and genital stages of psychosexual development. Erikson extended Freud's five developmental stages to eight (to include adulthood) and labeled stages after life crises. Watson argued that scientists must address observable behavior only, not mental activity. Behaviorism relies on two types of learning: classical conditioning and operant conditioning. Social cognitive theorists, such as Bandura, argue that much learning occurs by observing models and that children choose whether or not to engage in behaviors they have learned. Piaget studied how children form mental representations of the world and manipulate them. He hypothesized that children's cognitive development follows an invariant sequence of stages: sensorimotor, preoperational, concrete operational, and formal operational. Information-processing theory deals with the ways in which children encode information, transfer it to working memory, manipulate it, place it storage, and retrieve it from storage. The biological perspective refers to heredity and to developments such as formation of sperm and ova, gains in height and weight, maturation of the nervous system, and the way hormones spur the changes of puberty. Ethology involves instinctive, species-specific behavior patterns, termed fixed action patterns (FAPs). Many FAPs, such as those involved in attachment, occur during a critical period of life. Bronfenbrenner's ecological theory explains development in terms of the reciprocal interaction between children and the systems in which development occurs: the microsystem, mesosystem, exosystem, macrosystem, and chronosystem. Vygotsky's key concepts are the zone of proximal development (ZPD) and scaffolding.

LO3 Discuss controversies in child development.

Development would appear to reflect the interaction of nature (genetics) and nurture (nutrition, cultural and family backgrounds, and opportunities to learn about the world). Maturational, psychoanalytic, and cognitive-developmental theorists see development as discontinuous (occurring in stages). Aspects of physical development, such as the adolescent growth spurt, do occur in stages. Learning theorists tend to see development as more continuous. Bronfenbrenner and Bandura do not see children as entirely active or entirely passive. They believe that children are influenced by the environment but that the influence is reciprocal.

Key Terms

behaviorism Watson's view that science must study observable behavior only and investigate relationships between stimuli and responses.

maturation The unfolding of genetically determined traits, structures, and functions.

psychosexual development The process by which libidinal energy is expressed through different erogenous zones during different stages of development.

stage theory A theory of development that views changes as occurring in distinct periods of life.

psychosocial development Erikson's theory, which emphasizes the importance of social relationships and conscious choice throughout eight stages of development.

life crisis An internal conflict that attends each stage of psychosocial development.

identity crisis According to Erikson, a period of inner conflict during which one examines one's values and makes decisions about one's life roles.

classical conditioning A simple form of learning in which one stimulus comes to bring forth the response usually brought forth by a second stimulus by being paired repeatedly with the second stimulus.

operant conditioning A simple form of learning in which an organism learns to engage in behavior that is reinforced.

reinforcement The process of providing stimuli that follow responses and increase the frequency of the responses.

positive reinforcer A reinforcer that, when applied, increases the frequency of a response.

negative reinforcer A reinforcer that, when removed, increases the frequency of a response.

extinction The eventual cessation of a conditioned response in the absence of reinforcement.

social cognitive theory A cognitively oriented learning theory that emphasizes observational learning.

observational learning Acquisition of expectations and skills by observing others.

cognitive-developmental theory The stage theory that holds that the child's abilities to mentally represent the world and solve problems develop due to the interaction of experience and the maturation of neurological structures.

scheme An action pattern or mental structure that is involved in the acquisition and organization of knowledge.

adaptation The interaction between the organism and the environment, consisting of assimilation and accommodation.

assimilation The incorporation of new events or knowledge into existing schemes.

accommodation The modification of existing schemes to permit the incorporation of new events or knowledge.

equilibration The making of an equilibrium, or balance, between assimilation and accommodation.

ethology The study of instinctive, or inborn, behavior patterns.

fixed action pattern (FAP) A stereotyped pattern of behavior that is evoked by an instinct.

ecology The branch of biology that deals with the relationships between living organisms and their environment.

ecological systems theory The view that explains child development in terms of the reciprocal influences between children and environmental settings.

microsystem The immediate settings with which the child interacts, such as the home, the school, and peers.

mesosystem The interlocking settings that influence the child, such as the interaction of the school and the larger community.

exosystem Community institutions and settings that indirectly influence the child, such as the school board and the parents' workplaces.

macrosystem The basic institutions and ideologies that influence the child.

chronosystem The environmental changes that occur over time and have an effect on the child.

zone of proximal development (ZPD) Vygotsky's term for the range of tasks a child can carry out with the help of someone who is more skilled.

scaffolding Vygotsky's term for temporary cognitive structures or methods of solving problems that help the child as he or she learns to function independently.

L◯4 Describe ways in which researchers study child development, including the strengths and weaknesses of each.

Naturalistic observation is conducted in "the field"—the actual settings in which children develop. The case study is a carefully drawn account or biography of the behavior of a child. Correlation enables researchers to determine whether one behavior or trait is related to another. A correlation coefficient can vary between +1.00 and –1.00. Correlational studies reveal relationships but not cause and effect. In an experiment, an experimental group receives a treatment (independent variable), whereas another group (a control group) does not. Subjects are observed to determine whether the treatment has an effect. Longitudinal research studies the same children repeatedly over time. Cross-sectional research observes and compares children of different ages. Cross-sequential research combines the longitudinal and cross-sectional methods by breaking down the span of the ideal longitudinal study into convenient segments. Ethical standards prevent researchers from using methods that might harm children.

nature The processes within an organism that guide it to develop according to its genetic code.

nurture Environmental factors that influence development.

empirical Based on observation and experimentation.

naturalistic observation A method of scientific observation in which children (and others) are observed in their natural environments.

case study A carefully drawn account of the behavior of an individual.

standardized test A test of abilities in which an individual's score is compared to the scores of a group of similar individuals.

correlation coefficient A number ranging from +1.00 to –1.00 that expresses the direction (positive or negative) and strength of the relationship between two variables.

positive correlation A relationship between two variables in which one variable increases as the other increases.

negative correlation A relationship between two variables in which one variable increases as the other decreases.

experiment A method of scientific investigation that seeks to discover cause-and-effect relationships by introducing independent variables and observing their effects on dependent variables.

hypothesis A proposition to be tested.

independent variable A condition in a scientific study that is manipulated so that its effects can be observed.

dependent variable A measure of an assumed effect of an independent variable.

experimental group A group made up of subjects who receive a treatment in an experiment.

control group A group made up of subjects in an experiment who do not receive the treatment but for whom all other conditions are comparable to those of subjects in the experimental group.

longitudinal research The study of developmental processes by taking repeated measures of the same group of participants at various stages of development.

cross-sectional research The study of developmental processes by taking measures of participants of different age groups at the same time.

cohort effect Similarities in behavior among a group of peers that stem from the fact that group members are approximately of the same age.

cross-sequential research An approach that combines the longitudinal and cross-sectional methods by following individuals of different ages for abbreviated periods of time.

time lag comparison The study of developmental processes by taking measures of participants in different groups when they are the same age.

Learning Outcomes

LO1 Explain the influences of heredity on development, referring to chromosomes and genes, mitosis and meiosis, twins, and dominant and recessive traits.

Heredity defines one's nature, as determined by the biological transmission of physical traits from one generation to another. Heredity is also involved in many psychological traits. People normally have 46 chromosomes organized into 23 pairs. Each chromosome contains thousands of genes—the basic units that regulate the development of traits. Genes are segments of strands of DNA. In mitosis, strands of DNA break apart and are rebuilt in the new cell. Sperm and ova are produced by meiosis—or reduction division— and have 23 rather than 46 chromosomes. If a zygote divides into two cells that separate and each develops into an individual, we obtain monozygotic (MZ) twins, which are identical. If two ova are each fertilized, they develop into dizygotic (DZ) twins, which are fraternal. Traits are determined by pairs of genes. Mendel established that some traits result from an "averaging" of the genetic instructions carried by the parents. However, genes can also be dominant (as in the case of brown eyes) or recessive (blue eyes).

LO2 Describe the features and causes of various chromosomal abnormalities.

Intellectual deficiency is a result of many chromosomal abnormalities. Down syndrome is caused by an extra chromosome on the 21st pair. Children with Down syndrome have characteristic facial features, including a downward-sloping fold of skin at the inner corners of the eyes, and various physical health problems. Disorders that arise from abnormal numbers of sex chromosomes are called sex-linked. These include XYY males and girls with a single X sex chromosome.

LO3 Describe the features and causes of various genetic abnormalities.

Phenylketonuria (PKU) is a metabolic disorder transmitted by a recessive gene. Huntington's disease is a fatal progressive degenerative disorder and a dominant trait. Sickle-cell anemia is caused by a recessive gene and is most common among African Americans. Tay-Sachs disease is a fatal disease of the nervous system that is caused by a recessive gene and is most common among children in Jewish families of Eastern European origin. Cystic fibrosis is caused by a recessive gene and is the most common fatal hereditary disease among European Americans. Sex-linked genetic abnormalities are carried only on the X sex chromosome and include hemophilia, Duchenne muscular dystrophy, diabetes, and color blindness.

LO4 Discuss methods of detecting genetic abnormalities.

Prenatal testing procedures can determine the presence of various genetic and chromosomal abnormalities. Such tests include amniocentesis, chorionic villus sampling, ultrasound, and parental blood tests.

LO5 Describe methods of determining our genotypes and our phenotypes.

Our genotypes are the sets of traits that we inherit, but inherited traits vary in expression, depending on environmental conditions. One's actual set of traits is one's phenotype. Researchers study the extent to which a trait is inherited by observing its distribution among relatives who differ in degree of genetic closeness. Parents and children have a 50% overlap in

Key Terms

heredity The transmission of traits and characteristics from parent to child by means of genes.

genetics The branch of biology that studies heredity.

chromosomes Rod-shaped structures composed of genes that are found within the nuclei of cells.

gene The basic unit of heredity. Genes are composed of deoxyribonucleic acid (DNA).

polygenic Resulting from many genes.

deoxyribonucleic acid (DNA) Genetic material that takes the form of a double helix composed of phosphates, sugars, and bases.

mitosis The form of cell division in which each chromosome splits length-wise to double in number. Half of each chromosome combines with the appropriate bases to regain the original form and then moves to the new cell.

mutation A sudden variation in a heritable characteristic, as by an accident that affects the composition of genes.

meiosis The form of cell division in which each pair of chromosomes splits so that one member of each pair moves to the new cell. As a result, each new cell has 23 chromosomes.

autosome A member of a pair of chromosomes (with the exception of sex chromosomes).

sex chromosome A chromosome in the shape of a Y (male) or X (female) that determines the sex of the child.

monozygotic (MZ) twins Twins that derive from a single zygote that has split into two; identical twins. Each MZ twin carries the same genetic code.

dizygotic (DZ) twins Twins that derive from two zygotes; fraternal twins.

ovulation The releasing of an ovum from an ovary.

allele A member of a pair of genes.

homozygous Having two identical alleles.

heterozygous Having two different alleles.

dominant trait A trait that is expressed.

recessive trait A trait that is not expressed when the gene or genes involved have been paired with dominant genes.

carrier A person who carries and transmits a recessive gene but does not exhibit its effect.

multifactorial problems Problems that stem from the interaction of heredity and environmental factors.

Down syndrome A chromosomal abnormality characterized by mental retardation and caused by an extra chromosome in the 21st pair.

sex-linked chromosomal abnormalities Abnormalities that are transmitted from generation to generation and carried by a sex chromosome.

Klinefelter syndrome A chromosomal disorder found among males that is caused by an extra X sex chromosome and that is characterized by infertility and mild mental retardation.

testosterone A male sex hormone produced mainly by the testes.

Turner syndrome A chromosomal disorder found among females that is caused by having a single X sex chromosome and is characterized by infertility.

estrogen A female sex hormone produced mainly by the ovaries.

phenylketonuria (PKU) A genetic abnormality in which phenylalanine builds up in the body and causes mental retardation.

Huntington's disease A fatal genetic neurologic disorder whose onset is in middle age.

sickle-cell anemia A genetic disorder that decreases the blood's capacity to carry oxygen.

Tay-Sachs disease A fatal genetic neurological disorder.

cystic fibrosis A fatal genetic disorder in which mucus obstructs the lungs and pancreas.

hemophilia A genetic disorder in which blood does not clot properly.

sex-linked genetic abnormalities Abnormalities resulting from genes that are found on the X sex chromosome. They are more likely to be shown by male offspring (who do not have an opposing gene from a second X chromosome) than by female offspring.

muscular dystrophy A chronic disease characterized by a progressive wasting away of the muscles.

genetic counseling Advice concerning the probabilities that a couple's children will show genetic abnormalities.

prenatal Before birth.

genes, as do brothers and sisters, with the exception of MZ twins, who have 100% overlap. MZ twins resemble each other more closely than DZ twins on physical and psychological traits, even when reared apart. If adopted children are closer to their natural than to their adoptive parents on a physical or psychological trait, that trait is likely to have a strong genetic basis.

LO6 Describe the process of conception.

The process is the union of a sperm and an ovum—conception. Fertilization normally occurs in a fallopian tube. If the egg is not fertilized, it is discharged. Men typically ejaculate hundreds of millions of sperm. More boys are conceived than girls, but male fetuses have a higher rate of spontaneous abortion. Chromosomes from the sperm cell align with chromosomes in the egg cell, combining to form 23 new pairs.

LO7 Discuss the causes of infertility and alternate ways of becoming parents.

Male fertility problems include low sperm count and motility, infections, and trauma to the testes. Female fertility problems include failure to ovulate, infections such as PID, endometriosis, and obstructions. Fertility drugs stimulate ovulation. Artificial insemination can be done with the sperm from multiple ejaculations of a man with a low sperm count or with the sperm of a donor. In vitro fertilization (IVF) can be used when the fallopian tubes are blocked. An embryo can also be transferred into a host uterus when the mother cannot produce ova.

amniocentesis A procedure for drawing and examining fetal cells sloughed off into amniotic fluid to determine the presence of various disorders.

chorionic villus sampling A method for the prenatal detection of genetic abnormalities that samples the membrane enveloping the amniotic sac and fetus.

uterus The hollow organ within females in which the embryo and fetus develop.

ultrasound Sound waves too high in pitch to be sensed by the human ear.

sonogram An image of an embryo or fetus generated using ultrasound waves.

alpha-fetoprotein (AFP) assay A blood test that assesses the mother's blood level of alpha-fetoprotein, a substance that is linked with fetal neural tube defects.

genotype The genetic form or constitution of a person as determined by heredity.

phenotype The actual form or constitution of a person as determined by heredity and environmental factors.

canalization The tendency of growth rates to return to genetically determined patterns after undergoing environmentally induced change.

niche-picking Choosing environments that allow us to develop inherited preferences.

autism A developmental disorder characterized by failure to relate to others, communication problems, intolerance of change, and ritualistic behavior.

conception The union of a sperm cell and an ovum that occurs when the chromosomes of each of these cells combine to form 23 new pairs.

endometrium The inner lining of the uterus.

spontaneous abortion Unplanned, accidental abortion.

motility Self-propulsion.

pelvic inflammatory disease (PID) An infection of the abdominal region that may have various causes and that may impair fertility.

endometriosis Inflammation of endometrial tissue sloughed off into the abdominal cavity rather than out of the body during menstruation; the condition is characterized by abdominal pain and sometimes infertility.

artificial insemination Injection of sperm into the uterus to fertilize an ovum.

in vitro fertilization Fertilization of an ovum in a laboratory dish.

donor IVF The transfer of a donor's ovum, fertilized in a laboratory dish, to the uterus of another woman.

Learning Outcomes

LO1 Describe the key events of the germinal stage.

During the germinal stage, the zygote divides repeatedly but does not gain in mass. Before implantation, the dividing cluster of cells is nourished by the yolk of the original egg cell. Once implanted in the uterine wall, it obtains nourishment from the mother. The zygote travels through a fallopian tube to the uterus, where it implants. It then takes the form of a blastocyst. Layers of cells form within the embryonic disk. The outer part of the blastocyst differentiates into membranes that will protect and nourish the embryo.

FIGURE 3.1

The Ovarian Cycle, Conception, and the Early Days of the Germinal Stage

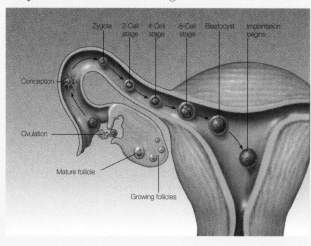

LO2 Describe the key events of the embryonic stage.

The embryonic stage lasts from implantation until the eighth week of development, during which the major organ systems differentiate. Development follows cephalocaudal and proximodistal trends. The outer layer of the embryonic disk develops into the nervous system, sensory organs, nails, hair, teeth, and skin. Two ridges form the neural tube, from which the nervous system develops. The heart begins to beat during the fourth week. Toward the end of the first month, arm and leg buds appear and the face takes shape. The nervous system has also begun to develop. By 5 to 6 weeks, the embryo has undifferentiated sex organs that resemble female structures. Testes produce male sex hormones that spur development of male genital organs and the male duct system. The embryo and fetus exchange nutrients and wastes with the mother through the placenta. The umbilical cord connects the fetus to the placenta. Many germs pass through the placenta, including those that cause syphilis and rubella. Some drugs also pass through, including aspirin, narcotics, and alcohol.

LO3 Describe the key events of the fetal stage.

The fetal stage lasts from the end of the embryonic stage until birth. The fetus begins to turn at the ninth or tenth week. The second trimester is characterized by maturation of organs and gains in size. By the end of the second trimester, the fetus opens and shuts its eyes, sucks its thumb, alternates between wakefulness and sleep, and responds to light and sounds. During the third trimester, the heart and lungs become increasingly capable of sustaining independent life. Newborn babies prefer their mother's voice to that of other women, apparently because of prenatal exposure.

Key Terms

neonate A newborn baby.

germinal stage The period of development between conception and the implantation of the embryo.

blastocyst A stage within the germinal period of prenatal development in which the zygote has the form of a sphere of cells surrounding a cavity of fluid.

embryonic disk The platelike inner part of the blastocyst that differentiates into the ectoderm, mesoderm, and endoderm of the embryo.

trophoblast The outer part of the blastocyst from which the amniotic sac, placenta, and umbilical cord develop.

umbilical cord A tube that connects the fetus to the placenta.

placenta An organ connected to the uterine wall and to the fetus by the umbilical cord. The placenta serves as a filter between mother and fetus for the exchange of nutrients and wastes.

embryonic stage The stage of prenatal development that lasts from implantation through the eighth week of pregnancy; it is characterized by the development of the major organ systems.

cephalocaudal From head to tail.

proximodistal From the inner part (or axis) of the body outward.

ectoderm The outermost cell layer of the newly formed embryo from which the skin and nervous system develop.

neural tube A structure that forms in the ectoderm during the embryonic stage, from which the nervous system develops.

endoderm The inner layer of the embryo from which the lungs and digestive system develop.

mesoderm The central layer of the embryo from which the bones and muscles develop.

androgens Male sex hormones.

amniotic sac The sac containing the fetus.

amniotic fluid Fluid within the amniotic sac that suspends and protects the fetus.

fetal stage The stage of development that lasts from the beginning of the ninth week of pregnancy through birth; it is characterized by gains in size and weight and by maturation of the organ systems.

stillbirth The delivery of a dead fetus.

teratogens Environmental influences or agents that can damage the embryo or fetus.

critical period In this usage, a period during which an embryo or fetus is particularly vulnerable to a certain teratogen.

syphilis A sexually transmitted infection that, in advanced stages, can attack major organ systems.

congenital Present at birth; resulting from the prenatal environment.

HIV/AIDS HIV stands for *human immunodeficiency virus,* which cripples the body's immune system. AIDS stands for *acquired immunodeficiency syndrome,* a condition in which the immune system is weakened and the body becomes vulnerable to a variety of fatal illnesses.

rubella A viral infection that can cause retardation and heart disease in the embryo. Also called German measles.

toxemia A life-threatening disease that can afflict pregnant women; it is characterized by high blood pressure.

premature Born before the full term of gestation. Also referred to as *preterm.*

Rh incompatibility A condition in which antibodies produced by the mother are transmitted to the child, possibly causing brain damage or death.

thalidomide A sedative used in the 1960s that has been linked to birth defects, especially deformed or absent limbs.

progestin A hormone used to maintain pregnancy that can cause masculinization of the fetus.

DES Diethylstilbestrol, an estrogen that has been linked to cancer in the reproductive organs of children of women who used the hormone when pregnant.

fetal alcohol syndrome (FAS) A cluster of symptoms shown by children of women who drank heavily during pregnancy, including characteristic facial features and mental retardation.

LO4 Describe environmental influences on prenatal development, including maternal nutrition, teratogens, infections, parental drug use, environmental hazards, and parents' age.

Maternal malnutrition has been linked to low birth weight, prematurity, stunted growth, retardation of brain development, and behavioral problems. Folic acid reduces the risk of neural tube defects. Exposure to particular teratogens is most harmful during critical periods—the times when certain organs are developing. Women who contract rubella may bear children who suffer from deafness, mental retardation, heart disease, or cataracts. Syphilis can cause miscarriage, stillbirth, or congenital syphilis. Babies can be infected with HIV in utero, during childbirth, or by breast feeding. Toxemia is characterized by high blood pressure and is connected with preterm or undersized babies. In Rh incompatibility, antibodies produced by the mother are transmitted to a fetus or newborn infant and cause brain damage or death. Thalidomide causes missing or stunted limbs in babies. Tetracycline can cause yellowed teeth and bone problems. DES leads to high risk of cervical and testicular cancer. High doses of vitamins A and D are associated with nervous system damage and heart defects. Maternal addiction to narcotics is linked to low birth weight, prematurity, and toxemia, and fetuses can be born addicted themselves. Cocaine increases the risk of stillbirth, low birth weight, and birth defects. Maternal use of alcohol is linked to death of the fetus and neonate, growth deficiencies, and fetal alcohol syndrome (FAS). Maternal cigarette smoking is linked with low birth weight, stillbirth, and mental retardation. Prenatal exposure to heavy metals threatens cognitive development. Prenatal exposure to PCBs is connected with babies that are smaller, less responsive, and more likely to develop cognitive deficits. Fetal exposure to radiation can cause neural and skeletal problems. Teenage mothers have a higher incidence of infant mortality and children with low birth weight. Women older than the age of 30 run an increasing risk of chromosomal abnormalities and of having stillborn or preterm babies. Advanced paternal age also poses risks.

FIGURE 3.3

Critical Periods in Prenatal Development

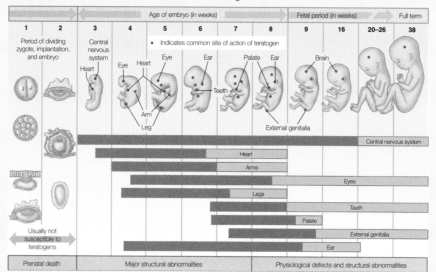

Learning Outcomes

LO1 Identify the stages of childbirth.

The initiation of labor may be triggered by secretion of hormones by the fetus. Maternal hormones stimulate contractions strong enough to expel the baby. The first stage of childbirth begins with the onset of regular uterine contractions, effacing and dilating the cervix. During transition, the cervix is nearly fully dilated and the head of the fetus moves into the birth canal. The second stage begins when the baby appears at the opening of the birth canal. It ends with the birth of the baby. When the baby is breathing on its own, the umbilical cord is clamped and severed. During the third stage, the placenta separates from the uterine wall and is expelled along with fetal membranes.

LO2 Examine different methods of childbirth.

General anesthesia puts the woman to sleep; regional or local anesthetics deaden pain in parts of the body. The Lamaze method teaches women to dissociate uterine contractions from pain and fear by associating other responses, such as relaxation, with contractions. A coach aids the mother in the delivery room. A C-section delivers a baby surgically through the abdomen. Herpes and HIV infections in the birth canal can be bypassed by C-section.

LO3 Discuss potential problems with childbirth.

Prenatal oxygen deprivation can be fatal if prolonged; it can also impair development of the nervous system, leading to cognitive and motor problems. A baby is preterm when birth occurs at or before 37 weeks of gestation. A baby has a low birth weight when it weighs less than 5 1/2 pounds (about 2,500 grams). The risk of having preterm babies rises with multiple births. Risks include infant mortality and delayed neurological and motor development. Sucking and breathing reflexes may be weak. The walls of air sacs in the lungs may stick together, leading to respiratory distress. Preterm babies usually remain in incubators. Preterm infants profit from early stimulation.

LO4 Describe the postpartum period.

Women may encounter the baby blues, postpartum depression, and postpartum psychosis. These problems probably reflect hormonal changes following birth, although stress can play a role. Research by Klaus and Kennell suggested that the first few hours after birth present a "maternal-sensitive" period during which women's hormone levels particularly dispose them to "bond" with their neonates. However, the study confounded the effects of extra time with their babies with special attention from health professionals.

Key Terms

full term The amount of time of a normal pregnancy: 266 days from the date of conception.

Braxton-Hicks contractions The first, usually painless, contractions of childbirth.

prostaglandins Hormones that stimulate labor contractions.

oxytocin A hormone that stimulates labor contractions.

efface Thin out.

dilate Widen or enlarge.

episiotomy An incision between the birth canal and anus that widens the vaginal opening to prevent random tearing during childbirth.

fetal monitoring Use of an electronic sensing device to track the fetus's vital signs during childbirth.

forceps An instrument that fits around the baby's head to pull the baby through the birth canal.

vacuum extraction tube An instrument that uses suction to pull the baby through the birth canal.

transition Initial movement of the baby's head into the birth canal.

midwife A trained person who helps women in childbirth.

anesthetics Agents that lessen pain.

general anesthesia Putting a person to sleep to prevent her or him from feeling pain.

tranquilizer A drug that reduces feelings of anxiety and tension.

local anesthetic A method that reduces pain in an area of the body.

natural childbirth A method of childbirth in which women use no anesthesia but are educated about childbirth and strategies for coping with discomfort.

Lamaze method A childbirth method in which women learn to relax and breathe to conserve energy and lessen pain and have a coach during childbirth.

cesarean section Delivery of the neonate through an incision in the mother's abdomen.

anoxia Lack of oxygen.

hypoxia Less oxygen than needed.

schizophrenia A psychological disorder characterized by disturbances in thought, perception and attention, motor activity, and mood.

breech presentation A position in which the fetus enters the birth canal buttocks first.

preterm Born at or before completion of 37 weeks of gestation.

small for dates Descriptive of full-term neonates who are unusually small for their age.

lanugo Fine, downy hair on the body of the neonate, especially preterm babies.

vernix An oily white substance that coats the skin of the neonate, especially preterm babies.

respiratory distress syndrome Breathing problems, including weak and irregular breathing, to which preterm babies are prone.

incubator A heated, protective container in which premature infants are kept.

postpartum period The period following childbirth.

postpartum depression (PPD) Severe, prolonged depression after delivery that is characterized by feelings of sadness, apathy, and worthlessness.

bonding The formation of feelings of attachment between caregiver and child.

Apgar scale A measure of a newborn's health that assesses appearance, pulse, grimace, activity level, and respiratory effort.

reflex An unlearned, stereotypical response to a stimulus.

visual accommodation The automatic adjustments made by the lenses of the eyes to focus on objects.

convergence The inward movement of the eyes to focus on a nearby object.

amplitude The height of sound waves; the greater the amplitude of sound waves, the louder the sound is.

pitch The highness or lowness of a sound, as determined by the frequency of sound waves.

rapid-eye-movement (REM) sleep A period of sleep during which we are likely to dream, as indicated by rapid eye movements.

non-rapid-eye-movement (non-REM) sleep Periods of sleep during which no rapid eye movements occur.

LO5 Describe the characteristics of a neonate.

The neonate's health is usually evaluated according to the Apgar scale.

TABLE 4.2
The Apgar Scale

POINTS	0	1	2
Appearance: Color	Blue, pale	Body pink, extremities blue	Entirely pink
Pulse: Heart rate	Absent (not detectable)	Slow—below 100 beats/minute	Rapid—100–140 beats/minute
Grimace: Reflex irritability	No response	Grimace	Crying, coughing, sneezing
Activity level: Muscle tone	Completely flaccid, limp	Weak, inactive	Flexed arms and legs; resists extension
Respiratory effort: Breathing	Absent (infant is apneic)	Shallow, irregular, slow	Regular breathing; lusty crying

The Brazelton Neonatal Behavioral Assessment Scale screens for behavioral and neurological problems. The rooting and sucking reflexes are basic to survival. Neonates are nearsighted. Neonates visually detect movement, and many track movement. Fetuses respond to sound months before they are born. Neonates are particularly responsive to the sounds and rhythms of speech. The nasal and taste preferences of neonates are similar to those of older children and adults. The sensations of skin against skin are also soothing and may contribute to formation of bonds of attachment. Neonates spend two-thirds of their time in sleep, and half of that in REM sleep (see Figure 4.5). Babies cry mainly because of pain and discomfort. SIDS is a disorder of infancy that apparently strikes while the baby is sleeping. SIDS is more common among babies who are put to sleep in the prone position, preterm and low-birth-weight infants, male infants, and infants whose mothers smoked during or after pregnancy.

FIGURE 4.5
REM Sleep and Non-REM Sleep

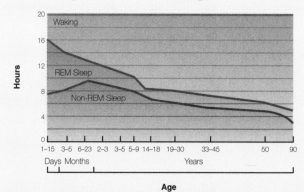

pacifier An artificial nipple, teething ring, or similar device that, when sucked, soothes babies.

sudden infant death syndrome (SIDS) The death, while sleeping, of apparently healthy babies who stop breathing for unknown reasons.

medulla A part of the brain stem that regulates vital and automatic functions such as breathing and the sleep-wake cycle.

Learning Outcomes

LO1 Discuss tendencies in physical growth in infancy.

Three key sequences of physical development include cephalocaudal, proximodistal, and differentiation. Infants usually double their birth weight in 5 months and triple it by the first birthday. Height increases by about half in the first year. Infants grow another 4 to 6 inches in the second year and gain another 4 to 7 pounds. The head diminishes in proportion to the rest of the body. Failure to thrive (FTT) impairs growth in infancy and early childhood. FTT can have organic causes or nonorganic causes, such as deficiencies in caregiver–child interaction. Breast milk is tailored to human digestion, contains essential nutrients and the mothers' antibodies, helps protect against infant diarrhea, and is less likely than formula to cause allergies.

LO2 Examine the development of the brain and neurons in infancy.

FIGURE 5.3
Growth of Body Systems as a Percentage of Total Postnatal Growth

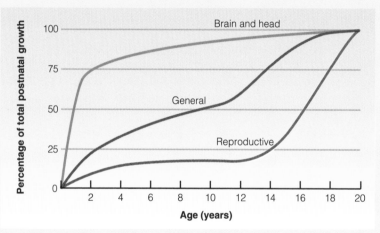

As the child matures, axons of neurons lengthen, dendrites and axon terminals proliferate, and many axons become wrapped in myelin, enabling them to function more efficiently. The brain triples in weight by the first birthday, reaching nearly 70% of its adult weight (see Figure 5.3). There are two major prenatal neural growth spurts: Neurons proliferate during the first growth spurt; the second spurt is due mainly to the proliferation of dendrites and axon terminals. Sensory and motor areas of the brain begin to develop because of maturation, but sensory stimulation and motor activity also spur development. Malnutrition is connected with a small brain, fewer neurons, and less myelination.

Key Terms

differentiation The processes by which behaviors and physical structures become specialized.

failure to thrive (FTT) A disorder of infancy and early childhood characterized by variable eating and inadequate gains in weight.

canalization The tendency of growth rates to return to normal after undergoing environmentally induced change.

nerves Bundles of axons from many neurons.

neurons Cells in the nervous system that transmit messages.

dendrites Short fibers extending from neurons that receive impulses from other neurons.

axon A long, thin part of a neuron that transmits impulses to other neurons through branching structures called axon terminals.

neurotransmitter A chemical that transmits a neural impulse across a synapse from one neuron to another.

myelin sheath A fatty, whitish covering that encases and insulates axons.

myelination The coating of axons with myelin.

multiple sclerosis A disorder in which hard fibrous tissue replaces myelin, impeding neural transmission.

medulla An area of the brainstem involved in heartbeat and respiration.

cerebellum The part of the hindbrain involved in coordination and balance.

cerebrum The part of the brain responsible for learning, thought, memory, and language.

ulnar grasp Grasping objects between the fingers and the palm.

pincer grasp Grasping objects between the fingers and the thumb.

locomotion Movement from one place to another.

toddler A child who walks with short, uncertain steps.

perceptual constancy Perceiving objects as maintaining their identity although sensations from them change as their positions change.

habituation Becoming used to a stimulus and therefore paying less attention to it.

L○3 Describe motor development in infancy.

Children gain the ability to move their bodies through a sequence of activities that includes rolling over, sitting up, crawling, creeping, walking, and running. The sequence remains stable, but some children skip a step. Both maturation (nature) and experience (nurture) play roles in motor development. Infants need some opportunity for experimentation before they can sit up and walk. Development of motor skills can be accelerated by training, but the effect is generally slight.

L○4 Discuss sensory and perceptual development in infancy.

Infants' acuity and peripheral vision approximate adult levels by the age of 6 months. Two-month-old infants fixate longer on the human face than on other stimuli. Some researchers argue that neonates prefer faces because they are complex images. Neonates direct their attention to the edges of objects, but 2-month-olds scan from the edges inward (see Figure 5.8).

FIGURE 5.8
Eye Movements of 1- and 2-Month-Olds

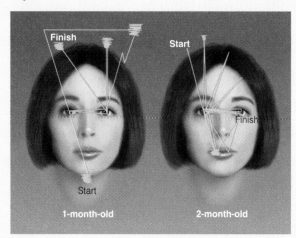

Most infants refuse to venture out over the visual cliff by the time they can crawl. Size constancy appears to be present by 2 1/2 to 3 months of age; shape constancy develops by age 4 to 5 months. Neonates reflexively orient their heads toward a sound. Infants discriminate caregivers' voices by 3 1/2 months of age. Early infants can perceive most of the speech sounds throughout the languages of the world, but by 10–12 months of age, this ability lessens. Neonates seem to be at the mercy of external stimuli, but later on, intentional action replaces capture. Systematic search replaces unsystematic search, attention becomes selective, and irrelevant information gets ignored. Sensory changes are linked to maturation of the nervous system (nature), but experience also plays a crucial role in perceptual development (nurture).

Learning Outcomes

LO1 Examine Jean Piaget's studies of cognitive development.

Piaget's sensorimotor stage refers to the first two years of cognitive development, during which changes are shown by means of sensory and motor activity. The first substage is dominated by the assimilation of stimulation into reflexes. In the second substage, primary circular reactions, infants repeat stimulating actions that occur by chance. In the third substage, secondary circular reactions, patterns of activity are repeated because of their effects. In the fourth substage, infants intentionally coordinate schemes to attain goals. In the fifth substage, tertiary circular reactions, infants purposefully adapt established schemes to specific situations. In the sixth substage, external exploration is replaced by mental exploration. Through the first 6 months or so, when a screen is placed between an object and an infant, the infant behaves as if the object is no longer there.

LO2 Discuss the information-processing approach.

Early infants use memory and imitation to process information. Older infants are more capable of encoding and retrieving information. Neonates reflexively imitate certain behaviors, such as sticking out the tongue. Infants later show deferred imitation, suggesting that they have mentally represented actions.

LO3 Identify individual differences in intelligence among infants.

The Bayley Scales of Infant Development (BSID) have mental-scale and motor-scale items that can suggest early signs of sensory or neurological problems, but the BSID does not predict school grades accurately. Visual recognition memory moderately predicts IQ scores in later childhood.

TABLE 6.1
Items from the Bayley Scales of Infant Development (BSID–II)

AGE	MENTAL-SCALE ITEMS	MOTOR-SCALE ITEMS
1 month	The infant quiets when picked up.	The infant makes a postural adjustment when put to examiner's shoulder.
2 months	When examiner presents two objects (bell and rattle) above the infant in a crib, the infant glances back and forth from one to the other.	The infant holds his or her head steady when being carried about in a vertical position.
5 months	The infant is observed to transfer an object from one hand to the other during play.	When seated at a feeding-type table and presented with a sugar pill that is out of reach, the infant attempts to pick it up.
8 months	When an object (toy) in plain view of the infant (i.e., on a table) is covered by a cup, the infant removes the cup to retrieve the object.	The infant raises herself or himself into a sitting position.
12 months	The infant imitates words that are spoken by the examiner.	When requested by the examiner, the infant stands up from a position in which she or he had been lying on her or his back on the floor.
14–16 months	The infant builds a tower with two cubes (blocks) after the examiner demonstrates the behavior.	The infant walks alone with good coordination.

Key Terms

primary circular reactions The repetition of actions that first occurred by chance and that focus on the infant's own body.

secondary circular reactions The repetition of actions that produce an effect on the environment.

tertiary circular reactions The purposeful adaptations of established schemes to new situations.

object permanence Recognition that objects or people continue to exist when they are not in view.

deferred imitation The imitation of an action that occurred in the past.

visual recognition memory The kind of memory demonstrated by an infant's ability to discriminate previously seen objects from novel objects.

prelinguistic Referring to vocalizations made by the infant before the development of language.

cooing Prelinguistic vowel-like sounds that reflect feelings of pleasure or positive excitement.

babbling The child's first vocalizations that have the sounds of speech.

echolalia The automatic repetition of sounds or words.

intonation The use of pitches of varying levels to help communicate meaning.

receptive vocabulary The number of words one understands.

expressive vocabulary The number of words one can use in the production of language.

referential language style Use of language primarily as a means for labeling objects.

expressive language style Use of language primarily as a means for engaging in social interactions.

overextension Use of one word to refer to things or actions for which a child does not have words.

telegraphic speech Type of speech in which sentences contain only the essential words.

holophrase A single word that is used to express complex meanings.

syntax The rules in a language for combining words in order to form sentences.

models In learning theory, those whose behaviors are imitated by others.

extinction Decrease in frequency of a response due to absence of reinforcement.

shaping Gradual building of complex behavior through reinforcement of successive approximations to the target behavior.

psycholinguistic theory The view that language learning involves an interaction between environmental influences and an inborn tendency to acquire language.

language acquisition device (LAD) An inborn tendency to acquire language, which primes the learning of grammar.

surface structure The superficial features of language, especially vocabulary and grammar.

deep structure The underlying set of rules for transforming ideas into sentences.

aphasia A disruption in the ability to understand or produce language.

Broca's aphasia An aphasia caused by damage to Broca's area and shown by difficulty in speaking.

Wernicke's aphasia An aphasia caused by damage to Wernicke's area and characterized by impaired comprehension of speech and difficulty producing the right word.

sensitive period The period from about 18 months to puberty when the brain is especially capable of learning language.

LO4 Examine language development in infancy.

Prelinguistic vocalizations include crying, cooing, and babbling. Children from different cultures initially babble the same sounds. The first word typically is spoken between 11 and 13 months. It may take another 3–4 months to achieve an expressive vocabulary of 10 to 30 words.

TABLE 6.2
Milestones in Language Development in Infancy

APPROXIMATE AGE	VOCALIZATION AND LANGUAGE
Birth	• Cries.
12 weeks	• Cries less. • Smiles when talked to and nodded at. • Engages in squealing and gurgling sounds (cooing). • Sustains cooing for 15–20 seconds.
16 weeks	• Responds to human sounds more definitely. • Turns head, searching for the speaker. • Chuckles occasionally.
20 weeks	• Cooing becomes interspersed with consonant-like sounds. • Vocalizations differ from the sounds of mature language.
6 months	• Cooing changes to single-syllable babbling. • Neither vowels nor consonants have fixed pattern of recurrence. • Common utterances sound somewhat like *ma, mu, da,* or *di.*
8 months	• Continuous repetition (reduplication) enters into babbling. • Patterns of intonation become distinct. • Utterances can signal emphasis and emotion.
10 months	• Vocalizations mixed with sound play, such as gurgling, bubble blowing. • Makes effort to imitate sounds made by older people with mixed success.
12 months	• Identical sound sequences replicated more often. • Words (e.g., *mama* or *dada*) emerge. • Many words and requests understood (e.g., "Show me your eyes").
18 months	• Repertoire of 3–50 words. • Explosive vocabulary growth. • Babbling consists of several syllables with intricate intonation. • Little effort to communicate information. • Little joining of words into spontaneous two-word utterances. • Understands nearly everything spoken.
24 months	• Vocabulary more than 50 words, naming everything in the environment. • Spontaneous creation of two-word sentences. • Clear efforts to communicate.

Source: Table items adapted from Lenneberg (1967, pp. 128–130).
Note: Ages are approximations. Slower development does not necessarily indicate language problems. Albert Einstein did not talk until the age of 3.

Children's first words are mostly nominals. Children with a referential language style use language mainly to label objects. Those with an expressive language style mainly seek social interactions. Infants' early sentences are telegraphic. Two-word sentences show understanding of syntax. Learning theorists explain language development in terms of imitation and reinforcement. But children do not imitate sentences that are inconsistent with their grasp of grammar. The nativist view holds that innate prewiring causes children to attend to and acquire language in certain ways. Key biological structures involved in language are based in the left hemisphere for most people. Damage to either Broca's area or Wernicke's area may cause a characteristic aphasia. Lenneberg proposes that plasticity of the brain provides a sensitive period for learning language that begins at 18–24 months and lasts until puberty.

Learning Outcomes

LO1 Describe the development of attachment in infants.

Children try to maintain contact with persons to whom they are attached. Most infants in the United States are securely attached. In the strange situation, securely attached infants mildly protest mother's departure and are readily comforted by her. The two major types of insecure attachment are avoidant attachment and ambivalent/resistant attachment. Securely attached infants are happier, more sociable, and more cooperative. They use the mother as a secure base from which to explore the environment. High-quality caregiving contributes to security. Parents of securely attached infants are more likely to be affectionate and sensitive to their needs. Security of attachment is also related to the infant's temperament. The initial-preattachment phase lasts from birth to about 3 months and is characterized by indiscriminate attachment.

The attachment-in-the-making phase occurs at about 3 or 4 months and is characterized by preference for familiar figures. The clear-cut-attachment phase occurs at about 6 or 7 months and is characterized by dependence on the primary caregiver. Behaviorists suggest that infants become attached to caregivers because caregivers meet their bodily needs. Psychoanalysts suggest that the primary caregiver becomes a love object. The Harlows' experiments with monkeys suggest that contact comfort is a key to attachment. Ethologists view attachment as an inborn fixed action pattern (FAP) which occurs during a critical period.

FIGURE 7.2
Development of Attachment

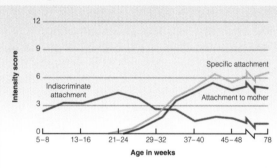

LO2 Discuss social deprivation, neglect, and other factors that influence attachment.

Rhesus infants reared in isolation confinement later avoid contact with other monkeys. Many institutionalized children who receive little social stimulation develop withdrawal and depression. Maltreated children are less intimate with peers and are more aggressive, angry, and noncompliant than other children. Exposure to violence in the home may lead children to accept family violence as the norm. Some parents rationalize that they are hurting their children "for their own good"—to discourage problematic behavior. Autism spectrum disorders (ASDs) are characterized by impairment in communication skills and social interactions, and repetitive, stereotyped behavior. Other features include intolerance of change, stereotypical behavior, mutism, echolalia, and self-mutilation. Genetic studies find higher concordance rates for autism among monozygotic than dizygotic twins.

Key Terms

attachment An emotional bond shown by seeking closeness with another and distress upon separation.

separation anxiety Fear of separation from an attachment figure.

secure attachment A type of attachment shown by exhibiting mild distress at leave-takings and being readily soothed by reunion.

avoidant attachment A type of insecure attachment shown by apparent indifference to leave-takings by and reunions with an attachment figure.

ambivalent/resistant attachment A type of insecure attachment shown by severe distress at leave-takings by and ambivalent behavior at reunions with an attachment figure.

disorganized-disoriented attachment A type of insecure attachment shown by confusion or disorientation and contradictory behaviors toward an attachment figure.

indiscriminate attachment The display of attachment behaviors toward any person.

initial-preattachment phase The first phase in development of attachment, characterized by indiscriminate attachment.

attachment-in-the-making phase The second phase in development of attachment, characterized by preference for familiar figures.

clear-cut-attachment phase The third phase in development of attachment, characterized by intensified dependence on the primary caregiver.

contact comfort The pleasure derived from physical contact with another.

ethologist A scientist who studies the behavior patterns characteristic of various species.

social smile A smile that occurs in response to a human voice or face.

critical period A period during which imprinting can occur.

imprinting The process by which some young nonhumans become attached to the first moving object they follow.

autism spectrum disorders (ASDs) Developmental disorders characterized by impairment in communication and social skills, and by repetitive, stereotyped behavior.

autism A disorder characterized by extreme aloneness, communication problems, preservation of sameness, and ritualistic behavior.

mutism Refusal to speak.

social referencing Using another person's reaction to a situation to form one's own response.

emotional regulation Techniques for controlling one's emotional states.

separation-individuation The process of becoming separate from and independent of the mother.

temperament Individual style of reaction and adaptation that is present early in life and remains fairly stable.

goodness of fit Agreement between the parents' expectations of a child and the child's temperament.

TABLE 7.1
Characteristics of Autism Spectrum Disorders (ASDs)

KEY INDICATORS

Does not babble, point, or make meaningful gestures by 1 year of age

Does not speak one word by 16 months

Does not combine two words by 2 years

Does not respond to name

Loses language or social skills

OTHER INDICATORS

Poor eye contact

Doesn't seem to know how to play with toys

Excessively lines up toys or other objects

Is attached to one particular toy or object

Doesn't smile

At times seems to be hearing impaired

Source: Adapted from Strock (2004).

LO3 Discuss the effects of day care on attachment.

Infants with day-care experience are more independent, self-confident, outgoing, affectionate, and cooperative with peers and adults. Children in high-quality day care outperform children who remain in the home in cognitive skills. Children in day care are also more aggressive. Children in day care show higher cortisol levels than children in the home, suggestive of stress—regardless of the quality of day care.

LO4 Examine the emotional development of infants.

Bridges proposed that we are born with one emotion—diffuse excitement—and that other emotions differentiate over time. Sroufe focused on the ways in which cognitive development can provide the basis for emotional development. Izard proposed that infants are born with several emotional states but that their appearance is linked to cognitive development and social experiences. Fear of strangers is normal in that most infants develop it at about the age of 6 to 9 months. Infants display social referencing as early as 6 months of age, when they use caregivers' facial expressions or tones of voice for information on how to respond in novel situations. Caregivers help infants learn to regulate their emotions. The children of secure mothers are more likely to regulate their emotions positively.

LO5 Examine the personality development of infants.

Findings using the mirror technique suggest that the self-concept develops by about 18 months of age. Thomas and Chess found that most infants can be classified as having easy, difficult, or slow-to-warm-up temperaments. Temperament remains moderately consistent from infancy through young adulthood. Female infants sit, crawl, and walk earlier than boys do. By 12 to 18 months of age, girls prefer to play with dolls and similar toys, whereas boys prefer transportation toys and gear.

TABLE 7.2
Types of Temperament

TEMPERAMENT CATEGORY	EASY	DIFFICULT	SLOW TO WARM UP
Regularity of biological functioning	Regular	Irregular	Somewhat irregular
Response to new stimuli	Positive approach	Negative withdrawal	Negative withdrawal
Adaptability to new situations	Adapts readily	Adapts slowly or not at all	Adapts slowly
Intensity of reaction	Mild or moderate	Intense	Mild
Quality of mood	Positive	Negative	Initially negative; gradually more positive

Sources: Chess & Thomas (1991) and Thomas & Chess (1989).

Learning Outcomes

LO1 Describe patterns of growth in early childhood.

Children gain about 2 to 3 inches in height and 4 to 6 pounds in weight per year in early childhood. Boys are slightly larger than girls. The brain develops more quickly than any other organ in early childhood, in part because of myelination. Myelination enhances children's ability to attend to and process visual information, enabling them to read and to screen out distractions. The left hemisphere is relatively more involved in logical analysis and problem solving, language, and mathematical computation. The right hemisphere is usually superior in visual–spatial functions, aesthetic and emotional responses, and creative mathematical reasoning. Nevertheless, the functions of the left and right hemispheres are not independent. Factors involved in the brain's plasticity are the growth of new dendrites and the redundancy of neural connections.

Key Terms

corpus callosum The thick bundle of nerve fibers that connects the left and right hemispheres of the brain.

plasticity The tendency of other parts of the brain to take up the functions of injured parts.

gross motor skills Skills employing the large muscles used in locomotion.

fine motor skills Skills employing the small muscles used in manipulation and coordination, such as those in the fingers.

sleep terrors Frightening dreamlike experiences that occur during the deepest stage of non-REM sleep, shortly after the child has gone to sleep.

FIGURE 8.1
Growth Curves for Height and Weight, Ages 2 to 6 Years

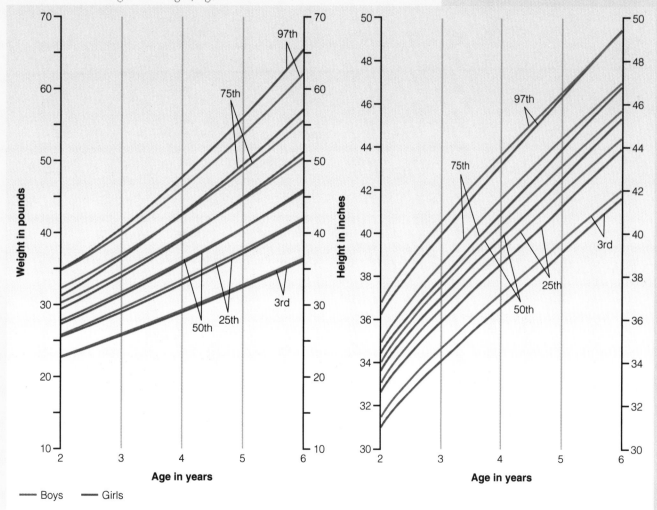

somnambulism Sleep walking.

enuresis Failure to control the bladder once the normal age for control has been reached.

bed-wetting Failure to control the bladder during the night.

encopresis Failure to control the bowels once the normal age for bowel control has been reached. Also called *soiling*.

LO2 Describe development of motor skills in early childhood, including drawing and handedness.

Preschoolers make great strides in the development of gross motor skills, which involve the large muscles. Girls are somewhat better at tasks requiring balance and precision; boys have some advantage in throwing and kicking.

TABLE 8.1
Development of Gross Motor Skills in Early Childhood

2 YEARS (24–35 MONTHS)	3 YEARS (36–47 MONTHS)	4 YEARS (48–59 MONTHS)	5 YEARS (60–71 MONTHS)
• Runs well straight ahead • Walks up stairs, two feet to a step • Kicks a large ball • Jumps a distance of 4–14 inches • Throws a small ball without falling • Pushes and pulls large toys • Hops on one foot, two or more hops • Tries to stand on one foot • Climbs on furniture to look out of window	• Goes around obstacles while running • Walks up stairs, one foot to a step • Kicks a large ball easily • Jumps from the bottom step • Catches a bounced ball, using torso and arms to form a basket • Goes around obstacles while pushing and pulling toys • Hops on one foot, up to three hops • Stands on one foot • Climbs nursery-school apparatus	• Turns sharp corners while running • Walks down stairs, one foot to a step • Jumps from a height of 12 inches • Throws a ball overhand • Turns sharp corners while pushing and pulling toys • Hops on one foot, four to six hops • Stands on one foot for 3–8 seconds • Climbs ladders • Skips on one foot • Rides a tricycle well	• Runs lightly on toes • Jumps a distance of 3 feet • Catches a small ball, using hands only • Hops 2 to 3 yards forward on each foot • Stands on one foot for 8–10 seconds • Climbs actively and skillfully • Skips on alternate feet • Rides a bicycle with training wheels

Note: The ages are averages; there are individual variations.

Fine motor skills develop gradually. The most active children generally show less well developed motor skills. Table 8.2 describes the development of fine motor skills in early childhood.

TABLE 8.2
Development of Fine Motor Skills in Early Childhood

2 YEARS (24–35 MONTHS)	3 YEARS (36–47 MONTHS)	4 YEARS (48–59 MONTHS)	5 YEARS (60–71 MONTHS)
• Builds tower of 6 cubes • Copies vertical and horizontal lines • Imitates folding of paper • Paints on easel with a brush • Places simple shapes in correct holes	• Builds tower of 9 cubes • Copies circle and cross • Copies letters • Holds crayons with fingers, not fist • Strings four beads using a large needle	• Builds tower of 10 or more cubes • Copies square • Prints simple words • Imitates folding paper three times • Uses pencil with correct hand grip • Strings 10 beads	• Builds 3 steps from 6 blocks, using a model • Copies triangle and star • Prints first name and numbers • Imitates folding of piece of square paper into a triangle • Traces around a diamond drawn on paper • Laces shoes

Note: The ages are averages; there are individual variations.

After 2 or 3 years of age, children become less restless and are more able to sustain attention during play. Boys tend to be more active than girls in large muscle activities. Boys are more fidgety and distractible, perhaps because they are less mature physically. Kellogg identified 20 scribbles that she considers the building blocks of art. She theorizes that children undergo four stages of progressing from scribbles to drawing pictures. By 6 months, most infants show clear-cut hand preferences, which become still more established during early childhood. More than 90% of children are right-handed.

LO3 Describe nutritional needs in early childhood.

The typical 4- to 6-year-old needs 1,800 calories a day, compared with 1,300 for the average 1- to 3-year-old. During the second and third years, children's appetites typically wane and grow erratic. Many children eat harmful amounts of sugar and salt.

LO4 Describe health problems in early childhood, focusing on minor and major illness and on accidents.

The incidence of minor illnesses, such as colds, nausea and vomiting, and diarrhea, is high. Although diarrhea is usually mild in the United States, it is a leading killer of children in developing countries. Diarrheal diseases are almost completely related to unsafe drinking water and lack of sanitation. Immunization and antibiotics reduce the incidence of serious childhood diseases. Air pollution contributes to respiratory infections. Lead poisoning causes neurological damage.

LO5 Describe sleep patterns and sleep disorders of early childhood.

Most 2- and 3-year-olds sleep about 10 hours at night and nap during the day. Sleep terrors and sleep walking usually occur during deep sleep. Sleepwalkers' eyes are usually open, and if they are awakened, they may show confusion and disorientation but are unlikely to be violent.

TABLE 8.3
Sleep Obtained by Children during a 24-Hour Period

	INFANCY	PRESCHOOLERS	YOUNGER SCHOOL-AGE CHILDREN	OLDER SCHOOL-AGE CHILDREN
Bottom 25%	11 hours or less	9.9 hours or less	9 hours or less	8.9 hours or less
Middle 50%	11.1–14.9 hours	10–11 hours	9.1–10 hours	9–9.9 hours
Upper 25%	15 hours or more	11.1 hours or more	10.1 hours or more	10 hours or more

Source: National Sleep Foundation (2009).

LO6 Describe elimination disorders, including their origins and possible treatment.

Most American children are toilet trained by about age 3 or 4 but continue to have "accidents" at night for another year or so. Enuresis is the failure to control the bladder once a child has reached the "normal" age for doing so—placed at 5 years of age by the American Psychiatric Association. Encopresis (soiling) is connected with physical immaturity, constipation, and stress.

Ten Things You Need to Know about Immunizations

1. Why your child should be immunized
Children need immunizations (shots) to protect them from dangerous childhood diseases. These diseases can have serious complications and even kill children.

2. Diseases that childhood vaccines prevent
Diphtheria
Haemophilus influenzae type b (Hib disease—a major cause of bacterial meningitis)
Hepatitis A
Hepatitis B
Measles
Meningococcal
Mumps
Pertussis (Whooping Cough)
Pneumococcal (causes bacterial meningitis and blood infections)
Polio
Rotavirus
Rubella (German Measles)
Tetanus (Lockjaw)
Varicella (Chickenpox)
Audio, text-only, and other language versions of the Vaccine Information Sheets are available. Go to http://www.cdc.gov/nip/publications/VIS/default.htm.

3. Number of doses your child needs
The following vaccinations are recommended by age two and can be given over five visits to a doctor or clinic:
4 doses of diphtheria, tetanus & pertussis vaccine (DTaP)
3–4 doses of Hib vaccine (depending on the brand used)
4 doses of pneumococcal vaccine
3 doses of polio vaccine
2 doses of hepatitis A vaccine
3 doses of hepatitis B vaccine
1 dose of measles, mumps & rubella vaccine (MMR)
3 doses of rotavirus vaccine
1 dose of varicella vaccine
2–3 doses of influenza vaccine (6 months and older) (number of doses depends on child's birthday)

4. Like any medicine, there may be minor side effects
Side effects can occur with any medicine, including vaccines. Depending on the vaccine, these can include: slight fever, rash, or soreness at the site of injection. Slight discomfort is normal and should not be a cause for alarm. Your health care provider can give you additional information.

5. It's extremely rare, but vaccines can cause serious reactions—weigh the risks!
Serious reactions to vaccines are extremely rare. The risks of serious disease from not vaccinating are far greater than the risks of serious reaction to a vaccination.

6. What to do if your child has a serious reaction
If you think your child is experiencing a persistent or severe reaction, call your doctor or get the child to a doctor right away. Write down what happened and the date and time it happened. Ask your doctor, nurse or health department to file a Vaccine Adverse Event Report form or call 1-800-338-2382 to file this form yourself.

7. Why you should not wait to vaccinate
Children under 5 are especially susceptible to disease because their immune systems have not built up the necessary defenses to fight infection. By immunizing on time (by age 2), you can protect your child from disease and also protect others at school or daycare.

8. Be sure to track your shots via a health record
A vaccination health record helps you and your healthcare provider keep your child's vaccinations on schedule. If you move or change providers, having an accurate record might prevent your child from repeating vaccinations he or she has already had. A shot record should be started when your child receives his/her first vaccination and updated with each vaccination visit.

9. Some are eligible for free vaccinations
A federal program called Vaccines for Children provides free vaccines to eligible children, including those without health insurance coverage, all those who are enrolled in Medicaid, American Indians and Alaskan Natives.

10. More information is available
General immunization questions can be answered by The CDC Contact Center at 1-800-CDC-INFO (1-800-232-4636)
English and Español
Questions about vaccines and vaccine-preventable diseases frequently asked by people calling the TTY Service Hotline can be viewed in American Sign Language at 1-888-232-6348 (TTY hotline) http://www.cdc.gov/vaccines/about/contact/default.htm

Source: Centers for Disease Control and Prevention (2007, January 10). Ten Things You Need to Know about Immunizations. Department of Health and Human Services. http://www.cdc.gov/nip/publications/fs/gen/shouldknow.htm

Learning Outcomes

LO1 Outline the cognitive developments of Piaget's preoperational stage.

Piaget's preoperational stage lasts from about age 2 to 7 and is characterized by the use of symbols to represent objects and relationships. Pretend play is based on the use and recollection of symbols or on mental representations of things. Preoperational thinking is characterized by egocentrism, precausal thinking, confusion between mental and physical events, and ability to focus on only one dimension at a time. Young children's thinking is egocentric, animistic, and artificialistic. In transductive reasoning, children reason by going from one instance of an event to another. Preoperational children do not show conservation, because conservation requires focusing on two aspects of a situation at once.

TABLE 9.1
Highlights of Preoperational Thought

TYPE OF THOUGHT	SAMPLE QUESTIONS	TYPICAL ANSWERS
Egocentrism (placing oneself at the center of things such that one is unable to perceive the world from another's point of view)	Why does it get dark out?	So I can go to sleep.
	Why does the sun shine?	To keep me warm.
	Why is there snow?	For me to play in.
	Why is grass green?	Because that's my favorite color.
	What are TV sets for?	To watch my favorite shows and cartoons.
Animism (attributing life and consciousness to physical objects)	Why do trees have leaves?	To keep them warm.
	Why do stars twinkle?	Because they're happy and cheerful.
	Why does the sun move in the sky?	To follow children and hear what they say.
	Where do boats go at night?	They sleep like we do.
Artificialism (assuming that environmental events are human inventions)	What makes it rain?	Someone emptying a watering can.
	Why is the sky blue?	Somebody painted it.
	What is the wind?	A man blowing.
	What causes thunder?	A man grumbling.
	How does a baby get in Mommy's tummy?	Just make it first. (How?) You put some eyes on it, then put on the head.

LO2 Discuss factors in cognitive development, focusing on Vygotsky's views and the effects of the home environment, early childhood education, and television.

Vygotsky's concepts include scaffolding and the zone of proximal development. Others include social and family factors such as family income, parents' educational level, family size, and the presence of stressful family events such as divorce, job loss, or illness. The children of responsive parents who provide appropriate play materials and stimulating experiences gain in social and language development. Head Start programs enhance economically disadvantaged children's cognitive development, academic skills, and readiness for school.

Key Terms

preoperational stage The second stage in Piaget's model of cognitive development, characterized by inflexible and irreversible mental manipulation of symbols.

symbolic play Play in which children make believe that objects and toys are other than what they are. Also called *pretend play.*

egocentrism Putting oneself at the center of things such that one is unable to perceive the world from another person's point of view.

precausal A type of thought in which natural cause-and-effect relationships are attributed to will and other preoperational concepts.

transductive reasoning Reasoning from one specific isolated event to another specific isolated event.

animism The attribution of life and intentionality to inanimate objects.

artificialism The belief that environmental features were made by people.

conservation In cognitive psychology, the principle that properties of substances such as weight and mass remain the same (are conserved) when superficial characteristics such as their shapes or arrangement are changed.

scaffolding Vygotsky's term for temporary cognitive structures or methods of solving problems that help the child as he or she learns to function independently.

zone of proximal development (ZPD) Vygotsky's term for the range of tasks a child can carry out with the help of someone who is more skilled.

theory of mind A commonsense understanding of how the mind works.

appearance-reality distinction The difference between real events on the one hand and mental events, fantasies, and misleading appearances on the other hand.

scripts Abstract generalized accounts of familiar repeated events.

autobiographical memory The memory of specific events; also called *episodic memory.*

rehearsal Mental repetition.

fast mapping A process of quickly determining a word's meaning, which facilitates children's vocabulary development.

whole-object assumption The assumption that words refer to whole objects and not to their component parts or characteristics.

contrast assumption The assumption that objects have only one label; also known as the *mutual exclusivity assumption*.

overregularization The application of regular grammatical rules for forming past tense of irregular verbs and plurals of irregular nouns.

pragmatics The practical aspects of communication, such as adaptation of language to fit the social situation.

inner speech Vygotsky's concept of the ultimate binding of language and thought. Inner speech originates in vocalizations that may regulate the child's behavior and become internalized by age 6 or 7.

TABLE 9.2
Scales of the HOME Inventory

SCALE	SAMPLE ITEMS
Parental emotional and verbal responsiveness	• The parent spontaneously vocalizes to the child during the visit. • The parent responds to the child's vocalizations with vocal or other verbal responses.
Avoidance of restriction and punishment	• The parent does not shout at the child. • The parent does not interfere with the child's actions or restrict the child's movements more than three times during the visit.
Organization of the physical environment	• The child's play environment seems to be safe and free from hazards.
Provision of appropriate play materials	• The child has a push or a pull toy. • The child has one or more toys or pieces of equipment that promote muscle activity. • The family provides appropriate equipment to foster learning.
Parental involvement with child	• The parent structures the child's play periods. • The parent tends to keep the child within her or his visual range and looks at the child frequently.
Opportunities for variety in daily stimulation	• The child gets out of the house at least four times a week. • The parent reads stories to the child at least three times a week.

LO3 Discuss development of theory of mind, including false memories, origins of knowledge, and the appearance-reality distinction.

As children's theory of mind develops, children come to understand that there are distinctions between external and mental events and between appearances and realities. By age 3, most children begin to realize that people gain knowledge through the senses. By age 4, children understand which sense is required to provide information about qualities such as color (vision) and weight (touch). Although Piaget believed that children do not differentiate reality from appearances or mental events until the age of 7 or 8, research finds that preschoolers can do so.

LO4 Discuss memory development during early childhood, including strategies for remembering.

Preschoolers recognize more items than they can recall. Autobiographical memory is linked to language skills. By the age of 4, children can remember events that occurred 1 1/2 years earlier. Young children seem to form scripts, which are abstract, generalized accounts of events. Factors affecting memory include what the child is asked to remember, interest level and motivation, the availability of retrieval cues, and the measure of memory being used. Preschoolers look, point, and touch when trying to remember things. Preschoolers can be taught to use strategies such as rehearsal and grouping of items that they might not use on their own.

LO5 Outline language developments during early childhood and explain the interactions between language and cognition.

Preschoolers acquire about nine new words per day. Word learning often occurs rapidly through fast mapping. During the third year, children usually add articles, conjunctions, possessive adjectives, pronouns, and prepositions. Between the ages of 3 and 4, children combine phrases and clauses into complex sentences. Preschoolers tend to overregularize irregular verbs and noun forms as they acquire rules of grammar. Piaget believed that children learn words in order to describe classes or categories they have created. Other theorists argue that children create classes to understand things that are labeled by words. Vygotsky believed that during most of the first year, vocalizations and thought are separate, but usually during the second year, cognition and language combine forces. To Vygotsky, private speech is the ultimate binding of language and thought.

Learning Outcomes

LO1 Describe the dimensions of child rearing and the styles of parenting.

Parental approaches to child rearing can be classified according to the dimensions of warmth–coldness and restrictiveness–permissiveness. Consistent control and firm enforcement of rules can have positive consequences for the child. Parents tend to use inductive methods, power assertion, and withdrawal of love to enforce rules. Inductive methods use "reasoning," or explaining why one sort of behavior is good and another is not. Authoritative parents are restrictive but warm and tend to have the most competent and achievement-oriented children. Authoritarian parents are restrictive and cold. The sons of authoritarian parents tend to be hostile and defiant; daughters are low in independence. Children of permissive parents show the least competence and maturity. Parents tend to prefer power-assertive techniques when they believe that children understand the rules they have violated and are capable of acting appropriately.

TABLE 10.1
Baumrind's Patterns of Parenting

PARENTAL STYLE	PARENTAL BEHAVIOR PATTERNS	
	RESTRICTIVENESS AND CONTROL	WARMTH AND RESPONSIVENESS
Authoritative	High	High
Authoritarian	High	Low
Permissive–Indulgent	Low	High
Rejecting–Neglecting	Low	Low

LO2 Explain how siblings, birth order, peers, and other factors affect social development during early childhood.

Siblings provide caregiving, emotional support, advice, role models, social interaction, restrictions, and cognitive stimulation. However, they are also sources of conflict, control, and competition. Younger siblings usually imitate older siblings. Firstborn and only children are generally more highly motivated to achieve, more cooperative, more helpful, more adult oriented, and less aggressive. Children learn social skills from peers—such as sharing, helping, taking turns, and coping with conflict. Peers foster development of physical and cognitive skills and provide emotional support. Preschoolers' friendships are characterized by

Key Terms

inductive Characteristic of disciplinary methods, such as reasoning, that attempt to foster understanding of the principles behind parental demands.

authoritative A child-rearing style in which parents are restrictive and demanding yet communicative and warm.

authoritarian A child-rearing style in which parents demand submission and obedience.

permissive-indulgent A child-rearing style in which parents are warm and not restrictive.

rejecting-neglecting A child-rearing style in which parents are neither restrictive and controlling nor supportive and responsive.

regression A return to behavior characteristic of earlier stages of development.

sibling rivalry Jealousy among brothers and sisters.

dramatic play Play in which children enact social roles.

nonsocial play Solitary forms of play.

social play Play in which children interact with and are influenced by others.

disinhibit To stimulate a response that has been suppressed by showing a model engaging in that response.

categorical self Definitions of the self that refer to external traits.

stereotype A fixed, oversimplified, conventional idea about a group.

gender role A cluster of traits and behaviors that a culture expects females or males to exhibit.

gender identity Knowledge that one is female or male.

gender stability The concept that one's sex is unchanging.

gender constancy The concept that one's sex remains the same despite changes in appearance or behavior.

gender-schema theory The view that one's knowledge of the gender schema in one's society guides one's assumption of gender-stereotyped preferences and behavior patterns.

psychologically androgynous
Having both stereotypical feminine and masculine traits.

shared activities and feelings of attachment. Parten followed the development of six types of play among 2–5-year-olds: unoccupied play, solitary play, onlooker play, parallel play, associative play, and cooperative play. Children show preferences for gender-stereotyped toys by 15 to 30 months of age. Boys in early childhood prefer vigorous outdoor activities and rough-and-tumble play. Girls are more likely to engage in arts and crafts. Preschool children generally prefer playmates of their own sex. Boys' play is more oriented toward dominance, aggression, and rough play. Prosocial behavior—altruism—begins to develop in the first year, when children begin to share. Girls show more empathy than boys do. The aggression of preschoolers is frequently instrumental or possession oriented. By age 6 or 7, aggression becomes hostile and person oriented. Impulsive and relatively fearless children are more likely to be aggressive. Social cognitive theory suggests that children become aggressive as a result of frustration, reinforcement, and observational learning. Observing aggressive behavior teaches aggressive skills, disinhibits the child, and habituates children to violence.

LO3 Discuss personality and emotional development during early childhood, focusing on the self, Erikson's views, and fears.

Self-definitions that refer to concrete external traits are called the categorical self. Children as young as 3 years can describe themselves in terms of characteristic behaviors and internal states. Secure attachment and competence contribute to the development of self-esteem. Preschoolers are most likely to fear animals, imaginary creatures, and the dark; the theme involves threats to personal safety. Girls report more fears than boys do.

LO4 Discuss the development of gender roles and sex differences.

Cultural expectations of females and males are called gender roles. Males are more aggressive and more interested in sex than females. Testosterone may specialize the hemispheres of the brain—more so in males than in females, explaining why females excel in verbal skills that require some spatial organization, such as reading. Males might be better at specialized spatial-relations tasks. Male sex hormones are connected with greater maze-learning ability in rats and with aggressiveness. Social cognitive theorists explain the development of gender-typed behavior in terms of observational learning and socialization. According to Kohlberg's cognitive-developmental theory, gender-typing involves the emergence of three concepts: gender identity, gender stability, and gender constancy. People with both stereotypical feminine and masculine traits are said to be psychologically androgynous.

Learning Outcomes

LO1 Describe growth patterns in middle childhood.

Children tend to gain a little over 2 inches in height and 5 to 7 pounds in weight per year during middle childhood. Children become more slender. Boys are slightly heavier and taller than girls through the ages of 9 or 10, when girls begin the adolescent growth spurt. At around age 11, boys develop relatively more muscle tissue and females develop more fatty tissue.

FIGURE 11.1
Growth Curves for Height and Weight

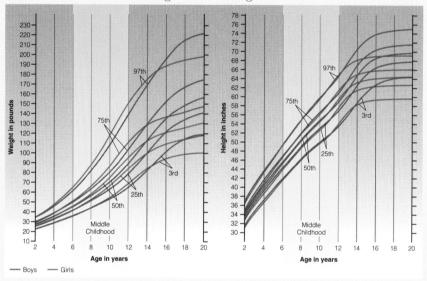

Source: Kuczmarski et al. (2000, Figures 9–12)

LO2 Discuss nutrition and overweight in childhood, focusing on incidence, origins, and treatment of the problem.

About one-sixth of American children are overweight, and the prevalence of being overweight has been increasing. Overweight children usually do not "outgrow" "baby fat." During childhood, heavy children are often rejected by their peers. Heredity plays a role in being overweight. Children with high numbers of fat cells feel food deprived sooner than other children. Overweight parents may encourage overeating by keeping fattening foods in the home. Sedentary habits also foster being overweight.

Key Terms

growth spurt A period during which growth advances at a dramatically rapid rate compared with other periods.

adipose tissue Fat cells.

reaction time The amount of time required to respond to a stimulus.

attention-deficit/hyperactivity disorder (ADHD) A behavior disorder characterized by developmentally inappropriate or excessive inattention, impulsiveness, and hyperactivity.

hyperactivity Excessive restlessness and overactivity; one of the primary problems in attention-deficit/hyperactivity disorder (ADHD).

stimulants Drugs that increase the activity of the nervous system.

dyslexia A reading disorder characterized by problems such as letter reversals, mirror reading, slow reading, and reduced comprehension.

learning disorders A group of disorders characterized by inadequate development of specific academic, language, and speech skills.

double-deficit hypothesis The theory of dyslexia which suggests that dyslexic children have biological deficits in *phonological processing* (interpreting sounds) and in *naming speed* (identifying letters—such as *b* versus *d*, or *w* versus *m*).

mainstreaming Placing disabled children in classrooms with nondisabled children.

FIGURE 11.2
Overweight Children in America

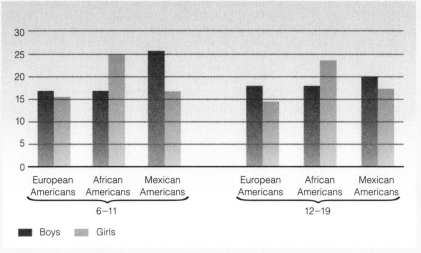

Source: American Heart Association (2007).

LO3 Describe motor development in middle childhood, focusing on sex differences, exercise, and fitness.

Middle childhood is marked by increases in speed, strength, agility, and balance. Children show regular improvement in gross motor skills and are often eager to participate in athletic activities, such as ball games that require movement of large muscles. Muscles grow stronger and pathways that connect the cerebellum to the cortex become more myelinated. Reaction time gradually decreases. Fine motor skills also improve, with 6–7-year-olds tying shoelaces and holding pencils as adults do.

Boys have slightly greater overall strength, whereas girls have better coordination and flexibility, which is valuable in dancing, balancing, and gymnastics. Boys generally receive more encouragement than girls to excel in athletics. Most children in the United States are not physically fit. One reason is the amount of time spent watching television.

LO4 Discuss the symptoms, possible origins, and treatment of attention-deficit/hyperactivity disorder (ADHD).

Attention-deficit/hyperactivity disorder (ADHD) involves lack of inattention, impulsivity, and hyperactivity. ADHD runs in families and coexists with other problems. Children with ADHD do not inhibit impulses that most children control, suggesting poor executive control in the brain. Stimulants are used to stimulate the cerebral cortex to inhibit more primitive areas of the brain. Stimulants increase the attention span and academic performance of children with ADHD, but there are side effects and the medications may be used too often.

LO5 Discuss the various kinds of learning disorders and their possible origins.

Learning disabilities are characterized by inadequate development of specific academic abilities, language, and speech skills. Children may be diagnosed with a learning disability when their performance is below that expected for their age and level of intelligence. Current views of dyslexia focus on the ways that neurological problems may contribute to perceptual problems. Genetic factors appear to be involved, because dyslexia runs in families. The double-deficit hypothesis suggests that dyslexic children have neurologically based deficits in phonological processing and in naming speed. Some studies suggest that disabled children achieve more when they are mainstreamed. Other studies suggest that many disabled children find regular classrooms overwhelming.

Learning Outcomes

LO1 Describe the developments in Piaget's concrete-operational stage, focusing on examples of decentration, such as conservation and seriation.

In the stage of concrete operations, children begin to show the capacity for adult logic with tangible objects. Concrete-operational thinking is characterized by reversibility, flexibility, and decentration. Concrete-operational children show understanding of conservation, transitivity, and class inclusion.

LO2 Discuss the theories of moral development of Piaget and Kohlberg.

Piaget theorized two stages of moral development: moral realism and autonomous morality. The earlier stage emerges at about the age of 5 and judges behavior as right when it conforms to rules. Five-year-olds see rules as embedded in the structure of things and believe in immanent justice. Children begin to show autonomous morality in middle childhood and come to view social rules as agreements that can be changed. Kohlberg believed that there are three levels of moral development and two stages within each level. In the preconventional level, children base moral judgments on the consequences of behavior. In the conventional level, right and wrong are judged by conformity to conventional standards. In the post-conventional level, moral reasoning is based on one's own values.

LO3 Discuss information processing in middle childhood, focusing on developments in selective attention and memory.

Selective attention—attending to the relevant features of a task—advances steadily through middle childhood. Many psychologists divide memory functioning into three major processes: sensory memory, working memory, and long-term memory. Maintenance of information in working memory depends on strategies such as encoding and rehearsing stimuli. Older children process information more efficiently. Information is transferred from short-term memory to long-term memory by rehearsal and elaboration. Children organize their long-term memory into categories. Awareness and conscious control of cognitive abilities is termed metacognition, as evidenced by ability to formulate problems, awareness of how to solve them, use of rules and strategies, ability to remain focused, and ability to check answers. By 6 or 7, children know to use rehearsal to remember things.

LO4 Discuss theories, measurement, and determinants of intelligence, and the relationship of intelligence to achievement and creativity.

Intelligence is a child's underlying competence or learning ability. Spearman suggested that the behaviors we consider intelligent have a common, underlying factor: *g*. But *s*, or specific capacities, account for some individual abilities. Thurstone used factor analysis to define several primary mental abilities. Sternberg proposes a three-pronged theory of intelligence: analytical intelligence, creative intelligence, and practical intelligence. Gardner believes that people have multiple "intelligences," each of which is based in a different part of the brain. The SBIS assumes that intelligence increases with age, so older children must answer more items correctly than younger children to obtain a comparable score—which Binet termed a mental age (MA). A comparison of a child's mental age with his or her chronological age (CA)—(MA/CA)—yields an intelligence quotient (IQ). The average IQ is defined as 100. The Wechsler scales group test questions into subtests that measure different types of intellectual tasks. Most psychologists and educational specialists believe that intelligence

Key Terms

concrete operations The third stage in Piaget's model of development, characterized by flexible, reversible thought concerning tangible objects and events.

decentration Simultaneous focusing on more than one aspect or dimension of a problem or situation.

transitivity The principle that if A > B and B > C, then A > C.

seriation Placing objects in an order or series according to a property or trait.

moral realism The judgment of acts as moral when they conform to authority or to the rules of the game.

objective morality The perception of morality as objective, that is, as existing outside the cognitive functioning of people.

immanent justice The view that retribution for wrongdoing is a direct consequence of the wrongdoing.

autonomous morality The second stage in Piaget's cognitive-developmental theory of moral development, in which children base moral judgments on the intentions of the wrongdoer and on the amount of damage done.

preconventional level According to Kohlberg, a period during which moral judgments are based largely on expectations of rewards or punishments.

conventional level According to Kohlberg, a period during which moral judgments largely reflect social rules and conventions.

sensory memory (sensory register) The structure of memory first encountered by sensory input. Information is maintained in sensory memory for only a fraction of a second.

working memory The structure of memory that can hold a sensory stimulus for up to 30 seconds after the trace decays.

encode To transform sensory input into a form that is more readily processed.

rehearse Repeat mentally.

rote learning Simple associative learning based on repetition.

long-term memory The memory structure capable of relatively permanent storage of information.

elaborative strategy A method for increasing retention of new information by relating it to well-known information.

metacognition Awareness of and control of one's cognitive abilities.

metamemory Awareness of the functions and processes involved in one's storage and retrieval of information.

intelligence Defined by Wechsler as the "capacity . . . to understand the world [and the] resourcefulness to cope with its challenges."

achievement That which is attained by one's efforts and presumed to be made possible by one's abilities.

intelligence quotient (IQ) (1) A ratio obtained by dividing a child's mental age on an intelligence test by his or her chronological age. (2) A score on an intelligence test.

mental age (MA) The months of credit that a person earns on the Stanford-Binet Intelligence Scale.

chronological age (CA) A person's age.

cultural bias A factor hypothesized to be present in intelligence tests that provides an advantage for test takers from certain cultural backgrounds.

culture-free Descriptive of a test in which cultural biases have been removed.

cultural-familial intellectual disability Substandard intellectual performance stemming from lack of opportunity to acquire knowledge and skills.

creativity A trait characterized by flexibility, ingenuity, and originality.

convergent thinking A thought process that attempts to focus in on the single best solution to a problem.

divergent thinking Free and fluent association to the elements of a problem.

heritability The degree to which the variations in a trait from one person to another can be attributed to genetic factors.

word-recognition method A method for learning to read in which children come to recognize words through repeated exposure to them.

tests are at least somewhat biased against African Americans and members of lower social classes. Intelligence tests reflect knowledge of the language and culture in which the test is administered. The first intellectual spurt occurs at about the age of 6 and coincides with entry into school. The second spurt occurs at age 10 or 11. Intellectual disability refers to limitations in intellectual functioning that are characterized by an IQ score of no more than 70 to 75. Giftedness involves outstanding abilities, high performance in a specific academic area, such as language or mathematics, or leadership, distinction in the arts, or bodily talents. Lower-class U.S. children obtain lower IQ scores than more affluent children. The relationship between intelligence test scores and measures of creativity are only moderate. The closer the relationship between people, the more alike their IQ scores.

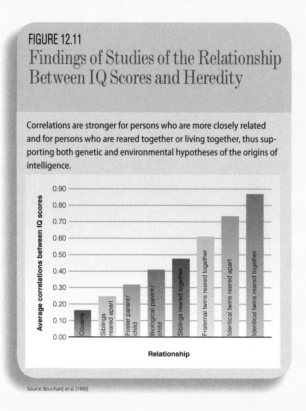

FIGURE 12.11
Findings of Studies of the Relationship Between IQ Scores and Heredity

Correlations are stronger for persons who are more closely related and for persons who are reared together or living together, thus supporting both genetic and environmental hypotheses of the origins of intelligence.

Source: Bouchard, et al. (1990).

LO5 Discuss language development in middle childhood, emphasizing vocabulary, grammar, reading, and bilingualism.

In middle childhood, language use becomes more sophisticated, including understanding that words can have multiple meanings. There are advances in articulation and use of grammar. Reading relies the integration of visual and auditory information. During the preschool years, neurological maturation and experience combine to allow most children to make visual discriminations between letters with relative ease. Children can generally separate two languages from an early age, and most Americans who first spoke another language in the home also speak English well.

phonetic method A method for learning to read in which children decode the sounds of words based on their knowledge of the sounds of letters and letter combinations.

sight vocabulary Words that are immediately recognized on the basis of familiarity with their overall shapes, rather than decoded.

bilingual Using or capable of using two languages with nearly equal or equal facility.

Learning Outcomes

LO1 Explain theories of social and emotional development in middle childhood.

Social development in middle childhood involves the development of skills, changes in interpersonal relationships, and the expansion of self-understanding. Freud viewed the period as the latency stage; Erikson saw it as the stage of industry versus inferiority. Social cognitive theorists note that children now increasingly regulate their own behavior. Cognitive-developmental theory notes that concrete operations enhance social development. In middle childhood, children become more capable of taking the role or perspective of another person. Selman theorizes that children move from egocentricity to seeing the world through the eyes of others in five stages. In early childhood, children's self-concepts focus on concrete external traits. In middle childhood, children begin to include abstract internal traits. Social relationships and group membership assume importance. Competence and social acceptance contribute to self- esteem, but self-esteem tends to decline because the self-concept becomes more realistic. Authoritative parenting fosters self-esteem. Children with learned helplessness tend not to persist in the face of failure. Some girls feel more helpless in math than boys do because of gender-role expectations.

LO2 Discuss the influences of the family on social development in middle childhood.

In middle childhood, the family continues to play a key role in socialization. Parent–child interactions focus on school-related issues, chores, and peers. Parents do less monitoring of children; "coregulation" develops. Children are likely to greet parental divorce with sadness, shock, and disbelief. Children of divorce fare better when parents cooperate on child rearing. Children appear to suffer as much from marital conflict as from divorce per se. Having both parents in the workforce may be related to relative lack of supervision. However, there is little evidence that maternal employment harms children.

LO3 Discuss the influences of peers on social development in middle childhood.

Peers take on increasing importance in middle childhood and exert pressure to conform. Peer experiences also broaden children. Peers afford practice in social skills, sharing, relating to leaders, and coping with aggressive impulses. Popular children tend to be attractive and mature for their age. Early in middle childhood, friendships are based on proximity. Between the ages of 8 and 11, children become more aware of the value of friends as meeting each other's needs and having traits such as loyalty. At this age, peers tend to discourage contact with members of the other sex.

Key Terms

latency stage In psychoanalytic theory, the fourth stage of psychosexual development, characterized by repression of sexual impulses and development of skills.

industry versus inferiority The fourth stage of psychosocial development in Erikson's theory, occurring in middle childhood. Mastery of tasks leads to a sense of industry, whereas failure produces feelings of inferiority.

social cognition Perception of the social world and the relationship between the self and others.

learned helplessness An acquired (hence, learned) belief that one is unable to control one's environment.

coregulation A gradual transferring of control from parent to child, beginning in middle childhood.

transsexual A person who would prefer to be a person of the other sex and who may undergo hormone treatments, cosmetic surgery, or both to achieve the appearance of being a member of the other sex.

Pygmalion effect The fulfillment of positive expectations due to the behavior of those who hold the expectations.

self-fulfilling prophecy An event that occurs because of the behavior of those who expect it to occur.

sexism Discrimination or bias against people based on their sex.

sexual harassment Unwelcome verbal or physical conduct of a sexual nature.

conduct disorders Disorders marked by persistent breaking of the rules and violations of the rights of others.

attributional style The way in which one is disposed to interpret outcomes (successes or failures), tending to place blame or responsibility on oneself or on external factors.

serotonin A neurotransmitter that is involved in mood disorders such as depression.

generalized anxiety disorder An anxiety disorder in which anxiety appears to be present continuously and is unrelated to the situation.

phobia An irrational, excessive fear that interferes with one's functioning.

separation anxiety disorder An extreme form of otherwise normal separation anxiety that is characterized by anxiety about separating from parents; SAD often takes the form of refusal to go to school.

school phobia Fear of attending school, marked by extreme anxiety at leaving parents.

LO4 Discuss the influence of the school on development in middle childhood.

Schools make demands for mature behavior and nurture positive physical, social, and cognitive development. Readiness for school is related to children's early life experiences, individual differences in development and learning, and the schools' expectations. An effective school has an energetic principal, an orderly atmosphere, empowerment of teachers and students, high expectations for children, and solid academics. Many girls suffer from sexism and sexual harassment in school. Math and science are generally stereotyped as masculine, and language arts as feminine.

LO5 Discuss social and emotional problems that tend to develop in middle childhood.

Children with conduct disorders persistently break rules or violate the rights of others. There may be a genetic component to such disorders, but sociopathic models in the family, deviant peers, and inconsistent discipline all contribute. Depressed children tend to complain of poor appetite, insomnia, lack of energy, and feelings of worthlessness. Depressed children tend to blame themselves excessively for shortcomings. Separation anxiety disorder (SAD) is diagnosed when separation anxiety is persistent and excessive and interferes with daily life. Children with SAD tend to cling to parents and may refuse to attend school. SAD is an extreme form of otherwise normal separation anxiety and may take the form of school phobia. But children can refuse school for other reasons, including finding school to be unpleasant or hostile.

Learning Outcomes

LO1 Describe the changes of puberty and its effects on adolescents.

G. Stanley Hall believed that adolescence is marked by "storm and stress." Puberty is a stage of physical development that is characterized by reaching sexual maturity. Sex hormones trigger the development of primary and secondary sex characteristics. Girls have their growth spurt sooner than boys do. Boys tend to spurt up to 4 inches per year, and girls, up to 3 inches per year. Boys' shoulders become broader, and girls develop broader and rounder hips. More of a male's body weight is made of muscle. Adolescents may look gawky because of asynchronous growth. Boys typically ejaculate by age 13 or 14. Female sex hormones regulate the menstrual cycle. Early-maturing boys tend to be more popular. Early-maturing girls become conspicuous, often leading to sexual approaches, deviant behavior, and a poor body image. Girls are generally more dissatisfied with their bodies than boys are.

LO2 Discuss emerging sexuality and the risks of sexually transmitted infections among adolescents.

Sexually transmitted infections (STIs) include bacterial infections such as chlamydia, gonorrhea, and syphilis; viral infections such as HIV/AIDS, HPV, and genital herpes. Factors that increase the likelihood of contracting an STI include sexual activity with multiple partners, without condoms, and substance abuse. Sharing hypodermic needles with an infected person can also transmit HIV. Prevention involves education about STIs, along with advice concerning abstinence or "safer sex."

LO3 Discuss adolescent health, including causes of death and nutritional issues.

Most American adolescents are healthy, but about one in five has a serious health problem. Most of which stem from their lifestyle. Death rates are greater for older adolescents and for male adolescents. Accidents, suicide, and homicide account for about three in four deaths among adolescents. The average girl needs about 2,200 calories per day, and the average boy needs about 3,000 calories. Adolescents need high quantities of elements such as calcium, iron, zinc, magnesium, and nitrogen. Adolescents usually need more vitamins than they take in, but less sugar, fat, protein, and sodium. Female adolescents are prone to anorexia nervosa and bulimia nervosa. Anorexia nervosa is characterized by fear of being overweight, a distorted body image, and refusal to eat. Bulimia nervosa is characterized by recurrent cycles of binge eating followed by purging. Eating disorders may develop because of fear of gaining weight resulting from cultural idealization of the slim female. Genetic factors may connect eating disorders with perfectionistic personality styles.

Key Terms

genital stage In psychoanalytic theory, the fifth and final stage of psychosexual development in which gratification is attained through sex with a person of the other sex.

puberty The biological stage of development characterized by changes that lead to reproductive capacity. Puberty signals the beginning of adolescence.

primary sex characteristics The structures that make reproduction possible.

secondary sex characteristics Physical indicators of sexual maturation—such as voice change and bodily hair—that do not directly involve reproductive structures.

asynchronous growth Imbalanced growth, such as the growth that occurs during the early part of adolescence and causes many adolescents to appear gawky.

secular trend A historical trend toward increasing adult height and earlier puberty.

semen The fluid that contains sperm and substances that nourish and transport sperm.

nocturnal emission Emission of seminal fluid while asleep.

gynecomastia Enlargement of breast tissue in males.

epiphyseal closure Turning to bone of the cartilage that separates the long end (epiphysis) of a bone from the main part of the bone.

mammary glands Glands that secrete milk.

menarche The onset of menstruation.

HIV/AIDS Human immunodeficiency virus (HIV) is the cause of acquired immunodeficiency syndrome (AIDS), a condition that cripples the immune system.

anorexia nervosa An eating disorder characterized by extreme fear of being too heavy, dramatic weight loss, distorted body image, and resistance to eating enough to reach or maintain a healthy weight.

bulimia nervosa An eating disorder characterized by cycles of binge eating and purging to prevent weight gain.

substance abuse A persistent pattern of use of a substance characterized by frequent intoxication and impairment of physical, social, or emotional well-being.

substance dependence A persistent pattern of use of a substance that is accompanied by physiological addiction.

tolerance Habituation to a drug creating a need to use increasingly higher doses to achieve similar effects.

abstinence syndrome A group of symptoms that results from a sudden decrease in the level of usage of a substance.

sedatives Drugs that soothe or quiet restlessness or agitation.

hallucinogenics Drugs that give rise to perceptual distortions.

LO4 Discuss substance abuse and dependence among adolescents.

Substance abuse is use of a substance despite the social, occupational, psychological, or physical problems it entails. Substance dependence is characterized by loss of control over the substance and is typified by tolerance and withdrawal symptoms. Depressants are addictive substances that slow the activity of the nervous system. Alcohol lowers inhibitions, relaxes, and intoxicates. Heroin can provide a strong euphoric "rush." Barbiturates relieve anxiety and tension. Stimulants accelerate the heartbeat and other bodily functions and depress the appetite. Nicotine is the stimulant in tobacco. The stimulant cocaine produces euphoria and bolsters self-confidence, but it occasionally causes respiratory and cardiovascular collapse. Adolescents use amphetamines to remain awake for cram sessions. Hallucinogenics give rise to perceptual distortions called hallucinations. Marijuana helps some adolescents relax and elevates the mood, but it impairs perceptual–motor coordination and short-term memory. LSD ("acid") produces vivid hallucinations. Most students have tried alcohol, and many use it regularly. About 30% of high school seniors have engaged in binge drinking. Substance abuse and dependence usually begin with experimental use. Adolescents may experiment because of curiosity, conformity to peer pressure, parental use, rebelliousness, and a desire to escape from boredom or pressure and to seek excitement or pleasure. Some individuals may have a genetic predisposition toward dependence on certain substances.

TABLE 14.5
Disapproval of Drug Use by Twelfth-Graders, 1978 versus 2008

DO YOU DISAPPROVE OF PEOPLE (WHO ARE 18 OR OLDER) DOING EACH OF THE FOLLOWING?	PERCENT DISAPPROVING, CLASS OF 1978	PERCENT DISAPPROVING, CLASS OF 2008
Try marijuana once or twice	33.4%	55.5%
Smoke marijuana regularly	43.5	79.6
Try LSD once or twice	85.4	85.5
Take LSD regularly	96.4	93.5
Try MDMA (Ecstasy) one or twice	—	88.2
Try cocaine once or twice	77.0	89.2
Take cocaine regularly	91.9	94.8
Try heroin once or twice	92.0	93.3
Take heroin regularly	97.8	95.9
Try amphetamines once or twice	74.8	87.2
Take amphetamines regularly	93.5	94.2
Try barbiturates once or twice	82.4	86.1
Take barbiturates regularly	94.3	94.3
Try one or two drinks of an alcoholic beverage (beer, wine, liquor)	15.6	29.8
Take one or two drinks nearly every day	67.7	74.5
Take four or five drinks nearly every day	90.2	89.8
Have five or more drinks once or twice each weekend	56.2	68.9
Smoke one or more packs of cigarettes per day	67.0	80.5
Take steroids	—	90.9

Source: Johnston et al. (2008a, Table 10). Retrieved from http://www.monitoringthefuture.org/data/08data/pr08t10.pdf.

Learning Outcomes

LO1 Describe the cognitive advances that define adolescent thinking.

In Western societies, formal operational thought begins at about the time of puberty. The major achievements of the stage involve classification, logical thought (deductive reasoning), and the ability to hypothesize. Adolescent thought is also characterized by the imaginary audience and the personal fable. The imaginary audience concept is the belief that others around us are concerned with our thoughts and behaviors, giving rise to the desire for privacy. The personal fable is the belief that our feelings and ideas are special and that we are invulnerable, which may underlie adolescent and risk taking. Females tend to excel in verbal ability. Males tend to excel in visual–spatial ability. Boys are more likely than girls to have reading problems. Sex differences in visual–spatial skills appear to be linked to biological factors and to gender stereotypes.

FIGURE 15.1
Examples of Tests Used to Measure Visual–Spatial Ability

a. Spatial visualization
Embedded-figure test. Study the figure on the left. Then cover it up and try to find where it is hidden in the figure on the right. The left-hand figure may need to be shifted in order to locate it in the right-hand figure.

b. Spatial perception
Water-level test. Examine the glass of water on the left. Now imagine that it is slightly tilted, as on the right. Draw in a line to indicate the location of the water level.

c. Mental rotation
Mental-rotation test. If you mentally rotate the figure on the left, which of the five figures on the right would you obtain?

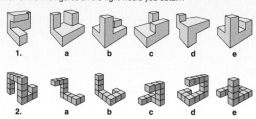

Answers: **a.** 1: Orient the pattern as if it were a tilted capital M, with the left portion along the top of the white triangle. 2: This pattern fits along the right sides of the two black triangles on the left. 3: Rotate this figure about 100° to the right, so that it forms a Z, with the top line coinciding with the top line of the top white triangle. **b.** The line should be horizontal, not tilted. **c.** 1: c; 2: d.

Go to 4ltrpress.cengage.com/cdev to access an interactive version of this figure.

Key Terms

formal operations The fourth stage in Piaget's cognitive-developmental theory, characterized by the capacity for flexible, reversible operations concerning abstract ideas and concepts, such as symbols, statements, and theories.

utopian Referring to an ideal vision of society.

imaginary audience The belief that others around us are as concerned with our thoughts and behaviors as we are; one aspect of adolescent egocentrism.

personal fable The belief that our feelings and ideas are special and unique and that we are invulnerable; one aspect of adolescent egocentrism.

postconventional level According to Kohlberg, a period during which moral judgments are derived from moral principles and people look to themselves to set moral standards.

reciprocity The principle that actions have mutual effects and that people depend on one another to treat each other morally.

LO2 **Describe and evaluate Kohlberg's view of the kinds of moral judgments made by many adolescents (and adults).**

In Stage 5's contractual, legalistic orientation, people weigh pressing human needs against society's need to maintain social order. In Stage 6's universal ethical principles orientation, people follow universal ethical principles and their own conscience, even if it means breaking the law. Postconventional thinking is nearly absent in developing societies, and infrequent in the United States. Gilligan challenges Kohlberg's view that males operate at higher levels of moral judgment than females do.

FIGURE 15.3

Age and Type of Moral Judgment

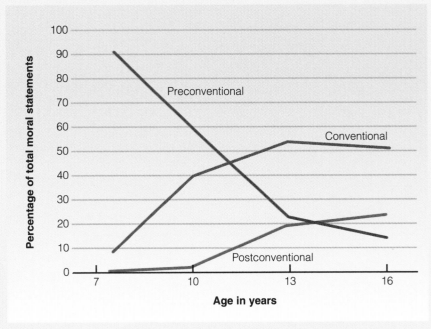

LO3 **Discuss the transition to high school and factors associated with dropping out.**

The transition to middle, junior high, or high school generally involves a shift from a smaller neighborhood elementary school to a larger, more impersonal setting. The transition is often accompanied by a decline in grades and a drop in self-esteem. High school dropouts are more likely to be unemployed and earn lower salaries. Dropouts are more likely to show delinquent behaviors. Truancy and reading below grade level predict school dropout.

LO4 **Discuss career development and the pluses and minuses of part-time work for high school students.**

Children's career aspirations are often not practical at first but become increasingly realistic as children mature and gain experience. Factors that influence choice of a career include abilities and personality traits. More than half of high school students hold part-time jobs during the school year. The benefits of adolescent employment include developing a sense of responsibility, self-reliance, and discipline, and learning to appreciate the value of money and education. But students who work also report lower grades and other problems.

Learning Outcomes

LO1 Discuss the formation of identity in adolescence.

Erikson's adolescent stage of psychosocial development is identity versus identity diffusion. The primary task of this stage is for adolescents to develop a sense of who they are and what they stand for. Marcia's identity statuses represent the four combinations of the dimensions of exploration and commitment: identity diffusion, foreclosure, moratorium, and identity achievement.

TABLE 16.1
The Four Identity Statuses of James Marcia

COMMITMENT	EXPLORATION	
	Yes	**No**
Yes	**Identity Achievement** • Most developed in terms of identity • Has experienced a period of exploration • Has developed commitments • Has a sense of personal well-being, high self-esteem, and self-acceptance • Cognitively flexible • Sets goals and works toward achieving them	**Foreclosure** • Has commitments without considering alternatives • Commitments based on identification with parents, teachers, or other authority figures • Often authoritarian and inflexible
No	**Moratorium** • Actively exploring alternatives • Attempting to make choices with regard to occupation, ideological beliefs, and so on • Often anxious and intense • Ambivalent feelings toward parents and authority figures	**Identity Diffusion** • Least developed in terms of identity • Lacks commitments • Not trying to form commitments • May be carefree and uninvolved or unhappy and lonely • May be angry, alienated, rebellious

LO2 Discuss relationships with parents and peers during adolescence.

Adolescents spend much less time with parents than children do. Although adolescents become more independent of their parents, they generally continue to love and respect them. The role of peers increases markedly during the teen years. Adolescents are more likely than younger children to stress intimate self-disclosure and mutual understanding in friendships. The two major types of peer groups are cliques and crowds. Adolescent peer groups also include peers of the other sex.

Key Terms

ego identity According to Erikson, one's sense of who one is and what one stands for.

psychological moratorium A time-out period when adolescents experiment with different roles, values, beliefs, and relationships.

identity crisis A turning point in development during which one examines one's values and makes decisions about life roles.

identity diffusion An identity status that characterizes those who have no commitments and who are not in the process of exploring alternatives.

foreclosure An identity status that characterizes those who have made commitments without considering alternatives.

moratorium An identity status that characterizes those who are actively exploring alternatives in an attempt to form an identity.

identity achievement An identity status that characterizes those who have explored alternatives and have developed commitments.

ethnic identity A sense of belonging to an ethnic group.

unexamined ethnic identity The first stage of ethnic identity development; similar to the identity status of diffusion or foreclosure.

ethnic identity search The second stage of ethnic identity development; similar to the identity status of moratorium.

achieved ethnic identity The final stage of ethnic identity development; similar to the identity achievement.

clique A group of five to ten individuals who hang around together and who share activities and confidences.

crowd A large, loosely organized group of people who may or may not spend much time together and who are identified by the activities of the group.

homosexual Referring to an erotic orientation toward members of one's own sex.

masturbation Sexual self-stimulation.

juvenile delinquency Conduct in a child or adolescent characterized by illegal activities.

LO3 Discuss sexuality during adolescence, focusing on sexual identity and teenage pregnancy.

Romantic relationships begin to appear during early and middle adolescence. Masturbation is the most common sexual outlet in adolescents. Some adolescents have a homosexual orientation. The process of "coming out" may be a long and painful struggle. Researchers have found evidence for genetic and hormonal factors in sexual orientation. Early onset of puberty is connected with earlier sexual activity. Adolescents who have close relationships with parents are less likely to initiate sexual activity early. Peer pressure is a powerful contributor to sexual activity. Many teenage girls who become pregnant receive little advice about how to resist sexual advances. Many misunderstand reproduction or miscalculate the odds of conception. Teenage mothers are more likely to have medical complications during pregnancy and birth, largely because of inadequate medical care. Teenage mothers have a lower standard of living and a greater need for public assistance.

LO4 Discuss the characteristics of juvenile delinquents.

Juvenile delinquency refers to illegal activities committed by a child or adolescent. Behaviors, such as drinking, that are considered illegal when performed by minors are called status offenses. Boys are more likely than girls to engage in most delinquent behaviors. Boys are more apt to commit crimes of violence, whereas girls are more likely to commit status offenses. Risk factors associated with juvenile delinquency include poor school performance, delinquent friends, early aggressive or hyperactive behavior, substance abuse, low verbal IQ, low self-esteem, impulsivity, and immature moral reasoning.

FIGURE 16.3

The Delinquency Case Rate per 1,000 Juveniles

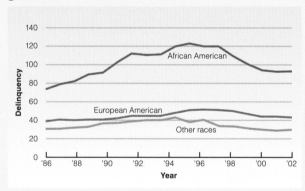

LO5 Discuss risk factors for adolescent suicide.

Suicide is the third or fourth leading cause of death among older teenagers. Most suicides among adolescents and adults are linked to stress, feelings of depression, identity problems, impulsivity, and social problems. Girls are more likely to attempt suicide, whereas boys are more likely to "succeed."

LO6 Discuss the (theoretical) stage of emerging adulthood.

Emerging adulthood is a period of development, spanning the ages of 18 to 25, in which young people engage in extended role exploration. Emerging adulthood can occur in affluent societies that grant young people the luxury of developing their identities and their life plans.

CONCEPT REVIEW
Comparison of Freud's and Erikson's Stages of Development

AGE	FREUD'S STAGES OF PSYCHOSEXUAL DEVELOPMENT	ERIKSON'S STAGES OF PSYCHOSOCIAL DEVELOPMENT
Birth to 1 year	**Oral Stage.** Gratification derives from oral activities, such as sucking. Fixation leads to development of oral traits such as dependence, depression, gullibility.	**Trust versus Mistrust.** The developmental task is to come to trust the key caregivers, primarily the mother, and the environment. It is desirable for the infant to connect its environment with inner feelings of satisfaction and contentment.
About 1 to 3 years	**Anal Stage.** Gratification derives from anal activities involving elimination. Fixation leads to development of anal-retentive traits (e.g., excessive neatness) or anal-expulsive traits (e.g., sloppiness).	**Autonomy versus Shame and Doubt.** The developmental task is to develop the desire to make choices and the self-control to regulate one's behavior so that choices can be actualized.
About 3 to 6 years	**Phallic Stage.** Gratification derives from stimulation of the genital region. Oedipal and Electra complexes emerge and are resolved. Fixation leads to development of phallic traits, such as vanity.	**Initiative versus Guilt.** The developmental task is to add initiative—planning and attacking— to choice. The preschooler is on the move and becomes proactive.
About 6 to 12 years	**Latency Stage.** Sexual impulses are suppressed, allowing the child to focus on development of social and technological skills.	**Industry versus Inferiority.** The developmental task is to become absorbed in the development and implementation of skills, to master the basics of technology, to become productive.
Adolescence	**Genital Stage.** Reappearance of sexual impulses, with gratification sought through sexual relations with an adult of the other sex.	**Identity versus Role Diffusion.** The developmental task is to associate one's skills and social roles with the development of career goals. More broadly, the development of identity refers to a sense of who one is and what one believes in.
Young adulthood		**Intimacy versus Isolation.** The developmental task is to commit oneself to another person, to engage in a mature sexual love.
Middle adulthood		**Generativity versus Stagnation.** The developmental task is to appreciate the opportunity to "give back." Not only are generative people creative, but they also give encouragement and guidance to the younger generation, which may include their own children.
Late adulthood		**Ego Integrity versus Despair.** The developmental task is to achieve wisdom and dignity in the face of declining physical abilities. Ego integrity also means accepting the time and place of one's own life cycle.

Jean Piaget's Stages of Cognitive Development

STAGE	APPROXIMATE AGE	COMMENTS
Sensorimotor	Birth–2 years	At first, the child lacks language and does not use symbols or mental representations of objects. In time, reflexive responding ends, and intentional behavior—as in making interesting stimulation last—begins. The child develops the object concept and acquires the basics of language.
Preoperational	2–7 years	The child begins to represent the world mentally, but thought is egocentric. The child does not focus on two aspects of a situation at once and therefore lacks conservation. The child shows animism, artificialism, and objective responsibility for wrongdoing.
Concrete operational	7–12 years	Logical mental actions—called operations—begin. The child develops conservation concepts, can adopt the viewpoint of others, can classify objects in series, and shows comprehension of basic relational concepts (such as one object being larger or heavier than another).
Formal operational	12 years and older	Mature, adult thought emerges. Thinking is characterized by deductive logic, consideration of various possibilities (mental trial and error), abstract thought, and the formation and testing of hypotheses.

Features of Preoperational Cognition

Symbolic Thought	• Child uses symbols to represent objects and relationships. • Child engages in symbolic play. • Symbolic play grows more frequent and complex. • Child may have imaginary friend(s). • Mental operations are inflexible and irreversible.
Egocentrism	• Child does not take viewpoint of others. • Child may be lacking in empathy for others. • Piaget used three-mountains test to assess egocentrism.
Precausal thinking	• Child believes things happen for a reason. • Child engages in transductive reasoning ("Should sleep because it's dark outside"). • Child shows animism (attributes life and will to inanimate objects). • Child shows artificialism (assumes environmental features are made by people).
Confusion of mental and physical events	• Child assumes thoughts reflect external reality. • Child believes dreams are real.
Focus on one dimension at a time	• Child does not understand law of conservation. • Child centers on one dimension at a time. • Child does not show appropriate class inclusion (may not include dogs as animals).

CONCEPT REVIEW
Highlights of Prenatal Development

FIRST TRIMESTER

Period of the Ovum First 2 weeks	• Dividing cluster of cells enters and moves around the uterus, living off the yolk of the egg cell. • Blastocyst becomes implanted in the wall of uterus, possibly accompanied by implantation bleeding. 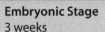
Embryonic Stage 3 weeks	• Head and blood vessels form. • Brain begins to develop.
4 weeks	• Heart begins to beat and pump blood. • Arm buds and leg buds appear. • Eyes, ears, nose, and mouth form. • Nerves begin to develop. • Umbilical cord is functional. • Embryo weighs a fraction of an ounce and is 1/2 inch long. 
5–8 weeks	• Hands and feet develop with webbed fingers and toes. • Undifferentiated sex organs appear. • Teeth buds develop. • Kidneys filter uric acid from the blood; liver produces blood cells. • Bone cells appear. • Head is half the length of the entire body. • Embryo weighs about 1/13th an ounce and is 1 inch long.
Fetal Stage 9–12 weeks	• All major organ systems formed. • Fingers and toes are fully formed. • Eyes can be clearly distinguished. • Sex of fetus can be determined visually (e.g., by ultrasound). • Mouth opens and closes; fetus swallows. • Fetus responds to external stimulation. • Fetus weighs 1 ounce and is 3 inches long.

continues

Highlights of Prenatal Development—continued

SECOND TRIMESTER

13–16 weeks
- Mother detects fetal movement.
- Many reflexes present.
- Fingernails and toenails form.
- Head is about one-fourth the length of the body.

17–20 weeks
- Hair develops on head.
- Fine, downy hair (lanugo) covers body.
- Fetus sucks its thumb and hiccups.
- Heartbeat can be heard when listener presses head against mother's abdomen.

21–24 weeks
- Eyes open and shut.
- Light and sounds can be perceived.
- Fetus alternates between periods of wakefulness and sleep.
- Skin looks ruddy because blood vessels show through the surface.
- Survival rate low if fetus is born.
- Fetus weighs about 2 pounds and is 14 inches long; growth rate is slowing down.

THIRD TRIMESTER

25–28 weeks
- Organ systems continue to mature.
- Fatty layer begins to develop beneath the skin.
- Fetus turns head down in the uterus.
- Fetus cries, swallows, sucks its thumb.
- Chances of survival good if born.
- Fetus weighs 3 to 4 pounds and is 16 inches long.

29 to 36–38 weeks
- Organ systems function well.
- Fatty layer continues to develop.
- Fetal activity level decreases in the weeks before birth as a result of crowding.
- Weight increases to an average of 7–7 1/2 pounds; boys are about half a pound heavier than girls; length increases to about 20 inches.